DIANA INQUEST

THE

Untold Story

John Morgan

PART 4:
THE BRITISH COVER-UP

First published by John Morgan and
printed in the UK by Lightning Source

ISBN: 978-0-9807407-3-8

Cover Picture:
Princess Diana's coffin as it left La Pitié Salpêtrière Hospital at 6.15 p.m. on
31 August 1997. The coffin is shrouded in the royal standard, the official flag
of the British royal family.
Why is this?
In August 1996 – precisely one year before the crash – the Queen had
removed Diana from the royal family, yet as soon as Diana died, she
immediately again became a royal. Prince Charles rushed across to Paris to
claim the body and the coffin was promptly draped with the royal standard.

Cover image reproduced from film footage in 2004 History Channel documentary,
Princess Diana   .

Diana Inquest: The Untold Story

Is dedicated

To

Diana, Princess of Wales

And

Dodi Fayed

Killed in a mindless tragedy

The crash in the Alma Tunnel, Paris, at 12.23 a.m., 31 August 1997

And

To those few in their and Henri Paul's families

Who have had the courage to fight for the truth to come out

Who have been confronted with an unconscionable
travesty of justice

Known as the official investigations

That commenced in Paris immediately after the crash

That concluded at 4.33 p.m. on 7 April 2008 in London's
Royal Courts of Justice

Other Volumes In This Series

Part 1: Diana Inquest: The Untold Story (2009)

Covers pre-crash events in the Ritz Hotel, the final journey and what happened in the Alma Tunnel

Part 2: Diana Inquest: How & Why Did Diana Die? (2009)

Covers possible motives for assassination and post-crash medical treatment of Princess Diana – including mistreatment in the ambulance

Part 3: Diana Inquest: The French Cover-Up (2010)

Covers the autopsies of the driver, Henri Paul, and the misconduct of the French investigation into the crash

Other Books by John Morgan

Cover-Up of a Royal Murder: Hundreds of Errors in the Paget Report (2007)

Flying Free: A Journey From Fundamentalism To Freedom (2005)

Table of Contents

CONTENTS

Preface

The collision that resulted in the deaths of Princess Diana and Dodi Fayed in Paris in the early hours of 31 August 1997 was possibly the most significant car crash of the 20th century.

But it also raised many questions, the primary one being: Was this just an ordinary car accident or was it actually an assassination?

The *Diana Inquest: The Untold Story* series of books has sought to answer that question, by closely analysing the vast amount of evidence heard during the 2007-8 inquest into the deaths. The books have also drawn on a huge volume of evidence from within the British police investigation – evidence that was withheld from the inquest jury by the judge, Lord Justice Scott Baker.

In the first volume, we studied the evidence that immediately surrounded the crash itself – the events at the Ritz Hotel, the final journey and the witness accounts of the crash in the Alma Tunnel.

Part 2 covered the possible motives for an assassination and the post-crash medical treatment of Princess Diana – *How & Why Did Diana Die?*

Part 3 addressed the questions involving the driver of the crashed Mercedes, Henri Paul, in particular claims that he was drunk at the wheel, and also important issues regarding the conduct of the French investigation.

This volume, Part 4, entitled *Diana Inquest: The British Cover-Up* deals with critical questions surrounding the post-death treatment of Princess Diana's body.

It specifically addresses the events that occurred in the 25 hours immediately following the official announcement of Diana, Princess of Wales' death, at 4.10 a.m. in Paris on 31 August 1997.

Events moved very quickly – it will be shown that by 4 a.m. in London the following day, Princess Diana's body had undergone a rushed repatriation, two post-mortems and two embalmings.

Who was making the early decisions that led to this extensive and invasive treatment of Diana's body – the body of a passenger who is supposed to have died in a routine traffic accident?

That question will be answered, but in achieving that, this volume will raise many other questions that have never previously been asked.[a]

A close analysis of the post-death events, as conducted in this volume, arrives at some shocking but inescapable conclusions:

- that there was a post-mortem of Diana's body held in Paris, just 1½ hours after her official time of death
- that a decision to embalm Diana's body in Paris was made in the UK, very soon after her death
- that the earliest events – during the first 25 hours – were being driven by the royals in Balmoral
- that the samples that were toxicology tested following the UK post-mortem were not from Princess Diana's body.

It will also be shown that the inquest jury – who were expected to arrive at a verdict on the cause of death – were prevented from having access to the post-mortem reports for the two people – Princess Diana and Dodi Fayed – whose deaths they were investigating.

Scott Baker's inquest jury were required to draw conclusions without being allowed to view some of the most basic documentation and without hearing any evidence from some of the most important witnesses.

Just as Parts 1, 2 and 3 revealed a jury that was kept in the dark on most of the key evidence, this was also the case in the evidence relating to the post-death events.

Out of 23 documents connected to the post-mortem of Princess Diana, the jury got to see just 2. Out of 14 key witnesses, the jury heard from just 3.

This current volume, Part 4, deals specifically with the British cover-up operation that took place during the initial hours following the deaths of Princess Diana and Dodi Fayed. Effectively, this series of books has also revealed that that cover-up continued right through the work of Operation Paget – culminating in the deeply flawed 2006 Paget Report[b] – and then into the six months of the 2007-8 London inquest, conducted by Lord Justice Scott Baker, a judge who has been shown to be corrupt.

This volume draws heavily from material in the 2010 book *Diana Inquest: The Documents the Jury Never Saw* – often simply referred to as *The Documents* book. Many of the witness statement excerpts labelled in this book as "Jury Didn't Hear" appear in full context in *The Documents* book. Generally the page number references from that book have been shown in the footnotes or endnotes in this volume. Some excerpts that were redacted from *The Documents* book have been included in Part 4 – this is because they are critical to specific aspects of the case. Where that has occurred the endnote

---

[a] The main questions are listed in the Conclusion chapter at the end of this book.

[b] The Paget Report was specifically dealt with in the 2007 book, *Cover-Up of a Royal Murder: Hundreds of Errors in the Paget Report*.

refers to the original document, however unredacted parts of the excerpt may still be viewable in their context in *The Documents* book.

Page numbers referenced to *The Documents* book relate to the UK edition. Readers who have the US edition of *The Documents* book will be able to locate the same excerpts within a few pages of the UK edition page number. For example, if the UK edition quote is from p300, it will appear before p310 in the US edition.

Extensive witness lists shown at the start of Part 1 have not been included in this book in an effort to save space. All witnesses mentioned in Part 4 have been included in the index, and of course are also mentioned in the lists in Part 1.[a]

I have deliberately included verbatim inquest testimony in this book – it reveals the words of the witnesses themselves as they describe what they saw or heard.

Diana Inquest: The Untold Story has also drawn heavily on the information – 7,000 pages of transcripts and other evidence – that are publicly available on the official inquest website: www.scottbaker-inquests.gov.uk All quotes throughout this book have been fully referenced, and I encourage readers to look up the website for the full transcript of any particular piece of witness evidence they need to view in its complete context.

Points to assist with the reading of *Diana Inquest* and accessing evidence:

Transcript quotes have been referenced through the book as follows:
Example:
Claude Garrec, Henri Paul's Closest Friend: 31 Jan 08: 124.15:
Hough: Q. Did he have any ambition to become the head of security?
A. No

Claude Garrec	= Witness name
Henri Paul's Closest Friend	= Witness' position or relevance
31 Jan 08	= Date of testimony at the inquest
124	= Page number – note that page numbers appear at the bottom of each page on the inquest website transcripts
15	= Line number on the page
Hough	= Lawyer doing the questioning – there is a list of lawyers and who they represent near the front of this book
Q	= Statement made by the lawyer or questioner
A	= Statement made by the witness or answerer

---

[a] There are some additional "witnesses not heard" listed near the front of this volume.

DIANA INQUEST: THE BRITISH COVER-UP

The official inquest website contains a large number of significant items of evidence: photos, documents, letters and so on. It is important to note that none of this evidence is stored in numerical or subject order – the easiest way to locate these items is by scrolling down the evidence list looking for the specific reference number you are seeking. The reference numbers, which always begin with the prefix code "INQ", will often be found in the footnotes or endnotes in this book.

In addition, the website has several interesting and useful videos that are available for viewing by the public. These are also not as easy to access as the transcripts. To reach the videos, click on "Evidence", then click on any date on the calendar, then scroll down or up until you come to an item of evidence that is obviously a video. When you click on that item, a page will open up that will give you access to all of the videos on the website.

Throughout this book underlining of words or phrases has been used as a means of emphasising certain points, unless otherwise stated.

"Jury Didn't Hear" appears in bold before:
1) Any evidence that was not heard during the inquest
2) Written documents from the Coroner not seen by the jury.

"Jury Not Present" appears in bold before any statement made in court where the jury wasn't present.

There are several people who have provided invaluable support that has helped enable these volumes to be completed. Full acknowledgements are included in Part 1 and the final volume.

Word usage:

"Autopsy" and "post-mortem" are synonymous – "autopsy" is generally used in France, whereas "post-mortem" is generally used in the UK.

KP = Kensington Palace, Diana's home.

Sapeurs-Pompiers = Paris Fire Service

BAC = Blood Alcohol Concentration

"Cours la Reine", "Cours Albert 1er", "Avenue de New York" and "Voie Georges Pompidou" are all names for the same riverside expressway that runs into the Alma tunnel. The parallel service road is also known as "Cours Albert 1er"

Fulham Mortuary = Hammersmith and Fulham Mortuary

Imperial College = Charing Cross Hospital[a]

---

[a] Imperial College operates 5 hospitals in the area of West London, of which Charing Cross is one. Throughout this case the terms "Imperial College" and "Charing Cross Hospital" have been used interchangeably.

The Witnesses Not Heard

Parts 1, 2 and 3 included lists of 176 witnesses not heard at the inquest. The following 45 witnesses should be added to that number, giving a new total of 221.[a]

Witness Name	Position or Relevance	French Investigation	British Investigation	Inquest
French Body Examinations of Diana and Dodi				
Anonymous Police Photographer	French Police Officer	Not interviewed	Not interviewed	No evidence heard
Photographer – Took photos during Lecomte examination of Diana's body				
French Embalming of Diana				
Jerald Pullins	Former European CEO of SCI	Not interviewed	Not interviewed	No evidence heard
Pullins – Claimed by Paget to have called Racine at 5 a.m. 31 August 1997				
Identity Unknown	President of Kenyons in 1997	Not interviewed	Not interviewed	No evidence heard
Kenyons' president – Called Racine at 5 a.m. 31 August 1997				
Hervé Racine	PFG President	Not interviewed	Not interviewed	No evidence heard
Racine – Called Chapillon after 5 a.m.				

---

[a] Of the additional 45 listed here, 37 have never been officially interviewed or heard from. When added to the Parts 1 to 3 lists of 84, this gives a new total of 121. 8 others had previously given official statements or reports which were not read out at the inquest. When added to the Parts 1 to 3 lists of 47, this gives a new total of 55. There are no others who had excerpts of their report or statement only read at the inquest but should have been cross-examined. That leaves the Parts 1 to 3 lists of 40 unchanged.

DIANA INQUEST: THE BRITISH COVER-UP

Witness Name	Position or Relevance	French Investigation	British Investigation	Inquest
Michel Chapillon	PFG French Director	Not interviewed	Not interviewed	No evidence heard
Chapillon – Called Plumet at 7 a.m.				
Sophie Hauffman	BJL Switchbrd/ Planner	Not interviewed	Not interviewed	No evidence heard
Hauffman – Called Amarger to do embalming at 9 a.m.				
Michel Lebreton	BJL Dry Ice Operative	Not interviewed	Not interviewed	No evidence heard
Lebreton – Alleged to have administered dry ice to Diana				
Patrick Launay	PFG Director	Not interviewed	1 Statement	No evidence heard
Launay – Attended the hospital and dealt with British embalmers				
Alain Caltiau	PFG Asst General Manager	Not interviewed	Not interviewed	No evidence heard
Caltiau – Attended the PFG office and dealt with phone calls				
René Deguisne	BJL Asst General Manager North, East, West France	Not interviewed	1 Statement	No evidence heard
Deguisne – General evidence on BJL operations				
Josselin Charrier	BJL Embalmer	Not interviewed	Not interviewed	No evidence heard
Charrier – Assisted Amarger with the embalming.				
Bernard Colsy	BJL Asst General Manager, Île-de-France	Not interviewed	Not interviewed	No evidence heard
Colsy – Boss of the embalmers				

THE WITNESSES NOT HEARD

Witness Name	Position or Relevance	French Investigation	British Investigation	Inquest
Theophie Le Couarec	Hospital Charge Nurse	Not interviewed	Not interviewed	No evidence heard
Le Couarec – Accompanied Amarger at the hospital				
Anonymous	Hospital Employee	Not interviewed	Not interviewed	No evidence heard
Anonymous employee – Informed Amarger that the British had required a female embalmer				
Jeanne Lecorchet	Hospital Nurse	Not interviewed	Not interviewed	No evidence heard
Lecorchet – Present in Diana's room with embalmers near start of embalming				
Dr Bernard Kouchner	French Minister of Health	Not interviewed	Not interviewed	No evidence heard
Kouchner – Viewed Diana's body at around 2 p.m.				
Two Anonymous Female Police Officers	Present Throughout the Embalming	Not interviewed	Not interviewed	No evidence heard
Repatriation				
David Green	UK Embalmer	Not interviewed	2 Statements	No evidence heard
Bill Fry	UK Embalmer	Not interviewed	Not interviewed	No evidence heard
Green & Fry – Witnessed repatriation; Experts on embalming; Green conducted UK embalming				
Keith Leverton	UK Funeral Director	Not interviewed	1 Statement	No evidence heard
Leverton – Involved in repatriation				
Mme Celadon	Police Admin Officer	Not interviewed	Not interviewed	No evidence heard
Celadon – Involved in repatriation documentation.				

Witness Name	Position or Relevance	French Investigation	British Investigation	Inquest
Jacques Dupont	PFG Employee	Not interviewed	Not interviewed[a]	No evidence heard
Dupont – Present at the IML during hold-up of Dodi's repatriation				
Daniel Tassell	Levertons Manager	Not interviewed	Not interviewed	No evidence heard
Tassell – Took first phone call from Mather regarding repatriation				
British Embassy				
Tim Livesey	Embassy Assistant	Not interviewed	Not interviewed	No evidence heard
Livesey – Assisted Jay, Moss and Tebbutt; Present at hospital				
Steve Gunner	Assistant Service Attaché	Not interviewed	Not interviewed	No evidence heard
Gunner – Involved in organising Charles' flight to Paris				
Catherine Bouron	Jay's Private Secretary	Not interviewed	Not interviewed	No evidence heard
Bouron – Witness to events at the Embassy				
Gillian Storey[b]	Consular Officer	Not interviewed	Not interviewed	No evidence heard
Storey – Produced "telephone report of death"				
Role of Royal Family & Household				
Supt Kingsmill	Head of Royalty Protection	Not interviewed	Not interviewed	No evidence heard
Kingsmill – Travelled to Paris early on 31 August 1997				

[a] The Paget Report mentions that a statement was taken from a "Jacques Dupont" working at the Paris Traffic Information and Control Centre on the night of 30 August 1997. Although the names are identical, this would appear to be a different person to the PFG witness regarding the repatriation. There are 17 listings for "Jacques Dupont" in the Telephone White Pages just for Central Paris, Department 75. See Paget Report, p393 and www.pagesjaunes.fr/pagesblanches

[b] Storey's role is addressed in the statement from Stephen Donnelly – see 17 Dec 07: 121.6 to 121.21.

THE WITNESSES NOT HEARD

Witness Name	Position or Relevance	French Investigation	British Investigation	Inquest
David Ogilvy[a]	Lord Chamberlain	Not interviewed	Not interviewed	No evidence heard
Ogilvy – At Buckingham Palace before 8.30 a.m. 31 August 1997				
Malcolm Ross	Lord Chamberlain's Office Comptroller	Not interviewed	Not interviewed	No evidence heard
Ross – Called Mather from Scotland at 6 a.m. 31 August 1997				
Peter Harding	Defence Services Secretary	Not interviewed	Not interviewed	No evidence heard
Harding – At Buckingham Palace before 8.30 a.m. 31 August 1997				
Lucy Dove	Buckingham Palace	Not interviewed	Not interviewed	No evidence heard
Dove – Spoke to Burton on morning of 31 August 1997				
Matthew Ridley	Lord Steward	Not interviewed	Not interviewed	No evidence heard
Ridley – Royal Coroner, John Burton, was answerable to him				
Stephen Lamport	Charles' Private Secretary	Not interviewed	Not interviewed	No evidence heard
Nick Archer	Charles' Staff Member	Not interviewed	Not interviewed	No evidence heard
Lamport & Archer – Witnesses to events at Balmoral on 31 August 1997				
Sandra Henney	Charles' Press Secretary	Not interviewed	Not interviewed	No evidence heard
Henney – On royal flight to collect Diana's body				
UK Post-Mortems				
Richard Wall	OCG MPS Officer	Not interviewed	1 Statement	No evidence heard
Wall – Operated as Exhibits Officer during the post-mortems				

[a] Earl of Airlie. Also known as Lord Airlie.

DIANA INQUEST: THE BRITISH COVER-UP

Witness Name	Position or Relevance	French Investigation	British Investigation	Inquest
Dennis Sharp	OCG MPS Officer	Not interviewed	1 Statement	No evidence heard
Sharp – Attended critical pre-post-mortems meeting at Scotland Yard				
Harry Brown	Coroner's Officer	Not interviewed	Not interviewed	No evidence heard
Brown – Carried out instructions from John Burton on 31 August 1997				
Police Officer Isted	Senior Photography Officer	Not interviewed	Not interviewed	No evidence heard
Isted – Received photo albums of Diana's post-mortem at 4 a.m. on 1 September 1997				
DC James Emeny	Paget Officer	Not interviewed	Not interviewed	No evidence heard
Emeny – Conducted critical interview with Richard Wall				
Neal Williams	Photo-grapher	Not interviewed	1 Statement	No evidence heard
Mark Taylor	Asst Photo-grapher	Not interviewed	1 Statement	No evidence heard
Williams & Taylor – Present during Diana's post-mortem				
Nigel Munns	Senior Mortuary Officer	Not interviewed	Not interviewed	No evidence heard
Munns – Present during the post-mortems; Boss of Robert Thompson				

The Lawyers & Representation

Name[a]	Status	Representing
Ian Burnett	QC[b]	The Inquest
Ian Croxford	QC	President, Ritz Hotel
Tom de la Mare		President, Ritz Hotel
Henrietta Hill		Mohamed Al Fayed
Nicholas Hilliard		The Inquest
Richard Horwell	QC	Commissioner of Police
Jonathon Hough		The Inquest
Lee Hughes		The Inquest
Jeremy Johnson		SIS (MI6) & Foreign & Commonwealth Office
Richard Keen	QC	Henri Paul's Parents
Edmund Lawson	QC	Commissioner of Police
Jamie Lowther-Pinkerton		Princes William & Harry
Alison MacDonald		Mohamed Al Fayed
Duncan MacLeod		Commissioner of Police
Lady Sarah McCorquodale		Spencer Family
Michael Mansfield	QC	Mohamed Al Fayed
Martin Smith[c]		The Inquest
Robin Tam	QC	SIS (MI6) & Foreign & Commonwealth Office
Robert Weekes		Henri Paul's Parents

---

[a] Alphabetic Order
[b] Queen's Counsel
[c] Solicitor to the inquest

The Organisations

Abbreviation	Name	Definition or Function
BCA	Bureau Central des Accidents	Central Accident Bureau – French police
BJL	Hygeco[a] or Bernard J. Lane	French embalming company – Subsidiary of PFG
	Brigade Criminelle	Department of French police dealing with murders, kidnappings and terrorism
CIA	Central Intelligence Agency	US Foreign Intelligence Service
DGSE	Direction Générale de la Securité	French Foreign Intelligence Service – French equivalent of MI6
DST	Directorate de Surveillance Territories	French Domestic Intelligence Service – French equivalent of MI5
	Elysée	Offices of the French Government
	Étoile Limousines	Provided chauffeured Mercedes to the Ritz as required
FBI	Federal Bureau of Investigation	Criminal investigative agency of the US Justice Department
FCO	Foreign & Commonwealth Office	UK Ministry of Foreign Affairs
FPA	Forensic Pathology Alliance	A division of LGC[b]

---

[a] Hygeco is actually the parent company of BJL, but the two names are at times used interchangeably in the witness evidence.

[b] Set up in collaboration with Forensic Pathology Services, a major group of Home Office pathologists.

TIMELINE OF EVENTS

8.15 a.m.	Monceau phones Hauffman instructing her to call a female embalmer – complying with the original request from Ross Meeting between Bestard and Coujard Coujard receives Lecomte's body examination reports for Diana and Dodi
8.20	Moss phones Donnelly with request for ice for Diana's body Henri Paul autopsy commences
8.30	Coujard issues burial certificates for Diana and Dodi
8.45	Mme Chirac views Diana's body with the Jays
9.00	Donnelly phones Caltiau of PFG requesting ice for Diana's body Hauffman calls Amarger to tell her she will be needed to carry out the embalming Monceau leaves his house heading to the hospital Launay phones his assistant, Dupont Chapillon phones Jauze to ask him to be ready to handle Dodi's repatriation Royal coroner, John Burton, calls Buckingham Palace and is told that Diana is being repatriated that day via RAF Northolt and it is likely she will be buried at Windsor Castle
9.20	A police Commissaire phones Plumet "a number of times" Lionel Jospin, PM, views Diana's body with Michael Jay
9.30	Mather arrives at Buckingham Palace
9.35	Monceau arrives at the hospital
9.45	Hauffman calls Amarger to give specific instructions to attend the hospital Moss phones Plumet to officially engage PFG for the repatriation
10.00	Monceau enters Diana's room for the first time Henri Paul autopsy concludes
10.05	Jauze arrives at work at PFG
10.15	Plumet calls Launay to confirm PFG are handling the case
10.30	Amarger leaves for the hospital First post-death phone call between Tony Blair and the Queen
10.45	Amarger arrives at the hospital
11.00	Plumet calls Jauze and tells him to go to the Ritz Hotel

	Clive Leverton meets with Keith and Tassell – they learn from Mather that they have to leave the UK at 2 p.m.[a]
	Royal Standard from Lord Chamberlain arrives at Levertons
	Levertons are told that the plane with Diana's body will arrive at RAF Northolt at 7 p.m. (8 p.m. French time)
	Amarger enters Diana's room for the first time
	Tony Blair's tribute to Diana – the "People's Princess"
11.15 a.m.	Charrier arrives at the hospital
11.30	Tebbutt and Burrell arrive at the hospital
	Plumet calls Launay to inform him a coffin will be arriving at Villacoublay and Charles will be coming on another plane, which will be met at Villacoublay by Jay, and they will come to the hospital
	Robert Thompson arrives at Fulham Mortuary and finds "several men in dark suits" who appear to be "police officers from Royalty Protection"
11.45	Launay calls Dupont to tell him to work on the Dodi body repatriation
	Tebbutt finds the room "getting hotter" and he is told Diana is "melting"
12.00 p.m.	Blankets are put up in Diana's room to shut out the media
	Air conditioners are put into Diana's room
12.15	Monceau talks with Moss
12.25	Charles' bodyguard, Peter Von-Heinz, and an advance officer enter Diana's room and put black sticky tape over the blinds
12.30	Commencement of embalming
	Royal family arrives at Crathie church for service that fails to mention Princess Diana
1.15	Launay leaves his house heading to the airport
1.30	Conclusion of embalming
1.45	Kingsmill arrives at the hospital
2.00	Launay arrives at Villacoublay Airport
	Dr Bernard Kouchner[b] views Diana's body
	Meeting at the hospital to organise security and media for Charles' visit
2.05	Clive Leverton, David Green and Bill Fry leave from RAF Northolt
3.22	Charles leaves Aberdeen on the royal flight

[a] French time.
[b] French Minister of Health.

TIMELINE OF EVENTS

3.30 p.m.	Plumet and Jauze arrive at the IML[a]
	Stoneham receives a call notifying him of the Scotland Yard pre-post-mortem meeting
3.40	Patrick Launay, Clive Leverton, David Green and Bill Fry arrive at the hospital
4.05	Repatriation of Dodi's body held up by Lecomte
4.15	Coffin porters arrive at the hospital
4.35	Dodi's body released from IML – witnessed by Jauze and Plumet[b]
4.40	Jauze and Plumet leave IML
4.50	Jauze and Plumet arrive at the hospital
5.00	Charles, Sarah and Jane's royal flight arrives at Villacoublay airport
5.15	Pre-post-mortem meeting held at New Scotland Yard – attended by Jeffrey Rees, Philip Stoneham, Richard Wall and Dennis Sharp
5.30	Keith Leverton leaves for RAF Northolt
5.40	Charles, Sarah and Jane arrive at the hospital
6.15	Diana's body leaves the hospital
6.25	Dodi's body arrives at Fulham Mortuary
7.00	Diana's body arrives at Villacoublay
6.00[c]	Commencement of Dodi's post-mortem
6.30	Remembrance service at St Paul's Cathedral
7.00	Diana's body arrives at RAF Northolt
7.13	Charles boards plane for return trip to Balmoral
7.15	Conclusion of Dodi's post-mortem
7.25	Dodi's coffin leaves Fulham Mortuary
7.35	Diana's body arrives at Fulham Mortuary accompanied by Sarah and Jane
7.55	Chain and 4 photographs removed from Diana's body
8.05	Chain and 4 photographs given to Michael Walker
8.15	Burgess and Keith Brown leave Fulham Mortuary heading home
8.21	Commencement of Diana's post-mortem
8.30	Departure from Fulham Mortuary of Sarah and Jane with Paul Mellor
11.20	Conclusion of Diana's post-mortem

---

[a] Events at the IML, particularly involving the movement of Dodi's body, have been covered in Part 3.

[b] See Part 3.

[c] From this point times are UK time. All previous times were Paris time.

11.40 p.m.	Diana's body moved to St James' Palace

Sep 1

12.30 a.m.	DS Richard Wall places head hair samples from Diana and Dodi into a locked safe at New Scotland Yard
1.00	Thompson leaves the Fulham Mortuary
4.00	Conclusion of UK embalming of Diana
9.50	Wall deposits the head hair samples into a sealed bag in the OCG store at New Scotland Yard

Introduction

Events moved very quickly following the death of Princess Diana in a Paris hospital in the early hours of 31 August 1997.

Within 25 hours Diana's body had been subjected to a quick autopsy and embalming inside the hospital; a rapid repatriation involving her ex-husband, Prince Charles; a full three hour post-mortem at a London mortuary and a four hour embalming at St James' Palace.

1   Autopsy[a] in Paris[b]

At 5.30 a.m. on 31 August 1997, precisely 1 hour and 20 minutes after Princess Diana's official death announcement, Dominique Lecomte, Head of the Paris IML[c], carried out an examination of her body.

Prof Bruno Riou, Senior Duty Anaesthetist, La Pitié: 7 Mar 06 Paget Description of Statement: **Jury Didn't Hear**:

"After about thirty minutes in the 'Recovery Room', the Princess of Wales was moved to the Operating Theatre, a little further down the corridor.... This would have been at about 0230hrs [2.30 a.m.].... There, they tried to save the Princess of Wales, but at 0400hrs, she was pronounced "life extinct". The body of the Princess of Wales was then moved to room 1S.012, also off the corridor.... In 1997, this was a quiet room that doctors used to use to speak with families of seriously ill or injured patients. This room has since changed shape and has had an extra wall put in. It is in this room, that Professor Lecomte conducted a physical, external examination of the Princess of Wales' body. The body lay to rest in this room until about 0700hrs [7.00 a.m.]." [2]

Maud Coujard, Deputy Public Prosecutor, Paris: 20 Nov 07: 15.1:

Burnett: Q. There was no need to have an autopsy of either passenger, but you decided, in consultation with the Public Prosecutor[d], to organise an external examination. Is that a fair summary?

A. I could add two sophistications. The one was that in August, we knew that the Princess of Wales had undergone extended medical examinations. The second thing that I would like to say, the fact that I was not the one who

---

[a] Throughout this chapter it is important to understand what an autopsy is. The terms autopsy and post-mortem are interchangeable. The Oxford definition of an autopsy is: "an examination of a dead body to discover the cause of death".

[b] This issue was first addressed in the Pregnancy chapter of Part 2 – see p199.

[c] Institute of Forensic Medicine.

[d] Gabriel Bestard.

made the decision. It is the Public Prosecutor that made it after discussion with me.

....Q. Did a time come a little later that morning when you were provided with the results of [Lecomte's] examinations?

A. Yes, I think it was at about 8/8.30 in the morning, but once again it is too long ago for me to remember precisely.

Q. Having received the results of the examination, did you produce a certificate releasing the bodies of Mr Al Fayed and the Princess of Wales for burial?

A. Yes, it meant that actually there were not any barriers to their burial.

Q. Did that mean that having issued your certificate, there was no legal reason for the bodies to be retained for forensic examination in France?

A. Well, it meant that there was no forensic reason to retain the bodies and it meant that the funeral formalities could start.

At 44.12: Mansfield: Q. The forensic examination that you requested in relation to Princess Diana. At the time that you authorised or ordered that, were you aware that there was to be, in the United Kingdom, a full autopsy?

A. No, I do not think so.

Maud Coujard: 15 Nov 06 Statement: **Jury Didn't Hear**:

"The question was never asked as to whether we should conduct an autopsy on Henri Paul, this was evident, as he was the driver. However, the decision to make during the night was whether to carry out post mortems on the Princess of Wales and Mr Al Fayed.

"As I had been present whilst the driver was being removed from the vehicle, we were certain that Henri Paul was the driver of the vehicle involved in the accident, and that there could not have been a change around. The two other deceased parties were therefore passengers. We therefore proceeded the way we normally do in relation to road traffic accidents and only ordered the autopsy of the driver, Henri Paul. Nevertheless the Public Prosecutor or I, without being any more precise, decided to request that an experienced forensic pathologist proceed with an external physical examination of the bodies of the Princess of Wales and Dodi Al Fayed. Professor Lecomte accepted this task, which she conducted, to my knowledge, early the next morning.

"The Sunday morning, I met up with the Public Prosecutor and to my recollection a deputy, and we discussed the accident.... A Judicial Police officer brought me the reports from Professor Lecomte. I speak from memory, as I have not seen the Dossier since. I think I can recall that Dodi Al Fayed had multiple trauma injuries and that he had a fracture of the spine or the spinal cord. Whereas the Princess of Wales, after cardiac massage that had been conducted and the operation she had, died of a rupture of the pulmonary vein. Having viewed these documents I issued the burial certificates." [3]

Maud Coujard: 15 Nov 06 Statement: **Jury Didn't Hear**:

"Question: Do you recall what instructions you gave to Professor Lecomte in relation to the examination of the bodies? What were the consequences of the conclusions of Professor Lecomte on your role as deputy Public Prosecutor?

"Answer: For us, Magistrates to the Prosecutor's office, ordering an external physical examination of a body has a precise significance: this signifies that the expert will conduct a meticulous and attentive examination of the body, describe all traces of injury from force or marks. Having examined the bodies thus, the expert will make conclusion as seen fit. I therefore gave no precise instructions to Professor Lecomte, the request for an external examination suffices in itself." [4]

Martine Monteil, Head of Brigade Criminelle: 15 Nov 06 Statement: **Jury Didn't Hear**:

"I should point out that in road traffic accidents, it is not usual to carry out a post mortem on the passengers because in most cases it is not relevant to the investigation. In the event, it was the Public Prosecutor's Department that decided to examine the bodies of both the Princess of Wales and of Dodi Al Fayed. It was the Public Prosecutor's Department, acting on the basis of an expedited police investigation at that time who, in the light of the results, decided to issue the burial certificates without any restrictions." [5]

Martine Monteil: 15 Nov 06 Statement: **Jury Didn't Hear**:

"I then also had to dispatch a team of officers to the Institute of Forensic Medicine to be present at the examinations of the bodies of the Princess of Wales and Dodi Al Fayed by Professor Lecomte. I also appointed an officer to be present at the post mortem on the driver, Henri Paul." [6]

Prof Dominique Lecomte, Pathologist and Head of IML, Paris: 9 Mar 05 Statement: **Jury Didn't Hear**:

"Question: Was a pregnancy test carried out on the mortal remains of Lady Diana Frances Spencer?

Answer: No, because that was not requested.

Question: Is that current practice?

Answer: I act in accordance with the task entrusted to me.

Question: Do you know whether a test for pregnancy was done before the examination which you carried out on Lady Diana's body at la Salpêtrière?

Answer: I have no knowledge of that at all.

Question: Do you know what the doctors did to the body beforehand?

Answer: No, when I arrived I made an external examination. I did not take any samples.

Question: Did you examine the uterus?

Answer: No, I did not make any internal examination.

Question: Do you know whether anyone else took samples from the body before your intervention?

Answer: I do not. As soon as my external examination was finished, I left the scene, then returned to the IML to draw up my report.

....Question: In France, after such an accident, can there be an autopsy?

Answer: It happens, but mainly as regards the driver. Nevertheless the identity of a victim, even a passenger, can be taken into account and justify an autopsy.

Question: Was Mr Al Fayed the subject of an external examination at la Salpêtrière?

Answer: Yes, it was I who examined him on his arrival at the IML at 6.45 a.m.[a] Again, that was an external examination.

....Question: Did you take notes at the time of the examination which you carried out on the Princess's body?

Answer: Yes, I always take notes." [7]

Prof Dominique Lecomte: 31 May 06 Statement: **Jury Didn't Hear**:

"On 31st August 1997 at 5.30 a.m., I examined the body of Princess Diana at the emergency department of the Pitié Salpêtrière hospital, as I have stated in my report dated 31/08/97. No samples were taken from the body of the Princess, in fact no request for autopsy or autopsy was conducted on this body. On 31/08/97 at 6.46 a.m., I examined the body of El Fayed recorded at the IML as No 2146.... In fact, no request for autopsy or autopsy was conducted on this body." [8][b]

---

[a] Lecomte has stated here that she "examined [Dodi] on his arrival at the IML at 6.45 a.m." This evidence indicates that Dodi's body arrived at the IML at 6.45 a.m. – almost 6½ hours after the crash. Henri Paul's "Receipt of Cadaver" form – reproduced in Part 3, Figure 1 – shows an arrival time at the IML of 3.40 a.m. This raises the question: Why did Dodi's body arrive approximately 3 hours later than Henri's? There was never any documentation provided to the jury regarding the movement of Dodi's body after the crash, and particularly nothing regarding his arrival at the IML. In his statement to the British police Jean-Claude Mulès, Brigade Criminelle Commander, said that he "gave the order at the scene that the bodies [of Dodi and Henri] could be removed to the IML by police transport". Mulès added that this was "for expediency". He said that the bodies "were transported using separate police vehicles" and Mulès recalled "both these vehicles departing the scene at the same time". So, we have the bodies of Dodi and Henri both being removed from the crash scene "at the same time" – Mulès – but Henri arriving at the IML at 3.40 a.m. – "receipt of cadaver" document – and Dodi arriving at about 6.45 a.m. – Lecomte. Source: Jean-Claude Mulès, Witness Interview, 19 July 2006, p3.

[b] It is interesting that Lecomte's claim that "No samples were taken" relates only to Diana – she doesn't claim this with regard to Dodi. This may be because there is documentary evidence – Mulès' police report, shown later – that samples were

Jean-Claude Mulès, Commander Brigade Criminelle: 5 Feb 08: 8.20:
Hilliard: Q. [Your 31 August 1997 report]: "Having been informed of the
death of the Princess of Wales, at 4 o'clock, I was instructed by my
department to go immediately to the La Pitié Salpêtrière Hospital ... to assist
Professor Dominique Lecomte, for observations on the body, the report of
which will be contained in a separate statement ...[a] I was also instructed to go
to the Institute of Forensic Medicine for the same purpose in respect of the
bodies of Dodi Al Fayed and Henri Paul." Do you see that?
A. Yes.
Q. Is that what you did?
A. It is what I wrote. When you work for the Criminal Brigade, what you
write, you do and what you do, you write.
Dr Eva Steiner, Inquest & Paget Expert on French Law: 21 Nov 07: 78.4:
A. According to article 74[b], when a sudden death has occurred, the Public
Prosecutor, with the assistance of the police officer, may go to the scene of
the death and take all measures which are required, which includes a report
by a medical doctor to check whether or not the death is suspicious, to
determine the cause of the death. But this is not – at the first stage, it is not a
post mortem, at this stage. It can be a post mortem if there is strong suspicion
that the death is caused by another thing than an accident, in case of a car
crash, but in this case I reckon there have not been such a procedure.
Hough: Q. Well, in this case, what happened was that there was a post
mortem ordered by the prosecutor on the body of driver, Henri Paul, but only
external examination of the others involved, specifically Princess Diana. To
what extent is that normal?
A. This is a routine procedure, I would say....[c]
Q. But whether somebody is the driver of a vehicle in a fatal accident or one
of the other occupants and sadly dies, is it purely a matter of the prosecutor's

---

indeed taken from Dodi. Such documentary evidence does not exist for the body of
Princess Diana.
[a] The words not read out are: "in the form of a sub-file". See INQ0000058 on inquest
website.
[b] Of the Code of Criminal Procedure.
[c] Despite the context, Steiner is not referring to the examinations of the passengers,
but the post-mortem on the driver. The rest of Steiner's answer is: "This is routine
procedure because the reason why, actually, there is a post mortem of the driver is
that obviously if the driver was driving under the use of alcohol or offensive drugs or
substances, we have to determine that because there might be – first of all, it will
determine the cause of the death, obviously – the cause of the accident, I should say –
and secondly there might be issues of civil liability arising from that. In this case, to
the best of my knowledge, the driver was an employee and was acting in the course
of his employment, so the passengers, whether alive or not, or their heirs, their
dependants, have to know what was the cause of the death for civil liability because
here, unfortunately, most of the people died."

discretion whether to order an examination and what kind of examination to order?

A. Yes. It is even the matter of the Public Prosecutor's discretion to authorise a post mortem of the driver. They do that in a routine way, but there is nothing in the Code of Criminal Procedure which says that we should have a post mortem for the driver. And I feel sorry for the passengers – usually, there is no post mortem for the passengers because it is completely irrelevant.

Dr Eva Steiner: 29 Sep 06 Statement: **Jury Didn't Hear**:

"Under article 74 of the Code of Criminal Procedure, the Public Prosecutor may, in the case of violent or suspicious death and 'if he considers it necessary', appoint an expert to ascertain the cause of the death. This, again, was done in this case, Dr Lecomte concluding that the death was not suspicious and was the result of the crash. At this stage the authorisation to embalm could legally proceed." [9]

Dr Robert Chapman, Pathologist, UK: 24 Feb 05 Statement: **Jury Didn't Hear**:

Commenting on findings in the later UK post-mortem: "There was no evidence of a formal postmortem examination having taken place." [10]

UK 41
D83

FORENSIC REPORT

stamped:]
SEEN AND
ATTACHED/Officer
of the Criminal
Investigation Police

[signed and seal]

Jean-Claude
MULES

I, the undersigned, Professor LECOMTE, a national expert, doctor of medicine at the University of Paris, based at the Institute of Forensic Medicine, 2 Place Mazas, Paris 12, at the request of Madam Prosecutor Coujard, acting on the authority of the State Prosecutor in accordance with article 74 of the Penal Procedural Code, having firstly sworn to serve the cause of justice faithfully and to the best of my ability, at 0530 hrs on 31.8.97 attended the Accident and Emergency Department of the Pitié Salpétrière Hospital in order to examine the body identified in the police investigation as that of Princess Diana. I noted :

- a sutured incision from a transversal thoracotomy;
- a sutured wound at the right paramedian forehead, plus an abrasion of the upper lip;
- a linear ecchymotic abrasion to the right of the neck;
- an abraded lateral upper right abdominal area;
- two sutured antero-external wounds to the right buttock, and multiple abrasions to the right leg and the left ankle;
- a haematoma to the left buttock and haematomas to the back of the right and left hands;
- massive crushing of the rib cage.

From my examination, I conclude that death was due to internal haemorrhaging as a result of crushing of the rib cage and to the phenomenon of deceleration, causing a rupture of the pericardium and a wound to the left pulmonary vein, upon which surgery was performed.

Paris, 31 August 1997
[Signature]

Professor Dominique LECOMTE
Institute of Forensic Medicine
2, Place Mazas
75012 PARIS

Figure 1

Professor Lecomte's official report of Diana's post-death examination. It is notable that it fails to specifically state that this examination was only external. Instead Lecomte does state that she was able to determine an internal cause of death "from my examination". This key document was not made available to the inquest jury.

Comment: The issues are:

1) Was it normal practice to carry out an examination on the body of a passenger in a car crash?

2) What was the nature of the examination that Lecomte conducted?

3) Why did the examination take place?

It is very significant that the inquest jury didn't see or hear:

a) any documentation relating to this examination of Diana's body in Paris[a]

b) any evidence from Professor Lecomte, the pathologist who conducted this critical body examination.[b]

The witness evidence describing the operation that was carried out is:

- Coujard: "an external physical examination" of both bodies[c]
- Monteil: "the examinations of the bodies"[d]
- Riou: "a physical, external examination"
- Lecomte: "an external examination" of both Diana and Dodi[e] – in 2005
- Lecomte: "no ... autopsy was conducted" on either Diana or Dodi – in 2006
- Mulès: "observations on the body"
- Chapman: "there was no evidence of a formal postmortem examination".

Of these the jury heard only the Mulès account: "observations on the body".

The jury also heard descriptions from the lawyers present: Burnett – "an external examination" and Mansfield – "the forensic examination".

It is significant that the only eye-witness of the Princess Diana examination to have ever been questioned about what took place is the pathologist, Dominique Lecomte.[f] Lecomte and Mulès are the only identified

---

[a] The issue of documentation is discussed later in this chapter.

[b] Part 3 has revealed how Lecomte refused to appear at the inquest and the judge, Scott Baker, subsequently withheld all of Lecomte's police statement evidence from the jury.

[c] Although Coujard has described the examination as "external", it is in the context of discussion relating to a post mortem: "the decision to make during the night was whether to carry out post mortems". A post-mortem determines cause of death – in the case of Diana, the cause of death was internal and could not be discovered from an external examination.

[d] Monteil also refers to the examination of the bodies in the context of the relevance of conducting "a post mortem on the passengers" in a road accident.

[e] Lecomte's evidence is discussed in more detail below.

[f] In Part 3 Lecomte was shown to have lied in her evidence on the autopsies of Mercedes driver, Henri Paul.

people present. Later evidence[a] will show that police photos were taken – Mulès, Monteil, Shepherd – and Monteil has stated that she "had to dispatch a team of officers".[b]

Mulès is the only police officer present to have ever been identified and – although Mulès indicated a report was raised – no police report on Diana's body examination has ever surfaced.[c]

Lecomte's report – reproduced above – <u>does not state that the examination was external</u>. Neither does her report of Dodi's body examination – shown later. The first documentary evidence that indicates either examination could have been external was from police commander Jean-Claude Mulès on 5 September 1997 – reproduced later.

Although Lecomte's witness evidence in 2005 is that these examinations were external, and in 2006 they were not autopsies, the documentary evidence – Lecomte's two reports, Mulès' 31 August 1997 report (see below), Mulès' report on Dodi – all completed on the day, indicates that autopsies did actually take place.

Lecomte's "forensic report" of Diana's examination clearly states: "<u>From my examination,</u> I conclude that death was due to ... a rupture of the pericardium and a wound to the left pulmonary vein, upon which surgery was performed."

In other words, on 31 August 1997, after conducting Diana's examination, Lecomte stated in writing that she had determined the cause of death "from my examination". I suggest that it is impossible to conclude that a person has a ruptured pericardium and a wounded left pulmonary vein by an external examination.[d] And, as mentioned earlier, Lecomte does not claim in that document that the examination was external – she calls it a "forensic report" and stated that her job was to "examine the body".

So, a clear conflict of evidence: Lecomte stating under oath to police in 2005 and 2006:
-    "I made an external examination"
-    "I did not make any internal examination"
-    "as soon as my external examination was finished"
-    "no ... autopsy was conducted on this body".

But in 1997, the form Lecomte completed on the day states that she made internal cause of death findings from that examination.

---

[a] Later in this chapter.
[b] Monteil stated that these officers were sent to the IML, whereas the examination of Princess Diana took place at La Pitié Salpêtrière Hospital.
[c] There is a police report for Dodi's body examination – reproduced later in this chapter.
[d] The nature of these injuries has been outlined in Part 2.

In Mulès' report on the day – read to the jury – he describes being "instructed ... to assist ... Lecomte, for observations on the body". Then Mulès adds: "I was also instructed to go to the Institute of Forensic Medicine for the same purpose in respect of the bodies of Dodi Al Fayed and Henri Paul."

In saying this, Mulès has stated that his attendance "in respect of the bodies of Dodi Al Fayed and Henri Paul" and "the Princess of Wales" was all "for the same purpose" – "to assist ... Lecomte, for observations on the body". We already know – see Part 3 – that what took place in respect of Henri Paul was a full autopsy.

In this 31 August 1997 report Mulès appears to have equated what took place in respect of Diana and Dodi with what occurred to Henri Paul.

I suspect that Mulès' examination report of Diana's body – which has never surfaced – would support this, along with the report completed by Professor Lecomte (discussed above) – indicating an autopsy took place.

At the inquest Mulès should have been cross-examined about the Princess Diana examination, but that never happened.

Why?

Jean-Claude Mulès, Commander Brigade Criminelle: 5 Feb 08: 17.4:
Hilliard: Q. Let's take blood for example. Once the sample of blood is taken from the body, can you help us with the procedure? What happens to the sample? What sort of container is it put in? How is it labelled? Where is it kept? Help us with the procedure that would be followed with an important item like that.
A. Before you start, before the physician takes the samples, he has at his disposal a few little bottles with reference numbers. So you take the blood from different places, from the heart, and the practitioner puts the cover onto those bottles. It is a system that is auto-blocking, self-blocking. You cannot open it anymore afterwards. Then the samples are put in a fridge for further examinations by biologists or toxicologists to be undertaken; as a matter of fact, in that hospital case, the expert being Mrs Lecomte.
Q. Can you help me, when does the label go on the sample bottle? Is the sample bottle there with a label already on it....
Comment: Mulès is being asked about procedures with autopsy blood samples, but appears to inadvertently mention the taking of blood samples "in that hospital case" by Lecomte. Mulès could not be referring to Henri Paul's autopsy, as that occurred at the IML.

I suggest that it would have been unusual for Lecomte – the head of the IML – to conduct a body examination in a hospital. But Lecomte did in the case of Princess Diana. And Mulès has already stated that he was present.

This could be an inadvertent reference by Mulès to blood samples being taken from Princess Diana's body at the La Pitié Salpêtrière Hospital on 31 August 1997.

Prof Alain Pavie, Cardiac and Thoracic Surgeon, La Pitié: 9 Mar 05

Statement: **Jury Didn't Hear**:

"Question: What actions were taken after the death [of Diana]?

Answer: Sutures were inserted over the incision in the same way as if she had been alive. That is called re-establishing skin integrity. Her body was placed in a large room. Mrs Leconte [sic], the medical examiner on duty, was called. With Mr Riou we explained to her what we had done, namely a right thoracotomy then a left and an incision at the sternum."[11]

Comment: Pavie has described a conversation occurring between Diana's death announcement – at 4.10 a.m. – and the commencement of Lecomte's examination – at 5.30 a.m.

There are three potential witnesses – Pavie, Riou and Lecomte.

Lecomte has said "No" she did not "know what the doctors did".

Riou was interviewed by Scotland Yard in March 2006. During a discourse on the events, he made no mention of this conversation.[a]

Pavie mentions it; Lecomte denies it; Riou ignores it.

Someone is lying.

This is a difficult issue – Parts 2 & 3 have already revealed that all three of these people have lied on various issues relating to this case. Lecomte is certainly the person with the most form for lying – see Part 3.[b]

Although Pavie is not specific, his testimony implies that Lecomte was called by the hospital: "Her body was placed in a large room. Mrs [Lecomte], the medical examiner on duty, was called.... We explained to her what we had done".

Maud Coujard has stated: "the Public Prosecutor or I ... decided to request that an experienced forensic pathologist proceed with an external physical examination.... Professor Lecomte accepted this task".

In her report on the day – shown earlier – Lecomte stated that she carried out the examination "at the request of Madam Prosecutor Coujard".

It would seem to be logical that an examination of Diana, Princess of Wales' body in Paris would have required some legal legitimacy – not simply a call from the hospital requesting that.

---

[a] Riou's full statement is included in *The Documents* book – see Interview, 7 March 2006. Regarding Lecomte's role, Riou said: "It is in this room, that Professor Lecomte conducted a physical, external examination of the Princess of Wales' body.": see p374, UK edition.

[b] Later evidence in this chapter will indicate that Lecomte may have had reason to lie about this conversation. It is possible that concerns were put to her – particularly by Riou – suggesting that the death of Diana may have been suspicious.

This raises an important issue: There has never been any disclosure of a written request from Coujard to Lecomte.

Why? Were Diana and Dodi's bodies examined without a formal written request?

The short answer is "not likely". This case file is littered with formal written requests from French authorities before procedures were carried out.[a]

I suggest that evidence in this chapter has and will show that such a written request may not have been for an external examination, but instead an examination to determine the cause of death.[bc] It was not possible to draw a cause of death conclusion on Diana's death without an internal examination.[d]

As this chapter progresses it will become clear that there are reasons why the authorities need this examination of Diana's body to be seen to be external, and not the autopsy that the evidence indicates it was.

I suggest that this is why the inquest jury saw and heard so little about this examination, and 90% of the evidence in this chapter is labelled "Jury Didn't Hear".

Jean Monceau, BJL Director and Embalmer, Paris: 18 Oct 05 Statement: **Jury Didn't Hear**:

"I produce as Exhibit JM/12e a copy of an example of a death certificate which would have been completed by the doctor who certified death in 1997." [12]

Prof Bruno Riou, Senior Duty Anaesthetist, La Pitié: 7 Mar 06 Paget Description of Statement: **Jury Didn't Hear**:

"DS Grater showed Professor Riou a copy of Mr Jean Monceau's exhibit JM/12 marked 'Certificat de Décès'. Professor Riou confirmed that he had completed a form similar to this one for the Princess of Wales at the time of

---

[a] The notable exceptions are: a) when unauthorised testing was carried out by Gilbert Pépin – see Part 3; b) the embalming documentation – see Chapter 2. That does not appear to be the case here – the evidence indicates that this examination request came from the Public Prosecutor's department.

[b] A close look at the body examination reports reveals that they draw conclusions on the cause of death – of both Diana and Dodi.

[c] i.e. an autopsy. The Oxford definition of an autopsy: "an examination of a dead body to discover the cause of death".

[d] Even if Lecomte has lied regarding the discussion Pavie said took place prior to the examination – see above – she would still have needed to conduct an internal examination if she were to fulfil a request for an autopsy.

[e] Both front and back of this exhibit are shown below.

her death. He explained that this was the type of Death Certificate used for administration purposes in France. He clarified that this document would not be held in the Princess of Wales' medical dossier, but that it would have been sent to the Mairie Paris XIIIe and the National Institute called INSERN [Public Records Office]. He acknowledged that this form does not show the time of death, however the Hospital records the death of a patient on their Admissions Sheet, known as "Fiche Individuel"[a]....

"On discussing the form JM/12 further, Professor Riou explained that he would probably have ticked 'OUI' [YES] box for "'Obstacle Medico-Legal (voir 2 au verso[b])', which translates as 'Medico-Legal issue'. Professor Riou clarified that by ticking the 'YES' box, it did in no way mean that a crime had occurred. He explained that the 'YES' box is normally always ticked when the death is not natural, anticipated through illness or disease, for example suicide, car crash etc... By ticking the 'YES' box, it means that a Legal Physician must examine the body prior to allowing it to be released for burial or cremation. This examination can be either external physical examination, as in the case of the Princess of Wales, or autopsy. It is this which led to the physical external examination of the Princess of Wales by Professor Lecomte on the morning of 31st August 1997." [13]

Comment: Both Monceau and Riou have given evidence that after the death of Princess Diana this "Death Certificate" form – labelled JM/12 by the British police – would have been and was completed.[c]

So, where is it?

The completed form has never surfaced in any police investigation and it was not presented at the inquest.

---

[a] This appears on p344 of *The Documents* book (UK edition).

[b] This translates as "see 2 overleaf" – see blank JM/12 form below.

[c] Riou completed another form, also a death certificate, which is reproduced on p676 of Part 2 – that one was available to the jury, in the original French. In completing that form – the English version of which appears in *The Documents* book p391 (UK edit.) – Riou appears to have signed a pre-printed document that states: "This patient did not ... pose any forensic medical problem." It is possible that this 2nd death certificate was completed after the conclusion of Lecomte's autopsy of Diana. Riou should have been challenged by the British police regarding the apparent conflict between the JM/12 form and this 2nd certificate, but that never happened. A third form was also discussed in the Riou interview (p375 of *The Documents* book): "DS Grater showed Professor Riou a copy of a document obtained via the Foreign and Commonwealth Office (FCO).... Professor Riou confirmed that this is the form on which he recorded the Princess of Wales' death and her time of death immediately after she was deceased. He also confirmed his signature. He explained that this is the form used for certification of death at the hospital and for hospital administration purposes." That form was also not shown to the inquest jury.

AUTOPSY IN PARIS

[TN: Printed form - relevant parts only translated]

JM/12

DEATH CERTIFICATE
In accordance with the decree of 24 December 1996

DEPARTMENT:

To be completed by the Doctor

DISTRICT:

The undersigned doctor of medicine certifies that the death of the person named opposite
on _____ at __ hrs is real and constant (see 1 overleaf)

_____ Post Code: [ ][ ][ ][ ][ ]

Medical legal obstacle (see 2 overleaf) ---------------------- [ ] YES [ ] NO

SURNAME:

Forenames:

Date of birth:_____ Sex: _____

Address :_____

_____

_____

FOR TOWN HALL USE ONLY

At _____ on

The serial number of death in the Register entered opposite must be reproduced overleaf

SERIAL NO
OF DEATH:
[ ][ ][ ][ ][ ]

Signature (legible surname) and doctor's stamp (mandatory)

Figure 2

Blank death certificate form – known as JM/12 in the police files. The reverse side of this form appears below. Bruno Riou stated that he completed this form in relation to the death of Princess Diana on 31 August 1997. There are several points: 1) If Riou did complete this form, it has never surfaced. 2) Describing Riou's interview, DS Philip Easton stated: "[Riou] acknowledged that this form does not show the time of death". Even a cursory look at the form shows that it does have provision for the time of death – the form reads: "The death of the person named opposite on [blank space] at [blank space] hrs is real and constant." On the reverse side the instructions say: "The date and time of death must be given". 3) Riou provided evidence regarding this form that appears to conflict with the account from Maud Coujard – see below. The jury did not get to see this blank form. (TN = Translator's Note).

[TN: Printed form – relevant parts only translated]

NOTES FOR COMPLETING THE ADMINISTRATION SECTION

IMPORTANT

1. The date and time of death must be given - where applicable, approximately. Do not quote the date of the report. However, in the event of a death that presents a medical legal obstacle, these details will be confirmed subsequently in the forensic expert's report.
2. Medical legal obstacle: suicide or suspicious death, the origin of which appears to be related to an offence. In this case, the body is at the disposal of the judicial authorities. The following funeral arrangements are suspended until authorisation is given by the judicial authority:
    -   Handing over of the body (article R363-10 of the Local Authority Code)
    -   Embalming (article 365-8 of the Local Authority Code)
    -   Transportation of the body to the home of the deceased or to a medical establishment prior to its placing in the coffin (article R363-6 of the Local Authority Code)
    -   Admission to a funeral parlour prior to placing in the coffin (articles R361-37 and R361-38 of the Local Authority Code)
    -   Taking samples with a view to investigating the cause of death (article R363-11 of the Local Authority Code)
    -   Closing the coffin (article 363-18 of the Local Authority Code)
    -   Burial (as a result)
    -   Cremation (article R361-42 of the Local Authority Code).

The same funeral arrangements are suspended when there is a claim linked to the cause of death (accident at work, occupational illness, or as a result of injuries for a person receiving a war pension).

Figure 3

Reverse side of JM/12 "Death Certificate" form shown above.

During Riou's 2006 police interview he stated "that he would probably have ticked 'OUI' [YES] box for ... 'Medico-Legal issue'[a]. Professor Riou clarified that by ticking the 'YES' box, it did in no way mean that a crime had occurred. He explained that the 'YES' box is normally always ticked when the death is not natural, anticipated through illness or disease, for example suicide, car crash etc... By ticking the 'YES' box, it means that a legal physician must examine the body prior to allowing it to be released for burial or cremation. This examination can be either external physical examination, as in the case of the Princess of Wales, or autopsy. It is this which led to the physical external examination of the Princess of Wales by Professor Lecomte on the morning of 31st August 1997."

---

[a] This shows on the form as "Medical Legal Obstacle".

This evidence raises several concerns:

1) Riou said that "ticking the 'YES' box ... did in no way mean that a crime had occurred", but the form's instructions say: "Medical legal obstacle: suicide or suspicious death, the origin of which appears to be related to an offence".

When one considers that Diana's death could not possibly have been a suicide – see Parts 1 and 2 – it becomes clear that Riou has stated the opposite to what the form says. According to the form if "YES" is ticked then the death is "suspicious" and "an offence" appears to have been committed. Whereas Riou has said that "YES" is ticked for a "car crash".

2) Riou states that "by ticking the 'YES' box, it means that a legal physician must examine the body". The reverse of the form actually states that ticking the 'YES' box puts "the body ... at the disposal of the judicial authorities".[a] It then goes on to preclude a long list of activities "until authorisation is given by the judicial authority".[b] Having said this, Riou may still be correct in saying an examination is inevitable – the reverse of the form states: "in the event of a death that presents a medical legal obstacle, these details [of date and time of death] will be confirmed subsequently in the forensic expert's report.[c]" It appears to be significant though, that Riou – who must have been familiar with the procedure as he had been a doctor for 21 years[de] – fails to mention the required involvement of the Public Prosecutor's Department.[fg]

3) The general evidence is that examinations are not carried out on the bodies of passengers in a car crash:[h]

---

[a] The general evidence shows that in this particular case the initial decisions regarding the bodies were made by the judicial authorities.

[b] It could be significant that the list of suspended activities includes "taking samples with a view to investigating the cause of death", yet there is no mention of external examinations.

[c] Lecomte's report doesn't include those details.

[d] 15 Nov 07:2.2

[e] At the time of this interview in 2006.

[f] This issue is addressed in the Conclusion section of this chapter.

[g] Issues relating to the JM/12 form are discussed further in the Conclusion section of this chapter.

[h] There are also indications in Coujard's evidence that she may have been aware that what occurred was not normal practice. When Coujard says in her statement – not heard by the jury – that it was normal to order an autopsy of the driver, she then adds "nevertheless" she or Bestard "decided to request that an experienced forensic

- Steiner – "usually, there is no post mortem[a] for the passengers because it is completely irrelevant"
- Monteil – "it is not usual to carry out a post mortem on the passengers because in most cases it is not relevant".[b]

In direct contrast, Riou has stated that: a) "the 'YES' box is normally always ticked when the death is not natural"; and b) "by ticking the 'YES' box, it means that a legal physician must examine the body".

The logical summary of those two statements (a and b) is that if a death is not natural (e.g. car crash) then the body must be the subject of examination – be it driver or passenger.

This is contrary to the general evidence that examinations are normally only carried out on the driver.

4) Coujard presented a completely different picture in her evidence – she said that "it is the Public Prosecutor that made [the examination decision] after discussion with me".

Coujard made no mention at all of a form completed by a doctor determining that an examination of the passengers must take place.

In summary, there are only three witnesses – Riou, Pavie, Coujard – who have provided accounts of the process that occurred after Princess Diana's death:

- Riou: the completion of Form JM/12 including ticking "YES" for "Medico-Legal issue" – this directly led to a required examination, which was external
- Pavie: the calling of Lecomte; a discussion between Riou, Pavie and Lecomte
- Coujard: a decision by Public Prosecutor Bestard to request an external examination – this request is made by Coujard to Lecomte[c], who "accepted" and conducted the examination.

---

pathologist proceed with an external physical examination" of Diana and Dodi's bodies. In her statement Coujard is cagey about disclosing who actually authorised this procedure: "the Public Prosecutor or I, without being any more precise". At the inquest Coujard stated that it was Bestard.

[a] Post-Mortem: Oxford definition: "an examination of a dead body to establish the cause of death". The Lecomte examination reports for both Diana and Dodi both conclude with a cause of death based on the results of the examination. This is discussed further in this current chapter.

[b] Monteil goes on to say: "In the event, it was the Public Prosecutor's Department that decided to examine the bodies". She doesn't appear to distinguish between the words "post mortem" and "examine". This is supported by the Oxford definition of a post mortem: "an examination of a dead body to establish the cause of death".

[c] Coujard said in her November 2006 statement: "I ... gave no precise instructions to Professor Lecomte, the request for an external examination suffices in itself."

Monceau supports Riou's account that the JM/12 form would have been completed and this would seem logical – why would this death certificate form exist if it was not filled out in the event of a death?

Coujard's evidence was: "the decision to make during the night was whether to carry out post mortems on the Princess of Wales and Mr Al Fayed".

Why did Coujard say this, when the evidence from Monteil and Steiner indicates that such an issue was normally "irrelevant"? This question will be dealt with shortly.

There are several reasons that have been put forward by witnesses to justify the decision to examine the bodies of Diana and Dodi:

-    Riou: "a Legal Physician must examine the body ... when the death is not natural ... for example suicide, car crash"

-    Coujard: "in August, we knew that the Princess of Wales had undergone extended medical examinations" – at the inquest

-    Lecomte: "the identity of a victim, even a passenger, can be taken into account and justify an autopsy".

It is significant that Bestard was not heard from at the inquest – Coujard stated that "I was not the one who made the decision – it is the Public Prosecutor that made it after discussion with me" – so Bestard is the obvious person to explain why. Since Coujard was there when he made the decision, she should be the next best witness on this subject.

Although Steiner did not directly put forward a reason for the examinations, her evidence on this point is significant. She stated at the inquest: "It can be a post mortem if there is strong suspicion that the death is caused by another thing than an accident, in case of a car crash, but in this case I reckon there have not been such a procedure."[a]

Steiner has put forward "strong suspicion that the death is caused by another thing than an accident" as a reason for a post mortem, but then strongly qualified that: "in this case I reckon there have not been such a procedure" – without going on to explain what she felt the procedure was in this case.

Steiner, who was the inquest's expert on French law, comes across as somewhat embarrassed that the body examinations of Diana and Dodi took place at all: "And I feel sorry for the passengers – usually, there is no post mortem for the passengers because it is completely irrelevant."

---

[a] Effectively, this appears to be a conflict of evidence: if the examination by Lecomte was to determine cause of death, which Steiner agrees it was, then it was a post-mortem, by definition – see earlier.

Riou's explanation for the examination – that it must occur after a car crash – flies in the face of the general evidence that it is not relevant to examine the bodies of dead passengers after a car crash. Riou appears to have come up with this to retrospectively justify ticking "YES" in the medico-legal issue box of the death certificate. This issue is dealt with earlier and later in this chapter.

Lecomte's reasoning that it was the identity of the passengers that determined having to examine their dead bodies after the event, I suggest lacks logic – however it may be closer to the mark than other suggestions. This aspect is further addressed towards the conclusion of this chapter.

As stated above, Coujard was present when the decision to carry out the body examinations was made – she has said that Bestard made the decision "after discussion with me".

The reason Coujard has submitted – "in August, we knew that the Princess of Wales had undergone extended medical examinations" – was actually volunteered by her.[a]

Now this is an amazing statement and there are a couple of significant points to note:

1) Burnett's question did not specifically relate to Diana – his question addresses "either passenger", that is both Diana and Dodi

2) Burnett asks if it is "a fair summary" that "there was no need to have an autopsy", but Bestard and Coujard "decided ... to organise an external examination". This question appears to draw Coujard into making two responses: a) she supplies the reason why the examination was ordered: "in August, we knew that the Princess of Wales had undergone extended medical examinations"; and, b) she distances herself from the decision and pins it on Bestard.[b]

Has Coujard, at the inquest, given a plausible reason for the body examination of Princess Diana?

The timing is that Diana's death officially occurred at 4.00 a.m. and Lecomte commenced her examination of Diana's body at 5.30 a.m. So there is a window of 1½ hours for the following events to occur:

1) Notification of Diana's death to Coujard
2) Coujard calls Bestard to discuss their next moves
3) Bestard instructs Coujard to request the examinations of Diana and Dodi's bodies

---

[a] Burnett, the inquest lawyer, did not directly ask Coujard why she requested the examinations. He was asking for confirmation of what took place – not why it took place.

[b] This is something Coujard had avoided doing in her carefully worded Paget statement – she stated then: "The Public Prosecutor or I, without being any more precise, decided to request ... an external physical examination".

4) Coujard contacts Lecomte, who is presumably asleep at home[a]
5) Lecomte travels to La Pitié Hospital
6) Lecomte meets with Riou and Pavie
7) Lecomte commences the examination of Princess Diana's body.

All of the above could have practically occurred in the 1½ hour period, but I suggest there is a problem with the acquisition of the knowledge of Diana's "extended medical examinations" in August 1997.

The question then is: How did Coujard come by this knowledge in the short interval between Diana's death – at 4 a.m. – and the making of the examination decision, probably by 5 a.m. at the latest?

Another question is: Why didn't one of the lawyers at the inquest ask Coujard: a) what she meant by this; b) how she acquired this information before 5 a.m. on 31 August 1997; and c) why that information would lead to a decision to examine the bodies of Diana and Dodi?

There may be some substance to Coujard's assertion.

Princess Diana made two known visits to doctors in the days immediately preceding her departure with Dodi for their final Mediterranean cruise on 22 August 1997.

Dr Peter Wheeler, Diana's GP: 28 Jun 06 Statement: **Jury Didn't Hear**:
"I was Diana, Princess of Wales's apothecary between January 1991 until her death on 31st August 1997. I last saw Diana, Princess of Wales on either 20th or 21st August 1997 I cannot now recall. Either way I can be certain that I saw her on the day she returned from holiday in Greece.[b] I visited her at Kensington Palace. My visit followed [a] telephone call from Diana, Princess of Wales in Greece the day previously. Diana, Princess of Wales was suffering from breakthrough bleeding[c], a condition that we had been trying to treat for approximately two months.... This condition was irritating Diana, Princess of Wales and therefore she had asked me to see her as soon as she returned to London." [14]

Dr Lily Hua Yu, Diana's Chinese Doctor: 6 Jan 05 Statement read out 20 Dec 07: 64.13:
"I am a medical doctor qualified in China.... I first started treating Diana, Princess of Wales in September 1996.... She initially came to me twice a week but, after a while, she would come to me once every two weeks.... The last time I treated Diana was on 21 August 1997, ten days before she died.... She had a close doctor and patient relationship with me."

---

[a] It is before 5.30 a.m. on a Sunday morning.
[b] This was 20 August 1997.
[c] This issue is addressed in the Pregnancy chapter in Part 5.

Comment: Dr Lily has stated that Diana would visit her "once every two weeks" – there is nothing in Lily's statement (which was read to the jury) that indicates this visit on August 21 was anything out of the ordinary.

Diana's visit to Dr Wheeler the previous day (August 20) does appear to be a special visit to address concerns over breakthrough bleeding – see Pregnancy chapter in Part 5.

It is certainly debatable whether these two doctor's visits – one of which is probably normal – could constitute "extended medical examinations", and I would suggest that it probably doesn't. Having said that, anyone monitoring Diana's phone calls – see Surveillance chapter of Part 2 – would have been aware of the Wheeler visit[a] ahead of time and possibly also the medical condition that was to be addressed.

There is a possibility that these doctor visits were known to the French authorities and the information had been exaggerated to "extended medical examinations".

One of the questions the lawyers should have asked Coujard (in the list above) was: Why would French knowledge that Diana had undergone extended medical examinations in August lead to a decision to examine the bodies of Diana and Dodi?

I suggest that in Diana's case – and Coujard only addressed evidence regarding Diana in her answer[b] – the most apparent connection between perceived extended pre-crash medical examinations and a post-death body examination would be a concern regarding pregnancy.

It could be that Bestard (via Coujard) ordered Lecomte to examine Princess Diana's body to establish if she was pregnant. It is possible that he requested the same examination procedure for Dodi to avoid arousing suspicion. Abnormal as it was to order an examination of passenger bodies – Steiner, Monteil – it would have been even more out of place to order an examination of Diana's body, but not Dodi's.[c]

---

[a] Wheeler said that he had received a "telephone call from Diana ... in Greece the day previously".

[b] Burnett was referring to both bodies in his question.

[c] The suggestion that the examination of Diana's body was more important to the French than that of Dodi's appears to be also borne out in the timing. There are two points: 1) Diana's examination occurs first, even though she died 3½ hours after Dodi. In other words, even though Dodi had died several hours earlier, it appears no decision was made to examine his body until after Diana had died. 2) A look at the earlier "Timeline of Events" shows that the examination of Diana took about 50 minutes – from 5.30 till 6.20 a.m. – whereas Dodi's only took 30 minutes – from 6.45 to 7.15 a.m. The timing of the conclusion of Diana's body examination is an estimate based on the following factors: a) it started at 5.30 a.m. at the hospital; b) Dodi's started at 6.45 a.m. at the IML; c) both were conducted by Lecomte; d) the distance between the hospital and the IML is about 1 km; e) Lecomte's evidence was

AUTOPSY IN PARIS

The police report for Dodi's body examination follows – it raises additional questions.

that she left the hospital straight after the conclusion of Diana's examination: "As soon as my external examination was finished, I left the scene, then returned to the IML to draw up my report."; f) The general evidence indicates that Dodi's body was already at the IML when Lecomte arrived; g) There is no reason to suggest there would have been a delay of more than 15 minutes between Lecomte's arrival at the IML and the commencement of Dodi's examination; h) The evidence from Riou was that Diana's body remained in the examination room until 7 a.m. – see earlier.

D 86 **UK 44**

qp

FRENCH REPUBLIC

_____

**POLICE
HEADQUARTERS**

_____

JUDICIAL POLICE
DEPARTMENT

_____

DEPARTMENT

**CRIMINAL
INVESTIGATION
DEPARTMENT**
36, Quai des Orfèvres
75001 PARIS

STATEMENT
_____

BC N° 288/97
Assistance of forensic
doctor for forensic
observations

Dodi AL-FAYED

MANSLAUGHTER

Against/ Persons
unknown

**Victim(s): Lady Diana,
AL FAYED, PAUL**

At six forty-five (06.45) hours on the thirty-first August nineteen hundred and ninety-seven,

I, **JEAN-CLAUDE MULÈS
POLICE MAJOR**

An Officer of the Judicial Police working at the CRIMINAL INVESTIGATION DEPARTMENT, continuing the investigation on the same legal basis,

Having **TRAVELLED** to the premises of the IML, 2, place Mazas in PARIS 12 for the purpose of **forensic observations** on the body of **Dodi AL FAYED,** registered at the IML under the reference 2147.

Where at the time indicated in the heading of the present sheet, we were shown the body of the person concerned. (1.75 m – 72 kg),

After having informed the forensic doctor summoned, **Professor Dominique LECOMTE,** of the circumstances of the death (fatal road traffic accident), recorded after resuscitation attempt by the emergency services deployed, **ASSIST** her in this operation.

IT IS AGREED with this practitioner that she will inform me of her conclusions at the end of her operation, which she did at **07.15 hours**, handing me the report and the sketch sheet thus drafted that I **ATTACH** the present sheet.

The following samples were taken:

- Blood,
- Urine,
- Other habitual samples.

I had **handed to me the victim's clothing** – cut for resuscitation – which will be retained in the department for possible return at the request of the family.

DULY NOTED AS AN OFFICIAL REPORT.

The Police Major
[signed and stamped]

Figure 4

This form, completed by Mulès, reveals that blood and other samples were taken from Dodi Fayed's body approximately 6 hours after the crash. A similar examination had been carried out earlier on Princess Diana's body, but no corresponding police report has ever surfaced.

AUTOPSY IN PARIS

...CTURE OF ...CE

...(RECTORATE ...THE JUDICIAL POLICE

BRIGADE
CRIMINELLE
36, Quai des
Orfevres,
75001 PARIS

STATEMENT

BC No. 293/97

Rectification,
following an mistake
caused by computer
error

INVOLUNTARY
MANSLAUGHTER,

Victim(s) : Lady
Diana, AL FAYED,
PAUL

On 5 September 1997,
at

I, JEAN-CLAUDE MULES
POLICE MAJOR
an officer of the Judicial Police attached to the BRIGADE CRIMINELLE,

in pursuance of the investigation and on the same legal basis,

State that in drafting of the statement concerning the attendance at the external medical-legal examination on the body of Emad (Dodi) AL FAYED at the Medical Legal Institute (Ref. Statement No 63 in respect of the dispatch concerning the expedited investigation), **a mistake, caused by a computer error was inserted in the text**, concerning the paragraph relating to the sampling. This prewritten paragraph, normally used to record this type of medical procedure, reads as follows

Samples were taken of:
- Blood
- Urine
- Other usual samples

I must make the point and confirm that, in line with the instructions given for this procedure, no sampling of any sort took place, the pathologist limiting his external examination to the body of the deceased.

Duly noted.

Police Major
[Signature and seal]

Figure 5

The above document, which was not presented at the inquest, was raised by Jean-Claude Mulès on 5 September 1997 – 5 days after the examination by Lecomte of Dodi Fayed's body. In this document Mulès reverses his statement – see Figure 4 – made on 31 August 1997, that blood, urine and "other usual samples" were extracted by Lecomte from Dodi's body. He blames a "computer error" that "inserted" these words into the text. Mulès notes that "the pathologist [limited] his external examination to the ... deceased" – yet the pathologist, Dominique Lecomte, is a "her" not a "his". Mulès fails to provide a credible explanation for why he would sign and seal an "official report" that states very clearly and specifically that these samples were taken, if in fact they weren't. Mulès was not asked about this at the inquest – he should have been. There has also never been an explanation for why there appears to be no "official report" for a similar examination undertaken by Lecomte, earlier the same morning, on the body of Princess Diana.

It is significant that no police report – similar to Dodi's – has ever surfaced for Diana's body examination. The evidence from Monteil was that she "had to dispatch a team of officers to ... be present at the examinations of the bodies". And there is strong evidence that the police took photos during Diana's examination – Mulès, Monteil, Shepherd[a] – so, why no police report?

There are two significant points regarding Mulès' report of Dodi's examination:

1) There is no claim in the report – written on 31 August 1997 – that this examination was external: it is called "forensic observations"

2) Mulès has stated that samples were taken – "blood, urine [and] other habitual samples": i.e. not just an external examination, contrary to witness evidence – Coujard, Lecomte.

On 5 September 1997 – 5 days after Dodi's examination – Mulès raised a new report (shown above) stating that his August 31 examination report was in error. Mulès said that "no sampling of any sort took place".

It could be significant that although the August 31 report makes no mention of the examination being only external, the September 5 report describes it as an "external medical-legal examination" and again an "external examination of the body".

So, in the official police examination report the examination is not described as "external", but "forensic". In a report 5 days after the event, intended to correct an error, the examination is twice described as "external".

The reality is that the first known evidence indicating that either Diana or Dodi's body examination were external did not appear until 5 days later – in this "correction" report drawn up by Mulès.

There is no mention of either examination being external in the following key documents:[b]

  a) Lecomte's examination report for Diana
  b) Lecomte's examination report for Dodi
  c) Mulès' examination report for Dodi.

In fact, the evidence is to the contrary:

-   in Diana's examination report Lecomte finds an internal cause of death "from my examination" – see earlier

-   in Dodi's examination report Mulès declares that samples were taken – see above.

In his September 5 report Mulès states that the extraction of samples listed in the August 31 report was a "prewritten paragraph" and was "a mistake, caused by a computer error ... inserted in the text".

---

[a] See later this chapter.

[b] The terminology used to describe the reports – the use of the word "forensic" – is addressed in the Conclusion section of this chapter.

There are several points:

1) A similar report form was completed by Mulès for the autopsy of Henri Paul.[a] A close comparison of the two reports raises several points:[bc]

- Dodi's report shows a description of the operation, on the left hand side – "Assistance of forensic doctor for forensic operations". This is completely missing on Henri's report.

- Dodi's report shows the name of the body, on the left hand side – "Dodi AL-FAYED". This is completely missing on Henri's report.

- Dodi's report reads towards the end of the form "<u>DULY NOTED AS AN OFFICIAL REPORT</u>"[d]. This is completely missing on Henri's report.

This raises the issue: Just how much of the information on these forms is "prewritten" or computer generated, as has been claimed by Jean-Claude Mulès?[e]

2) It should have been a simple matter for Mulès to attach a copy of the computer-generated form template to his 5 September 1997 statement. If what he says is correct, the list of samples taken would have shown on the template.

3) This August 31 police report is a simple and brief overview of what transpired during the examination. It seems amazing that two of the most important factors describing the examination – there is no mention of it being only external; the samples taken are listed – are completely wrong according to Mulès' September 5 statement.

In his September 5 report Mulès says: "I must make the point and confirm that, <u>in line with the instructions given</u> for this procedure, no sampling of any sort took place, the pathologist limiting <u>his</u> external examination to the body of the deceased."

This raises two additional questions:[f]

---

[a] Viewable on the inquest website: INQ0041596.

[b] Both reports have been translated by the British police from the original French – that is a drawback, that we are unable to study the original forms, which have never been made available. It is obvious that the British police should have provided the original French documents in the case of significant items of evidence, such as these police reports.

[c] The same person authored both reports – Jean-Claude Mulès.

[d] Underlined on the report.

[e] A detailed examination of the reports reveals other differences, but it may be argued that they could be put down to variations in the translation.

[f] There is a third question which may not be so significant: Why does Mulès say the pathologist limited the examination "to the body of the deceased"? As far as I know, no one has suggested Lecomte was examining anything other than the body of Dodi Fayed during this examination.

1) Where are "the instructions given"? These instructions – which were from the Public Prosecutor's Department – have never surfaced. I suggest that there is a possibility that the reason these instructions haven't appeared is that they may have required the pathologist to determine a cause of death – i.e. not a request for an external examination. This suggestion is based on logic: if one looks at the examination reports for Diana and Dodi[a] compiled by Lecomte on 31 August 1997[b] they: a) do not state the examination was external; and b) do conclude with the cause of death.[c]

2) Why has Mulès used the word "his" when the pathologist who conducted the examination – Dominique Lecomte – was female?

As Parts 1 and 3 have shown, the words – written or verbal – of Jean-Claude Mulès cannot be taken at face value. As the commander responsible for much of the investigation into the crash, he has extensive form for lying. There is no reason to suggest that the completion by Mulès of this report on 5 September 1997 is any different.

Why hasn't the equivalent police report on the body of Diana, Princess of Wales ever surfaced?[d] Why were the jury provided with a form for Dodi but not a form for Diana?

I suggest that the reason could be that a similar "error" occurred in that report – i.e. it would include a list of the samples taken. It would not be a good look for the French police to have made the identical "mistake" on both reports.

The issue of samples that may have been taken during the Diana examination is much more significant and will be discussed later in this book and in Part 5.

As stated earlier, the first mention of either Diana or Dodi's examinations being only external was on 5 September 1997, in Mulès' "correction" report – shown above.

On 20 October 1997 – seven weeks after the crash – Judge Hervé Stéphan presented the following assignment to Dominique Lecomte: "... [To provide] any information likely to assist in establishing whether or not the lesions observed or noted on the bodies of Diana Spencer, Henri Paul and Imad Al Fayed were of the type to cause the immediate deaths of the persons concerned." [15e]

---

[a] Diana's is shown earlier; Dodi's appears on p397 of *The Documents* book – UK edition.

[b] Reports drawn up in response to "the instructions given".

[c] As discussed earlier, in the case of Diana the cause of death as stated in Lecomte's report could not have been determined without an internal examination.

[d] Monteil said that she sent "a team of officers ... to be present at the examinations of the bodies of the Princess of Wales and Dodi Al Fayed" – see earlier.

[e] Appears in document on p402 of *The Documents* book (UK edit).

There has never been any explanation for why Stéphan asked this of Lecomte – it does not appear to have any obvious relevance to the issues facing the investigation.[a] In fact, it was already widely known that Princess Diana's death had not been declared until 4 a.m.[b] and that both Dodi Fayed and Henri Paul had died immediately after the crash. In light of the fact that Lecomte had made no mention in her 31 August 1997 reports that her examinations of Diana and Dodi's bodies were only external – see earlier – it could be significant that she used this opportunity to outline that:
-   re Dodi: "an external examination only was conducted on the body of Imad Al Fayed"
-   re Diana: "the question cannot be answered from external examination" and "the organs [were] not explored by the single external examination".[16c]

When one considers the significance of Lecomte's examinations of Diana and Dodi's bodies, her examination reports are very short.[d] In December 2006 Operation Paget asked Dr Richard Shepherd to examine the photos[e] and reports from these examinations. In his assessment[f], Shepherd described Lecomte's reports as "brief 'Forensic Reports'" and said "Lecomte describes briefly, or very briefly, the injuries". Later in his report Shepherd again mentions "albeit brief reports prepared by Professor Lecomte".[17] Shepherd makes no mention of the Lecomte examinations being external – he describes them as "examinations".

Even though in March 2005 the police did not ask Professor Lecomte whether the examination of Diana was external or internal, we find her stipulating:
-   "I made an external examination"
-   "I did not make any internal examination".

When the subject of Dodi's examination came up, the police did ask if an "external examination" took place. This time Lecomte reinforces this with: "Again, that was an external examination".

---

[a] These have been dealt with thoroughly in Parts 1 to 3.

[b] Over 3½ hours after the crash.

[c] On page 2 of this same report, Lecomte stated in reference to Princess Diana: "We can say that death was not immediate as on the arrival of the SAMU at the scene, the patient was conscious but in a very serious haemodynamic state as her blood pressure could not be assessed." The evidence presented in Part 2 shows that this is clearly untrue as assessments of Diana's blood pressure were made in the car and the ambulance. See Chapter 9 of Part 2.

[d] Diana's report is shown earlier; Dodi's report is shown on p397 of *The Documents* book.

[e] The photographs taken are discussed below.

[f] This can be viewed on p405 of *The Documents* book – UK edition.

Lecomte's answers given through this short piece of interview – not heard by the jury – are quite revealing:

-   When the police asked if it was "current practice" not to perform a post-death pregnancy test, instead of answering the question, Lecomte replied: "I act in accordance with the task entrusted to me."

When the police directly asked: "Do you know what the doctors did to the body beforehand?" Lecomte answered "No" but then voluntarily added two pieces of unsolicited material: 1) "when I arrived I made an external examination"; 2) "I did not take any samples". Both of these statements had no direct connection to the question asked.

In his book, *A Royal Duty*, Diana's butler Paul Burrell described what occurred after travelling from Paris to London with Diana's body:

Paul Burrell, Diana's Butler: 2003 Book Excerpt: **Jury Didn't Hear**:
"We arrived at an undertaker's in London[a], and the next person I saw was the princess's doctor, Dr Peter Wheeler....

"'I have to attend an autopsy now' he said....

"'Why does she need another autopsy?' I asked, knowing she had already undergone one in Paris.

"'The one performed in Paris was conducted on French soil, under French law. For our government's satisfaction, we have to do the same", he said, mentioning something else about forensic inspections and necessary procedures." [18]

Comment: In his book Burrell describes viewing Diana's body twice and spending several hours at the hospital on the day – it is likely that during that period he had discovered that an autopsy had already been conducted. This supports the above evidence that the examination conducted by Lecomte was not just an "external examination".

The above excerpt from Burrell's book indicates that Wheeler also already knew a Paris autopsy had occurred.

Paul Burrell, Paget Statement: **Jury Didn't Hear**:
"I understand [Diana] had a medical examination in France but I do not understand autopsies.... I believe there is a report concerning an autopsy, which was kept in the Kensington Palace safe along with some other documents (of which Lady Sarah[b] is aware)."[19]

Michael Messinger, Commander, MPS: 21 Mar 06 Statement: **Jury Didn't Hear**:
"We drew up a policing plan to facilitate the repatriation of Diana Princess of Wales.... I spoke with Detective Superintendent Jeff Rees ... and instructed him that should there be any video or photographs of the post mortem that I

---

[a] This was the Fulham Mortuary where the post-mortems of Diana and Dodi were conducted – see later.

[b] McCorquodale – Diana's sister.

understood had taken place in France, he was to secure them in a locked safe and to know of their location at all times. I am not sure at this time why I came to believe there may be some photographic or video material. I cannot recall who may have told me this." [20]

Jeffrey Rees, Head of Early Crash Investigations, British Police: 17 Dec 07: 70.17:

Mansfield: Q. What did you think might have come back [from France]?

A. Obviously at some stage the bodies would be returning to the United Kingdom, there would have to be further post-mortem examinations and so forth.

Comment: The critical evidence from the French is that it was known that the Lecomte examination of Diana's body established the cause of death:

- the examination form itself concludes with the cause of death
- Coujard: "the Princess of Wales ... died of a rupture of the pulmonary vein. Having viewed these [examination] documents I issued the burial certificates"
- Monteil: "in the light of the results, [the Public Prosecutor's Department] decided to issue the burial certificates without any restrictions".

It is particularly significant that none of these documents or witness accounts were viewable by the jury. The jury only heard evidence showing that what took place was merely an "external examination".

The evidence that the examination determined the cause of death – i.e. was an autopsy or post-mortem – is supported by:

1) the copy of Mulès' examination report on Dodi Fayed which showed blood, urine and other samples being taken

2) the examination report itself, which gave an internal cause of death

3) Riou's ticking the "YES" box for medico-legal issues in the death certificate

4) Burrell's accounts that what took place in France was an autopsy

5) Messinger's account that he understood a "post mortem ... had taken place in France"

6) Rees' statement that "there would have to be <u>further</u> post-mortem examinations" in the UK

7) the withholding from the inquest jury of any documentation relating to Lecomte's examination of the body of Diana, Princess of Wales.

On the other hand, Robert Chapman, who conducted the later UK post-mortem of Princess Diana, stated: "There was no evidence of a formal postmortem examination having taken place."

This did not appear in Chapman's evidence until 2005 – it was not in his report which was written up following the post-mortem. I suggest that normally a comment of this nature – stating that something wasn't witnessed

– would not be made, and it is interesting that Chapman has included this in his 2005 statement.

It will be shown in the later UK Post-Mortems chapter of this book that Chapman is an unreliable witness.

Chapman's account must be viewed in the light of the extensive evidence in the UK Post-Mortems chapter – showing his unreliability – and also the evidence in this chapter – suggesting a post-mortem.

The balance of the evidence indicates that a post-mortem was conducted by Dominique Lecomte on Diana's body.

Some photos were taken around the time of the examination of Princess Diana's body.

Jean-Claude Mulès: 19 Jul 06 Paget Report Description of Statement: **Jury Didn't Hear**:

"In respect of the photographs of the external examination of the Princess of Wales, Mulès stated that he recalled that after they were printed he went to collect them, placed them into a sealed envelope and then handed them personally to Monteil who he saw place them into her office safe. He did not personally see the photographs and did not know if the negatives were contained within the envelope or whether they had remained with the photographic unit.

"In respect of any photographs that were taken of the external examination of Dodi Al Fayed, Mulès could not recall specifically whether or not photographs had been taken, but thought it likely they would have been." [21]

Martine Monteil, Head of Brigade Criminelle: 19 Jul 05 Written communication with Paget: **Jury Didn't Hear**:

Question: "We are informed that a number of sensitive photographs relating to this enquiry, were stored in your safe at the time of the investigation. Do you know where they are now? (They are not with the Brigade Criminelle or the Photographic Branch). If not, what do you recall of the nature of these photographs? (Hospital[a], paparazzi, scene?)"

Answer: "All the photographs that were taken in this matter are in the proceedings."[22]

Martine Monteil: 15 Nov 06 Statement: **Jury Didn't Hear**:

"Question: Do you know the nature of the photographs taken of the Princess of Wales during her external examination at the Pitié Salpêtrière hospital and do you know where they are now?

Answer: All the photographs taken during this procedure were passed to the Examining Magistrate and must be in the file. I should add the negatives must be stored and filed as is always the case with the Police Photographic Branch [Identité Judiciaire]." [23]

---

[a] Photos at the hospital should include those taken around the time of the Diana body examination.

Prof Richard Shepherd, Expert Inquest Pathologist, UK: 16 Jul 07 "Operation Paget" Report: **Jury Didn't Hear**:

"On the 6th and 8th December 2006 I examined copies of photographs of Henri Paul (PCE/20), Dodi Al Fayed (PCE/19) and Diana, Princess of Wales (PCE/18) taken during the examinations performed by Professor Lecomte on 31st August 1997....

"I can see no significant discrepancies between the photographs and the, albeit brief, reports prepared by Professor Lecomte. Not all of the injuries described by Dr Chapman to Dodi Al Fayed and to Diana, Princess of Wales are clearly represented in these sets of photographs...."[24]

Comment: Monteil describes despatching "a team of officers to the Institute of Forensic Medicine to be present at the examinations of the bodies of the Princess of Wales and Dodi Al Fayed" – see earlier.

That account raises several issues:

1) Diana's examination took place at the hospital, not the IML.

2) Only Mulès has ever claimed to be present at Diana's examination and there is no record of any other police being there. In Lecomte's report of the examination there is no mention of anyone else attending.[a]

3) There is no police report of Diana's examination.

Monteil and Mulès have provided evidence that there were photos taken and Shepherd states that he has seen and studied the photos. There is no evidence of: a) how many photos there were; or, b) who took them.

Mulès stated that he "did not personally see the photographs" but "went to collect them, placed them into a sealed envelope and then handed them personally to Monteil who he saw place them into her office safe." Monteil – who appears to have played "hard to get" over these photos – was asked by the British police: "Do you know the nature of the photographs taken of the Princess of Wales during her external examination...?" Monteil actually failed to answer this question – instead focusing only on the second part of the question: "Do you know where they are now?"

As was amply shown by the evidence regarding the photos relating to the 2nd autopsy of Henri Paul[b], there is no guarantee that photos were taken during a particular operation or examination. In this case, the photos of Princess Diana's examination could just as easily have been taken prior to the examination and we would be none the wiser. The only person who has ever

---

[a] It should though be noted that Lecomte made no mention of anyone else being present at the examination of Dodi Fayed's body, yet Mulès claimed to be there and did compile a report – see earlier.

[b] See Part 3.

claimed to have seen any of these photos is Professor Richard Shepherd in December 2006.

There are two points:

1) Shepherd stated: "Not all of the injuries described by Dr Chapman [in the UK post-mortems[a]] to Dodi Al Fayed and to Diana, Princess of Wales are clearly represented in these sets of photographs."

2) As with the photographs of the Henri Paul autopsies[b] the French police have been very reticent to release photos of Diana and Dodi's autopsies to the British authorities. Messinger appears to have knowledge of the existence of photos on 31 August 1997, yet the interview of Monteil by Operation Paget in November 2006 indicates that over 9 years later they still hadn't seen these photos.[c] Shepherd viewed the photos the following month, December 2006 – just eight days before the Paget Report was published.[d]

Even though Mulès was present during Dodi's examination he "could not recall specifically whether or not photographs had been taken". Shepherd states that he has viewed photos from that examination in a file called "PCE/19".

There is no record of photos being taken in either of Lecomte's reports[e] – reports which she claims were written up on the day.

One could ask: Why wasn't the person or persons who took the photos at these examinations heard from at the inquest?[f] The fact is that they have never been identified or interviewed by any police investigation.

Conclusion

The three issues raised near the beginning of this chapter were:
1) Were the examinations normal practice?
2) What was the nature of the examinations?
3) Why did they take place?

I believe it is common sense that to carry out a body examination – external or otherwise – on a dead passenger from a road crash is not normal practice in any country. This common sense view is supported by Steiner and Monteil who both stated that such an examination was not relevant to any investigation. Even Coujard – who was directly involved in ordering the

---

[a] See later chapter.

[b] See Part 3.

[c] This is amazing when one considers they were photos taken by the French police of the dead body of the most popular British princess of the modern era.

[d] Shepherd said he viewed the photos on the 6th and 8th of December and the Paget Report was published on the 14th.

[e] Both Diana and Dodi's examinations.

[f] Not necessarily in the form of a cross-examination, but simply a reading of their statements may have been sufficient.

examination – indicated by her evasiveness in her statement testimony, that she was aware that this was unusual behaviour.

It is significant that none of this evidence – Steiner, Monteil, Coujard's police statement – was heard by Baker's inquest jury.

The evidence that these examinations were not normal practice naturally raises the obvious question: Why did they occur? This will be addressed shortly.

With the knowledge that examinations were made of the bodies of Princess Diana and Dodi Fayed outside of normal procedure, it would obviously be more acceptable to interested parties – i.e. family – that these were simply external and not more invasive.

The witness evidence – Riou, Coujard, Lecomte – is that: the examinations were external.[a]

The documentary evidence from the day of the examinations indicates otherwise:

- Lecomte's examination report for Diana, a) does not say the examination was external; b) states in conclusion an internal cause of death deduced "from my examination"
- Mulès' examination report for Dodi declares that samples including blood and urine were taken.

Other documents that must – or did – exist are missing:

- the formal request to Lecomte from the Public Prosecutor's Department for the conduct of the examinations
- the police report for Diana's examination.

Although the general evidence shows that at the time the purpose of the examinations was apparently to determine cause of death, this has never been admitted in witness evidence. Instead, witnesses have come up with other reasons for the examinations:

- Coujard: "the Princess of Wales had undergone extended medical examinations"
- Riou: "a Legal Physician must examine the body ... [after a] car crash"
- Lecomte: "the identity of a victim, even a passenger, can ... justify an autopsy".

---

[a] Although witnesses – in some cases repeatedly – stated that these examinations were only external, no one has ever been able to put forward a credible explanation showing what practical benefit can be achieved by externally examining the body of a dead passenger in a car crash. My understanding is that the normal reason for a body examination in these circumstances is to establish cause of death – but that would not necessarily be determined from an external examination.

These explanations have been addressed earlier in the chapter – I suggest that the witnesses have not provided us with the true picture.

The question then is: An examination of passengers in a car crash was not normal procedure, so why then were body examinations called for in this particular case?

I suggest there are two possible reasons and both may have played a role in arriving at this unusual decision to conduct examinations. Both reasons relate directly to the examination of Princess Diana – as suggested earlier, I believe that the examination of Dodi Fayed may have occurred in order to not draw explicit attention to the reason(s) Princess Diana's body was examined.[a]

The first reason I suggest is closely linked to the completion of the death certificate form (JM/12[b]) by Bruno Riou following the death of Diana – this is a form that has since gone missing and has never resurfaced.

The main significance of this form is that Riou has stated to the British police that he ticked "YES" in the box for "medical legal obstacle" – see earlier. The reverse of this form – shown earlier – states that when "YES" is ticked, it means that the death is a "suicide or suspicious death, the origin of which appears to be related to an offence".

According to Riou this form is "used for administration purposes in France" and "would have been sent to the ... National Institute ... [Public Records Office]."

This evidence conflicts with the instructions on the reverse of the form which states that when there is a medical legal obstacle "the body is at the disposal of the judicial authorities".

I suggest that after Riou completed this form, following the death of Princess Diana, a copy of it would have been immediately faxed or delivered to the "judicial authorities" – i.e. the Public Prosecutor's office, or Maud Coujard.

From that point on, I suggest that the issue of conducting a body examination of Princess Diana would have been a foregone conclusion. Coujard and Bestard were presented with an official death certificate completed by the officiating doctor stating that he had concerns that the circumstances of the death of Diana, Princess of Wales were suspicious.

Enter: Professor Dominique Lecomte – an expert pathologist who has already been shown in Part 3 to be dishonest and deceitful in her conduct of Henri Paul's autopsy. She was earlier in the morning enlisted to carry out Diana's body examination. Lecomte found the cause of death to be connected to the torn pulmonary vein – see earlier.

---

[a] In other words, I believe the French had little or no interest in examining Dodi but did it in order to not draw specific attention to the fact they had examined Diana.
[b] See earlier.

Why then did Professor Bruno Riou tick "YES" for medical legal obstacle?

Part 2 has already shown that on the night of the crash the team at La Pitié Salpêtrière Hospital – led by Riou – performed as best they could in a vain but desperate attempt to save the life of Princess Diana. There is no reason at all to suggest that those people were in any way part of a conspiracy to eliminate Princess Diana – quite the opposite, they tried valiantly to save her life. There is however quite a bit of evidence in Part 2 that testimony provided by senior doctors Riou and Pavie in the years following the crash has assisted in covering up regarding the delay in getting Diana to the hospital.[a]

At the time, the circumstances of Diana's death must have been all too clear to Bruno Riou, who was involved right from the first phone call to the hospital from Dr Lejay at 1.25 a.m. He may have even been aware that the crash had occurred just before 12.30 a.m. The evidence in Part 2 indicates that there was communication between ambulance doctor Martino and Riou at the time of Diana's arrival.[b]

One of the first actions by Riou[c] – after Diana's arrival at 2.06 a.m. – was to order X-rays of Diana's chest and pelvis area. That revealed a haemothorax – there was a major haemorrhaging of blood in the thorax. An external examination of Diana would have revealed the thoracic trauma that had already been noted by Martino when he first undressed Diana in the ambulance soon after 1.06 a.m., approximately one hour earlier. Plus, Diana's blood pressure was very low and by the time she arrived at the hospital 1 hour and 43 minutes after the crash, the princess was unconscious. Riou – who took the Lejay phone call at 1.25 a.m. – must have realised, as soon as he saw the thoracic trauma, that he hadn't been told about it during the earlier phone call. Surely, he would have wondered why.

I suggest that there are a critical set of factors that on the night would have raised serious questions in the mind of Riou, and also to a lesser extent[d], Pavie[e]:

-   the thoracic trauma that was externally evident but was not communicated to the hospital ahead of arrival

---

[a] This is addressed at length in Part 2.

[b] See Part 2, p647.

[c] Events are summarised here – the full evidence of what occurred is shown in Part 2.

[d] Pavie was not there at the arrival – see Part 2.

[e] Pavie gave evidence that he and Riou spoke to Lecomte ahead of her examination of Diana – see earlier.

- the inordinate delay in getting to hospital given the combination of thoracic trauma and low blood pressure – i.e. it would have been known in the ambulance that Diana's life could not be saved outside of a hospital
- Diana had arrived unconscious and stopped breathing 6 minutes after that arrival[a] – yet the crash had occurred 1 hour and 43 minutes earlier.[b]

It may be significant that even though the body examination took place 1½ hours after any attempted life-saving activity had finished[c], both Riou and Pavie stayed around and spoke with Lecomte ahead of the examination – see Pavie's earlier evidence. It may be that they communicated genuine concerns to Lecomte regarding Diana's treatment in the ambulance. Riou – who is a specialist in anaesthetics and resuscitation[25] – or Pavie, may have been suspicious enough to specifically suggest samples to be taken.[d]

It is not completely known what occurred inside the ambulance during the 5 minutes that it stopped close to the gates of the La Pitié Salpêtrière Hospital.

Part 2 however has already revealed <u>what is known</u>:
- that the ambulance did stop for 5 minutes close to the hospital
- that the ambulance was seen to be rocking by a journalist witness, Thierry Orban
- that there were 5 people (excluding Diana) in the ambulance at that stage – a driver and 4 in the back[e]
- that of the 4 people in the back, 2 remained unidentified at the inquest and have never been interviewed by the police, and only 2 were cross-examined at the inquest

---

[a] Diana's effective time of death was 2.12 a.m. – see Part 2.

[b] At the hospital press conference held at 5.55 a.m. Riou said: "Tonight the Princess of Wales was the victim of a high-speed car accident. The Paris ambulance service took charge and tried at once to resuscitate her. But when she arrived here, she was haemorrhaging very badly from the thorax – and then her heart stopped.": Diana: The Night She Died, Channel 5 Documentary, 2003.

[c] Diana's official time of death was 4 a.m. and the examination commenced at 5.30 a.m. – see earlier.

[d] It may be significant that Lecomte appeared to deny that any contact with the doctors took place: "Question: Do you know what the doctors did to the body beforehand? Answer: No, when I arrived I made an external examination. I did not take any samples." If suggestions had been put to Lecomte during this conversation that Diana's death was suspicious, this could give rise to a situation where she would deny the conversation ever took place – which is what has happened. There would not appear to be any benefit in Lecomte denying the conversation if it had only been about the surgical actions taken by the doctors.

[e] This is based on the evidence in Part 2 and also what is revealed in The Documents book – Martino's 12 May 2005 statement and the Ambulance Report.

- that both of the witnesses who were cross-examined – Martino and Derossi[a] – have a) lied in evidence they have given, and b) carried out actions (or inaction) in the ambulance that reduced Diana's chances of survival

- that Martino's evidence to Lienhart and Lecomte[b] was that he stopped the ambulance and increased the dopamine drip.

What if the rocking ambulance – which has never been explained[c] – was because Princess Diana was still alive and physically put up a struggle against her "treatment"?

What if, instead of increasing the dopamine outside the hospital, Martino had administered a substance that sped up Diana's deteriorating situation?

I am not suggesting that Riou was aware of the circumstances of the 5 minute stoppage, or even that it actually happened.

He didn't need to be.

Riou was definitely aware of the earlier three factors – the combination of external thoracic trauma with low blood pressure; the huge delay in arrival; the death occurring 6 minutes after arrival.

I suggest that this should have been enough to raise the question of suspicion in the mind of an experienced doctor, as Riou was.[d]

I further suggest that, based on the circumstances Professor Bruno Riou was confronted with, he did the only decent thing that was in his power to do – he ticked "YES" in the medical legal obstacle box on Diana's death certificate.

There is no question that Riou's subsequent evidence on the reason he ticked "YES" is illogical – he has said that "the 'YES' box is normally always ticked when the death is not natural ... for example suicide, car crash etc": thus requiring "a Legal Physician [to] examine the body".

This statement runs directly counter to:

a) what it states on the reverse of the form – see earlier

b) the evidence of Monteil and Steiner that body examinations are not relevant for car crash passengers

c) common sense, which tells us that it would be ridiculous for body examinations to be conducted on dead passengers in all car crashes.

I suggest that Riou knows that this statement is false and has been pressured – by the French authorities – to lie, as a part of the wide-ranging cover-up that has occurred in France since 31 August 1997.[a]

---

[a] Derossi has stated that he was not in the ambulance but the evidence in Part 2 indicates that he was.

[b] They conducted an investigation into the medical treatment in 1998 – see Part 2.

[c] The rocking ambulance evidence was not even mentioned at the inquest, outside of the reading of Orban's statement.

[d] In 1997, Riou had 12 years experience as a doctor: 15 Nov 07: 2.2.

None of this detracts from the reality of what occurred on the night.

I suggest that:

1) Riou ticked "YES" in the medical legal obstacle box on Diana's death certificate

2) Coujard received that death certificate – probably within minutes, by fax

3) Coujard consulted Bestard, telling him of the situation

4) Bestard decided that Lecomte needed to conduct a body examination to determine cause of death

5) Coujard formally requested Lecomte to conduct the examination

6) Riou and Pavie spoke with Lecomte after her arrival at the hospital, but before she conducted the examination

7) Lecomte carried out the examination in the presence of an unidentified police photographer – who took photos – and Jean-Claude Mulès.

Most of the evidence of what occurred was withheld from the Baker inquest jury. It is particularly significant that: a) the completed JM/12 form cannot be "found"; b) the jury never got to hear about the existence of the JM/12 form – blank or completed; and c) the jury never got to hear what Riou had to say on this subject.

This evidence – that Riou may have believed Diana's death was suspicious – is supported by the terminology used on the three key known body examination documents: the Lecomte examination reports for Diana and Dodi and the police report for Dodi.

The heading on Lecomte's report for Diana – shown earlier – reads: "FORENSIC REPORT". Dodi's report heading[b] reads: "FORENSIC MEDICAL REPORT". In his report – shown earlier – Mulès describes Dodi's examination as "forensic observations".

All three key known reports describe these examinations as "forensic" – not "external".[c] The Oxford dictionary definition for "forensic" reads: "relating to the use of scientific methods <u>to investigate crime</u>".[d]

This evidence indicates that the examination of Princess Diana's body was conducted as a result of concerns raised by Professor Bruno Riou[e], early on 31 August 1997, that a crime had been committed.[f]

---

[a] See earlier volumes, particularly Part 3.

[b] Shown in *The Documents* book, p397 (UK edit).

[c] The absence of the word "external" in these reports has been discussed earlier.

[d] It is also notable that in Mulès' 5 September 1997 report – shown and covered earlier – the word "forensic" is missing. Instead the word "external" is used for the first time, twice.

[e] When he completed form JM/12 – see above.

[f] As suggested earlier, a similar examination was conducted on Dodi Fayed's body so as not to draw specific attention to the fact an examination had been conducted on the body of Princess Diana.

This evidence is also supported during the cross-examination of Maud Coujard at the inquest. Coujard confirmed that the Diana and Dodi examinations' results "meant that actually there were not any barriers to their burial". When questioned further by Burnett, Coujard confirmed that after the results of the examinations came in and the consequent issuing of burial certificates, "there was [now] no forensic reason to retain the bodies" of Princess Diana and Dodi Fayed.

There is evidence that indicates there may have been an additional reason for the conduct of the Lecomte examination of Princess Diana.

As has been shown earlier, when the subject of body examinations came up at the inquest, Maud Coujard immediately added an unsolicited "sophistication": "in August, we knew that the Princess of Wales had undergone extended medical examinations".

As discussed earlier, this evidence could be seen to point to a concern about pregnancy – mainly because it's difficult to imagine any other topic that could link these three factors: the death of the princess; extended medical examinations; and a post-death body examination.[a]

I suggest that pregnancy would not have been a concern to the French, but it may have been an issue for parts of the British Establishment.[b] Evidence in the following chapter – on the Embalming – will show that the British were involved in the decisions that were being made in the La Pitié Salpêtrière Hospital following the death of Princess Diana. The logic is: If the British were involved with the embalming – and the evidence will show that they were – then why wouldn't they have been involved with the body examination?

The conduct by Lecomte of a body examination would have been an opportunity to carry out sampling of blood and urine, which could have been tested at the hospital to establish – or dismiss – pregnancy.[c] Pavie said to British police in March 2005 – in the context of the medical treatment at the hospital – "In view of the seriousness of the situation, no blood test was carried out to determine pregnancy. She had practically none of her own blood left, because of the many drips."[26]

In light of this evidence – that Diana may not have had her own blood in her body after she died – a sample of urine may have been more accurate as a test for pregnancy. Later evidence will show that in the context of the

---

[a] Remembering that Diana's final visit to her GP, Dr Wheeler, was to address a problem with breakthrough bleeding – see earlier evidence.
[b] This subject is dealt with in the Motives section of Part 2.
[c] Earlier evidence – the police report – has already shown that blood and urine samples were taken from the body of Dodi Fayed. It could be significant, in the light of that evidence, that the police report on Diana's examination is missing.

embalming in Paris and the post-mortem in London, urine takes on increased significance.

So why has there been a major suppression of documentation surrounding these body examinations?

Why is it that after 5 years of investigation there are still documents that the author of this book has not seen – the official request by the Public Prosecutor's Department for the conduct of the examinations; the police report of Princess Diana's examination; the completed JM/12 death certificate; the death certificate kept by the FCO[a][b]?

Why is it that the jury were not shown any of those documents and also were prevented from seeing the other documents reproduced in this chapter: Lecomte's examination report for Diana; the blank JM/12 death certificate form; Mulès' September 5 correction report? And also Lecomte's examination report for Dodi?[c]

Why is it that out of a total of at least 9 documents[d] relating to the body examinations, the jury only saw one – the police report of Dodi Fayed's examination? 1 out of 9. Why?

Why is it that out of the players who were involved in the examinations – Lecomte, Coujard, anonymous police photographer, Riou[e], Bestard, Monteil, Mulès[f] – the evidence of only one, Coujard, was heard at the inquest? 1 out of 7[g]. Why?[h]

Why is it that out of 25 items of witness evidence in this chapter, 20 are marked "Jury Didn't Hear" – the jury heard only five? 5 out of 25. Why?

This chapter dealt with a French examination of the body of Britain's Princess Diana. Why did the British inquest get to hear so little about such a major operation?

I suggest that the answer to all of these questions is that it was not in the interests of the British authorities for evidence to be seen by the jury indicating that early on 31 August 1997 the officiating doctor had serious concerns that the death of Princess Diana occurred under suspicious circumstances.

---

[a] Mentioned in Riou's evidence, quoted in earlier footnote.
[b] Foreign & Commonwealth Office.
[c] Reproduced in *The Documents* book.
[d] 8 have been listed above.
[e] Riou was cross-examined at the inquest, but not about the body examination or the JM/12 form.
[f] Mulès was cross-examined at the inquest, but not about the body examinations.
[g] At least 7 – this list does not include the anonymous "team" that Monteil stated she sent to the Diana examination.
[h] If the jury only hears the evidence of one person, this prevents them from being able to compare evidence and see possible conflicts between witness accounts.

Additionally I suggest it was not in the interests of the British authorities to see evidence – which will be supported by additional evidence in Part 5 – indicating that an opportunity was possibly taken to conduct a pregnancy test on samples from the body of Princess Diana.

I suggest that is damning evidence on its own: If the examination of Princess Diana's body by Professor Lecomte was just a "normal" external examination, why was it that the jury were not provided with most of the evidence relating to it?

As with every aspect of this case so far, no one event should be seen as a stand-alone, but must be viewed in the context of the surrounding events.

The examination conducted by Lecomte at 5.30 a.m. must be looked at along with the embalming that took place in Paris later that day and eventually should also be seen in the context of the final post-mortem, conducted by Robert Chapman in London at 8.21 p.m.[a] that evening.

It is only when these events are viewed as a complete package that one can understand the full significance of each individual event that took place.

This will become clearer as the amazing story revealed in this book unfolds....

---

[a] London time.

2   French Embalming[a]

Coroner: Summing Up: 31 Mar 08: 50.6:
"You may think, having heard so many witnesses on the topic, that there is really no doubt at all that the embalming was entirely innocent."

---

[a] The evidence in this chapter needs to be viewed in the light of other chapters: Royal Control and UK Post-Mortems in this book and the Pregnancy chapter in Part 5.

Several hours after the autopsy by Lecomte, the body of Princess Diana was embalmed at La Pitié Salpêtrière Hospital. This operation was carried out by employees from a Paris company called BJL.[a]

The main issue around the French embalming of Princess Diana relates to the following question: Why was Diana's body embalmed in Paris, when it was already known that she would be repatriated to the UK later that day?[b]

The full significance of this will become clearer as this book progresses.

Choice of Hospital Room

The evidence will reveal it was the placement of Princess Diana's body in a hospital room without air conditioning[c] that appeared to eventually lead to the decision to embalm Princess Diana.

Paget Report, p532: **Jury Didn't Hear**:

"The Princess of Wales was pronounced dead at 4 a.m. following emergency surgery at the Pitié Salpêtrière Hospital in Paris. Her body, after an external[d] examination by a court appointed medical expert, was taken to a private room within the hospital, close to the emergency reception area."

Paget Report, p532: **Jury Didn't Hear**:

"Professor Bruno Riou ... has shown Operation Paget the locations in which the Princess of Wales received her immediate treatment; where she underwent emergency surgery; where she was externally examined by the pathologist; and finally the room in which she lay that day, before her body was returned to the United Kingdom. This room, a standard three-bedded hospital room, was on the first floor of the Emergency wards of the Pavillon Gaston Cordier, overlooking Avenue de la Nouvelle Pitié.

"[Riou] stated that the Princess of Wales was not taken to the hospital mortuary as it was felt inappropriate to transport her body across the hospital grounds at that time because of the media interest in such a V.I.P. The hospital mortuary and the emergency reception areas are at opposite ends of the hospital grounds."

Prof Bruno Riou: 7 Mar 06 Paget Description of Statement: **Jury Didn't Hear**:

"The body of a person deceased on this ward would then normally have been taken to the Hospital Morgue ... but the hospital administration decided that this building was too far away, and that because of the media interest and the

---

[a] More details about BJL are revealed later.
[b] Later evidence will reveal that the repatriation was known about well before the embalming took place.
[c] The crash occurred in summer.
[d] This examination was not just external – see earlier.

fact the Princess of Wales was a VIP, she was moved to the emergency wards on the first floor of the Pavillon Gaston Cordier, which was controllable and secure.

"The body of the Princess of Wales was taken along the ... one below ground floor corridor, to the lifts ... and taken to the first floor emergency wards, opposite those lifts.... The Emergency Care Ward was a fourteen-bed unit.... The room in which the body of the Princess of Wales was taken, Room 1.006, had three beds, but was used solely for her, and she was placed on the bed on the right hand side of the door, as you enter the room.... It is in this room that the body of the Princess of Wales was laid to rest until her departure for England." [27]

Comment: This evidence shows that Princess Diana was moved several times within la Pitié Salpêtrière Hospital.

The locations were:
1) room of "immediate treatment"[a]
2) theatre of "emergency surgery"[b]
3) room where the Lecomte examination was carried out – see earlier
4) room where her body lay throughout the day, prior to repatriation – see later.

This evidence confirms that Diana wasn't moved to the final room (where the embalming took place – see later) until after the Lecomte examination, which had commenced at 5.30 a.m.[c] Riou's earlier evidence showed that "the body lay to rest in this [examination] room until about 0700hrs [7.00 a.m.]." [d]

There are several relevant points:

1) There is a window of time that indicates the Diana examination may have lasted around 45 minutes or so.[ef]

2) Until about 7.00 a.m. Diana's body was under ground level (one floor down) – Riou

3) At around 7.00 a.m. Diana was moved from completely out of view of the media to a room that could be within their view – see later.

It may be significant that Diana was moved from the underground floor to one floor above ground at around sunrise – in Paris on 31 August 1997 sunrise was at 7.06 a.m.[28]

---

[a] Recovery room – see Part 2.

[b] Part 2 showed that some surgery occurred in the place of initial treatment, then Diana was moved – under Dr Pavie's direction – to the operating theatre, for further surgery.

[c] See earlier in Lecomte's report.

[d] See "Autopsy in Paris" chapter.

[e] Lecomte only provides a starting time of 5.30 a.m. in her report, with no finishing time.

[f] Timings relating to the examinations are addressed in Chapter 1.

This new 1st floor room did not have air conditioning and on what was to become a hot Paris summer's day – the temperature that day climbed to 30.3 degrees Celsius[29a] – the atmosphere inside the room soon became very warm.

Keith Moss, British Consul General, Paris: 22 Nov 07: 18.9:

Hough: Q. Was there then a press conference at just before 6 o'clock in the morning?

A. Yes, there was.

Q. At that stage, I think the body of the Princess was still in the intensive care unit.

A. It could have been, yes.

Q. Was it moved shortly afterwards?

A. Well, it was moved at some point – I cannot precisely remember the times, but it was relocated from the re-animation centre, the A&E centre, up to where I was at some time after that.

Q. That was in the same building? It was moved to another room in the same building?

A. Yes, it was.

At 19.19: Q. While you were in the room for that early part of time, were you aware of any air-conditioning unit which was in the room?

A. No, I was not.

Q. Can you describe what the heat in the room was like?

A. I suppose, to begin with, it was a fairly comfortable ambient temperature, but as the day progressed – and bearing in mind this is Paris in August – the temperature, the outside temperature began to increase and with it, therefore, the risk of the temperature in the room in which the Princess's body had been placed increasing as well.

Stephen Donnelly, British Vice Consul, Paris: 22 Sep 05 Statement read out 17 Dec 07: 120.17:

"On the morning of Sunday 31st August at about 8.15 a.m. to 8.20 a.m., I received a telephone call ... from the Consul General, Keith Moss.... [He] had told me that the Princess of Wales' body was in a room next to where he was and that it was extremely hot and that he had asked the hospital to provide ice to put around the body, but that the hospital had told him that they did not have any. So he asked me to try to find some ice. I had no idea where to start. I expected that the hospital would have some. It was Sunday morning. On reflection, I decided to call PFG, one of the funeral directors that are recommended to bereaved families, to see if they could point me in the right direction.... I was surprised to be put through to a man who introduced himself [as] the president of the company, but I cannot recall his name. It

---

[a] 86.5 degrees Fahrenheit.

would be fair to say that this call, to the best of my recollection, would have been made around 9 a.m. I spoke in French to the president of PFG and told him that I was calling in respect of the death of Diana, Princess of Wales. He told me that he was aware of her death. It was as if he had been expecting my call. I explained the problem of the heat at the hospital and that there was no ice. I told him which hospital and I asked him if he could help. I do not recall his exact words, but he informed me that he could help and that he would deal with it."

Colin Tebbutt, Diana's Driver and Security: 26 Nov 07: 89.18:

Hough: Q. At what time, roughly, did you arrive at the hospital?

A. It would have been before midday[a], sir....

Q. I think you went in the hospital to the corridor where the room was where the Princess's body was being kept. Is that right?

A. I first went to see Mr Moss, who again was calm, collected and totally in control. It was chaos and I had a great deal of time for the way he dealt with everything.

Q. Did Mr Moss take you up to that sealed corridor and to the room where the Princess lay?

A. Yes, sir. His room was right on the end of the sealed corridor.

Q. When you arrived, around midday, what was the temperature like in the room?

A. When I actually went into the room, the whole part of that hospital was very warm. It was a hot day and in the room it was extremely hot.

Q. When you arrived, were there any air conditioners in the room?

A. No.

.... Q. We have heard from Mr Moss that the decision was taken to put up some makeshift curtains, some sheets up at the windows of the room. Were you involved in that decision?

A. Yes, I was, sir, because the message came, if you looked out the window, the press were climbing over the roofs, sir. There were no sort of things up at

---

[a] Tebbutt left London with Burrell by plane at about 6.30 a.m. local time – 7.30 a.m. in Paris. After arriving they first visited and had coffee with British ambassador Michael Jay, then proceeded to the Ritz Hotel – in search of Diana's possessions – before moving on to the hospital: see Tebbutt cross-examination from 88.6 and Paul Burrell's 2003 book *A Royal Duty* pp286-8. There are minor conflicts over the order of events between Burrell and Tebbutt, but I suggest – especially considering Burrell's relationship with the truth (see Part 2) – that it is reasonable to accept Tebbutt's account that they arrived at the hospital before midday. This also is supported by Gibbins who was at Kensington Palace in London – he said he went home for a break at around 7.45 a.m. (8.45 a.m. in Paris) and returned to the office at around 11.15 a.m. (12.15 p.m. in Paris). Gibbins said he received a call from Tebbutt about the hot room crisis sometime after 12.15 p.m. Paris time: 21 Nov 07:7.21 to 9.1.

the window, so they had a direct passage in. I suppose I could have used sheets, but we only were given blankets, which I suppose increased the heat unfortunately. But, yes, I put blankets up at the window.

At 123.10: Horwell: Q. It was very hot in that room, was it not?

A. Oh, extremely, sir.

Colin Tebbutt: Jul 04 Statement: **Jury Didn't Hear**:

"It was a hot day and I noticed the room was extremely hot.... All the while the hospital room was getting hotter. I spoke to the hospital funeral directors.... I was informed that the body would start to deteriorate quite rapidly. This was also the opinion of the nursing staff, as it was just so hot....The information that I had been given was that the Princess was melting."[30]

Michael Gibbins, Diana's Private Secretary: 21 Nov 07: 8.14:

Burnett: Q. Once you were back in the office after 11 to 11.30, did Colin Tebbutt call ever?

A. Several times, yes.

Q. Do you remember having any discussion with him about the presentability of the body of the Princess?

A. Yes, I do. He rang on one occasion and said that the room in which the Princess was was hot and there was overhead lighting and he was concerned that there was some deterioration in the Princess's body and that steps should be taken to make it presentable for the people who were flying from the UK, the Princess's family and indeed Prince Charles, to make it presentable for them when they arrived.

Keith Moss, British Consul General, Paris: 22 Nov 07: 19.4:

Hough: Q. Now we have heard from others that there was some suggestion of curtains or sheets being put up at the windows of the room where the Princess was. Were you aware of that taking place?

A. Yes, by way of background at some point – and by then, it must, I am sure, have been daylight – the hospital staff, I think a nurse or a couple of nurses, approached me to say that the room in which the Princess's body had been placed had large picture windows, and in the distance, way beyond the hospital compound were high-rise buildings, and they were concerned about the possibility of long-range cameras being directed into the room to try to take photographs. They therefore asked me if it would be appropriate to put curtains up to prevent that from happening and I agreed.[a]

---

[a] In Moss' statement he said: "On my agreement, the nursing staff set up curtains at the windows." Moss said that the nurses notified him of the problem "not long after the Princess of Wales' body had been moved to the room". This does not fit with the recollection of Tebbutt that the windows were covered not long before the

Huguette Amarger, French Embalmer: 8 Mar 05 Statement read out 22 Nov 07: 93.24:

"This [embalming] took place in the large room with the Princess's bed and big air conditioners to cool it. It was terribly hot."

Jean Monceau, BJL Director and Embalmer, Paris: 20 Nov 07: 70.24:

Burnett: Q. The body of the Princess was, as you have told us, in an ordinary room and this was August 31st. Was it hot in there?

A. It is hard to remember. I guess the temperature was not fit to preserve the body as such without doing anything, but I do not know whether it was really hot or not.

At 84.5: Mansfield: Q. When you arrived at the hospital, did you expect to find the Princess's body in the mortuary rather than in a room or a ward?

A. When you take care of VIPs such as a president, a king, et cetera, very often the bodies of such personalities are not put in a mortuary room because those rooms, you know, do not look very good.

Clive Leverton, Royal Funeral Director: 22 Nov 07: 79.25:

Hough: Q. In your view, would it have been necessary to embalm within 24 hours?

A. It is difficult for me to say because I do not know what she was like prior to the embalming.

Q. What we have heard was that she was not in the mortuary.... She is in a room with no air conditioning, and she is not in the mortuary and so on. Does that help at all?

A. It would not, no. The obviously place for a deceased person would be in a mortuary refrigerator.

Q. I am not going to pursue the details of that.

Alan Puxley, Vice-President Operations, Kenyon International[a]: 16 Jun 04 Statement: **Jury Didn't Hear**:

"The usual practice is to store the deceased in a refrigerator in a mortuary or another cool place".[31]

Jean Monceau: 18 Oct 05 Statement: **Jury Didn't Hear**:

"I suggested [to British Consul-General, Keith Moss] arterial injections to preserve the body from the proliferation of bacteria (odours and change of colour), especially given that the heat in the room where the body was, being so high, was a contributory factor." [32]

Paget Report, p557: **Jury Didn't Hear**:

"The Princess of Wales' body was not refrigerated. She was lying in a hot hospital room."

---

embalming – see earlier and later. Source: Keith Moss, Witness Statement, 22 October 2004, reproduced in *The Documents* book, p651 (UK Edition)

[a] Kenyon's were Funeral Directors for the Royal Family until the early 1990s: Alan Puxley, Witness Statement, 16 June 2004, reproduced in *The Documents* book, p462 (UK Edition)

Comment: There are initially two key questions:
1) Why was Diana's body taken to a non-air conditioned room rather than a refrigerated mortuary room?
2) Who was responsible for that decision?

Several reasons have been given to support the failure to send Diana to the hospital's own mortuary:

a) Riou: "it was felt inappropriate to transport her body across the hospital grounds ... because of the media interest in such a V.I.P."

b) Riou: "the hospital administration decided that [the mortuary] was too far away"

c) Riou: the 1st floor room "was controllable and secure"

d) Monceau at the inquest: "VIPs such as a president, a king, et cetera – very often the bodies of such personalities are not put in a mortuary room because those rooms ... do not look very good".[a]

Out of these four reasons, three were not heard by the jury – they only heard Monceau's account.

When it was put to the royal funeral director, Clive Leverton, that Diana was "in a room with no air conditioning and ... not in the mortuary" he replied that "the obvious place for a deceased person would be in a mortuary refrigerator". This is supported by the evidence of Alan Puxley, not heard by the jury.

Leverton's evidence is significant because of who he is – the royal funeral director – he obviously has experience in dealing with the bodies of dead royals.[b] Leverton's evidence directly contradicts Monceau's account – the only reason heard by the jury (see above) – "very often the bodies of such personalities are not put in a mortuary room". This may be why Hough quickly responded to Leverton: "I am not going to pursue the details of that".

Whatever the case, I suggest that Leverton and Puxley's accounts are common sense – it is common sense that protection of the body through cool temperatures would override any concerns about the body being in a room that does "not look very good".

Riou stated that the 1st floor room "was controllable and secure" – by implication, the hospital mortuary was not. This raises the obvious question: why would a ward in a hospital be more secure than that hospital's mortuary?

No explanation has ever been provided for that question and I suspect there may not be one. Common sense may suggest the opposite is true:

---

[a] Monceau also said in his 2005 statement: "A decision was taken that she would not be going to the mortuary": Jean Monceau, Witness Statement, 18 October 2005, p5.

[b] Although Diana was not a royal at the time of her death – see Part 2 – she was quickly treated as a royal after her death. This will become a clear theme of the evidence in this volume.

hospitals are not generally required to store dead bodies in their wards, whereas for a mortuary it is their everyday business.

Riou also stated that Diana's body wasn't taken to the mortuary because of fear of the media interest. When one considers that Diana was moved from a below ground floor – not visible to the media – to a 1st floor room which was visible (see Tebbutt and Moss) – this reason also does not appear to make sense.

Another reason from Riou was that the mortuary "was too far away".

The general gist of the evidence – Monceau, Riou – is that they are clutching at straws. None of these four reasons given for the move have credibility. The reader should bear in mind that the movement of dead bodies to mortuaries in large hospitals is a very common occurrence – it happens on a daily, possibly hourly, basis.

Lecomte's examination of Diana's body would have been completed by around 6.30 a.m. at the latest – see earlier. That would have left over half an hour of darkness or twilight before sunrise at 7.06 a.m. It seems amazing that hospital officials couldn't have worked out a plan to get Diana into the mortuary at that time.

The question of course is: If there is a genuine reason why Diana was placed in a non-air conditioned room, then why is it that we have been provided with four different reasons that lack credibility?

The real reason why Diana was placed at 7 a.m. into a room that was guaranteed to heat up through the day will become increasingly apparent as this chapter progresses.

The other question was: Who was responsible for this move?

The answer appears to lie in the timing – this move doesn't take place until around 7 a.m. – so three hours after the surgical team had given Diana up as dead, at 4 a.m. It occurs after the body examination by Lecomte, which started at 5.30 a.m. and would have concluded before 6.30 a.m.[a] – Lecomte commenced the examination of Dodi's body at 6.45 a.m. at a different but nearby location, the IML.

Paget stated that Riou showed them "where [Diana] was externally examined by the pathologist" – see earlier. This indicates that Riou may have been still present at the time of the examination and this makes sense when one considers that he was the receiving doctor and also took charge of the surgical team – see Part 2.[b]

---

[a] Professor Shepherd stated in his December 2006 report that Lecomte "reported her findings to Major Mulès at 05.45" a.m.: p8. This would appear to be an error – there are 3 points: a) Shepherd agrees the examination commenced at 5.30 a.m.; b) Lecomte stated that she was able to establish an internal cause of death – see chapter 1; c) Shepherd does not appear to quote a source for this.

[b] Riou also spoke at a press conference held at the hospital at 5.55 a.m.

Pavie also described a meeting between himself, Riou and Lecomte ahead of the body examination.

So, there were three senior French figures who we know were present at the time of, or not long before, Diana's transfer to the private room at around 7 a.m. – Professor Dominique Lecomte, Professor Alain Pavie and Dr Bruno Riou.

Later evidence will show there were also senior British officials present at the hospital – Consul-General, Keith Moss, and Ambassador, Michael Jay.

I suggest the decision to not transfer Princess Diana's body to the hospital mortuary was made by a combination within this group of 5 senior personnel: Riou, Pavie. Lecomte, Jay and Moss.[abc]

The question is: Why? Why did they not transfer Diana to the mortuary?[d]

Leverton, Puxley and common sense suggest that that would have been the only reasonable move – so why didn't that happen?

The answer will become increasingly apparent as this chapter progresses. What happened next?

The general evidence indicates that after sunrise – just after the move – the room where Diana was being held started heating up:

- Moss: "as the day progressed ... the outside temperature began to increase and with it ... the risk of the temperature in the room ... increasing as well"
- Donnelly: "Keith Moss... told me ... that it was extremely hot" – at 8.20 a.m.
- Tebbutt (at inquest): "in the room it was extremely hot" – around 12.00 p.m.
- Tebbutt (in 2004): "the hospital room was getting hotter ... it was just so hot"
- Gibbins: Tebbutt "said that the room ... was hot"
- Amarger: "it was terribly hot" – around 12 p.m.
- Monceau (at inquest): "I do not know whether it was really hot or not" – around 11 a.m.
- Monceau (in 2005): "the heat in the room ... being so high".

Of the witnesses who have spoken on this, only four actually entered the room on the day – Tebbutt, Amarger, Monceau and Moss[a].

---

[a] Monceau gave evidence in his statement – not heard by the jury – "A decision was taken that she would not be going to the mortuary" – see later.

[b] Lecomte, who was an experienced pathologist – see Part 3 – would have been fully aware of the detrimental effect of placing a dead body in a hot room.

[c] There is a possibility of input also from Balmoral – it will be shown later in this book that key decisions during this day were being made by the royals at Balmoral.

[d] Also, why have no hospital staff ever been interviewed about the move of Diana to a non-airconditioned room?

Of those, only two, Amarger and Tebbutt, testified to the inquest that it was hot in the room. Monceau stated that he didn't know and Moss would only say to the jury that there was "a risk of the temperature ... increasing".

In direct contrast to those two accounts:

a) Donnelly, who was not cross-examined, provided a statement account of Moss telling him as early as 8.20 a.m. that the room was already "extremely hot"

b) Monceau stated in 2005 – not heard by the jury – that the "heat in the room" was "high".

It seems odd that at the inquest Monceau (a French embalmer) couldn't remember if the room was hot, since that was apparently the very reason the embalming was called for – see later.

As this book progresses, it will be shown that Moss – who had a central role in events at the hospital – has played an integral part in the British cover-up. Suffice it to say at this stage that there is a huge gap between Moss' inquest account – "the risk of the temperature in the room ... increasing"[b] – and Donnelly's account of what Moss told him at 8.20 a.m. on the day – "it [is] extremely hot".

The witness evidence reveals several factors that contributed to the increasing room heat and its potential to have an effect on the body:
- the room had no built-in air conditioning
- the hospital had no dry ice – Donnelly
- the overhead lighting in the room – Gibbins
- the use of blankets instead of sheets to block out the media - Tebbutt.

Needless to say, had Diana's body been transferred to the hospital mortuary, as was the normal procedure, then none of these problems could have arisen.

The evidence really is overwhelming that the room where Princess Diana's body was held was extremely hot, over a period from after 8.00 a.m. through to about lunchtime when the embalming commenced.[c]

The question then is: What was – or wasn't – done about it?

---

[a] Moss actually has testified that he never entered the room, but the general evidence indicates that he did – see later.

[b] At one point Moss mentioned Monceau referring to "the heat in the room":22 Nov 07:24.3. In his 2004 statement Moss indicated that he didn't view the body before the embalming: "I had not at this stage seen the body" – talking about the period when he spoke with Monceau, not long before the embalming. If this is true, it means that Moss set up his room – next door to where Diana's body was brought to – at the hospital, but didn't view her body for a period of at least 6 hours – from around 7 a.m. when she was transferred to his area until the conclusion of embalming around 1.30 p.m.

[c] The timing of the embalming is addressed later.

The Donnelly phone call reveals that by 8.20 a.m. the room was already "extremely hot" and:

    a) Moss "had asked the hospital to provide ice ... but ... the hospital ... did not have any"

    b) Moss "asked [Donnelly] to try to find some ice".

Donnelly phoned PFG[a] and was told by Caltiau[b] "that he would deal with it" – later evidence will show that Caltiau appears to have actually done nothing. It will also be revealed that dry ice was never applied to the body of Princess Diana.

The next evidence of any action occurring was the installation of air conditioners, but according to Tebbutt these were not present when he arrived after 11.30 a.m.

Colin Tebbutt: 5 Jul 04 Statement: **Jury Didn't Hear**:
"The room was starting to get even hotter and Mr Moss and I put air conditioning units into the room to try to keep it cool. When I switched one of the units on I noticed the Princess of Wales' hair and eyelashes move." [33]

Comment: Amarger has confirmed that air conditioners were in the room while she carried out the embalming, which commenced at about 12.30 p.m.: "[The embalming] took place in the large room ... and big air conditioners to cool it". She also indicates they hadn't been there for long: "It was terribly hot."

In summary, Moss was aware that the room was "extremely hot" from before 8.20 a.m. when he called Donnelly. The first evidence of anything being done about it was after the arrival of Tebbutt at 11.30 a.m. – the installation of portable air conditioners.[c]

The question then is: What was Moss doing for the period of over three hours between 8.20 and 11.30 a.m.?

Surely as British Consul General, present at the scene since 2.15 a.m., his primary concern should have been for the welfare and protection of Princess Diana's body. Yet the evidence indicates that he made the 8.20 a.m. phone call to Donnelly then washed his hands of it – even refusing at the inquest to admit that the room had been hot: there was "the risk of the temperature in the room ... increasing".

What was Moss doing during the morning of Sunday 31 August 1997 that was more important than taking care of the welfare of Princess Diana's body?

---

[a] French funeral directors.

[b] See later.

[c] It should be noted that the air conditioners were apparently ineffective according to Tebbutt's evidence. He states a couple of paragraphs later: "All the while the hospital room was getting hotter." Colin Tebbutt, Witness Statement, 5 July 2004, reproduced in *The Documents* book, p440 (UK Edition)

This issue was not addressed at Scott Baker's "thorough" inquest.

The significance of the evidence regarding the choice of room is connected to the evidence – already seen in Part 2 – that Princess Diana may have been up to a week pregnant at the time of her death. If that was the case, there would have been knowledge of it at La Pitié Salpêtrière Hospital on the morning of 31 August 1997 – primarily from the results of blood tests taken after her arrival at the hospital and probably confirmed from blood and urine samples taken during the Lecomte autopsy (see previous chapter).

In the light of this possible knowledge of a pregnancy, there is clear evidence – see later – of an early decision[a] taken by British authorities to embalm Diana's body while it was still in Paris. That decision could have been the result of an effort to suppress knowledge of a pregnancy – there is evidence that suggests embalming can influence autopsy results.[b]

The placement of Princess Diana's body in an extremely hot environment – see earlier – may have been a deliberate move to facilitate conditions that would demand an embalming take place to preserve her body for presentation purposes – see later.

The embalming of Princess Diana in Paris is a major issue in this case and the evidence of what occurred will become clearer as this chapter progresses.

---

[a] Well before 8.15 a.m.
[b] See Part 2 Pregnancy chapter and the UK Post-Mortems chapter in this volume.

French Evidence Table[a]

Witness Name	Position[b]	Role in Events	Inquest	Paget Report	Police[c] Statement
Jean Monceau	BJL[d] Director	Supervised events	Cross-examined[e]	Excerpts included	Yes
Huguette Amarger	BJL Embalmer	Embalmed Diana	Statement only heard[f]	No	Yes
Sophie Hauffman	BJL Switchbrd & Despatcher	Received and made calls	Not heard	No	No
Bernard Colsy	BJL Asst General Manager[g]	Boss of embalmers	Not heard	No	No
Josselin Charrier	BJL Embalmer	Assisted with embalming	Not heard	No	No
Michel Lebreton	BJL Dry Ice Operative	Allegedly Applied Dry Ice to Diana[h]	Not heard	No	No

[a] This table lists the French witnesses, all of whom were employed by PFG – the funeral directors – or BJL, the embalming company, or were employed by SCI, the company that owned PFG.
[b] Full names of companies are shown in the Company Structure below.
[c] All police statements were taken by Paget – the French investigation completely omitted the entire subject of embalming.
[d] Embalming company.
[e] Police statement not read out – as was usually the case at this inquest when witnesses were cross-examined.
[f] Parts of Amarger's statement were omitted during the inquest reading – see later.
[g] Colsy directly controlled the Île-de-France area, which included Paris: René Deguisne, Witness Statement, 9 May 2005, reproduced in *The Documents* book, p450 (UK Edition)
[h] Later evidence will show that this didn't actually take place.

DIANA INQUEST: THE BRITISH COVER-UP

Witness Name	Position[b]	Role in Events	Inquest	Paget Report	Police[c] Statement
Name Unknown	Kenyons' President	Initiated early phone calls	Not heard	No	No
Jerald Pullins	SCI Executive VP Intl Operations[a]	Allegedly initiated early phone calls[b]	Not heard	No	No
Hervé Racine	OGF President	Phoned PFG	Not heard	No	No
Michel Chapillon	PFG French Director	Organised response	Not heard	No	No
Jean-Claude Plumet	PFG Director	Attended the hospital	Not heard	No	Yes
Gérard Jauze	PFG Director	Attended the hospital	Not heard	No	Yes
Patrick Launay	PFG Director	Attended the hospital	Not heard	No	Yes
Alain Caltiau	PFG Asst General Manager	Handled phones	Not heard	No	No
René Deguisne	BJL Asst General Manager	Head of North, East & West France	Not heard	No[c]	Yes

The above table helps to reveal just how ineffective the inquest was in covering the French witness evidence regarding the embalming of Princess Diana.

Out of 13 key witnesses[a] to various aspects of the embalming related events on the day, only one – Jean Monceau – was cross-examined at the

---

[a] Paget describes Pullins as "former European Managing Director". On 14 August 1997 it was announced that he had been promoted to Executive Vice-President International Operations. This is explained in the section on Malcolm Ross in the Early Royal Control chapter.

[b] This is according to the Paget diagram. It will be shown later that the initial call to Racine was made by the president of Kenyons.

[c] The Paget Report included a short quote made by Monteil, but from Deguisne, in her statement – see Paget Report, p546.

inquest. When it came to the person who actually carried out the embalming – Huguette Amarger – the jury only heard the reading of her statement.[b] The inquest heard no evidence at all from the remaining 11 French embalming witnesses.

In light of this huge "oversight" by the inquest coroner, Scott Baker, it is also significant that the embalming evidence[c] from Jean-Claude Plumet, Gérard Jauze and Patrick Launay was excluded from the Paget Report. This has led to a situation where the British police evidence from these three key witnesses was not made public until the publishing of the 2010 book *Diana Inquest: The Documents the Jury Never Saw.*

As this chapter progresses, two important themes will develop:

1) The statement made by Monceau under oath to the British police in late 2005 is in serious conflict with important areas of his evidence provided, also under oath, to the Baker inquest.

2) Key areas of Jean Monceau's evidence are in conflict with the police statement evidence of the other 4 witnesses who have been interviewed – Amarger, Plumet, Jauze and Launay.

The fact that Monceau's evidence conflicts with that of other witnesses, and himself, is particularly poignant because at the inquest the jury were forced to rely on Monceau's account – he was the only witness cross-examined.

This approach by Scott Baker has led to great difficulties in establishing precisely what did occur in Princess Diana's room at La Pitié Salpêtrière Hospital on 31 August 1997.

---

[a] There are 15 witnesses in the above table. Deguisne, although interviewed by Paget, admitted that he was not a witness to the events – see later. Later evidence will also show that Pullins may not have been a witness.

[b] Parts of her statement were not read out – see later.

[c] In the form of police statements or interviews.

Company Structure: 1997

To fully understand the significance of events on the day, it is important to realise that in 1997 there was a financial linkage between the French funeral directors (PFG) and the French embalming company (BJL).

This is a critical fact that was not made known to the inquest jury.

The diagram on the following page reveals the company structure at the time of the Paris crash, in 1997.

FRENCH EMBALMING

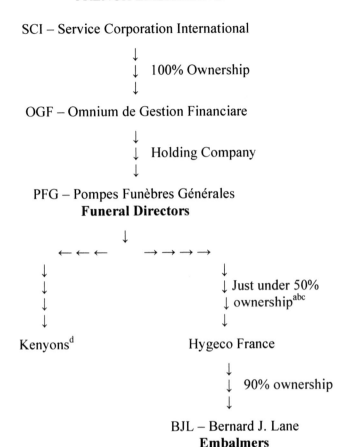

SCI – Service Corporation International

↓
↓ 100% Ownership
↓

OGF – Omnium de Gestion Financiare

↓
↓ Holding Company
↓

PFG – Pompes Funèbres Générales
Funeral Directors

↓

← ← ←   → → → →

↓   ↓
↓   ↓ Just under 50%
↓   ↓ ownership[abc]
↓   ↓

Kenyons[d]   Hygeco France

↓
↓ 90% ownership
↓

BJL – Bernard J. Lane
Embalmers

Figure 6

---

[a] See "Conseil de la Concurrence", Décision No. 97-D-28 29 April 1997: www.afif.asso.fr/francais/conseils/97d28.pdf . Scroll down to Heading "B – Les Pratiques", point 1.

[b] The understanding that BJL was closely related to PFG is supported by statement evidence – not heard by the jury – from Gérard Jauze, a PFG Director: "From memory, with the exception of the [BJL] embalmers, I think that we were the only representatives from PFG at the hospital to arrive before the coffin." : Gérard Jauze, Witness Statement, p6.

[c] A company is not a subsidiary of its parent company unless the parent owns a majority of its shares. Therefore, because PFG's shareholding in Hygeco France was just less than 50% – the "Conseil de la Concurrence" report (see earlier footnote) says "nearly 50%" – BJL was not a full subsidiary of PFG. There was however a significant financial connection between the two companies.

[d] The relationship between PFG and Kenyons is addressed in the Malcolm Ross section of the Royal Control chapter.

Pre-Embalming Events

Chronology of involvement of French embalmers and funeral directors

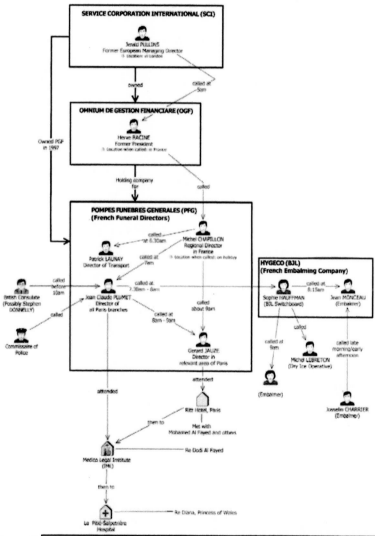

Figure 7 Diagram drawn up by Operation Paget showing French interaction regarding embalming and the transfer of Dodi Fayed's body. On the left side where it states that SCI "owned PGF", that should read "PFG". The person shown as "Embalmer" called at 9 a.m. was Huguette Amarger – see below. This document, found on p563 of the Paget Report, was not made available to the inquest jury.

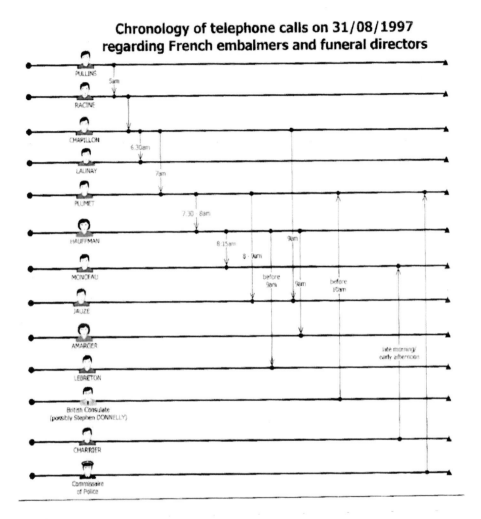

Chronology of telephone calls on 31/08/1997
regarding French embalmers and funeral directors

Figure 8

Diagram drawn up by Operation Paget showing timing of French
phone calls regarding embalming and the transfer of Dodi Fayed's
body (covered in Part 3). Although these two Paget documents give a
general understanding of the communications, a fuller and more
accurate presentation – based on witness and documentary evidence –
appears in the following table that details the phone calls made on 31
August 1997. The above document, found on p564 of the Paget
Report, was not made available to the inquest jury.

91

Phone Calls: 31 August 1997[a]

Time (a.m.)	From		To		Purpose
bc	Name d	Position	Name e	Position	
4.30	Ross	LCO[f] Comp-troller	Unknown	Kenyons' President	Enlist Services for Repatriation and Embalming[g]
5.00	Unknown	Kenyons' President	Racine	OGF President	Order for Repatriation and Embalming[h]
5.30	Racine	OGF President	Chapillon	PFG France Regional Director	Order for Repatriation and Embalming

[a] This chart is based on an overview of the evidence on a very complicated subject. There are conflicts with the Paget view, which has been shown on the previous pages – these are explained through the chapter. Where the evidence is not completely defined, informed estimates have been made. The reader will become more familiar with the story as it develops through this book.

[b] Some of the timings have been estimated, based on information from the Paget Report, inquest evidence and official documents.

[c] Times are Paris local time. UK time is one hour behind: 5.30 in Paris = 4.30 in London.

[d] Surnames only.

[e] Surnames only.

[f] Lord Chamberlain's Office.

[g] Although there is no specific documentary or witness evidence of this call, the general evidence will show that it would have triggered the 5 a.m. call from the Kenyons president to Racine.

[h] There is evidence of Operation Paget informing PFG director, Patrick Launay, about this call. It is also mentioned in the statements of other PFG directors, Jean-Claude Plumet and Gérard Jauze. It is not known how Paget was made aware of the call and its timing. Source: Patrick Launay, Witness Statement, 21 March 2006, reproduced in *The Documents* book, p511 (UK Edition); Jean-Claude Plumet, Witness Statement, 11 November 2005, reproduced in *The Documents* book, p469 (UK Edition); Gérard Jauze, Witness Statement, 21 March 2006, reproduced in *The Documents* book, p477 (UK Edition).

FRENCH EMBALMING

Time (a.m.)	From		To		Purpose
	Name	Position	Name	Position	
7.00	Chapillon	PFG France Regional Director	Plumet	PFG Paris Director	Order for Repatriation and Embalming
7.45	Plumet	PFG Paris Director	Monceau[a]	BJL Embalmer & Director	Order for Embalming by Female
8.15	Monceau	BJL Embalmer & Director	Hauffman	BJL Switchbrd & Despatch	To Organise Embalmer[b]
8.20	Moss	British Consul General	Donnelly	British Vice Consul	Request Dry Ice
8.45	Hauffman	BJL Switchbrd & Despatch	Lebreton	BJL Dry Ice Operative	Inform Services Needed[c]
9.00	Hauffman	BJL Switchbrd & Despatch	Amarger	BJL Embalmer	Inform Services Needed
9.00	Donnelly	British Vice Consul	Caltiau	PFG Asst General Manager	Request Dry Ice
9.45	Hauffman	BJL Switchbrd & Despatch	Amarger	BJL Embalmer	Specific Instructions Given

[a] Paget has shown this call being to Hauffman, with Hauffman later calling Monceau. Evidence in this book will show the call was made directly to Monceau, with Monceau later calling Hauffman.

[b] Monceau's account is that this was a call from Hauffman to himself regarding a request for dry ice. Monceau will be shown in this book to be a liar and the evidence will show that embalming would have been discussed.

[c] Evidence will show that this call never occurred.

Time (a.m.)	From		To		Purpose
	Name	**Position**	**Name**	**Position**	
9.45	Moss	British Consul General	Plumet	PFG Paris Director	Formally Enlist PFG for Repatriation
9.45	NA	Brigade Criminelle Commis-saire	Plumet	PFG Paris Director	Authorised Repatriation[a]
10.30[b]	Charrier	BJL Embalmer	Monceau	BJL Embalmer & Director	Offering Services

It is very significant that the content of the two Paget diagrams[c] was withheld from the jury.

The diagrams reveal:

1) An early morning call from London to Hervé Racine, President of the PFG holding company.[d] The evidence will show that this call set in motion a series of other calls – Racine to Chapillon; Chapillon to Plumet; Plumet to BJL.

The question this raises is: What event would trigger a call to be made from London to Racine at 4 a.m.[e] on a Sunday morning?

This phone call occurred at 5 a.m. Paris time – approximately 50 minutes after the official announcement of the death of Princess Diana.[f]

The timing of this call – extremely early on a Sunday morning – indicates that there was some very important business-related news to be passed on to Hervé Racine.

The evidence in this chapter will reveal that this call included notification that PFG had been requested by a British authority to carry out an embalming on Princess Diana, using a female embalmer.

---

[a] Plumet said he rang "a number of times" – see later. It will be shown from the evidence that these calls probably never took place.

[b] Monceau timed this call at around 12 noon in his account, but later evidence in this book will show that, if this call took place, it must have been much earlier.

[c] Reproduced on the previous pages.

[d] The diagram shows this call being made by the former European CEO of SCI – the company that owned PFG and BJL – Jerald Pullins. Later evidence in this book will show that this is not correct – this call was made by the president of Kenyons, a subsidiary of PFG.

[e] London time – 5 a.m. in Paris. London is one hour behind.

[f] Announced at 4.10 a.m.

The question is: Why was knowledge of the existence of this phone call withheld from the jury during the inquest that "examined [the evidence] in the minutest detail"? [34]

2) There was a phone call from Jean-Claude Plumet, Paris director of PFG to BJL[a] at around 7.45 a.m.[b] – this is approximately 1¼ hours before PFG was called by Donnelly[c] and about ½ an hour prior to Moss' call to Donnelly notifying that he needed ice to cool Diana's body.

This is important because it indicates that communication to BJL – the embalming company connected to PFG – occurred prior to the hot-room crisis (see earlier) that was the official reason for the embalming.

Although later evidence will show that these calls – to Racine and BJL – did not actually occur in the precise way described by Paget, it is nevertheless true that early calls were being made.

That is a critical point that, it will become clear, was withheld from the jury.

As stated earlier, embalming related evidence at the inquest was heard from only two French witnesses: Monceau – cross-examined[d]; Amarger – statement read. As these two witnesses were providing evidence on the same events, it was important that the jury were in a position to easily compare their evidence, but that is not what happened.

Monceau was cross-examined on Tuesday, 20 November 2007 – his evidence concluded at 3.10 p.m.[35e] This left plenty of time for the reading of Amarger's statement which would only take around 8 minutes. Instead of doing that, Baker decided to close the inquest early that afternoon and sent the jury home.

Amarger's statement wasn't read out until two days later – on Thursday, November 22, just prior to the close of the inquest for the weekend.[f] In the intervening two days the jury had heard evidence on various subjects, including a substantial amount of general evidence relating to the embalming. The issue though is that it was only Monceau and Amarger's evidence that could and should have been subjected to direct comparison by the jury, but Baker prevented this from happening.

---

[a] PFG had as financial connection with BJL – see earlier.

[b] This is just 39 minutes after sunrise which was at 7.06 a.m. – see earlier.

[c] Donnelly stated his call took place at about 9 a.m.

[d] Complicating things even further, it will be shown that Monceau, the only French witness cross-examined, has lied repeatedly throughout his testimony on the events.

[e] Inquest days often finished around 4 p.m. – sometimes earlier, sometimes quite a bit later.

[f] Inquest weeks generally lasted 4 days and concluded on Thursdays.

When a comparison of Monceau and Amarger's testimony is carried out, it turns out that there are major conflicts of evidence on some of the most critical aspects.

Huguette Amarger, BJL Embalmer: 8 Mar 05 Statement read out 22 Nov 07: 90.23:

"On 31st August 1997, I was working for Hygeco. My company called me very early in the morning, about 9 a.m. It was the person dealing with planning who called me, but I forget who it was. I was told 'Don't leave home, your services are going to be required, listen to the radio'. I understood it was about the accident to Diana. I must say that I did not have a mobile phone, and stayed at home waiting for the second call.

"Question: Why did your company call you? Did they think they were going to be dealing or had they already been called in?

"Answer: I think that since I was rung, it was because my company had already been called in.

"So I was rung again during the morning, shortly after the first call. I left home between 10 and 11 o'clock. As it was, I lived in the 14th district. It was the person from planning who gave me the order to go to La Pitié Salpêtrière. Later on, during the following week, discussing the matter with some people from the hospital, I learned that the British wanted it to be a woman to take care of giving the treatment.

"Question: What instructions were you given?

"Answer: I was told to go to the mortuary room of La Pitié Salpêtrière...."

Jean Monceau, BJL Director and Embalmer, Paris: 20 Nov 07: 63.1:

Burnett: Q. Did you get a telephone call from Sophie Hauffman, an employee of the company, alerting you to the situation regarding the Princess of Wales?

A. Yes. Sophie Hauffman was the one who was on duty that day at the call centre.

Q. Had an order been placed in the name of the Princess of Wales for dry ice?

A. Yes. Exactly.

Q. Were you informed that the place at which the Princess was lying was La Pitié Salpêtrière Hospital?

A. Yes.

Q. But at this stage, did you know who had made the request for dry ice?

A. Well, it was the person on duty – it was called the "amphitheatre of death" – at the hospital of La Pitié Salpêtrière.

Q. At this stage, had any request been made for an embalmer?

A. Do you mean to ask had a request, a specific request, for embalming services been made at that stage?

Q. At that stage, yes.

A. No.

Q. So the request at that stage was limited to dry ice. What was your immediate reaction to that when you were told of it?

A. Well, no reaction, but one of agreement. If we are asked to do something, we go and do it.

Q. In 1997, and indeed now, was there any legal procedure in place for the application of dry ice to the body of a deceased person?

A. Yes. It was a block of ice under the neck, two on the thorax, two on the abdomen and the last one on the pubis, on the pelvic area.[a]

Q. Now, my question was whether the application of dry ice required any legal procedures to be followed.

A. No, none at all.

Q. Does dry ice assist in making the body of a deceased person look presentable for those who wish to view it?

A. No, not at all.

Q. Is dry ice a product which itself can cause damage to the body of a deceased person?

A. Yes, it burns the skin.

Q. If it was considered necessary – and we will come to this in a moment – but just hypothetically, to prepare a body to make it presentable, is dry ice the procedure that should be used?

A. No, quite the opposite, as a matter of fact. You place dry ice when you want to preserve the body temporarily, but not also that it would be presentable.

Q. Did the time come when you left your home and went to the hospital?

A. Yes.

Q. Did you arrive for a trainee, a student, to join you?

A. No, I asked the person who had the ice to join me.

Q. I see. Did you ask Mrs Hauffman to make contact with anyone else within your company to obtain equipment?

A. Yes, I called my trainee because he was the one who had my equipment, but he could not get it to me, so I called another embalmer who lived nearby, close to the hospital, namely Mrs Amarger.

Q. Your equipment was with your student, your pupil, and is that because you were about to travel abroad to Indonesia?

A. Yes.

Q. So you asked Madame Amarger to join you at the hospital with her embalming equipment?

A. Yes.

Q. At this stage, if I understand your evidence, Mr Monceau, no one had yet asked that the Princess be embalmed. Is that correct?

---

[a] This indicates that Monceau was reasonably familiar with the process.

A. When I asked for embalming equipment, that request had already been made.

Q. By whom?

A. No, it was not a request as such. It was just that the representative of the Consulate of Great Britain asked me whether it was enough to place dry ice because Prince Charles, the Princess of Wales' sister, the President were to come and the body was to be presentable and I said "No, not at all. It is not what it is meant for".

Q. Can I take this –

A. So he asked me what could be done in order for the body to be presentable when the family would come, and I said that there are specific preservation treatments that can be done. So he said to me, "Well, if you can do it, do it".

Q. Now you are describing events that happened at the hospital, I think. I was asking you a question about events long before you got to the hospital, M Monceau. So can we take it very slowly, stage by stage?

A. Well, then, if you take it stage by stage, I did not ask for that equipment before I arrived at the hospital.

Q. Can I take you to one or two passages in your statement to see if I have understood this? I wonder if it could be interpreted. In your statement, when describing the telephone call that you had from Sophie Hauffman, you said this: "Already in my mind, as an embalmer, and knowing the public status of the Princess of Wales, I knew that dry ice would not be enough to make the body presentable."

A. As a matter of fact, the difference between what you think and what you eventually do because you are asked to do it.

Q. So, coming on then to how Mrs Amarger became involved, can I simply read you a passage from your statement? "At the time I had a student who I was training. As I was due to leave for Indonesia, my pupil had my equipment but he was not at home. I therefore asked Madame Hauffman to contact someone else who might have embalming equipment and who did not live far from the hospital. Mrs Hauffman therefore contacted Mrs Amarger." Is that right?

A. Yes, and I directly contacted Mrs Amarger too.

Q. Thank you. So we are now just coming to the point at which you travel to the hospital. So we will take the next stage, if we may, again quite slowly. Now, you went to the hospital and, when you got there, you reported to the police, I believe. Is that right, Mr Monceau?

A. Yes.

Jean Monceau: 18 Oct 05 Statement: **Jury Heard Part Only**:

"On 30 and 31 August 1997 I was on call, but this was implicit, and if staff needed to contact someone, it was me. The following Monday, I was due to leave for Indonesia. I was packing my bags for Indonesia. Sophie Hauffman, a BJL employee who was manning the phones on the switchboard at the company's head office ... and dispatching the embalmers phoned me and told me what was happening. All the calls are noted down on a message pad, which serves as an order form for the work. It is a form listing details of the deceased, the contact details, and the name of the person placing the order, which in this case was PFG. The order form could still be in existence today. I have contacted BJL, who inform me that the order form has been lost, but there is still an accounting document which shows that we were engaged for this matter. However, this document does not show who telephoned Sophie Hauffman. Only Sophie Hauffman could tell you who she spoke to that day.

"The order form had the name of the Princess of Wales, the place – *la Pitié Salpêtrière* – and the first thing was a request for dry ice. It also had the details of the company that called us, namely the General Funeral Service[a], but not the name of the employee. They did not ask us for an embalmer, they simply asked for dry ice. This order form was also marked 'Recommended' in order to highlight its importance.

"I have been asked if I remember the time that Sophie Hauffman received the first call. I do not remember. It was very early in the morning, 0730 [7.30 a.m.] to 0800hrs perhaps, as my wife was still asleep.

"Sophie Hauffman phoned me at possibly 0815hrs, at my home, to ask me: "What should we do?" I said to her: "What have they requested by way of work?". She told me that the funeral directors had asked for dry ice. Already in my mind, as an embalmer, and knowing the public status of the Princess of Wales, I knew that dry ice would not be enough to make the body presentable.

"In 1997, requests for dry ice were a regular feature and we did roughly twenty applications of dry ice per day. But dry ice is very cold, it burns, and the preservation is very temporary, for about 20 hours. And what is more, a public figure with fractures cannot be presented naked. However, because I did not want any trouble in my work, I told her that we had to respect the person placing the order and that we would do as we had been asked. The application of dry ice was the most conservative of the courses of action that the funeral directors could have undertaken. It was the most basic thing, not requiring any

---

[a] PFG.

authorisation, and not even subject to French law. I told her to dispatch someone to apply dry ice to the hospital.

"You have asked me if anyone other than the PFG could have called upon our services. Yes, sometimes it can be the family of the deceased or other embalming companies.

"You have asked me if I know who asked PFG to contact us. No, but I imagine that PFG must also have an order form.

"You have asked me if the person from PFG who called Mrs Hauffman called from the hospital. It is possible. I think they were in the mortuary and called BJL. In my experience, the mortuary in that hospital is not equipped for the task of preparing someone of that status for presentation.

"After the telephone call from Sophie Hauffman, I got dressed and got my car in order to go to the hospital. I wanted to see if there were any problems, and to establish what condition the body was in, in order to make certain that dry ice was the best way to proceed. I must have left home at around 0900hrs [9.00 a.m.] and I got to hospital at around 0930 to 0940hrs.

"You have asked me if Mrs Hauffman or I contacted anyone else from BJL. At the time, I had a student, who I was training. As I was due to leave for Indonesia, my pupil had my equipment, but he was not at home. I therefore asked Mrs Hauffman to contact someone else who might have embalming equipment and who did not live far from the hospital. We did not choose that person specially, I simply needed the equipment she had. Mrs Hauffman therefore contacted Mrs Huguette Amarger." [36]

Comment: The initial issues regarding the embalming relate to how it came about:

1) Who was it that decided Princess Diana should be embalmed?

2) Why was Princess Diana embalmed?

To establish the answers to these questions, it is essential to know the timing of the events that occurred on the day.

The critical timing question is: Was the definite decision to embalm Diana made before discussions between the British Consul (Moss) and French embalmer (Monceau)? This meeting apparently included discussions relating to the potential condition of the body, as a result of the hot room.[a]

If it can be shown that there was a definite decision to embalm well before the hospital conversation between Monceau and Moss, then that raises the

---

[a] The content of these discussions – which took place at the hospital – is covered later, but the official evidence indicates that Moss okayed the embalming procedure during that conversation.

possibility that there was a reason other than the hot room crisis[a] that triggered the process of embalming Diana.[b]

It is therefore very significant that in the evidence heard from Jean Monceau during his inquest cross-examination, he provided no information at all regarding timing. No lawyers asked him about timings of the events he described, and he did not volunteer the information.[c]

Because of this incredible "oversight", the jury heard no evidence from Monceau on: a) the time of the initial call requesting BJL's services; b) the time he arrived at the hospital; and c) the time that Monceau claimed it was decided embalming must be carried out and he directed the equipment be brought to the hospital.

In her evidence Huguette Amarger – who carried out the embalming, see later – does provide some limited information relating to timing:
-   "My company called me very early in the morning, about 9 a.m.... I was told 'Don't leave home, your services are going to be required, listen to the radio'." Amarger added: "since I was rung, it was because my company had already been called in."
-   "I was rung again during the morning, shortly after the first call."
-   "I left home between 10 and 11 o'clock ... to go to La Pitié Salpêtrière."

Amarger added: "During the following week, discussing the matter with some people from the hospital, I learned that the British wanted it to be a woman to take care of giving the treatment."

In summary, Amarger's timing evidence is:
1)   At 9 a.m. Amarger was told: "your services are going to be required"
2)   Before 10 a.m. Amarger had received a second call with specific instructions: "I was told to go to the mortuary room of La Pitié Salpêtrière"
3)   Before 11 a.m. Amarger had left home, heading to the hospital.[d]

Patrick Launay, PFG Repatriation Director: 21 Mar 06 Statement: **Jury Didn't Hear**:
"On the weekend of 30 to 31 August 1997 I was not working, but I could be called in.... Mr Chapillon, who at the time was our Regional Director, called me at home at around 630hrs [6.30 a.m.] to tell me that the Princess of Wales

---

[a] Discussed earlier.

[b] Later evidence will also show that no embalming decision could be legal, unless it had been instigated by or had the approval of the representative of Diana's relatives.

[c] The third person statement excerpts from Monceau shown in the Paget Report also made no mention of the timing of pre-embalming events. This is despite the fact that Monceau did give timings in the original transcript of his statement to the British police – not made public until *The Documents* book was published in 2010.

[d] The conflicts in evidence between Monceau and Amarger will be covered later.

and Dodi Al Fayed had died in a car accident in Paris. He told me that he was on holiday.... He told me to be on standby in case my services were required.... I was not given any instructions, I was simply asked to be available to carry out an assignment. The first thing I did was to switch the television on in order to get some news....

"In the meantime, at 0900hrs, I had called a colleague, Mr Jacques Dupont, my assistant, so that he could be ready to intervene. At around 1000 or 1030hrs I got a call from Mr Plumet, the Director of the Paris agencies and assistant to Mr Chapillon, telling me that he was dealing with the funeral arrangements of the Princess of Wales and Dodi Al Fayed. I asked him if he would need me. He told me that Gérard Jauze, the Director of the Saint-Cys branch, was organising the funeral with him and that he would get back in touch with me when he had more information on the repatriations....

"I should explain that Mr Plumet was Mr Chapillon 's deputy. Mr Jauze in turn was Mr Plumet 's deputy. Mr Dupont was my deputy. 1 reported to Mr Chapillon in the management chain, but in this case my instructions came from Mr Plumet, who was the person in charge on an operational level for the two repatriations.

"In the company hierarchy there was also Mr Alain Caltiau, who was the company representative at all levels, as well as being Mr Chapillon's superior, but I do not know what his involvement was in this case....

"You ask me if a paper or computerised record was made in respect of this matter. I do not know, and I do not have any record. I did not deal with the formalities, I was helping out.

"You ask me if I have any personal notes on this matter. I do not.

"You ask me if I remember getting a call from Mr Steven Donnelly of the British Consulate on Sunday 31 August 1997. I knew Mr Donnelly well, but I do not remember such a call. It is possible that there was contact, but I have no recollection of it....

"You ask me if anyone from PFG contacted BJL Hygeco that day. I for my part did not contact them and I did not have any administrative or personal involvement in the preparations....

"You ask me if I went to the IML that day. No. I sent Mr Jacques Dupont to the IML."[37]

Jean-Claude Plumet, PFG Director of Paris Agencies[a], Paris: 4 Nov 05
Paget description of Statement: **Jury Didn't Hear**:
[Note: Plumet's evidence is a third person account written by DS Easton. Easton stated: "Mr Plumet had explained that he did not wish to provide a

---

[a] The Paget Report describes his position: "He worked for Paris Undertakers ... PFG". Plumet was not just an employee but a director of an organisation that employed 6,000 people in France in 1997: Jean-Claude Plumet, Witness Statement, 11 November 2005, p2.

formal statement". I suggest that is a concern – that Plumet was not prepared to provide evidence under oath.[a]]

"On the weekend of 30th and 31st August 1997, Mr Plumet was at home. He was not 'on-call'.... On the morning of Sunday 31st August 1997, Mr Plumet was asleep.... He was awoken by a telephone call from Mr Chapillon at around 0700hrs [7.00 a.m.], who informed him of the incident in the Alma underpass, and asked him to go into his office to deal with arrangements required for the Princess of Wales.... Mr Chapillon was on holiday.... Mr Plumet has since been made aware that Mr Chapillon had himself been informed of the incident by telephone by Mr Racine. Mr Racine is believed to have been at his home in Paris, and had in turn been telephoned by the company President of the United Kingdom based affiliate.... Mr Plumet then made his way to his office.... At some point before 1000hrs, Mr Plumet received a telephone call at his office from a man from the British Consulate in Paris. Mr Plumet does not recall the name of the person who telephoned him. The caller appointed Mr Plumet and PFG to undertake the necessary arrangements for the transfer of the Princess of Wales. This person explained that this would be for the Princess of Wales' body to be taken from the Pitié Salpêtrière Hospital to the airport at Villacoublay. Other than these details, this person did not give any specific instructions on how this task should be carried out....

"Around the same time, a male 'Commissaire de Police' also telephoned him a number of times at his office. Mr Plumet does not recall the name of this 'Commissaire', but he appeared to be in charge and appeared to have been appointed to liaise directly with PFG.

"For the comprehension of the reader, and upon clarification by Mr Plumet, the rank of 'Commissaire' in the French Police, is equivalent to the rank of Commander in the Metropolitan Police Service. Because on Sunday the Town Hall and the Police Administration Offices were closed, Mr Plumet asked the 'Commissaire' to produce a statement declaring that he authorised Mr Plumet to have the body moved to the United Kingdom. In Mr Plumet's opinion, this 'Commissaire' would have probably also given authority to embalm, and would also have dealt with all the issues surrounding the body of Dodi Al Fayed....

---

[a] It is a further concern that Easton wrote: "This statement is produced as a result of what Mr Plumet said during this discussion, whilst the events are still fresh in my mind and using handwritten notes that I made at the time of our meeting." One wonders why Operation Paget does not use tape recorders when interviewing witnesses. Source: Jean-Claude Plumet, Witness Statement, 11 November 2005, reproduced in *The Documents* book, p468 (UK Edition).

"When asked, Mr Plumet stated that he did not recall making contact with the embalmers B.J.L. on that Sunday morning. When asked to clarify, he explained that it was possible that he had made contact with B.J.L., as the body would be leaving France without a lead lined coffin and in his opinion the body would therefore need to be embalmed, and he simply could not remember. He explained that if he had contacted B.J.L. he would have needed to have a member of the deceased's family or representative to complete documentation for the Police Administration Offices. However, no such member was present. When asked, Mr Plumet stated that he did not recall making a request for dry ice. He explains that this is possible, but he simply could not remember. He also explained that in his opinion, a requirement for dry ice would probably have been dealt with by the hospital.

"To recap, on Sunday 31st August 1997, Mr Plumet received a telephone call at home from Mr Chapillon informing him of the incident and telling him to go into his offices. He subsequently received telephone calls from the British Consulate in Paris and a Police 'Commissaire'. In addition, he does not remember telephoning the embalmers, B.J.L.

"During the course of that morning, the 'Directeur General Adjoint', Deputy General Director of the company, in charge of the 'Île-de-France' region, a Mr Alain Caltiau attended the PFG offices ... and sat at Mr Plumet's desk. Mr Plumet believes that Mr Caltiau informed Mr George Baudon, the Head of Logistics, to organise vehicles and personnel for the day, but other than this he did not have any other involvement in the events surrounding the Princess of Wales and Dodi Al Fayed. He told Mr Plumet that he was simply there in case any problems arose."[38]

Gérard Jauze, PFG Branch Director, Paris: 21 Mar 06 Statement: **Jury Didn't Hear**:

"On Sunday, 31 August 1997, I was at home having a shave when I heard on the radio that the Princess of Wales had died. I had gone out jogging and, when I got back, my wife told me that M. Michel Chapillon, a regional director of PFG, had phoned me at around 0900 hrs [9.00 a.m.]. My wife told me that I should call M. Chapillon and that I would be dealing with the funeral arrangements for the Princess of Wales and Dodi Al Fayed. I phoned M. Chapillon, who informed me that he was on holiday.... He asked me to wait and to be ready to act if I got a call from the Ritz Hotel and/or the British Embassy in Paris. It was also possible that neither of them would call. I just had to be on standby in case we were asked to deal with the funeral arrangements. It seemed logical to me that PFG would be in charge for this type of assignment: we were and still are one of the foremost funeral directors in France and are a point of contact for consulates, embassies and VIPs. We have a structure in place to deal with this kind of situation....

"As soon as the call came in from M. Chapillon ... I decided to go to my office in Saint-Cyr to get my things ready in case I was called to the Ritz

Hotel. I knew that I had to act fast. I took my motorbike and gathered up a few things. I got to my office at 1000 to 1015hrs. On the Sunday, no one was on duty in my office. At around 1100hrs, I got a call from M. Plumet, who was in the regional office in the Boulevard Richard Lenoir, which was the duty branch for Sundays. He told me that he had received a call from the Ritz Hotel and that I should head over there. Things started to hot up....

"You ask me if I know or if I knew Mr Steven Donnelly from the British Consulate in Paris. No. You inform me that Mr Steven Donnelly states that he telephoned the President of PFG that day. If that is the case, he must have called him on his mobile, as I cannot imagine the President working in his office on a Sunday. If not, he must have called the switchboard and they gave him the number for the office in the Boulevard Richard Lenoir, the only office providing coverage on a Sunday. If he phoned our office, he must have spoken to the Assistant General Manager, M. Alain Caltiau, who came into the office on his own initiative to deal with the telephone calls and to assist M. Plumet and me. M. Alain Caltiau has retired, but if you find it helpful, I could find his contact details for you."[39]

René Deguisne, BJL Asst General Manager North, East, West France: 9 May 05 Statement: **Jury Didn't Hear**:

"Question: Who contacted Hygeco[a] following the death of the Princess of Wales? And at what time?

Answer: It was Mr Plumet of Pompes Funèbres Générales [undertakers]. In fact I did not know that. I called Mr Monceau who gave me the information. I do not know at what time that call was made; we no longer have any records for 1997. Our oldest ones go back to 1999.

Question: Do you know who took the telephone call at Hygeco?

Answer: No.

Question: What was Mr Monceau's role?

Answer: He was responsible for the commercial and quality of service sector.

Question: Is it possible that it was he who took the call?

Answer: No, but it was he who gave the instructions.

Question: Do you know who asked Pompes Funèbres[b] to act in this way?

Answer: Yes, it was Mr Moss, the British Consul. He asked for this treatment in expectation of the arrival of the Prince of Wales who wished to see the body. I hand you a copy of the invoice which we sent in the first place to Mr Moss, 45 rue du Faubourg Saint Honoré, Paris 8, a copy of the credit note which cancelled that invoice and a copy of the new invoice addressed to the Embassy of Great Britain, Consular Section, 16 rue Anjou, Paris 8."[40]

---

[a] BJL was owned by Hygeco – see earlier.
[b] PFG.

Comment: Monceau's evidence is that the first event to occur was the placement of "an order ... in the name of the Princess of Wales for dry ice".[a]

In Monceau's statement – not heard by the jury – he outlined the details of this order:

- it was "telephoned [to] Sophie Hauffman"
- it was made "very early in the morning, 0730 [7.30 a.m.] to 0800hrs perhaps"
- it was received by phone and "noted down on a message pad, which serves as an order form for the work"
- "the name of the 'person' placing the order ... was PFG", but the order "does not show who telephoned" it through
- "the person from PFG ... I think they were in the [hospital] mortuary and called BJL" [b]
- "the order form had the name of the Princess of Wales"
- "the place [was] la Pitié Salpêtrière"
- "the first thing was a request for dry ice"
- "they did not ask us for an embalmer"
- "this order form was also marked 'recommended' in order to highlight its importance".

Deguisne has provided an account, based on what Monceau has told him[c], of this same phone call:

- "it was Mr Plumet" of PFG, who made the call
- it is not known "who took the telephone call" at BJL – it was not Monceau
- it was to request embalming: "this treatment in expectation of the arrival of the Prince of Wales" for which Deguisne produced the invoice for the work carried out.[d]

When Plumet was asked about this, he first stated that "he did not recall" contacting BJL. When Paget queried this: "he explained that it was possible" as "in his opinion the body would ... need to be embalmed, and he simply could not remember".

Plumet has really provided an indefinite account: "he did not recall"; "it was possible"; "he simply could not remember".

---

[a] Confirmed to Burnett.

[b] There are two problems with this point: a) The general evidence is that Princess Diana's body was never in the mortuary – see earlier Choice of Room section; b) This would place someone from PFG in the hospital before 8.00 a.m. Later evidence will show that there was no one at the hospital from PFG until Patrick Launay arrived at 3.40 p.m.

[c] "I called Mr Monceau who gave me the information."

[d] This invoice is discussed later in the Role of the British Embassy section of this chapter.

Later evidence will reveal that Plumet – who it will be shown was not present at the hospital until hours after the embalming had been completed – linked himself to the embalming by saying that "he felt that he had all the necessary authorities to proceed".[41ab]

Given that Plumet was not involved in the embalming operation itself, it appears logical that his role could have included passing on the instruction to embalm to BJL, and this is certainly supported by Deguisne: "it was Mr Plumet".

Why would Plumet attempt to distance himself from making this phone call?

The evidence that is revealed later in this chapter will show that the embalming of Princess Diana was a sinister action, which was carried out quickly, and as embalmings go, ineffectively. It will be shown that a major cover-up has taken place to suppress information that could reveal the true purpose of the embalming.

Outside of Plumet's involvement in the pre-embalming process and his claim of dealings with a Commissaire[c], his actions on the day appear to be quite normal for a funeral director. This indicates that Plumet's decision to refuse to provide sworn evidence in a formal statement – see earlier – may show that he is uncomfortable about his role in that pre-embalming process.

Although Deguisne was not an eye-witness and has relied on Monceau for his account – "I called Mr Monceau who gave me the information" – his evidence is significant because he was the first witness to be interviewed on this subject.[d]

There is substantial conflict between the accounts of Monceau and Deguisne:

a) the caller: Monceau – the order "does not show who telephoned" it through; Deguisne – "it was Mr Plumet"

---

[a] There are other comments included in Plumet's statement that link him to the embalming – this is covered later in the section on the Role of Plumet.

[b] Plumet indicated in his statement that he had knowledge of the embalming before it occurred: Plumet was asked if he knew there would be a post-mortem in the UK. "Plumet ... clarifies that if he had been told of this, he would have asked the [police] 'Commissaire' what he should do next, and what he should do about the embalming.": Jean-Claude Plumet, Witness Statement, 4 November 2005, reproduced in *The Documents* book, pp475 (UK Edition)

[c] Later evidence will reveal that Plumet's account of interaction with a Commissaire is fictional – see Repatriation chapter.

[d] Deguisne was interviewed on 9 May 2005; Monceau on 18 October 2005; and Plumet 4 November 2005.

b) the person called: Monceau – it was "telephoned [to] Sophie Hauffman"; Deguisne – it is not known, it was not Monceau

c) the purpose of the call: Monceau – "a request for dry ice"; Deguisne – embalming "treatment".

There are only three aspects of this phone call that Deguisne reveals – caller, person called, purpose of call – and all three conflict with Monceau's evidence, yet Deguisne got his information from Monceau.

Either Deguisne is lying or Monceau is lying, but both accounts cannot be correct. There is also the possibility that Monceau lied to Deguisne prior to Deguisne's police interview.[a]

As this chapter progresses, it will become increasingly apparent that Jean Monceau has lied repeatedly in his evidence – both in his police statement and at the inquest – regarding this embalming of Princess Diana.

As discussed above, Plumet's own evidence – his indefinite account regarding the call, his admission of involvement with the embalming – when seen in the light of Deguisne's definite account, indicates that it was Plumet who made this 7.45 a.m. phone call to BJL.

Monceau has stated that Hauffman took the call. It is significant that no evidence whatsoever has been taken from Sophie Hauffman – she has never been interviewed by police and was not heard from at the inquest.

Deguisne has said that the call was not taken by Monceau, but he has been provided that evidence by Monceau himself. Later evidence will indicate that it was Monceau who took this call from Plumet, and not Hauffman.

Monceau has stated that the call was to request dry ice. Later evidence will reveal that dry ice was never administered to Princess Diana's body and there never was a request from PFG for BJL to use dry ice.[b] The evidence will instead indicate that this call was to instruct BJL to embalm Princess Diana, as stated by Deguisne.

The full evidence on these points will become clearer as this chapter proceeds.

In October 2005 – 8 years after the crash – Monceau has provided very clear and specific information on what was written on this order form. But Monceau also tells us that "the order form has been lost" – this of course means that his account cannot be verified by the actual document itself.[c] And of course, as shown above, Monceau's account cannot be compared to Hauffman's evidence, because she has never been asked to give her account.

Of the remaining two PFG employees who the police interviewed – Launay and Jauze – only Launay was asked about this call: "I for my part did

---

[a] Deguisne was interviewed 5 months earlier than Monceau.

[b] This is despite a 9 a.m. request from Donnelly to PFG – see later.

[c] It's not just that the order form was lost by 2005 – the question is: Why didn't the French or British police seize this document – if it existed – in 1997?

not contact [BJL] and I did not have any administrative or personal involvement in the [embalming] preparations".

In light of the above evidence, it becomes significant that at the inquest Monceau changed his account on who made this early "dry ice" order: the dry ice order came from "the person on duty – it was called the 'amphitheatre of death' – at the hospital of La Pitié Salpêtrière".

In Monceau's 2005 statement the order was from PFG[a], but two years later, at the inquest, it was from the duty officer at the hospital.[b]

The timing of these various witness accounts is critical: Monceau's statement was made in October 2005; Plumet, the following month, in November 2005 and Launay and Jauze, both in March 2006. Then when Monceau was cross-examined at the inquest the following year – in November 2007 – he had changed his evidence.

Why?

I suggest that Monceau initially stated that PFG made the order, but when this was not supported by the PFG accounts – made after Monceau's – then Monceau changed his account to reflect that lack of supporting evidence from PFG. His new evidence instead reflected a comment made by Plumet in November 2005: "a requirement for dry ice would probably have been dealt with by the hospital".

It is significant that Burnett, who formulated his cross-examination questions based on Monceau's statement that he had in front of him, failed to confront Monceau on this critical change of evidence.

In his statement Monceau said that Hauffman was "manning the phones on the switchboard at the company's head office ...[c] and dispatching the

---

[a] In that statement Monceau appears to have inadvertently made a reference to a request from "an authority", without saying who the authority was: "You have asked me if you need authorisation to apply dry ice. No.... The death had been announced on television at 0400hrs [4.00 a.m.], and an authority had called upon our services. Afterwards, we applied the dry ice as this is a non-invasive procedure. There was no need for authorisation.": Jean Monceau, Witness Statement, 18 October 2005, reproduced in *The Documents* book, p411.

[b] The inquest also heard the following exchange between Hough and Keith Moss, the British Consul General:
Hough: "Now the information from M Desguine [sic] of that company is that BJL was called in by the undertakers, PFG. Does that accord with what you understand?"
Moss: "I would not dispute it. I do not specifically recall it but I am sure that is correct": 22 Nov 07: 22.21. Deguisne's account – which conflicts with what Monceau told the inquest – came from a statement that wasn't tabled at the inquest (see earlier).

[c] Monceau included the full street address here: "20, Boulevard de la Muette, BP 64 (95142) Garges les Gonesse".

embalmers". By the inquest Monceau had reduced Hauffman's role to "the one who was on duty that day at the call centre".

The Paget communications diagram – see earlier – shows Amarger being called by Hauffman, "BJL Switchboard". Amarger's actual evidence was that it was "the person dealing with planning who called me, but I forget who".

If it was Hauffman that called Amarger – and Monceau's statement admission that she was "dispatching the embalmers"[a] indicates that it would have been – then Hauffman's role ("dealing with planning") is a far cry from what the inquest heard: "on duty ... at the call centre".

The importance of Hauffman's role makes it unbelievable that she has never been interviewed and was not heard from at the inquest.

There is an additional key point that raises doubts about Monceau's evidence regarding the 7.45 a.m. call to BJL:

In his 2005 statement Monceau said: "I have been asked if I remember the time that Sophie Hauffman received the first call. I do not remember. It was very early in the morning, 0730 [7.30 a.m.] to 0800hrs perhaps, as my wife was still asleep."

Monceau was asked about the timing of the initial call to Hauffman, and has supplied a time – 7.30 to 8.00 – based on the information: "my wife was still asleep".

The question is: What has Monceau's wife being asleep got to do with a call being received by Hauffman at the BJL office? This appears to be an inadvertent admission by Monceau that the initial call was actually to him at home – not to Hauffman. It could be that the next call Monceau mentions: "Sophie Hauffman phoned me at possibly 0815hrs, at my home", may have instead been from Monceau to Hauffman, to pass on instructions.

Later evidence will reveal that there is good reason to suggest that Monceau was contacted early, but not about dry ice.

Monceau's evidence is:
- "a specific request, for embalming services" had not been made when the dry ice was ordered – inquest
- "they did not ask us for an embalmer, they simply asked for dry ice" – statement
- "I knew that dry ice would not be enough to make the body presentable" – statement
- "I told [Hauffman] to dispatch someone to apply dry ice to the hospital" – statement
- "I asked the person who had the ice to join me" at the hospital – inquest
- "my pupil had my equipment but he was not at home" – statement
- "I called my trainee because he was the one who had my equipment, but he could not get it to me" – inquest

---

[a] Not heard by the jury.

- "I therefore asked Madame Hauffman to contact someone else who might have embalming equipment and who did not live far from the hospital. Mrs Hauffman therefore contacted Mrs Amarger" – statement
- "I called another embalmer who lived nearby, close to the hospital, namely Mrs Amarger" – inquest
- confirmed that he "asked Madame Amarger to join [him] at the hospital with her embalming equipment" – inquest
- "I directly contacted Mrs Amarger too" – inquest
- "I did not ask for that [embalming] equipment [from Amarger] before I arrived at the hospital" – inquest.

There are then additional conflicts between Monceau's 2005 statement and his 2007 inquest account:[a]

a) In 2005: "I told [Hauffman] to dispatch someone to apply dry ice to the hospital"

At the inquest: "I asked the person who had the ice to join me" at the hospital.

In his 2005 statement Monceau asked Hauffman to organise the dry ice operative, but at the inquest he did it himself.

b) In 2005: "I therefore asked Madame Hauffman to contact someone else.... Mrs Hauffman ... contacted Mrs Amarger"

At the inquest: "I called another embalmer who lived nearby, close to the hospital, namely Mrs Amarger".

In 2005 he asked Mrs Hauffman to find another embalmer with the equipment who lived close to the hospital – Monceau did not know which embalmer Hauffman would choose. In other words, Monceau gave Hauffman the two criteria – equipment and location – and left it up to Hauffman to find the right person.[b]

By 2007 this had changed to Hauffman being left out of the equation and Monceau instead calling Amarger direct from the hospital. At the inquest, as soon as Monceau realised there was a conflict, he tried to adjust his 2005 account: "Yes, and I directly contacted Mrs Amarger too."

Amarger made no mention of being phoned by Monceau, who she calls "my boss" in her evidence – see later.

c) In 2005: "My pupil had my equipment but he was not at home"

At the inquest: "I called my trainee because he was the one who had my equipment, but he could not get it to me".

---

[a] These conflicts occurred despite Burnett appearing to use a method of questioning that prompted Monceau from his 2005 statement.

[b] It also had to be someone who was willing or available to work on Sunday.

In 2005 Monceau could not locate the trainee, but at the inquest the trainee appears to have been contacted but "could not get" the equipment to Monceau.

So in summary Monceau's key general evidence at this stage is:

1) An order was placed with BJL for dry ice

2) At that stage "a specific request for embalming services" had not been made

3) "I said [to Moss] that there are specific preservation treatments that can be done. So he said to me, 'Well, if you can do it, do it'." [a]

4) Monceau only considered using another embalmer when he was unable to access his own equipment

5) Monceau stated that he didn't seek his equipment until after his conversation with Moss at the hospital

6) The reason Amarger was chosen as the embalmer was because she "did not live far from the hospital".

At this point it is important for the reader to understand that Monceau's evidence is that he made no moves to seek out his embalming equipment until he had the go ahead from Moss to conduct the embalming. This took place at the hospital.[b]

This Monceau evidence then indicates that the following phone calls occurred after Monceau had arrived at the hospital and conversed with Moss:[c]

- Monceau to his student trainee
- Monceau to Hauffman[d]
- Hauffman to Amarger
- Monceau to Amarger.

When analysed closely, the conflict between Monceau and Amarger's evidence is stark. Amarger appears to be describing a situation where by 9 a.m. the British have requested an embalming that needed to be carried out by a woman – "since I was rung, it was because my company had already been called in" and "the British wanted it to be a woman to take care of giving the treatment".

In other words, Amarger is saying that the fact that she, the embalmer, was rung at 9 a.m. indicated that an embalming must have already been

---

[a] The Moss-Monceau conversation is addressed in detail later.

[b] Monceau clarified this in his inquest evidence: "I did not ask for that equipment before I arrived at the hospital".

[c] This will become clearer when the Moss-Monceau conversation is dealt with later in this chapter.

[d] This is Monceau's call to Hauffman seeking an embalmer, as told in his 2005 statement.

requested – and she later found out that the British had specifically asked for a female embalmer.[a]

This evidence indicates that the reason Amarger was called in to conduct the embalming was because the "British wanted it to be a woman".

Monceau makes no mention of this: he states that the reason Amarger was chosen was because he couldn't get his equipment[b], and secondarily, because Amarger lived close to the hospital.

The other major conflict between Monceau and Amarger relates to the timing of the events – again, all of Monceau's evidence heard at the inquest was devoid of timing.[c] This point will be dealt with later.

Before the timing conflicts are addressed, it is important to understand the significance of Monceau's evidence regarding dry ice.

Dry Ice

The evidence from Donnelly – see earlier – was that he was called by Moss "at about 8.15 a.m. to 8.20 a.m.". Moss told him that "he had asked the hospital to provide ice to put around the body, but that the hospital had told him that they did not have any. So he asked me to try to find some ice."[d] Donnelly states that at "around 9 a.m." he called PFG and was "put through to a man who introduced himself [as] the president of the company". Donnelly said that "it was as if he had been expecting my call". Donnelly went on to tell the person that ice was needed and the man replied that "he could help and that he would deal with it".

Jean-Claude Plumet, PFG Paris Director, stated that "at some point before 1000hrs [10.00 a.m.] [he] received a telephone call at his office from a man from the British Consulate in Paris. Mr Plumet does not recall the name of the person who telephoned him. The caller appointed Mr Plumet and PFG to undertake the necessary arrangements for the transfer of the Princess of Wales."

---

[a] Amarger should have been asked who at the hospital she talked to, and they should have been interviewed by police and cross-examined at the inquest.

[b] In his statement Monceau pointed out: "We did not choose [Amarger] specially, I simply needed the equipment she had." It could be significant that his evidence was taken 7 months after Amarger's (March 2005 and October 2005).

[c] I suggest that the lack of timing in Monceau's inquest evidence is not a coincidence, but is deliberate. This may become more apparent when the evidence is reviewed in the "Conclusions" section of this chapter.

[d] When one considers that dry ice is used widely in the medical industry for preserving organs, the question is raised: How is it that a hospital in late 20th century Paris didn't have dry ice, or access to it?

In their diagram Paget have suggested this call could have been from Stephen Donnelly. I suggest that that is not possible: a) Plumet is far removed from being the "president" of PFG; b) the content of the calls is completely different – Donnelly was asking for ice, whereas Plumet spoke to a man who was authorising PFG to organise Diana's repatriation; c) In a 2005 communication with Paget, Monteil stated: "Let us remember that PFG had themselves been called upon by Mr Moss, British Consul to Paris".[42]

It makes sense that this call to Plumet could have come from Moss – and Moss should have been asked about it at the inquest, but wasn't.[ab]

In this light, it is significant that Paget did not ask Plumet about the Donnelly phone call during his interview. They did however ask the other two PFG directors who gave evidence. Jauze, who was a branch director, said: "If [Donnelly] phoned our office, he must have spoken to the Assistant General Manager, M. Alain Caltiau, who came into the office on his own initiative to deal with the telephone calls".

Launay's evidence was that Caltiau "was the company representative at all levels, as well as being Mr Chapillon's[c] superior" – this places Caltiau two rungs above Plumet in the company hierarchy and without a doubt the most senior PFG person present on the day.[d]

Each of the three witnesses gives Caltiau a different title: Launay – "company representative at all levels"; Jauze – "Assistant General Manager"; Plumet – "Deputy General Director". Given that French is not Donnelly's first language, I suggest that it is possible that he made the ice request to Caltiau and perceived he was talking to the president of PFG – this is what the balance of the evidence indicates.

Caltiau should have been interviewed by the police or the inquest. This has never happened.

-----

[a] The jury were not even made aware of this call because Plumet's statement was not read out.

[b] In his statement Moss said: "Part of [Donnelly's] duties included liaison with 'Pompes Funèbres Générales'.... I do not recall how the decision to instruct this firm, above any other, came about." Plumet has said that he recalls a call from the British Consulate. Neither Moss nor Donnelly claim to have made that call. The general evidence shows that PFG's services had already been requested at the same time as BJL's were – before 9 a.m. – see earlier. It appears that the later call, described by Plumet, was a more specific confirmation that PFG's services would be required. Source: Keith Moss, Witness Statement, 22 October 2004, reproduced in *The Documents* book, p652 (UK edition).

[c] Chapillon was French Regional Director.

[d] Plumet stated that "Caltiau ordered lunch" for the staff at the office: Jean-Claude Plumet, Witness Statement, 11 November 2005, p4.

Despite Donnelly being told that "he would deal with it", there does not appear to be any evidence of Donnelly's 9 a.m. request for ice being followed up.

According to Monceau, an order for dry ice was submitted to BJL between 7.30 and 8 a.m. – this is over an hour before Donnelly's call to Caltiau.[a] Monceau states that Hauffman then called him at 8.15 a.m.

The detail of the dry ice order – as described by Monceau – has been dealt with earlier in this chapter. There were several important inconsistencies in the evidence and it remains that Monceau's account of this order is not supported in any other evidence – documentary or witness.

The inquest jury heard Monceau say that the order was made by the hospital.[b] The content of the call from Moss to Donnelly at around 8.20 a.m. indicates that the hospital had not told Moss that they would order dry ice: "the hospital had told him that they did not have any – so he asked me to try to find some ice."

And when Donnelly calls Caltiau at around 9 a.m., he is not told that the issue is already being dealt with – Caltiau instead told Donnelly that "he would deal with it".

There are several points:

1) Hospital staff should have been interviewed to establish if an order was made – this never occurred. No hospital staff member has ever been interviewed in connection with any aspect of the embalming.

2) This call is not included in Paget's comprehensive listings of calls made – see earlier diagrams. This is because the hospital call only entered Monceau's evidence at the inquest and was not included in his Paget statement – see earlier.

3) Normally there is paperwork associated with a commercial order of this nature, but no documentation supporting Monceau's assertion that the hospital (or PFG) ordered dry ice has ever surfaced.

---

[a] This timing difference must be seen in the context of events at the hospital – Diana was moved into the final room at around 7.00 a.m. and sunrise was at 7.06 a.m. It makes sense that the heat in Diana's room would not have become an issue until well after that time. Moss said: "To begin with, it was a fairly comfortable ambient temperature, but as the day progressed ... the outside temperature began to increase". It is a long stretch to connect a dry ice order received by BJL between 7.30 and 8.00 a.m. with a heating room. The timing of Moss' phone call to Donnelly – 8.15 to 8.20 a.m. – is more realistic. Donnelly then spent some time contemplating what to do, and didn't phone PFG until another ¾ of an hour, at "around 9 a.m." Meanwhile, Monceau said he "must have left home at around 0900hrs [9.00 a.m.]".
[b] This conflicted with his statement evidence – not heard by the jury – that the order was made by PFG.

4) The only evidence relating to dry ice being applied to Diana's body comes from Monceau – this is covered below.[a]

In his evidence Monceau has made categorical statements regarding the usage of dry ice – that evidence needs to be subjected to scrutiny.

Monceau was asked very specific questions at the inquest:
- "Does dry ice assist in making the body of a deceased person look presentable for those who wish to view it?" Monceau: "No, not at all."
- "Is dry ice a product which itself can cause damage to the body of a deceased person?" Monceau: "Yes, it burns the skin."
- "To prepare a body to make it presentable, is dry ice the procedure that should be used?" Monceau: "No, quite the opposite, as a matter of fact."

This evidence from Monceau is incredible for two reasons:

a) Monceau personally claims to have supervised the application of dry ice to Princess Diana's body – see later

b) in his statement – not heard by the jury – Monceau said: "In 1997, requests for dry ice were a regular feature and we [BJL] did roughly twenty applications of dry ice per day".

The question for now is: Is what Monceau says here about dry ice correct?

I entered the words "dry ice funeral directors" into Google Search[b] - it gave 67,200 results. When I conducted the research on what sites say about dry ice, I found that it is widely recommended as a means for preserving bodies for presentation purposes – particularly where relatives of the deceased do not wish the body to be intrusively contaminated with powerful embalming fluids, and also when bodies are viewed outside of funeral parlours, e.g. in the home.

The following sites or articles are a sampling of those that refer to the use of dry ice, generally for presentation purposes:
- "Most funeral homes have coolers. Refrigeration is also done with dry ice....": Last Rights of Central Pennsylvania[43]
- "One of the options funeral directors can use to preserve a body for viewing or transport is dry ice or refrigeration": The-Daily-Record.com[44]
- "Ice or dry ice can be used to preserve the body until burial": www.greenyour.com[45]
- Funeral Directors where packages including dry ice are encouraged:
  Shalom Funeral Service, Denver, USA[46]
  Neyagawa City Funerals, Neyagawa, Japan[47]
- "Thresholds[c] uses dry ice to slow decomposition until the body is taken to be buried or cremated": Home Funeral.info[48]

---

[a] See below cross-examination of Monceau which is discussed in the Comment following it.
[b] On 6 December 2009.
[c] A company that helps people to conduct home funerals.

- In North America "when specified by state ordinance (usually within 24 hours of death) refrigeration, chilling or dry ice can usually be legally substituted for embalming": Wikipedia: Natural Burial[49]
- "Lots of dry ice, or even ice packs, works fine in keeping bodies cool enough" for inter-state transportation: Greensprings Natural Cemetery Preserve[50]
- "To gain a place on the [Green Burial Council] list the funeral homes must ... use refrigeration or dry ice to preserve the deceased": Grave Matters[51]
- "Transfer the deceased to the place of viewing.... Dry ice is recommended to keep the deceased cool.... You will need to purchase approximately 30 lbs of dry ice placed in a plastic bag and then cloth bag....": Funeral Ideas.com[52].

This evidence raises serious concerns regarding Monceau's expert evidence to the inquest. Monceau: a) denied that dry ice can "assist in making the body of a deceased person look presentable"; b) stated that dry ice shouldn't be used to make a body presentable; and c) stated that dry ice "burns the skin" of the deceased body.

The truth would appear to be the opposite of what Monceau told the jury: dry ice can be used to make a body look presentable; there is no convincing reason why dry ice shouldn't be used to make a body presentable and dry ice doesn't burn the skin, if it is enclosed in a cloth bag – as indicated on the Funeral Ideas site above.

Returning to the issue of the content of the Hauffman-Monceau phone call that Monceau described taking place at 8.15 a.m. – the evidence (see earlier) indicates that the conversation could not have been about an order for dry ice from the hospital or PFG.[a] It is also more likely that the call was placed by Monceau – see earlier.[b]

This raises the question: What was that 8.15 a.m. conversation about?

I suggest that the answer lies in the content of the call made by Hauffman to Amarger at around 9 a.m. – Hauffman told Amarger: "Don't leave home, your services are going to be required, listen to the radio".

This is where the stark timing difference between Amarger and Monceau's evidence comes to light: Amarger's evidence shows that at some point before 9 a.m. it had been decided that an embalming was going to be carried out by a female operative, and Amarger was chosen.

---

[a] Since Hauffman has never been interviewed, the only evidence that this 8.15 a.m. phone call took place is from Monceau.
[b] Earlier evidence indicated that Plumet called Monceau around 7.45 a.m. and Monceau would have then called Hauffman at around 8.15 a.m.

I suggest a possible scenario: Amarger's evidence would fit with the 8.15 a.m. call from Monceau stating to Hauffman that the British had requested an embalming in France and that it needed to be carried out by a female.

This scenario would account for why Diana's body lay in the hospital room for several hours after sunrise without receiving an administration of dry ice[a] – because from Monceau's point of view this was never about dry ice, but instead the conduct of an embalming requested of him by the British.[b]

This would also account for why Monceau's evidence was so critical of dry ice as an option – because Monceau has been placed in a position where he has to defend his actions carried out on the day. Those actions were the ordering of an embalming, which meant that any blood samples taken during the later British post mortem would not be credibly testable (see later).

There is a major conflict of evidence from Monceau – between his statement and the inquest – regarding the sequence of events once he arrived at the hospital. This is dealt with later, but suffice it to say at this stage that with regard to timing, Monceau's evidence is that Amarger wasn't called at anywhere close to the time that Amarger has said.

Amarger states she was called about 9 a.m., but Monceau says that he didn't arrive at the hospital until at least 9.30 a.m. and didn't seek another embalmer until well after that. The precise timing differences will become clearer as this chapter develops.

Jean Monceau, BJL Director and Embalmer, Paris: 20 Nov 07: 67.21:
Burnett: Q. Now, you went to the hospital and, when you got there, you reported to the police, I believe. Is that right, Mr Monceau?
A. Yes.
Q. Did you see the Prefect of Police, Mr Massoni, in the corridor in the hospital?
A. Yes.
Q. Did you tell him that you had been called to apply dry ice to the body of Princess of Wales?
A. I do not remember that.
Q. Well, again, that is in the statement that you made two years ago, and no doubt you thought carefully about the content of your statement.
A. Yes.
Q. Does that generally represent your best recollection of events?
A. What?
Q. Does the content of the statement represent your best recollection of

---

[a] Monceau has stated that dry ice was administered but that is not supported by any other witness accounts. This issue is dealt with later.
[b] Probably directly requested by Plumet, who would have been passing on information from Chapillon, Racine and originally the president of Kenyons, who was in the UK – see earlier and later.

events?

A. Yes. Yes, of course, yes.

Jean Monceau: 18 Oct 05 Statement: **Jury Didn't Hear**:

"When I arrived at the hospital, I reported to the police. I saw the Prefect of Police, Massoni, in a corridor in the hospital very close to the entrance, together with some senior officers. I told the Prefect that I had been called to apply dry ice to the body of the Princess of Wales and that I would report back to him later."[53]

Philippe Massoni, Prefect of Police, Paris: 14 Nov 06 Statement read out 21 Nov 07: 60.2:

"I do not have any recollection of being involved in the decision to embalm the Princess of Wales....

Question: "M Monceau, an embalmer, recalls speaking to you. Do you remember this conversation?

Answer: "Not at all."

Jean Monceau: 20 Nov 07: 68.16:

Burnett: Q. Did you go to the room in which the body of the Princess of Wales was lying?

A. Yes. A nurse guided me.

Q. Was it an ordinary room within the hospital?

A. Yes, it was a bedroom.

Q. At that time, were there any representatives from the British authorities present in the room?

A. No.

Q. No one. Was there a dry ice operative there?

A. No.

Q. Can you remember when he arrived?

A. It is really difficult to remember ten years later if the person came half an hour or an hour later. I know he was not there when I got there. I stood there trying to start examining the body, looking at the stitches, et cetera, and what I could do. I know that at some point in time a young man, Michel Lebreton, arrived.

Q. Was the dry ice there when you arrived?

A. No.

Q. How did that arrive? Was it with Mr Michel Lebreton?

A. Yes, because Michel Lebreton was the person in charge of applying dry ice to bodies.

Q. Were you present in the room when he started to apply dry ice to the body?

A. Yes.

Q. Now again, can I simply remind you of what you said in your statement? I appreciate it is extremely difficult to remember the detail after ten years, but you said this: "Michel Lebreton, the dry ice operative, was already in the room. He was alone." Then you describe the room.

A. Well, it is not what I remember.

Q. It is not what you remember now. Let's go on. At some stage Michel Lebreton began to apply dry ice to the body. Is that right?

A. Yes.

Q. Was it necessary to deal with bandages and compresses and things of that sort before doing so?

A. Yes.

Q. He began to put dry ice on the body and you started to describe that to us earlier. Is that the process you were describing?

A. Yes.

Q. Without giving us any details of what you saw, was it your view that the body of the Princess was fit to be viewed by her family and the President of France and others who might be coming later?

A. [If] the question was with dry ice only, the body could be presentable? The answer is not at all.

Q. Did you in fact come to the conclusion that the dry ice should be removed?

A. Well, my idea was to explain what would happen if we were to just use dry ice to present the body. Obviously I thought that had to be removed if we were to apply another treatment to the body, but it was not removed at that very moment.

Q. The body of the Princess was, as you have told us, in an ordinary room and this was August 31st. Was it hot in there?

A. It is hard to remember. I guess the temperature was not fit to preserve the body as such without doing anything, but I do not know whether it was really hot or not.

Q. Did you come to the conclusion that the body of the Princess needed to be embalmed?

A. Well, it is not the way it was decided. As a thanatopractitioner, I am always in favour of preservation treatment because I know that it works and I know that it makes the body presentable. But did I explain to the representatives, the different representatives that were present, that it was necessary to proceed to embalming procedures? No.

Q. I think again you may be getting ahead of me. I am taking it stage by stage. At this stage, you are in the room, having been there with Michel Lebreton dealing with the dry ice, and I am simply asking the question whether, in your professional judgment – leave aside anyone else – in your professional judgment, you thought that there was a need to embalm the body.

A. Yes.

Q. Now in your statement, you say precisely that, that it was your feeling "... that we had to embalm the body" and that you would convince people that you had to perform embalming. Do you remember saying that?

A. You are saying that you want to proceed stage by stage, and concerning the stage that you are talking about, I am alone with Michel Lebreton in the room and so I cannot try to convince anyone.

Q. I am trying not to be controversial. I just wish to show you what you said in your statement. So what you are saying is that you were not in a position to convince anyone at that stage because only Mr Lebreton was with you?

A. That is right.

Q. Forgive me. That was my fault, I am sure. You then had a meeting with various people from the funeral directors, that is Mr Plumet and M Jauze, and you spoke to them about the need to embalm. Is that right?

A. Yes, that is right.

Q. You asked them about seeking the necessary authorisations to embalm; is that right?

A. Well, if you want to take it stage by stage, I talked to those two people, the funeral directors, of the possibility of embalming before I talked about it to the representatives of the British authorities.

Q. Thank you.... Where we have reached in the process is that you had discussed the possibility of embalming with the funeral directors and, at that stage, had you had any discussions with anyone from the British authorities or did that come later?

A. Well, I first went to discuss the matter with the representative of the British Consulate and I had not met anybody yet because actually, when I arrived at the hospital, I was just walked to the room by a nurse.

Q. I think there is no disagreement here, at least in the way I am putting the questions to you and your answers. Again, what you say in your statement is that the people from the funeral service introduced you to the Consul General, Mr Moss.

A. Yes, that is true, yes.

Q. So that was after you had had a discussion with the people from the funeral service about the general topic of embalming?

A. Yes.

Q. Thank you. It was about this time, I think, that your colleague, Madame Amarger, arrived at the hospital. Do you remember that?

A. I think it was at around that time. Whether it was at precisely that time, I could not tell you.

Q. Do you remember having a discussion with Mr Moss, the British Consul General in Paris?

A. Yes.

Q. Were you aware by this time that it was expected that various members of the Princess's family and also the President of France and others would wish to pay their respects to the late Princess that day?

A. Yes, I was told that the Prince was expected at about 5 o'clock, at Villacoublay, the airport.

Q. Did you have a discussion with Mr Moss about the subject of presenting the body of the Princess of Wales to those who wished to pay their respects?

A. Yes.

Q. What did you suggest to him?

A. Well, he told me to do what was necessary, and it was very obvious to me that it was not possible to present the body in the state that it was; that is, without any clothes on and not at all prepared, with just dry ice applied to it.

Q. I do not need the details from you, but did you explain to him the basic embalming procedure that you had in mind?

A. Yes, in a basic way, like we do with a family anyway. With members of the family of the deceased, you never go into the details.

Q. No. We, I am sure, all understand that it involves introducing chemicals, but also in such gestures as washing the hair of the deceased person, making sure that blemishes are covered up and matters of that sort?

A. Yes, exactly.

Q. I think you said a moment or two ago that essentially Mr Moss said to you to do whatever was necessary to make the Princess presentable to those who were coming later that afternoon.

A. Yes.

Q. At about that time, did another embalmer from your firm, M Charrier, make contact with you and you asked him to join you at the hospital?

A. Yes.

....Q. Did you speak to Madame Martine Monteil who was the head of the Brigade Criminelle?

A. Yes.

Q. She was somebody who you knew, at least by reputation; is that right?

A. Sure.

Q. What did she say to you when you explained the process that you were proposing to undertake?

A. Well, I did not exactly explain to her the actual process. I just presented to her the situation, what the situation was, that Mr Chirac was going to come, that Prince Charles was going to come, and I said that, as such, the body was not presentable. So she gave me her personal mobile phone number and she said "Do what is necessary, and if you have any problems, then you can call me".

Q. Did she tell you that everything would be in order and the authorisations would be given?

A. Yes, she said that the authorisations would be issued.

Q. Did you take that as official authority to proceed?

A. No. I could not say that I took it as an official authorisation. I took it for what it was, that is somebody representing the police authorities, telling me to do what was necessary to present the body as well as possible.

Q. Thank you.

A. Because I had conversed with the Prefect of Police and the British General Consul. So that was a number of people with whom I had discussed the matter and who had, all of them, the same opinion.

Q. I should emphasise, Mr Monceau, that I do not believe anyone is offering any criticism of the way you acted. That is not my understanding at the moment.

.... Q. Well now, just to ask you a few final questions to make sure that I have understood your evidence correctly. Is it right that no one asked you to embalm the Princess's body? In fact, you suggested it and then Mr Moss agreed?

A. Yes, it is true.

Q. Was the single reason for wishing to embalm the body of the Princess to make her body presentable to those who would be viewing it later that day?

A. The general idea is that everything that was done was to make the body presentable.

Jean Monceau: 18 Oct 05 Statement: **Jury Didn't Hear**:

"After [meeting with Massoni] I went up to the first floor, where the Princess of Wales was in a wing where there were no patients. It must have been around 1000hrs [10.00 a.m.]. I met the departmental supervisor and some other people from the police, but I don't know who they were. The Princess of Wales was in a room that they pointed out to me. There were no representatives from the British authorities or from the funeral service at that stage.

"Michel Lebreton, the dry ice operative, was already in the room. He was alone. The Princess of Wales was on a hospital bed. It was a ward for four people, but there was just her bed. The body had been left under a sheet, but Michel Lebreton was already working, and the body was undressed on the hospital bed. Mr Lebreton was in the process of sponging the blood: he was changing the absorbent bandages and the compresses, as she had come out of the operating theatre. He had started putting on the dry ice, but as soon as I saw the physical condition of the body, I told Michel Lebreton to remove the dry ice. I did not know how she was going to be presented, but in view of the injuries, the blood on her thigh, regurgitation from the mouth and the nose due to pulmonary problems, I said to myself that dry ice was inadequate. We therefore removed the dry ice together. There were already two pieces of dry ice on the abdomen, two pieces on the thorax and one piece at the back of the neck. Dry ice is pre-cut into 15cm x 15cm and 1.5cm thick pieces. The dry ice had not yet burnt the tissue.[a]

"You have asked me how I was dressed that day. I imagine that I would have arrived in a shirt and tie, and I got changed into a white coat. From memory, I think that Michel Lebreton was wearing a white coat, but I do not know. Later on, when I did the embalming with Huguette Amarger, we donned white coats and gloves etc.

"It was not a normal day. I was constantly going in and out. I spoke to a number of people. It must have been between 1030 and 1045hrs.

"You have asked me if you need authorisation to apply dry ice. No. As soon as death is declared real and constant, and the body has waited a while before going to the mortuary – it is a legally stipulated period in the event that the person might be alive – the body is taken to the mortuary and placed in a refrigerator. But this was not the case here. A decision was taken that she would not be going to the mortuary. As far as I was concerned, that legal deadline had passed. The death had been announced on television at 0400hrs, and an authority had called upon our services. Afterwards, we applied the dry ice as this is a non-invasive procedure. There was no need for authorisation.

"After removing the dry ice, we dealt with the body. We raised the head in order to avoid cadaveric lividity forming in the head. I had asked to see someone from the funeral authorities to explain the problems with the dry ice, so there was a lot of waiting around. My feeling was that we had to embalm the body, but I was in no position to act. Furthermore, at that time, Mrs Amarger had not yet brought the equipment. I knew already that I would convince the people that we had had to remove the dry ice, which we had removed, and that we had to perform embalming.

"I met Paul Burrell, the butler.... He had been given a room in the corridor. He was in that room crying....

"After that, I met the people from the funeral directors, PFG, Mr Plumet and Mr Jauze. It must have been around 1130hrs. I told them about my intention to request authorisation to carry out embalming, as the dry ice was not going to be adequate. They told me that you need

---

[a] This raises the issue: Why didn't Lebreton apply the dry ice with a cloth bag to prevent burning, as is the normal practice – see earlier and later.

all sorts of authorisations. I told them that we had to see who the authority was to sign a request for authorisation to carry out embalming.

"Meanwhile, I released Michel Lebreton. Mrs Amarger had arrived at the hospital. It must have been around 1130 to 1200hrs, or even 1300hrs, but earlier than afternoon. I decided that it would be Mrs Amarger who would do the embalming, but we were waiting for authorisation. I asked how the body was to be presented, the schedule for the family's visit, when the body was to be taken away, etc. in order to find out how to proceed. These conversations were with people from the funeral service, and they in turn introduced me to the British Consul-General in Paris, Mr Keith Moss....[a]

"During this time [talking to Moss] another embalmer, Josselin Charrier, phoned me. He asked me if I needed any help. I said the more the better. He arrived at the hospital at around 1330hrs [1.30 p.m.]. He was my equivalent within the company, in charge of the transport department. Later on, it would be him that did the embalming with Mrs Amarger, whilst I took care of the liaison with the other people....

"I saw the Superintendent from the Brigade Criminelle, Mrs Martine Monteil. I explained what was happening to her. She told me not to worry, and that everything would be in order and the authorisations would be given. She left me her mobile phone number and told me that I could call her if there were any problems. I took this authority to carry out the embalming as being from the Prefect, which is explained by the Statutory Order at Exhibit JM/7. There was nothing strange that the lady Superintendent, who was so well known in France, should give authority for me to proceed....

"You have asked me what was the single reason for proceeding with embalming. It was to make the body as presentable as possible to the family. Embalming is intended to delay thanatomorphosis, i.e. all the signs that change a body immediately after death. It is for the presentation of the deceased to the family and friends, so that when they come to see the body they do not find it with the mouth open or in a state that is not presentable. In the case of the Princess, she was a public figure and she had fractures and was bleeding: it was imperative that she be presented properly. It was not necessarily to preserve the body although I did not know if she was going to

---

[a] The statement evidence of the Monceau-Moss conversation appears later.

be presented in an open coffin I thought that this was possible and that in such a case embalming is necessary....

"You have asked me if it was my decision and my decision alone to proceed with the embalming. Nobody asked me to embalm the Princess of Wales. It was me who suggested the embalming in order to make the body as presentable as possible under the circumstances and there was no external influence. As an expert in embalming, I did not do anything illegal or wrong or inappropriate that day....

"You have asked me how many bodies I and my colleagues had embalmed before the 31st August 1997. It is between 100 and 120 bodies per month. In my case, roughly 13,000 bodies. Josselin Charrier has done rather less because he worked in the provinces and it will be less still for Mrs Amarger as she was newer to the profession.[a]" [54]

Martine Monteil, Head of Brigade Criminelle: 15 Nov 06 Statement: **Jury Didn't Hear**:

"Reply to question: [b] I do not have any recollection of a conversation with Monsieur Monceau, the embalmer.... As a general rule, once the burial certificate has been signed, there is no reason for the investigators to be informed about the type of funeral or of the embalming to be carried out. They do not usually therefore have any contacts with those organisations or with any embalmers that might be involved." [55c]

---

[a] This evidence raises the question: Why did Monceau use an embalmer who was less experienced for such an important embalming? The answer lies in Amarger's evidence, where she states that the British had requested a female embalmer.

[b] We are not told what the question was.

[c] Sixteen months previous to this Monteil had provided an answer to Paget that appears to conflict with this: "Question: Enquiries made with Hygeco, the company who affected this [embalming] procedure, has highlighted that this was authorised by Mr Moss the British Consul General, with your authority.... What do you remember of the decision taken to embalm the Princess' body?" "Answer: We should at this point recall the answers given by a witness, in the presence of British investigators ... Mr René Desguine [sic] (statement taken 09/05/2005) Assistant Managing Director of the company Hygeco, hired by the French Funeral Directors PFG to undertake conservation care; let us remember that PFG had themselves been called upon by Mr Moss, British Consul to Paris: 'I must however point out that preservation techniques are always carried out in the presence of or with the consent of a police authority. For the Princess of Wales, we had the agreement of Mrs Martine Monteil, head of the Crime Squad at the time, before proceeding with the treatment requested by the Consul of Great Britain. There was in any case no reason for any objection; on 31 August 1997 the inquiry being carried out only concerned a traffic accident.'" Monteil failed to directly answer the question: The question was: "What do you remember...?" She answered by quoting from Deguisne. Monteil then made no comment on the accuracy of Deguisne's account. It is significant that Deguisne was

Huguette Amarger, BJL Embalmer: 8 Mar 05 Statement read out 22 Nov 07: 91.20:

"Question: What instructions were you given?

"Answer: I was told to go to the mortuary room of La Pitié Salpêtrière and I was accompanied by a charge nurse. I think that his name is Theophie Le Couarec, something like that. He is Breton and retired to the South of France. I was to treat the body. At the hospital I met a colleague, Mr Jean Monceau, who at that time was my superior, also an embalmer. I remember that among ourselves, we did not speak of the Princess of Wales by her proper name, but we called her 'Patricia'. I do not know where that name came from or where the decision to call her that came from, but obviously I knew which person I was going to be dealing with. So Theo, the charge nurse, took me to the department where she was. I think she was in the resuscitation department.

"I remember that there were a lot of people in that department, including persons from the French Government and the British authorities. My boss came with the Princess's majordomo. His name was Burrell; I remember because his name was in the media subsequently over selling some of the Princess's letters. He was crying a lot and I asked him to bring some clothes to dress the Princess in after the treatment which I was going [to] apply to her. He told me he would deal with it."

Comment: Monceau's evidence is that the first thing he did after arriving at the hospital was to report to Massoni, Prefect of Police, to inform him that he "had been called to apply dry ice to the body of Princess of Wales"[a][b].

Massoni denied this outright: He said "Not at all".

---

not involved in the events – he said in his statement: "I must say that I did not have to deal with the case of Princess Diana personally." Deguisne instead stated that he had been provided information from Monceau: "I called Mr Monceau who gave me the information." Monceau will be shown in this book to have lied about the events that occurred on 31 August 1997. In summary: Monteil was asked a direct question in writing. She has time to consider her reply and chooses to indirectly answer the question by quoting from the statement of a person who wasn't present on the day. That indirect answer conflicts directly with Monteil's official statement: "I do not have any recollection of a conversation with Monsieur Monceau, the embalmer." Sources: Martine Monteil, Email Reply sent to DS Easton (in response to undated letter from "Lord Stevens of Kirkwhelpington"), 19 July 2005, pp1-2; René Deguisne, Witness Statement, 9 May 2005, p2.

[a] This – about the dry ice – was in Monceau's police statement, but he said he didn't remember it at the inquest.

[b] Later in his inquest cross-examination, Monceau appeared to inadvertently forget about this meeting with Massoni: "actually, when I arrived at the hospital, I was just walked to the room by a nurse".

Monceau further stated that Monteil "gave me her personal mobile phone number and she said 'Do what is necessary, and if you have any problems, then you can call me'." And: "she said that the authorisations would be issued".

Monceau made additional references to these meetings in his statement:

- "[Monteil] told me not to worry, and that everything would be in order and the authorisations would be given. She left me her mobile phone number and told me that I could call her if there were any problems." – see above (p6 of statement).

- "Superintendent of Police Madame Monteil also told me not to worry when I asked her if I might have problems in respect of the documents required to proceed with embalming and she left me her mobile telephone number telling me that I could call her at any time in case of problems" – p8.

Monteil stated: "I do not have any recollection of a conversation with Monsieur Monceau, the embalmer".

Monceau said later in his statement: "It was not my place to refuse [to embalm], even the Prefect of Police[a] was present at the hospital" – see later (p8).

The question is: What would Monteil and Massoni be doing at the hospital, when their priority presumably would have been to set up and run a major police investigation into the crash?

Outside of Monceau, there is no evidence that Monteil was present at the hospital on that day.[b]

Both Plumet and Launay have said they saw Massoni at the hospital, but they themselves didn't arrive there until later in the afternoon – Launay at 3.40 p.m.; Plumet at 4.50 p.m. – and Launay describes Massoni being there for the visit by Prince Charles and Diana's sisters.

- Launay: "We then waited for Prince Charles and the Princess's two sisters to arrive.... I saw ... Mr Massoni, the Prefect of Police, there."

- Plumet: "The President of the French Republic, the Police Prefect and the Minister for the Interior were all present".

Plumet arrived at the hospital just under an hour before the Charles visit, which occurred at around 5.40 p.m. – see later.

Diana's driver, Colin Tebbutt, who was present at the start of the embalming, stated at the inquest that "immediately [after the Moss-Monceau conversation] the funeral directors[c] changed into what appeared to be

---

[a] Massoni.

[b] Mulès gave evidence that he "recalled that after [the Diana examination photos] were printed he went to collect them ... and then handed them personally to Monteil who he saw place them into her office safe." – see Chapter 1. Although this probably occurred on August 31, it is not stated.

[c] Tebbutt called the embalmers "funeral directors" – see later.

protective clothing and they went about their work" – see later. Monceau's sequence of events is that the Monteil authorisation occurred after the Moss conversation. This is further witness evidence that the Monteil authorisation never happened.

The general evidence indicates that Monceau's meetings with Massoni and Monteil never actually occurred. This evidence has implications regarding the legality of Monceau's actions – this is addressed later.

Monceau has also stated that he discussed dry ice with Moss, but that is not mentioned in Moss' evidence – see later for both accounts of that conversation.

The inquest heard an elaborate account from Monceau, describing the application of dry ice to Princess Diana after his arrival at the hospital.

There are however several concerning factors:

1) Lebreton, the dry ice operative who is stated by Monceau to have administered the dry ice, has never been interviewed by any police investigation and was not heard from at the inquest.[a]

2) At the inquest Monceau stated that Lebreton was not in Diana's room when he arrived: "I know he was not there when I got there."

In Monceau's 2005 statement he said the opposite: "Michel Lebreton, the dry ice operative, was already in the room. He was alone."

3) The inquest heard three times that it was Monceau's account that he and Lebreton were alone in the room with Diana's body when the dry ice was administered:

a) Lebreton "was alone" when Monceau arrived – Monceau statement quoted.[b]

b) "I am alone with Michel Lebreton in the room" – Monceau

c) "only Mr Lebreton was with you" – Burnett to Monceau.

No other witnesses have described being alone in the room at any time.[c]

---

[a] The Paget diagrams show a phone call from Hauffman to Lebreton before 9 a.m. Neither Hauffman nor Lebreton have ever been interviewed – it is therefore not known how Paget came by this information.

[b] The statement read: "Michel Lebreton, the dry ice operative, was already in the room. He was alone."

[c] The closest anyone gets to saying this is Plumet who gave this account: "[Plumet] states that he looked into the room where the Princess of Wales' body was; she was on a bed and had been dressed. The embalming had taken place, and no one else was in the room." Plumet describes looking into the room, but not entering it. I suggest that if he had entered it, he may have been closely followed by police who were guarding the room from the outside. Source: Jean-Claude Plumet, Witness Statement, 11 November 2005, p6.

Amarger clearly describes the situation during the time she did the embalming: "I was never alone in the room. There were always some French policemen and authorities who came to gather their thoughts. This took place in the large room.... The head of the French police officers, in uniform, asked that only women stayed with me, and I found myself in the quiet again with my assistant who had arrived in the meantime.... He was the only man in the room, with two policewomen."[a]

Amarger has stated that throughout the period of the embalming – which lasted about an hour, see later – there was a constant police presence. This guarding process was apparently considered so critical that even during the period of embalming – which involved a procedure where Diana's body would have been naked and exposed – there were two female police officers present in the room.[b]

I suggest that it is common sense that Princess Diana's body was under constant police guard, possibly from as early as her 2.06 a.m. arrival at La Pitié Hospital.[c]

Yet Monceau has asked us to believe that this police guard was dispensed with whilst he and Lebreton administered the dry ice.

The resulting question is: Why would there be a police guard throughout the embalming, but not during the application of dry ice?

4) Outside of Monceau, there is absolutely no witness – or other – evidence that dry ice was applied to Diana's body. It is not just that there is no evidence of the administration of the dry ice itself, but there are no references to it whatsoever – nothing about any preparation before administration, nothing about any aftermath of the presentation, no evidence from anyone that Lebreton was even present, and no mention of discussion of any intention to apply dry ice or anything about it at all.[d]

I suggest that it is very convenient that Monceau has stated there was no one else present in the room when he and Lebreton administered the dry ice – convenient, because it "fits" with there being no witnesses.

Moss and Tebbutt should have been asked about this at the inquest, but weren't.

---

[a] See Amarger's statement, later.

[b] The British had earlier requested a female to perform the embalming operation – see earlier.

[c] Keith Moss also said in his statement: "Teams of police officers permanently guarded the corridor.": Keith Moss, Witness Statement, 22 October 2004, reproduced in *The Documents* book, p651 (UK Edition)

[d] Monceau also stated – see earlier – that dry ice causes burns to the body. If that testimony was true, why has there never been any mention of such burns from the post mortem conducted in the UK? The UK post mortem is covered later in this volume.

5) Monceau gave evidence – see earlier – that dry ice shouldn't be used "to prepare a body to make it presentable", yet he claims to have supervised the application of dry ice to Diana's body.

6) Monceau was asked by Burnett: "Did you in fact come to the conclusion that the dry ice should be removed?" Monceau replied: "Well, my idea was to explain what would happen if we were to just use dry ice to present the body. Obviously I thought that had to be removed if we were to apply another treatment to the body, but it was not removed at that very moment." [a]

Monceau's reply raises three issues:

a) Monceau appears to suggest that he administered the dry ice in order to "explain what would happen if we were to just use dry ice to present the body". In other words, he applied the dry ice in order to show those who needed to see – presumably Moss and other authority figures present – how ineffective dry ice was in the situation. [b]

I suggest that this is an amazing comment, and in line with the evidence in point 4 (above) there is absolutely no evidence of Monceau showing Diana's body – after dry ice had been administered – to any people.

b) Monceau's inquest account was that dry ice "burns the skin" – see earlier. When this is viewed in the light of his account that the dry ice "was not removed at that very moment" [c], the indication is that Monceau has admitted to deliberately carrying out a post-death action that would have damaged the body of Princess Diana. [d]

c) Monceau states: "Obviously I thought [the dry ice] had to be removed if we were to apply another treatment to the body, but it was not removed at that very moment."

This account conflicts directly with Monceau's statement: "[Lebreton] had started putting on the dry ice, but as soon as I saw the physical condition

---

[a] Later in his inquest account Monceau states – in relation to his conversation with Moss (see later) – "it was very obvious to me that it was not possible to present the body in the state that it was; that is, without any clothes on and not at all prepared, with just dry ice applied to it." This is further confirmation of Monceau's inquest evidence that the dry ice was not removed straightaway – the conversation with Moss took place at around 12.00 noon.

[b] Elsewhere Monceau has stated that the dry ice was applied because it was asked for: "If we are asked to do something, we go and do it" – see earlier.

[c] See also previous footnote indicating the dry ice was still on when Monceau spoke with Moss.

[d] When dry ice is applied, a cloth bag is used to prevent burning (see earlier), but Monceau failed to mention that in his evidence – instead saying that dry ice "burns the skin".

of the body, I told Michel Lebreton to remove the dry ice.... We therefore removed the dry ice together."

So in the statement the dry ice was removed even before it had been fully applied. At the inquest the dry ice is fully applied and not removed until later.

There is no evidence from any witness – other than Monceau – that dry ice was removed from Diana's body at any point.

7) Tebbutt said in his statement – see later: "I also noticed three hospital funeral directors[a], two male and one female, were present when I was in the room." Other evidence shows that these   three people must have been Monceau, Amarger and Charrier.[b] If Lebreton had been there, then Tebbutt should have seen four people.[cd]

8) The general evidence is that Diana's body was in a state of potential deterioration prior to the embalming being carried out – Tebbutt: "the Princess was melting". Tebbutt arrived around 11.30 a.m. – 2½ hours after Donnelly's call to Caltiau and 3¼ hours after Monceau's call to Hauffman.[e]

I suggest it would be common sense that if the dry ice had been applied the process of "melting" would have been arrested. There is however no evidence of that happening pre-embalming.

At the inquest Monceau was asked what his reaction was to the dry ice order: "If we are asked to do something, we go and do it."

---

[a] Tebbut calls the embalmers "funeral directors".

[b] Charrier assisted Amarger throughout the embalming – see later.

[c] One could argue that Lebreton had already left after administering the dry ice. Tebbutt times this observation soon after his arrival – see later – before noon and before the Monceau-Moss conversation. Monceau's inquest account was that the dry ice remained on until after his conversation with Moss. If Lebreton had been there, it would seem logical that he would have stayed for any removal of the dry ice. Tebbutt's account of three people indicates that he was not there.

[d] One could also argue that Charrier hadn't arrived yet. I suggest that if a fourth embalmer had suddenly appeared, Tebbutt would have probably said so. Monceau does place Charrier's arrival well after his conversation with Moss – it will be shown later that this helps Monceau to claim a later embalming (2 p.m.). Amarger's evidence will indicate that Charrier was there for the complete embalming, which started straight after the Moss conversation (Tebbutt). There is really no credible evidence indicating that the third person Tebbutt saw wasn't Charrier. Obviously both Charrier and Lebreton should have been interviewed by police or at the inquest. This has not occurred in either case.

[e] Gibbins – who was in London and relied on information from Tebbutt – said "there was some deterioration in the Princess's body". The later general evidence will show that deterioration had not yet set in, but the hot room had created a situation where Diana's body could have deteriorated if nothing had been done.

The reality appears to be quite the opposite: they were asked to supply dry ice[a], but did not "go and do it".

The general evidence indicates that the embalming didn't commence until about 12.30 p.m. – see later.[b]

This evidence means that there was a period of over 3 hours – from 9 a.m., when PFG was made aware of the need for dry ice, until about 12.30 p.m. – during which no action was taken by PFG or BJL to cool the body of Princess Diana.

Timing of Events

The overall evidence from Jean Monceau was that the following sequence of events occurred after he arrived at the hospital:

- Monceau reported to Massoni, Prefect of Police, to tell him he "had been called to apply dry ice"[c] – after 9.40 a.m.
- a nurse guided Monceau to Diana's room
- Monceau examined Diana's body – after 10.00 a.m.
- Lebreton arrived and administered the dry ice[de]
- Monceau meets with Plumet and Jauze, directors from PFG[f] – 11.30 a.m.
- Plumet and Jauze introduce Monceau to Moss
- Amarger arrives
- Monceau talks to British Consul General Keith Moss[g]
- Charrier phones Monceau who asks him to come to the hospital[h]
- Monceau meets with Monteil who provides verbal authorisation to conduct the embalming[i]
- Embalming commenced – 2 p.m.

Amarger also related the events that occurred:

---

[a] Donnelly asked Caltiau (of PFG) for "ice" – there is no credible evidence that that order was passed on to BJL – see earlier.

[b] Monceau states that the embalming didn't commence until after 2 p.m., but this is not supported by the general evidence – this is discussed later.

[c] This meeting appears to be fictional – see earlier.

[d] There is reason to believe this never occurred – see earlier.

[e] In Monceau's 2005 statement, Lebreton was already there when Monceau arrived.

[f] This never occurred – neither Plumet nor Jauze were in the hospital until nearly 5 p.m. – see later.

[g] There is conflict over the content of this discussion – see below.

[h] The evidence will show that Charrier was there before the embalming commenced at around 12.30 p.m. If this call occurred, it would have been earlier.

[i] Monteil has denied that this occurred – see earlier and later.

- Amarger attended to the hospital mortuary accompanied by Theophie Le Couarec (Theo)[a]
- Amarger is met at the mortuary by Monceau
- Theo takes Amarger to the room where Diana's body is
- Monceau comes into the room with Burrell
- Amarger asks Burrell to bring some clothes to dress Diana with
- Embalming commenced.

This draws us back to the issue of timing – as stated before, Monceau gave no timing evidence before the jury and the statement heard from Amarger provided very little.

Amarger stated earlier: "I left home between 10 and 11 o'clock." Amarger lived in Paris' 14th department and La Pitié Salpêtrière is in department 13 – the two departments are adjacent.[b] It is therefore possible that Amarger could have arrived around 11.00 a.m. or earlier – so not too far removed from the arrival time of Tebbutt which could have been around 11.30 a.m.

The difference of course is that Amarger's instruction was to report to the mortuary – not to the area where Diana's body was being held. From her evidence it appears that she arrived accompanied by a hospital employee, Theo, and met with Monceau in the mortuary.

It is possible that Monceau discussed issues regarding the embalming at the mortuary and it is here that Amarger states: "We did not speak of the Princess of Wales by her proper name, but we called her 'Patricia'."

These two factors – meeting in the mortuary and use of the name "Patricia" – indicate that there was secrecy involved in the actions of the embalmers.

The question is: Why? If there was nothing to hide regarding the embalming of Diana, then why the secrecy?

Monceau's record of the sequence of events is quite different to Amarger's.

In Monceau's earlier inquest evidence he said:
- "I did not ask for that [embalming] equipment [from Amarger] before I arrived at the hospital"
- "when I asked for embalming equipment, that request [for Diana to be embalmed] had already been made"
- "so [Moss[said to me, "Well, if you can do [the embalming], do it".

Based on these statements, the sequence of events is: a) Monceau arrives at the hospital; b) Monceau talks to Moss who authorises the embalming; c) Monceau requests the embalming equipment from Amarger.

In Monceau's later inquest evidence he is cross-examined by Burnett, who is asking questions based on Monceau's Paget statement:

---

[a] It is possible that Amarger was picked up and driven to the hospital by "Theo".

[b] Monceau gave evidence that Amarger lived close to the hospital – see earlier.

- Burnett states that after administering the dry ice at the hospital, Monceau "had a meeting with ... Mr Plumet and M Jauze", which Monceau confirmed
- Burnett states: "You say in your statement ... that the people from the funeral service [Plumet and Jauze] introduced you to the Consul General, Mr Moss" – which Monceau affirmed
- Burnett then states, still using Monceau's statement: "It was about this time ... that ... Madame Amarger arrived at the hospital" to which Monceau replied: "I think it was at around that time. Whether it was at precisely that time, I could not tell you."
- Burnett next asks: "Do you remember having a discussion with Mr Moss...?" Monceau: "Yes".

So the sequence of events based on Burnett's reading of Monceau's statement[a] is:

a) administration of dry ice
b) discussion at the hospital between Monceau and Plumet and Jauze
c) arrival of Amarger
d) discussion between Monceau and Moss.

The major conflict is that:

- in Monceau's earlier inquest evidence he has stated that contact was not made with Amarger until after his discussion with Moss, in which the embalming process was approved
- in Monceau's Paget statement – used by Burnett in the later inquest cross-examination – Amarger arrived at the hospital with her equipment before the Moss discussion.

The significance of this conflict will become clearer later, when the evidence pertaining to the nature of the conversation between Moss and Monceau is covered.

As mentioned above, Monceau, in his statement, describes a meeting with the PFG funeral directors. He stated: "After that [applying the dry ice and meeting Burrell], I met the people from the funeral directors, PFG, Mr Plumet and Mr Jauze. It must have been around 1130hrs [11.30 a.m.]. I told them about my intention to request authorisation to carry out embalming, as the dry ice was not going to be adequate. They told me that you need all sorts of authorisations. I told them that we had to see who the authority was to sign a request for authorisation to carry out embalming.... We were waiting for authorisation. I asked how the body was to be presented, the schedule for the family's visit, when the body was to be taken away, etc. in order to find out how to proceed. These conversations were with people from the funeral

---

[a] This fits with Monceau's statement evidence – see earlier.

service, and they in turn introduced me to the British Consul-General in Paris, Mr Keith Moss."

At the inquest Monceau confirmed that this conversation took place: "I talked to those two people [Plumet and Jauze] ... of the possibility of embalming before I talked about it to the ... British authorities".

The problem here for Monceau is that both Plumet and Jauze have no recall of this conversation ever taking place:

Jean-Claude Plumet, PFG Director of Paris Agencies, Paris: 4 Nov 05 Paget description of Statement: **Jury Didn't Hear**:

"In addition, when questioned, Mr Plumet does not recall being present during a conversation between Mr Moss and Mr Monceau.

"When asked if he recalled Mr Monceau informing himself and Mr Jauze that it was his intention to seek authorisation to embalm the Princess of Wales, Mr Plumet stated that he does not remember seeing or speaking with Mr Monceau at the hospital. He explains that he could have written this episode out of his memory, because as far as he was concerned, he was dealing with his own responsibilities and felt under pressure.

"When asked if he handed Mr Monceau an authorisation form, that in normal circumstances is the deceased's family's authorisation for the embalmer to proceed, and which Mr Monceau is believed to have completed his section as the embalmer, Mr Plumet explains that it is possible, but again that he could not remember as this was not important to him. If Mr Monceau's recollection of this is right however, Mr Plumet explains that this document would have been filed with Mrs Celadon at the Bureau des Operations Mortuaires, at the Prefecture de Police." [56]

Gérard Jauze, PFG Branch Director, Paris: 21 Mar 06 Statement: **Jury Didn't Hear**:

"You ask me if I remember speaking to M. Jean Monceau. I certainly do not recall speaking to him in the room where the Princess of Wales was. Otherwise it is possible, but I do not remember.

"You have read over the following paragraph to me from the statement of M. Jean Monceau [mostly as quoted above[a]].... That is the first I have heard of that. At 1130hrs [11.30 a.m.], I was either at the Ritz Hotel or I was leaving there to return to Boulevard Richard Lenoir. It is possible that I met him later on, but I do not remember the conversation. I did not deal with that, other

---

[a] Paget appears to have made a change to Monceau's original statement: Jauze reads: "I spoke to them about my request that consideration be given to embalming....", whereas the original statement (shown above) reads: "I told them about my intention to request authorisation to carry out embalming...." In the original statement Monceau reveals a more definite intention to embalm – in the doctored copy given by Paget to Jauze, this intention has been watered down to a process of consideration. Source: Gérard Jauze, Witness Statement, 21 March 2006, reproduced in *The Documents* book, p484 (UK Edition)

than during my presence at the hospital. I did not have time. It is possible that it was M Plumet who saw him." [57]

Comment: The reality is that both Plumet and Jauze were involved in other activities through the day – see earlier and Part 3[a] - and did not go to the hospital until after Dodi Fayed's body was released from the IML at about 4.35 p.m.[b]

Their schedules – which were very busy through that day – preclude a hospital meeting with Monceau at any time before the embalming. The jury did not get to hear about this – the jury members heard only Monceau's account and would have presumed that this conversation must have taken place.[c]

The evidence from Plumet and Jauze, when added to the earlier denials from Massoni and Monteil – also not heard by the jury – indicates that Monceau has lied repeatedly about conversations which never actually occurred on the day. This issue will be addressed later.

The issue at hand is: At what point did the British authorities request or authorise the embalming of Princess Diana? Put another way: Was the embalming request made by British Consul General, Keith Moss, during his pre-embalming conversation with Jean Monceau, or was it made earlier in the day by a British authority – not necessarily Keith Moss?

---

[a] Part 3 shows their presence at the IML in the afternoon.

[b] This is supported in the PFG statements: Jauze: "You ask me if I remember the British funeral directors arriving at the hospital. No. They must have been amongst all the other people at the hospital.": Gérard Jauze, Witness Statement, 21 March 2006, p7. Plumet: "Mr Plumet does not recall at what time they arrived at the hospital, other than he arrived before the HRH the Prince of Wales, President Chirac and others.": Jean-Claude Plumet, Witness Statement, 4 November 2005, p5. The UK funeral director and embalmers arrived at 3.45 p.m. and Prince Charles arrived at about 5.40 p.m. – see later for both. Jauze and Plumet arrived at around 4.50 p.m. – between the two.

[c] The jury also heard Monceau confirming that "the people from the funeral service [Plumet and Jauze] introduced you to the Consul General, Mr Moss". This has been denied by both Jauze and Plumet in their statements. Jauze: "You ask me if I remember speaking to the British Consul General in Paris, Mr Keith Moss. I do not remember. I do not know if he would have wanted to speak to us, but I cannot tell you, I'm not sure. You ask me if I remember speaking to any English people. Once again, I do not remember.": Gérard Jauze, Witness Statement, 21 Mar 06, p7; Plumet: "When asked about a conversation ... with Mr Keith Moss ... Plumet states that he does not remember. He also does not remember whether he was introduced to Mr Moss or not.... Mr Plumet does not recall being present during a conversation between Mr Moss and Mr Monceau.": Jean-Claude Plumet, Witness Statement, 4 Nov 05, p6.

We have already seen the evidence from Amarger that indicates a female embalmer was requested by the British before 9 a.m. In contrast, Monceau's statement evidence indicates that the conversation with Moss – where embalming was initially addressed with a British authority – took place at a point after 11.30 a.m.[a]

Monceau-Moss Conversation

During Monceau's inquest cross-examination the substance of the Monceau-Moss conversation at the hospital was effectively glossed over. What was mentioned is included in the excerpt of Burnett's questioning – earlier – and Mansfield's questioning – below. This issue was however addressed in more detail in Monceau's Paget statement, which the jury didn't hear.

Jean Monceau, BJL Director and Embalmer, Paris: 20 Nov 07: 83.6:
Mansfield: Q. I want to ask you a little bit about the contact with Mr Moss, the English Consul General. Do you remember talking to him?
A. Yes, yes, of course I remember talking to him.
Q. This was before the embalming had taken place?
A. Of course, yes.
Q. Did Mr Moss say to you that in fact there would have to be a full autopsy in the United Kingdom?
A. Not at all.
Q. Did Mr Moss indicate to you that Princess Diana would be returning to the United Kingdom that very day – that is Sunday 31st August?
A. Yes.
....Q. With regard to the same conversation with Mr Moss, did you get the impression that he did not understand what you were saying about the level of embalming you expected to undertake?
A. No, not at all.
Jean Monceau: 18 Oct 05 Statement: **Jury Didn't Hear**:
"It was the first time I had met Mr Moss. I explained to him that it was not possible or appropriate to present the Princess of Wales to the President of France, or to her sisters or her family, in the state she was in. He got me to explain what dry ice is. I also told him what I recommended, i.e. embalming, whilst explaining that it was not like Egyptian embalming, which is not allowed under French law. We spoke in French and English, but in French we did not speak about embalming but thanatopraxie [thanatopraxis], which is a treatment involving the injection of preservatives into the arterial circuit and the

---

[a] This timing is supported in Tebbutt's evidence – see later.

recovery of veinous blood from the right of the heart and from the main veins.

"I also explained the various levels of embalming to him: dry ice; the next level, which consists of mortuary cleansing, i.e. packing with gauze, suturing the mouth, covering the eyes, and make-up. I also explained to him that because of the fractures and sutures, this level would not be adequate. I suggested arterial injections to preserve the body from the proliferation of bacteria (odours and change of colour), especially given that the heat in the room where the body was, being so high, was a contributory factor....

Following this explanation, Mr Moss told me that he thought that it was a good idea to proceed in this fashion for the arrival of the family of the Princess of Wales. However, he told me that he must first resolve the problems surrounding the authorisations....

"I have been asked if I can remember any other British people with the Consul. Yes, but they were not introduced to me....

"You have asked me how this case differs from a normal case. On that day, I was told that Prince Charles was coming to Paris and that he was bringing with him some British embalmers. This led me to believe that he wanted the Princess to be embalmed. Furthermore, Mr Keith Moss, who as far as I was concerned, was the person with authority to deal with the funeral of the deceased, gave me verbal authorisation to proceed with the embalming.... As I have already explained to you, in order to be able to proceed with embalming, a member of the family or any other person having the capacity to deal with the funeral of the deceased must sign a request for authorisation to proceed with embalming." [58]

Keith Moss, British Consul General, Paris: 22 Nov 07: 23.1:

Hough: Q. When M Monceau introduced himself to you or was introduced to you, what title did he give for himself?

A. Well, I thought at the time that he described himself as an "embaumeur", which according to my dictionary is the French for an embalmer, the English word deriving from the French. But it transpired that it was called a "thanatopracteur", but I think the difference between the two is broadly the same.

Q. Did you discover that he was called a thanatopracteur after these events from the invoice?

A. He may have described it to me himself as a thanatopracteur. I do not actually recall that on the day, but I did notice it when we got the invoice from the company some time later billing us for his services, in which he was described as that.

Q. At the time that all this was happening though, were you aware of the technical differences between "embaumement" and "thanatopraxie"?

A. No.

Q. Were you aware of what a thanatopracteur did at all?

A. Well, he briefed me on what he was intending to do, so yes.

Q. What did he tell you he was going to do?

A. He told me that in view of the condition in which he found the Princess of Wales' body and the conditions in which it was kept, that it was very –

Q. Are you referring there to the heat?

A. The heat in the room, yes. In his opinion it was essential for two reasons for his services to be used. But the first reason was – and I suppose primary reason in a sense – was a presentational reason because I think, at that time, we knew that Prince Charles would be coming out from the UK, along with the Princess of Wales' two sisters and others, and that there would also be high-level visits from the French side. So from a presentational point of view, it was essential that the Princess's remains should be made to look as presentable as possible and to provide some dignity, I suppose, to her. The second reason was to – I am not quite sure of the words, but maybe to control a process of decomposition which otherwise her remains may have been subjected to, given the circumstances.

Q. Looking back now, do you think that the procedure was presented as anything special or unusual?

A. The procedures I do not think were. The circumstances of course were unique – this was the Princess of Wales, a very, very important public figure – but I think the interventions that were carried out by M Monceau were fairly standard.

Q. The special circumstance was the one that you have referred to, namely that she was going to be visited by some very senior officials?

A. And the person herself, yes.

Q. At the time, when you were told about this procedure by Mr Monceau, did you consider at all the effect the procedure might have on the ability to carry out a post-mortem examination in the UK?

A. No.

Q. At that stage, were you aware that the Princess would undergo a post-mortem examination in the UK?

A. No.

Q. Did you know at that time that the procedure that was going to be performed by M Monceau could cause a post-mortem pregnancy test to produce a false positive?

A. Absolutely not.

Q. That was the kind of technical information that you did not have, was it?

A. Not at all.

Q. After M Monceau had provided you with this information and his reasons, what did you respond about what he should do?

A. I have given a great deal of thought to this because I understand its importance. There were consultations – I cannot now remember with whom – but as far as I recall, either I or somebody else connected with our emergency unit, if you like to call it that, in the hospital made contact with somebody in the UK. Bearing in mind that it was very disparate, you had people all over the place, family in various locations, it was extremely difficult to be precise about who was going to take these sorts of decisions. But it was very clear upon the information that we had received from M Monceau, the thanatopracteur, that what he was proposing was essential in view of the circumstances. So at some point an authority was made, was given, possibly by somebody in London, probably by somebody in London, for us to go ahead on that basis.

Q. Did you have personal contact with the people in London from whom you were seeking authorisation?

A. I had so many contacts that day on such a scale, I honestly cannot, with all integrity, answer the question. I am sure I must have done, but I cannot remember with whom.

Q. In all those discussions, what reasons were given by you or by anybody else for this procedure to be undertaken?

A. As I said before, the primary reason was a presentational one, to ensure that the Princess's remains, which were very badly damaged, we were told – I was told by the hospital staff, as a result of the accident, and that she was in no condition – her body was in no condition to be seen by members of her family or others if left untreated.

Coroner: Do you have any recollection of any reference to dry ice at any time?

A. Dry ice?

Coroner: Yes.

A. Well, Steven Donnelly, I understand, recalls a telephone call in which I asked him if dry ice could be provided. I do not myself recall that conversation, but I have absolutely no doubt of Steven's integrity in this and that it probably was requested, yes.

Q. Do you know for what purpose dry ice was requested or why it might have been requested?

A. I think it was to do with the conditions in the room, the ambient temperature, and it was an idea that arose at an early stage – I think it was, for dry ice to be applied in order to slow down a process of decomposition.

Q. Now we have heard from M Monceau that dry ice could certainly not have preserved the body for the length of time that he wanted to preserve it for.[a]

---

[a] Hough has quoted something that Monceau did not say to the inquest – Monceau's evidence was that dry ice would not make the body presentable and made no direct

Was that something he discussed with you?

A. He could well have done. I do not honestly remember.

At 54.8: Mansfield: Q. In relation to your information about what the French embalmer was doing, did you not appreciate that he in fact was doing what he might call a complete embalming?

A. My recollection, as I think I referred to earlier, of that exchange, based on what the hospital authorities and he had seen of the Princess of Wales' remains[a], was that he needed to conduct, if you like, a series of procedures which – again, I cannot remember the details, but I think it was not specific. He did not go into great detail. It was just a general description of what he was proposing to do with the objectives, as I have stated earlier.

Q. Well, I am not going to take time on this. It is just this: he certainly thought that you were under no misapprehension about the fact that it was going to be a complete embalming.

A. That may be the case. As I say, I cannot remember the precise details now.

Q. In relation to that, whatever your understanding was, and for whatever purpose – I am not suggesting anything improper, may I make that perfectly clear – what I am going to ask you is obviously about consent and authority. Obviously you appreciate it was invasive, the treatment that he was doing?

A. I must have done. As I say, I cannot recall the precise details.

At 63.16: Horwell: Q. This is your meeting with the thanatopracteur. You say this in your statement: "He talked about the decomposition of the body and said that the remains would be in a real mess and that he was there to make it as presentable as possible for the family. I had not, at this stage, seen the body and I assumed that the Princess of Wales' body would not be in a fit state for presentation. I therefore saw this service as a perfectly legitimate thing to do."

A. Yes.

Q. And you agree with that?

A. Yes.

Q. Secondly at page 10, please, again just above halfway. "I have been asked whether I would have let the thanatopracteur carry on with his work if I had known that he would introduce chemicals into the Princess of Wales' body. My train of thought now is that I would have probably asked whether this was standard procedure. If I had been informed that this was standard practice, then I would undoubtedly have told him to carry on. If this procedure was the norm and I had told him not to proceed, I would have been held personally responsible." Again, do you agree with that?

---

reference to its qualities of preservation in this case. The closest he got to what Hough has said was: "You place dry ice when you want to preserve the body temporarily, but not also that it would be presentable." : 20 Nov 07: 64.22.

[a] Moss has stated that he hadn't viewed Diana's body at the time he spoke to Monceau.

A. Yes, I do.

Q. Could it have been the case, Mr Moss, that in fact you authorised Mr Monceau to carry on his work, bearing in mind the difficulty of the situation, the confusion, the chaos and the need obviously for some expedition?

A. I think that is possibly the case, yes.

Keith Moss: 22 Oct 04 Statement: **Jury Heard Part Only**:

"At some point during the day a representative from B.J.L. Service Parisiens d'Hygiène Funéraire attended to prepare the Princess's remains for viewing by the Royal party. I subsequently learnt from his invoice, dated 7th October 1997, that this person was called a 'Thanatopracteur'. The nearest word in the English language that would describe the role this person undertook, would be an embalmer. I'm not sure at what time he was called to attend or what time he arrived at the hospital. I do not recall whether he had been called by the hospital, by the 'Pompes Funèbres Générales'[PFG], or by Steven Donnelly, although the latter is rather unlikely.

"The 'Thanatopracteur' must have been introduced to me, but I can't recall how. It is my recollection that the hospital staff knew him. He couldn't just have walked in to the hospital and then made his way to my floor. There were too many checkpoints. He would have been with the Staff Nurse or Doctors. I don't remember his name, but I would describe him as a white Caucasian male, with dark hair, very soberly dressed, about five foot ten inches tall, in his fifties, carrying a little bag which I assumed were the tools of his trade.

"I would like to clarify that in my report[a], paragraph twelve; I have used the words 'Embalming Team', to describe the 'thanatopracteur'. In addition to this, having subsequently seen a copy of the invoice on the FCO files, I noted that the invoice used the word 'thanatopracteurs' – in the plural. My recollection is that there was only one individual, however I cannot discount the possibility that he had an assistant.

"He talked about the decomposition of the body, and said that the remains would be in a real mess and that he was there to make it as presentable as possible for the family. I had not at this stage seen the body and I assumed that the Princess of Wales' body would not be in a fit state for presentation. I therefore saw this service as a perfectly legitimate thing to do.

"Additionally I was aware that there were plans made to allow the wife of President Chirac and Mme. Jospin to pay their last respects. As I recall, Mme. Chirac attended with Sir Michael and Lady Jay at 0845hrs [8.45 a.m.], which could suggest that the 'Thanatopracteur's work had already been completed by then. But I am really not sure. I recall that Prime Minister Lionel Jospin accompanied by Sir Michael Jay went to pay his last respects at

---

[a] This report has never been made available and was not shown to the jury.

143

0920hrs, and that a bouquet of flowers from former President Giscard d'Estaing was also left. But I really cannot be sure of precisely when the 'Thanatopracteur' attended. I had not come across his type of role before, although I had been involved as a Consular Officer with arrangements for dealing with British citizens who had died overseas.

"This was a unique case. The circumstances were so special, with the heir to the British throne coming out to Paris to accompany his former wife's body back to the United Kingdom. Although the FCO has a manual in several volumes, covering Diplomatic Service Procedure, including Royal matters, they would give guidance on protocol for dealing with State Visits, Private Visits, etc.... However, they were never intended to cover the death of a former member of the Royal Family, in a foreign country without the Embassy's knowledge. With this in mind, decisions were made as they unfolded, sticking to the principles of common sense and the basic requirements of a British national in need of Consular assistance.

"When the 'Thanatopracteur' told me he was here to make the Princess of Wales' body look as presentable as possible for viewing by her next of kin, I asked him what this involved. He said, washing her hair, cleaning her body, applying make-up to reduce the impact of shock to the next of kin. I asked him if he needed me there and he said no. I thanked him, and left him to get on with it.

"This conversation was conducted in French in my Office on the corridor I have described. I can't remember if anyone else was present, possibly a nurse. If there had been someone there who I didn't know, I would have remembered. I don't recall if Paul Burrell, the Princess of Wales' butler, or Colin Tebbutt, the Princess of Wales' driver, were there when all this took place....

"I have been asked whether I know what 'embalming' means. I don't fully know I am not an expert, but I am aware that this was a procedure that was undertaken in Ancient Egypt to preserve bodies for the afterlife. With regards to what was undertaken on the body of the Princess of Wales, I understood it was not in order to preserve her in perpetuity, but for her to be made presentable for her family.

"After the 'Thanatopracteur' had completed his work, he asked me to check what he had done. I had not been in to see the Princess of Wales' body before then. I went into the dimly lit room[a], and all I saw was her face, with the rest of her body covered up to the neck in bed linen. I thanked him for his work.

---

[a] This contrasts with the evidence from Gibbins at the inquest: "There was overhead lighting and [Tebbutt] was concerned that there was some deterioration in the Princess's body". Tebbutt made no mention of the lighting in his account.

"I have no experience of embalming and I do not know precisely what the 'Thanatopracteur' had done. I do know that I was satisfied that he was there to undertake preparation of her remains for viewing.

"I have been asked whether I know exactly what the 'Thanatopracteur' had in the bag that he was carrying. I do not know.

"As a Consular Officer my experience of dealing with the death of British nationals overseas was primarily to insure that the wishes of the next of kin were taken fully into account.... In accordance with the wishes of a family, appropriate arrangements would be made for the repatriation of the body to either the UK or another country of the family's choice. Although I have not witnessed such procedures, I would assume that part of this process could involve the stabilisation of the body for transportation back to the UK. Given this experience, the procedure described to me by the 'thanatopracteur' appeared a perfectly legitimate thing to do under the circumstances....

"I have been asked whether I would have let the 'Thanatopracteur' carry on with his work if I had known he would introduce chemicals into the Princess of Wales' body.

"My train of thought, now, is that I would have probably asked whether this was standard procedure. If I had been informed that this was standard practise then I would undoubtedly have told him to carry on. If this procedure was the norm, and I told him not to proceed, I would have been held personally responsible.

"At about 1400hrs [2 p.m.], Doctor Bernard Kouchner, the founder of Médecins Sans Frontière and Minister for Health, attended the hospital and came to my room. He asked whether he would be allowed to pay his final respects to the Princess of Wales, describing himself as a personal friend. I checked with Sir Michael Jay who agreed that this would be acceptable as long as he was accompanied by one of the nurses." [59]

Comment: There are two important issues:

1) What was Moss' perception of the procedure Monceau was going to carry out?
2) Did Moss authorise Monceau to carry out the embalming?

At the inquest Monceau was only asked about this conversation (by Burnett) in passing – the gist of his evidence was "[Moss] told me to do what was necessary", see earlier – but he gave a full account in his 2005 statement, which was not heard by the jury.

In summary, Monceau testified in his statement:

- Monceau "explained ... it was not ... appropriate to present the Princess of Wales ... in the state she was in"

- Monceau "explained the various levels of embalming to [Moss]" [a]
- "I suggested arterial injections"
- "Moss told me that he thought that it was a good idea to proceed in this fashion"
- Moss "told me that he must first resolve the problems surrounding the authorisations"
- "Moss ... gave me verbal authorisation to proceed with the embalming"
- "Nobody asked me to embalm the Princess of Wales. It was me who suggested the embalming".

Moss' evidence from his 2004 statement – mostly not heard by the jury – was: "When [Monceau] told me he was here to make the Princess of Wales' body look as presentable as possible for viewing by her next of kin, I asked him what this involved. He said, washing her hair, cleaning her body, applying make-up to reduce the impact of shock to the next of kin. I asked him if he needed me there and he said no. I thanked him, and left him to get on with it."

The key points of Moss' statement account are:

1) Moss is not describing Monceau asking for Moss' authorisation – Moss makes a statement of fact: "[Monceau] told me he was here to make the Princess of Wales' body look as presentable as possible".

2) Moss indicates that Monceau told him what he was about to do to Diana's body – but Moss does not say Monceau described the embalming process. Instead it was: "washing her hair, cleaning her body, applying make-up" – i.e. not the injecting of chemicals.

There is a major conflict here between the two accounts – yet they are the two parties describing the exact same conversation.

The main areas of conflict are:
- Monceau said he "explained the various levels of embalming" and "suggested arterial injections"; Moss said Monceau described "washing her hair, cleaning her body, applying make-up"
- Monceau said Moss "told me that he must first resolve the problems surrounding the authorisations" and "gave me verbal authorisation to proceed with the embalming"; Moss indicated that authorisation was not an issue – Monceau came to do the job and was just informing Moss what he was up to.

The reality is that these two statement accounts to Paget could hardly be more conflicting on the central issues:
- Monceau described embalming – Moss didn't
- Monceau said Moss authorised it – Moss indicates authorisation wasn't needed.

The most important point is that the jury didn't get to hear either of these accounts.

---

[a] This included dry ice – see earlier discussion.

Why?

By the time we get to the inquest, Moss' account of the conversation has changed considerably – but even then, Moss presents two completely different stories to the lawyers cross-examining him:

- to Hough: "Either I or somebody else connected with our emergency unit ... in the hospital made contact with somebody in the UK.... At some point an authority was made, was given, possibly by somebody in London, probably by somebody in London, for us to go ahead on that basis." [a]

- to Horwell: Horwell asked Moss: "Could it have been the case ... that in fact you authorised Mr Monceau to carry on his work, bearing in mind the difficulty of the situation, the confusion, the chaos and the need obviously for some expedition?" To which Moss confirmed: "I think that is possibly the case, yes."

So to Hough, Moss has said that authorisation to embalm was sought from "somebody in the UK".

To Horwell, Moss confirms that he himself "authorised Mr Monceau to carry on his work" – no mention of needing UK approval.

Keith Moss, the British Consul General to Paris, has therefore presented three completely different and conflicting accounts of what transpired during his conversation with Jean Monceau at the hospital – first in his 2004 statement, second to Burnett at the inquest and third to Horwell.

The question is: What actually was said in this Monceau-Moss conversation?

The biggest difficulty in getting to the truth on this is that both men – Monceau and Moss – are evidently liars.[b] In saying this, I suggest that the reason Moss has come up with three stories of a conversation he was a full participant in, is because he is not telling a true account of what occurred. I also suggest that by the time of the inquest, it had become paramount to the cover-up that Moss was seen to be the person who authorised the embalming.

Why do I say this? Because I believe the evidence shows that Amarger, in her statement, has told the truth as she saw it. Her account was that the British had requested the embalming procedure before 9 a.m. This also fits with Moss' 2004 statement testimony that Monceau didn't seek his authorisation, but was just informing Moss of what he had come in to the hospital to carry out.

---

[a] Moss states: "somebody in the UK"; "somebody in London"; "somebody in London" – he makes no attempt to explain who this "somebody" might be and what's possibly more important, nobody asks him. Why is this?

[b] Monceau has been shown as a liar in his earlier accounts on the dry ice and Amarger's role on the day. Monceau's level of credibility is addressed in the Conclusions section of this chapter.

This evidence, of an early British request for embalming, completely changes the scenario – it indicates that the real reason for embalming had nothing to do with the expected deterioration of the body due to the hot room – this was a cover. This issue is dealt with in the Conclusions section of this chapter.

I suggest that Moss gave a statement account that Monceau did not describe an embalming procedure because Moss did not wish to be linked in any way to the embalming of Princess Diana.

There is a critical difference between the Paget investigation and the inquest that forced Moss into changing his position.

That difference is Huguette Amarger, the embalmer.

Amarger's evidence was completely excluded from the Paget Report – she was not even named in the script of the report[a] and there was no mention that Paget had taken a statement from her. When it came to the inquest, although Amarger wasn't cross-examined, her statement was read out.

It is Amarger's statement that made the time and point of embalming authorisation an issue. Because her statement was left out of the Paget Report, it meant that at that time Moss was able to distance himself from the authorisation and his evidence was not significant.

Once Amarger's statement was decided to be included at the inquest, it then meant that a later authorisation point had to be "proven" to counter her passing (but clear) evidence that it was known before 9 a.m. that "the British wanted it to be a woman to take care of giving the treatment". I suggest that this was when it must have been decided that Moss was the man to do this. Moss was then forced into changing his story – he now took on the role of authoriser of the embalming, but only after "I or somebody else ... made contact with somebody in the UK ... possibly ... somebody in London, probably ... somebody in London".[b]

One could ask: Well why did they include Amarger's statement at the inquest?

Baker has always claimed his inquest was thorough, but I suggest that Baker has always been more concerned about a public perception of thoroughness, rather than the inquest actually being thorough. If Baker had gone ahead with the embalming evidence at the inquest without including any testimony from the person who did the embalming – Amarger – then it would have been difficult to maintain a perception of thoroughness – to the

---

[a] Amarger's name appears once in the entire report: in the second embalming diagram (shown earlier) – this may have been inadvertent, as her name appears to be deliberately excluded from the first diagram (also shown earlier).

[b] This was to Hough. By the time Horwell got to Moss – over an hour of cross-examining later – Moss had forgotten about the need to get authorisation from London: Moss confirmed he "authorised Mr Monceau to carry on his work".

jury or to the public. Therefore Baker did the very minimum required – he included Amarger's statement[a], but ensured that she was not cross-examined.

Had Amarger been cross-examined at the inquest, on the basis of her 2005 statement, the jury would have witnessed evidence that flew directly in the face of the account put by Monceau – see earlier – and to a lesser extent, Moss.

This was not a prospect that Baker could countenance.

Moss stated that he "was told by the hospital staff" that the "princess's remains ... were very badly damaged ... as a result of the accident".[b]

This evidence indicates that Moss hadn't viewed Diana's body himself and this is supported by his account to Paget: "I had not at this stage[c] seen the body". As mentioned in an earlier note, the suggestion here is that Moss – who set up an incident room next door to where Diana's body was moved to,

---

[a] Not all of Amarger's statement was read out – see later.

[b] I suggest that this may not be true. It has always been known that Princess Diana's main injury was internal and her face sustained minimal damage in the crash. There is a photo in Part 2 of Diana in the Mercedes after the crash that confirms this. Amarger said in her statement – this part not heard by the jury – that "she was unrecognizable, like any person killed in a road accident, at least by comparison with what I knew of her in the magazines. She had a wound on her right shoulder, I think, and another on her right hip, and a lot of bruises on the legs, as well as on the face...." :Huguette Amarger, Witness Statement, 8 March 2005, p3. Tebbutt, who saw Diana's body around noon, stated at the inquest: "She looked old, her mouth was down, not a lot of damage to her face". Burrell was with him and said on pp288-9 of *A Royal Duty*: "What I witnessed before me was indescribable, and it is not appropriate to explain further. But, regardless of how she looked, I wanted to hold her...." In contrast, David Green a British embalmer, who first saw Diana at about 4 p.m. said: "There was [a] small cut to her forehead that had been concealed with makeup and her hair brushed down over it." David Green, Witness Statement, 13 July 2004, reproduced in *The Documents* book, p503 (UK Edition). Clive Leverton, the British funeral director, who saw Diana at the same time, said at the inquest: "She had a bit of a bang on her forehead which [the French embalmers] covered a bit and she looked quite peaceful actually.": 22 Nov 07: 75.21. Moss gave evidence in his statement that Diana had been viewed by dignitaries prior to the embalming: "Mme. Chirac attended with Sir Michael and Lady Jay at 0845hrs [8.45 a.m.].... I recall that Prime Minister Lionel Jospin accompanied by Sir Michael Jay went to pay his last respects at 0920hrs....": Keith Moss, Witness Statement, 22 October 2004, reproduced in *The Documents* book, p653 (UK Edition) This issue is addressed further in the Head Injury section of the UK Post-Mortems chapter.

[c] The stage of the discussion with Monceau.

after his 2.15 a.m. arrival – hadn't gone next door to view the body between 7 a.m.[a] and 12.00 p.m.[b]

In contrast, during Moss' inquest cross-examination, Hough asked him: "While you were in the room for that early part of time, were you aware of any air-conditioning unit which was in the room?" Moss replied: "No, I was not." Then Hough: "Can you describe what the heat in the room was like?" Moss: "I suppose, to begin with, it was a fairly comfortable ambient temperature...."

So when Moss is asked questions that related to early conditions in the room – well before the 12.00 p.m. discussion with Monceau – he doesn't say "I don't know. I wasn't there." Instead, he answers both questions as though he had been there:

- "No, I was not" aware of any air-conditioning unit in the room
- the temperature in the room started out "fairly comfortable ambient".

This evidence is also supported by Stephen Donnelly's account of an 8.20 a.m. phone call – see earlier: "Keith Moss ... told me that the Princess of Wales' body was in a room next to where he was and that it was extremely hot".

Further to this, at the inquest Tebbutt was asked: "Did Mr Moss take you ... to the room where the Princess lay?" Tebbutt replied: "Yes, sir." [c]

It is really common sense that Moss – who was effectively the British representative in charge at the hospital, and had been there from before Diana even arrived in the room – would have visited the room next door and viewed Diana's body.

I suggest that the comment by Moss that indicated he had not seen the body at any time during the 5 hour period (7.00 to 12.00 p.m.) is a lie – possibly an attempt to distance himself from involvement in the embalming decision. If Moss hadn't even viewed the body, how could he be held responsible for the unwanted distinction of authorising the embalming? In saying this, I am not suggesting that Moss did authorise the embalming at 12.00 p.m. – the general evidence is that the embalming was in fact ordered much earlier in the day (see earlier).[d]

Nevertheless, Moss' answers to Hough indicate that he had been in the room and would have had firsthand knowledge of the state of Princess Diana's body.

---

[a] This is approximately when Diana's body was placed in the final room – see earlier.

[b] The approximate time of the Monceau-Moss conversation.

[c] See later. This occurred just after Tebbutt arrived at 11.30 a.m. but before the Moss-Monceau conversation which occurred around 12 noon.

[d] If Moss had really been the one who was responsible for authorising the embalming – as was suggested at the inquest – then why wouldn't he have just nipped next door to view the situation with his own eyes, before making such a momentous decision?

The Paget Report suggested that Moss' inability to understand French led to a misunderstanding by Moss of what Monceau was saying.

Paget Report, p539: **Jury Didn't Hear**:

"Jean Monceau clearly believed that he explained to Keith Moss that the Princess of Wales required the highest level of embalming because of the fractures and sutures. However this conversation appears to have taken place in French and, as Keith Moss later described, he believed he was agreeing to a less intrusive form of treatment in order to make the Princess of Wales presentable for her family when they arrived at the hospital."

Keith Moss, British Consul General, Paris: 22 Nov 07: 4.20:

Hough: Q. Turning to the reasons for your appointment in January 1995 to Paris, I think you were then – I am sure you still are – a fluent French speaker.

A. Perhaps a bit less fluent now than I was.

Keith Moss: 22 Oct 04 Statement: **Jury Didn't Hear**:

"I believe the reason I had been posted to Paris, as Consul General, was down to my ability to speak French.... I became fluent in French and I was able to speak, read, and understand, but I always found writing difficult.... During my career I also benefited from speaking French in Douala, and in Vienna, where French and English are the working languages of the United Nations."[60]

Keith Moss: 22 Oct 04 Statement: **Jury Didn't Hear**:

"This conversation [with Monceau] was conducted in French in my Office on the corridor I have described."[61]

Colin Tebbutt, Diana's Driver and Security: July 04 Statement: **Jury Didn't Hear**:

"Mr Moss ... then spoke to the Hospital Funeral Directors in French...."[62]

Comment: At the inquest Hough pointed out that Moss was appointed in January 1995 – therefore he had been Consul General in Paris for over 2½ years at the time of the crash. He also indicates that his fluency in French was a reason for his appointment, and that is confirmed by Moss: "among other reasons".[63]

This evidence – along with what Moss said in his statement – indicates that Moss should have had no difficulty in understanding what Monceau was saying and Moss himself has never claimed that there was any difficulty.

Monceau however said in his statement: "We spoke in French and English, but in French we did not speak about embalming but thanatopraxie, which is a treatment involving the injection of preservatives into the arterial circuit and the recovery of veinous blood from the right of the heart and from the main veins."

There are two issues with this account:

1) Monceau has stated that the conversation was in "French and English" but other evidence suggests that it was only in French:

a) Tebbutt: "Moss ... then spoke to the Hospital Funeral Directors in French" [a]

b) Moss: "I thought at the time that he described himself as an 'embaumeur'"

c) Moss: "this conversation was conducted in French"

d) Moss made no mention in his statement or at the inquest of English being spoken

e) Moss was fluent in French – see above

f) there are general references during Moss' cross-examination that refer to him as being a French speaker – see 34.17 and 59.18.

The question is: Why would Moss need to talk in English to Monceau when he had been talking French in his role as British Consul General for 2½ years?

2) Monceau differentiates between embalming and thanatopraxie: "in French we did not speak about embalming but thanatopraxie". Monceau then defines thanatopraxie: "the injection of preservatives into the arterial circuit and the recovery of veinous blood from the right of the heart and from the main veins".

Monceau goes on in his statement to describe "the various levels of embalming"[b] – the third of which is "arterial injections to preserve the body from the proliferation of bacteria".

What Monceau fails to do is explain the difference between thanatopraxie – "the injection of preservatives into the arterial circuit" – and the "third level" of embalming – "arterial injections to preserve the body".

I suggest that they are one and the same.

This is supported by Moss in his evidence:

- at the inquest: "at the time that he described himself as an 'embaumeur' ... but it transpired that it was called a 'thanatopracteur', but I think the difference between the two is broadly the same"

- in his statement: "this person was called a 'thanatopracteur' – the nearest word in the English language ... would be an embalmer".

It appears that Moss had looked the words up in the dictionary and found that they were virtually one and the same – dictionaries translate both words, "embaumeur" and "thanatopracteur", as the English: "embalmer".

---

[a] Tebbutt thought they were funeral directors but he is referring to the embalmers – see later.

[b] Monceau describes three levels of embalming – dry ice, mortuary cleansing, arterial injections – yet later in his statement he says that what took place was "complete embalming – partial embalming does not exist."

At the inquest – despite Moss' claim that the words had essentially the same meaning – Hough, during his cross-examination of Moss, attempted to perpetuate the "differences":

- "Were you aware of the technical differences between 'embaumement' and 'thanatopraxie'?"

- "Were you aware of what a thanatopracteur did at all?"

Why then did Monceau, and later Hough, attempt to suggest that two French words – "embaumement" and "thanatopraxie" – that essentially had the same meaning, were actually different?

I believe the answer to this can be found on page 539 of the Paget Report: "Jean Monceau clearly believed that he explained to Keith Moss that the Princess of Wales required the highest level of embalming.... However this conversation appears to have taken place in French and, as Keith Moss later described, he believed he was agreeing to a less intrusive form of treatment...."

In other words, I suggest that Monceau, whose statement was taken a year after Moss', has used the language issue (French and English) and definition of terms – thanatopraxie and embaumement – in a crude attempt to explain why Moss got a completely different perception of the conversation: they were talking at cross-purposes because they were different nationalities and didn't have the same understanding of the terms used.

At the inquest Hough latched onto this[a], asking Moss: "Were you aware of the technical differences between 'embaumement' and 'thanatopraxie'?" I suggest that if someone had asked Hough this same question, he wouldn't have been able to provide an answer because effectively there are no differences – they are just two words that mean the same thing.

In the end, this could only have assisted in adding to any pre-existing confusion that the jury already had on the embalming issue.

Tebbutt-Gibbins Role

Colin Tebbutt, Diana's Driver and Security: 26 Nov 07: 90.17:
Hough: Q. When you arrived, were the French funeral directors present?
A. Yes.
Q. What were they doing?
A. Just standing in the corridor, sir.[b]

---

[a] At the inquest Moss' evidence was actually more closely aligned to Monceau's and the jury did not get to hear the widely divergent statements – see earlier.

[b] The French funeral directors didn't arrive at the hospital until about 4.50 p.m. – see earlier and later. Tebbutt here must have been referring to the embalmers – Monceau, Amarger and Charrier – who were at the hospital before Tebbutt. This fits with Tebbutt not realising that it was an embalming that had taken place.

Q. Did you call Mr Gibbins from there?

A. Yes, I set up a communications room, sir. Mr Moss gave me a room to set up three lines; one to Balmoral, one to Mr Gibbins and a general line for me.

Q. When you first spoke to Mr Gibbins, what instructions did he give you?

A. I gave him as full and comprehensive a report as I could, but the message came over very quickly: just leave everything alone with the Princess.

Q. How do you mean "leave everything alone"?

A. Well, that Levertons, the Royal undertakers, would be here to take care of everything. The only problem I could see was they were arriving very late in the day.

Q. When were they due to arrive?

A. 5 o'clock, sir.[a]

.... Q. So you were there, Levertons were due to arrive around 5 o'clock in the evening, you thought. What view did you form about the state of the body and what should be done in view of the heat?

A. Sir, it is a very emotional time, to walk in and see your boss lying like she was. She looked old, her mouth was down, not a lot of damage to her face, but she had that "I do not want to be here" look, and I have to say that it went back to my mother who died, who was a beautiful woman, and when my mother died, she looked old and did not want to be there, and before my daughter saw my mother, a funeral director did her hair and did make-up, and when I went back to see my mother, she was my mother, she was beautiful. In my mind, and my mind only, was the family were coming, His Royal Highness[b] was coming, other members were coming, and I would not have wanted to see the lady in that condition. My only concern was to make her face look a little bit better.[c]

Q. Who did you speak to about that concern?

A. I spoke to Mr Gibbins. I also considered the heat in the room was not doing the Princess any good.

Q. You say you spoke to Mr Gibbins. Did you speak to anybody in the hospital first before you spoke to him?

A. I spoke to Mr Moss. I cannot remember the actual – we discussed it. It was playing on my mind a bit, the heat of the room and the fact that you and I would have been in a fridge, but there was Her Royal Highness lying in a bed in a very, very hot room. I considered she was starting to melt, but I am no

---

[a] The evidence from the funeral directors is that they actually arrived at the hospital at about 3.45 p.m. – see later.

[b] Prince Charles.

[c] Amarger, the embalmer, said in her 2005 statement (this part, not heard by the jury): "She was unrecognizable, like any person killed in a road accident, at least by comparison with what I knew of her in the magazines. She had a wound on her right shoulder, I think, and another on her right hip, and a lot of bruises on the legs, as well as on the face....": Huguette Amarger, Witness Statement, 8 March 2005, p3

expert.

Q. You say this[a]: "I spoke to the hospital funeral directors through Mr Moss. I asked about the condition of the body under these circumstances and what the condition of the body would be when the Prince of Wales and the family attended. I was informed that the body would start to deteriorate quite rapidly. This was also the opinion of the nursing staff as it was just so hot. I had to force this issue because of my concerns for the family's attendance and I rang Mr Gibbins."

....Q. When you say you had to force the issue –

A. Well, "force" is perhaps the wrong word.... I had to go through Mr Moss and try and make people understand that I did not want His Royal Highness and the two ladies[b] to see the Princess lying in a bed in the state she was.

At 124.19: Horwell: Q. You ... refer[c] to your speaking to Mr Moss, who was of course with you in Paris, and told him: "If we don't do something, the body is going to be in a state."

A. Yes, there was a general conversation on that, sir.

Q. And a little later...: "The funeral directors were also in the room, I said, 'Would you kindly do whatever you do to prepare the body for when the family arrives'." Mr Moss then spoke to them in French and immediately afterwards, the funeral directors changed into what appeared to be protective clothing and they went about their work?

A. Correct, sir.

Colin Tebbutt, Diana's Driver and Security: 5 Jul 04 Statement: **Jury Didn't Hear**:

"When we arrived at the Hospital the scene outside was quite amazing; there were thousands of people outside.

"The Hospital was secured by a Uniformed Police presence up to the floor where the Princess of Wales was being kept. The Consul General, Mr Moss, who is an Embassy employee to the Foreign Office and responsible for making important decisions, had set up office in a small room at the entrance of the corridor where the Princess of Wales was being kept.... The corridor was in turmoil. There were a lot of people milling around. Mr Moss, the Consul General, was calm and appeared in total control. French Police Officers in plain clothes were pointed out to me, and were situated two at each end of the corridor. There appeared to be access to this secure area, but the people present could have been Doctors; I also believe the French Minister for Health was there. There were French Officials walking into the

---

[a] In his Paget statement.
[b] Diana's two sisters: Jane Fellowes and Sarah McCorquodale.
[c] In his Paget statement.

Princess' room and bowing at the end of the bed. I ... felt this was inappropriate. I then introduced myself to everybody present and everyone appeared pleased to see us as members of the Princess of Wales' staff.

"I was introduced to a female nurse I now know as Jeanne Lecorchet, who appeared to do more than the other female nurse who may have been 'Dominique' that Paul Burrell later spoke of in his book.

"Mr Moss introduced me to a few of the people present and pointed out the Police Officers. Jeanne Lecorchet then said, "Would you like to see the Princess?" in English. Paul and I were taken to the first room on the right. We went in to see the Princess of Wales. Paul collapsed and I held him up. The Princess of Wales was in a bed and the bedclothes were arranged up to her neck and bedding neatly done up to her face. She looked older but peaceful. There appeared to be lacerations to the right hand side of her face and her neck seemed to be swollen, but the left hand side seemed okay. It was a hot day and I noticed the room was extremely hot. I also noticed three Hospital Funeral Directors, two male and one female, were present when I was in the room. At this time they were not doing anything with the body. I started using my past experience as a Police Officer, and did the best I could; I was given a room and I asked for three separate telephone lines.

"On one line I rang Mr Gibbins and made this his extension number. I gave him a comprehensive explanation of what I was doing and what was going on. He told me to take any action that I deemed necessary, but not to allow anyone touch the body until Levertons, the Royal Undertakers, arrived.

"On one of the other lines I rang the Queen's Police Officer, Chief Superintendent Robinson. When I spoke to him, I tried to put him at ease. There was a conversation about the Princess of Wales' personal belongings, but I don't recall the exact details of that conversation. I made this Mr Robinson's extension number.

"The third line, I maintained as a general line.

"Paul Burrell who was in a very distressed state at this time, I placed into this office with two Priests, one French and one English, I believe, who were also in attendance.

"I formally produce my original notes.... These notes and plans were made around the time of the incident, on the plane on my return to London, and again when I got home....

"Paul remained with me throughout, but was in shock and in a very highly emotional state. Paul Burrell used the phone to make calls from 'my office' and I am aware that the Prince of Wales called us and spoke to Paul....

"After a while we received a telephone call stating that the Press were on the roof of a nearby building. Fearing Press intrusion and photographs of the Princess of Wales through the Hospital room windows, Paul Burrell, the nurses and I erected blankets up at the windows. The room was starting to get even hotter and Mr Moss and I put Air Conditioning Units into the room to try to keep it cool. When I switched one of the Units on I noticed the Princess of Wales' hair and eyelashes move. This shocked me momentarily and I shed a tear. But I had to be in control and I soon regained my composure.

"I had received word from Mr Gibbins that Levertons, the Royal Undertakers were due to arrive at around 5 p.m., and that no-one should do anything until such time as they got here. In the corridor were the same Hospital Funeral Directors as I have spoken about earlier, and I expressed to everyone present that no one was allowed to touch the Princess of Wales' body. I gave this instruction in English and I believed that everyone there could understand what I was saying. If there were any communication difficulties, Mr Livesey would translate.

"All the while the Hospital room was getting hotter. I spoke to the Hospital Funeral Directors through Mr Moss and I asked about the condition of the body under these circumstances and what the condition of the body would be when the Prince of Wales and the family attended. I was informed that the body would start to deteriorate quite rapidly. This was also the opinion of the nursing staff, as it was just so hot.

"I had to force this issue because of my concerns for the Family's attendance and I rang Mr Gibbins. I told him that, as I understood it, if we waited for Levertons to arrive with a coffin at 5 p.m., the information that I had been given was that the Princess was melting. I asked him to find out what to do. I was aware that the Prince of Wales was due to arrive shortly after 5 p.m. and from what French Funeral Directors had mentioned, it would take approximately one and a half hours to prepare the body for the Prince's arrival.

"Mr Gibbins rang me back and said that, 'If you think, they will do a good job. Then Yes.' He expressed that if they were proper Funeral Directors employed by the Hospital and if Mr Moss was in agreement they should be allowed to carry on. I was quite relieved by this decision, as I did not wish the Princess of Wales' family to see her body in a state of deterioration.

"I then spoke to Mr Moss and told him, 'If we don't do something the body is going to be in a state', this was opinion from my experience of dealing with dead bodies....

"The Funeral Directors were also in the room and I said 'Would you kindly do what-ever you do to prepare the body for when the family arrives'. Mr Moss who had been present, standing next to me in the office when I was speaking to Mr Gibbins, then spoke to the Hospital Funeral Directors in French, and as far as I am aware he asked the Funeral Directors to prepare the body for when the family arrived. At that point the Funeral Directors immediately went into a side room and got dressed in what appeared to be protective clothing.

"Before they were allowed into the Hospital room, Inspector Peter Von-Heinz, the Personal Protection Officer for Prince Charles and his advance, went into the room to look at where the Prince of Wales would be taken. I explained the circumstances to him and he then spoke with the local French Police. He was a fluent French speaker.

"The Hospital Funeral Directors were wearing gowns and facemasks. Paul Burrell then handed over the dress and shoes we had obtained from Lady Jay at the Embassy. The Funeral Directors went into the room and were joined by two female nurses Jeanne Lecorchet and another. I don't recall if they were gowned, and there was possibly one other, again I am not sure.

"Paul Burrell and I took this opportunity to go for some food at the Hospital cafeteria, while the Funeral Directors carried on with whatever they had to do....

"Time flew. After about forty minutes to an hour, we returned to the corridor....

"I have been asked whether I was aware that the Princess of Wales had been embalmed. I did not know anything about an embalming process and I was unaware until now that such a procedure had taken place. I just presumed that they had got on with whatever they do. I have never watched anybody prepare a body.

"I continued making telephone calls. As far as I was aware Mr Gibbins was still in overall charge, but I had to make arrangements for transport upon our return to England. I had heard that Paul Burrell and I were not going to be allowed to return to England on the Royal plane and I was concerned about the continuity of the Princess of Wales' body in respect of her return to London. Common sense told me that a Coroner's Enquiry would take place and I felt I should accompany the body back to London. I asked Paul to organise for us to return on the Royal flight.

"I have been asked whether I was aware that the Princess of Wales was going to be subject of a Post-Mortem examination at the Fulham Mortuary. I would say that at no stage was I aware of this. And it was only when I met Mr Gibbins at RAF Northolt that I was aware of our final destination, Fulham Mortuary....

"I was now becoming worried. Levertons were due to arrive and were expecting to prepare the body and that I would now have to tell them that preparation had already been done on the authority of Mr Gibbins." [64]
Michael Gibbins, Diana's Private Secretary: 21 Nov 07: 9.2
Burnett: Q. Did [Tebbutt], in any sense, pass on to you what was being discussed or suggested by the hospital authorities at that end?
A. I think no more than said that it was felt that steps should be taken to make the body presentable.
Q. What was your reaction to that?

A. I think I said that if that was the advice from the hospital, then that should be done.

At 43.8: Horwell: Q. This is what you said in your statement of 1st September 2004..... "I have been asked if the word 'embalming' was ever used. I cannot remember. I had so many calls. I can however state that I never gave Colin Tebbutt directions to have the Princess embalmed. I was never aware that the Princess had undergone or was about to undergo any form of embalming process. The issue was to make the Princess look presentable for the arrival of the family."

A. That is correct.

Michael Gibbins, Diana's Private Secretary: 1 Sep 04 Statement: **Jury Didn't Hear**:

"I think Colin [Tebbutt] told me that he had been into a room to see the Princess's body and that there was damage to one side of her face....

"There was some question of the hospital authorities trying to preserve the Princess. My recollection of this conversation with Colin was that the family were due to arrive and that the Princess needed to be made to look presentable. I said Colin 'Thank you for reporting that, you must follow what the hospital authorities say and go with it'....

"It was never a thought of a medical preservation process. I have never had any dealings with the embalming of a body. It would not have been my place to deal with this. A lot of the decisions that Colin Tebbutt was asking me to make needed to be made by the relatives, but I had no one to call. I couldn't ring His Royal Highness Prince Charles or the Princess of Wales' mother.[a] I was in London, what could I do, but to say to Colin to do what he thought was best in the circumstances. My reaction was, if the people on the ground felt that this was the right thing to do then let them get on with it.

"Throughout that day I do not recall receiving directions from either the Foreign Office or our embassy in Paris." [65]

Comment: Colin Tebbutt was certainly present in the hospital when these events occurred – earlier evidence indicated that he arrived somewhere around 11.30 a.m.[b] Tebbutt also was a witness to the expectation that Diana's condition could deteriorate.

---

[a] Issues regarding the notification of Diana's family are dealt with later.

[b] Gibbins – see earlier – gave evidence that he was out of the office returning around 11.00 to 11.30 a.m. UK time. This indicates that the phone calls from Tebbutt to Gibbins would have taken place after 12 noon Paris time. This timing could fit with the embalming starting at around 12.30 p.m. as other evidence indicates.

If one looked at Tebbutt and Gibbins' evidence alone, one could be led to think that they were calling the shots regarding the embalming decision – that the embalmers[a] were acting in reaction to Tebbutt's "forcing" the issue.

Other evidence – see earlier – shows that the decision to embalm was made by British authorities much earlier in the day. It appears to be a coincidence that Tebbutt and Gibbins were discussing the situation and taking a stand at approximately the same time that the embalmers were ready to commence their work.

Non-Existent Documentation

René Deguisne, BJL Assistant General Manager: 9 May 05 Statement: **Jury Didn't Hear**:
"Question: Who contacted Hygeco following the death of the Princess of Wales? And at what time?
Answer: It was Mr Plumet of Pompes Funèbres Générales [undertakers].[b] In fact I did not know that. I called Mr Monceau who gave me the information. I do not know at what time that call was made; we no longer have any records for 1997. Our oldest ones go back to 1999."[66]
Comment: Monceau stated: "I have contacted BJL, who inform me that the order form has been lost, but there is still an accounting document which shows that we were engaged for this matter."
There are three points:
1) the jury never got to hear about the order form or the accounting document
2) the accounting document has never been shown to the police or inquest
3) this evidence conflicts with Deguisne's account.
Monceau: "there is still an accounting document", or Deguisne: "we no longer have any records for 1997".
Someone is lying – they can't both be right. Or, are they both lying?
Monceau certainly has the most form for lying – see earlier and later.
But later in Deguisne's interview, in order to "prove" a point[c], he produced BJL documentation from 1997: "I hand you a copy of the invoice

---

[a] Tebbutt calls them funeral directors.

[b] This evidence has already been addressed in an earlier footnote in the "Pre-Embalming Events" section.

[c] The point Deguisne is trying to "prove" is that an order to embalm was made from Moss to PFG. As Deguisne was not a witness to the events and was not heard at the inquest, his evidence on this has less relevance. The general evidence from Moss and PFG – Plumet, Jauze, Launay – was that there was no contact between Moss and PFG. The full statements of these witnesses are shown in *The Documents* book. It has been indicated earlier that Plumet could have received a call from Moss to confirm PFG's involvement in the repatriation – see earlier and later.

which we sent in the first place to Mr Moss ... a copy of the credit note which cancelled that invoice and a copy of the new invoice addressed to the Embassy of Great Britain".[67]

I suggest that both men – Monceau and Deguisne have lied, but on different points.

Deguisne has clearly lied – he said: "we no longer have any records for 1997", yet he later produced invoices from 1997.

The evidence also shows that Monceau has lied – he insists that "there is still an accounting document" for an order from PFG for dry ice.

Well, if this exists, where is it? No one has seen it. The general evidence – see earlier – is that there never was such an order placed on BJL from PFG.

There is of course no question that BJL carried out the embalming of Princess Diana but no documentation has ever been produced to support Monceau's accounts[a] of an order for dry ice. There has also never been any corroboration from any other witness.

It is notable that there has been no documentation forthcoming from PFG.
Gérard Jauze, PFG Branch Director, Paris: 21 Mar 06 Statement: **Jury Didn't Hear**:

"You ask me if I remember the documents that were generated after we were instructed. I have no knowledge of the documents. After getting the call from M. Chapillon, everything happened very quickly.

"You ask me if there are still any documents following the conversation with PFG on 31 August 1997. From what I have been told, I do not think so. Logically there should be a file because when I met Mr Mohamed Al Fayed[b] on 31 August 1997 I opened a file.[c] The documents and the invoices should be in that file, but I do not know if they are still in existence today. In 1997, we had an office on the boulevard Richard Lenoir in Paris, but the agency relocated and that perhaps explains why the documents cannot be found now. What is certain is that we did not work with lots of documents. It was a unique situation and we had to work very quickly. They were VIPs, and there were international ramifications, and we found ourselves caught up in the unfolding events." [68]

Jean-Claude Plumet, PFG Director of Paris Agencies, Paris: 4 Nov 05 Paget description of Statement: **Jury Didn't Hear**:

---

[a] Monceau had two different accounts – one in his 2005 statement and a different one at the inquest: see earlier.
[b] Jauze was in charge of the handling of Dodi Fayed's body in France.
[c] This is supported in Jauze's account when he described his communication with Mohamed Al Fayed: "Mr Mohamed Al Fayed came into the office to talk to me. I noted his wishes in writing.": Gérard Jauze, Witness Statement, 21 March 2006, reproduced in *The Documents* book, p478 (UK Edition)

"When asked, Mr Plumet explained that he did not complete any documentation after this telephone call. He explains that there was a dossier at PFG, but that since 1997 the offices at 42 Boulevard Richard Lenoir flooded and the dossier was lost." [69]

Patrick Launay, PFG Repatriation Director: 21 Mar 06 Statement: **Jury Didn't Hear**:

"You ask me if a paper or computerised record was made in respect of this matter. I do not know, and I do not have any record. I did not deal with the formalities, I was helping out.

"You ask me if I have any personal notes on this matter. I do not." [70]

Comment: Three different PFG witnesses were asked about documentation – or the lack thereof – and three different accounts were forthcoming:

- Jauze: "the agency relocated and that perhaps explains why the documents cannot be found now"
- Jauze: "what is certain is that we did not work with lots of documents"
- Jauze: "it was a unique situation and we had to work very quickly"
- Jauze: "they were VIPs, and there were international ramifications, and we found ourselves caught up in the unfolding events"
- Plumet: "he did not complete any documentation after this telephone call" – this call was from the British Consulate appointing PFG to carry out Diana's repatriation
- Plumet: "there was a dossier at PFG, but that since 1997 the offices at 42 Boulevard Richard Lenoir flooded and the dossier was lost"
- Launay: "I do not know [if there are any records], and I do not have any record"
- Launay: "I did not deal with the formalities".

What becomes clear is that there are no records regarding the involvement of PFG, the funeral directors who controlled the arrangements on the day.

The point is that this has to be one of the most significant deaths that PFG have ever been involved with[a] – so why is there no paperwork to record it?

We have been provided with 3 main reasons from the three witnesses:

1) the documentation was never completed in the first place
2) relocation of premises
3) the premises were flooded.

If the documents were never completed at the time, then this raises the question: Why wasn't retrospective documentation completed to get the records straight[b] – particularly on such an important case?

---

[a] When Jauze was interviewed he provided a copy of "a document given to me by PFG as a souvenir of this episode": Gérard Jauze, Witness Statement, 21 March 2006, p9.

[b] In this connection, Plumet stated the following: "Because on Sunday the Town Hall and the Police Administration Offices were closed, Mr Plumet had to contact Mme Celadon at the 'Operations Mortuaires de la Prefecture de Police', which translates as

If the documents were completed but then later lost, why was it that this particular file was lost – or were all of PFG's files lost?

I suggest that the reasons proffered do not necessarily "add up" – of particular concern is that different reasons for the non-existent documentation have been provided by all three witnesses.

When this is viewed in the context of Monceau's conflicting accounts regarding his interaction with PFG – a dry ice order that doesn't exist[a], a key conversation at the hospital that is denied by both PFG "participants" – it becomes very significant that none of this evidence was heard by the jury.

Is PFG covering up the evidence?

The evidence provided in this chapter indicates that Plumet may have been the person who directly enlisted the services of Jean Monceau and BJL – not for dry ice, but for embalming; not at midday, but at about 7.45 a.m.

If this was the case, then there may well be PFG documentation connecting that company to early orders from British authorities – possibly originally through Kenyons[b] – for an embalming to be carried out on Princess Diana's body.

That could be the reason why PFG witnesses – in unison – have declared that there is no documentation available in the case of the death of Diana, Princess of Wales.[c]

---

the Police Administration Offices for Funeral Issues, on Monday 1st September 1997. This was in order that the relevant documentation could be 'regularised', that is, to have it completed retrospectively." Although Plumet doesn't specify which documents he is referring to, the context indicates they are the documents that were legally required before repatriation – and not internal PFG documents. Source: Jean-Claude Plumet, Witness Statement, 4 November 2005, p3. This was supported in Launay's account: "Normally you have to have authority for the transportation of the body issued by the Prefecture of Police and also a death certificate issued by the Town Hall of the place of death. However, given the speed of the repatriation, the fact that it was a Sunday (with all government offices closed) and the presence of the Prefect at the time of departure, it was taken as read that all the documents would be regularised the following day, which was the case. Under normal circumstances, for a person other than a VIP, the body would not be transported until the Monday. However, on that day all the French authorities required for the repatriation of the body were present at the hospital.": Patrick Launay, Witness Statement, 21 March 2006, p5.

[a] Monceau even said in his 2005 statement, with reference to the non-existent dry ice order: "I imagine that PFG must also have an order form" – see earlier.

[b] It will be shown later that the 5 a.m. phone call to Racine came from the president of Kenyons in London.

[c] The lack of embalming documentation is covered later in the section called "Was It Legal?"

Stephen Donnelly, British Vice Consul, Paris: 22 Sep 05 Statement read out 17 Dec 07: 119.20:

"Another role [for the vice-consul] is dealing with requests from UK coroners to obtain documents from the French authorities relating to the deaths of British citizens in France. The reason that this is a consular function is because the French authorities do not accept requests under the Convention of Mutual Legal Assistance from Coroners. The original formal request from the Coroner to the French authorities in this case was in fact made by the consular section. We received the formal request from the Coroner, from which I drafted a 'note verbale', which I think was then signed by the Consul General at the time, Keith Moss, as I am not able to do so myself."

Comment: Donnelly has stated that a "formal request ... was in fact made by the consular section" for documents relating to the deaths. He says: "We received the formal request from the Coroner, from which I drafted a 'note verbale'" which was signed by Moss.

The questions are:
1) Where are the copies of this "formal request" and signed "note verbale"?
2) What was the French response to this request?

It will be shown at the conclusion to this chapter that there are several significant documents that are missing, particularly in connection to the embalming of Princess Diana.

Role of René Deguisne

The most significant point about the role of René Deguisne is that on the day, 31 August 1997, he actually had no role. However, Deguisne's "role" took on a life of its own in subsequent "evidence" relating to the embalming.

Deguisne, a senior BJL executive, was interviewed by the UK police, but his statement was withheld from the inquest jury.

René Deguisne, BJL Assistant General Manager: 9 May 05 Statement: **Jury Didn't Hear**:

"I must say that I did not have to deal with the case of Princess Diana personally, since in 1997 I was already the assistant general manager, I was responsible for a sector, dealing with the north, east and west of France, but not the Île-de-France. I have been responsible for that since 1999.

Question: Who was responsible for the Île-de-France at that time?

Answer: The assistant general manager in post at the time, and in charge of the Île-de-France was Mr Bernard Colsy, and the manager who went to the scene at La Salpêtrière, with the embalmer, Mrs Amarger, was Mr Jean Monceau."[71]

Jean Monceau: 18 Oct 05 Statement: **Jury Didn't Hear**:

"René Desguine [sic] came in as Managing Director of Hygeco after 1997. Within the firm's hierarchy, I was subordinate to Mr Desguine [sic]."[72]

Comment: In his statement to the British police, Monceau implied that René Deguisne was his boss at the time of the crash: "I was subordinate to Mr Desguine".

This conflicts with the clear evidence of Deguisne: "I did not have to deal with the case of Princess Diana.... I was responsible for a sector, dealing with the north, east and west of France, but not the Île-de-France." Deguisne testified that Bernard Colsy was "in charge of the Île-de-France" – the Île-de-France includes Paris, where the embalming occurred.

The reality is that Deguisne didn't have control over the Île-de-France area until 1999: "I have been responsible for that since 1999" – when he became Managing Director. At the time of the crash in 1997, Deguisne had no direct line of authority over Monceau, but Colsy did.

In this light, it is very significant that:

a) Operation Paget interviewed Deguisne – who "did not have to deal with the case of Princess Diana" and neglected to interview Colsy, who did deal with the case

b) Monceau failed to mention Colsy in any of his evidence.

Martine Monteil, Head of Brigade Criminelle: 19 Jul 05 Email to Paget:
Jury Didn't Hear:
"We should at this point recall the answers given by a witness ... Mr Rene Desguine [sic] (statement taken 09/05/2005) Assistant Managing Director of the company Hygeco, hired by the French Funeral Directors PFG to undertake conservation care...."[73a]

Keith Moss, British Consul General, Paris: 22 Nov 07: 22.21:
Hough: Q. Now the information from M Desguine [sic] of that company is that BJL was called in by the undertakers, PFG. Does that accord with what you understand?
A. I would not dispute it. I do not specifically recall it but I am sure that is correct.[b]

Comment: It does not appear to be a coincidence that in all three of the above pieces of evidence – Monceau in his October 2005 statement; Monteil in her July 2005 email; Hough at the inquest – the name Deguisne is misspelt in exactly the same way: "Desguine" – the "s" has been moved from the 6th letter to the 3rd letter in the word.

In Monceau's case, he has stated that he was "subordinate to Mr Desguine". The fact that Monceau has failed to spell Deguisne's name

---

[a] Monteil quoted Deguisne's account to avoid directly answering a question regarding the authorisation of the embalming. The full text of Monteil's account in this email has been included in a previous footnote in the section on "Dry Ice".

[b] This issue is covered in an earlier footnote in the "Pre-Embalming Events" section.

correctly supports the above understanding that Deguisne was not Monceau's boss.

In the other two instances – Monteil; Hough – they are quoting directly from Deguisne's May 2005 statement.

There is no question that Deguisne spelt his own name correctly in his statement – it is reproduced on p449 of *The Documents* book.[a]

The point is that Monceau has referred to Deguisne and Paget have interviewed him, yet Deguisne – by his own admission – had no relevance to the case, and in fact told Paget that he got his evidence from Monceau[b]: "I called Mr Monceau who gave me the information"; "I have all that [information] from Mr Monceau".[74]

Yet that knowledge didn't stop inquest lawyer, Jonathon Hough, from quoting Deguisne to Moss, as though he was a witness to the events, and his evidence was relevant. Moss has replied: "I am sure that is correct". In doing this – not mentioning that Deguisne was not a witness of the events – I suggest that Hough has deceived the jury, and possibly Keith Moss.

Monteil made use of Deguisne's evidence in a similar way – this is addressed in the earlier footnote in the "Dry Ice" section.

This evidence raises the question: Why did Paget interview Deguisne and not Colsy? Colsy may have had knowledge about how decisions were arrived at on the day.

The effect of interviewing Deguisne was that his evidence could potentially be used to support Monceau's account – you end up with two people saying the same thing, rather than just Monceau on his own.

I suggest that Deguisne's evidence wasn't read out at the inquest, because it would have become quickly evident to the jury that what he had to say had no relevance: "I did not have to deal with the case of Princess Diana".

The way things transpired, certain parts of the evidence of Deguisne was able to be introduced as evidence, without the entire Deguisne statement being subjected to scrutiny. Hough did this at the inquest and Monteil did it through her email to Paget.[c]

The other significant question is: How is it that Monceau, Monteil and Hough all got the spelling of Deguisne's name wrong, and all made the identical mistake?

---

[a] In October 2009 René Deguisne was the President of the French Institute for Thanatopraxy. The correct spelling of Deguisne's name is verified by references to him on the internet. Check Google Search.

[b] Monceau has been shown in this book to be an unreliable witness.

[c] In the final analysis, this had little impact on the inquest evidence – Monteil's evidence was not heard anyway; Hough only quoted a minor point – but because Deguisne was interviewed in this way, it certainly created a greater potential for misleading the jury.

This question raises the issue of how both Monteil and Hough came by their information.[a] If they had been using the original statement of Deguisne – which had the correct spelling – it seems an incredible coincidence that both would have transposed the "s" in exactly the same way.

Embalming Process

Huguette Amarger, French Embalmer: 8 Mar 05 Statement read out 22 Nov 07: 92.21:
"Question: What does the term 'treatment' mean in your profession?
Answer: It is the fact of treating a dead body for the purposes of hygiene and presentation. It is a matter of watching[b] and shampooing the body. A formalin-based product, that is to say a disinfecting product, is then injected in order to delay the disinfection of the body."
Jean Monceau, BJL Director and Embalmer, Paris: 20 Nov 07: 79.15:
Burnett: Q. Was the single reason for wishing to embalm the body of the Princess to make her body presentable to those who would be viewing it later that day?
A. The general idea is that everything that was done was to make the body presentable. So that is why, among other things, that we proceeded to something that is called "thanato-aesthetics". It is a final treatment that ends the process of thanatopraxy.

Who Did It?

The embalming process was carried out by Huguette Amarger.
Huguette Amarger, French Embalmer: 8 Mar 05 Statement read out 22 Nov 07: 92.21:
"Mr Monceau was present at the beginning of my work, then he came and went a few times.... The head of the French police officers, in uniform, asked that only women stayed with me, and I found myself in the quiet again with my assistant who had arrived in the meantime. I do not remember his name. He no longer works for Hygeco either; he was the only man in the room, with two policewomen."
Jean Monceau, BJL Director and Embalmer, Paris: 20 Nov 07: 78.4:

---

[a] Presumably Monceau made the mistake because he was personally not that familiar with Deguisne. Having said that, Deguisne became Managing Director in 1999 – and therefore boss of Monceau, but two levels up. Monceau left Hygeco BJL in August 2001. Sources: René Deguisne, Witness Statement, 9 May 2005, reproduced in *The Documents* book, p450 (UK Edition); Jean Monceau, Witness Statement, 18 October 2005, reproduced in *The Documents* book, p407 (UK Edition).
[b] This should be "washing".

Burnett: Q. Who, in fact, performed the embalming process?

A. Mrs Amarger, Josselin Charrier and myself, Jean Monceau.

Jean Monceau: 18 Oct 05 Statement: **Jury Didn't Hear**:

"You have asked me how I was dressed that day.... Later on, when I did the embalming with Huguette Amarger, we donned white coats and gloves etc."[75]

Jean Monceau: 18 Oct 05 Statement: **Jury Didn't Hear**:

"During this time [talking to Moss] another embalmer, Josselin Charrier, phoned me. He asked me if I needed any help. I said the more the better. He arrived at the hospital at around 1330hrs [1.30 p.m.]. He was my equivalent within the company, in charge of the transport department. Later on, it would be him that did the embalming with Mrs Amarger, whilst I took care of the liaison with the other people."[76]

Comment: There is a clear conflict in Monceau's evidence.

At the inquest: "Mrs Amarger, Josselin Charrier and myself, Jean Monceau" performed the embalming.

In his statement – not heard by the jury – Monceau presents two conflicting pictures:

1) "I did the embalming with Huguette Amarger"
2) Charrier "did the embalming with Mrs Amarger, whilst I took care of the liaison".

Amarger has said that "Mr Monceau was present at the beginning of my work, then he came and went a few times" – Monceau was "present", but at no point has Amarger suggested that Monceau participated in the embalming itself.

PFG director Gérard Jauze has also stated that Amarger was "the embalmer" – see later.

Earlier evidence revealed that in response to an early British request for a female embalmer, Amarger was chosen to carry out the embalming. The balance of the evidence – Amarger, Monceau, Jauze – supports the fact that Amarger was the embalmer. The evidence from Amarger and Monceau also shows that Amarger had an assistant[a] – Monceau names him as Charrier, but there is no other account to support that.

Charrier has never been interviewed by any investigation and also was not heard at the inquest – he should have been.

---

[a] Tebbutt also supports this in his statement. Describing events soon after his arrival: "I also noticed three Hospital Funeral Directors, two male and one female, were present when I was in the room." Tebbutt apparently thought the embalmers were funeral directors. The funeral directors didn't arrive at the hospital until later in the afternoon – see later.

Monceau, who has already been shown in this book to be a liar, has included himself as one of the embalmers – "I did the embalming" – but this account: a) conflicts with other evidence in his statement – "I took care of the liaison", and b) is not supported by any other witnesses.

What is clear is that the jury only heard the account – given under cross-examination – that Monceau was one of the embalmers. As the general evidence is that he was Amarger's boss, this account may have effectively countered – in the jury's eyes – Amarger's statement evidence that she was chosen because "the British wanted it to be a woman to take care of giving the treatment"[a] – see earlier.

This issue goes to the very heart of who was responsible for ordering the embalming and when that occurred. If it could be shown at the inquest that Monceau was an integral part of the physical embalming process, then that tends to undermine Amarger's account that the British requested a female embalmer.

It is significant that the jury never got to hear Monceau's conflicting account stating that he was not part of the embalming team.

Monceau said in his statement: "In my case, [I had embalmed] roughly 13,000 bodies. Josselin Charrier has done rather less because he worked in the provinces and it will be less still for Mrs Amarger as she was newer to the profession."

So we have three embalmers present in the hospital at the time of the embalming:
- Monceau: very experienced – "roughly 13,000 bodies"
- Charrier : "has done rather less"
- Amarger: "less still ... as she was newer to the profession".

On the day, Monceau – the senior embalmer present – handed over the embalming of Diana, Princess of Wales, to a far less experienced embalmer.[b]

---

[a] This evidence from Amarger was significant in showing that the embalming was ordered early by UK authorities – see earlier and later.

[b] In Gérard Jauze's 2006 statement – not heard by the jury – he said: "You ask me if I have ever met Mme Amarger. Yes, and I knew that she and M. Monceau were very well respected and that they had worked on VIPs and important figures." The question was specifically about Amarger, yet Jauze has brought Monceau into the answer. This appears to confirm that Amarger generally played a subordinate role and indicates that although Amarger may have "worked on VIPs and important figures", it was only in a secondary role to Monceau. Source: Gérard Jauze, Witness Statement, 21 March 2006, p6.

If this wasn't because the British had asked for a female, then why was it? Why was Amarger, a person who "was newer to the profession", chosen to carry out one of the most significant embalmings BJL had ever been called on to do?

This was a question that the jury should have heard asked. They didn't.

Not only did the jury not hear that question, but they also never heard: a) that Amarger "was newer to the profession" and b) that Monceau stated that Charrier "did the embalming with Mrs Amarger, whilst I took care of the liaison".

The jury were never put in a position where they could compare the level of experience between Amarger and Monceau – but then they wouldn't have thought it was relevant because they heard Monceau state on live videolink[a] under oath, that he had participated in the embalming, alongside Amarger and Charrier.

As stated above, Monceau's statement evidence was that during the embalming "I took care of the liaison with the other people". The jury never heard this.

The question is: Who were "the other people"?[b]

Monceau has not said. He should have been asked at the inquest. Also, why didn't the UK police ask him?

There is no known evidence from any other person that Monceau "liaised" with them during the embalming period. The evidence from the funeral directors – Plumet and Jauze – is that they can't recall having anything to do with Monceau on the day.

Amarger's evidence is that Monceau "came and went a few times".

Where was Monceau when he wasn't in the room? Evidence in this book will indicate that Monceau – in a similar way to Henri Paul, Claude Roulet, Jean-Marc Martino and Arnaud Derossi[c] – may have been taking instructions from an additional employer, possibly based in the UK.

As this book progresses, it will become increasingly clear that, as part of the police investigations, Monceau's phone records and bank accounts should have been checked.

This never occurred.

Procedure

There are several key areas of conflict regarding the embalming process.
Jean Monceau, BJL Director and Embalmer, Paris: 20 Nov 07: 85.1:

---

[a] Between Paris and London.

[b] This is similar to an earlier statement by Monceau, also not heard by the jury: "I was constantly going in and out. I spoke to a number of people. It must have been between 1030 and 1045hrs." – see earlier.

[c] See Parts 1 and 2.

Mansfield: Q. Would it be right to say that what was done in relation to Princess Diana was full embalming, complete embalming, not partial embalming?

A. Well, it depends on what you mean by "complete" and "partial" because anyway in France you never talk in terms of embalming. We don't take anything away from the bodies. We leave everything that is inside. Embalming, according to the French term, would be complete anyway.[a]

Q. I think you told the British police that partial embalming, as far as you are concerned, does not exist.[b]

A. Yes, because of the way we understand the word in French. Anyway, in France, you talk about thanatopractitioning, thanatopractice with thanatopractitioners, and when you train someone in that field, you tell that person that actually it consists in, well, recovering the blood – you inject product that has preservation qualities and you recover as much blood from the veins as possible.

Q. Could you give us an estimate in this case of how many litres of fluid was used in relation to Princess Diana?

A. I think we must have used three 2-litre bottles, so that would make 6 litres all in all of fluids with water.

Huguette Amarger, BJL Embalmer: 8 Mar 05 Statement read out 22 Nov 07: 94.20:

Hough: "There was then a question about how the treatment was carried out chronologically and about what quantities and what products were injected and the witness [Amarger] gave a very detailed explanation. I think the only piece of information that needs to be given, because it related to a question earlier, is that about 10 litres of formalin was used; that is to say four 25-litre[c] jars."

Huguette Amarger, BJL Embalmer: 8 Mar 05 Statement: **Jury Didn't Hear**:

---

[a] BJL Managing Director, René Deguisne, testified to the British police: "There are two levels of treatment: washing and dressing comprise the first level, and presentation treatment with washing and dressing the second level. The presentation treatment consists of injecting the arteries with a preservative liquid which spreads throughout the body and rehydrates it. The princess's body was therefore given the second level.": René Deguisne, Witness Statement, 9 May 2005, reproduced in *The Documents* book, p452 (UK Edition)

[b] Alan Puxley, Kenyon Vice-President of Operations, testified to Paget: "There is no definition of the term 'partial embalming', there are different degrees.": Alan Puxley, Witness Statement, 16 June 2004, reproduced in *The Documents* book, pp461 (UK Edition).

[c] This should read "2.5 litre".

"Question: How was the treatment carried out, chronologically?

"Answer: I combed the hair to remove the pieces of glass and other dirt, and I washed the body superficially to begin with. It is always the same procedure that I follow. I made incisions at four points, in the two carotid arteries and the two femoral arteries. Separately, I injected the formalin-based liquid[a] into each of the arteries with a cannula[b].

"Question: What quantities, and what products did you inject?

"Answer: .... I injected about 10 litres of formalin, that is, one two-and-a-half litre jar into each artery which goes to remake the blood circuit. I then massaged each limb in order to move the product along and push out the blood which goes out towards the suction jar. I then withdrew the cannulas and made a general puncture in the rib cage and the abdominal cavity. Everything is drawn out into the same jar. (intestines, stomach, lungs). Before stitching up the incisions and to avoid discharges, I apply white powder. This is called incision powder. I am not sure whether I used any that day. I then place cotton wool in each incision and I plug each orifice (nostrils and mouth).... I then stitch up each incision in the arteries and also the mouth. I place transparent plastic disks under each eyelid to stop it opening. I then put one litre of pure, colourless formalin into the chest and abdominal cavities. I withdraw the trocar[c] and stitch up the incision.

"I then washed the body and the hair again. I dried the body and the hair, and blow-dried it. I dressed the body in a black dress which my colleague Monceau brought me and which I learned immediately belonged to the wife of the British ambassador, like the black shoes.

"I must make the point that what I did was in no way specific to the Princess. That is how I always proceed.

"The formalin which I injected into the arteries was praline pink in colour. It is mixed with lanolin and is pink-coloured to give the tissues a slight tint.

"I knew that account had to be taken of the fact that the date of the funeral was not known.

"The formalin is diluted 15 or 20 per cent with water. It is I who do the mixing, as I see to it that the body stays looking natural. That is how I always proceed. The mixture of formalin depends on the state of putrefaction of the body. At that time, the body was all right.

---

[a] Alan Puxley, Kenyon Vice-President of Operations, testified to Paget: "Formaldehyde is a gas and has to be dissolved in water as a solution. Normally it is purchased as a solution of various percentages of formaldehyde, for example 26% is typical. It is placed in a tank, mixed with water and at final injecting into the deceased it may be reduced to 3 to 4%.": Alan Puxley, Witness Statement, 16 June 2004, reproduced in *The Documents* book, pp460-1 (UK Edition).

[b] Tube used to administer or drain off fluid.

[c] Special long metal tube.

"I knew that the subsequent exposure of the body abroad had to be taken into account and I thought that the body might change coffins. I therefore put in more formalin than usual.

"As the law requires, a specimen of the mixture injected into the arteries is sealed to the ankle of the body. There is a label with the name of the company which makes the product. My signature is not there. It was Hygeco that supplied the product...." [77]

Philip Easton, Paget Investigator: 19 Jul 05 Statement[a]: **Jury Didn't Hear**: "On 8th March 2005 I was present at the Brigade Criminelle Headquarters in Paris, in company of Detective Inspector Jane Scotchbrook, when Captain Isabelle Deffez took a statement from Mrs Huguette Amarger.... During the course of the statement taking process, which was conducted in the French language, DI Scotchbrook and I asked Mrs Amarger a number of questions, which Captain Deffez recorded, along with the answers given....

"Mrs Amarger describes how ... the contents of the Princess of Wales' abdominal cavity were suctioned into a jar. Captain Deffez has recorded that this included intestines, stomach, and lungs. Further to this, and still fresh in my memory, I can state that DI Scotchbrook and I also asked whether this included urine. Mrs Amarger confirmed that urine was also suctioned into this same container for disposal." [78]

Philip Easton, Paget Investigator: 9 Nov 05 Email to Monceau: **Jury Didn't Hear**:

"Further to your visits to London[b], I have a few additional questions to ask:
• Is urine removed from the body at the time of embalming?
• Do you recall whether the Princess of Wales' urine was removed when she was embalmed?

"For your information Mrs Huguette Amarger told us: 'I then withdrew the cannulas and made a general puncture in the rib cage and the abdominal cavity. Everything is drawn out into the same jar. (intestines, stomach, lungs).'"[79]

Jean Monceau, BJL Director and Embalmer, Paris: 11 Nov 05 Email to Easton: **Jury Didn't Hear**:[c]

"I have just returned to Madrid, I therefore reply to your E-mail: ...
'• *Is urine removed from the body at the time of embalming?*'
• Yes, if there is urine at the time of the abdominal punction;

---

[a] This statement was omitted from *The Documents* book due to the sensitive nature of its contents.
[b] Two visits, during which Monceau made statements to Operation Paget.
[c] The questions from Easton are shown in *italics*.

'• *Do you recall whether the Princess of Wales' urine was removed when she was embalmed?'*
• It is difficult to know if urine passes into the tube at the time of aspiration; unless the bladder is full, under these circumstances, it is clear. I did not myself conduct this punction, I therefore do not have an answer to this precise question; you should ask Mrs Amarger or Mr Jocelyn Charrier who were present.
'For your information Mrs Huguette Amarger told us: "I then withdrew the cannulas and made a general puncture in the rib cage and the abdominal cavity. Everything is drawn out into the same jar. (intestines, stomach, lungs)." '
THIS IS TRUE[a],[80]

Dr Robert Chapman, Pathologist, UK: 10 Sep 97 Post-Mortem report: **Jury Didn't Hear**:
"Lungs: Both lungs showed evidence of widespread patchy contusion[b].
Three wide bore puncture holes were noted.... These punctures appeared related to the embalming process.... Brownish soft material and fluid were present within the airways.
"Abdomen: .... Post-mortem wide bore needle damage was also noted to the lesser curve of the stomach.... The stomach contained a large quantity of fluid and partly digested food matter.... Patchy bruising was noted to the hepatic flexure of the colon[c]....
"Bladder...: The bladder was empty and showed no evidence of trauma or natural disease." [81]

Dr Susan Paterson[d], Toxicologist, UK: 28 Sep 04 Statement: **Jury Didn't Hear**:
"Re: Female (Fulham 31897) (deceased) Lab No. 676/97
"The following analyses were performed:
.... The stomach contents were screened for salicylate and paracetamol.... Neither was detected....
The preserved blood, stomach contents and vitreous humor were screened for common basic drugs... No drugs were detected.
"Conclusion: .... No drugs were detected in stomach contents, preserved blood or vitreous humor."[82]

Comment: There are critical conflicts between Amarger's report of Princess Diana's embalming – as recorded by the British police – Monceau's inquest

---

[a] Use of capitals for emphasis appears to be in Monceau's original email.
[b] Bruising.
[c] Main part of the large intestine.
[d] Dr Susan Paterson carried out the toxicological testing on samples obtained by Robert Chapman from the bodies of Princess Diana and Dodi Fayed.

evidence, Monceau's email account and Diana's post-mortem report drawn up by Robert Chapman.

It is important to understand that the embalming occurred during the afternoon of 31 August 1997, concluding around 1.30 p.m.[a] The British post-mortem, conducted by Chapman, didn't commence until nearly 8 hours later at 8.20 p.m. UK time – 9.20 p.m. in Paris.

Amarger stated: "Everything is drawn out into the same jar. (intestines, stomach, lungs)." Although this statement appears ambiguous – was she referring to the organs or their contents? – the context is in connection with the use of cannulas, which are tubes used for draining fluid. Therefore Amarger could only be referring to the organ contents.[bc]

Easton, who interviewed Amarger, has confirmed that the contents of that container were set aside "for disposal". So the fluid contents of Diana's lungs, stomach and intestines were, according to Amarger, removed and disposed of in Paris.

When Monceau was asked about this in an email from Easton, he responded: "THIS IS TRUE".[d]

Yet when it came to the inquest, Monceau stated: "We don't take anything away from the bodies. We leave everything that is inside."[e] This agrees with Monceau's original statement, where he gave an elaborate account of the embalming process, but completely ignores the removal of organ contents.[f]

---

[a] The timing is addressed later.

[b] This was confirmed during the post-mortem – Chapman found the lungs, stomach and intestines still inside the body.

[c] General research on modern embalming methods reveals that the internal organs are not removed from the body. That did though occur during the embalming process in ancient Egypt.

[d] Emphasis is Monceau's.

[e] I suggest that Monceau specifically volunteered this information – he was not directly answering the question, which related to the level of embalming. The question, put by Michael Mansfield, was: Was "what was done ... full embalming ...?" Monceau eventually describes the process: "You inject product that has preservation qualities and you recover as much blood from the veins as possible."

[f] Monceau's statement: "You have asked me to describe the embalming of the Princess. We wash the natural cavities and orifices. We disinfect the body. We restitch the visible wounds, after packing them with gauze. We then took out two common right and left carotid arteries. Then a right external femoral. We inject a solution of conserving product containing formaldehyde, phenol, methanol, glycerol and amaranth. These fluids are mixed in the form of arterial fluid which itself is diluted in the order of 2500 cc of water to 300 cc of solution. A draining, anti-coagulant product is added to this mixture. We clamp the left carotid artery and the right femoral artery. We inject the common right carotid in the direction of the body.

On 18 October 2005 Monceau leaves out organ content removal, then – when confronted with Amarger's account of organ content removal – reverses his evidence just 24 days later on November 11. Then in 2007, at the inquest, Monceau returns to his original position – "we don't take anything away from the bodies". Language acrobatics – two 180° turns.

At the inquest:

- Amarger was not cross-examined
- the part of Amarger's statement describing organ content removal is not read out[a]
- Easton's statement regarding urine removal is not read out
- Monceau's email to Easton confirming organ content removal is not read out
- Monceau was heard saying: "We don't take anything away from the bodies" – unchallenged.

The jury are then left with the impression that organ contents remained untouched during the embalming – the urine is not touched. Nothing could be further from the truth – the evidence will show that the only aspect of this embalming that was successfully carried out was the removal of the urine.

We temporarily ligature the upper part of the carotid in order to avoid the return of the fluids. When we have injected 3 litres of solution we insert a puncture tube under the xiphoid appendix in the direction of the right atrium of the heart. We then proceed with the exsanguino-transfusion of the body. We injected a second 3 litre jar of solution. We stopped the left carotid injection. We injected the right femoral in the direction of the leg. Then we proceed with the extraction from the external left femoral and inject the left leg. We make a puncture in the thoracic cavity and then in the abdominal cavity. We inject the left carotid in the direction of the head and we await the return from the Willis arterial polygon via the right carotid. We then insert the inspiration catheter in the arterial trachea in order to free the upper arterial passages. We suture all the arteries and re-close the incisions. We pack the nasal and mouth cavities with gauze. We place eye covers over the eyelids. We suture the inferior maxilla. We insert an injection tube in the sealing holes which served for the aspiration of the body to inject and diffuse 250 cc of pure fluid into the thoracic cavity and 250 cc into the abdominal cavity. We pack the rectal and vaginal cavity with gauze. We suture the sealing point. On all the sutures we apply a collodion varnish to avoid leaks. We then move onto the dressing, which I think was done by Hugette Amarger and Jocelyn Charrier, followed by make-up and hairdressing. The body is then presented on the hospital bed. The hands are then joined together above the sheet. Following this, we presented her to Paul Burrell to ask him if it was alright. We then waited outside for the visit of the family.": Jean Monceau, Witness Statement, 18 October 2005, p10. Monceau then went on to say that what he had described was a full embalming: "You have asked me if the procedure that I have just described to you could be described as partial embalming. No. It is complete embalming. Partial embalming does not exist.": p11.

[a] 22 Nov 07: 94.20.

It is significant that Isabelle Deffez, of the French police, failed to record Amarger saying that "urine was also suctioned into this same container for disposal" – a point that was specifically stated 4 months later by Easton and confirmed during the UK post-mortem: "the bladder was empty".

Why did Deffez[a] leave out the removal of urine from Diana's body during the embalming? It's not just that it was left out once, but it was left out twice: Easton stated: "DI Scotchbrook and I also asked whether this included urine. Mrs Amarger confirmed that urine was also suctioned...."

So Deffez left out both the question and the answer relating to urine. Why?

Easton's evidence indicates that the Amarger interview was not electronically recorded – "still fresh in my memory" – and I suggest that that is astounding for a 21st century 1st world police force (French or British).[b]

The relevance of urine is that it can be tested to establish whether a person is pregnant.[c] It is actually normal practice in the modern embalming process to remove urine and other fluids because they start to decompose after death. Embalming.net describes a process of "suctioning fluids out of the internal organs in the abdomen and thoracic cavity".[83] I suggest that this is a process that would have been known to the British authorities who requested the embalming – see earlier.

There is a further conflict in the evidence. Amarger stated that the stomach and lung contents – and Easton added the urine – were "drawn out into the same jar" yet Chapman describes:

- "the stomach contained a large quantity of fluid[d] and partly digested food matter"

---

[a] In 1997 Deffez was a Brigade Criminelle lieutenant. She has already been listed in the "Witnesses Not Heard" table in Part 1, under "Henri Paul".

[b] The interview took place at the Brigade Criminelle Headquarters in Paris.

[c] Part 2 included a 2000 report from Janusz Knepil, showing that pregnancy testing on urine contaminated by embalming fluid could produce an incorrect result. I suggest that in 1997 that information would not necessarily have been known to the people making the decisions on the handling of Diana's body. See Part 2, Pregnancy chapter, under "Embalming and Post-Mortem".

[d] Some might think this was embalming fluid, but there is no evidence to suggest that. In the post-mortem report, Chapman does state that there was "considerable embalming fluid ... present within the chest cavity". Thompson – who had worked at the mortuary since 1984 (Affidavit, 13 June 2001, p1) – said that he believed the fluid in the stomach "was alcohol, not formaldehyde". Chapman differed: he said "the [stomach] material did not smell of alcohol". Paterson carried out tests on the stomach contents, but makes no mention in her statement of there being embalming fluid in the sample. She did not test the stomach contents for alcohol. There is also no

- "fluid [was] present within the airways" of the lungs
- "the bladder was empty".[a]

The question then is: How is it that the contents of the stomach, lungs and bladder were all suctioned out, then 8 hours later "the stomach contained a large quantity of fluid", "fluid [was] present within the airways" of the lungs but "the bladder was empty"?

We have a situation where:

- Amarger has claimed the contents of the stomach, lungs, intestines and bladder were suctioned out
- Deffez has omitted to record mention of the bladder being suctioned
- the bladder – which holds the urine – is actually the only organ that has been confirmed at post-mortem to have been fully suctioned.[b]

The post-mortem revealed the following:

- Lungs: "three wide bore puncture holes[c] ... [that] appeared [to be] related to the embalming"
- Stomach: "wide bore needle damage ... to the lesser curve of the stomach"
- Bladder: "no evidence of trauma".

There is a major conflict.

How is it that the stomach and lungs both show embalming puncture marks, but have fluid still in them, whilst the bladder has no puncture marks, but has no urine inside it?

There are several possible explanations[d], but I suggest the most likely scenario is that Amarger inserted the trocar[a] but failed to wait until all the fluid was removed from the stomach and lungs, but did get all the urine out.

---

evidence of Amarger inserting embalming fluid into the stomach area. This issue is addressed further in the UK Post-Mortems chapter.

[a] In the post-mortem report, Chapman did not comment on the contents of the intestines, which Amarger also claimed had been suctioned out.

[b] Chapman stated that "the bladder was empty" and Easton said: "Mrs Amarger confirmed that urine was also suctioned into this same container for disposal." This suctioning process for the bladder is confirmed on the Embalming.net website: "The sharp blades on the trocar [special long metal tube] are used to pierce through the abdomen near the belly button. From this entry point the embalmer directs the trocar towards and pierces all the internal organs, [and allows] the trocar to remain in each organ long enough to suction off the fluids.": www.embalming.net under "Cavity Embalming". Cavity embalming is part of the process involved in a full embalming.

[c] The fact that there is not just one puncture mark could be a reflection on Amarger's apparent inexperience – see earlier – or that the embalming was rushed – see later – or both.

[d] The other explanations are: 1) Chapman is lying about there being puncture marks on the lungs and stomach and the absence of marks on the bladder; 2) Easton has lied about the urine being suctioned and Chapman has lied when he said the bladder was empty; 3) Chapman and Thompson have both lied about fluid in the stomach.

There are three points:

a) this fits with evidence that reveals this embalming was a rush job (see later)

b) this fits with the possibility that Amarger had been specifically instructed to ensure that she completely cleared the bladder of urine

c) this indicates that Chapman has lied by omission, when he has neglected in his post-mortem report to mention the presence of puncture marks on the bladder.

I suggest that the following could be what occurred: Amarger was instructed – probably by the British, but through Monceau – to ensure that the bladder was emptied during the embalming.[b] When Amarger was interviewed 7 years after the event, she said that the stomach and lungs were also suctioned[c], but this process appears to have not been effective. During the recording of this interview Deffez, a Brigade Criminelle Capitaine – probably acting on instructions from higher up – deliberately left out Amarger's evidence that the bladder was also suctioned. This omission was possibly an attempt to cover-up the deliberate removal of urine from Diana's body to hide evidence of pregnancy. When Chapman carried out the post-mortem about 8 hours after the embalming, he deliberately omitted mentioning puncture mark(s) on the bladder and instead stated that it "showed no evidence of trauma".

The final act in this chain of events was the withholding from the inquest jury of all relevant evidence:

- virtually all references in Amarger's statement pertaining to the embalming procedure[d]
- the addition to Amarger's statement submitted by Easton, stating that the urine was suctioned
- the post-mortem report of Robert Chapman[e] (see later).

---

[a] Special long metal tube.

[b] This may have even been one of the primary focuses of the embalming – later evidence will show that the embalming carried out was rushed and substandard. This is supported by the fact that the stomach contents were not suctioned – a process that occurs during a normal embalming, to slow decomposition.

[c] This evidence is supported by puncture marks observed by Chapman at the post-mortem.

[d] The jury heard much of Amarger's statement, but the lawyer broke off when it came to her evidence on the embalming procedure – see earlier.

[e] How is it that the jury who are investigating the circumstances and nature of the death of a person, Princess Diana, aren't provided access to, or a reading of the post-mortem conducted on the body of that person? This is discussed later in the Post-Mortem chapter.

Dr Robert Chapman, Pathologist, UK: 24 Feb 05 Statement: **Jury Didn't Hear**:

"No urine was present in the bladder. A sample would have been obtained if available for toxicology studies. This would, if obtained, be tested for alcohol and drugs. Had urine been present I would not have tested it for pregnancy. It is not normal practice to carry out either blood or urine tests for pregnancy following post-mortem and I have never carried out such a test." [84]

Comment: Dr Robert Chapman has stated: "I have never carried out such a [post-mortem pregnancy] test".

Chapman is a pathologist. It is the toxicologist – in this case, Paterson – who carries out the testing on samples.

Level and Quality

What level of embalming was carried out and just how effective was it?

Huguette Amarger, BJL Embalmer: 8 Mar 05 Statement read out 22 Nov 07: 93.7:

"Question: Were you given any instructions in writing?

"Answer: No, but there was a panic on. There were a lot of people. My boss told me to be quick because Prince Charles was arriving in the afternoon and it went without saying that he should see the Princess in a presentable condition....

"Before I could start my work, I was put out by seeing the Scotland Yard police officers putting black sticky tape over the blinds lowered over the windows. There was therefore only a very little light and I was going to be hampered in my work."

Jean Monceau, BJL Director and Embalmer, Paris: 20 Nov 07: 80.4:

Burnett: Q. Do you remember the British funeral directors arriving at the hospital later that afternoon?

A. With the Prince of Wales, yes.[a]

Q. Can you remember the conversation that you had with them?

A. Well, they came with their equipment to embalm the body of the Princess and they realised that we had already undertaken the embalming process, so we invited them to control the work that we had undertaken. We told them how many arteries we had injected with which fluids and they thanked us, the men, and they kissed the young thanatopractitioner, female thanatopractitioner, that was there.

Q. I think they told you that you had done a good job.

A. Yes, of course.

Jean Monceau: 18 Oct 05 Statement: **Jury Didn't Hear**:

---

[a] The embalmers arrived two hours ahead of Prince Charles. This is addressed later.

"The British funeral directors, who arrived at around 1700 hrs [5 p.m.] ... told me that they had come to embalm the Princess and that we had done a good job and they were happy because we had helped them gain some time." [85]

David Green, Embalmer, UK: 13 Jul 04 Statement: **Jury Didn't Hear**:

"In my opinion and experience she was nicely presented, her hair had been brushed and cosmetics applied to her face. There was [a] small cut to her forehead that had been concealed with makeup and her hair brushed down over it.

"I spoke to two of the French embalmers in broken English and they told me that they had done some embalming. They did not tell me specifically what embalming they had done and ... the vessels they had used to inject the fluids into the body.[ab]

"They handed me two Phials of samples of the fluid they had used.... I was not aware what type, make or strength the fluid was as they were unlabelled and the embalmer did not specifically tell me....

"The embalming carried out by the French may have been only sufficient for viewing. The French only can answer what they did, and upon whose instruction. I did not see her naked sufficient to say where and how much embalming they had done until after the post mortem. Even then I couldn't give my opinion of exactly what they had done because [any] incisions could have been theirs, the pathologist's or a surgeon's, and at the time of my embalming it was not a concern, I just carried out my work.

"In my opinion what embalming had been carried out was only for the purpose of the viewing and to tidy up her appearance. The closing of eyelids and open mouths, the addition of makeup and some injection of embalming fluids around the areas of visible injuries following traumatic death is quiet normal....

"When we placed her in the coffin Bill[c] and I agreed that the embalming was insufficient for long term preservation i.e. until the funeral, and we agreed that I would have to carry out full embalming after the post mortem. She was a fresh body.... I had no immediate concerns of decomposition that had to be

---

[a] This and below – "I was not aware what type, make or strength the fluid was" – appears to conflict with Monceau's account above: "We told them how many arteries we had injected with which fluids...."

[b] Clive stated: "There were a couple of embalmers, one of which I was introduced to. I didn't discuss anything with them; I needed to take the lead. I did not receive any information from these French embalmers as to what they had done. The question of embalming never cropped up." Clive Leverton, Witness Statement, 13 July 2004, reproduced in *The Documents* book, p492 (UK Edition).

[c] Bill Fry – a fellow embalmer who has never been interviewed by police and was not heard at the inquest.

addressed.... At about 11 to 11.30 p.m., I went to the Chapel at St James' Palace to carry out the embalming.... I did not need to nor was asked to note the embalming points on the body enough to give any opinion as to the extent or how well the embalming was done.... It took about five hours to carry out the work to my satisfaction."[86]

David Green, Embalmer, UK: 17 Sep 04 Statement: **Jury Didn't Hear**:
"I learnt that she had received some embalming treatment by the French upon our arrival at the Salpêtrière Hospital, and the French, for the family's viewing ... may have carried this out.... I cannot comment on the exact extent of the embalming the French carried out.... Upon arrival she had already been embalmed to some extent."[87]

Dr Robert Chapman, Pathologist, UK: 26 Nov 2007: 45.17:
Mansfield: Q. Was there any discussion [with Lecomte in June 1998[a]] about embalming?

A. Yes, I think there was.

Q. Right. Can I deal with that? Do you remember what the thrust of that discussion was?

A. I think the point that I would have made is that the embalming had been thorough in the sense that most of the body tissues had been affected by the embalming, that there had been damage related to the use of cannulae or trocars with installation of embalming fluids, and that this had impinged upon, slightly at least, the area of injury to the heart of Princess Diana.

....Q. Now, the embalming in this case was a full embalmment, was it not, as far as you could tell?

A. Yes.

Q. Which meant that the blood that you took from any part of the body was likely to be contaminated?

A. Yes.

Q. Of course, the reason I ask is in relation to blood tests that can on occasion be done in relation to pregnancy.

A. Yes.

Q. But in your view, even the blood that you took was likely to have been contaminated?

A. Yes.

At 64.23: Horwell: Q. Do you have any comment to make on the proficiency of the embalming of the Princess of Wales?

A. It was a very efficient and proficient procedure. It had done what it set out to do.

Dr Robert Chapman, Pathologist, UK: 24 Feb 05 Statement: **Jury Didn't Hear**:

---

[a] At a meeting in London – see later.

"There were various incisions clearly resulting from embalming and from resuscitation and treatment....

"The body was fully embalmed. The embalming process appeared thorough with widespread use of a trocar or wide needle to drain and instil fluid....

"All of the available blood was contaminated or even largely replaced by the embalming fluid making any sample rather unreliable for toxicology testing."[88]

Robert Thompson, Fulham Mortuary Manager: 13 Jun 01 Affidavit: **Jury Didn't Hear**:

"I also noticed that Princess Diana's body had been partially embalmed before arrival at the mortuary, and the embalming had been done extremely badly." [89]

Robert Thompson: 9 Nov 04 Statement: **Jury Didn't Hear**:

"As soon as the coffin was opened I could see that the Princess had been embalmed and that it had been done particularly badly.... During my profession within the mortuary business I experienced many embalmed bodies. In the case of Diana, Princess of Wales I could see that cotton wool had been stuffed into her neck. This is done in order to prevent body fluid coming up to the face but the way in which it had been done gave her the appearance of having a very swollen neck, like a goitre. It was also clear to me that they had soaked wadding, which is usually cotton wool or towel, and put it into the cavities. In addition to the neck, it is usually the thoracic and pelvic cavities that are also packed with wadding. This is what I call gross embalming. By this, I mean that it has not been done in a complete way.... The embalmers had obviously not bothered embalming the whole of her body, just bits and it seemed as though it had been done in a hurry. This became even more apparent to me once the post mortem examination was underway as I could see that some organs were still red, whereas they should have been green had the embalming fluid taken its full effect." [90]

Dr Susan Paterson, Toxicologist, UK: 28 Sep 04 Statement: **Jury Didn't Hear**:

"As the body had been embalmed, both preserved blood and vitreous humor were screened for drugs and ethanol.... There was no evidence to show that the blood had been contaminated with embalming fluid." [91]

Comment: There are two main questions that need to be addressed:

1) What was the level of embalming that was carried out?
2) How effective and professional was the standard of the job done by Amarger?

There is conflict regarding the level:

- Green: "the embalming ... may have been only sufficient for viewing" – statement [a]
- Green: "in my opinion what embalming had been carried out was only for the purpose of the viewing and to tidy up her appearance" – statement
- Green: "some embalming treatment" – statement
- Green: "the embalming was insufficient for long term preservation, i.e. until the funeral" – statement
- Green: "I would have to carry out full embalming" – statement
- Chapman: "the embalming had been thorough in the sense that most of the body tissues had been affected" – inquest
- Chapman: "the embalming in this case was ... full" – confirmed to Mansfield – inquest
- Chapman: "it was a very efficient and proficient procedure" – inquest
- Chapman: "the body was fully embalmed" – statement
- Thompson: "Princess Diana's body had been partially embalmed" – affidavit.

So effectively there are 3 witnesses who have commented on the level of embalming:[b]

- Green: "the embalming was insufficient"
- Chapman: "the embalming ... was ... full"

---

[a] It is evident that Bill Fry, the embalmer who accompanied Green, should have been heard from at the inquest as well. He has never been interviewed by any of the investigations.

[b] Clive Leverton – an experienced funeral director – was also present with Green when they arrived at the hospital. In his statement, he ducked when this issue came up: "I still did not know if she had been embalmed at this stage, she had a sheet laid over her. David [Green] would be in the best position to comment on what embalming had been carried out." – see later. Colin Tebbutt said in his statement: "I spoke to the gentleman in charge who I believe to be Mr Leverton and informed him of what had been done [by the French embalmers] and the reasons. Mr Leverton went in to the room and came out shortly after. He said, 'They've done a very good job', referring to the French Funeral Directors. I was relieved by this comment. Mr Leverton explained that they would have to retouch the facial make-up and lipstick." This also was brought up by the police lawyer, Richard Horwell, at the inquest – see 26 Nov 07: 125.9. I suggest that Tebbutt's evidence that Clive said the embalmers had "done a very good job" – although focused on by Horwell – is not necessarily an accurate reflection of Clive's view. Even if Clive had thought the job done was atrocious, he would not be likely to convey that to an interested bystander. It is significant that Horwell – when he cross-examined Clive – failed to ask him about this, even though he had Tebbutt's statement account – see 22 Nov 07: 81.14.

- Thompson: the "body had been partially embalmed".

Therefore out of the 3 witnesses, two – Green, Thompson – have indicated that the embalming was partial, and one – Chapman – has said that the embalming was full.

It is very significant that the jury only heard the evidence of Chapman – that the embalming was full.

At the inquest, Monceau was specifically asked if it "was full embalming ... not partial embalming", but failed to directly answer this: "Well, it depends on what you mean.... Embalming, according to the French term, would be complete anyway." [a]

If the jury had attempted to interpret Monceau's cryptic answer, I suggest they could have concluded that his evidence was that the embalming was full – particularly after hearing Monceau confirm to Mansfield that "partial embalming ... does not exist". This account would have then supported Chapman's evidence.

Amarger, in her statement, described the embalming process – this was not heard by the jury[b] – and she was never asked to comment on whether the embalming was full or partial.

Amarger did however say – see earlier: "I knew that account had to be taken of the fact that the date of the funeral was not known.... The mixture of formalin depends on the state of putrefaction of the body. At that time, the body was all right. I knew that the subsequent exposure of the body abroad had to be taken into account and I thought that the body might change coffins. I therefore put in more formalin than usual." [c]

Without directly addressing the full/partial issue, Amarger appears to be indicating a full embalming took place – "I ... put in more formalin than usual." There is however evidence from Amarger – discussed below – that conflicts with this impression.

Amarger's account also appears to directly conflict with the evidence from Green who stated: "the embalming was insufficient for long term preservation i.e. until the funeral".

The evidence from the two witnesses - Green, Thompson – who indicated the embalming was partial, was not heard by the jury.

Why is this?

Who is telling the truth? Is it Chapman, Monceau and Amarger, or is it Green and Thompson?

---

[a] See earlier for the complete answer.
[b] Amarger's statement was read out, but this part of it was left out.
[c] This was not heard by the jury.

Once again we are faced with a completely inadequate level of cross-examination at the Baker inquest: of these 5 witnesses, 3 were never cross-examined. I suggest that it is no coincidence that of those there are 2 people – Green, Thompson – whose evidence indicates the embalming was incomplete. It is also no coincidence that the jury never even got to hear what they had to say in their statements.

There is evidence from Amarger – the person who carried out the embalming – that highlights factors which could have affected her ability to perform a full and effective embalming:

-   "there was a panic on ... my boss told me to be quick because Prince Charles was arriving"

-   "I was put out by seeing the Scotland Yard police officers putting black sticky tape over the blinds lowered over the windows. There was therefore only a very little light and I was going to be hampered in my work."

Amarger has therefore stated that the embalming was conducted under difficult circumstances: "there was a panic" and "there was therefore only a very little light".

In her statement Amarger doesn't mention any solution to the lighting problem – this indicates that not only had Diana's body been placed in a room without air conditioning, but it also had poor artificial lighting.

I suggest that these two factors – the panic and the poor lighting – may have placed Amarger (who was much less experienced than Monceau) under increased pressure and could have affected both the level and quality of the embalming.

Chapman has said:

-   confirmed to Mansfield: "the blood that you took from any part of the body was likely to be contaminated" – inquest

-   confirmed to Mansfield again: "even the blood that you took was likely to have been contaminated" – inquest

-   "all of the available blood was contaminated or even largely replaced by the embalming fluid, making any sample rather unreliable for toxicology testing" – statement.[a]

---

[a] There is an apparent conflict between Chapman's inquest account: "the embalming had been thorough in the sense that most of the body tissues had been affected" and his earlier statement: "all of the available blood was contaminated". In the statement Chapman describes complete contamination, but at the inquest this appears to be modified to "most of the body tissues".

Monceau has been shown to be a liar – see earlier. By the time the UK post-mortem evidence is analysed, later in this book, Chapman also will be shown to have covered up the truth on critical issues. In addition, Amarger's evidence on this subject is possibly conflicting – on the one hand, "I ... put in more formalin than usual" and on the other, "there was a panic" and "there was ... only a very little light".[a]

We are left with a situation where the balance of the credible evidence appears to reveal that the embalming was not full, but partial – Green, Thompson.

Why has Chapman repeatedly insisted that the embalming was full? And why is it that the two witnesses who indicated the embalming was not full were not heard from at the inquest?

These two questions are closely related to each other.

A full embalming automatically would preclude the possibility of a UK testing of Diana's blood for pregnancy – if the blood could be shown to be contaminated with or replaced by embalming fluid, then any testing for pregnancy would have been of questionable value.

There is conflicting evidence on the standard of the embalming:

- Monceau, confirmed to Burnett at the inquest: the British embalmers said that they "had done a good job"
- Monceau statement: "the British funeral directors ... told me ... that we had done a good job"
- Chapman at the inquest: "it was a very efficient and proficient procedure – it had done what it set out to do"
- Green statement: "I cannot comment on the exact extent of the embalming"
- Green statement: "she had already been embalmed to some extent"
- Thompson affidavit: "the embalming had been done extremely badly"
- Thompson statement: "[the embalming] had been done particularly badly".

Monceau has stated that the British – including Green – told him it was a "good job", but Green's evidence is much more circumspect: "I cannot comment" and she was "embalmed to some extent".

Thompson is forthright: it was "done extremely badly".

---

[a] Amarger's account should also be viewed in light of the earlier evidence that Diana's internal organs were not emptied or filled with embalming fluid.

Again, we have Chapman and Monceau painting a completely different picture to that of Green and Thompson.

Again, in the light of the earlier and later evidence that both Monceau and Chapman will or have been shown to be liars, and the embalming was instead carried out in a dimly lit panic by a less experienced operator, it would appear to be safe to conclude that the embalming conducted on the body of Princess Diana was not of a high standard.

In summary, there are then several reasons to believe that the embalming was neither full nor professional:

1) The only two people – Monceau and Chapman – who have stated that the embalming was full, have been or will be shown to be liars.

2) Green and Thompson have both indicated the embalming was partial and inadequate.

3) Thompson has given very specific evidence on the poor job done: "the appearance of having a very swollen neck"; "just bits" of the body were embalmed; "some organs were still red"

4) Both the post-mortem and toxicology reports indicate that the contents of internal organs[a][b] – with the exception of the bladder – were not fully suctioned[c] and the organs were not refilled with embalming fluid.[d]

5) Amarger was the least experienced of the three embalmers present – see earlier

6) The embalming was carried out in a situation of "panic" and Amarger was instructed to "be quick" – this is supported by Thompson: "it seemed as though it had been done in a hurry"

7) Amarger indicated that the embalming was conducted under poor lighting conditions

8) Amarger appears to have presented conflicting evidence: extra formalin used[e], but conducted under difficult conditions – see above

---

[a] The toxicology report refers specifically only to the stomach.

[b] The relevance of the toxicology report is doubtful as it will be shown in the Post-Mortem chapter that the samples tested were not from Princess Diana.

[c] This conflicts with Amarger's evidence that she did fully suction the internal organs – see earlier.

[d] www.embalming.net under "Cavity Embalming": "The trocar is ... pierced into the organs and the cavity [embalming] fluid flows into them by simple gravity. Usually two bottles of full strength fluid are used to treat the entire thoracic and abdominal cavities."

[e] The quantity used is covered below.

9) Chapman described "wide bore needle damage ... [on] the lesser curve of the stomach" and "damage related to the use of cannulae or trocars".[a]

There is also conflict over the amount of embalming fluid used in the embalming of Diana:

- Amarger: "I injected about 10 litres of formalin, that is, one two-and-a-half litre jar into each artery which goes to remake the blood circuit.... The formalin is diluted 15 or 20 per cent with water. It is I who do the mixing...."[b]
- Monceau: "we must have used three 2-litre bottles, so that would make 6 litres all in all of fluids with water"
- www.embalming.net: "the embalmer must inject about one gallon of fluid for every 50 pounds of body weight".[92] This converts to 4.55 litres[c] to 22.7 kg[d]. If Diana was a normal weight for her height[e] then there would have been a requirement for 14 litres of embalming fluid to be used for a complete embalming.[f]

There is a wide divergence between Monceau's assessment – Monceau has conducted thousands of embalmings, see earlier – that 6 litres was used "all in all", and the amount that would have been required to carry out a complete embalming, about 14 litres.

Why has Monceau, the most experienced embalmer present at the scene, understated the formalin amount required for a normal human being by about half?

There appear to be two main ways of interpreting this evidence:

1) Amarger is correct and Monceau is wrong. This would suggest that the embalming fluid used would have been approximately enough to carry out a full embalming and replace, or at least contaminate, all the blood.

---

[a] It is possible that this is normal with embalming, but the use of the term "damage" indicates it may not have been normal. It appears to conflict with Chapman's account that "it was a very efficient and proficient procedure".

[b] This could be read two different ways: 1) 10 litres total after including the water; or 2) 10 litres of formalin plus 15 to 20% water, making a total of 11.5 to 12 litres.

[c] 4.55 litres per gallon.

[d] 2.2 pounds per kilogram.

[e] Diana's height was 5 ft 10½ ins, or 179 cm.

[f] There is no evidence of what Diana's weight actually was, but I believe it is fair to presume that based on her figure, she would have been close to the optimum weight for her height. Optimum weight calculators give a weight of approximately 69 kg for Diana's height, which was 179 cm. This would equate to the need for about 14 litres of embalming fluid required for a complete embalming. Source: www.healthchecksystems.com

2) Monceau is correct and Amarger is wrong. This would suggest that nowhere near enough fluid was used to carry out a full embalming.

The earlier evidence – that the embalming was only partial – indicates that Monceau's account may be more likely to be correct. It does though reveal a surprising conflict within Monceau's evidence. On the one hand Monceau has indicated that the embalming was full, but on the other hand he is stating that only 6 litres of embalming fluid was used.

I suggest that it would be naïve to say that Monceau could have made an innocent mistake in his calculation of the embalming fluid used – according to his evidence he is the veteran of 13,000 embalmings: see earlier.

The most likely explanation could be that Monceau has inadvertently told the truth when he claimed that only 6 litres of embalming fluid was used.

In this light, Amarger's evidence – not heard by the jury – appears to paint a picture of a fuller embalming: "account had to be taken ... [that] the date of the funeral was not known"; "I ... put in more formalin than usual"; "about 10 litres of formalin ... diluted 15 or 20 per cent with water". Yet the earlier evidence actually points to this not being the case.

The logical conclusion is that Amarger has falsely presented a picture of a full embalming. It is difficult to establish what Amarger's motive might have been – it could simply be that she does not want to be known as the person who carried out an inadequate embalming on the body of Diana, Princess of Wales.

It may be that Amarger was instructed to indicate a full embalming before her statement was made in 2005.

The evidence indicates that during the embalming procedure priority was given to removing the urine from the bladder, but other organs were ignored. This is consistent with an attempt to cover-up for a possible pregnancy – it meant that the now non-existent urine could no longer be tested.

In contrast, the blood was not fully replaced or contaminated by embalming fluid. This is not consistent with covering up for possible pregnancy.

This situation could occur if a blood sample taken during the Lecomte autopsy at 5.30 a.m. had tested negative for pregnancy, but a urine test had tested positive. This could reflect the evidence that the blood in Diana's body may no longer have been hers. Pavie has stated: "she had practically none of her own blood left" – see earlier.

If this was the case, it could lead to a situation where the embalmers had to rid the body of urine, but did not need to do a thorough job with the blood.

Jean Monceau: 18 Oct 05 Statement: **Jury Didn't Hear**:

"You have asked me whether, if I had known that the Princess of Wales was going to undergo an autopsy prior to carrying out the embalming, I would have done anything different. No, because the embalming does not affect the autopsy. In France, we often carry out autopsies after embalming and the experts recognise the puncture points. This is why we leave a flask of fluid with the body." [93]

Comment: This appears to be another set of lies from Monceau.

Monceau says: "the embalming does not affect the autopsy".

This is from the same person who has said: "Partial embalming does not exist." [94]

All the evidence shows that a full embalming has a major effect on the ability to conduct a normal autopsy – the blood will be contaminated or replaced, the contents of organs are removed.

In this particular case the bladder was drained during the embalming – this meant that no urine sample could be taken during the London post-mortem[a].[b]

Timing

There is conflicting evidence regarding both the time the embalming started and the length of time it took to carry out.

Jean Monceau, BJL Director and Embalmer, Paris: 20 Nov 07: 79.23:
Burnett: Q. Can you remember how long the embalming process took to complete, Mr Monceau?
A. Well, I suppose I can remember at least two hours.
Q. Is it right that you started the process at around 2 o'clock, 14.00 hours?
A. Yes.

Jean Monceau: 18 Oct 05 Statement: **Jury Didn't Hear**:
"The embalming itself takes about an hour and a half, but you need at least 8 hours to get all this [legal procedures] done."[95 c]

Jean Monceau: 18 Oct 05 Statement: **Jury Didn't Hear**:
"You have asked me at which time the embalming was carried out on the Princess of Wales. From memory we started at around 1400 hrs and the embalming last two and a half hours. You have asked me if it is possible that the Princess of Wales's body was embalmed before

---

[a] Post-mortem or autopsy.
[b] The issue of the impact of embalming on the post-mortem is addressed in full in the UK Post-Mortems chapter.
[c] Refer section on "Was It Legal?"

1400 hrs. No, this is not possible. I was with the body and furthermore, the arteries were intact and the body was losing blood.[a] Impossible."[96]

Jean Monceau: 18 Oct 05 Statement: **Jury Didn't Hear**:

"I had asked to see someone from the funeral authorities to explain the problems with the dry ice, so there was a lot of waiting around. My feeling was that we had to embalm the body, but I was in no position to act. Furthermore, at that time, Mrs Amarger had not yet brought the equipment. I knew already that I would convince the people that we had had to remove the dry ice, which we had removed, and that we had to perform embalming."[97]

Colin Tebbutt, Diana's Driver and Security: 26 Nov 07: 90.17:

Hough: Q. When you arrived, were the French funeral directors present?
A. Yes.
Q. What were they doing?
A. Just standing in the corridor, sir.[b]

At 95.4: Hough: Q. Did you ever become aware of how long it would take?
A. I went for lunch or to try to get something to eat and they started whatever they were doing, and then when I came back about 40 minutes later, they were still in there, so they had an hour, hour and a half.

At 123.13: Horwell: Q. And do you continue [in your statement] with a reference to the French funeral directors, saying that it would take them about an hour and a half to prepare the body for the arrival of the Prince of Wales?
A. Well I have read that now, sir. It was about an hour/hour and a half because I was up at lunch.
Q. From what the French funeral directors had mentioned, it would take approximately one and a half hours to prepare –
A. If it is there, but I can't pick that up.
Q. It is there.
A. If it is there, sir, yes.
Q. So the French funeral directors were making it clear this they would require about an hour and a half to prepare the Princess's body for presentation?
A. Yes.[c]

---

[a] Monceau appears to be stating this as evidence that the embalming hadn't taken place before 2 p.m. – indicating the embalming process would damage the arteries and remove the blood. Suggesting that Diana's "body was losing blood" seems a strange thing to say as this (2 p.m.) was now 10 hours after her official time of death – at 4 a.m.

[b] Tebbutt is referring to embalmers, not funeral directors – see earlier footnote.

[c] Tebbutt said in his statement: "I was aware that the Prince of Wales was due to arrive shortly after 5 p.m. and from what French Funeral Directors had mentioned, it would take approximately one and a half hours to prepare the body for the Prince's

....Q. [In your statement]: "The funeral directors were also in the room, I said, 'Would you kindly do whatever you do to prepare the body for when the family arrives'." Mr Moss then spoke to them in French and immediately afterwards, the funeral directors changed into what appeared to be protective clothing and they went about their work?

A. Correct, sir.

Colin Tebbutt: 5 Jul 04 Statement: **Jury Didn't Hear**:

"The Funeral Directors went into the room and were joined by two female nurses Jeanne Lecorchet and another. I don't recall if they were gowned, and there was possibly one other, again I am not sure.

"Paul Burrell and I took this opportunity to go for some food at the Hospital cafeteria, while the Funeral Directors carried on with whatever they had to do. This was about two hours before the Prince of Wales arrived.

"Time flew. After about forty minutes to an hour, we returned to the corridor. It was about 4 p.m. Prior to going for food I hadn't noticed the Hospital Funeral Directors carrying any chemicals into the room, however upon our return the room smelt of chemicals and it was an awful smell. A mortuary type smell I recognised from the post-mortems I had been to as a Police Officer. There were still many people walking around in the corridor....

"When Paul Burrell and I looked at the body, on returning at around 4 p.m., the Princess of Wales still looked the same, but the French Funeral Directors did not know how to do her hair and I noticed that her lips were pointing slightly downwards. She didn't look like the Princess that I had known and this started to worry me somewhat. Paul had a photograph of the Princess of Wales and the Funeral Directors re-arranged her hair with his help."[98]

Keith Moss, British Consul-General, France: 22 Oct 04 Statement: **Jury Didn't Hear**:

"I was aware that there were plans made to allow the wife of President Chirac and Mme. Jospin to pay their last respects. As I recall, Mme. Chirac attended with Sir Michael and Lady Jay at 0845hrs [8.45 a.m.], which could suggest that the 'Thanatopracteur's work had already been completed by then. But I am really not sure. I recall that Prime Minister Lionel Jospin accompanied by Sir Michael Jay went to pay his last respects at 0920hrs, and that a bouquet of flowers from former President Giscard d'Estaing was also left. But I really cannot be sure of precisely when the 'Thanatopracteur' attended."[99]

Keith Moss: 22 Oct 04 Statement: **Jury Didn't Hear**:

"At about 1400hrs [2 p.m.], Doctor Bernard Kouchner, the founder of Médecins Sans Frontière and Minister for Health, attended the hospital and

---

arrival.": Colin Tebbutt, Witness Statement, 5 July 2004, reproduced in *The Documents* book, p441 (UK Edition) came to my room. He asked whether he would be allowed to pay his final respects to the Princess of Wales, describing himself as a personal friend. I checked with Sir Michael Jay who agreed that this would be acceptable as long as he was accompanied by one of the nurses.

"I had sole control of who entered the room...." [a][100]

Clive Leverton, Royal Funeral Director: 13 Jul 04 Statement: **Jury Didn't Hear**:

"We arrived at [the hospital at] about 1530 [3.30 p.m.] to 1545 hours.... I didn't know at that time if she had been embalmed or not. When we arrived outside the front of the hospital we spoke to a senior Royal Air force officer in uniform. I do not recall his name. I went inside... The RAF officer showed me upstairs where I was introduced to Paul Burrell and another man whom I cannot recall the name of. I am not sure who he was. I went into the room where the Princess was laid, I cannot recall if it was with Burrell and the other man or not. Here I saw Diana Princess of Wales on a bed. There were others and members of staff present. I still did not know if she had been embalmed at this stage, she had a sheet laid over her. David [Green] would be in the best position to comment on what embalming had been carried out."[101]

Patrick Launay, PFG Repatriation Director: 21 Mar 06 Statement: **Jury Didn't Hear**:

"I do not remember seeing anyone performing any embalming in the hospital that day." [102]

Jean-Claude Plumet, PFG Director of Paris Agencies, Paris: 4 Nov 05 Paget description of Statement: **Jury Didn't Hear**:

"Mr Plumet clarifies that upon his arrival at the hospital, he asked to see the 'Commissaire'. He explains that he and Mr Jauze then went up onto the floor where the Princess of Wales body was. It was around the middle of the afternoon.[b] He states that he looked into the room where the Princess of Wales' body was; she was on a bed and had been dressed. The embalming had taken place, and no one else was in the room."[103]

Gérard Jauze, PFG Branch Director, Paris: 21 Mar 06 Statement: **Jury Didn't Hear**:

"There was a police officer in the room and Mme Huguette Amarger, the embalmer. She told me that she had been doing the embalming for six hours....

"You inform me that the senior embalmer, M. Monceau, said that the embalming started at around 1400hrs. All that I can tell you is what I

---

[a] Moss gives this evidence immediately following his lengthy testimony on the embalming.

[b] Plumet arrived around 4.50 p.m. – see earlier. Sunset in Paris on 31 August 1997 was at 8.35 p.m.: Sunrise and Sunset for France – Paris – August 1997, www.timeanddate.com

remember. The mention of six hours certainly did not shock me. In the case of a victim of multiple injuries, the restoration can take a long time. Indeed, two hours seems a bit short to me, but I'm no specialist. I know that for a natural, non-traumatic death, the embalming can even take one hour, and that Mme Amarger, having told me that the Princess of Wales had sustained injuries, two hours would seem very short to me." [104]

David Green, Embalmer, UK: 17 Sep 04 Statement: **Jury Didn't Hear**: "Clive and I knew that the Prince of Wales, and the Princesses' two sisters were en route to view her very soon after our arrival. Therefore had I been told to start any embalming and to carry out a complete job it would not have been possible because of the time limitation. I would have needed three hours to do this." [a]

Comment: There is a considerable variation of evidence on how long this embalming of Princess Diana may have taken:
-   Monceau: "at least two hours" – inquest
-   Monceau: "about an hour and a half" – statement
-   Monceau: "two and a half hours" – statement
-   Tebbutt: "an hour, hour and a half" – inquest
-   Tebbutt: "about forty minutes to an hour" – statement[b]
-   Jauze: Amarger "told me that she had been doing the embalming for six hours" – statement
-   Jauze: "two hours seems a bit short to me" – statement
-   Jauze: "for a natural, non-traumatic death, the embalming can even take one hour" – statement
-   Green: "I would have needed three hours to do this" – statement.

So the evidence ranges from "about forty minutes to an hour" – Tebbutt – to "six hours" – Jauze.

Monceau, as is his way, has provided conflicting accounts – he has given three estimates of the time taken and they are all different: about 1½ hours; at least 2 hours; 2½ hours.

---

[a] Green also talked about his general embalming experience, earlier in his statement: "Many of the bodies I have embalmed have been [the] subject of a post mortem examination involving the removal of internal organs. This means that there is a loss of circulation, so I have to locate the necessary arteries in the limbs and head to inject the embalming fluid. It is [a] longer job: 2-3 hours compared with 1 to 2 hours on an intact body to carry this embalming out." This appears to be a more general estimate, whereas the 3 hours quoted here is a more specific assessment regarding the case of Princess Diana on 31 August 1997. Source: *The Documents* book p502.
[b] Also in his statement Tebbutt said that the embalmers had estimated it "it would take approximately one and a half hours to prepare the body".

Wikipedia – which has an extensive article on embalming – states: "a typical embalming takes several hours to complete".[105] This fits with the evidence of Green – a very experienced embalmer[a] – who said it should take "three hours".

Amarger does not comment on the length of time the embalming took her, but Jauze has quoted her as saying "six hours". This figure is significantly different to all other evidence on this subject.[b]

The general evidence indicates – see earlier timeline – that Amarger arrived at the hospital at around 10.45 a.m. and Jauze arrived at about 4.50 p.m. Other evidence shows that the embalming couldn't have started earlier than 11.30 a.m. and didn't finish later than 3.45 p.m. – see below.

This reveals that the embalming must have taken considerably less than 6 hours and this is supported by the other witness evidence – see above.

Jauze actually arrived at the hospital approximately 6 hours after Amarger. I suggest that it is possible that Amarger told him that she had been there for 6 hours, but Jauze misunderstood this and thought that Amarger had told him that the embalming had taken 6 hours.

At this point, the question is: At what time did the embalming commence?[c]

Monceau said in his statement: "we started at around 1400 hrs [2.00 p.m.] and the embalming last two and a half hours". When it was suggested to him that the process could have been carried out before 2.00 p.m., Monceau was adamant: "No, this is not possible. I was with the body and furthermore, the arteries were intact and the body was losing blood. Impossible."

This evidence raises questions – but not questions the jury would have been asking, because they never heard the evidence.

The questions are:

1) What is it that prompted Paget to suggest that the embalming could have been done by 2.00 p.m.?

2) Why was Monceau so adamant that it was impossible for the embalming to have occurred before 2.00 p.m.?

It is clear from the evidence of Launay and Clive Leverton that by the time they arrived at the hospital – "1530 [3.30 p.m.] to 1545 hours" – the embalming had already occurred – "she had a sheet laid over her".[d] Green,

---

[a] Green stated: "I would say that I have embalmed around about 8,000 bodies whilst with my current employer alone.": David Green, Witness Statement, 13 July 2004, reproduced in *The Documents* book, p501 (UK Edition)

[b] It is important to understand that Jauze was not a direct witness to the embalming – he arrived at the hospital well after it had been completed.

[c] The events discussed here, that assist in determining the timing of the embalming, are all included in the "Timeline of Events" at the start of chapter 1.

[d] The fact that Leverton states that Diana had a sheet over her indicates that the embalming was not in progress – it had either not yet started, or it was finished. If the

who arrived with them, stated: "I learnt that she had received some embalming treatment by the French upon our arrival at the Salpêtrière Hospital" – see earlier.[a]

This shows that once again Monceau's evidence has been found wanting. According to his main evidence[b] on this, the embalming commenced at 2 p.m. and would have concluded at 4.30 p.m. – over ¾ of an hour after the arrival of Launay, Leverton and Green.

As revealed earlier, there were three embalmers present – Monceau, Amarger and Charrier. Monceau has said in his statement: "During this time [talking to Moss] another embalmer, Josselin Charrier, phoned me.... He arrived at the hospital at around 1330hrs [1.30 p.m.]." There is no supporting evidence for this.

Amarger said that Charrier[c] "had arrived in the meantime" – prior to the commencement of the embalming.

The evidence from Tebbutt reveals that after arriving he "went in to see the Princess of Wales". Tebbutt goes on in his statement to say: "I also noticed three Hospital Funeral Directors[d], two male and one female, were present when I was in the room." The general evidence shows that the three people Tebbutt described were Monceau, Amarger and Charrier – see earlier. Earlier evidence also shows that Tebbutt arrived around 11.30 a.m.

This evidence places Charrier's arrival in the hospital before 11.30 a.m. – i.e. at least two hours earlier than Monceau has said. Charrier has never been interviewed and wasn't heard at the inquest.

It appears that Monceau has given the 1.30 p.m. arrival time for Charrier to support his insistence that the embalming didn't commence until 2 p.m.

Monceau describes several events occurring after Amarger's arrival – approximately 10.45 a.m. – and before the commencement of embalming: a meeting with Moss; a phone call from Charrier; a meeting with Monteil. Of these, there is no other witness support for the meeting with Monteil.[e]

Tebbutt, who arrived about 11.30 a.m., also refers to events that occurred prior to the embalming (an estimated timing for each event is shown beside it):

---

embalming had occurred after their arrival, then it would have been done by Green and Fry, not the French embalmers.

[a] Green also commented on the quality of the embalming – see earlier.

[b] In other statement evidence Monceau has said "the embalming itself takes about an hour and a half", but he appears to have been talking about embalming in general – not specifically Princess Diana's embalming.

[c] Amarger couldn't remember Charrier's name and described him as "my assistant".

[d] Tebbutt describes the embalmers as funeral directors – see earlier.

[e] Monteil denied this took place – see earlier.

- "I then introduced myself to everybody present" – statement – 3 minutes
- on arrival French funeral directors[a] were "standing in the corridor" [bc] – inquest – 3 minutes
- "we went in to see the Princess of Wales" – statement – 5 minutes
- "I rang the Queen's Police Officer, Chief Superintendent Robinson" – 3 minutes
- "I rang Mr Gibbins" – statement – 3 minutes
- "Paul Burrell, the nurses and I erected blankets up at the windows" – statement – 7 minutes
- "Mr Moss and I put air conditioning units into the room" [d] – statement – 10 minutes
- "I expressed to everyone present that no one was allowed to touch the Princess of Wales' body" – statement – 1 minute
- "I spoke to the hospital funeral directors through Mr Moss" – statement – 2 minutes
- "I rang Mr Gibbins" – statement – 2 minutes
- "Mr Gibbins rang me back" – statement – 2 minutes
- "I then spoke to Mr Moss" – statement – 2 minutes
- "Mr Moss ... spoke to the hospital funeral directors" – statement – 3 minutes
- "the Funeral Directors immediately went into a side room and got dressed" – 5 minutes

---

[a] Pre-embalming references by Tebbutt to funeral directors are referring to the embalmers: Amarger, Monceau and Charrier. Other evidence clearly shows that the earliest funeral directors didn't arrive until after 3.30 p.m. By his own admission Tebbutt stated that he did not realise an embalming had taken place – see earlier. At the inquest Tebbutt should have been asked if one of the "funeral directors" was female, but this never occurred.

[b] Monceau said in his statement: "There was a lot of waiting around. My feeling was that we had to embalm the body, but I was in no position to act." Monceau though is referring to a period before the arrival of Amarger – 10.45 a.m. Tebbutt cannot be describing the same period because he arrived approximately 45 minutes after Amarger, at 11.30 a.m.

[c] One could ask: What were the embalmers waiting for? Monceau has stated he was waiting for "authorisation" but this has been denied by Monteil, Plumet and Jauze – see earlier. There is no evidence to suggest Monceau was waiting to talk to Moss, although a conversation with Moss did take place at around 12 p.m. Moss' earliest evidence – in his statement – was that Monceau didn't seek authorisation, but was merely informing Moss what he was there to do (see earlier). There is a possibility that if samples were taken by Lecomte at the earlier autopsy of Diana, the embalmers may have had instructions to wait for sample test results prior to commencing the embalming.

[d] These were in the room when Amarger conducted the embalming – see earlier.

- "Inspector Peter Von-Heinz, the Personal Protection Officer for Prince Charles and his advance, went into the room" – 5 minutes
- "Paul Burrell then handed over the dress and shoes" – 1 minute
- "the [embalmers] went into the room" – 1 minute.

The estimated timings of each event reveal that all up the sequence Tebbutt described could have taken around an hour[a] – bearing in mind that a) it's just an estimate; b) there could have been gaps between some events; and c) some events may have occurred concurrently – e.g. the installing of air conditioners and the putting up of blankets.

After describing the conversations with the "funeral directors" at the inquest, Tebbutt confirmed to Horwell: "immediately afterwards, the funeral directors changed into what appeared to be protective clothing and they went about their work".

Tebbutt then stated to Hough: "I went for lunch ... and they [the embalmers] started whatever they were doing".

Amarger also describes an event that occurred pre-embalming: "Before I could start my work, I was put out by seeing the Scotland Yard police officers putting black sticky tape over the blinds lowered over the windows".

The main evidence on the sequence of pre-embalming events comes from Tebbutt, with confirmation from other witnesses:

- the conversation between Moss and Monceau is corroborated by both Moss and Monceau
- the call to Gibbins is corroborated by Gibbins
- the covering of the windows is corroborated by Moss
- the presence of air conditioners is corroborated by Amarger
- the entrance of Von-Heinz and an advance into the room is corroborated by Amarger[b].

Tebbutt appears to also have a recall which links events: e.g. the embalmers were standing around when he arrived; he went to lunch at the time the embalming started; the embalming commenced straight after the conversation between Moss and Monceau.

On this issue, there is however a timing conflict when Tebbutt's inquest evidence is compared to what he said in his 2004 statement to the British police: "Paul Burrell and I took this opportunity to go for some food at the hospital cafeteria, while the funeral directors carried on with whatever they had to do. This was about two hours before the Prince of Wales arrived. Time

---

[a] The total comes to 58 minutes.
[b] This issue is addressed in the Repatriation Issues chapter – see the section on Presence of British Police.

flew. After about forty minutes to an hour, we returned to the corridor. It was about 4 p.m."

There is a critical time difference here:
- at the inquest: "I went for lunch or to try to get something to eat"
- in his statement: "Paul Burrell and I took this opportunity to go for some food at the hospital cafeteria.... This was about two hours before the Prince of Wales arrived".

So, at the inquest, it was lunch-time; in 2004 to the police, it was about 3.40 p.m.[a]

Which is correct?

There are four reasons why the statement account of a 3.40 p.m. commencement of the embalming could not be correct:

1) Evidence from Clive Leverton and David Green indicates that the embalming was completed before 3.45 p.m.[b]

2) There is no indication in Tebbutt's evidence that he filled in 4 hours – from 11.30 a.m. to 3.40 p.m. – before getting something to eat. The events that are described above – the air conditioning units; phone calls; putting blankets up; conversations; viewings of Diana's body – could easily have all occurred in the space of an hour – there is nothing to indicate that they could have taken 4 hours.

3) According to Tebbutt, Diana was already "melting" at around 12 noon – there is no evidence to indicate that they then waited another 3½ hours or so before commencing the embalming

4) In his statement, Tebbutt goes on to say: "Time flew. After about forty minutes to an hour, we returned to the corridor. It was about 4 p.m." There is an immediate conflict here: Tebbutt has stated that the embalming started two hours before Charles' arrival, which was at 5.40 p.m. – so 3.40 p.m. But then, when he returns from eating, it is only 4 p.m.

There is a possibility that it is Tebbutt's recollection that Charles arrived around 5 p.m.[cd] – this would then show Tebbutt indicating commencement of the embalming at around 3 p.m. and concluding around 4 p.m.

A close analysis of Tebbutt's statement[e] reveals that despite his evidence that he still had his "notes and plans [that] were made around the time of the incident", he is actually very scant on the timing of events from his arrival in

---

[a] Charles arrived at 5.40 p.m.

[b] Leverton states: "I didn't know at that time if she had been embalmed or not", but evidence from Green, who arrived at the same time showed that the embalming had been completed: "I learnt that she had received some embalming treatment by the French upon our arrival at the Salpêtrière Hospital" – see earlier.

[c] This would be an incorrect recall – the evidence is overwhelming that Charles arrived at the hospital around 5.40 p.m. – see later.

[d] Tebbutt's statement: "The Prince of Wales was due to arrive shortly after 5 p.m."

[e] The full text is reproduced in *The Documents* book, starting page 428.

Paris through to the end of that day, 31 August 1997. I suggest this is unusual for an ex-policeman with 34 years experience.[106a]

Although Tebbutt spent 8 pages[b] describing those events, he includes very limited timings relating to that whole period:
- "when we boarded the plane it was about 7 a.m."[107] – Tebbutt produced the air ticket[c]
- "Levertons ... were due to arrive at around 5 p.m."
- "we waited for Levertons to arrive with a coffin at 5 p.m."
- "the Prince of Wales was due to arrive shortly after 5 p.m."
- "I took this opportunity to go for some food.... This was about two hours before the Prince of Wales arrived"
- "we returned to the corridor. It was about 4 p.m."
- "I looked at the body, on returning at around 4 p.m."

An analysis of the timings mentioned – completely listed above – reveals an amazing focus on 4 p.m. and 5 p.m. – particularly when one considers that Tebbutt was apparently referring to his notes (see above) and that the 7 a.m. timing would have been supported by the airline ticket.

Tebbutt includes no timings in his statement for any of the events between the 7 a.m. departure from London and the 3.40 p.m. – "two hours before the Prince of Wales arrived" – commencement of the embalming and departure for food.[d] This is supported by three mentions by Tebbutt of people from the UK arriving around 5 p.m.

Then, emphasising that timing period, "we returned ... [at] about 4 p.m." – the embalming now basically finished. And just in case we never got that: "I looked at the body, on returning at around 4 p.m."

The earlier four reasons show that this 4 p.m. completion of a "forty minutes to an hour" embalming could not possibly be correct.

Why is it then, that Tebbutt has not just indicated that it ended around 4 p.m., but has focused on that period in his statement timings?

There are three facets to this:

1) No mention of any other timings between 7 a.m. and 3.40 p.m. – many events occurred, but no timings

---

[a] At the inquest Tebbutt revealed that he prides himself on punctuality – in other words, he is very conscious of time: "I am always on time" to which Hough replied: "I think we are getting that impression from you, Mr Tebbutt": 26 Nov 07: 84.9.

[b] *The Documents* book, pp437-445.

[c] Tebbutt's statement: "I exhibit the air ticket for Flight BA332 S that day as CHT/2.": Colin Tebbutt, Witness Statement, 5 July 2004, reproduced in *The Documents* book, p437 (UK Edition)

[d] I suggest it is no coincidence that at the inquest Tebbutt was not asked about timings for events during this period, and none were forthcoming.

2) There appears to be a deliberate focus of timings related to the embalming period – indicated in the statement to have occurred between 3.40 and about 4 p.m.

3) No mention of any other timing of events from 5 p.m. to the conclusion of the evening – at the Fulham Mortuary.

Why?

I suggest that there has been police "involvement" in the compilation of the timings in Tebbutt's 2004 statement. As mentioned earlier, Tebbutt had been a long-serving police officer himself.

It is very significant that:

a) Tebbutt's original notes from the period have never been made available and were not shown to the jury

b) Tebbutt was not questioned on the timing of the embalming under cross-examination and the jury never saw his statement.

Under cross-examination Tebbutt was asked: "Did you ever become aware of how long [the embalming] would take?" Tebbutt answered: "I went for lunch or to try to get something to eat and they started whatever they were doing, and then when I came back about 40 minutes later, they were still in there, so they had an hour, hour and a half."[a]

It looks like the word "lunch" has slipped out – it was not there in the statement. Tebbutt appears to quickly try to correct it: "lunch or to try to get something to eat".

I suggest that at the inquest Tebbutt has inadvertently timed the start of the embalming – the word "lunch" times it. This conflicts seriously with his statement account – about 3.40 p.m.

Next, Tebbutt proceeds to further correct the "lunch" mention: "when I came back about 40 minutes later, they were still in there, so they had an hour, hour and a half".

Again, a conflict with his statement:[b] "After about forty minutes to an hour, we returned to the corridor.... When Paul Burrell and I looked at the body, on returning at around 4 p.m., the Princess of Wales still looked the same, but the French Funeral Directors did not know how to do her hair.... The Funeral Directors re-arranged her hair with [Burrell's] help."

In the statement: Tebbutt and Burrell went in and "looked at the body" and Burrell helped with Diana's hair.

At the inquest: "they were still in there" and continued on for another ½ to ¾ of an hour.[c]

---

[a] This issue of time taken was first raised above.

[b] I suggest that to remember the "40 minutes" at the inquest, Tebbutt may have had his statement in front of him.

[c] Tebbutt indicates "an hour, hour and a half" all up – roughly take away the "40 minutes" that Tebbutt and Burrell (inquest evidence) were having lunch.

I suggest that Burrell and Tebbutt would have not been allowed into the room if the embalming had still been in progress on their return. So, in other words, the embalming was effectively complete by the time they returned – in the statement.

The difference is that at the inquest the embalming period has been extended by Tebbutt – maximum now 1½ hours. In his statement the maximum was one hour. Quite a difference, if you consider that he appears to have his statement in front of him – see earlier footnote.

I suggest that if the jury had been allowed to see Tebbutt's notes, they would have revealed Tebbutt had included timings of events throughout this most critical of days.[a] I believe the notes would reveal that the embalming took place close to lunchtime – not 3 to 4 p.m.

As it turned out, the jury never even knew that the Tebbutt notes existed, let alone seeing them.

Tebbutt's statement was taken in July 2004, whereas Monceau – who also insisted on a finish to the embalming around 4 p.m.[b] – was not interviewed until later the following year, in October 2005.

This indicates that it was actually not Monceau who first came up with a later timing on the embalming, but I also suggest that the idea didn't originate from Tebbutt.

Instead I believe it was included in Tebbutt's account at the suggestion of the British police. It was in the interest of the British authorities to be distanced from the decision to embalm. The later in the day that the embalming was timed – and as close to the arrival of Charles and the British embalmers as possible – the harder it is to pin the embalming decision on the British authorities. If it can be shown that Monceau and his team were waiting around for hours trying to obtain elusive authorisations – something

---

[a] In Tebbutt's statement he includes specific dates and times of events that had less relevance. He: a) reveals the exact date he wrote to Stevens offering his assistance to Paget – 8 January 2004; b) the precise date he met Princess Diana – "the night she got engaged ... in 1981"; c) the exact date of Diana's divorce – 28 August 1996 – and the exact time she walked out of the ballet school that day as Princess Diana – 10.28 a.m.; d) correctly recalls the exact date of Diana's return from holiday with Rosa Monckton – 20 August 1997; e) the time he was due to collect Diana on her return to Stansted from the final holiday – 2 p.m. on 31 August 1997; f) the timing of his arrival at Kensington Palace in the middle of the night after the Paris crash – 2.30 to 3 a.m. on 31 August 1997; g) the time for a call from Gibbins the next day – at 4 p.m. on 1 September 1997. See *The Documents* book, pp428-448. At the inquest Tebbutt appeared to recall the time Gibbins announced that Diana had died: "about 3 o'clock" (UK time) 26 Nov 07: 87.17.

[b] A timing that doesn't match the events on the day – see earlier.

which never actually happened[a] – then the focus is completely removed from the reality of what occurred: an order for the embalming from British authorities prior to 9 a.m. – Amarger.

Tebbutt has gone along with the later timing in his statement, but I doubt that he would have had any idea of the significance of or implications involved in this change of evidence.

Monceau has completely gone along with this in his evidence, going so far as to put his own hand up for the embalming, in his statement[b] and at the inquest.[c]

Moss has stated that "at about 1400hrs [2 p.m.], Doctor Bernard Kouchner, the founder of Médecins Sans Frontière and Minister for Health ... asked whether he would be allowed to pay his final respects to the Princess of Wales.... Sir Michael Jay ... agreed that this would be acceptable...."[d] This evidence – which appears to have come from Moss' notes at the time[e] – shows that at about 2 p.m. it was possible to view Diana's body.

This evidence indicates that the embalming was already completed by 2 p.m. Given the earlier evidence that Diana was "melting" by about 12 p.m. it would seem unlikely that outside visitors – like Kouchner – would have been allowed to view her prior to the administration of the embalming.

Tebbutt has stated that the embalming took "an hour, hour and a half" – inquest and "40 minutes to an hour" – statement. The above discussion indicates that the statement evidence is likely to be more accurate.[f] Tebbutt's statement records that afterwards Burrell had helped rearrange Diana's hair.

---

[a] See earlier.

[b] In his statement Monceau said: "Nobody asked me to embalm the Princess of Wales. It was me who suggested the embalming...."

[c] At the inquest Burnett asked: "Is it right that no one asked you to embalm the Princess's body? In fact, you suggested it and then Mr Moss agreed?" Monceau: "Yes, it is true."

[d] Moss has also said: "Mme. Chirac attended with Sir Michael and Lady Jay at 0845hrs [8.45 a.m.], which could suggest that the 'Thanatopracteur's work had already been completed by then". That is obviously impossible because Amarger didn't arrive until well after that – see earlier. Moss does admit: "I am really not sure.... I really cannot be sure of precisely when the 'Thanatopracteur' attended."

[e] On 1 September 1997 Moss completed a report detailing events surrounding the crash – see Embassy chapter in Part 5. At the start of his statement Moss said: "I am using a copy of this report in order to refresh my memory of the events". This appears to be why he is specific on timing of certain events. In that light, it appears amazing that he didn't see it as relevant to include the timing of the embalming in his report. Source: Keith Moss, Witness Statement, 22 October 2004, reproduced in *The Documents* book, p648 (UK Edition).

[f] Tebbutt may have come up with "an hour, hour and a half" to extend the embalming period after he appears to have slipped earlier in the same answer by indicating it occurred around lunchtime.

So, if we then took the outer limit of Tebbutt's statement timing, we could conclude the embalming took approximately one hour.

The general evidence – see above – indicates that a full embalming would normally take significantly longer than that: Wikipedia says "several hours"; Jauze said "two hours seems a bit short".[a] Green said "three hours".

I suggest that Tebbutt's one hour fits with the earlier evidence: the embalming was conducted in a panic, was only partial and was of poor quality.

Although the balance of the evidence points to a very quick embalming, it is difficult to establish precisely why this is what occurred.

Amarger stated: "My boss told me to be quick because Prince Charles was arriving in the afternoon". Yet at the inquest Monceau stated that by the time he spoke to Moss – 12 noon and pre-embalming – he had been "told that the Prince was expected at about 5 o'clock, at Villacoublay, the airport".[bc]

So at that stage there was still over 5 hours before Charles was due to arrive at the hospital. Given that a full embalming only takes around three hours, why then did Monceau tell Amarger to be quick?

It may be significant that Amarger says she was only told "Prince Charles was arriving in the afternoon" – even though Monceau had a specific time: after 5 p.m.

In summary, when the witness evidence is pieced together – Monceau, Amarger, Moss, Tebbutt, Gibbins – it seems that the embalming is most likely to have started around 12.30 p.m.[d]

Regarding the duration of that embalming the credible[e] evidence is:
- there was a panic – Amarger
- it was only partial – Green, Thompson
- it was a substandard job – Green, Thompson

---

[a] After studying all the steps involved in the conduct of a full embalming it would seem to me that if one knew what one was doing it would take approximately 3 hours, if it wasn't rushed.

[b] This fits with the evidence that Charles and Diana's sisters arrived at the hospital at 5.40 p.m.

[c] This also fits with the evidence from Levertons (UK funeral directors) that they knew by 11 a.m. French time that Diana's body would be landing back at RAF Northolt at 8 p.m. French time – see later.

[d] Tebbutt said "immediately [after the Moss-Monceau conversation] the funeral directors changed into what appeared to be protective clothing and they went about their work". So, no delay. Contrary to this, Monceau declared that there was a delay while he sought authorisation for the embalming from Monteil, but Monteil has denied this. Monceau has form for lying and Tebbutt doesn't – at least not to the same extent.

[e] I suggest that Monceau is not a credible witness – see earlier.

-    it lasted for approximately 40 minutes to an hour – Tebbutt.

This evidence indicates that the embalming would have commenced around 12.30 p.m., was rushed, and then concluded by 1.30 p.m.[a] – over two hours ahead of the arrival of the British embalmers, at around 3.45 p.m.

The reality is that before 12.30 p.m. Amarger was in the hospital room with her equipment ready to do the embalming.

Monceau, though, has stated that the embalming didn't commence until 2 p.m.

Monceau's statement account was: "Mrs Amarger had arrived at the hospital. It must have been around 1130 to 1200hrs, or even 1300hrs [1 p.m.], but earlier than afternoon. I decided that it would be Mrs Amarger who would do the embalming, but we were waiting for authorisation."

Monceau's overall timeline evidence becomes clearer:

1) "we were waiting for authorisation" – "around 1130 to 1200hrs, or even 1300hrs [1 p.m.]"

2) Monceau eventually got "authorisation" from Moss and Monteil – see earlier

3) the embalming commenced "at around 2 o'clock" – confirmed to Burnett.

Why does Monceau state the embalming took place from 2 p.m. when all the timing evidence indicates it was already completed by 2 p.m.?

It is ridiculous to suggest that Amarger and Monceau waited around for a further 1½ hours – from 12.30 to 2 p.m. – while Diana's body continued to risk deterioration in the sweltering conditions. There were now also blankets covering the windows, increasing the heat.

I suggest that had Monceau and Amarger done that, they would have faced an additional 1½ hours of increasingly desperate pressure from the people present – nurses, Tebbutt, Burrell, Moss – to take some sort of action to sustain the condition of the body.

There is no evidence of that occurring.

The evidence instead indicates that the conversation with Moss occurred and very soon after that, the embalming process commenced – at around 12.30 p.m., and not at 2.00 p.m. as insisted upon by the unreliable Monceau.

Monceau may have been adamant on the later 2 p.m. start to fit with his evidence that he waited around for the authorisations – see earlier. The reality is that Monteil, Plumet and Jauze have all denied that Monceau sought authorisation, and Moss' statement evidence was that Monceau told him what he was going to do – not that Monceau sought authorisation for his actions.

---

[a] There is additional support for this timing in the Repatriation Issues chapter – section on Presence of British Police – where it is shown that Kingsmill arrived at the hospital after the embalming (Tebbutt) but was present for a 2 p.m. meeting (Moss).

It is significant that the jury heard none of this – no evidence from Monteil, Plumet or Jauze, and Moss' statement evidence was also not read out.

There is the additional point – mentioned earlier – that it was in the British authorities' interests for the embalming to have been timed as occurring later in the day. Monceau was interviewed by the British police[a] – the 2 p.m. timing may have been a collaboration between the police and Monceau.

Why was the embalming done in an early afternoon panic, when it was known by Monceau that Charles wasn't arriving until at least 5 p.m.?

Only Monceau can answer this, but this is a question he has never been asked.

A possible reason is that it may have been decided to get the embalming over before members of Diana's family – or other critical people, like Mohamed Al Fayed – got wind of what was being done. Later evidence will show that Diana's immediate family were not notified ahead of the embalming.

The truth about this embalming of Princess Diana's body is that the only part of it that was done effectively was the removal of all urine.

Did Monceau receive instructions that the urine had to be removed and no other aspects of the embalming were important?

If this was the case – and if Pavie was correct that at this stage the blood in the body was no longer Diana's – it would be further evidence that the embalming was all about the removal of evidence that Diana may have been pregnant.

Why is it that Huguette Amarger – the woman who conducted this embalming – was not cross-examined at Baker's "thorough" inquest?

Evidence of Jean Monceau

The French witnesses whose evidence was sought by Operation Paget – between 2004 and 2006 – were generally interviewed in Paris by French police with Scotland Yard officers present. This was not the case with Jean Monceau.

Jean Monceau made two trips to London in October/November 2005 and gave a statement on each occasion. The French police were not present for either statement. Both of these statements are among the critical documents that were withheld from the jury.

---

[a] See below.

There was also important email correspondence during the same period, between Monceau and Paget – this was all withheld from the inquest jury.[a]

In an email from DS Easton to Monceau on 9 November 2005, Easton mentions "your visits to London" – plural. At the inquest Monceau confirmed: "I made two statements – I went back [to London] another time".[108]

Monceau's second statement – made in London sometime between 18 October and 9 November 2005 – has never been officially disclosed by the British police. It is evident from the inquest transcripts that the cross-examining lawyer, Ian Burnett, also did not have access to that second statement.[109]

What does this second statement say? Why did the British police withhold it from the inquest?

When it came time for Jean Monceau to provide evidence to the inquest, there was pressure to minimise the amount of time he was subjected to cross-examination.

Judge Baker prepared the court for this late in the morning before Monceau was due to provide his afternoon evidence: "The message that I have received is that M Monceau is going to be available, no doubt at considerable inconvenience to himself, to give evidence from half past one our time, but it is essential that he starts at half past one."[110]

At the close of Monceau's inquest evidence, Baker said to Monceau: "M Monceau, we are very grateful to you for coming and for changing your arrangements. I am sorry that there was a muddle about the time for which you were summoned, but we are extremely grateful to have had evidence from you which is very helpful. Thank you."[111]

In the end, Monceau was in the witness stand – conducted by videolink – for about 1½ hours. Questions and answers had to be translated, so this actually equates to about 45 minutes of normal cross-examination time.

When one considers that Monceau was the only French embalming witness out of 15 – see earlier table – to be cross-examined, it seems unbelievable that even he was not subjected to a proper and thorough period of questioning.

It becomes very evident that the issue of embalming was "too hot to handle" as far as the British authorities were concerned. The extremely light treatment of embalming at the inquest reflects a reticence to deal with this issue, despite its critical importance to the overall case – as shown in this chapter.

Why is this?

---

[a] The correspondence and the first statement (18 October 2005) are reproduced in *The Documents* book, pp406-427.

I suggest it is because the British authorities were involved with the embalming process right from early on 31 August 1997.

Their suppression of the critical evidence on the subject continues to this day.

When all this is seen in the light of the evidence regarding Tebbutt's testimony – that he appears to have altered his account on timing of the embalming to fit with what is acceptable to the British authorities – it would seem that Monceau has been required to do similar.

Both witnesses – Tebbutt and Monceau – have given evidence of an embalming that finished around 4 p.m., when the general evidence is that the embalming must have occurred very early in the afternoon – see earlier.

I suggest that it is no coincidence that at the inquest neither Tebbutt nor Monceau gave – or were asked about – the timing of events through the day.

Role of Jean-Claude Plumet

In his testimony, French funeral director, Jean-Claude Plumet, revealed that he had an involvement in the embalming.

Jean-Claude Plumet, PFG Director of Paris Agencies, Paris: 4 Nov 05 Paget description of Statement: **Jury Didn't Hear**:

"A male 'Commissaire de Police' also telephoned him a number of times at his office.... In Mr Plumet's opinion, this 'Commissaire' would have probably also given authority to embalm....

"When asked, Mr Plumet stated that he did not recall making contact with the embalmers B.J.L. on that Sunday morning. When asked to clarify, he explained that it was possible that he had made contact with B.J.L., as the body would be leaving France without a lead lined coffin and in his opinion the body would therefore need to be embalmed, and he simply could not remember. He explained that if he had contacted B.J.L. he would have needed to have a member of the deceased's family or representative to complete documentation for the Police Administration Offices. However, no such member was present....

"We asked Mr Plumet whose authority would have been required to embalm. He explained that because he was aware that the body of the Princess of Wales was due to be moved, and that he believed the funeral would not be held until a few days later, and that she might be moved to a different coffin upon her return to the United Kingdom, it seemed very normal that she would need to be embalmed. Under normal circumstances, the family or a family representative would ask the undertakers about what was needed to proceed. From there the undertakers would draw up the appropriate paperwork and get the family to sign these, before forwarding the documentation to the Police Administrative Offices, and then on to the embalmers B.J.L. On this day, there was no paperwork, however the President of the French Republic, the Police Prefect and the Minister for the Interior were all present. Furthermore, he explains that he was working to a Police official who was a 'Commissaire'. He does not believe anything was being done contrary to the French Law. He felt that he had all the necessary authorities to proceed....

"When asked whether he or anybody else at PFG made a direct request of BJL to have the Princess of Wales embalmed, Mr Plumet explained that he could not remember....

"When asked whether it was ever brought to his attention that the Princess of Wales would be subject to a post-mortem on her return to the United Kingdom, Mr Plumet replied that it had not. He clarifies that if he had been told of this, he would have asked the 'Commissaire' what he should do next, and what he should do about the embalming."[112]

Comment: When Plumet was directly asked he "stated that he did not recall making contact with the embalmers BJL on that Sunday morning."

The general evidence is that Plumet spent the morning preparing for and organising the repatriation of Diana, then after lunch in the office[113], attended the IML with Jauze, arriving at around 1.45 p.m. Plumet and Jauze oversaw the departure of Dodi's body, then moved onto the hospital, arriving there at around 4.50 p.m. – over three hours after the completion of the embalming of Diana's body.

Yet despite this evidence – no recall of phoning BJL; not at the hospital until after the embalming – in his statement Plumet shows that he had prior knowledge of and an element of involvement in the embalming.

When Plumet was asked if he had prior knowledge of the UK post-mortem, he replied "that if he had been told of this, he would have asked the 'Commissaire' ... what he should do about the embalming."

This shows that Plumet knew ahead of time that the embalming was going to take place.

So, how did Plumet know this? He: a) didn't work for BJL; b) wasn't present at the hospital; and c) has said that he can't recall phoning BJL.

According to Monceau, the embalming decision was made on the run, as events developed at the hospital – the hot room, after the application and removal of dry ice, and after approval from Moss and Monteil.[a]

Plumet also showed that he has knowledge of some of the circumstances of the embalming:

- "on this day, there was no paperwork" – how does Plumet know this?
- "he does not believe anything was being done contrary to the French Law"
- "he felt that he had all the necessary authorities to proceed".

---

[a] This evidence has been shown to be false – see earlier.

In this account Plumet has revealed that he believes he had substantial knowledge of what occurred, and even appears to take ownership for the action itself: "he felt that he had all the necessary authorities to proceed".

Plumet is saying that before the embalming took place he had the authorisation organised.

The general evidence shows that there was actually no official authorisation for this embalming – not from the family, the police, or the British Embassy – see earlier and later. Instead, the order – which came from the British authorities before 9 a.m. – has never been officially disclosed.

Plumet's account does fit though with the earlier evidence on the series of phone calls that took place early on 31 August 1997. If the order had come from a British authority in the UK to the president of Kenyons, who was in the UK, to Racine, then Chapillon to Plumet, then Plumet calls Monceau around 7.45 a.m. requesting an embalming to be carried out by a female embalmer.

There is nothing that would have necessarily appeared sinister at the time. The British were requesting PFG to organise an embalming of Princess Diana, ahead of her return to the UK.

It is possible that Monceau was given a contact number to receive additional instructions directly – Monceau talks in his evidence of taking "care of the liaison with the other people" (see earlier).[a]

It's interesting that Plumet doesn't deny calling BJL: "he did not recall making contact". In fact, it is a notable feature of Plumet's evidence that he doesn't outrightly deny anything to do with the embalming, including Monceau's lies:

-   dry ice: "he did not recall making a request for dry ice. He explains that this is possible, but he simply could not remember"
-   a direct request of BJL to embalm: "he could not remember"
-   witnessing the Moss-Monceau conversation: "does not recall"
-   seeing or speaking with Monceau pre-embalming: "does not remember" and "he explains that he could have written this episode out of his memory"
-   handing Monceau an embalming authorisation form: "it is possible, but ... he could not remember as this was not important to him".

This evidence shows that when Plumet is asked about Monceau's version of events[b] that occurred pre-embalming at the hospital – events that it would have been impossible for Plumet to have been involved in or witness,

---

[a] Not heard by the jury.
[b] Monceau was interviewed on 18 October 2005 and Plumet just over two weeks later, on 4 November.

because he wasn't there until hours later – Plumet doesn't deny, but instead sits on the fence.

Monceau has said Plumet was there – the evidence shows he couldn't have been – but rather than hang Monceau out to dry, Plumet has kind of half gone along with it.[a]

Why?

I suggest it is because Plumet is involved with the embalming – that he was the PFG link to BJL on the morning of the crash – and is aware that the embalming was carried out illegally (see later) and possibly is aware that there were sinister motives behind it.

In light of this, it is significant that:

a) Plumet refused to make a formal, sworn statement – see earlier
b) there is no mention in his statement of Plumet agreeing to give sworn testimony to the British inquest.[b]

There is no question that Plumet's evidence should have been heard at the inquest. Not only was Plumet not cross-examined, but Baker, who was in possession of Plumet's statement, withheld it from his own jury.

In the end, the inquest jury heard no evidence at all from Jean-Claude Plumet and would not have even been aware of his existence.

Why?

Gérard Jauze, PFG Branch Director, Paris: 21 Mar 06 Statement: **Jury Didn't Hear**:

"It is logical that someone instructed BJL to carry out the embalming. BJL would have gone to the hospital at our request, but I do not know who instructed them. It must have been M. Plumet or M. Caltiau, the deputy general manager, as they were both in the office in Boulevard Richard Lenoir, and they alone could have given the authority to proceed."[114]

Comment: Jauze appears to support Plumet's account that PFG were involved in the decision to embalm.

---

[a] This contrasts with Jauze's response to similar questions. Although Jauze also made comments like "I do not remember", when he is confronted with Monceau's account of meeting with Jauze and Plumet prior to the embalming, Jauze replies: "That is the first I have heard of that. At 1130hrs [11.30 a.m.], I was either at the Ritz Hotel or I was leaving there to return to Boulevard Richard Lenoir. It is possible that I met [Monceau] later on, but I do not remember the conversation. I did not deal with that, other than during my presence at the hospital.": Gérard Jauze, Witness Statement, 21 March 2006, reproduced in *The Documents* book, pp483-4 (UK Edition)

[b] Both Launay and Jauze agreed to appear at the inquest, but Plumet's statement does not include a reference to this. See *The Documents* book, p486 (Jauze); p517 (Launay).

Was the Embalming Legal or Expected?

This is a major issue: Did BJL director Jean Monceau order an illegal embalming of Princess Diana's body?

Jean Monceau, BJL Director and Embalmer, Paris: 20 Nov 07: 82.14: Mansfield: Q. Was it also your understanding in France that prior to embalming, there had to be a notice in writing from the family of the deceased or someone having authority to organise the funeral, but it has to be in writing. Were you aware of that?

A. Well, in France you have to be authorised to do it by the members of the family or anyone having authority. Considering the fact that I had talked about the subject with the different authorities present on site, including the people – the head of the funeral body in France, I thought that basically I had received enough authority.

Q. Yes. The question is: did you see any written authority at any time?

A. No, but what I saw was Prince Charles, in the late afternoon, with two people getting ready to embalm the body of the Princess.[ab]

Q. I understand that.

At 87.2: Horwell: Q. As an expert, Mr Monceau, do you consider that you did anything illegal or wrong on that day?

A. Yes, because otherwise you would not ask me all these questions.

Q. Mr Monceau –

A. Yes, because what I did wrong was that I did the thing that I did. If I had known at the time that it would lead to such investigations, to my being questioned so many times, I would have waited until the next Monday. I would have waited until I would have received all the necessary official authorisations.

Q. All right. I am going to ask you a much more specific question, Mr Monceau. Did you at the time, on 31st August 1997, think that you were

---

[a] Charles actually arrived two hours after the two embalmers – see earlier Timeline of Events .

[b] This was Monceau's answer under pressure from Mansfield. When Monceau was asked earlier about the purpose of the embalming by the inquest lawyer, Ian Burnett, he replied: "The general idea is that everything that was done was to make the body presentable.": 20 Nov 07: 79.18. This is supported by earlier evidence that showed the heat in the room could have led to presentational problems. It is interesting that when under pressure over why the embalming was carried out without proper authorisation, the presentation issue goes out the window and Monceau comes up with the arrival of Charles and the UK embalmers later in the day. The issue of Monceau's answers to Mansfield is addressed again later in this section on Legality.

doing anything wrong or illegal?

A. No, not at all.

At 76.5: Burnett: Q. Did you understand, having had the Consul General's approval in the way that you have described it to the course you proposed[a], that that was sufficient for the purposes of getting consent for French law from someone responsible for the funeral arrangements?

A. No.

Q. So what did you want for that?

A. Well, the normal way, the way things would have taken place normally, would have been to get the authorisation from the town hall of the district on call, on duty that Sunday, that was the town hall at the 4th district of Paris, but you have to bear in mind that it was the Princess of Wales and that it was not the normal procedure that was followed.

Jean Monceau: 18 Oct 05 Statement: **Jury Didn't Hear**:

"Generally, for a body that died in normal circumstances, when there are no medico-legal problems, in order to be able to carry out an embalming you need a family member or any other person having the capacity to deal with the funeral of the deceased to sign for us an authority to proceed. Once that request has been made, you go to the Town Hall and you present this request for authorisation to carry out embalming, together with the death certificate, stating that there are no medico-legal obstacles, and that there is no requirement for immediate placing within a coffin, to the Mayor of the Commune where the death took place (the Registrar), who grants it. You then go to the office of Mortuary Operations at the Prefecture of Police, who issue an official embalming report, the equivalent of the authorisation for embalming. You then go [to] the police station for the arrondissement where the embalming is to be performed and you make an appointment for the time it will be done. At the appointed time, the police meet the embalmer at the place where the embalming is to be performed. The embalmer carries out the embalming and the police ensure that a flask containing at least 50 ml of the product used is deposited with the body. The embalming itself takes about an hour and a half, but you need at least 8 hours to get all this done. If there is a medico-legal problem you cannot proceed with embalming until you get a release order from the Public Prosecutor.

"In Paris on the weekends not all town halls of the arrondissements are open. In this case, you go to the town hall for the 4th arrondissement, which is the duty town hall for weekends or when it is not open you go to the Office of Mortuary Operations at the Prefecture of Police. You submit the request for authority to embalm and it is granted. You then go to the police station for the arrondissement, who arrange an appointment with the embalmer. The rest of the procedure is the same as under normal circumstances. On the Monday,

---

[a] The discussion between Monceau and Moss is covered earlier.

the Town Hall for the 4th arrondissement or the Prefecture of Police informs the Town Hall for the arrondissement and a messenger from the embalming company has to go to the Town Hall to sign the register. Once this has been done, the procedure is in order and the Town Hall can issue the 'Acte de Décès' [Record of Death] (which is used for inheritance purposes).

"When I became a director of BJL, I produced a set of standard operating procedures for the employees of the company so that they did not make any mistakes. I produce as Exhibit JM/6 a copy of the standard operating procedures, which I produced and which were in effect in 1997; these were inspired by the statutory order that I produce at Exhibit JM/7, which was in force in 1997. In this statutory order, it is explained that you cannot proceed with an operation to conserve the body of a deceased person without the authorisation of the Mayor of the Commune of the place of death, and in Paris by the Prefect of Police. I should explain that in practice it is never the Mayor or Prefect of Police that give this authorisation but one of their representatives.

"I also produce as Exhibit JM/8 a photocopy of the regulations concerning the authority for transportation and other matters from the Code of Mortuary Operations.

"You have asked me how this case differs from a normal case. On that day, I was told that Prince Charles was coming to Paris and that he was bringing with him some British embalmers. This led me to believe that he wanted the Princess to be embalmed. Furthermore, Mr Keith Moss, who as far as I was concerned, was the person with authority to deal with the funeral of the deceased, gave me verbal authorisation to proceed with the embalming. Similarly, Superintendent of Police Madame Monteil also told me not to worry when I asked her if I might have problems in respect of the documents required to proceed with embalming.... The law says that you need the request for authorisation from the family or their representative and the authority from the Prefecture of Police. On that day I had verbal agreements, but under those exceptional circumstances this was enough to proceed with embalming on the understanding that everything would be regularised. It was not my place to refuse, even the Prefect of Police was present at the hospital.

"As I have already explained to you, in order to be able to proceed with embalming, a member of the family or any other person having the capacity to deal with the funeral of the deceased must sign a request for authorisation to proceed with embalming. This authorisation sheet contains a section that has to be completed by the embalmer. On 31 August 1997, P.F.G. gave me that part which I completed and I returned it to them. The part of the authorisation meant to be completed by the family had not been filled in. However, it went without saying that this would be regularised.

"You inform me that there is a burial certificate signed by Mrs Coujard, the Public Prosecutor, in the case papers. I was not aware of this and this authority does not affect the procedure in respect of embalming. This authority would have been given in order to allow the body to be buried. It is the final document that the Public Prosecutor would issue and therefore the body could leave France....

"You have asked me what French legislation governs embalming. It is the notices in the Official Journal of the French Republic.

"You have asked me if it is mandatory to embalm a body before it is repatriated. Yes. Any body that leaves French soil has to have undergone embalming. This is stipulated by the French Public Hygiene Committee so that germs are not taken to other countries. This is achieved thanks to the bactericidal, viricidal and fungicidal action of the products used (formaldehyde). Even if the body is repatriated in a lead lined coffin, the law requires embalming." [115]

Jean Monceau: 18 Oct 05 Statement: **Jury Didn't Hear:**

"Mrs Amarger had arrived at the hospital. It must have been around 1130 to 1200hrs, or even 1300hrs, but earlier than afternoon. I decided that it would be Mrs Amarger who would do the embalming, but we were waiting for authorisation. I asked how the body was to be presented, the schedule for the family's visit, when the body was to be taken away, etc. in order to find out how to proceed. These conversations were with people from the funeral service, and they in turn introduced me to the British Consul-General in Paris, Mr Keith Moss....

"I saw the Superintendent from the Brigade Criminelle, Mrs Martine Monteil. I explained what was happening to her. She told me not to worry, and that everything would be in order and the authorisations would be given. She left me her mobile phone number and told me that I could call her if there were any problems. I took this authority to carry out the embalming as being from the Prefect, which is explained by the Statutory Order at Exhibit JM/7. There was nothing strange that the lady Superintendent, who was so well known in France, should give authority for me to proceed....

"You have asked me what was the single reason for proceeding with embalming. It was to make the body as presentable as possible to the family.... In the case of the Princess, she was a public figure and she had fractures and was bleeding: it was imperative that she be presented properly. It was not necessarily to preserve the body although I did not know if she was going to be presented in an open coffin I thought that this was possible and that in such a case embalming is necessary....

"You have asked me if it was my decision and my decision alone to proceed with the embalming. Nobody asked me to embalm the Princess of Wales. It was me who suggested the embalming in order to make the body as presentable as possible under the circumstances and there was no external influence. As an expert in embalming, I did not do anything illegal or wrong or inappropriate that day." [116]

Comment: The evidence of Jean Monceau again raises several important issues.

One critical question is: Did Monceau himself believe that he acted within the law, when he instructed Amarger to conduct the embalming?

When Monceau was asked: "if it was my decision and my decision alone to proceed with the embalming", he volunteered in his answer: "I did not do anything illegal or wrong or inappropriate that day". This statement had no connection to the question.

Monceau was asked by Horwell at the inquest: "Do you consider that you did anything illegal or wrong on that day?" – Monceau replied: "Yes, because what I did wrong was that I did the thing that I did."

Horwell didn't get the answer he wanted, so he asked again: "Did you at the time ... think that you were doing anything wrong or illegal?" Answer: "No, not at all."

So again we have conflicting evidence – in Monceau's statement: not illegal; at the inquest: illegal, then next answer, not illegal.

So did Monceau think what he did was illegal?

Unfortunately for Monceau, when under cross-examination he backed up his first account – that what he did was illegal – with an explanation: "I would have waited until the next Monday.[a] I would have waited until I would have received all the necessary official authorisations."

This shows that Monceau went ahead with the embalming with the full knowledge that he didn't have "all the necessary official authorisations".

In other words, Monceau knew at the time that what he did was illegal, and he has lied twice – once in his statement and once at the inquest – when he said that it wasn't illegal.

Why would Monceau act illegally?

This evidence adds to the earlier and later evidence that Monceau wasn't making the decisions here, but was acting on instructions from unidentified persons outside of the known players. Monceau has possibly been paid well –

---

[a] Later evidence will show that if Monceau had gotten cold feet and not carried out this embalming, a backup plan was already in place: headed to the Paris hospital were two British embalmers who would have carried out the embalming, had it not already been done by Amarger.

probably by a British authority – to supervise the embalming and provide false evidence to the police and the inquest.

In his statement – not heard by the jury[a] – Monceau did provide a defence for his illegal actions: "On that day I had verbal agreements, but under those exceptional circumstances this was enough to proceed with embalming on the understanding that everything would be regularised. It was not my place to refuse – even the Prefect of Police was present at the hospital."

There are several problems with Monceau's defence:

1) Monceau states that "the Prefect of Police was present". The prefect of police – Philippe Massoni – was not present at the hospital during the embalming – see earlier[b]

2) Monceau said: "I had verbal agreements" or authorisations.[c] Monceau actually had nothing of the sort: a) The earlier evidence shows that although Monceau met with Moss, he never sought Moss' authorisation for the embalming – Monceau simply informed Moss of what he had come to do: the embalming; b) Monteil denied that Monceau talked to her and this is supported by the evidence from Tebbutt[d] – see earlier; c) Plumet and Jauze also denied that they spoke with Monceau – see earlier.

3) Monceau states: "everything would be regularised". There is no evidence that that ever occurred. Instead, at the conclusion of Monceau's 2005 statement[e] it reads:

"During my statement you have shown me the following documents:
OD137 (folder 24) – full copy of the *'Acte de Décès'* [Record of Death]
OD137 (folder 24) - authorisation to close the coffin
OD137 (folder 24) – mortuary pass
I can inform you that you are missing:
- the Death Certificate, which you could obtain from the Town Hall of the 13th arrondissement.
- the request for authorisation to embalm together with the declaration by the embalmer that you can obtain from the registrar of deaths in the Town Hall of the 13th arrondissement or from the Office of Mortuary Operations at the Prefecture of Police.
- the authority for embalming treatment (which also summonses the police, which you can obtain from the Registrar of Deaths at the Town Hall of the

---

[a] Most of the witness evidence regarding the legality – or more correctly, illegality – of the embalming, was not heard at the inquest.

[b] The earlier evidence indicates that Massoni was only at the hospital late in the afternoon, for the visit of Prince Charles.

[c] Monceau is referring to authorisations from Moss, Monteil, Plumet and Jauze – see earlier.

[d] Tebbutt testified that the embalming commenced immediately after the conversation with Moss.

[e] Not heard by the jury.

13th arrondissement or at the Office of Mortuary Operations at the Prefecture of Police.

- an official report of embalming[a] which you can obtain from the police station of the 13th arrondissement where the duty officer of the Judicial Police would have been on the day in question." [117]

The point here is that out of the above 7 documents listed by Monceau, it appears that only one – the death certificate[b] – was available to the inquest jury.

Why is this?

Monceau has listed 4 missing documents: 1) the request for authorisation to embalm; 2) the embalmer's declaration; 3) the embalming authority; 4) the embalming report.

If this embalming documentation exists:

a) why didn't the British police obtain copies of it after taking Monceau's statement in 2005?

b) why were there not copies of it at the inquest?

c) why did the jury not even get to hear that this documentation should have existed?[c]

The most likely answer to these three questions appears to be that the embalming documentation may not actually exist.

Why is it that when Monceau's short defence for his actions is analysed, virtually every aspect of it is found to be predicated on false evidence? Massoni was not present; there never was any verbal authorisation; and it appears that the embalming documentation never was "regularised".

Monceau has stated: "On 31 August 1997, P.F.G. gave me that part [of the embalming authorisation form] which I completed and I returned it to them. The part of the authorisation meant to be completed by the family had not been filled in. However, it went without saying that this would be regularised."

The evidence – see earlier – shows that there was no one from PFG present at the hospital until well after the embalming had been

---

[a] In an apparent direct contradiction of this, Monceau had stated earlier in the same statement: "You have asked me if I made out an embalming certificate. No, that does not exist, but at the bottom of the form requesting authorisation to embalm, signed by the family or a representative, I make a statement. This is done before the embalming and even before the request at the town hall.": Jean Monceau, Witness Statement, 18 Oct 05, p11.

[b] Shown in Figure 19 of Part 2.

[c] Monceau's statement, from which this information is derived, was not read out to the jury.

completed. Plumet – who Monceau earlier claimed to have spoken with prior to the embalming – was asked about Monceau's account regarding the form. The Paget record of Plumet's response: "Mr Plumet explains that it is possible, but again that he could not remember as this was not important to him. If Mr Monceau's recollection of this is right however, Mr Plumet explains that this document would have been filed with Mrs Celadon at the Bureau des Operations Mortuaires, at the Prefecture de Police."[118]

Plumet "could not remember" it, but if it did happen the "document would have been filed with Mrs Celadon".[a] This interview with Plumet was conducted in Paris[119], so why then is there no evidence of the Paget officers going to the "Bureau des Operations Mortuaires" to recover a copy of the document?

I suggest the answer again is: because this document does not actually exist.

One document that apparently does exist is the burial certificate, but it was not shown to the jury[b] and has never been made public. Monceau said in his statement: "You inform me that there is a burial certificate signed by Mrs Coujard, the Public Prosecutor, in the case papers. I was not aware of this and this authority does not affect the procedure in respect of embalming."

This evidence is in direct conflict with Maud Coujard's testimony at the inquest: "That [burial] certificate is obviously issued before any embalming procedure starts.... What is sure is that [embalming] cannot start before that [burial] certificate is issued."[120]

What Monceau fails to explain in his testimony is: at what point is it legally okay in France to start the process of seeking authorisation for an embalming? Not only that, but Monceau specifically states that the burial certificate is not part of that process.

I suggest that it is common sense that the burial certificate would be required before embalming could commence and particularly in a case where the officiating doctor has stated the death was suspicious – see earlier.

---

[a] Monceau also claimed to have met with PFG employee Gérard Jauze at the hospital. Jauze's response, after reading Monceau's account, was: "That is the first I have heard of that."- see earlier.

[b] As with other key documents in this case, how is it that Baker can decide that the jury are not entitled to see the burial certificate of the person whose death they are meant to be investigating?

It seems that Monceau, an experienced embalmer who must be familiar with the procedures, has lied again.

Why?

Monceau also said in his statement: "If there is a medico-legal problem you cannot proceed with embalming until you get a release order from the Public Prosecutor."

It is possible that Monceau – particularly if he was giving evidence under outside instructions – categorically denied the relevance of the burial certificate to embalming to distance this particular case from any implication that there was a medico-legal problem – i.e. that the death was suspicious.

Earlier evidence has shown – see Chapter 1 – that there was a medico-legal problem.

Jean Monceau: 20 Nov 07: 72.23:

Burnett: Q. The procedure, the legal process, before you can embark on an embalming includes getting the permission of someone authorised to organise the funeral. Is that right?

A. Yes.

Q. And also to get official authority from the Mayor or the Prefect or someone speaking for them?

A. Well, the authority of the mayor of the district of Paris that is on duty that Sunday, not the Prefect of Police because the Police Prefect department is closed on Sundays.

Q. Yes, although you had the Police Prefect in hospital with you?

A. Obviously, and unfortunately for the Prefect of Police, it is not the Prefect of Police who signs this kind of authority.

Q. I do not need to get into a technical debate with you about who needs to sign what. We have a French lawyer coming for that tomorrow.

Comment: This is an amazing piece of cross-examination.

Monceau starts with: "not the Prefect of Police because the Police Prefect department is closed on Sundays". When Monceau is reminded by Burnett that his evidence is: "the Police Prefect [was] in hospital with you", Monceau replies: "it is not the Prefect of Police who signs this kind of authority".

Then, probably in an attempt to avoid further embarrassment, instead of challenging Monceau on what is an obvious conflict of evidence – the Prefect signs, then the Prefect doesn't sign – Burnett backs off: "I do not need to get into a technical debate...."

Earlier evidence has shown that Monceau has lied in his claim that Massoni was present at the hospital at the time of the embalming. This period of cross-examination appears to confirm that – the question being: If it was the responsibility of the Prefect of police to provide authority for the embalming and he was conveniently present at the hospital, then why didn't Monceau get Massoni to sign this form?

The general evidence appears to reveal that the form Monceau is referring to was never actually created.

Jean Monceau has provided varying accounts on the role of the Prefect or Prefecture of Police:

- "the authority of the mayor of the district of Paris that is on duty that Sunday [is required], <u>not the Prefect of Police</u> because the Police Prefect department is closed on Sundays" – inquest
- "it is <u>not the Prefect of Police</u> who signs this kind of authority" – inquest
- "you then go to the office of Mortuary Operations at the <u>Prefecture of Police</u>, who issue an official embalming report, the equivalent of the <u>authorisation for embalming</u>" – statement
- "in Paris on the weekends ... you go to the town hall for the 4th arrondissement ... or when it is not open you go to the Office of Mortuary Operations at the <u>Prefecture of Police</u>. You submit the request for <u>authority to embalm</u> and it is granted" – statement
- "you cannot proceed ... without the <u>authorisation</u> of the Mayor of the Commune ... and in Paris by the <u>Prefect of Police</u> ... [or] one of their representatives – statement
- "you need the request for authorisation from the family or their representative and the <u>authority from the Prefecture of Police</u>" – statement
- "it was not my place to refuse, even the Prefect of Police was present at the hospital" – statement
- "I took this authority [from Monteil] to carry out the embalming as being from the Prefect" – statement
- "I could not say that I took [Monteil's approval] as an official authorisation" – inquest
- "I had conversed with [Monteil], the Prefect of Police and the British General Consul ... all of them [had] the same opinion" – inquest.

There are two issues:

1) What is the law?
2) What occurred in the case of Princess Diana?

Monceau – who had conducted 13,000 embalmings[a] – has changed his evidence regarding the law.

In his 2005 statement Monceau has categorically testified under oath: "you cannot proceed ... without the authorisation of the Prefect of Police"; "you need ... authority from the Prefecture of Police".

At the inquest, also under oath, Monceau presents the opposite situation: "it is not the Prefect of Police who signs this kind of authority".

---

[a] See earlier.

The exact opposite.

In Monceau's statement: "I took this authority [from Monteil] to carry out the embalming as being from the Prefect".

At the inquest: "I could not say that I took [Monteil's approval] as an official authorisation".

So, in 2005, the authorisation from the Prefect was essential, and Monceau took Monteil's approval as the equivalent.[a]

In 2007, at the inquest, Monteil's approval is not "an official authorisation".

I suggest the difference might be that in 2005 Monceau didn't have Moss saying he authorised the embalming. At the inquest Moss' evidence had significantly changed (see earlier) – Moss is by then talking about authorisation being given from London (to Hough) and by himself (to Horwell).

This evidence[b] – which ignores the legal requirements – changed the away from the need for police authorisation, which was never given anyway, to authorisation by the British, via Moss.[c]

Burnett told Monceau that "we have a French lawyer coming ... tomorrow" to outline the legal situation of the embalming.

This was Eva Steiner. What did she say?

Dr Eva Steiner, Inquest & Paget Expert on French Law: 21 Nov 07: 68.14: Hough: Q. In order to perform those [embalming] kinds of operations, is it right that you primarily need an authorisation from the mayor of the municipality where the death occurred or where the preservation is to take place?

A. Yes, you need this authorisation.... In the circumstances where somebody dies on a Sunday or Bank Holiday, the town halls in France are closed and the mayors are not available, or their substitute, to give this type of

---

[a] In the same statement Monceau has claimed that "the Prefect of Police was present at the hospital", but fails to explain why he went to Monteil instead. The general evidence – see earlier – is that he went to neither: not Massoni or Monteil.

[b] Moss was cross-examined on 22 November 2007, two days after Monceau on the 20th. Pre cross-examination statements were taken from many witnesses, so the gist of their evidence was known ahead of time. I suggest that Monceau would have had some awareness of what Moss was going to say, before he took the stand. In other words, I am suggesting that it is not a coincidence that Monceau's evidence has changed, and it is also no coincidence that Moss' evidence changed as well. This all appears to be connected to the fact that Amarger's evidence was heard for the first time at the inquest – see earlier Comment on the Monceau-Moss conversation.

[c] The earlier evidence from Amarger indicated that authorisation came from the British authorities early in the day. I suggest that is the true account.

authorisation. A common practice is that you have to get all the relevant authorisations to the Prefecture, where you always have a person on duty, usually a substitute for the Prefet, and the Prefet, being the head of police, understood in a wide sense, usually it is a senior police officer who will be on duty on Sundays and Bank Holidays as well. So the practice is to ask for the substitute the authorisation in these type of cases.

....Q. One needs three things in order to obtain the authorisation of the Mayor. Is that right?

A. Yes. Well, we need – the authorisation of the Mayor has to be based on first either a written expression of the last will of the deceased, which is not the case here, I suppose, or a request by the person having the quality to organise the funeral. So this is the expression which is used. It may mean either a member of the family or, in his absence or her absence, a person what has been nominated to take over. So it can be any kind of person actually.... I would suggest that, for example, for an ordinary citizen who dies in similar circumstances on foreign soil, the consul or the vice-consul would be this type of person.

....Q. What is the second thing?

A. The second thing is that there should be a statement describing the procedure of embalming. This, of course, reading to the best of my knowledge, reading the documents I have been provided with, this condition has been fulfilled. So this follows again normal medical procedure.

Q. When you say a statement describing the procedure, that is the embalming or thanatopraxy procedure?

A. Yes, the product which has been used and the way it has been done.

Q. Now the third thing that is required when you get the authorisation of the Mayor, what is that?

A. It is a medical certificate establishing that the circumstances of the deaths do not give rise to further investigation of a medical forensic nature. So we want to make sure here that the person has died either of natural causes or, if it is an accident, that the death is not suspicious.

Q. Now those are the rules in abstract. Can we now apply them to this case? We have heard from Madame Coujard, who is the prosecutor, that after external examination of the Princess by Professor Lecomte, she issued a certificate releasing the bodies for burial. Now, the other thing that you need to look at is a certificate of death by Dr Riou which is being put up on the screen behind you now.... This is a certificate of the death of the Princess, signed by Bruno Riou who administered care to her.[a] As you will see, it contains the phrase "... ne posait pas de probleme medico-legal". Is that a certificate that was no medico-legal obstacle, which is the third requirement

---

[a] This death certificate can be viewed in the inquest website: INQ0002108. It has also also been reproduced in Part 2, Figure 19.

for bringing to the Mayor of the district or the Prefect?

A. Yes, it is actually. It is very clear: " ... did not give rise to any issues of a forensic legal nature."

....Q. M Monceau told us yesterday that he obtained authorisation from Mr Moss, the British Consul General, who, at least from his point of view, was in charge of repatriation and funeral arrangements at that stage. Now do you think, as a matter of French law, that he was entitled to rely upon that authorisation in order to comply with the first of the requirements?

A. Yes, I do. I mean, everything to do with private matters such as death, births, adoption, are dealt with the Consulate. I mean, the Ambassador has nothing to do with that.

....Q. Now, we have also heard from Mr Monceau that after going through the stages that we have just gone through, he explained to Madame Monteil, the head of the Brigade Criminelle, that he proposed performing a procedure to make the body presentable, and that she then told him to do whatever was necessary and that all necessary formal authorisations would be issued.... Do you consider that that was adequate authorisation on behalf of the Mayor or the Prefect?

A. It was.

....Q. Now, we heard yesterday that M Monceau in retrospect was worried, partly because he was being asked so many questions, that he might have done something not quite by the book. Do you think, having heard everything that I have explained and with your knowledge of French law, that he acted legally in performing the procedure?

A. I think he did. I think he did. I cannot – well, it is difficult for me to take a view on the status of Princess Diana at that time. If we say that she was an ordinary citizen, British citizen, then I think the procedure is the procedure which would have been followed for any other ordinary citizen dying on the French soil – I mean foreign citizens dying on French soil. Now, provided that she was not an ordinary citizen but a public figure – I mean, it is difficult for me to answer this point because obviously maybe the British Ambassador had a word to say on that, but this is not for me to decide, whether or not she was considered as a private or a public citizen.

Q. You certainly don't know what part, if any, the British Ambassador played?

A. Not at all.

Q. If there was some failure to comply technically with the French legal provisions, do you think that M Monceau did his best in the circumstances to comply?

A. I think he did. I mean, these are exceptional circumstances.

....Q. If a body is to be transported within the first 24 hours or in a sealed coffin, is it not obligatory to embalm?

A. No, it is not.

Dr Eva Steiner: 29 Sep 06 Statement: **Jury Didn't Hear**:

"I have been asked to re-examine the question of the legality in French law of the embalming of Diana, Princess of Wales following her death in Paris.

"I am aware that, in this respect, a legal action has been lodged by Mr M. Al-Fayed and copy of the written conclusions submitted by him to the Paris court investigating magistrate has been communicated to me.

"I would like to refer to my previous report dated 23 March 2006[a] where, at paragraph VI, I have already considered the legality of the process of embalming.

1-On the process of embalming:

.... The process [of embalming] is prohibited in circumstances where, following medical examination, the doctor appointed by the authorities finds that there are suspicious circumstances relating to the injuries necessitating further investigation of a medical forensic nature....

2- On the validity of the authorization to embalm:

A- The authority to embalm

.... The Mayor is vested with the general power to authorize embalming.... The power of the *Préfet* to substitute for the Mayor is even truer in Paris where his power is generalised.... Usually the most senior police officer in the Department acts as a substitute for the *Préfet*.

.... I note that the authorisation to embalm was given here by the *Préfet's* representative on duty in Paris on the day where the embalming took place which, in the circumstances described on the documents provided to me ... is in accordance with French laws and procedures.

B-the necessary requirements prior to obtaining the authorisation to embalm:

(i) I can only repeat here that in the absence of the last will of the deceased 'the person having capacity to organise the funeral' can make the request to the competent authorities. This person can be a family member or anybody being responsible for the funeral arrangements. Here the Consul general of the British Embassy, acting as a representative of the British State in France in circumstances where a member of the British Royal family was involved, qualified under the terms of article R 2213-2 CGCT[b] as 'a person having capacity to organise the funeral'.

(ii) On the description of the process of embalming further required by the law, it appears from the documents provided that, in accordance with the law,

---

[a] No reports from Steiner were provided to the jury and I also have not seen her 23 March 2006 report.

[b] Code Général des Collectivités Territoriales.

Mr Jean Monceau, from the embalming company, has prior to his intervention described at length the procedures he was about to carry out. (iii) The issue of the medical certificate: what is required by article R 2213-2 is a medical certificate concluding that after examination of the body there are no suspicious circumstances necessitating further investigation of a forensic nature. I note ... that this procedure was carried out by Doctor Lecomte and, subsequently, Dr Riou. I should add here that, under article 74 of the Code of Criminal Procedure, the Public Prosecutor may, in the case of violent or suspicious death and 'if he considers it necessary', appoint an expert to ascertain the cause of the death. This, again, was done in this case, Dr Lecomte concluding that the death was not suspicious and was the result of the crash. At this stage the authorisation to embalm could legally proceed."[121]

Coroner: Summing Up: 31 Mar 08: 87.3:

"In Dr Steiner's view everything was done to comply with French law."

Comment: Baker has failed to tell the jury that Steiner had reservations.

Inquest lawyer, Jonathon Hough, asked the critical question twice: "Do you think ... [Monceau] acted legally ...?" Steiner: "I think he did. I think he did. I cannot – well, it is difficult for me...." And Steiner moves on to question Princess Diana's status – the procedure is different for a royal than a commoner: "this is not for me to decide, whether or not she was considered as a private or a public citizen".

Hough – not content with this answer: "If there was some failure to comply technically with the French legal provisions, do you think that M Monceau did his best in the circumstances to comply?"

Now the question has changed. Hough has accepted that Monceau may not have followed the law, so "do you think that M Monceau did his best"?

Steiner: "I think he did. I mean, these are exceptional circumstances."

Steiner's view was that Monceau "did his best" considering the "exceptional circumstances".

That is quite different to Baker's "everything was done to comply with French law".[a]

Steiner's account to the inquest – "this is not for me to decide, whether or not she was considered as a private or a public citizen" – contrasts starkly with her statement account, defending the embalming decision: "here ... in circumstances where a member of the British Royal family was involved".

---

[a] Baker goes on to tell the jury: "Be that as it may, you may think that everyone concerned acted in good faith and did their best in unusually trying circumstances.": 31 Mar 08:87.4. The reality is that Baker has misrepresented the position of Dr Eva Steiner, his own expert.

So at the inquest "not for me to decide" if she was a royal; in Steiner's 2006 statement, categorical: "a member of the British Royal family".

I suggest that it is ridiculous that one of the inquest's legal experts is unsure of the status of the person whose death is being investigated. The rest of the civilised world knew the status of Princess Diana: she had clearly been stripped of her royal status by the Queen in August of 1996 – 12 months before the crash.[a]

I suggest that Steiner has lied on two occasions – in her statement, where she said Diana was a royal; and secondly at the inquest, where she indicated that Diana's status was not known.

French Embalming Law: General Codes of Territorial Collectivities (CGCT): **Jury Didn't Hear**:

"Civil Code: Funeral Operations:

Embalming

Article R2213-2

"The embalming of a deceased person cannot proceed without an authorisation given by the Maire of the area where the death took place or the area where the embalming takes place.

To obtain this authorisation, you should produce:

1) a written notice expressing the wishes of the deceased or a request from any person having authority to proceed with funeral arrangements, justifying his position and home address.

2) A declaration identifying the method of embalming, the chemicals to be used, the location and time of the operation, as well as the name and address of the person who will undertake the embalming or the embalming company to be used.

3) A certificate from the Doctor authorised to certify death, confirming that there are no legal reasons why this procedure cannot proceed.

Article R2213-4

"The Police employee designated in Article L2213-14[b] of the General Codes of Territorial Collectivities, to be present during these operations must, prior to this, be presented with the authorisation mentioned in Article R2213-2...."[122]

Comment: The evidence relating to the French law – Steiner's statement; Steiner's inquest account; the CGCT excerpt – shows what is practically required before an embalming can take place:

Authorisation from the mayor or the Prefect of police, or their representative.

To obtain that authorisation, there are three requirements:

---

[a] The significance of the status of Princess Diana is addressed later in the Royal Control chapter.

[b] It is not known how this police officer is designated.

1) Authorisation in the last will of the deceased. Failing that, written authorisation from a family member. Failing that, written authorisation from a person who "has been nominated [by the family] to take over".

2) "A statement describing the procedure of embalming", in writing.[a]

3) "A medical certificate establishing ... that the death is not suspicious".

The official authorisation document is then presented to the police officer present at the embalming.

To simplify this further: 6 things were required ahead of time to legalise the embalming process:

- authorisation from Diana's will or her family or someone representing her family

- a description of the embalming procedure

- a medical certificate showing the death was not suspicious

- the above three items needed to be shown to the mayor or the Prefect or one of their representatives

- authorisation from the mayor, Prefect or representative

- presentation of the authorisation to the police present at the embalming.

What occurred, point by point, in the case of the embalming of Diana, Princess of Wales?

1) Family authorisation.

There is absolutely no evidence of any attempt to get hold of a copy of Diana's will to find out what her "will" might be regarding a potential embalming.

Failing that, there is then absolutely no evidence of an attempt by anyone – Moss, Monceau, Tebbutt, Gibbins – to make contact with any member of Diana's family.[bc]

Because there was no attempt to contact the family, it becomes evident that there was then no person appointed to represent her family and give the authorisation.

So, no – point 1 was not fulfilled.

Steiner has stated that this was fulfilled:

In her statement: "Here the Consul general [Moss] ... in circumstances where a member of the British Royal family was involved, qualified".

---

[a] Although the law does not specifically use the term "in writing" it is clear from the nature of what is required – "the location and time of the operation, as well as the name and address" of the embalmer – that it is referring to a written document.

[b] Prince Charles was not a member of Diana's family – they were divorced on 28 August 1996.

[c] Issues regarding notification of the family members are dealt with later in this chapter.

This appears to be false on two counts: a) Diana was not "a member of the British Royal family", and b) Moss' police statement reveals that he didn't authorise the embalming – see earlier.

At the inquest Steiner avoided the royal issue, merely confirming that Monceau "was entitled to rely upon [Moss'] authorisation".

The reality, though, is that, even if Moss had authorised this embalming, he was in no position to – Moss had not been appointed to represent Diana's family.

When Mansfield asked Monceau if he was aware that this authorisation "had to be a notice in writing" he ducked the question, instead explaining "I thought that basically I had received enough authority" from the "the different authorities present".[a] Mansfield had to repeat the question and Monceau then replied: "No, but what I saw was Prince Charles, in the late afternoon, with two people getting ready to embalm the body of the Princess."

The point here is that the embalmers and Charles arrived well after the completion of the embalming – that had nothing to do with the issue of why Monceau never sought proper authorisation. The evidence – Amarger, who carried out the embalming – shows that the embalming was "authorised", or ordered, by British authorities much earlier in the day.

I suggest that Monceau never got legal authorisation because he had been told much earlier that: a) the job had to be done by a woman; b) Monceau had to supervise it; c) it would all be "regularised" later; d) that whatever investigations would be carried out in the future, he would be provided immunity from prosecution over his role in the events; and e) he would be paid well for his role in the events.

2)   Embalming statement.

Steiner says in her statement: "It appears from the documents provided that, in accordance with the law, Mr Jean Monceau ... has prior to his intervention described at length the procedures he was about to carry out."

At the inquest: "Reading the documents I have been provided with, this condition has been fulfilled."

It is interesting that in both her statement and inquest evidence, Steiner has qualified her account with "the documents I have been provided with" – as though Steiner is aware there may be other documents she might not have been provided with.

---

[a] This was denied by the French authorities – Massoni, Monteil and the funeral directors, Plumet and Jauze – see earlier. British consul-general, Moss, agreed that he spoke to Monceau, but Moss' statement evidence reveals he didn't give authorisation – see earlier.

It may be significant that we have not been told precisely which documents Steiner had been given.[a] Steiner may have only had Monceau's statement of what occurred.[b] We already know that Moss' account differs considerably from that – see earlier.

The legal reality is that even if Monceau had told the truth about what he told Moss – and I suggest he hasn't (see earlier) – there would have still been no written document to be presented to the Prefect's representative outlining the embalming procedure.[c] So the second requirement still would not have been fulfilled anyway – contrary to Steiner's statement and inquest accounts.

So again, I suggest, despite Steiner's evidence, point 2 has not been fulfilled.

3) Medical Certificate.

Steiner's statement: "This, again, was done in this case, Dr Lecomte concluding that the death was not suspicious".

At the inquest the evidence – between Hough and Steiner – was quite different. This time there is no mention to the jury that Lecomte's examination was to determine the "death was not suspicious". Hough mentions the "external examination" in passing, but then proceeds to show a pre-printed death certificate[d], signed by Riou, stating (in French) that Diana's death "did not give rise to any issues of a forensic legal nature". In other words, it was not suspicious.

It is very significant that in doing this, Hough and Steiner failed to mention Riou's clear evidence to Paget – see Chapter 1 – that "he had completed" Form JM/12 and "would probably have ticked 'OUI' [YES] box for 'Obstacle Medico-Legal'". They also neglected to include in their evidence that the completed Form JM/12 has since gone missing and has never resurfaced.

As suggested in an earlier footnote, it is very possible that the death certificate shown to the jury was completed after the conclusion of Lecomte's autopsy of Princess Diana.[ea] There is certainly no evidence to suggest that this form played a role in the events.

---

[a] If Steiner had the embalming statement, presumably she would have said. The general evidence is that it does not exist, and never did.
[b] As was pointed out at the conclusion of Monceau's statement – see earlier – Paget had no embalming documentation at all. There has never been any evidence to suggest that they obtained any documents subsequent to that.
[c] The law is that the three items being discussed are presented to the Prefect's representative (in lieu of the mayor or Prefect) for his/her authorisation.
[d] See inquest evidence: INQ0002108. It has also been reproduced in Part 2, Figure 19.
[e] See Chapter 1.

Coujard's evidence was: "A Judicial Police officer brought me the reports from Professor Lecomte.... Having viewed these documents I issued the burial certificates."[b] Embalming could not occur without a burial certificate.[c]

Hough introduced a document that was not part of the critical process that occurred leading up to the embalming. Steiner fell quickly into line, accepting this document as part of the authorisation to embalm and ignoring her statement evidence that the authorisation was predicated on the Lecomte examination.[d]

So, yes, in this case the medical certificate was produced by Lecomte[e] – that's not, though, what the jury heard.

Point 3 was fulfilled.

4) and 5) Visit to Prefect's representative and subsequent authorisation.

In Steiner's statement: "The authorisation to embalm was given here by the Préfet's representative".

At the inquest: Steiner confirmed to Hough that Monteil's conversation with Monceau "was adequate authorisation on behalf of the Mayor or the Prefect".

---

[a] In support of this, Steiner has stated: "The issue of the medical certificate ... concluding that after examination of the body there are no suspicious circumstances necessitating further investigation of a forensic nature. I note ... that this procedure was carried out by Doctor Lecomte and, subsequently, Dr Riou."

[b] See Chapter 1. This was confirmed at the inquest: Burnett: "Having received the results of the [Lecomte] examination, did you produce a certificate releasing the bodies of Mr Al Fayed and the Princess of Wales for burial?" Coujard: "Yes, it meant that actually there were not any barriers to their burial.": 20 Nov 07:15.23.

[c] Maud Coujard: "That [burial] certificate is obviously issued before any embalming procedure starts.... What is sure is that [embalming] cannot start before that [burial] certificate is issued.": 20 Nov 07:45.2.

[d] In the process, the closest the jury ever got to hearing that the Lecomte examination could have been called for to allay concerns of a suspicious death was a generalised comment from Eva Steiner, later in her cross-examination: "According to article 74 [Code of Criminal Procedure] when a sudden death has occurred, the Public Prosecutor, with the assistance of the police officer, may go to the scene of the death and take all measures which are required, which includes a report by a medical doctor to check whether or not the death is suspicious, to determine the cause of the death. But this is not – at the first stage, it is not a post mortem, at this stage. It can be a post mortem if there is strong suspicion that the death is caused by another thing than an accident, in case of a car crash, but in this case I reckon there have not been such a procedure." Just in case any of the jury might have thought this could have anything to do with what actually happened in Diana's case, Hough quickly chipped in with the official version of what occurred: "Well, in this case, what happened....": 21 Nov 07: 78.4.

[e] Just three hours later this same pathologist, Dominique Lecomte, would be in control of the fraudulently conducted autopsy of the driver, Henri Paul – see Part 3.

What the jury didn't hear was Monteil's statement evidence: "I do not have any recollection of a conversation with Monsieur Monceau, the embalmer".

There are 3 points:

a) Monteil has denied this conversation ever took place

b) it is common sense that Monteil would not be standing around the hospital, when she was in charge of the Brigade Criminelle investigation

c) there is an accumulation of evidence that Jean Monceau has lied about the events of that day.

I suggest that it would seem most unlikely that this conversation between Monceau and Monteil ever actually took place.[a]

So, no, the evidence is that the Prefect representative's authorisation was not given. Points 4 and 5 were not fulfilled.

6) Presentation to police.

Even though Steiner is an expert on French law, she neglected to mention – in her statement or at the inquest – that it was a requirement for the authorisation to be shown to the police present.

It is obvious that point 6 was not fulfilled because there never was any written authorisation – point 5 – as required by the law.

The above analysis shows that out of 6 steps – all of which were required for a legal embalming to take place – only one was actually fulfilled. 1 out of 6.

In other words, the embalming of Princess Diana was carried out illegally under French law.

How is it then that the inquest's expert in French law, Eva Steiner, was able to tell the inquest that the embalming was legal?

The short answer is: she didn't.[b]

There are several points:

1) At the inquest, Steiner never actually said the embalming was legal – see discussion above regarding Baker's summation

2) Steiner qualified her comments – at the inquest she said: "reading the documents I have been provided with" regarding the embalming statement

3) In answers Steiner diverted attention away from the main issue. When she was asked whether Moss' authorisation would have been valid, Steiner said: "Everything to do with private matters such as death, births, adoption,

---

[a] This issue has also been addressed earlier.

[b] In contrast, in Steiner's statement she indicated the embalming was legal – "At this stage the authorisation to embalm could legally proceed" – but the jury did not hear that.

are dealt with the Consulate [Moss]. I mean, the Ambassador [Jay] has nothing to do with that."

The reality is that issue was nothing to do with Moss v Jay. The issue was whether consul-general Moss, as the British representative in Paris – it could just as easily have been ambassador Jay – had the right to authorise the embalming, on behalf of Diana or her family.

4) It has already been shown that Steiner was prepared to lie to the jury[a] – see earlier. As shown above, Monceau failed to attain 5 out of 6 requirements for legality. When Steiner's evidence is closely analysed it can be seen that the jury was misled, and she was an active participant in achieving that. For example, Steiner, a legal expert, must have been aware that documents would have been required for a legal authorisation – yet there is no documentation for four of the steps. It would have been impossible for the Prefect's representative – allegedly, Monteil – to have legally authorised this embalming without seeing the form completed by a representative of the family.[b] Steiner must have realised that, yet the transcript shows her leaving the jury with the impression that what occurred was okay.

Effectively, by the time Baker in his Summing Up had stated that "Steiner's view [was] everything was done to comply with French law", the jury had been completely misled – between the combined efforts of Baker, Hough and Steiner.

The inquest employed a French legal expert, Eva Steiner, and the jury were told that she had prepared "independent reports on French legal matters for the purposes of ... these inquests[c]".[d]

When it comes to the topic of embalming[e], and you scrutinise what actually occurred on 31 August 1997, then compare that to what was told to the inquest – only one out of 13 witnesses were cross-examined[f], and that was Jean Monceau, a compulsive liar. Add Eva Steiner to the mix[g] – a comprehensively illegal embalming is made to appear legal – and one can see

---

[a] Regarding Diana's status.

[b] Monceau's earlier evidence was that he acquired this form from Plumet and Jauze, but they have both denied that they even met Monceau on the day, and the general evidence shows that they were not at the hospital until after the embalming was finished – see earlier.

[c] Technically there were two inquests – one for Diana, one for Dodi – but practically it was conducted as a single inquest.

[d] 21 Nov 07: 64.25

[e] Embalming was the main issue addressed by Eva Steiner.

[f] See earlier table.

[g] Part 3 shows that the evidence regarding Henri Paul's autopsies was scrutinised by several experts. This did not occur with the evidence of the embalming of the princess – there was just the one "independent" expert, Eva Steiner. There does not appear to have been any peer-based scrutiny of her evidence.

that what was shown to the jury was smoke and mirrors: they never heard what really occurred on the day and they had a judge summing up to them that it was all within the law.

Nothing could have been further from the truth.

In her inquest evidence Steiner brought up the issue of "whether or not [Diana] was considered as a private or a public citizen". The embalming evidence shows that in death, Princess Diana was treated far worse than a private citizen – a private citizen would have been treated with a legal embalming – six out of six.

Diana, Princess of Wales was accorded one out of six – and even the "one" was a medical statement from a dodgy practitioner.[a]

Why was there an illegal embalming on the body of Princess Diana?

Although much of what follows is evidence-based, it also includes speculation about what may have occurred.

Huguette Amarger, who carried out the embalming, was asked: "Were you given any instructions in writing?" She answered: "No, but there was a panic on."

The general evidence – this was discussed earlier – is that the embalming was conducted in a rush. Earlier evidence also showed that it was known before 9 a.m. that an embalming had to be carried out – at the request of the "British".

Amarger arrived at the hospital before 11 a.m., but Monceau stated that he believed Charles wasn't coming until 5 p.m. Monceau therefore had a window of approximately 6 hours to carry out the embalming.

Yet, it appears that Monceau rushed Amarger, to the point where she went ahead with the embalming even though there was no documentation to support it. In other words, the embalming was illegal – not authorised (see earlier) – but it may be that Amarger agreed to do it anyway, because of a "panic" created by Monceau.

There is even a possibility that Amarger may have objected to conducting an embalming without any documentation to authorise it. Monceau may have overridden objections by telling Amarger that Charles was coming in the "afternoon"[b], instead of what he knew – that Charles wasn't coming until 5 p.m.[c]

As suggested earlier, I believe Monceau was instructed before 9 a.m. to have the embalming carried out. But it is possible he had to wait on

---

[a] Professor Dominique Lecomte – see Part 3.
[b] See Amarger's earlier evidence.
[c] Charles actually arrived at 5.40 p.m. – see later.

confirmation of results from samples of urine and blood taken during Lecomte's earlier autopsy of Princess Diana.[a]

An analysis of the conduct of the embalming – as done earlier in this chapter – shows that the only effective and thorough action in this quick embalming was the removal of urine from the bladder.[b] It may be that the results from the Lecomte autopsy sample tests showed a positive on pregnancy for urine, but a negative in the blood[c] – as Pavie indicated earlier, the blood may no longer have been Diana's.

The manner in which the embalming was conducted – and the subsequent interview of Amarger (see earlier) – indicate that the extraction of the urine was certainly the main focus of it.

It has long been suspected by believers in the conspiracy, that the primary purpose of the embalming was to remove the ability for pregnancy to be checked through later samples.[d]

I suggest that the balance of the evidence supports this, but I also stress that there is no "smoking gun" or direct evidence that points to it. My conclusion is wholly based on a considerable amount of circumstantial evidence, not least of which is the actions taken at the hospital on the day, the lack of documentation and the subsequent cover-up of information in the police investigations and coroner's inquest.

All of this evidence needs to be viewed in the light of the chapter on Pregnancy in Part 2 and also the Pregnancy chapter that appears later in Part 5.

Many have said that it was irrelevant whether Diana was pregnant – all that was needed as a motive was a perception that she could have been, or could become pregnant to Dodi. I agree with that. Nevertheless, I believe that if it was discovered, through testing conducted at La Pitié Salpêtrière Hospital on 31 August 1997, that Diana actually was pregnant, then that would have created a situation where authorities could have been determined to remove that evidence.

I suggest that British authorities may have become aware that Diana was pregnant prior to 5 a.m.[e] on 31 August 1997 and I further suggest that this information could have led them to order the embalming of Diana, Princess of Wales to take place later that day.

---

[a] I suggest that if the embalming had been avoidable, it wouldn't have been conducted – even at 11 a.m. Diana could have been transferred to the much cooler hospital morgue.

[b] This will be confirmed in the later UK Post-Mortems chapter.

[c] The evidence regarding pregnancy is assessed in the Part 5 Pregnancy chapter.

[d] Knepil – see Part 2 – gave evidence that embalming fluid in urine can create a false test result. I suggest that this would not have been known in 1997, and it was considered safer by the perpetrators to remove the urine altogether.

[e] UK time.

I believe Monceau received that order and was told the embalming didn't need to be authorised and that everything would later be "regularised" – which it wasn't – and that Monceau would be well paid for his services and would be provided with future immunity from prosecution for his role in the events that took place.

Burial Certificate

The general evidence – see earlier – shows that there was a sequence of events:
- Riou completed the JM/12 death certificate, ticking YES for Medico-Legal problem
- Bestard and Coujard ordered an autopsy on both Diana and Dodi
- Lecomte conducted the autopsies and found the death of Diana was due to a torn pulmonary vein
- Coujard received the Lecomte reports
- Coujard issued burial certificates
- Monceau and Amarger carry out the embalming of Princess Diana.

Maud Coujard, Deputy Public Prosecutor, Paris: 20 Nov 07: 44.24:
Mansfield: Q. Do you know whether you signed the burial certificate before the embalming had taken place or after the embalming or don't you know?
A. Well, that certificate is obviously issued before any embalming procedure starts, but anyway, I do not remember any kind of embalming procedure being performed that night, before the morning. But anyway, what is sure is that it cannot start before that certificate is issued.

Maud Coujard: 15 Nov 06 Statement: **Jury Didn't Hear**:
"Did you make any decisions concerning the embalming that was performed on the Princess of Wales? ....
"Answer: No. I was not consulted on this matter. I do not know if I heard talk of embalming that would be conducted on the body of the Princess of Wales before or after signing the burial certificate. What I can say, is that, had I deemed it necessary for the investigation, that the body remain intact, I would have made mention of this on the burial certificate, forbidding all post mortem treatment or cremation. I had no reason to make such restrictions, as I have already indicated to you." [123]

Martine Monteil, Head of Brigade Criminelle: 15 Nov 06 Statement: **Jury Didn't Hear**:

"[Question:] We are grateful for your e-mail response of 19 July 2005.[a] Can you confirm that you authorised the embalming and what authority you were acting on?

"[Answer:] I should point out that in road traffic accidents, it is not usual to carry out a post mortem on the passengers because in most cases it is not relevant to the investigation. In the event, it was the Public Prosecutor's Department that decided to examine the bodies of both the Princess of Wales and of Dodi Al Fayed. It was the Public Prosecutor's Department, acting on the basis of an expedited police investigation [*flagrance*] at that time who, in the light of the results, decided to issue the burial certificates without any restrictions.

"If my memory is correct, it was the British Consul, Mr Moss, who made known the wish for embalming to be carried out on the body of the Princess of Wales. From the moment that the Public Prosecutor's Department had signed the burial certificate without restrictions, there was no reason to object. I am not sure, but I think that embalming may be necessary anyway when a body has to be repatriated to another country.[b]

"It was not the French authorities that called in the Funeral Service and an embalmer.

"Reply to question: I do not have any recollection of a conversation with Monsieur Monceau, the embalmer....

"Reply to question: As a general rule, once the burial certificate has been signed, there is no reason for the investigators to be informed about the type of funeral or of the embalming to be carried out. They do not usually therefore have any contacts with those organisations or with any embalmers that might be involved." [124]

Comment: There are several points regarding Monteil's account, which was not heard by the jury.

1) Monteil was asked to confirm authorising the embalming – in the July 2005 email she had indirectly answered, quoting Deguisne (see earlier) – but she failed again to directly answer.

This time Monteil went back to the decision to do the post-mortem, correctly pinning this onto the "Public Prosecutor's Department".

Why though, in Monteil's mind, is there a connection between the post mortem and the embalming?

Earlier in this book it has been suggested that the way the embalming was carried out could have been tied to the result of tests conducted from post-mortem samples.

---

[a] This is the email where Monteil quoted Deguisne saying Monteil had authorised the embalming – see earlier.

[b] This issue is dealt with in a later section of this chapter.

2) Monteil then states: "It was the Public Prosecutor's Department, acting on the basis of an expedited police investigation [*flagrance*] at that time who, in the light of the results, decided to issue the burial certificates without any restrictions."

The key words here appear to be: "expedited police investigation".

Monteil's testimony raises the automatic question: If there hadn't been an "expedited police investigation", would the burial certificates not have been issued "without any restrictions"?

And what does Monteil mean by "expedited police investigation" – the French investigation into the crash went on for two years?

The burial certificates were issued at around 8.30 a.m. – see earlier timeline of events. Were the burial certificates expedited because it was known Charles would be coming over that day?

Were the burial certificates issued "without any restrictions" because the British had already requested an embalming? It is known from Amarger's earlier evidence that before 9 a.m. plans were in place for an embalming to be carried out.

3) Monteil appears definite that the French didn't order the embalming – she concludes her answer to the authorisation question: "It was not the French authorities that called in the Funeral Service and an embalmer."

This supports Amarger's evidence – also not heard by the jury – that the British ordered the embalming.

Monteil says "if my memory is correct, it was ... Moss". The evidence in this chapter has shown that was not the case – the embalming decision was made well before Moss was informed of it at around noon.

Both Monteil and Coujard emphasise the importance of the burial certificate with regard to embalming:

- Monteil: "from the moment that the Public Prosecutor's Department had signed the burial certificate without restrictions, there was no reason to object" to embalming
- Coujard: "what is sure is that [embalming] cannot start before that certificate is issued".

In this light, Coujard said: "I do not know if I heard talk of embalming that would be conducted on the body of the Princess of Wales before or after signing the burial certificate." This indicates that Coujard did hear "talk of embalming" but doesn't know if that was "before or after signing the burial certificate".

The timing – that Amarger was already phoned "about 9 a.m." – indicates that it was already known by the authorities well before that time that an embalming would be conducted.

239

Since the burial certificate was issued at around 8.30 a.m., I suggest that Coujard "heard talk of embalming" before she issued the burial certificates.

Then, at the inquest – just one year after providing her Paget statement, Maud Coujard changed her evidence.

Maud Coujard: 20 Nov 07: 17.7:

Burnett: Q. Were you aware on 31st August 1997 that the body of the Princess of Wales had undergone a process of embalming?

A. I do not remember whether I was made aware of that that particular day. Maybe that was later on. I have no memory of being made aware of that particular piece of information at any particular moment.

At 45.8: Mansfield: Q. Your recollection, is this right, is that you don't recall being told anything about embalming? Is that the position?

A. I do not remember having been told about it during the night or during the day on 31st August 1997.

Comment: In November 2006, in Coujard's statement, the issue was whether she heard about the embalming "before or after signing the burial certificate". The implication from that is that Coujard accepted that she did hear about it on the 31 August 1997.

At the inquest, in November 2007, Coujard has completely changed her account – now she says she does "not remember having been told about" the embalming on 31 August 1997.

Why has Maud Coujard changed her evidence?

Coujard appears to have tried to distance herself from early knowledge of the embalming, possibly because, as a member of the Public Prosecutor's Department, she must know that it was carried out illegally – see earlier.

As has been shown above, where embalming occurs there is a connection with the burial certificate – the embalming cannot take place without the burial certificate.

It was Maud Coujard who signed the burial certificate, ahead of the embalming.

Why was the burial certificate of Princess Diana not shown to the inquest jury who were investigating her death?

Notification of Family

Prof Dominique Lecomte, Pathologist and Head of IML, Paris: 9 Mar 05 Statement: **Jury Didn't Hear**:

"Question: Who took the decision as to the embalming of Lady Diana's body?

Answer: The procedure is that the family makes the request for that to the Magistrate, who agrees or does not. In this case, I do not know what was done."[125]

Gérard Jauze, PFG Branch Director, Paris: 21 Mar 06 Statement: **Jury Didn't Hear**:

"It would have been up to the family to decide if they wanted the body embalmed, and PFG's job[a] to get the necessary authorisations."[126]

Comment: The family can only "decide", if they are notified ahead of time.

   Was there any notification to Princess Diana's family ahead of the embalming?

Michael Gibbins, Diana's Private Secretary: 21 Nov 07: 38.15:

Mansfield: Q. Were you ever asked to make contact with the Princess's family to see whether they were agreeable to any form of invasive treatment that may be required?

A. I was not asked to, but I felt that it would have been the right thing to do, if it were possible.

Q. Yes. So as far as you recollect, therefore, you were never asked to make any enquiries along those lines?

A. I do not recollect being asked.

Michael Gibbins: 1 Sep 04 Statement: **Jury Didn't Hear**:

"I have never had any dealings with the embalming of a body. It would not have been my place to deal with this. A lot of the decisions that Colin Tebbutt was asking me to make needed to be made by the relatives, but I had no one to call. I couldn't ring His Royal Highness Prince Charles or the Princess of Wales' mother. I was in London, what could I do, but to say to Colin to do what he thought was best in the circumstances....

"Throughout that day I do not recall receiving directions from either the Foreign Office or our embassy in Paris." [127]

Anthony Mather, Asst Comptroller, Lord Chamberlain's Office: 22 Nov 07: 87.12:

Hough: Q. Did you ... liaise with the Princess of Wales' private secretary, Mr Gibbins, from whom we have heard?

A. I remember not, but I am sure – the telephone did not stop, so I am sure "yes" is the answer.

René Deguisne: 9 May 05 Statement: **Jury Didn't Hear**:

"Question: Do you know whether the Princess of Wales's family were aware of the decisions taken as to the preservation treatment of Lady Diana's body?

Answer: I do not, but I imagine Mr Moss was in touch with Prince Charles.

Question: Do you know whether Mr Moss signed a document by which he had the power to act, to take decisions on behalf of the family of the deceased?

Answer: No, I do not."[128]

---

[a] As shown earlier BJL was financially connected to PFG at the time. On the day, it was the job of BJL – Monceau – to secure the required authorisations. This is addressed earlier.

Lucia Flecha de Lima, Friend of Diana and Wife of Brazilian Ambassador, USA: 1 Sep 04 Statement: **Jury Didn't Hear**:
"When I heard about the accident I prepared to go to Paris.... I ... called Kensington Palace to get hold of Paul Burrell. He was not there but they got a message to him. When Michael Gibbins phoned me from Kensington Palace and told me Princess Diana was dead, I got on a plane to London."[129]
Comment: When Paget interviewed René Deguisne, they referred to a document which, had it been properly completed, could have given Moss "the power to act, to take decisions on behalf of [Diana's] family".

The problem is that this document has never been seen and the general evidence shows that contact was not made with Princess Diana's family – in other words, this document does not exist and never has.

Michael Gibbins' evidence is significant regarding Princess Diana's family's knowledge of events.

There are two main points:

1) Gibbins stated that he "was not asked to" contact Diana's family about the embalming. The question is: Why did he have to wait to be asked? Gibbins was not asked that.

2) Gibbins admitted "that it would have been the right thing to do if it were possible".

Gibbins stated – in evidence not heard by the jury – "A lot of the decisions that Colin Tebbutt was asking me to make needed to be made by the relatives, but I had no one to call. I couldn't ring His Royal Highness Prince Charles or the Princess of Wales' mother. I was in London, what could I do?"

This evidence raises important questions:

Why hasn't Gibbins – who after all, was Princess Diana's private secretary – got contact numbers for any of the following:

a) Sarah McCorquodale or Jane Fellowes – Diana's sisters

b) Frances Shand-Kydd – Diana's mother

c) Raine Spencer – Diana's step-mother

d) Earl Spencer – Diana's brother

e) Prince Charles, who was the father of his boss' children

f) Princes William or Harry – his boss' own sons

g) Balmoral, which is where Charles, William and Harry were holidaying?

When Gibbins testified to Paget that he couldn't remember "if the word 'embalming' was ever used", he stated that the reason was: "I had so many calls."[130]

The question then is: Who were all these calls to or from? Gibbins wants us to believe that none of them were to or from any of Diana's family – "I had no one to call".

Lucia's evidence – not heard by the jury – reveals that even though Gibbins failed to call immediate family members living in the UK, he managed to phone her in the USA.

Why is this?

Tebbutt gave the following evidence at the inquest: "Mr Moss gave me a room to set up three lines: <u>one to Balmoral</u>, one to Mr Gibbins and a general line for me".

How is it that Tebbutt was able to have a dedicated line to Balmoral from the Paris hospital, yet Gibbins – "I couldn't ring ... Charles" – is unable to call Balmoral from the comfort of his own office in London?

It is clear that the people who should have been making the embalming decision – particularly Diana's mother, step-mother, sisters or brother – were never consulted on the day.

But not only that, Gibbins appears to have given evidence that helps to cover-up the real reason why these people were not contacted.[a] Gibbins has stated that he was <u>not able to</u> contact people that common sense alone tells us he would have been able to contact. Gibbins' evidence appears to be that he never even tried to make contact with any of the above listed people or locations.

Why is this?

Gibbins should have been asked, but he never was.

There is a possibility that Gibbins was warned early in the day not to make contact with Princess Diana's family – that all of that would be handled by Buckingham Palace, Balmoral, the British Embassy or the British Government. Gibbins appears to have provided cover for the Establishment in his evidence on this subject.[b]

Later evidence will show that there must have been early contact between members of Diana's family and Balmoral in order to arrange Charles' – accompanied by Diana's sisters – visit to Paris to pick up the body. This issue is addressed later.

There is evidence of an early call from Raine Spencer to Keith Moss – see below.

Stephen Donnelly, British Vice Consul, Paris: 22 Sep 05 Statement read out 17 Dec 07: 118.2:

---

[a] I suggest that the reason is because the decision to embalm had already been made earlier in the day by other people.

[b] It appears to not be a coincidence that three months later Michael Gibbins was awarded an LVO – Royal Victorian Order, Lieutenant – in the New Year's Honours List announced 31 December 1997. Source: Life Peers to Order of the Companion of Honour, BBC News, 31 December 1997, p4.

"I have been working as British Vice-Consul since 1987.... I ... deal with assisting the families of the bereaved and this was my function in August of 1997.... For those [British nationals in] hospital, the first responsibility is tracing and informing the next of kin. This is exactly the same for hospital cases as well as deaths. For a death, this is done in conjunction with the Foreign and Commonwealth Office and the British police. Once traced, we would guide the families to the proper authorities in France to arrange the repatriation of the body to the United Kingdom."

Keith Moss, British Consul General, Paris: 22 Nov 07: 6.23:

Hough: Q. Did consular work extend to helping those concerned when a British citizen died in France?

A. Yes.

Q. What would the Consul normally do when that occurred?

A. The role of the Consulate is first of all to ensure that the family and next of kin are informed....

At 25.21: Q. After M Monceau had provided you with this information [about the embalming procedure] and his reasons, what did you respond about what he should do?

A. I have given a great deal of thought to this.... It was very disparate, you had people all over the place, family in various locations. It was extremely difficult to be precise about who was going to take these sorts of decisions.[a]

At 55.3: Mansfield: Q. What I am going to ask you is obviously about consent and authority. Obviously you appreciate it was invasive, the treatment that [Monceau] was doing?

A. I must have done. As I say, I cannot recall the precise details.

Q. You make it very clear in your statement that one of your concerns was in fact to ensure that the wishes of the family are taken into account; "next of kin" in fact was how you put it.

A. Yes. Sorry, where in my statement does that sit? Can you refer me?

Q. It is page 9 at the bottom. I will just read the sentence ...: "As a consular officer, my experience of dealing with the death of British nationals overseas was primarily to ensure that the wishes of the next of kin were taken fully into account." Now, of course it may be done in a variety of ways, but in this particular instance, whatever your level of understanding was of what was happening, what contact was had about this treatment with the next of kin?

A. Well, I think I referred to this in an earlier answer to a previous question. There must have been communications, telephone calls with people in the UK, but I cannot – and I have tried to trawl my memory a great deal because I know these are important issues, but I cannot be precise about what form those communications took or with whom they took place.

Q. So do we have – and again, I am really not going to pursue it with you if

---

[a] The full text of this part of Moss' testimony has been shown earlier.

you cannot give an answer – you don't know what next of kin gave consent and you don't know actually who authorised all of this, is that right?

A. To the question of whether the Princess of Wales' –

Q. Next of kin?

A. No, the Princess of Wales' body should be prepared for viewing?

Q. Yes. Sorry.

A. Well, as I say, I cannot – I have tried a lot to think about this, to help, to be more precise, but I really cannot remember the precise details of those conversations, other than that, at a point, it was recognised and generally agreed that something had to be done. We could not leave her as she was because of the condition in which her body –

Q. That is totally appreciated. It is the further question. Appreciating a situation in which you were placed, is the answer that you really cannot help as to which next of kin was contacted about this or who actually authorised it, at the end of the day, from the British end?

A. From the UK end, no, I cannot remember that.

Q. All right. Did you ever know?

A. No, I do not.[a]

Comment: There are just two options:

1) There were "conversations" regarding authorisation "with people in the UK"

2) There were no "conversations" regarding authorisation "with people in the UK".

Moss has stated under oath, answering a question regarding next of kin: "there must have been communications, telephone calls with people in the UK", then: "I cannot be precise about ... with whom they took place". Moss explains: "I have tried to trawl my memory a great deal".

Then later under Mansfield's continued cross-examination: Mansfield: "Did you ever know ... which next of kin was contacted about this or who actually authorised it ... from the British end?" Moss: "No, I do not."

Moss has given two conflicting positions. Take your pick:

1) "there must have been" contact "with people in the UK" and I am trawling my memory about who it was that was contacted

2) I have never known who it was that was contacted or "who actually authorised it".

The first position is that contacts were made, but Moss just can't remember with whom. The second position is that Moss has never known who was contacted.

Which is true?

---

[a] After this Mansfield moved straight on to a new topic.

245

Earlier evidence has revealed that Moss made no references in his statement to seeking authorisation from anyone.[a] Further to that, earlier evidence also revealed that the decision to embalm had been made by the "British" much earlier in the day.

This indicates that on the day, practically speaking, the decision to embalm was not in Moss' hands, and it may well be that Moss already had instructions to that effect prior to his conversation with Monceau.

Keith Moss, British Consul General, Paris: 22 Nov 07: 15.19:

Hough: Q. At what time of the morning were you informed that the Princess had died?

A. That would have been – I think it was around about 4 o'clock.

....Q. Did you then pass on that information?

A. Yes, we did.

Q. To whom?

A. The kind of contacts I have mentioned previously, members of the [Royal] Household, the Foreign Office and so on.

Q. Did you also pass the information to the Princess's own family?

A. I do not recall, but I may have done. I certainly don't recall speaking to any of them individually other than – I have made a note. If I may refer to my statement?

Coroner: Yes, of course.

Q. It is page 6, I think, around the middle of page 6.

A. Countess Spencer, who I think at the time was the Princess of Wales' stepmother – is that correct? Because she had contacted me. She got my mobile phone number from somewhere and contacted me direct while the Princess was still alive to find out what was going on. So I phoned her back once we had received this information of her death.

Keith Moss: 22 Oct 04 Statement: **Jury Didn't Hear**:

"At around 0400hrs [4.00 a.m.] ... we were again joined up by the doctor who had headed up the medical team. He informed us that they had ... to switch off her life support system at 0345hrs.

"Following this briefing we informed; Balmoral, number 10 Downing Street, the Elysée Palace, the FCO ... [and] Countess Spencer, who was in Venice at the time.

"Following consultation with the above parties, it was agreed to convene a press conference."[131]

Comment: There are two separate issues regarding family notification: first, the death of Diana around 4 a.m., and second, the embalming of Diana later in the day.

The above evidence raises several points:

---

[a] See section on Monceau-Moss conversation. Moss' evidence changed at the inquest.

1) Moss has stated at the inquest that after the death of a British citizen in France, "the role of the Consulate is first of all to ensure that the family and next of kin are informed".

2) When Moss is initially asked by Hough, who he notified about the death, Moss cannot even remember if any family were told – "I do not recall".

3) In Moss' statement he lists the apparent order of notification[a] after the death of Diana:

    a) Balmoral – Queen, Charles[b], William, Harry[c]

    b) Downing St – Prime Minister Tony Blair

    c) Elysée Palace – French Government

    d) FCO – Foreign & Commonwealth Office, British Government

    e) Countess Spencer – Raine Spencer, Diana's stepmother.[d]

There is no mention of making any contact with Diana's immediate adult family in the UK – her mother, Frances Shand-Kydd; her sisters, Sarah and Jane.[e]

Some may argue that it was not Moss', or the consulate's, job to do that – that would be done by the FCO. But that is not Moss' evidence – Moss himself stated: "the role of the Consulate is first of all to ensure that the family and next of kin are informed".

Except, apparently, in the case of Princess Diana.

Raine Spencer was informed by Moss, but at the inquest it became apparent that this only occurred because Raine had called Moss while Diana

---

[a] Even if this wasn't the actual original order of notification, it is the order in which it came to Moss' mind – either by recall or from his notes – when he completed his statement.

[b] Neither the Queen nor Charles was Diana's family – this is discussed later.

[c] At the time of the crash William was 15 and Harry was 12. They were both minors and not in a position to be involved in important decisions regarding repatriation and embalming. At the inquest when the issue of family notification of the death is brought up, Moss refers to his statement – notably he doesn't see "Balmoral" as notification of family, but only "Countess Spencer". This indicates that calling Balmoral may not have been about William and Harry, but instead primarily to notify the Monarch, and possibly Charles. When the issue of notification was first brought up by Hough at the inquest, Moss lists off "members of the household, the Foreign Office and so on". Moss is presumably referring to the royal household. William and Harry do not appear to figure in Moss' thinking at all.

[d] Although Moss has said family notification comes "first", it is notable that Raine appears last on Moss' statement list.

[e] Diana's brother, Charles – Earl Spencer – was in South Africa at the time of the crash.

was still alive.[a] Moss explicitly says that: "because she had contacted me – she got my mobile phone number from somewhere".

Moss comes across almost as though he is apologising – "OK, I know I shouldn't have notified her, but she had already phoned me, so I had to – I don't know how she got my number."

Why? Why is it that when Princess Diana dies the family notification system doesn't apply?

Does the communication improve when it comes to the decision to embalm?

It has already been shown earlier that an embalming conducted without the approval of the family – or the family's nominated representative – would be illegal. This then would require the notification of at least one family member, prior to the commencement of any embalming procedure.

We already now know that Moss had the phone number for Raine Spencer – not Diana's closest blood relative, but certainly a person who was a close family member of Diana's prior to her death.[b] Raine may well have known how to make contact with other family members, if Moss did not have that information.[c]

Did Moss call Raine to seek approval for the embalming?

Less than 1½ hours after Moss had been reminded that he had called Raine after Diana's death, Moss told the inquest: "I have tried to trawl my memory a great deal ... but I cannot be precise[d] about ... with whom [communications] took place."

I suggest that if Moss had phoned Raine about the embalming the "trawl" of his memory would have revealed that, given the earlier reference to calling Raine during his cross-examination.

Moss appears to become noticeably uncomfortable when Mansfield pursues the issue of family notification of the embalming – he tries to change the subject to whether it needed to be done: "something had to be done – we could not leave her as she was".

Moss clearly had the means to contact the next of kin – he had Raine's phone number – but just as clearly, Moss never dialled that number prior to the embalming.

Why wouldn't he phone Raine?

---

[a] Raine was cross-examined at the inquest – on 12 December 2007, about 3 weeks after Moss – but was not asked about this. She should have been.

[b] See Part 2.

[c] In this light, as indicated earlier, Gibbins – Diana's private secretary, based at Kensington Palace – would have had contact details for Diana's family. I suggest this is also common sense.

[d] Moss says he can't be "precise", but he also is unable to even give general evidence regarding this.

I suggest it is because Moss knew that the embalming decision had already been made well ahead of time. Had Moss phoned to notify the family, he may have been acting against other instructions.

To bring family into a decision-making role would have been an additional complication that the British authorities did not want or need.

The evidence in this section appears to destroy any perception that Moss may have acted as the representative of Princess Diana's family. The only family contact that Moss appears to have had was with Raine, and there is certainly no evidence of the issue of representation or authorisation being discussed in those two conversations – only one of which occurred after the official time of death.

Patrick Launay described what normally occurs when a British citizen dies in France, unaccompanied by family.

Patrick Launay, PFG Repatriation Director: 21 Mar 06 Statement: **Jury Didn't Hear**:

"When there was a death [in France] and ... the family were not at the place of death, the Consulate would be informed by the [French] authorities and would contact the family in the UK. At that juncture, the family would contact a funeral director's, normally in England, and that firm in turn would contact their opposite numbers in France."[132]

Comment: Launay outlined several basic steps:
1) French authorities inform the British Consulate
2) Consulate contacts the family
3) Family contacts a UK funeral director
4) UK funeral director contacts a French funeral director.

Point 1 occurred – the British Embassy was notified by the Élysée Palace.[a]

Point 2 partially occurred – Raine was contacted but no other adult family.

Point 3 – there is no evidence of this occurring. Later evidence will show knowledge of the death of Diana by the president of Kenyons in London, before 5 a.m., but it is not officially known how he came by this. That person should have given evidence at the inquest, but that never occurred.

Point 4 occurred – later evidence shows the Kenyons president contacted Racine at around 5 a.m.

Was It Required By Law?

Was embalming legally required ahead of repatriation of Princess Diana's body to the UK?

Jean Monceau, BJL Director and Embalmer, Paris: 20 Nov 07: 78.16:

---

[a] This is covered in Part 5.

Burnett: Q. What was your understanding at the time about the requirements for embalming before a body might be repatriated to the United Kingdom?
A. Well, my feeling about what?
Q. Did you believe that in fact it was mandatory for there to be embalming before a body could be returned to the United Kingdom?
A. Well, the information that is available to the public in France, there is the Association Francaise d'Information Funeraire, AFIF – that is the French Association of Funeral Information – that has rules, among which it says that Great Britain is one of the countries for which it is recommendable to proceed to such treatments before repatriating the body.
Q. So that is your professional body then, is it, that recommends that?
A. No, they provide information for the attention of professionals working in the field of funerals.
At 81.2: Mansfield: Q. May I ask you first of all about the rules or your understanding of the rules from your association about repatriation?
A. Yes.
Q. Is the association indicating that it is a recommendation only or obligatory that bodies repatriated to the United Kingdom are embalmed?
A. Well, it publishes a list of countries that impose – that make it obligatory to proceed to preservation treatments before repatriation and Great Britain was in the list.
Q. If that is what the list is saying, that it is obligatory, can you explain why Dodi Al Fayed was not embalmed?
A. Well, I am not being heard to talk about Dodi Al Fayed. I have no relationship whatsoever with what happened to Dodi Al Fayed's body. I was at the Pitié Salpêtrière Hospital taking care of the Princess of Wales' body. I did not go or work at the Institute of Forensic Medicine where the body of Dodi Al Fayed and that of the driver were, so I am not at all concerned with that matter.
Q. All right. Have you discovered at any stage that the association's rules to which you refer are in fact merely guidelines and are not indicating an obligation? Have you ever discovered that?
A. Yes, it is true. Well, you asked me a question, I answer.
Q. I am very happy. Thank you. Could you let us know when it was that you discovered it was not obligatory? When did you discover that?
A. When Scotland Yard questioned me about the matter and I told them about the association, its rule, and then I consulted colleagues who told me that maybe it was not obligatory to proceed to embalming before repatriation to the UK. So that is when I discovered it.
Jean Monceau: 18 Oct 05 Statement: **Jury Didn't Hear**:
"You have asked me if it is mandatory to embalm a body before it is repatriated. Yes. Any body that leaves French soil has to have undergone embalming. This is stipulated by the French Public Hygiene Committee so

that germs are not taken to other countries.... Even if the body is repatriated in a lead lined coffin, the law requires embalming."[133]

Jean Monceau: 18 Oct 05 Statement: **Jury Didn't Hear**:

"I produce as Exhibit JM/11 a copy of a document from the French Association of Funeral Information (AFIF).... This document shows that in France we are advised that the United Kingdom requires embalming for repatriation. This was also the case in 1997."[134]

Jean Monceau: 19 Oct 05[a] Email to Easton: **Jury Didn't Hear**:[b]

"Having made enquiries with the Funeral Association (AFIF), the document listing countries that require "**compulsory**" embalming prior to repatriation (this is the document on which I had based my statement and my answers to your questions), **does not imply a notion that this is compulsory !!! ???** This, according to them, implies that countries that normally use embalming (this is the case in the UK), expect that the country of departure ensures embalming for the good of public hygiene,

But there is absolutely no Law stating that embalming is compulsory."[135]

Huguette Amarger, BJL Embalmer: 8 Mar 05 Statement read out 22 Nov 07: 92.21:

"Question: What does the term 'treatment' mean in your profession?

"Answer: It is the fact of treating a dead body for the purposes of hygiene and presentation.... I must say that in order that a body can leave French territory, it is compulsory for embalming treatment to be applied."[c]

Gérard Jauze, PFG Branch Director, Paris: 21 Mar 06 Statement: **Jury Didn't Hear**:

"If the UK had required embalming, it would have been done; embalming was not obligatory. It would have been up to the family to decide if they wanted the body embalmed, and PFG's job to get the necessary authorisations."[136]

René Deguisne, BJL Assistant General Manager: 9 May 05 Statement: **Jury Didn't Hear**:

"Question: Are there any agreements between France and the United Kingdom for the [embalming] procedure to be followed when repatriating bodies to the United Kingdom?

Answer: Yes, there are recommendations; the United Kingdom authorities wish treatment to be carried out on bodies brought back to their country. Thus there are inter-professional agreements to put these recommendations

---

[a] This is the day following Monceau's statement made in London to Paget.

[b] Emphasis in **bold** is either by Monceau or Easton.

[c] Amarger later confirmed this opinion: "I repeat, my [embalming] work was compulsory for the body to be able to leave France": 22 Nov 07: 95.17.

into practice; these are quite simply conventions for the transporting of mortal remains."[a]

Dr Eva Steiner, Inquest & Paget Expert on French Law: 21 Nov 07: 77.5:
Hough: Q. M Monceau was asked yesterday about whether it was obligatory to embalm a body for it to be transported out of France. What I was asking you was: if a body is to be transported within the first 24 hours or in a sealed coffin, is it not obligatory to embalm?
A. No, it is not.

Martine Monteil, Head of Brigade Criminelle: 15 Nov 06 Statement: **Jury Didn't Hear**:
"I am not sure, but I think that embalming may be necessary anyway when a body has to be repatriated to another country."[137b]

Comment: As with almost every aspect of this case, the evidence is quite mixed. Even on a point where the legal situation should be quite clear – either embalming is required, or it is not – the evidence is clouded by testimony that appears, in some cases, to protect witnesses' – or lawyers' – positions.

Eva Steiner, the French legal expert, states that the embalming was not obligatory, or required.

But Jonathon Hough, the inquest lawyer – who referred back to Monceau's inquest evidence – has slipped qualifications into his question: "within the first 24 hours" and "in a sealed coffin". Of particular interest here is the reference to "24 hours".

There is no reference to these qualifications, introduced by Hough, during the earlier cross-examinations of Monceau by both Burnett and Mansfield. In the full email from Monceau to Easton in October 2005[c], which outlines the legal requirements, there is no reference to "24 hours" or any other time restriction.[de]

---

[a] Deguisne, who to this day still works for Hygeco, has indicated there are legal agreements in place to enforce "recommendations" for embalming. He failed to point out there was no legal requirement – it is in Deguisne's interests for BJL to have been seen to have done the right thing legally on the day. All the better if the embalming could be shown to be the fulfilment of an existing "convention" or "agreement".

[b] This evidence from Monteil is not mentioned in the Comment below, but is included here for completeness. Monteil gives a diffident opinion – "I am not sure, but I think". It may be that Monteil has mentioned this as a defence for what was actually an illegal embalming – see earlier. The general evidence will show that embalming was not required for repatriation.

[c] This can be viewed in *The Documents* book, pp421-4.

[d] There is a reference to the type of coffin.

[e] Had there been a 24 hour restriction, I suggest that Monceau would have mentioned it, because it would improve his position re the embalming – see below.

The point here is that Hough appears to have deliberately introduced a false qualification to the embalming requirements. If Hough was correct, then it provides a timing justification for the embalming – carry out the embalming on 31 August 1997, just in case repatriation doesn't actually occur until after the 24 hour limitation. In this case, a 24 hour window would have expired at 4.00 a.m.[a] on 1 September 1997. This would make it perfectly logical to carry out the embalming on August 31, thus enabling a possible repatriation in the morning of September 1.

Hough therefore has introduced to the jury a new plausible reason to embalm on August 31, except that the evidence – Monceau's cross-examination; Monceau's email[b] – indicates that it is based on a lie.

I suggest that if Steiner was providing true and full evidence – as one would expect from a legal expert – she should have clarified the true position, but this never occurred.

Monceau's evidence appears to reflect his normal testimony acrobatics:

- "any body that leaves French soil has to have undergone embalming" – statement
- "there is absolutely no law stating that embalming is compulsory" – email
- "Great Britain is one of the countries for which it is recommendable to proceed to [embalming] before repatriating" – inquest, to Burnett
- "a list of countries that impose – that make it obligatory to proceed to [embalming] before repatriation and Great Britain was in the list" – inquest, to Mansfield
- "maybe it was not obligatory to proceed to embalming before repatriation to the UK" – inquest, to Mansfield.

As stated above, embalming before repatriation to the UK is either obligatory or it is not obligatory. At the inquest, Monceau had two positions on this – a) it is "obligatory" and b) it is "not obligatory".

When the subject is initially introduced by Burnett, Monceau states that the AFIF says in "information that is available to the public" that for repatriation to the UK "it is recommendable to proceed to" embalming of the body. Apparently seeking confirmation of this, Burnett asks if the AFIF "recommends that". Monceau replies: "No, they provide information for the attention of professionals".

Burnett then moves on to a new subject.

If Monceau and Burnett were intending to confuse the jury, I suggest they have probably succeeded.

---

[a] 24 hours after Diana's official time of death.
[b] Not heard by the jury.

Monceau starts with an AFIF recommendation that is open to the public, for embalming. Within one question, this has changed to: not a recommendation but "information", and not open to the public, but "for the attention of professionals".

Then Burnett leaves that conflict hanging and moves on.

It's not as though this issue was not central to the case – there are many unanswered questions regarding the embalming and I suggest that the jury were entitled to have answers.

When Mansfield introduces the topic, Monceau changes his evidence again – this time: the AFIF lists countries, including the UK, "that impose – that make it obligatory to proceed to [embalming] before repatriation".

Next Mansfield questions why Dodi was not embalmed, but Monceau doesn't back off and suggest that it's not actually legally required – the UK doesn't "impose" or "make it obligatory" – which would have been the truth. Instead Monceau says: "I am not at all concerned with that matter".

Mansfield – who appears to be aware of the Monceau email – then has to suggest that Monceau knows better – that the rules "are not indicating an obligation".

Monceau had already stated in his 2005 email that "there is absolutely no law stating that embalming is compulsory", but his inquest evidence shows that he had no intention of sharing that with the jury.

Why? I suggest because his actions on the day to embalm Princess Diana look a whole lot better if it can be shown that this was a legal requirement anyway.

The general evidence – Steiner, Jauze, Monceau's email – shows that embalming is not legally required before repatriation to the UK.

Amarger, also in 2005 evidence heard by the jury, said: "I must say that in order that a body can leave French territory, it is compulsory for embalming treatment to be applied".

Amarger's evidence is that by 2005 she had been "in business for myself"[138] as an embalmer for 5 years. It seems strange that she too would not understand the law regarding repatriation. I suggest that, just like Monceau, she has manufactured a legal requirement for embalming to justify her actions on the day.

In the end, the jury heard three accounts:
a) definite evidence from Amarger that embalming was "compulsory"
b) a confusing acrobatic jumble from Monceau
c) evidence from Steiner that embalming was not required "if a body is to be transported within the first 24 hours".

The true evidence is that embalming was not required and there was no related time pressure – but I suggest that the jury would not have been left with that impression.

Expectation of Embalming

Aside from the legality discussed above, what was the expectation that Princess Diana's body – repatriated to the UK within 16 hours[a] – would have been embalmed prior to departure from French soil?

Clive Leverton, Royal Funeral Director: 22 Nov 07: 79.25:

Mansfield: Q. In your view, would it have been necessary to embalm within 24 hours?

A. It is difficult for me to say because I do not know what she was like prior to the embalming.

Dr Robert Chapman, Pathologist, UK: 26 Nov 2007: 26.1:

"Embalming is a common procedure in the United Kingdom. It is usual for bodies being repatriated to the UK from abroad via air transportation."[b]

At 46.4: Mansfield: Q. Did you communicate [to Lecomte in June 1998] any view about your view as to the necessity for embalming in this case?

A. I do not recall. I do not recall.

Q. Because you can certainly look at one of your statements in relation to this issue. It is the one dated 24th February 2005 and it is under the heading of, "Embalming".... "It is quite possible that I asked why the body had been embalmed."

A. Yes.

Q. "I was quite surprised that there had been time for this process to take place, and given the rapid return of Diana, Princess of Wales' body to the United Kingdom, such a process would not have been necessary for preservation purposes prior to the post-mortem examination."

A. Yes.

Q. Now when you expressed that view, did you go on to communicate it to the French in 1998, although you were expressing the view in 2005 –

A. No, I do not recall having expressed it before this statement.

Q. Is that your view?

A. It is my view that it would not have been necessary for preservation, given that the examination was going to take place very rapidly upon her arrival back in the UK, certainly.

Q. Does that depend on where the body had been, as it were, housed in France, before it came back?

A. Yes. If the body is appropriately housed and refrigerated –

Q. There would be no need?

A. Indeed.

Q. But if it is not?

---

[a] Official time of death was 4 a.m. and arrival in UK was at 8 p.m. Paris time.

[b] Excerpt from 24 February 2005 statement read out.

A. If it is held somewhere warm and there is no appropriate refrigeration, then yes, it may be necessary.

Dr Robert Chapman, Pathologist, UK: 24 Feb 05 Statement: **Jury Didn't Hear**:

"I do have a very wide experience of the examination of embalmed bodies because of the requirement to carry out postmortem examinations on cases referred to the Coroner involving deaths abroad."[139]

Robert Thompson, Fulham Mortuary Manager: 9 Nov 04 Statement: **Jury Didn't Hear**:

"Any body coming back to the UK from abroad must be embalmed and during my profession within the mortuary business I experienced many embalmed bodies."[140]

David Green, Embalmer, UK: 13 Jul 04 Statement: **Jury Didn't Hear**:

"Had there been no viewing in Paris of such a well know person and by Prince Charles and family then it is possible no embalming would have taken place. We wouldn't have embalmed her knowing there was going to be a post mortem, and moreover not without authority from the Lord Chamberlain."[141]

David Green, Embalmer, UK: 17 Sep 04 Statement: **Jury Didn't Hear**:

"Other reasons I would not embalm a body would be, if there was no authority to embalm by the family or their representative, religious beliefs, infectious cases and severe bodily trauma where viewing is not appropriate. In my opinion there is no difference concerning the embalming requirement and the authority for embalming of a body coming into the UK from abroad, including France, to a body in our care in London. This would also apply when there is or is not a Coroner's Inquest and a post mortem examination. The same authority and decision to embalm or not should be considered....

"However our company a couple of times a month do collect bodies from airports such as Heathrow and preservation care commences upon our receiving them. Bodies coming into the UK are embalmed more often than not."[142]

John Burton, Royal Coroner, 1997[a]: 16 Jun 04 Statement: **Jury Didn't Hear**:

"As a coroner I would normally be dealing with approximately 2500 deaths/ post mortems a year. As the coroner for Heathrow I was involved in the inquest of numerous bodies that were repatriated to England. I attended a lot of these post mortems. In all such cases the bodies were embalmed to some degree....

"Later that morning I spoke to Levertons the undertakers in order to make arrangements for the post Mortem... I did not give them any other instructions nor was the subject of embalming mentioned. I would have ... assumed that the body transported by air would have been embalmed....

---

[a] Burton died in December 2004.

"The undertakers arrived with the coffin holding the body of Mr Dodi Al Fayed... I assisted in the removal of the body from the coffin and was surprised that the body did not appear to have been embalmed as is usual for bodies subject to air transportation. I took no active part in this post mortem apart from my cleaning duties....

"I could see and smell that the body of Diana Princess of Wales had clearly been embalmed. I fully expected that her body would have been embalmed in keeping with bodies that are flown back to England."[143]

Patrick Launay, PFG Repatriation Director: 21 Mar 06 Statement: **Jury Didn't Hear**:

"You ask me if it was strange for the Princess of Wales to have been embalmed before being repatriated to England. No. This kind of embalming is only for the presentation of the body. Moreover, 99% of bodies repatriated from France to the UK are embalmed."[144]

Gérard Jauze, PFG Branch Director, Paris: 21 Mar 06 Statement: **Jury Didn't Hear**:

"Even if the body were to be returned to a distant country, it would not automatically be embalmed."[145]

Comment: There is conflicting witness evidence on whether the embalming of Princess Diana would have been expected, ahead of repatriation:

- Clive Leverton: "it is difficult for me to say" – inquest
- Chapman: "it is usual for bodies being repatriated" – statement heard
- Chapman: "I was quite surprised that there had been time for [embalming]" – statement heard
- Chapman: embalming "would not have been necessary" – statement heard
- Chapman: "if [the body] is held somewhere warm ... [embalming] may be necessary" – inquest
- Thompson: "any body coming back ... from abroad must be embalmed"
- Green: "bodies coming into the UK are embalmed more often than not"
- Green: "we wouldn't have embalmed her knowing there was going to be a post mortem"
- Burton: "in all [repatriation] cases the bodies were embalmed"
- Burton: "I would have ... assumed that the body transported by air would have been embalmed"
- Burton: embalming "is usual for bodies subject to air transportation"
- Burton: "I fully expected that [Diana's] body would have been embalmed"
- Launay: "99% of bodies repatriated from France to the UK are embalmed"
- Jauze: a body repatriated "would not automatically be embalmed".

Considering that this evidence is from 7 people involved in the death industry, it seems odd that there is such a wide disparity on such a simple point – did they expect Diana would be embalmed?

There are three people that appear to believe that Diana's embalming was inevitable ahead of repatriation. These are:
-   Thompson: "any body ... must be embalmed"
-   Launay: "99% of bodies ... are embalmed"
-   Burton: "in all cases the bodies were embalmed".

The other four witnesses are nowhere near as definite:
-   Chapman: embalming "would not have been necessary"
-   Green: "bodies ... are embalmed more often than not"
-   Jauze: a body "would not automatically be embalmed"
-   Leverton: "it is difficult for me to say".

There are three points regarding the evidence from the witnesses who were definite:

1) It may be that Thompson is commenting on his understanding of the law – he states that repatriated bodies "<u>must</u> be embalmed". If that is the case, Thompson is clearly wrong on this – see the preceding section on legality.

2) Of all the 7 witnesses who have commented on this subject of expectation, the evidence of John Burton would appear to be the most unusual. In his statement, Burton appears to have gone out of his way to make this point – that all bodies repatriated by air are embalmed. Burton has effectively said the same thing at four different times in his statement.

When this is viewed in the light of evidence in Part 3 that Burton appeared to deliberately alter a part of this same police statement, in connection with a critical post-crash phone call[a], it seems that Burton cannot be viewed as a completely reliable witness.

Referring to his experience, Burton has stated that "in all [repatriation] cases the bodies were embalmed". Yet on the night of the 31 August 1997 Burton was present during the post mortem of Dodi Fayed, who was not embalmed.

Burton appears to be suggesting that the body of Dodi Fayed must have been the first repatriated body he had ever seen that was not embalmed. It may then be significant that when Burton comes to discussing Dodi Fayed's body in his statement, he tones down the language – it is no longer "all" repatriated bodies that are embalmed: it is now "usual" for those bodies to be embalmed.

---

[a] Refer to Burton's evidence on the phone call he received on 31 August 1997 from Jeffrey Rees. See Comment pp623-641 Part 3 (UK edition).

3) There is a possibility that Launay – who still worked for a PFG-related company at the time of his statement[a] – was attempting to normalise Diana's embalming by stating that "99% of bodies repatriated ... to the UK are embalmed". It may have been in his interests to defend the actions taken by BJL – a company closely related to PFG – on the day.

Launay's colleague, Gérard Jauze – who also still works as a director of PFG[146] – does not subscribe to the same belief. Jauze said: "Even if the body were to be returned to a distant country, it would not automatically be embalmed".

The evidence of the 4 witnesses – Jauze, Chapman, Green, Leverton – who don't insist that embalming for repatriated bodies was universal, appears to fit with common sense. I suggest it is common sense that if embalming on bodies repatriated to the UK from France was not legally required – and it wasn't (see earlier) – then there would be at least a segment of the population that would not be embalmed.

No witness has put forward a specific reason why repatriated bodies would all be embalmed, but there have been reasons given for why they wouldn't:

-   Leverton: "what she was like prior to the embalming" – by this, Leverton has indicated that if the body was in good condition[b], then why would you embalm her?

-   Chapman: "given the rapid return" – Chapman indicates that if the repatriation is quick – which it was in this case – embalming "would not have been necessary"

-   Green: "knowing there was going to be a post mortem" – Chapman appears to agree with this: embalming "would not have been necessary ... given that the examination was going to take place"[c]

-   Green: "I would not embalm a body ... if there was no authority to embalm by the family or their representative, religious beliefs, infectious cases and severe bodily trauma".

The evidence in this book shows – see earlier and later – that there has been a massive cover-up of the evidence surrounding the embalming. One could argue that if embalming was carried out on all bodies repatriated to the

---

[a] Launay was interviewed in March 2006 – 8½ years after the crash – and at that time was a director of OGF, the holding company for PFG: Patrick Launay, Witness Statement, 21 March 2006, reproduced in *The Documents* book, p509.

[b] Other evidence has indicated that if a body is kept cool – as most bodies are – then they would not require embalming in the first 24 hours, at least.

[c] The issue regarding prior knowledge of the UK post-mortem occurring will be dealt with shortly. The impact of an embalming on the conduct of and results from a post-mortem is covered in the UK Post-Mortem chapter.

UK from France, such a cover-up would not have been required. The cover-up itself – for which there is substantial proof – indicates that something unusual has occurred here: a rushed and illegal embalming conducted on a body that was repatriated in less than 24 hours of the death occurring, ahead of a full post-mortem examination.

Prior Knowledge of a British Post-Mortem[a]

Was it known in advance that a post-mortem would be conducted on the body of Princess Diana in the UK?[b]

John Macnamara, Al Fayed Director of Security: 14 Feb 08: 80.1:
Burnett: Q. At some stage, did you become aware that there was at least the likelihood – which in due course it became obvious was the need – for a post-mortem examination in England?
A. Well, yes. I knew that once [Dodi's] body came back to England, there would have to be a post mortem.
....Q. In 1983, the courts here had said that if a death occurs abroad and the body comes back to the United Kingdom, there has to be an inquest – if it is England and Wales, if the circumstances were such, that an inquest would happen here. You probably would not have been aware of that sort of detail.
A. I was not aware of the Act, although I did understand that there would have to be an inquest.
Q. That was because the death of Dodi, just as the death of Diana, was a violent or unnatural death because it had happened in a crash.
A. I accept that.
Q.... Do you remember whether, in your discussions with Mr Burgess that day, he explained that there had to be inquests because these were violent or unnatural deaths?
A. I do not think he went into that detail, but he certainly pointed out that there would have to be an inquest, yes.[c]
Michael Burgess, Royal Coroner, 2002 to Present[d]: 16 Aug 04 Statement:
Jury Didn't Hear:

---

[a] The evidence in this section should be viewed in the light of the evidence in the UK Post-Mortem chapter on the effect of embalming on post-mortem test results.
[b] This information has particular relevance to the embalming – it will be shown later in the UK Post-Mortem chapter that embalming can affect the post-mortem results.
[c] Macnamara's account is supported by the statement of Michael Burgess – see *The Documents* book, p536: "I told [Macnamara] that the coroner had duties because of section 8 (1) of the Coroners Act. I explained to him the necessity for a post mortem."
[d] Burgess remains royal coroner in 2011. Elizabeth Butler-Sloss became deputy royal coroner in order to conduct the inquest. Butler-Sloss' successor, Scott Baker, became deputy coroner for inner west London before taking on the inquest. Coronial succession is dealt with in Part 5.

"Around 9.45 a.m. I received a call from Peter Fahy the Assistant Chief Constable of Surrey Police. He informed me that the body of Dodi Fayed was being brought back for burial at Brookwood Cemetery before sunset. He asked me if I would become involved. I advised him that due to the case of Helen Smith and Section 8 (1) of the Coroners Act, there was a requirement for a post mortem and an inquest, I would be taking jurisdiction of the body of Dodi Fayed."[147]

John Burton, Royal Coroner, 1997: 16 Jun 04 Statement: **Jury Didn't Hear**:

"Early on the morning of Sunday 31st of August 1997, I was at home when I heard of the news of the death of Diana Princess of Wales and Mr Dodi Al Fayed via the radio....

"I telephoned the switchboard of Buckingham Place and spoke to a person who identified himself as being the Lord Chamberlain. He was unable to assist much further at this stage and it was agreed that I should phone back later.

"I again phoned the Buckingham Palace switchboard and spoke to a young lady who ... was able to tell me that Levertons undertakers were dealing....

"[Diana] had ... died an unnatural death. I was unaware if a post mortem had taken place in France.... I knew that I would require a post mortem to be carried out because I had an unnatural death and no evidence from a [previous] post mortem.

"Later that morning I spoke to Levertons the undertakers in order to make arrangements for the post mortem to be carried out at the Hammersmith and Fulham mortuary.[a] I did not give them any other instructions.... I believe that I did inform Levertons that I was intending to have a post mortem.

"I phoned one of my coroner's officers Harry Brown and asked him to make arrangements for the post mortem to be held at the Hammersmith and Fulham mortuary and place the duty home office pathologist on standby.

"Around midday Michael Burgess the coroner for the county of Surrey and also my deputy as the coroner for the Royal Household phoned."[148]

Clive Leverton, Royal Funeral Director: 22 Nov 07: 80.18:

Mansfield: Q. Were you aware that as a matter of course, I am using that language, an autopsy would have to take place?

A. No, not then. It was not –

Q. Not in France. I mean in England.

A. No. I was not really – I was just concentrating on doing the job in hand, as it were.

---

[a] The Hammersmith and Fulham Mortuary is generally referred to as simply the Fulham Mortuary in this book.

Q. Yes, I do understand. Obviously, trying to put ourselves in your position, it is very difficult. So it did not occur to you and, would this be right, in your presence, no one else said, "Look, there has to be an autopsy in England"?

A. No. We were just simply concentrating on doing what we had to do.

Keith Leverton, Royal Funeral Director: 27 Oct 04 Statement: **Jury Didn't Hear**:

"During that day Mather communicated with me over the phone.... I received calls from my brother when he was on the way to the hospital in Paris and later when he had left the hospital to let him me know he was on the way back. I had no specific requests or instructions to give to him. There were no instructions from the Lord Chamberlains office for me to pass onto Clive. I recall [being] informed that Diana, Princess of Wales was to go to Fulham Mortuary, this would have been most likely by Mather. I therefore understood there was to be a post mortem here."[149]

David Green, Embalmer, UK: 13 Jul 04 Statement: **Jury Didn't Hear**:

"When we placed [Diana] in the coffin Bill [Fry] and I agreed that the embalming was insufficient for long term preservation, i.e. until the funeral, and we agreed that I would have to carry out full embalming after the post mortem.... We knew that she was to be taken to Fulham Mortuary for a post mortem and that we would have to wait for further instructions of where and when we were to do this.ª"[150]

David Green, Embalmer, UK: 17 Sep 04 Statement: **Jury Didn't Hear**:

"Further to my first statement given to the police, [they] have revisited me to ask further questions concerning certain points in that statement. I have been asked to comment on, *'we wouldn't have embalmed her knowing there was going to be a post mortem, and moreover not without authority from the Lord Chamberlain'.* I learnt that she had received some embalming treatment by the French upon our arrival at the Salpêtrière Hospital, and the French for the family's viewing as I previously mentioned may have carried this out. As previously stated I cannot comment on the exact extent of the embalming the French carried out. I did not know on the way out to Paris whether there was going to be a post mortem examination or not.... In my experience, had I known that there was going to be a post mortem examination on any deceased person then any incisions or removal of fluids would change the state of the body and therefore it would not be the same as it was at the time of death.... When we placed her in the coffin Bill and I agreed that the embalming was insufficient for long term preservation i.e. until the funeral, and we agreed that I would have to carry out full embalming after the post mortem."[151]

Colin Tebbutt, Diana's Driver and Security: 26 Nov 07: 96.9:

ª Green is referring here to the instructions for the UK embalming – this is addressed later.

Hough: Q. Did you know at that time that the Princess of Wales might undergo a post-mortem examination in the UK?

A. That was in my mind because we do have post mortems when people come back, when they die abroad.

Q. Was there any discussion of that with Mr Moss or with the French funeral directors?

A. Not as I can remember, sir.

At 119.13: Mansfield: Q. Were you aware, when you were there, that there would have to be an autopsy here in the United Kingdom or not?

A. I think my – yes, I am sure I did, sir, and I think I put it in my statement, about a post mortem. I am pretty sure in my mind that it crossed my mind that day that they post-mortem people that come back into the country. So, yes, I was aware.

Q. The reason I ask you – and it is a small point – was anybody in Paris saying to the French, "Look, there has to be an autopsy"?

A. I did not hear that.

Q. You did not hear that. And you did not say it?

A. No, I did not.

Q. Because the way you have put it in your statement.... "I have been asked whether I was aware... " Do you see that?

A. Yes, sir.

Q. " ... whether I was aware that the Princess of Wales was going to be subject to a post-mortem examination at the Fulham mortuary. I would say that at no stage was I aware of this. And it was only when I met Mr Gibbins at RAF Northolt... "[a] Is that your recollection of your state of mind at the time?

A. My state of mind was in a dreadful state. I was trying to take a lot on board. I am sure in my mind, something said there would be an autopsy but if I have written that, I have written it for a reason. Hindsight is a –

Q. It is.

A. When you look back at things, there was so much happening that day. There was nothing untoward.

Q. No, no, I am not suggesting it. I am just assessing the state of mind of various people and the chronology of it. So do you think the statement is a reflection, or do you just not know any more, about what you thought about an autopsy?

A. I doubt if anybody put that question to me the way you have done it. They

---

[a] The full sentence is: "And it was only when I met Mr Gibbins at RAF Northolt that I was aware of our final destination, Fulham Mortuary.": Colin Tebbutt, Witness Statement, 5 July 2004, reproduced in *The Documents* book, pp442-3 (UK Edition).

probably said did you know there was an autopsy. When you put it in that way, then I probably had a memory flash that, "Christ, there probably will be one when we get back" –

Q. Well, I did not, my learned friend[a] did actually.

A. I cannot argue one way or the other on that, sir.

Michael Gibbins, Diana's Private Secretary: 21 Nov 07: 10.7:

Burnett: Q. Did you at any stage during the course of that day learn that a post-mortem examination was to be carried out?

A. I think I was told that at the mortuary by, I think it was, Dr Burton.

Keith Moss, British Consul General, Paris: 22 Nov 07: 25.5:

Hough: Q. At the time, when you were told about this procedure by Mr Monceau, did you consider at all the effect the procedure might have on the ability to carry out a post-mortem examination in the UK?

A. No.

Q. At that stage, were you aware that the Princess would undergo a post-mortem examination in the UK?

A. No.

Jean Monceau, BJL Director and Embalmer, Paris: 20 Nov 07: 83.12:

Mansfield: Q. Did Mr Moss say to you that in fact there would have to be a full autopsy in the United Kingdom?

A. Not at all.

Jean Monceau, BJL Director and Embalmer, Paris: 18 Oct 05 Statement: **Jury Didn't Hear**:

"You have asked me whether I knew that the Princess of Wales was going to undergo an autopsy upon her return to the United Kingdom. The British funeral directors, who arrived at around 1700 hrs [5 p.m.], informed me of this. We discussed the different techniques and they told me that this was the norm in the U.K. I was not previously aware of this."[152]

René Deguisne, BJL Assistant General Manager: 9 May 05 Statement: **Jury Didn't Hear**:

"Question: Did Hygeco know that an autopsy was going to be carried out on the body either in France or in Great Britain?

Answer: No.... Since we had the agreement of the Criminal Investigation Police, through Mrs Monteil, we assumed that there would not be an autopsy."[153]

Jean-Claude Plumet, PFG Director of Paris Agencies, Paris: 4 Nov 05 Paget description of Statement: **Jury Didn't Hear**:

"When asked whether it was ever brought to his attention that the Princess of Wales would be subject to a post-mortem on her return to the United Kingdom, Mr Plumet replied that it had not."[154]

---

[a] Mansfield is referring to Hough – see above.

Huguette Amarger, French Embalmer: 8 Mar 05 Statement read out 22 Nov 07: 95.14:

"Question: Did you know that an autopsy was going to be carried out on the body?

Answer: No, and in any case that would not have made any difference to my work. And I repeat, my work was compulsory for the body to be able to leave France."

Prof Dominique Lecomte, Pathologist and Head of IML, Paris: 9 Mar 05 Statement: **Jury Didn't Hear**:

"Question: Did you know at that time whether an autopsy would take place in England later?

Answer: I did not but I suspected it would take place.

Question: Did you suggest it?

Answer: It is not up to me to do so, that is the Magistrate's province."[155]

Maud Coujard, Deputy Public Prosecutor, Paris: 20 Nov 07: 44.12:

Mansfield: Q. This concerns the forensic examination that you requested in relation to Princess Diana. At the time that you authorised or ordered that, were you aware that there was to be, in the United Kingdom, a full autopsy?

A. No, I do not think so.

Comment: The issue of early knowledge of the UK post-mortem of Princess Diana is very important – it will be shown later in this book that embalming can significantly affect post-mortem sample test results.

There are two sides to this issue – first, what was known in France and second, what was known in the UK.

Dominique Lecomte – an experienced pathologist, who had already conducted her own post-mortem on Diana's body[a] – has stated that she "suspected it would take place". Then when asked if she had suggested it at the time, Lecomte backs off and states: "that is the Magistrate's province".

Lecomte, who was heavily involved in these early events[b], must have been aware that there was no magistrate appointed until 2 September 1997[156] – two days after the embalming took place. I suggest that it is mischievous for Lecomte to deny responsibility for this – "it is not up to me to do so" – and shift it onto a non-existent magistrate. The reality is that pathology is Lecomte's field of expertise: if anyone was to know – a) that a post-mortem was likely to occur in London; and b) the significance of that with regard to prior events in Paris – it was Dominique Lecomte.

Lecomte has admitted that she "suspected [a UK post-mortem] would take place". This raises the question: Why didn't Lecomte – after her 5.30 a.m.

---

[a] See Chapter 1.

[b] See Chapter 1 of this book and Section 1 of Part 3.

autopsy[a] – pass that information on to Maud Coujard, whose responsibility it was to sign the burial certificate?

If that had occurred, Coujard would have still been able to sign the burial certificate, but with the proviso that no embalming would be conducted prior to the holding of the UK post-mortem.

The evidence from the other French witnesses – Monceau[b], Amarger, Deguisne[c], Coujard, Plumet – was that they were not aware there would be a UK post-mortem. This appears to be the case – there is no evidence that indicates otherwise.

The significant point here is that the embalming was ordered early by the British authorities – not the French – see earlier. It may have been in British interests that the French were only given information on a need-to-know basis[d] – had there been French knowledge of a UK post-mortem, there may have been an unwanted attempt by someone at the hospital to prevent the embalming from occurring.

When Colin Tebbutt – who was present in the hospital – was asked about this at the inquest, he replied, "yes, I was aware" and says: "I think I put it in my statement, about a post mortem".

Actually Tebbutt's statement categorically says the opposite: "I would say that at no stage was I aware of this", and he goes on to specifically state when he became aware and who told him: "It was only when I met Mr Gibbins at RAF Northolt that I was aware of our final destination, Fulham Mortuary".

There is a clear conflict in Tebbutt's evidence:
- in his 2004 statement: "at no stage was I aware of this"
- at the inquest: "yes, I was aware".

As has been suggested earlier in this book, Colin Tebbutt, who had been a long-standing police officer, may have compromised his evidence under pressure from the British police. When one considers his police experience, it would seem logical that he could have understood there would probably be a post-mortem – Tebbutt stated at the inquest: "we do have post mortems when people come back". Had Tebbutt acknowledged in his statement that the UK post-mortem was likely, this would have cast more doubt on the motives for embalming – doubt that was not in the interests of the Paget investigation.

---

[a] See Chapter 1.

[b] Monceau has said that he didn't know about a UK autopsy ahead of the embalming – he found out when the British arrived – this was at 3.40 p.m.

[c] Deguisne – who was not an eye-witness of events (see earlier) – has given a strange logic for BJL's lack of expectation of a UK post-mortem: "since we had the agreement of ... Monteil, we assumed that there would not be an autopsy". Deguisne appears to be suggesting that Monteil would not have agreed to the embalming if she had known about a UK post-mortem. Earlier evidence has shown that Monteil didn't agree to the embalming.

[d] This is how MI6 operates – see Part 5.

I suggest that at the inquest, Tebbutt had forgotten what he had said in his earlier statement, and when asked on this topic, gave a true response: "Yes, I was aware".

When Tebbutt is challenged on this by Michael Mansfield, he appears to bluster: "if I have written that, I have written it for a reason". I suggest the reason was to fit Tebbutt's evidence into the story that Paget wanted to promote[a] – that there was no prior knowledge by people in the hospital at the time of the embalming, that there would be a UK post-mortem.

Were the British funeral and embalming personnel – Clive and Keith Leverton, Green, Fry – told about the post-mortem ahead of time?

Royal coroner at the time, John Burton, has stated in evidence not heard by the jury: "Later that morning I spoke to Levertons the undertakers in order to make arrangements for the post mortem to be carried out at the Hammersmith and Fulham mortuary.... I did inform Levertons that I was intending to have a post mortem."

Later evidence will reveal that Clive Leverton did not leave from RAF Northolt – heading to Paris – until 1.05 p.m.[b]

Burton has been reasonably clear with his timing and sequence of events:
- "early on the morning ... I heard of the news of the death"
- "I telephoned ... Buckingham Palace ... and it was agreed that I should phone back later"
- "I again phoned ... Buckingham Palace ... and ... a young lady ... was able to tell me that Levertons undertakers were dealing" with the deaths
- "later that morning I spoke to Levertons"
- "I phoned ... Harry Brown and asked him to make arrangements for the post mortem"
- "around midday Michael Burgess ... phoned".

This evidence places the call to Levertons ahead of Harry Brown and then the Burgess call comes in at midday. This appears to suggest the Leverton call could have been at around 11 a.m. – "later that morning".

This indicates then that around two hours before Clive Leverton left for Paris – at 1.05 p.m. – Burton had made arrangements with Levertons "for the post mortem to be carried out at the Hammersmith and Fulham mortuary".

What is the evidence from the British funeral-embalming personnel?[c]

---

[a] The book *Cover-Up of a Royal Murder: Hundreds of Errors in the Paget Report* reveals the methods used by Operation Paget to arrive at a finding that the crash was an accident, when the evidence continually pointed to assassination.
[b] UK time.
[c] If it can be shown that the British funeral team knew about the UK post-mortem before flying from RAF Northolt, this would raise issues over why two embalmers were on board. It will be shown later that embalming affects post-mortem test results.

- Fry has never been interviewed and wasn't heard from at the inquest
- Green: "when we placed [Diana] in the coffin Bill and I agreed ... that I would have to carry out full embalming after the post mortem" – July 2004 statement
- Green: "we knew that she was to be taken to Fulham Mortuary for a post mortem" – July 2004 statement
- Green: "I did not know on the way out to Paris whether there was going to be a post mortem examination or not" – September 2004 statement
- Keith Leverton: "I recall [being] informed that Diana ... was to go to Fulham Mortuary, this would have been most likely by Mather. I therefore understood there was to be a post mortem here"[a]
- Clive Leverton: "it did not occur to you and ... in your presence, no one else said, 'Look, there has to be an autopsy in England'" – confirmed to Mansfield.[b]

Clive Leverton, the head of the three person team that travelled to France, has effectively denied outright that he had any knowledge that there would be a post-mortem held in the UK – "I was just concentrating on doing the job in hand".

This is in direct conflict to the late John Burton's account: "Later that morning I spoke to Levertons ... to make arrangements for the post mortem".

Green has acknowledged that "when we placed [Diana] in the coffin" he already knew there would be a post-mortem. This would have been sometime around 4 p.m. – Green arrived at the hospital at about 3.40 p.m.

Keith Leverton remained behind in England, but his evidence is significant because he was the sole communication link between the team heading to France and what was happening in the UK.[c]

Keith describes just two times of communication with Clive during the entire Paris trip – between their departure from England (at 1.05 p.m.) to their return to England (at 7 p.m.)[d]. Keith has specifically stated: "I had no specific requests or instructions to give to [Clive]", when Clive called "on the way to the hospital in Paris and later when he had left the hospital".

This evidence shows that the knowledge of the team didn't change from when they left RAF Northolt in England to when they returned 6 hours later.

This means that if David Green was aware that there was to be a post-mortem at the time Diana was placed in the coffin in the hospital, then he also must have known that before he left England.

---

[a] Keith does not reveal at what stage he was told about this.

[b] Clive Leverton appears to have avoided this subject in his earlier police statement.

[c] This is confirmed by Anthony Mather in his statement: "I communicated with Keith Leverton over the telephone to his office in Camden. He communicated with his brother Clive Leverton who went to Paris.": Anthony Mather, Witness Statement, 23 August 2005, reproduced in *The Documents* book, p662 (UK Edition)

[d] Both times are UK time.

This of course fits with the evidence of John Burton.

It is significant that David Green was reinterviewed in September 2004 – two months after his initial statement – over precisely this issue: prior knowledge of the UK post-mortem. In his July statement, Green had said: "We wouldn't have embalmed [Diana] knowing there was going to be a post mortem". Paget evidently weren't happy about this as it indicates the truth – that Green did know "there was going to be a post mortem".

It appears that Green was asked to recant and this time Paget would have been far more content with: "I did not know on the way out to Paris whether there was going to be a post mortem examination or not".

But, as shown above, that new statement from Green does not fit the facts of the case and I suggest that Green has been encouraged by Operation Paget officers to lie under oath.[ab]

Monceau also stated: "The British funeral directors ... informed me of [the UK post-mortem].... I was not previously aware of this." Although Monceau has been shown to be an incredibly unreliable witness, there does not appear to be any reason for him to lie on this issue.

In summary, there are three points of evidence that reveal that Clive Leverton and his team were aware before they left London for Paris:

1) Burton's evidence that he told Levertons at around 11 a.m.
2) Green's account that he knew there would be a later post-mortem
3) Monceau's evidence that he heard about the UK post-mortem from the British team.

The significance of this evidence is that it raises the critical question: Why were two embalmers – Green and Fry – despatched to Paris[c], when it was

---

[a] It is interesting to note that Paget was comfortable with Green's account that he knew about the post-mortem at the time of placing Princess Diana in the coffin. Green actually repeats this part of the July statement in the new September account. I suggest Paget didn't challenge this because it didn't show knowledge of a UK post-mortem prior to take off from RAF Northolt. This only becomes an issue when it is seen in the light of the Keith Leverton and Mather statements, both of which were taken after Green's second statement. Keith was interviewed a month later, on 27 October 2004, and Mather the following year, on 23 August 2005.
[b] The interviews with Green took place after John Burton whose statement was taken in June 2004. Burton was reinterviewed in August – a month before Green's second statement. I imagine that Paget may have been intending to get a third interview with Burton, but it appears his health declined and he died just 4 months after his second interview, in December 2004. It may be that Paget would have been hoping that Burton's statements would never be seen, but they were published in 2010 in *The Documents* book.
[c] The early involvement of the two British embalmers is addressed in the Repatriation Issues chapter.

already known: a) that a post-mortem would be held in the UK; b) that if Diana was embalmed, any post-mortem test results would be adversely affected[a]?

If one considers Tebbutt's evidence (see above) – and this will be shown and confirmed later – the UK law required an inquest after arrival on British soil in precisely these circumstances – an unnatural death overseas. Although an inquest does not necessarily require a post-mortem, it certainly indicates that a post-mortem would have been likely.[b] It seems incomprehensible that these extremely experienced experts in their fields[c] would be unaware of the law in an area that directly impacted on their work.

Burton's evidence tends to confirm this – Burton wasn't just ringing Levertons to advise them there would be a post-mortem, but he was telling them where it would be held: "at the Hammersmith and Fulham mortuary".

Logistically this information was crucial to Levertons – when they landed with Princess Diana's body at RAF Northolt that evening, they had to know where to take it. And it was just as important from Burton's point of view – if he was to organise the site for the post-mortem, Hammersmith and Fulham, he had to be completely confident that Levertons would take Diana's body to that site after landing.

I suggest that its common sense that discussions of this nature would take place well ahead of time, in order to avoid possible misunderstandings. Given this, it is very telling that Clive, Keith and Green have all avoided mention of the 11 a.m. Burton call in their evidence. It is common sense that Clive Leverton had to know where to take the body after landing – if he didn't receive this information from Burton before leaving, then where and when did he get it.[d]

It is particularly significant that the only evidence that the inquest heard regarding the prior knowledge of the British team was from Clive Leverton, who straight out denied knowledge.

The evidence from all the other players – Burton, Keith Leverton, Green, Fry – was suppressed at Scott Baker's "thorough" inquest.

---

[a] This point will be addressed later.

[b] This is covered in the Post-Mortems chapter.

[c] In 1997, Clive and Keith Leverton were the two sole directors of Leverton and Sons Ltd, a company that had been in the funeral business for over 200 years: 22 Nov 07: 67.11 and 68.3. David Green said: "I have embalmed around about 8,000 bodies whilst with my current employer alone": David Green, Witness Statement, 13 July 2004, reproduced in *The Documents* book, p501 (UK Edition). Bill Fry has never been interviewed.

[d] Keith Leverton said the information "would have been most likely by Mather". Mather has never confirmed this – it is Burton who categorically stated that he called Levertons with the information.

The inquest jury would have had no reason not to believe Clive Leverton – yet his account that they heard was the opposite of the truth.

Role of the British Embassy

The role of Keith Moss, British Consul-General in Paris, has already been addressed, but there was at least one other key person in the British Embassy on 31 August 1997.

Michael Jay

Michael Jay, British Ambassador to France, 1996-2001, Paris: 11 Feb 08: 112.9:

Burnett: Q. It has been suggested that you personally ordered the embalming of the body of the Princess of Wales on the instructions of MI6 to conceal the fact that the Princess was pregnant with Dodi's child. You are aware of that?
A. I am aware of that allegation.
Q. The way I put it simply summarises what one reads in a witness statement from Mr Al Fayed.... What is your reaction to the allegations that were made?
A. There is no truth in them whatsoever.

Michael Jay: 31 Aug 97 Diary read out 11 Feb 08: 106.1:
"There are endless little problems, for example about undertakers – French law does not let foreign undertakers work here apparently, but neither we nor the French authorities let any of this become a problem."

Michael Jay: 13 Dec 05 Statement: **Jury Didn't Hear**:
"I have been asked whether I gave any instructions to anyone authorising the embalming of the Princess' body at the Pitié Salpêtrière hospital on 31/08/1997. I understand that after the death of the Princess of Wales her body had undergone an "embalming" process. I also understand that this is a not uncommon practice. I do not know at what stage I acquired this information, and I think that it was not until relatively recently. I do not believe that I was aware at the time the Princess' body had been embalmed, and I certainly gave no instructions to that effect or even in the most general terms as to the manner in which her body should be prepared."[157]

Keith Moss, British Consul General, Paris: 22 Nov 07: 28.1:
Hough: Q. To the best of your recollection and memory, was Sir Michael Jay involved in the decision to carry out this [embalming] procedure?
A. No, not at all.

Keith Moss: 22 Oct 04 Statement: **Jury Didn't Hear**:
"Throughout the day I gave verbal briefings to Sir Michael Jay, Tim Livesey and contacts in the UK, on a strict need to know basis. We wanted to keep all information as tight as possible."[158]

Keith Moss: 22 Oct 04 Statement: **Jury Didn't Hear**:

"At about 1400hrs [2 p.m.], Doctor Bernard Kouchner, the founder of Médecins Sans Frontière and Minister for Health, attended the hospital and came to my room. He asked whether he would be allowed to pay his final respects to the Princess of Wales, describing himself as a personal friend. I checked with Sir Michael Jay who agreed that this would be acceptable as long as he was accompanied by one of the nurses."[159]

Stephen Donnelly, British Vice Consul, Paris: 22 Sep 05 Statement read out 17 Dec 07: 124.10:

"I also remember speaking to Mr Al Fayed, although I do not recall at what time. I had received a call, probably from the Embassy, telling me that Mr Al Fayed was seeking assistance. Before returning the call, because Mr Mohamed Al Fayed is a non-British national, I spoke to the Ambassador, Michael Jay, and asked for clearance to do so. In principle we do not give consular assistance to non-British nationals, but under the circumstances it was agreed that I should give any help that I could.... I had been following the developments on Sky News. I saw that a military aircraft was about to leave the UK with a coffin and that members of the Princess of Wales' family were coming over to France as well. I remember phoning Sir Michael Jay with this news. He was at the Embassy at this time and I am not sure whether he was aware of this."

Keith Moss, British Consul General, Paris: 22 Nov 07: 30.16:

Hough: Q. Did you have a conversation at some point during the day with a senior French police officer?

A. Yes, I did.... He described himself as being a member of the French equivalent of the Diplomatic Protection Group in the UK.

At 35.2: Mansfield: Q. Did you report this conversation to anyone?

A. I did. I mentioned it shortly afterwards in the same place to the Ambassador.

Q. Sir Michael Jay?

A. Yes.

.... Q. In the report you wrote up the following day, did you mention this contact with somebody who purported to be a member of the French police?

A. No, I did not.

Comment: Michael Jay has stated, in evidence not heard by the jury: "I do not believe that I was aware at the time the Princess' body had been embalmed", and this: "I do not know at what stage I acquired this information [about the embalming], and I think that it was not until relatively recently."

Jay, who was British ambassador to France at the time, was the man in overall charge of the Paris end of the British dealings in the post-crash events. Consul-General, Keith Moss, was answerable to him – "I answered directly to the Ambassador Sir Michael Jay"[160] – as was the Vice-Consul, Stephen Donnelly.[a]

There is evidence of communications between Moss and Donnelly and Jay on the day:

- Moss: "Throughout the day I gave verbal briefings to Sir Michael Jay" – statement

- Moss: "I checked with Sir Michael Jay" about Kouchner visiting Diana – statement

- Moss: "I mentioned [a conversation with a senior police officer[b]] shortly afterwards ... to the Ambassador"[c] – inquest

- Donnelly: "I spoke to the Ambassador, Michael Jay, and asked for clearance" to help Mohamed Al Fayed

- Donnelly: "I remember phoning Sir Michael Jay with this news" that Charles was coming.

This evidence reveals that there was a reasonably regular level of communication between Moss and Donnelly and Jay on the day – and I suggest this is what one would expect. Donnelly, who was two rungs lower in the chain of command, even felt free to call Jay to tell him what he had seen on the TV news.

Moss gave "verbal briefings" and even appears to have been required to call Jay to approve visiting rights for individuals.

Michael Jay expects us – not the jury, as they didn't hear any of this[d] – to believe that Moss had to get specific clearance from Jay for Minister of Health, Bernard Kouchner, to visit Diana, but no clearance was required for people who were going to spend an hour or so removing and injecting fluids into, or making alterations to, Princess Diana's body.

Unless, of course, Jay and Moss were already made aware – by British authorities, who had earlier ordered the embalming[e] – that an embalming was going to take place.

Whichever way, I suggest that Jay's denial – not heard by the jury – is a bridge too far.

---

[a] Donnelly was not directly subordinate to Jay, but was to Moss, then to Jay.

[b] This was a conversation where the officer said that if the French had been notified of Diana's presence in advance, the police could have conducted "discreet surveillance or security coverage during the time of her visit". See full transcript on inquest website.

[c] Moss did not apparently consider this conversation important enough to include in his report – see above.

[d] The jury heard Donnelly's statement, but not those of Jay or Moss.

[e] See earlier.

Jay doesn't just deny knowledge of the embalming at the time, but states that he only "acquired this information ... relatively recently". Jay made this statement in late 2005 – over 8 years after the embalming occurred. So Jay is not saying he found out about the embalming just after the event – he is saying he found out about it years after the event. "Relatively recently" I suggest could be say, a couple of years ago, maybe in 2003.[a]

If this evidence were true, it would indicate that knowledge of the embalming – which occurred virtually under the nose of Jay's underling, Moss – has been withheld from Moss' boss, Jay, for a period of around 6 years.

How could this happen?

Moss has said that he "gave verbal briefings to Sir Michael Jay ... on a strict need to know basis" through the day.[b]

This indicates then that the visit of Kouchner was "need to know" but the injection of fluids into Diana's body wasn't "need to know".

I suggest that Michael Jay has lied on oath to the British police. I am not suggesting that Jay ordered the embalming – earlier and later evidence indicates an order from British authorities in the UK to the president of Kenyons – but I am suggesting that Jay was made aware on the day that the embalming occurred. I suggest that it is fanciful for Jay to state under oath, that he was unaware of the embalming until years later.

The reality is that the main issue of the day, for Jay, was that the 36 year old Diana, Princess of Wales had died in the middle of his territorial responsibility. Surely one of his primary pressing concerns would then be the protection of the body that belonged to such a famous and dearly-loved British citizen.

The question is: How is it that in Baker's thorough inquest, the most senior British official in Paris – Michael Jay – was not asked about his knowledge of the embalming?

Evidence from Donnelly – see below – reveals that the invoice for the embalming was held up for payment for two years after the crash. Did this delay occur without the knowledge of Jay?

Why is it that Donnelly was not cross-examined at the inquest?

Moss testified about the embalming authorisation: "there must have been communications, telephone calls with people in the UK". Did these calls take place behind Jay's back?

Why is it that Moss has never been asked – by police or at the inquest – if he told Jay about the embalming?

---

[a] Jay appears to provide conflicting evidence: "I do not know at what stage I acquired this information, and I think that it was not until relatively recently." Jay says he doesn't know when he found out, then goes on to say it was "relatively recently".
[b] One could ask: Why was Moss providing information to his boss on a "strict need to know" only basis. Who instructed Moss to do this?

Jay said in his diary on the day that "French law does not let foreign undertakers work here". The team that was headed over by plane consisted of three people – a funeral director and two embalmers. What sort of "work" did Jay have in mind, if it was not to carry out an embalming?[a]

Why has Jay denied knowledge of the embalming?

It will be revealed in Part 5 that Michael Jay and all his embassy staff have provided a blanket denial that they even knew Diana was in France before the crash. This will be shown to be a convenient denial: How can a person be involved in orchestrating a murder, if they have no knowledge that the victim was anywhere near the location of their death?

In a similar way, I suggest that Jay's amazing denial of any knowledge of the embalming – until years after it occurred – is a very convenient way to distance himself from that embalming.

If Jay had no knowledge of any embalming, how then could he have had any involvement in the decision for it to take place? How could Jay have been privy to early knowledge of it – prior to 9 a.m. on the day – if he didn't even know it had occurred until years later?

Stephen Donnelly

Stephen Donnelly, British Vice Consul, Paris: 22 Sep 05 Statement read out 17 Dec 07: 118.2:
"I have been working as British Vice-Consul since 1987 in what has become titled the protection section.... I am the head of the protection section reporting directly to Her Majesty's Consul General..... I ... deal with assisting the families of the bereaved and this was my function in August of 1997.... Another role is dealing with requests from UK coroners to obtain documents from the French authorities relating to the deaths of British citizens in France.... I have been asked when I first became aware that the Princess of Wales had been embalmed..... Even when I saw the bill from BJL, I knew that they had undertaken something, but I did not know that the Princess of Wales had been embalmed. I think it was only recently that I became aware that the Princess of Wales had been embalmed, I believe as a result of documents I have seen since being asked to give this statement. I subsequently researched what embalming actually is and now know that it involves injecting chemicals into the body. I have been asked if I know what the French term 'Soins de thanatopraxie' or 'thanatopracteur' means. I did not know in August 1997. I remember 'services d'hygiene' being used in the bill from BJL and that this referred to hygiene. I thought that 'thanatopracteur' was just a fancy name...."

---

[a] The presence of British embalmers is addressed later.

Comment: British Vice-Consul, Stephen Donnelly, has given a remarkable account of his lack of knowledge of: a) the embalming of Diana; and b) embalming in general.

Donnelly has stated that at the time of the crash he was "head of the protection section" and he had been working in that section "since 1987" – about ten years. Part of Donnelly's role was in "assisting the families of the bereaved".

Despite this extensive experience, Donnelly tells us: "Even when I saw the [embalming] bill ... I knew that they had undertaken something, but I did not know that the Princess of Wales had been embalmed." In a similar vein to ambassador Michael Jay (see above), in 2005 – 8 years after the embalming – Donnelly claims: "it was only recently that I became aware that the Princess of Wales had been embalmed". Donnelly says that recently he has "researched what embalming actually is".

By 2005 – when Donnelly finally gave his evidence – he had 18 years of experience in a department of the consulate that helps bereaved families of British citizens that died in Paris. Generally the bodies of these British citizens would be transferred back to the UK for burial or cremation. The general evidence – see earlier – shows that often these bodies would be subjected to embalming prior to repatriation.[a]

I suggest that Donnelly's evidence does not make sense: he has spent up to 18 years in a job that includes "assisting the families of the bereaved", yet hasn't known what embalming is until "only recently".

It may be that Donnelly has given evidence that distances him from the embalming, as have several other crucial witnesses, including his bosses Moss and Jay – see earlier.

Delayed Payment

Payment of the embalming account was delayed by about two years.
Stephen Donnelly, British Vice Consul, Paris: 22 Sep 05 Statement read out 17 Dec 07: 124.10:
"I have been asked whether I spoke with anybody from a company called BJL on 31st August 1997. I do not recall speaking with them. I do recall months later seeing a bill from this company which had been addressed to Keith Moss. I did not know of BJL's involvement prior to this. This bill was forwarded to the Royal Matters Section so that it could be dealt with. I also remember receiving a telephone call from the company many months later stating that the bill had not been paid and a further request was forwarded to the Royal Matters Section. I am aware that it took maybe two years for the

---

[a] Most bodies are not repatriated the same day as the death as happened in the cases of Princess Diana and Dodi Fayed – often there can be a delay of several days.

bills to be paid.... My concern was not with the content of this bill, but the fact that it had not been paid, nor had the bill from PFG."

Keith Moss: 22 Oct 04 Statement: **Jury Didn't Hear**:

"The Consulate received an invoice from the 'Thanatopracteur' dated 7th October 1997.... The company name: B.J.L. Service Parisiens d'Hygiène Funéraire; B.J.L. standing for Mr Bernard J. Lane....

"This invoice is placed on the FCO file, along with the Consular Report...."[161]

René Deguisne: 9 May 05 Statement: **Jury Didn't Hear**:

"Question: Do you know who asked Pompes Funèbres[a] to act in this way? Answer: Yes, it was Mr Moss, the British Consul. He asked for this treatment in expectation of the arrival of the Prince of Wales who wished to see the body. I hand you a copy of the invoice which we sent in the first place to Mr Moss, 45 rue du Faubourg Saint Honoré, Paris 8, a copy of the credit note which cancelled that invoice and a copy of the new invoice addressed to the Embassy of Great Britain, consular section, 16 rue Anjou, Paris 8."[162]

Comment: Why was it two years before the invoices for embalming and repatriation were paid?

There is no evidence that answers this question.

The evidence from Deguisne reveals that there was an initial embalming invoice addressed to Keith Moss, but this was later cancelled and a new invoice was raised, this time "addressed to the Embassy of Great Britain".

It would be normal practice for the embalming invoice to be payable by the person or organisation that ordered it.

This would indicate that whoever paid for this invoice would be accepting responsibility for the illegal embalming of Diana, Princess of Wales.

The initial invoice was addressed to Keith Moss. I suggest that Moss would not have been happy to get this invoice in his name – the evidence (see earlier) indicates that Moss did not order the embalming.

Moss probably called BJL and asked for a credit note and a new invoice to be addressed to the British Embassy: this is what occurred – Deguisne.

The Embassy got the invoice, but still it did not get paid.

The invoice "was forwarded to the Royal Matters Section" – Donnelly. Did the royal matters section try and extract payment from the royal family?[b]

Was there an attempt to get the payment from whoever it was in the UK that ordered the embalming?

In the end – "maybe two years" – the invoice was paid, but there is no evidence of who paid it.

---

[a] PFG.

[b] Also, was there an attempt to get the royal family or Diana's family to pay for the PFG invoice relating to repatriation?

It is already publicly known that the repatriation was carried out by the royal family (Charles) but there is evidence – see later[a] – that indicates the order to embalm also came from the royal family. I suggest that the payment delay may have been due to a reticence by the royal family to admit to their role in the embalming, and therefore their liability for the invoices.

Conclusion

Coroner: Summing Up: 31 Mar 08: 50.6:
"You may think, having heard so many witnesses on the topic, that there is really no doubt at all that the embalming was entirely innocent."
Comment: Although Scott Baker included embalming – "the circumstances in which Diana's body was embalmed"[163] – as one of only eight "issues or questions that would need to be explored at these inquests"[164b], he actually spent only 700 of his 80,000 word[c] Summing Up addressing this critical issue.

Baker stated that his jury had "heard so many witnesses" on the embalming – yet the embalming occurred in France, but of the 15 French witnesses listed in the evidence table near the start of this chapter, only one was cross-examined – Monceau, and the statement of only one was read out – Amarger. There was no evidence at all heard from the remaining 13 – this is despite the fact that Baker had been given official police statements from at least 4 of those.

In other words, Lord Justice Scott Baker deliberately withheld key embalming-related evidence that could have greatly increased his own jury's understanding of the events that transpired.

On top of this, the inquest heard no evidence at all from the hospital staff and police officers that were present around the time of the embalming.[d]

It has been shown in this chapter that the person who Baker did use to provide the main supply of evidence on the embalming to the jury, French embalmer Jean Monceau, has lied repeatedly on critical issues throughout his evidence.[e]

The reality is that the assertion by Baker that his jury had "heard so many witnesses on the topic" of embalming, is a joke, if it weren't so serious: the embalming of the body of Princess Diana within 9 hours of her official time of death.

---

[a] Early Royal Control chapter.
[b] Baker reiterated these issues at the start of his Summing Up: 31 Mar 08: 56.3.
[c] Less than 1%.
[d] None of these people appear to have ever been interviewed by any of the police investigations.
[e] See later footnote for the list of Monceau's lies.

When one assesses the evidence that the jury were actually allowed to hear on the embalming issue, compared to the overall evidence that should have been available, the results are appalling. Out of 168 items of witness evidence in this Embalming chapter, only 63 – under 40% – were heard by Baker's inquest jury.

Why is this?

I suggest it is because the full embalming evidence raises issues and questions which Scott Baker – who was provided all of the evidence from Operation Paget's files – did not want his jury to be probing.

Coroner: Summing Up: 31 Mar 08: 84.22:

"Embalming can only conceivably be a relevant issue in these proceedings if Diana was pregnant when she died, for it was said that her body was unlawfully embalmed by the French on the instructions of the British Establishment for the express purpose of covering up pregnancy. If you conclude that Diana was not pregnant, you can forget about the embalming aspect of the case."

Coroner: Summing Up: 31 Mar 08: 87.6:

"There is simply no basis for concluding that embalming was performed in furtherance of a conspiracy to hide pregnancy."

Comment: There are several serious concerns regarding these directions Baker has given to his jury:

1) Baker has directly tied the relevance of embalming to an allegation: "that [Diana's] body was unlawfully embalmed by the French on the instructions of the British Establishment for the express purpose of covering up pregnancy".

Since when does a jury limit its deliberations on a subject because of an allegation? The jury should have been advised to assess the relevance of embalming based on the facts surrounding the embalming.

The allegation was that the embalming was ordered to cover-up pregnancy. Whether that allegation is true or not should not be the limiting factor governing the jury's deliberations on embalming.

For example: What if the embalming had been ordered to cover-up harmful substances that could have been administered in the ambulance? If that were the case, then that would be an example of a sinister embalming with no connection to the allegation of pregnancy.

2)   Baker has said that embalming is only relevant "if Diana was pregnant". He goes on to direct the jury: "If you conclude that Diana was not pregnant, you can forget about the embalming aspect of the case."

Baker probably felt on safe ground saying this, because the evidence that the jury heard probably would have led them to believe Diana wasn't pregnant. Evidence in Part 5 will show that Diana could have been pregnant at the time of her death – based on a more complete evidence picture than the jury were allowed by Baker to see.

Irregardless of this, it is quite wrong for Baker to direct his jury in this way. In saying it, Baker appears to have attempted to divert the attention of the jury away from embalming and onto pregnancy. As shown above, there are possible reasons for embalming that would not involve pregnancy.

An honest judge would have directed the jury to evaluate the evidence relating to the embalming, and would not have withheld 60% of that evidence – see above – from that jury.

3) By connecting the embalming solely to pregnancy, Baker precludes the jury from considering the critical possibility that on 31 August 1997 there could have been a perception of pregnancy.

Irregardless of whether Diana was actually pregnant, there is a real possibility that even a perception of pregnancy could have led to an embalming. Baker should have pointed this out to his jury.

4) Baker states: "<u>If you conclude</u> that Diana was not pregnant, you can forget about the embalming aspect of the case" – at this stage Baker is allowing the jury to draw its own conclusions – "if you conclude".

Two or three minutes later, Baker says: "There is <u>simply no basis for concluding</u> that embalming was performed in furtherance of a conspiracy to hide pregnancy" – Baker is now telling the jury what to conclude – "there is simply no basis for concluding".

The jury – who were appointed to draw conclusions on the circumstances of the deaths – should have been left by Baker to draw their own conclusions.

The jury were shown <u>no documentation at all</u> relating to the embalming of Diana, Princess of Wales.

The relevant documents – which are either missing or were never completed – are:

1) Death certificate – form JM/12 showing a medico-legal problem[a] – completed by Bruno Riou around 4.20 a.m.
2) Burial certificate for Diana – issued by Maud Coujard at around 8.30 a.m.[b]
3) Record of the request for the embalming of Diana from PFG

---

[a] This indicates suspicious circumstances of death – see earlier.

[b] Patrick Launay revealed to Paget – see later in Repatriation chapter – that he saw two copies of the burial certificate: "I asked Mr Jauze for the documents relating to the repatriation. I was provided with the burial certificate.... I produce a copy of this document as my exhibit PL11.... I think that the original of the burial certificate accompanied the coffin back to the United Kingdom. It is likely that I gave it to the English funeral directors." This evidence shows that Launay passed the copy of the burial certificate onto Paget. Why has this never been acknowledged by Paget? And why did the jury not get to see a copy of this critical document?

4) Record of receipt of request for embalming which should have been completed by BJL
5) Authorisation from Diana's family or a representative of her family
6) Statement describing the procedure of embalming
7) Medical certificate showing the death was not suspicious
8) Authorisation from the mayor, prefect or a representative.

As stated above, most of the evidence – witness and documentary – relating to the embalming was withheld from the jury. On top of this, a lot of the evidence the jury did hear was from the lying Jean Monceau.

This drought of honest evidence placed the jury in a position from which it would have been impossible to determine what actually occurred in La Pitié Salpêtrière Hospital on 31 August 1997.

Although the documentary evidence has not been made available to the author of this book, a lot of the missing witness evidence has been included in the pages of this chapter.

What are we able to ascertain from the evidence that is available, and has now been published?

The general evidence indicates that the decision to embalm Princess Diana was made in the UK, very soon after her death in the early hours of Sunday, 31 August 1997. That decision was conveyed to the president of Kenyons[a] prior to 4 a.m. (UK time).

An order to embalm was eventually relayed to Jean-Claude Plumet, a director of PFG, who passed it on to Jean Monceau, a director of BJL, by phone at around 7.45 a.m. Included in this order was a request for the embalming to be conducted by a female operator.

In the meantime, at about 7 a.m. – very close to sunrise – Princess Diana's body had been shifted into a room with no air-conditioning. From that point on, her body would be subjected to warming conditions, which became very hot as the day progressed.

At about 8.15 a.m. Monceau telephoned Sophie Hauffman – the BJL employee on duty responsible for organising the embalmers – requesting that she find a female embalmer who could carry out the embalming of Princess Diana at La Pitié Hospital.

Around this time, Keith Moss, the British Consul-General, who at 2.15 a.m. had set up a control room close to what became Diana's room, called his Vice-Consul, Stephen Donnelly. Moss asked Donnelly to find some dry ice to counter the effects of the warming room on the condition of Diana's body.

At about 9 a.m. Hauffman phoned BJL embalmer Huguette Amarger, requesting her to stand by as her "services are going to be required".

---

[a] The involvement of the president of Kenyons will be addressed in the next chapter.

Meanwhile, Donnelly had phoned PFG, where he was connected to Alain Caltiau, the Assistant General Manager and most senior person present on the day. Donnelly requested dry ice and Caltiau assured Donnelly this would be seen to. In actual fact this request was denied, because it had already been decided that the princess would be embalmed and events were in train to ensure that occurred.

At the same time – about 9 a.m. – Monceau was leaving for the hospital. He arrived after 9.30 a.m. and Amarger, after being phoned a second time, arrived with her embalming equipment over an hour later, at around 10.45 a.m. Monceau met Amarger in the hospital mortuary where they discussed the procedure that needed to be carried out. Amarger then proceeded to the heating room where Diana's body was being held.

Josselin Charrier, the second embalmer, arrived half an hour later, at about 11.15 a.m.

Diana's driver and butler, Colin Tebbutt and Paul Burrell, arrived 15 minutes later, close to 11.30 a.m. They visited the body and concerns about the effect of the heat on the body were raised – nurses told Tebbutt that Diana was "melting".

In response to concerns by hospital staff, blankets were put up to cover the windows in the room, in an attempt to shut out the prying cameras of the media. At 12 noon mobile air conditioners were brought into Diana's room and switched on.

Amidst the concerns of the heating room, Monceau – who introduced himself as an embalmer – talked to Moss, telling him that his job was to make Diana's body presentable for the forthcoming visit of Prince Charles and Diana's relatives.

At 12.30 p.m. Amarger and Charrier commenced the embalming, after Monceau had told Amarger to be quick because Prince Charles was coming in the afternoon.

Amarger, who was relatively inexperienced, completed the embalming quickly, under pressure and with poor lighting – as a result of the blankets covering the windows. The embalming was completed within an hour, by 1.30 p.m.

Post-embalming evidence shows that the embalming was only partial and was very poorly done – the one aspect that was apparently successful was the complete suctioning out of the urine from the bladder. It is significant that that was the very part of the embalming that was left out of Amarger's statement – specifically omitted when the statement was drawn up by French police Captain Isabelle Deffez.

It will be shown in the Pregnancy chapter in Part 5 that the significance of removal of the urine from the bladder is that it was no longer able to be tested for pregnancy.

There is a huge variation between the true story of what occurred – shown above – and the story that was presented to the jury.

The main areas of concern are:

1) The embalming was ordered by the British within an hour of the official death of Princess Diana.[a]

The jury got to hear that the embalming was only decided on later in the day – as a result of the potential deterioration of the body that had been stored in a non-airconditioned room. There is no question that the placement of Princess Diana's body in a warm environment did create a situation where work needed to be carried out to prevent deterioration.

That is not the problem, but there are two critical issues here:

a) Why was Diana placed in a non-airconditioned room that was going to heat up during the day?

b) The embalming decision was made at about 4.30 a.m.[b] – around 3½ hours earlier than it could have been known the room was heating up – by people who were in the UK, far removed from the Paris hospital room.

The evidence points to:

- an early embalming decision which is made to appear as though it was arrived at much later

- a deliberate early decision to place Diana's body in a warm room, to create a pretext for embalming that would fit with a later decision.

This makes the timing of the events of supreme importance – the heating room did not become a major factor until well after sunrise. It has been shown – in evidence not heard by the jury – that important calls were being made as early as 5 a.m., over two hours before sunrise.

In this context it is particularly noticeable – as shown earlier – that Monceau's inquest evidence was completely devoid of timing information. Given that Monceau was the only French witness cross-examined, this becomes very significant – no times given and no times asked of the only cross-examined French witness.

I suggest that this is not a coincidence – it was part of a coordinated approach by Baker to ensure the jury were not in a position to determine the full significance of the embalming evidence.

The creation of the hot room situation fits with the decoy methodology that was used to orchestrate the events surrounding the crash: the decoy plan to use a third car from the hotel – see Part 1; the plan to use Chez Benoît as a decoy restaurant when the Ritz was the intended destination – see Part 1; the

---

[a] Additional evidence regarding the British involvement in the embalming decision will be revealed in the next chapter.

[b] 2½ hours ahead of the movement of Diana's body to the room where she was embalmed.

testing of samples from a body other than the driver, Henri Paul's – see Part 3; and now, the embalming of Diana's body because of deterioration from the hot room when the real reason may have been something completely different.[a]

2) The jury heard that BJL responded to a request for dry ice and administered it to the body of Princess Diana in the hospital.

The evidence reveals that this did not occur – that there was a request from the British Consulate, but this was ignored by PFG and no dry ice was applied by BJL to Diana's body.

3) The jury heard that the embalming of Diana was full, thorough and well-executed.

The evidence shows quite the opposite – the embalming was partial, poorly carried out under pressure, in a rush, with poor lighting, by a relatively inexperienced embalmer. In the final analysis, the only part of the embalming process that was successfully executed was the complete removal of all urine from Princess Diana's body.

It is this massive cover-up of the evidence relating to the embalming that leads to the inevitable question: Why?

Why did Baker go to such lengths to ensure that the jury heard less than half of the evidence?

Why did the French investigation not interview any of the embalming witnesses – none of the 15 French witnesses listed in the earlier table, and also not Keith Moss, not Michael Jay, not Stephen Donnelly, not Colin Tebbutt, not Paul Burrell?[b]

Why have none of the hospital employees or police officers present during the embalming ever been interviewed by any police investigation? Why were they not heard at the inquest?

Why did the French embalmer, Jean Monceau, tell repeated lies under oath to both the British police and inquest?[c]

---

[a] The reason for the embalming is discussed later.

[b] This major omission led to a situation where the earliest evidence taken from these witnesses was by Operation Paget, 7 years after the embalming took place.

[c] Jean Monceau said that:
- he met with Philippe Massoni on arrival at the hospital – he didn't
- dry ice was applied to Princess Diana's body – it wasn't
- he met with Jean-Claude Plumet and Gérard Jauze ahead of the embalming – he didn't
- he got authorisation for the embalming from Martine Monteil – he didn't
- dry ice can't be used effectively – it can
- dry ice burns the body – it doesn't if it is applied professionally
- the embalming was full – it wasn't
- embalming does not affect the autopsy results – it does
- the embalming occurred from 2 p.m. – it occurred much earlier than that

FRENCH EMBALMING

Why is it that Monceau's evidence conflicted directly with that of several other witnesses – Martine Monteil, Philippe Massoni, Jean-Claude Plumet, Gérard Jauze – yet none of those witnesses were cross-examined at the inquest? Why did Baker – who possessed statements from all of these witnesses – fail to have them read to his jury?

Why is it that Monceau's inquest evidence conflicts so heavily with his 2005 statement, taken only 2 years earlier? Why was Monceau's police statement not heard by the jury?

Why was the most central person to this embalming, Huguette Amarger[a], not cross-examined at Baker's thorough inquest? Why was Amarger's statement omitted from the Paget Report?

Why was Jean-Claude Plumet – the most critical PFG witness, who phoned BJL early on the Sunday morning – not heard from at the inquest? Scott Baker had possession of Plumet's statement – why did he withhold it from his own jury?

Why are there so many key witnesses that have never been interviewed by the police and were not heard from at the inquest – people like:

a) Sophie Hauffman – she was involved in crucial phone calls on the day

b) Josselin Charrier – he assisted Amarger with the embalming

c) Michel Lebreton – he was supposed to have carried out the administration of dry ice

d) Bernard Colsy – he was Monceau's direct boss at BJL and must have been privy to information regarding the events that took place

e) the president of Kenyons – he phoned Hervé Racine at the unearthly hour of 5 a.m. on the Sunday morning

f) Michel Chapillon – although he was enjoying a holiday, he appears to have taken charge of the PFG response and woke people up with important phone calls on the Sunday morning

g) Alain Caltiau – he appears to be the PFG director who received Donnelly's phone call requesting dry ice, yet failed to act on it, despite assuring Donnelly that he would.

Add to these 7 witnesses the accounts of Plumet and Amarger – mentioned above – and we have the evidence of 9 witnesses, who, if Baker had allowed their evidence to be heard, could have contributed immensely to the jury's understanding of what actually occurred.

But no, these people were not heard.

-    the embalming lasted 2½ hours – it lasted maximum 1 hour
-    a BJL embalming doesn't take anything away from the body – it does
-    partial embalming does not exist – it does.

[a] Amarger's evidence also conflicts with Monceau's accounts.

And yes, we see evidence of a huge cover-up of the evidence relating to the embalming of Diana, Princess of Wales in Paris on 31 August 1997.

But why?

Because the evidence shows the embalming was not straightforward – not as it was portrayed to the jury: ordered by Monceau; authorised by Moss and Monteil; conducted at around 2 p.m.; to preserve Diana's body for later presentation to Prince Charles and Diana's sisters.

I believe there are three possible reasons why an embalming could have been ordered early in the morning by the British authorities:

1)   To cover up a possible pregnancy.

The complete removal of the urine points to this, as urine is tested for pregnancy. The blood was not completely replaced in this embalming, but evidence has already been shown that by the time the embalming occurred the blood in Diana's body may no longer have been hers – I suggest that the embalmers would have been aware of this.

This point is followed up in the Part 5 Pregnancy chapter.

2)   To cover up a possible poisoning inside the ambulance.[a]

This scenario would fit with the finding by Professor Bruno Riou that the death was suspicious[b] – see earlier. It could also fit with the removal of urine during the embalming. Later evidence – in the UK Post-Mortems chapter – will show that Princess Diana's UK post-mortem samples were switched ahead of toxicology testing.[c]

3)   A combination of points 1 and 2.

The evidence that has been addressed in this chapter should be viewed in the light of later chapters – Royal Control, UK Post-Mortems and Pregnancy (Part 5).

---

[a] The ambulance treatment issues are covered in Part 2. The evidence there shows that the actions of the doctors – Martino and Derossi – were sinister and there was plenty of opportunity for the administration of poison.

[b] Riou was not asked about this at the inquest.

[c] This aspect could also fit with the pregnancy possibility.

3   Early Royal Control

Although the events – embalming and preparation for repatriation of Diana – were happening in Paris, there is substantial evidence indicating that they were being controlled by people based in the UK.

It has already been shown that the embalming was carried out as a result of an order from the UK, prior to 9 a.m. on 31 August 1997.

Before looking into the nature of the forces at work in the UK in the hours following the death of Diana, it is necessary to deal with two significant issues:

1)   The status of Princess Diana after her divorce on 28 August 1996
2)   The royal power structure that was in operation on the morning of 31 August 1997.

Post-Divorce Status of Princess Diana

There is conflicting evidence on Diana's status at the time of her death. **Buckingham Palace**: Press Release: Status and Role of the Princess Of Wales: 28 Aug 96: **Jury Didn't Hear**:

"The Princess of Wales, as the mother of Prince William, will be regarded by The Queen and The Prince of Wales as being a member of the Royal Family."[165]

Tony Blair, Prime Minister: 2010 Book: **Jury Didn't Hear**:

"The refusal [by the Queen] to lower the flags at Windsor Castle and the Tower of London [after Diana's death] was because Diana was no longer technically a member of the royal family, having been stripped of her HRH title."[166]

Miles Hunt-Davis, Private Secretary to Prince Philip: 13 Dec 07: 82.6:

"The Princess was no longer a member of the Royal Family after the divorce in August 1996."[a]

---

[a] As though to emphasise his point, Hunt-Davis repeated this sentiment: 81.14: "The lady concerned ceased to be a member of the Royal Family"; 86.25: "once the divorce had happened, what Princess Diana did was not relevant to the mainstream of the Royal Family".

Anthony Mather, Asst Comptroller, Lord Chamberlain's Office: 23 Aug 05
Statement: **Jury Didn't Hear**:
"There are plans in place for funerals of any member of the Royal Family....
There was never a separate plan for the funeral arrangements of Diana,
Princess of Wales, as she was not at the time of her death a member of the
Royal Family.[a] Because of this, an existing plan that was already in place for
the funeral arrangements of a member of the Royal Family, was adapted."[b167]
John Burton, Royal Coroner, 1997: 16 Jun 04 Statement: **Jury Didn't
Hear**:
"I ... phoned the Buckingham Palace switchboard and spoke to a young lady
who informed that they were experiencing problems, as there were no
contingency plans for the death of Diana Princess of Wales."[168]
Keith Moss: 22 Oct 04 Statement: **Jury Didn't Hear**:
"This was a unique case. The circumstances were so special.... Although the
FCO has a manual in several volumes, covering Diplomatic Service
Procedure, including Royal matters ... they were never intended to cover the
death of a former member of the Royal Family, in a foreign country without
the Embassy's knowledge."[169]
Comment: The press release, which was issued by the Queen's press
secretary, reveals that the Queen still viewed Princess Diana as "a member of
the Royal Family".

That is in conflict with the view of her Prime Minister, Tony Blair:
"Diana was no longer technically a member of the royal family".

The evidence from Miles Hunt-Davis – who had been Philip's private
secretary for 14 years[c] – shows that his view was also quite different to that
of the Queen's press secretary: Diana was "no longer a member of the Royal
Family".

The view of Miles is supported by the evidence from the people on the
ground, dealing with the aftermath of Diana's death on 31 August 1997:

-   Mather – involved in organising Diana's repatriation (see later) – "she
was not at the time of her death a member of the Royal Family"

-   Burton – who had to decide if Diana's body came under his
jurisdiction (see later) – "there were no contingency plans for the death of
Diana"

-   Moss – involved in organising events in Paris (see earlier) – FCO
procedures "were never intended to cover the death of a <u>former member</u> of
the Royal Family".

---

[a] Mather says "there was never a separate plan for ... Diana", but there must have
been one when she was a royal. There was no plan at the time of Diana's death.
[b] Later evidence will show that Operation Overstudy was employed to repatriate
Princess Diana.
[c] At the time of the inquest – 13 Dec 07: 44.20.

Mather specifically revealed in his evidence that "there are plans in place for funerals of any member of the Royal Family", but there wasn't for Diana.

This evidence reveals that although the Queen had publicly stated on 28 August 1996 that she still regarded Diana as "a member of the Royal Family", behind the scenes action was later taken to remove Diana from the royal family list of planned funerals.

When this is seen in the light of the evidence of Miles and Mather – both key members of the royal household and well-positioned to know the makeup of the royal family – it becomes clear that by the time of her death, Diana had effectively been removed from the royal family.

In addition to this witness evidence, I suggest that there are other common sense factors that indicate Diana was no longer a royal:

-    the public perception was that by removing the HRH title, the Queen had removed Diana from the royal family[a]

-    it was the marriage to Charles that had made Diana a royal, so the termination of that marriage effectively removed her from the royal family

-    it can be normal for a divorce to remove a person from the spouse's family, regardless of the terms of settlement[b] or presence of children. It often is seen as a time when the person becomes independent from the spouse and sets about creating a new life for themselves – Diana appears to have been no different in this (see Part 2).

I suggest that even though the Queen's publicly stated view was that Diana was still a royal, her actual view – revealed by the Queen's actions, e.g. removal of the HRH title, removal of a specific funeral plan[c] – appears to have been that she no longer saw Princess Diana as a member of the royal family.[d]

---

[a] Blair indicates this in his book: "Diana was no longer technically a member of the royal family, having been stripped of her HRH title".

[b] Diana's settlement involved retaining accommodation in Kensington Palace as "a central and secure home for the Princess and the children": Buckingham Palace Press Release: 28 August 1996.

[c] This is not just that there was no plan at the time of Diana's death. The reality is that there would have been a plan when Diana was a member of the royal family, but in the relatively short period of 12 months between the divorce and Diana's death, the Queen has had that plan removed.

[d] There are other events that have occurred over the years which support the belief that the Queen no longer sees Princess Diana as a royal: According to author Christopher Andersen, Buckingham Palace staff were told after the divorce that Diana's name was "never again to be spoken in the presence of the Queen". Already in July 1996, the *London Gazette*, on the Queen's instructions, had published letters patent deleting Diana's name from prayers for the royal family in churches throughout Christendom. Earlier, in 1993, after Diana and Charles' separation and

Royal Power Structure: 31 August 1997

On the morning of the crash, 31 August 1997, the key royal – family and household – figures were in various locations throughout the UK.

See diagram on the following page.[ab170]

---

four years before Diana's death, Buckingham Palace had deleted Diana's name from the *Court Circular*, which lists official royal engagements. Following Diana's death, the Queen instructed that her name was not to be mentioned during the Sunday morning service at Crathie Kirk, near Balmoral. The Queen stated that no prayers were to be spoken in remembrance of Diana. The minister instead gave his original prepared sermon about the joys of moving house, including jokes by Billy Connolly. By 2007, 10 years after her death, Diana postcards were banned from sale at royal shops and palaces. Sources: Christopher Andersen, The Day Diana Died, 1998, p57; Anthony Holden, Charles at Fifty, 1998, pp328,352; Ken Wharfe with Robert Jobson, Diana: Closely Guarded Secret, 2002, p205; Andrew Morton, Diana: Her True Story – In Her Own Words, 1997, p276; Richard Palmer, Diana is Still Loved ... But Her Palace Postcards are Banned, Daily Express, May 8 2007.

[a] Locations are shown directly under the name of the individual.

[b] The evidence of only two of these key people was heard at the inquest: Fellowes and Mather. Another six – the Queen, Janvrin, Ogilvy, Ross, Harding, Ridley – have also never been interviewed by any of the police investigations. Burton gave a police statement which was not read out at the inquest.

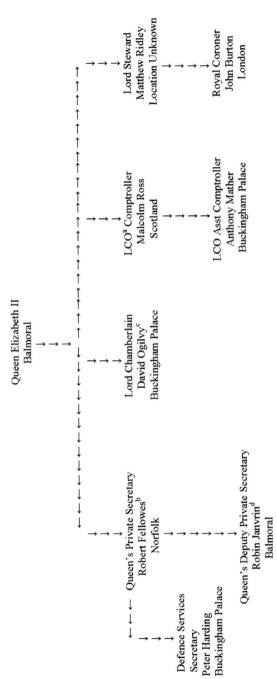

Figure 9

---

[a] Lord Chamberlain's Office.

[b] Brother-in-law to Princess Diana.

[c] Earl of Airlie. Also known as Lord Airlie.

[d] Mary Francis was "Assistant Private Secretary" to the Queen at the time of the crash. Francis' location is not known, but she does not appear to have played a role in the events.

291

Role of the Lord Chamberlain's Office

The Lord Chamberlain's Office – based at Buckingham Palace – played a key role in the events of 31 August 1997.

Anthony Mather, Asst Comptroller, Lord Chamberlain's Office: 22 Nov 07: 85.1:

Hough: Q. Would you rely upon the undertakers, in this case Levertons, to determine whether any operations were necessary to preserve the body?

A. I think one would, yes. They were more experienced than we were.

Q. Would you, as a general matter, leave it to them to decide on any action, either to preserve the body or to seal the coffin?

A. Yes.

Q. Now turning to the events of 31st August 1997, were you at home when you were first informed of the events in Paris?

A. I was.

Q. I think you were informed by Lieutenant Colonel Malcolm Ross.

A. Indeed. He was the comptroller.

Q. Did he contact you at about 6 o'clock in the morning?

A. Yes.

Q. Did you arrive in Buckingham Palace at about half past 8?

A. About then, yes.

Q. And once there, were you responsible for communications between the Palace and Balmoral, where members of the Royal Family were resident?

A. I would not say I was responsible, but I was in contact with them. It was a Sunday morning, it was a Bank Holiday, there were a few people around. When I got into the Palace, the Lord Chamberlain was in, as was the defence services secretary. We each took our particular roles and got on with our jobs.

Q. Your role involved some organisation of the repatriation operation?

A. We started operation – or I started Operation Overstudy and then turned to what happened when the body got back to Northolt.

Q. I think it was you who called in Levertons by communicating with Keith Leverton.

A. Yes.

Q. We have already heard from Clive Leverton earlier today about their involvement.[a] Now did you yourself, at any stage, communicate with any

---

[a] This is a typical example of the minimalist approach to seeking evidence at the Baker inquest. It will be shown in this chapter that Levertons' role is of critical importance and of particular significance is the relationship between Levertons and Mather. Hough here effectively removes any possible light that Mather could have shone on this subject. It is pretty basic to any search for the truth that the evidence of all relevant witnesses is taken, compared and analysed – it is very foolish to presume that every witness is speaking the truth, or has an accurate recall. This is additional

officials in France about the repatriation or about the arrangements for the body?

A. None, none whatsoever.

Q. Did you or anyone else in the Lord Chamberlain's office or the Palace have any involvement in the decision to embalm the Princess of Wales?

A. No.

....Q. Did you ... liaise with the Princess of Wales' private secretary, Mr Gibbins, from whom we have heard?

A. I remember not, but I am sure – the telephone did not stop, so I am sure "yes" is the answer.

....Q. Now, were you at any stage personally aware who at the British Embassy in Paris was coordinating that end of things.

A. No. From the Lord Chamberlain's office, we had no communications with France.

Q. Are you aware of anybody at the Palace having any communication with the British Embassy in Paris?

A. I can only assume that the private secretaries were, but I can only assume that.

Q. Not certainly from your end in terms of organising the arrangements for the body and its repatriation?

A. None at all.

Anthony Mather, Asst Comptroller, Lord Chamberlain's Office: 23 Aug 05 Statement: **Jury Didn't Hear**:

"In 1997 Lord Airlie was the Lord Chamberlain, and Lieutenant Colonel Malcolm Ross CVO, OBE was the Comptroller. My role as Assistant Comptroller meant that I spent 75% of my time concerned with honours and awards, and 25% of my time concerned in arrangements for funerals, ceremonial programmes, state visits, and garden parties at the Palace. My responsibility for funerals within the Lord Chamberlains office was for all members of the Royal Family, excluding the Monarch.

"The Monarch's funeral is the responsibility of the Earl Marshal, because it would always be a state funeral....

"In August 1991 Levertons ... became the undertakers to the Royal Family.... My contacts within Levertons in 1997 were and still are to this present day the brothers Keith and Clive Leverton....

"There are plans in place for funerals of any member of the Royal Family. Within those plans Operation Overstudy is a Royal Air Force plan to repatriate any member of the Royal Family following their death abroad,

---

evidence that there was no thorough search for the truth at the Diana inquest – as has been amply shown in this series of books.

back to the United Kingdom. I was involved in the operational plan named 'Operation Overstudy' from 1991 until 1999. During that time I was involved in updating and reviewing it on a regular basis in conjunction with the RAF....

"In 1997 Operation Overstudy was utilised to repatriate the Princess of Wales. Within this plan Levertons staff would travel on a separate aircraft to any member of the Royal Family, and arrive at the destination airfield in advance of the coffin.[a]

"Levertons ... would consider whether embalming was initially necessary upon their arrival and liaise with us....

"In my experience embalming is a requirement following the death of a member of the Royal Family for the purpose of preservation and presentation prior to the funeral taking place. The specifics of how the deceased should be prepared, and under what conditions the coffins are kept is not contained within Operation Overstudy. The undertakers take responsibility for this....

"On Sunday 31st August 1997 Lieutenant Colonel Malcolm Ross was at his home in Scotland. He contacted me at 0600 hours [6.00 a.m.] at my home, as a result of which I went straight to Buckingham Palace arriving at 0830 hours. Here I established a telephone link between the Palace and Balmoral where the Queen, and the Prince of Wales were in residence. Lord Airlie[b] was already at the Palace. From my recollection an RAF BAe 146 was sent to Aberdeen from RAF Northolt to collect the Prince of Wales. Subsequently Operation Overstudy was requested by me, as this was the most logical method of repatriating Diana, Princess of Wales.

"My responsibility was co-ordinating the staff involved with the repatriation operation and the reception in the United Kingdom.... I communicated with Keith Leverton over the telephone to his office in Camden. He communicated with his brother Clive Leverton who went to Paris. If they had any doubts or questions they would have contacted me for advice. I was in effect their point of contact within the staff at Buckingham Palace. The Lord Chamberlains office took instructions from the Prince of Wales' and the Queen's private secretaries. I did not communicate with the French authorities, and I did not speak to anyone about the decision or authority to embalm Diana, Princess of Wales' body. To the best of my knowledge and belief the Lord Chamberlains Office had no involvement in the decision to embalm Diana, Princess of Wales.

"I understand that Sir Malcolm Ross and Dr Burton were involved in communicating with the Princess of Wales' Family. Following the post

---

[a] The evidence will show that Levertons travelled with the coffin, not "in advance of" it.

[b] Lord Chamberlain – David Ogilvy.

mortem examination in the United Kingdom[a] I was aware that the undertakers had to carry out final preparations including the embalming of the body of Diana, Princess of Wales at The Chapel Royal, St James's Palace.

"I attended Fulham Mortuary on Sunday 31st August 1997 in company with Lady Sarah McCorquodale and Lady Jane Fellowes. I took them to the office area where Dr Burton spoke to them concerning his role and the post mortem examination....

"I would ... have been leasing with Diana, Princess of Wales' Private Secretary Mr Michael Gibbins. I cannot remember if any representative of the Lord Chamberlains office was on the Royal flight, or the undertaker's flight that day[b]....

"There was never a separate plan for the funeral arrangements of Diana, Princess of Wales, as she was not at the time of her death a member of the Royal Family. Because of this, an existing plan that was already in place for the funeral arrangements of a member of the Royal Family, was adapted.

"I was not aware personally who was co-ordinating actions at the British Embassy in Paris and their actions would not have been under my control. I do not recall communicating with any one there on that day.

"The repatriation procedures laid out in Operation Overstudy were followed and although things were rather hectic and chaotic during the course of the day, there were no major problems.

"I did not make any notes of what happened that day. I would have been writing notes, names and the like on the Sunday, and later a file note would have been made and kept within the Palace.

"On Tuesday 23rd August 2005 Detective Constable Emeny and Detective Sergeant Grater came to Buckingham Palace to obtain this statement from me. I showed them, and have allowed them access to correspondence and papers held by the Lord Chamberlains Office with regard to the events of Sunday 31st August 1997. This correspondence and papers includes the file note made on the 1st of September 1997 summarising the events of the previous day. The remainder of correspondence and papers refers to the

---

[a] It is possible that Mather has described this as the "post mortem examination in the United Kingdom" to distinguish it from the earlier post-mortem in France, described in chapter 1.

[b] There is no evidence of any passengers other than the undertaker and embalmers being on the flight, and it is not known why Mather has included this in his statement. It introduces the question:Why would someone think that there could have been a representative from the LCO on the flight?

funeral and those attending. These files are currently retained at the Palace, and will in future be placed within the Royal Archive."[171a]

Comment: In evidence not heard by the jury, Mather describes "the file note made on the 1st of September 1997 summarising the events" and "correspondence and papers ... with regard to the events".[b]

The question is: Why weren't these notes, correspondence and papers shown to the inquest jury that was investigating the events they related to?

The truth is that not only were these critical documents not shown to the jury, but the document that revealed they existed – Mather's statement – was also not shown.

The jury would have had no knowledge that this documentation existed. Why?

Communication with Gibbins

Colin Tebbutt, Diana's Driver and Security: 26 Nov 07: 91.1:
Hough: Q. When you first spoke to Mr Gibbins, what instructions did he give you?
A. I gave him as full and comprehensive a report as I could, but the message came over very quickly: just leave everything alone with the Princess.
Q. How do you mean "leave everything alone"?
A. Well, that Levertons, the Royal undertakers, would be here to take care of everything. The only problem I could see was they were arriving very late in the day.
Q. When were they due to arrive?
A. 5 o'clock, sir.
.... Q. When you did speak to Mr Gibbins, what was the conversation you had with him and what was his response?
A. Well, it was still not to do anything until Levertons came, but after we all described – I described to him my thoughts – I cannot remember the exact words, but he agreed that something should be done.
Q. Did he seek authorisation from anyone else before he said that to you?
A. I do not know, sir. I think he might have spoken to Mr Moss.
Colin Tebbutt, Diana's Driver and Security: 5 Jul 04 Statement: **Jury Didn't Hear**:
"On one line I rang Mr Gibbins.... He told me to take any action that I deemed necessary, but not to allow anyone touch the body until Levertons, the Royal Undertakers, arrived....

---

[a] Just 3 months after the events, Anthony Mather was awarded a CVO – Royal Victorian Order, Commander – from the Queen, announced in the New Year's Honours List, 31 December 1997. Source: Life Peers to Order of the Companion of Honour, BBC News, 31 December 1997, p4.
[b] Mather states that he showed these to Paget officers on 23 August 2005.

"I had received word from Mr Gibbins that Levertons, the Royal Undertakers were due to arrive at around 5 p.m., and that no-one should do anything until such time as they got here.... "I rang Mr Gibbins. I told him that, as I understood it, if we waited for Levertons to arrive with a coffin at 5 p.m., the information that I had been given was that the Princess was melting. I asked him to find out what to do....

"Mr Gibbins rang me back and said that, 'If you think, they will do a good job. Then Yes.' He expressed that if they were proper Funeral Directors employed by the Hospital and if Mr Moss was in agreement they should be allowed to carry on."[172a]

Michael Gibbins, Diana's Private Secretary: 21 Nov 07: 6.16:
Burnett: Q. Do you recollect receiving a call to inform you of the death of the Princess?
A. Yes, I do.
Q. Where did that telephone come from?
A. It came from Balmoral.
Q. Are you able now to recall who made the telephone call?
A. I think it was Robin Janvrin, who was the deputy private secretary to the Queen.
....Q. You had been in the office all night essentially. Did you return home for a short break?
A. I did.
Q. Was that at about half past 7 or 8 o'clock in the morning?
A. I would think so, yes.
Q. But did you return to the office at some point in the mid-morning at 11 or 11.30?
A. Yes, I did.
Q. Are you able to give us an indication generally of the atmosphere in the office and what was happening?
A. Well, I think everyone was very upset indeed. The telephones were constantly ringing from all sorts of places; from the media, from friends of the Princess and indeed from Paris.
Q. Was your principal function then to be fielding telephone calls?
A. Amongst the other members of staff, yes.
Q. Once you were back in the office after 11 to 11.30, did Colin Tebbutt call ever?
A. Several times, yes.
....Q. Was there any other motive in suggesting that something should be

---

[a] The full text of this portion of the statement has been shown earlier in the Tebbutt-Gibbins Role section of the Embalming chapter.

done, other than the presentability of the Princess's body before people came to see her?

A. None at all.

Q. Did you have any discussion that you can now recollect about the detail of what was proposed should happen?

A. None at all.

Q. At what stage did you learn that the Princess's body was to be repatriated that day?

A. I think some time in the afternoon, I cannot be more precise than that, when I received a call from, again, Robin Janvrin in Balmoral to suggest that I should go to Northolt to be in the receiving line.

Q. And that is what you did?

A. I did.

....Q. At that stage, did you learn that the body of the Princess was to be conveyed to Fulham mortuary?

A. I did.

Q. Did you at any stage during the course of that day learn that a post-mortem examination was to be carried out?

A. I think I was told that at the mortuary by, I think it was, Dr Burton.

Michael Gibbins, Diana's Private Secretary: 1 Sep 04 Statement: **Jury Didn't Hear**:

"There was some question of the hospital authorities trying to preserve the Princess.... I said Colin 'Thank you for reporting that, you must follow what the hospital authorities say and go with it'....

"A lot of the decisions that Colin Tebbutt was asking me to make needed to be made by the relatives, but I had no one to call....[a]

"Throughout that day I do not recall receiving directions from either the Foreign Office or our embassy in Paris."[173]

Comment: When it comes to contacts between Paris and London on the day, there are several major issues in the evidence.

When Tebbutt, in Paris, first contacts Gibbins, in London, "the message came over very quickly: just leave everything alone with the Princess". Then: "Levertons ... would be here to take care of everything".

Tebbutt's statement – not heard by the jury – was more specific: Tebbutt was told by Gibbins "not to allow anyone touch the body until Levertons ... arrived".

Later, Tebbutt rang Gibbins back to say that something had to be done to prevent the deterioration of Princess Diana's body – "the Princess was melting". In his statement Tebbutt next says: "I asked him to find out what to do.... Mr Gibbins rang me back and said...."

---

[a] The full text of this portion of the statement has been shown earlier in the Tebbutt-Gibbins Role section of the Embalming chapter.

At the inquest, Tebbutt changed his evidence: "I described to him my thoughts ... [and] he agreed that something should be done". Hough then specifically asked: "Did he seek authorisation from anyone else before he said that to you?" Tebbutt: "I do not know, sir. I think he might have spoken to Mr Moss."

In Tebbutt's statement we see two phone calls – 1) Tebbutt to Gibbins, asking "him to find out what to do"; and 2) Gibbins to Tebbutt, giving the response.[a]

This evidence reveals that Gibbins sought authorisation from someone in between the phone calls.

At the inquest, just the one phone call: Tebbutt to Gibbins – no delay: "he agreed that something should be done". When questioned on the authorisation, Tebbutt says "I do not know" and suggests Gibbins might have talked to Moss.

There are two reasons why Moss would not have been the person Gibbins spoke to:

1) Tebbutt's statement reveals that Gibbins spoke to someone else before calling back and that Tebbutt was aware when he called, that Gibbins would need to get authorisation – Tebbutt asked Gibbins: "to find out what to do". Moss was in the hospital with Tebbutt – if Gibbins had needed authorisation from Moss, then Tebbutt would have put Moss on the line. i.e. one phone call.

2) Gibbins passed on the authorisation to Tebbutt with conditions – one of those conditions was: "if Mr Moss was in agreement". This shows that Gibbins left it up to Tebbutt to check that Moss was in agreement.[b]

The obvious question is: Whose authorisation did Gibbins need to seek before he called Tebbutt back?

I suggest it is the same person who had earlier been in contact with Gibbins instructing him "not to allow anyone touch the body until Levertons ... arrived".

Was it the Lord Chamberlain's Office Assistant Comptroller, Anthony Mather?

At the inquest Mather was asked if he liaised with Gibbins on the day. Mather replied: "I remember not, but I am sure – the telephone did not stop, so I am sure 'yes' is the answer". In his statement – not heard by the jury – Mather was far more definite on this: "I would ... have been liaising with Diana, Princess of Wales' Private Secretary Mr Michael Gibbins."

---

[a] The response was to okay the embalming procedure as long as "they were proper Funeral Directors" and "Moss was in agreement".

[b] Tebbutt's response at the inquest indicates that he wasn't expecting Hough to ask him about the authorisation that was implied in his statement.

It is significant that in the evidence from Gibbins, he has avoided mention of any contact with Mather or the Lord Chamberlain's Office.

In fact Gibbins' account – in a similar vein to his evidence on contact with Diana's relatives (see earlier) – is notable for his failure to have any prior knowledge of any key events:

- discussion on the "detail of what was proposed should happen" to Diana's body: "none at all"
- repatriation that day – "some time in the afternoon, I cannot be more precise"
- destination of Fulham mortuary – after his arrival at RAF Northolt
- UK post-mortem – "I was told that at the mortuary".[a]

In his statement, Gibbins – who was awarded an LVO three months after the crash[b] – volunteers: "Throughout that day I do not recall receiving directions from either the Foreign Office or our embassy in Paris".

Gibbins' claims of lack of prior knowledge of key events – listed above – create a picture of Gibbins on the day, at Kensington Palace, but stranded on an island of ignorance. This fits with Gibbins' earlier family notification evidence: "I had no one to call.... I was in London, what could I do".

The above evidence from Tebbutt reveals that this perception is a lie – on three counts:

- Tebbutt "had received word from ... Gibbins that Levertons ... were due to arrive at around 5 p.m."
- Tebbutt was told by Gibbins "not to allow anyone touch the body until Levertons ... arrived"
- when Tebbutt "asked [Gibbins] to find out what to do", Gibbins then consulted an unnamed person for instructions before he "rang [Tebbutt] back".

Tebbutt's evidence reveals that Gibbins was receiving information and instructions from some source. Gibbins has specifically stated: "I do not recall receiving directions from either the Foreign Office or our embassy in Paris" but in saying this, Gibbins notably fails to mention Buckingham Palace or Balmoral.[c]

---

[a] In saying this, Gibbins has indicated that he found out at RAF Northolt that they were heading to Fulham Mortuary with Diana's body, but he had no knowledge of why he was making this trip. The sole purpose of attending the mortuary was for the post-mortem, but Gibbins waited until after arriving at the mortuary to be told a post-mortem of Diana was going to be carried out.

[b] See earlier footnote in Family Notification section of the Embalming chapter.

[c] This could be an indication that from Gibbins' point of view post-death decisions relating to Diana were being controlled by the royals, not the civil authorities. It will be shown later that this is what occurred. The assassination of Princess Diana may have been carried out by the intelligence agencies – see Part 5 – but the post-death decisions were handed over to be controlled by the royal family and royal household.

In contrast, Mather – who was at Buckingham Palace – has admitted he liaised with Gibbins (see above).

I suggest that Gibbins' failure to mention contact with Mather on the day is a lie by omission. Gibbins should have been directly asked about contact with Mather, but he wasn't.

At the inquest Mather confirmed that he "called in Levertons by communicating with Keith Leverton". Mather added in his statement: "If they had any doubts or questions they would have contacted me for advice. I was in effect [Levertons'] point of contact within the staff at Buckingham Palace."

In other words, Mather enlisted Levertons for the job – repatriation and embalming[a] – and he was effectively their employer for the day, and ultimately responsible for their actions.

The above evidence from Tebbutt indicates that Gibbins had been provided information regarding Levertons' movements, their expected arrival time at the hospital, instructions that Diana was not to be touched by anyone ahead of Levertons' arrival and later, clearance, after consultation, that the embalming could go ahead.

When one puts this evidence together – Mather, Tebbutt, Gibbins' evasiveness – it seems logical that Gibbins was in communication with Mather and was receiving information and instructions from him. I suggest that Gibbins called Mather to receive clearance to communicate to Tebbutt that it was okay for the embalming to proceed. The reason Gibbins would have called Mather is because Mather would have been the person who earlier had clearly instructed him "not to allow anyone touch the body until Levertons ... arrived".

Mather has categorically denied this: "I did not speak to anyone about the decision or authority to embalm Diana, Princess of Wales".[b]

I suggest Mather is yet another person who has attempted to distance himself from what was an illegal and despicable event[c] – the BJL embalming of Diana, Princess of Wales.

The evidence pointing to this will become clearer as this chapter develops. This fits with the overall theme of the general evidence that will emerge through this volume: Princess Diana was ousted from the royal family in August 1996, but precisely a year later, on 31 August 1997, in death, she was immediately reclaimed as a royal.

[a] In the team of three people sent to Paris on the day, two were embalmers. This is dealt with later.

[b] Both Mather's and Gibbins' phone records should have been examined during the police investigation – this never occurred.

[c] Mather's activities through the day are discussed in more detail later.

The general evidence will point to Mather giving instructions relating to the embalming. It will be shown later that Mather authorised the despatch of two UK embalmers – Green and Fry – to Paris as a back-up plan. If the illegal French embalming had been prevented from taking place, then the British embalmers had the equipment with them to carry out a quick embalming prior to repatriating Diana back to the UK.

Role of Levertons[a]

Anthony Mather contacted Levertons early on Sunday 31 August 1997.
Clive Leverton, Royal Funeral Director: 22 Nov 07: 68.24:
Hough: Q. Your contact at the Lord Chamberlain's office in 1997 was Lieutenant Colonel Anthony Mather, from whom we will be hearing this afternoon.
A. Correct.
Q. His official title was "assistant comptroller"?
A. Correct.
Q. Is it right to say that for members of the Royal Family, you have a general operational plan for the repatriation of their bodies in case they should unfortunately die overseas?
A. We have some plans for some members of the Royal Family and there is an overall operational plan involving repatriation if there is a death abroad....
Q. How many of you and your staff does that plan allow for?
A. Three broadly.
Q. Who would that be expected to be?
A. Well, myself or my brother, who is now retired, two others, one of whom would be an embalmer and a third person.
....Q. When you had to deal with the death of the Princess of Wales, did you consider it necessary to seal the coffin using its hermetic seal function?
A. We did not consider it necessary. We were under extreme pressure time-wise and we knew that the – sorry, can you say that again, please?
Q. Did you have to seal the coffin hermetically?
A. No, we did not consider it necessary.
Q. Is it right to say that the following members of your staff were involved.... First of all, there is Daniel Tassell, who I think was the resident duty manager.
A. Correct.
Q. Is it right to say that he was the first person who took the phone call because he was responsible for taking phone calls out of hours?
A. Yes, he was our resident manager at our head office in Camden and he took the first call.

---

[a] Witness evidence in this section is also referred to in the Use of British Embalmers section in the Repatriation Issues chapter.

Q. Is it right to say that he contacted your brother, who then contacted you?
A. That is correct, yes.
Q. The second member of your staff involved, David Green.
A. Yes.
Q. Now, who is he and what is his function?
A. He is a full-time qualified embalmer.
Q. Do you have any other embalmers on your staff?
A. No.
Q. Was another embalmer involved called Bill Fry?
A. Yes, in the event, I had to try to get hold of Bill because it was a bank holiday Sunday in August. David Green was camping on a farm in Dorset and we were having a hell of a job to get hold him and getting him back to London, so I had to get hold of another embalmer in case I could not get hold of David.
Q. So going back to the events on 31st August, 1997, where were you when you first heard about the crash and the death of the Princess of Wales?
A. My mother-in-law's in Cheltenham.
Q. What time did you receive the call?
A. I think it was 6.45 [a.m.] I think that rings a bell.
Q. That is what you say on page 4 of your statement.
A. Yes, 6.45.
Q. Now, what did you do when you received that first call?
A. I asked my brother to repeat what he told me over the phone, I think words to the effect of "the Princess of Wales had been killed, Dodi Al Fayed had been killed in a car accident in Paris". I could not believe what he said. He said it again and I said, "Right, I am on my way back to London".
Q. Your home in London is, I think, about an hour and a half by car from Cheltenham where you were.
A. I did exceed the speed limit.
Q. We have heard of a number of people doing that in this case. Is it right to say that you met up with your brother, Keith, and Mr Tassell, the duty manager, at 10 o'clock in the morning?
A. Yes, I went home and I went straight down to Camden.
Q. By the time you met them and, in fact, before you went out to France, did you know whether the Princess had been embalmed or whether any process had been carried out to preserve her body?
A. I had not a clue what we were going into, which is why I took the embalmers. We had no idea of the situation we were going into.
Q. Had you been given any instructions about any procedures to carry out on the body?
A. None whatsoever.

Q. You have just mentioned that you decided to take the embalmers.... Can you explain why you took those, despite having no specific instructions to embalm?

A. I just used my common sense, basically. As I said, I had trouble getting hold of David Green. That is why I contacted Bill Fry, who kindly came down. They were the two chaps. We were under a lot of pressure time-wise because we had to be at the airport by 1 to get out to Paris and we had no time at all.

Q. So you get to the airport at 1 o'clock, is that right?

A. Ish. I think we were a bit late.

Q. And that is you, Mr Green and Mr Fry?

A. Yes.

Q. Before you set off, had you received any specific instructions about preservation, care or repatriation at all?

A. Absolutely none, other than obviously we were going to have to bring her back. But that is all.

At 74.6: Q. I think you arrived at Pitié Salpêtrière at about half past three to quarter to four. I think that is in your statement.

A. Yes.

Q. When you were en route to the hospital, did you receive any information about the condition of the Princess or what you might have to do?

A. No.

Q. Now I think you entered the hospital by the main entrance –

A. Yes.

Q. – and the embalmers, with their equipment and the coffin, went in through a more discreet entrance.

A. Yes.

Q. When you got to the room where the Princess was, did you know at that stage whether any procedure had been carried out on her body?

A. No.

Q. At that stage, did you receive any instructions?

A. No.

....Q. What did you do with the body [after arriving at the hospital]?

A. I – we knew by now that time was getting very short. We knew that Prince Charles and her sisters were on the way to identify her and pay their respects, so we placed the coffin – by which time that had come into the room – on our trolley. We had a folding trolley. We moved her from the bed into the coffin and made her look as presentable as possible for her family.

At 78.22: Mansfield: Q. You indicated at the start of your evidence that – you used these words: you were under considerable, you used the word "extreme" pressure timewise from the beginning?

A. Right, yes.

Q. Because you knew you had to do everything that day, is that it?

A. No. We had to get out to Paris quickly. We were under pressure getting our staff assembled.

Q. But had somebody said, "Look, you have to do this as quickly as possible"?

A. No.

Q. But you just felt you had to?

A. I put myself under the pressure, to get things done.

Q. Just going forward: By the time you got there, you said you had not gone with the specific instruction to embalm?

A. Correct.

Q. And is this right, you did not gather whether or to what extent she had been embalmed?

A. I did not. When I entered the room, somebody introduced themselves – I think it was a lady and a man – as the embalmers. But to be quite honest, my concern was the poor lady on the bed and I saw that she was looking not too bad and the subject of embalming really never –

Q. Crossed your mind?

A. It was not important.

At 81.17: Horwell: Q. Your instruction was a single one, which was to repatriate the Princess?

A. In essence, yes.

Q. You had never received any instruction to embalm her?

A. Never.

Q. And the decision to take embalmers with you to Paris was yours and yours alone?

A. Yes and my brother's; ours.

Q. Yours and your brother's alone, and the only reason why that decision was made was on the principle of "just in case"?

A. Exactly. I had no idea of the situation we were going into.

Clive Leverton, Royal Funeral Director: 13 Jul 04 Statement: **Jury Didn't Hear**:

"The Lord Chamberlains' officers are the only people we receive our instructions from in the event of a death within the Royal Family. The contact there in 1997 was Lieutenant Colonel Anthony Mather O.B.E who was the Assistant Comptroller. The Lord Chamberlain is amongst other things, directly responsible to the Monarch who entrusts funeral arrangements to him, his comptroller, and then assistant comptroller.

"For members of the royal family there is an operational plan for Royal Air Force involvement, and our part in it, to repatriate the body....

"It refers to the undertaker (myself or Keith) two assistants, the repatriation coffin, and equipment such as for embalming, being flown to the destination in one air force aircraft, and for us to return with the body to an RAF airfield on the Royal Flight. We do not travel out with the Royal flight, we go before it, but the coffin does come back with the funeral director on the Royal flight. We would go out, for example, by RAF Hercules transport plane, and return on a Royal Flight aircraft. The main difference with the Royal family and regular clients is that we do not speak at all directly with any member of the royal family. We do not have any company documents or standard procedures concerning arrangements for repatriation or embalming concerning the Royal family, we get on with the task based upon our experience, knowledge and instructions at the time....

"At the time of the death of Diana Princess of Wales on the 31st August 1997, the following staff were involved. Daniel Tassel.... He was the first person contacted at Levertons on the Sunday morning by the Lord Chamberlains Assistant Comptroller. Daniel then contacted my brother that morning, and he contacted me.

"David Green has worked for us for about 15 years; he was at the time and still is our full time embalmer. Bill Fry was the other person involved he is another embalmer whom we know. He is the co-owner of Clarke and Strong of Coventry, who supply inside soft material sets for coffins. So we used him as a backup in these circumstances. David and Bill are both members of B.I.E, the British Institute of Embalmers. The reason I took David and Bill was because if the deceased required embalming they would carry it out for me.

"At the time of the request to repatriate the Princess I did not know whether she had been embalmed or not from what my brother had told me. I did not know where in Paris she was, or the condition of her body. We were not told whether any preparation or embalming had been carried out. We were not told to go out embalm and return her, we were given no instructions as to how to prepare her. Because we were not in contact with the family, either Diana's, namely Lady Sarah and Lady Jane, nor Prince Charles or any member of the Royal Family we were only to take instructions from the L.C.O. (Lord Chamberlain's Office). I therefore did not discuss preparation care, or indeed anything with the family, as I would normally do.

"There were pressures and time constraints placed upon us in these circumstances. Likewise I did not receive instructions from the police, the coroner nor the coroners' officer at all concerning preservation care or the repatriation. We didn't know until we reached the hospital in Paris what, if any, funeral directors had been involved with the care of the Princess of Wales.

"I took David and Bill because I didn't know what embalming if any, had been carried out, nor whether any was necessary at all. By taking the embalmers we would be prepared and able to carry out embalming if necessary in Paris. No specific instructions were given and so I made arrangements with my brother for myself, David, Bill, the first call coffin and our equipment to go immediately to the RAF Airfield, which in this case was Northolt. This was for us to repatriate the Princess in the coffin.

"I did not speak to Lt Col Mather nor did I receive any instructions from him. He spoke to my brother who was in communication with me.

"I had received a call at about 0645am on the Sunday morning whilst I was in Cheltenham. So I then travelled to my house in Crouch End, a 1 and ½ hour journey, and from there went to our office in Camden. I met up with Keith and Daniel at about 1000 am, I then learnt that we were to fly to France at 1pm. We didn't have much time to make arrangements and we had real trouble getting David back to the office from Dorset or Hampshire where he was at the time. He arrived just before we were due to leave the office. Bill was given a police escort part of the way from his home to our office.

"The Royal standard for placing on the coffin was now in our possession. The transportation was all arranged, and therefore our work started from when we arrived in France."[174]

Keith Leverton, Royal Funeral Director: 27 Oct 04 Statement: **Jury Didn't Hear**:

"The Lord Chamberlains' officers are the only people we receive our instructions from in the event of a death within the Royal Family. The contact there in 1997 was Lieutenant Colonel Anthony Mather O.B.E who was the Assistant Comptroller. The Lord Chamberlain is amongst other things, directly responsible to the Monarch who deputises down funeral arrangements to him, his comptroller, and then the assistant comptroller.[a] The main difference with the Royal family and regular clients is that we do not communicate with or receive instructions direct from any member of the family....

"At the time of the death of Diana, Princess of Wales on the 31st August 1997, the following staff were involved.[b] Daniel Tassell, the resident duty manager at the time. Daniel was the first person contacted at Levertons on the Sunday morning by the Lord Chamberlains[c] Assistant Comptroller Lt. Colonel Anthony Mather. Daniel was informed that there had been a death in Paris and it was not the Queen Mother.

---

[a] These 65 words of Keith's statement are almost identical to Clive's earlier statement – shown above. There are only two minor changes: Keith has changed "entrusts" to "deputises down" and has added "the" in front of "assistant comptroller". This issue of a copied statement is addressed in the following Comment.

[b] This sentence has been copied directly from Clive Leverton's statement. While Clive went on to describe the staff involved, Keith only mentions Daniel Tassell.

[c] The previous 15 words have been copied directly from Clive Leverton's statement.

"The message I received from Daniel at about 0630 hours [6.30 a.m.] that Sunday morning was that I telephone Mather immediately at his home, not at Buckingham Palace.

"I called him from my home and he informed me that Diana, Princess of Wales had died in Paris as a result of a car accident and that Dodi Al Fayed had also been killed. He instructed that we utilise Operation Overstudy to return her body to the United Kingdom. He said his thought at the time was that she would eventually be at St Georges Chapel, Windsor, but beyond that there were no instructions where the burial would be. There was nothing else discussed or instructed during this conversation. There were no other written procedures that we had to comply with. We undertook the task based upon our experience. At this stage we were only involved in the repatriation with the Royal Air Force.

"The Lord Chamberlain at the time was Lord Airlie. At a briefing conference chaired by the Comptroller Lieutenant Colonel Malcolm Ross at Buckingham Palace on Monday 1st September 1997, he explained there was to be a Service at Westminster Abbey followed by burial on Saturday 6th September 1997. 1 did not communicate with Malcolm Ross on Sunday 31st August 1997. Mather I considered as the contact at the Lord Chamberlains office, he was the individual who sent our company to carry out the instructions, and he was our contact on behalf of the families. Thereafter my sole contact was with Mather during the day.

"I was Mather's contact at Levertons and I communicated by telephone with Clive throughout the day. I was not informed by anyone what condition of Diana, Princess of Wales' body was in, nor was I told if any preparation or embalming had been carried out in Paris. The question of embalming never cropped up with the Lord Chamberlains office, or anyone else. Had this been required or requested by any one I would have referred the question back to Mather. We were not given any specific instructions of how to prepare in any way Diana, Princess of Wales' body. David Green and Bill Fry were to go to Paris with Clive to assist him and fulfil the role of embalmers only if it was required. Clive took them because we didn't know if embalming had been carried out or not, nor whether any was necessary. By taking the embalmers we would be prepared.

"I was not in contact with the family, either Diana's, namely Lady Sarah and Lady Jane, nor Prince Charles or any member of the Royal Family. We were not in a position to ask the appropriate person about the preservation care of the deceased. I therefore did not discuss preparation care, or indeed anything with any family member before Clive and the others travelled, as I may have done with a normal person's death. Until later that evening when Diana, Princess of Wales arrived at Fulham Mortuary I had no communication with or instruction from the British Police or the Coroner's office.

"I contacted Clive by telephone and informed him what I had been told by Mather. We agreed to meet at our office at Camden as soon as possible. I phoned David Green our embalmer and Clive contacted Bill Fry the other embalmer. I arrived at our office later that morning and met with Clive. We agreed that I would remain in London and he would go to Paris. The Royal standard arrived at our office. This was to be placed on the coffin. Clive, David, Bill, and the first call coffin and their equipment went to RAF Northolt.

"During that day Mather communicated with me over the phone. He told me that the flight with Clive, David and Bill was going out at 1300 hours [1 p.m.]. He also during the day instructed me to arrange for two wreaths and the hearse to be at RAF Northolt, to meet the Royal flight that was due in from Paris at 1900 hours. I received calls from my brother when he was on the way to the hospital in Paris and later when he had left the hospital to let ... me know he was on the way back. I had no specific requests or instructions to give to him. There were no instructions from the Lord Chamberlains office for me to pass onto Clive. I recall [being] informed that Diana, Princess of Wales was to go to Fulham Mortuary, this would have been most likely by Mather. I therefore understood there was to be a post mortem here."[175]

David Green, Embalmer, UK: 13 Jul 04 Statement: **Jury Didn't Hear**:
"On Sunday the 31st August 1997 I was away in Hampshire when Keith Leverton contacted me. He informed me that Diana Princess of Wales had died in Paris and I should return to our office in Camden immediately. This I did and met up with Clive Leverton and Bill Fry whom I was to travel with on the RAF flight. I believe they used Bill as a backup in case I couldn't return in time for the 1pm flight out. Bill however did come with us to assist in any case; he is also a qualified embalmer. I took with me a large case containing all the items required for embalming which I keep ready for use at any time. I also took a toolbox with other items used for other aspects of funeral directing such as sealing the coffin.... At that time we did not know what condition the body of the Princess was in, nor whether she had been, nor whether embalming was required to be done by me. So I went prepared to carry out whatever duties were required of me. We took with us the first call coffin. I took my instructions from Clive and Keith. I was given no instruction what to do before we left for France. I knew what would be required when I arrived and any instructions to carry out specific tasks such as embalming would come from the Lord Chamberlain via Clive."[176]

David Green, Embalmer, UK: 13 Jul 04 Statement: **Jury Didn't Hear**:
"We wouldn't have embalmed her [in France] knowing there was going to be a post mortem, and moreover not without authority from the Lord Chamberlain."[177]

David Green, Embalmer, UK: 17 Sep 04 Statement: **Jury Didn't Hear**:
"We follow the instructions of the family or their representative. We also follow the instructions of the Coroner. In the case of Diana, Princess of Wales we followed the instructions [from] the Lord Chamberlains office."[178]
Comment: Parts of Keith Leverton's statement have been copied from his brother, Clive's account. Where this has occurred, it has been pointed out in footnotes throughout Keith's statement. This indicates that when Keith completed his statement on 27 October 2004 – 3½ months after Clive – the police have supplied him with a copy of Clive's statement, to assist him in compiling his testimony.

This raises a very serious question over Scotland Yard's procedures during its investigation into the deaths of Princess Diana and Dodi Fayed. It is normal police procedure that when a witness is interviewed they supply their independent account of events – they shouldn't be given access to other witness accounts. I suggest that this is also basic common sense.

In this way the police are able to compare various witness accounts – maybe reinterview certain witnesses – and hopefully arrive at an accurate assessment of what actually occurred.

If the police provide certain witnesses with other witness accounts – as appears to have occurred in this case – then this very basic process becomes seriously compromised. As a consequence, it becomes harder to arrive at the truth of what occurred.

The natural question is: Just how determined was Operation Paget to seek out the truth during this investigation?[a][b]

Not only has Keith copied from Clive's statement, but he and the police have failed to then properly check what Keith has written. Keith exactly copied the words: "At the time of the death of Diana Princess of Wales on the 31st August 1997, the following staff were involved." While Clive, in his statement, then goes on to describe the staff involved – Tassell, Green and Fry – Keith does not. Keith only mentions Tassell, and then moves on to another topic.[c]

So Keith states that he will describe the "following staff [who] were involved", but then fails to do so.

---

[a] Police statement procedures in this case are also addressed in Part 5.
[b] The book *Cover-Up of a Royal Murder: Hundreds of Errors in the Paget Report* addresses many of the failings in the Paget investigation.
[c] The full statements can be viewed in *The Documents* book: Clive's from p487 and Keith's from p497 (UK edition).

Out of the 6 UK-based witnesses directly involved in the Leverton activities – Mather, Clive, Keith, Tassell, Green, Fry – the jury heard from just two – Clive and Mather.[a]

When Jonathon Hough cross-examined the Lord Chamberlain's Office Assistant Comptroller, Anthony Mather, at the inquest, he went through the events of 31 August 1997 chronologically. After Mather's 8.30 a.m. arrival at Buckingham Palace, Hough introduces Levertons: "it was you who called in Levertons". This approach may have confused the jury – they had heard earlier from Clive that it was 6.45 a.m. when he had received a call.

Hough's questioning was based on Mather's statement account: Malcolm Ross, the Comptroller, "contacted me at 0600 hours [6.00 a.m.] at my home, as a result of which I went straight to Buckingham Palace arriving at 0830 hours".

Mather then outlined a series of events that took place:
- "I established a telephone link between the Palace and Balmoral"[b]
- "an RAF BAe 146 was sent to Aberdeen from RAF Northolt to collect the Prince of Wales"
- "Operation Overstudy was requested by me"
- "I communicated with Keith Leverton over the telephone to his office in Camden".

In summary, Mather has indicated that the fourth action he took, after arriving at Buckingham Palace at 8.30 a.m., was to contact Keith Leverton, who by that time was in his office. There is no urgency conveyed in this account from Mather.

The evidence from Keith Leverton presents a different story altogether: "Daniel [Tassell] was the first person contacted at Levertons on the Sunday morning by ... Mather.... The message I received from Daniel at about 0630 hours [6.30 a.m.] that Sunday morning was that I telephone Mather immediately at his home, not at Buckingham Palace. I called him from my home...."

Keith has stated:

---

[a] The general evidence – see earlier and later – reveals that there were other witnesses too: Fellowes, Ross, Ogilvy, Harding. Of these, only Fellowes was cross-examined.

[b] At the inquest Mather was asked about this: Hough: Q. "Were you responsible for communications between the Palace and Balmoral, where members of the Royal Family were resident?" Mather: A. "I would not say I was responsible, but I was in contact with them." This appears to be a conflict with his statement, where Mather appeared to claim responsibility: "I established a telephone link between the Palace and Balmoral where the Queen, and the Prince of Wales were in residence."

- he received the message "at about 0630 hours [6.30 a.m.]" – not well after 8.30 a.m. as indicated by Mather
- he was asked to "telephone Mather immediately" – conveys a sense of urgency, not mentioned by Mather
- Mather was "at his home, not at Buckingham Palace" – Mather said he was already at Buckingham Palace
- "I called him from my home" – not at "his office" as stated by Mather.[a]

Clive's inquest account supported Keith's timing – Clive was contacted at his mother-in-law's at 6.45 a.m.[b]

In his statement, Mather appears to have deliberately conveyed an impression that events were not rushed or urgent and that Levertons were contacted over two hours – after 8.30 a.m. instead of before 6.30 a.m.[c] – later than what actually occurred.[d]

This general evidence continues through to Mather's inquest account, where far less detail of Mather's early activities was supplied to the jury.

Why would Mather misrepresent the evidence – conveying a later, relaxed timing for contacting Levertons?

There are two significant issues here:
1) the time at which events were set in train
2) whether Levertons were placed under time pressure, and if so, where was the pressure coming from?

Family Consultation

The point about family consultation – Diana's family – is that there's no evidence of any early consultation.

---

[a] It is true that Mather initially called the office and got Tassell, who was the "resident manager": Clive at the inquest. Tassell notified Keith who called Mather back from his home. Mather must have been aware that Keith was at home at 6.30 a.m. on a Sunday morning. By definition, contacting people at home early on a Sunday morning intimates a sense of urgency – this is not a picture that Mather was interested in supporting, for reasons that will become clearer as this book progresses.
[b] Green doesn't provide the early timing in his account and Fry has never been interviewed.
[c] Tassell called Keith "at about 0630 hours [6.30 a.m.]". The original call from Mather to Tassell would have been after 6 a.m. – when Mather was called by Ross – but before 6.30 a.m.
[d] In his statement Mather said: "I went straight to Buckingham Palace". The evidence from the Levertons shows that this is wrong – Mather talked to Levertons from his home before leaving.

There was evidently communication with Diana's sisters – Sarah and Jane – to enable them to be present during Charles' cross-Channel dash to collect Diana's body.[a]

At 6.30 a.m. Keith Leverton was told by Anthony Mather that "[Diana] would eventually be at St Georges Chapel, Windsor". Later evidence will show that Sarah and Jane told royal coroner John Burton, at Fulham mortuary later that evening, that the funeral would be at Althorp.

The evidence from the Levertons is:
- Keith: "I was not in contact with the family"
- Keith: "we were not in a position to ask the appropriate person about the preservation care of the deceased"[b]
- Keith: "I ... did not discuss preparation care, or indeed anything with any family member before Clive and the others travelled, as I may have done with a normal person's death"
- Clive: "we were not in contact with the family"
- Clive: "I ... did not discuss preparation care, or indeed anything with the family, as I would normally do"
- Green: "We [normally] follow the instructions of the family or their representative. We also follow the instructions of the Coroner. In the case of Diana, Princess of Wales we followed the instructions [from] the Lord Chamberlains office."
- Keith: "[Mather] was our contact on behalf of the families. Thereafter my sole contact was with Mather during the day".

No contact between funeral directors and the family of the deceased. Instead Keith says: "[Mather] was our contact on behalf of the families".

According to Mather – unless he has lied by omission – his earliest contact with the family of Diana was to take her sisters to Fulham Mortuary, after 8 p.m.: "I attended Fulham Mortuary ... in company with Lady Sarah McCorquodale and Lady Jane Fellowes. I took them to the office area where Dr Burton spoke to them concerning his role and the post mortem examination."[179]

It was at this meeting with Burton that the sisters told him the funeral would be at Althorp – see later.

---

[a] The reason that their presence on this trip was needed – for royal purposes – is discussed later.

[b] The general evidence reveals that Clive Leverton returned with the coffin on the same flight as Charles, Jane and Sarah. Later that night – at around midnight – Levertons carried out a four hour embalming of Diana's body. The question is: Why didn't Clive Leverton consult with Sarah and Jane about the UK embalming on that flight?

Mather does state: "I understand that Sir Malcolm Ross and Dr Burton were involved in communicating with the Princess of Wales' Family."

Burton's communication was at the mortuary – see above. Ross' evidence has never been taken by the police or the inquest. There is no reason to indicate that his communication with the family would have been anything other than arranging the flight to Paris with Charles.[a]

I suggest that the general evidence that the royals were saying early on that the burial of Diana would be on royal land[b] – Keith Leverton, John Burton (see later) – also indicates that there had been no early consultation on this with Diana's family.

Jean-Claude Plumet, PFG Director of Paris Agencies, Paris: 4 Nov 05 Paget description of Statement: **Jury Didn't Hear**:

"In the case of special clients and VIPs, it was Mr Plumet's role to deal with the relatives in person."[180]

Comment: Plumet's role was to "deal with the relatives" of "special clients and VIPs", yet in the case of Princess Diana there is no evidence of any attempt by Plumet – or anyone in PFG – to even make contact with any relatives.

Instead what we see is Plumet not appearing at the hospital to even view Diana's body until around 4.50 p.m., less than an hour ahead of Diana's sisters, Sarah and Jane, who accompanied Charles – see later. After Sarah and Jane arrived, there is then no evidence of any communication between them and Plumet, or any other PFG employee.

This evidence indicates that Plumet had been instructed not to fulfil his normal role of liaising with the relatives.

Speed of Repatriation

Clive Leverton, who was in charge of the trip to Paris, has provided evidence on the level of time pressure on the day:

- "I did exceed the speed limit" – at inquest, describing his trip from Cheltenham to his London home
- "we were under a lot of pressure time-wise because we had to be at the airport by 1 [p.m.]" – inquest, regarding leaving for Paris
- "we had no time at all" – inquest, regarding leaving for Paris
- "we had to get out to Paris quickly – we were under pressure getting our staff assembled" – inquest
- "we didn't have much time to make arrangements" – statement, regarding leaving for Paris

---

[a] This flight is addressed in detail later.

[b] The reason why the royals were saying this is addressed later in the Royal Coroner section of this chapter.

- "we were under extreme pressure time-wise" – inquest, regarding not sealing the coffin in Paris
- Levertons did not have "to do everything that day" – inquest, to Mansfield
- "I put myself under the pressure, to get things done" – inquest, to Mansfield
- "there were pressures and time constraints placed upon us in these circumstances" – statement
- "the requirement for all concerned [was] to carry out a ... very fast repatriation"[181] – statement
- "this embalming process[a] lasted till about 4 a.m. in the morning. I returned home and then came back to work at 7 a.m. for a later briefing conference at 4 p.m. the same day" – statement[182].

David Green also mentioned time pressure:
- "had I been told to start any embalming and to carry out a complete job, it would not have been possible because of the time limitation"
- "due to the tight timetable of the viewing and the return flight I had no immediate concerns of decomposition"[183]
- "we were required to return her quickly and that was what we were there to do"[184].

The evidence from Green is consistent – "the time limitation"; "the tight timetable" – and he indicates that the timetable was not set by Levertons: "we were required to return her quickly".

Clive provides conflicting evidence on this: in his 2004 statement he said: "there were pressures and time constraints placed upon us", but at the inquest, when confronted by Mansfield, Clive changed this: "I put myself under the pressure".

In 2004 the time pressure was "placed upon us", but three years later the pressure was self-administered, from Clive.

Which is the true account?

The clear evidence from Green – supported by Clive's statement – indicates that Clive has lied under oath at the inquest.

Earlier, when Hough asked Clive: "Did you consider it necessary to [hermetically] seal the coffin?", Clive responded in the negative[b], explaining: "we were under extreme pressure time-wise and we knew that the" – then immediately checked himself with: "sorry, can you say that again, please?"

---

[a] This is the UK embalming that took place late on August 31 and into the next day. This second embalming is covered later in this book.
[b] "We did not consider it necessary."

But I suggest it was too late for Clive to say he didn't understand the question – he had already answered it. Clive understood the question the first time.

When Hough repeated the question, Clive then repeated his initial short answer, almost word for word: "we did not consider it necessary".[a]

It appears that Clive had momentarily forgotten to leave the false impression that they were not under time pressure in Paris. Mansfield seemed to pick up on this and challenged him on it – see above.

In contrast, Green revealed that they were under pressure all day – "we were required to return her quickly" – and this is supported in Clive's original statement, referring to the events of the day: "there were pressures and time constraints placed upon us". Clive's statement even revealed that the pressure continued into the next day: "I returned home [at about 4 a.m.] and then came back to work at 7 a.m."

Neither of these accounts – Green and Clive's statements – was heard by the jury.

Instead the jury heard Clive lying under oath: Levertons did not have "to do everything that day" and "I put myself under the pressure, to get things done".

Why did Clive mislead the jury on this? The answer will emerge as this topic develops.

The evidence then is that Levertons was under time pressure, which was exerted from outside.

Who was pressuring Levertons?

Throughout the day – 31 August 1997 – Levertons was provided with three deadlines – Clive calls them "time constraints"; Green calls it a "tight timetable".

1) 1 p.m. at RAF Northolt for the flight to Paris: Clive: "I made arrangements ... to go immediately to the RAF Airfield, which in this case was Northolt"[b] and "we had to be at the airport by 1 [p.m.] to get out to Paris"[cd]

2) The visit by Prince Charles and Diana's sisters, Sarah and Jane, to view the body at the hospital in Paris.

---

[a] He added the word "no" this time.

[b] In statement.

[c] At inquest.

[d] This is also supported in other evidence: Clive's statement – "we were to fly to France at 1 p.m."; Keith – "the flight with Clive, David and Bill was going out at 1300 hours [1 p.m.]"; Green – "the 1 p.m. flight out".

Green called this the "tight timetable of the viewing". He elaborated: "I knew that the Prince of Wales, and the Princess's two sisters were en route to view her very soon after our arrival".[a]

At the inquest Clive was asked: "What did you do with the body [after arriving at the hospital]?" He replied: "I – we knew by now that time was getting very short. We knew that Prince Charles and her sisters were on the way to ... pay their respects".[b]

Both Green and Clive have stated that there wasn't much time between their arrival and the expected arrival of Charles, Sarah and Jane – "very soon after" and "time was getting very short".

The evidence from Moss is that "the Royal Flight was due to arrive at 1700hrs [5 p.m.]"[185] and "at around 1740hrs HRH Prince of Wales and the ... two sisters ... arrived at the hospital".[186] This fits with Monceau's inquest account: "I was told that the Prince was expected at about 5 o'clock, at Villacoublay, the airport" – the drive from the airport to the hospital being about 40 minutes.

This evidence shows that after Clive, Green and Fry's arrival at the hospital – which was at about 3.40 p.m.[c] – they were faced with the next deadline: the arrival of Charles and the sisters at 5.40 p.m.

3) 7 p.m. at Villacoublay airport with Diana's body, for the repatriation.

Green described this as "the tight timetable of ... the return flight". Clive stated: "we had to be back at Villacoublay at 7 p.m. for the return flight".[187]

This fits with the evidence of Keith Leverton, who said: "[Mather] also during the day instructed me to arrange for two wreaths and the hearse to be at RAF Northolt, to meet the Royal flight that was due in from Paris at 1900 hours [7 p.m.]."[d]

The above evidence shows that Levertons were pressured with a rushed timetable and tight time constraints throughout this critical day. It also reveals that a plan appears to have been put in place to ensure that Princess Diana was returned to UK soil on the same day as the crash, Sunday 31 August 1997. It also fits with the understanding of the embalmer, Huguette

---

[a] Clive supported this in his statement: "I was aware the Prince of Wales and the family members would arrive soon to view the deceased in the open coffin".

[b] This was prior to Clive being challenged on this time pressure issue by Mansfield. Clive later changed his evidence, saying: "I put myself under the pressure" – see above.

[c] See earlier Timeline of Events and Clive's inquest account: "about half past three to quarter to four".

[d] The royal flight with Diana's coffin aboard left Villacoublay at about 7 p.m. Paris time and arrived at RAF Northolt at about 7 p.m. London time – there is about a one hour time difference (Paris is ahead) and the flight takes around one hour.

Amarger – remember her evidence: "There was a panic on.... My boss [Monceau] told me to be quick because Prince Charles was arriving in the afternoon...."

Who was setting this plan and creating this tight timetable that Levertons were forced to adhere to?

This question will be addressed shortly.

Was it "normal" behaviour for Diana's repatriation to be rushed in this way?

Stephen Donnelly, British Vice Consul, Paris: 22 Sep 05 Statement read out 17 Dec 07: 129.19:
"I was surprised to find out that both Diana, Princess of Wales and Dodi Al Fayed were repatriated to the UK on 31st August 1997. The normal procedure, including the administrative processes, take between five to seven days, but I was not involved in this process so I do not know how the repatriation took place."

Jeffrey Rees, Head of Early Crash Investigations, British Police: 22 Jan 98 Report read out 17 Dec 07: 46.4:
"It had been anticipated by the British authorities that both bodies would remain in Paris that day, but at approximately 2 p.m. the OCG [Organised Crime Group] were informed that both bodies would be flown to London shortly."

Jeffrey Rees: 17 Dec 07: 70.22:
"I know that we did not envisage the bodies returning so quickly to the United Kingdom."

David Veness, MPS Asst Commissioner Specialist Operations, UK: 15 Jan 08: 93.13:
A. On that Sunday, as events were moving forward with some rapidity in that the post-mortems had been arranged at relatively short notice, which for certain reasons that appeared to be a highly desirable state of affairs, and that the bodies were returning to the United Kingdom, there was a need to move with expedition in order to have an able officer in order to conduct –
Mansfield: Q. Conduct what?
A. In order to conduct – assist to conduct the post-mortems.

Charles Ritchie, Military Attaché British Embassy, Paris: 12 Feb 08: 145.25:
Burnett: Q. It is fair to say I think that you were intimately involved in making a large number of arrangements, particularly for the Queen's Flight aircraft to come into a military airport and to ensure that everything was done appropriately from the point of view of the Embassy's military staff and also the French.
A. That is correct. We had to do two major matters. The first was to get the French Air Force to open Villacoublay which is the equivalent of RAF Northolt, to open it up, get it fully manned. Then a variety of telephone calls

were made, mainly to RAF Lyneham where the Royal Air Force regiment bearer party were based, also that we understood that a Hercules was coming in with the coffin. And then a completely separate arrangement was made to welcome Prince Charles and Princess Diana's two sisters and make all the necessary arrangements for them. All the protocol side had to be looked at and even I remember Lady Jay making us all black armbands as at one stage it looked as though we were not going to be able to get the Royal Air Force regiment bearer party and so we telephoned all the way round Army, Navy and Air Force to come in, who were there, ready to act as an informal bearer party.

Patrick Launay, PFG Repatriation Director: 21 Mar 06 Statement: **Jury Didn't Hear**:

"I should like to add that the speed with which the Princess was repatriated did not shock me, all the more so given that Dodi Al Fayed was himself repatriated even more quickly than the Princess. The request made by the two families that day was to repatriate the two bodies as quickly as possible."[188]

Comment: The earlier evidence from Green and Clive indicates that the speed was not normal. These men – who are experienced in their field – have testified that it was "extreme pressure"; they "had no time"; the repatriation was "very fast".

This view is supported by the accounts of Rees, Veness, Donnelly and Ritchie – all heard by the inquest jury.

Rees and Veness refer to "the bodies" – indicating that Dodi's repatriation was also rapid. This is true, but the general evidence shows that in Dodi's case there was a religious requirement for his body to be buried before sunset on the day of the death. The reasons for Diana's rapid repatriation – which will be discussed in due course – were completely different: there was no religious requirement.

These four witnesses – Rees, Veness, Donnelly, Ritchie – view what occurred from varying perspectives.

Rees and Veness are senior police officers. Rees says "the British authorities [thought] that both bodies would remain in Paris that day".

Donnelly, who has had substantial experience dealing with repatriations (see earlier), said a normal repatriation should take "between five to seven days".

Ritchie, who appears to have been intimately involved in enabling this rapid repatriation to occur, gives special insight into some of the hurdles that had to be jumped in order for this to happen:

- "to get the French Air Force to open Villacoublay ... to open it up, get it fully manned"

-   "to welcome Prince Charles and Princess Diana's two sisters and make all the necessary arrangements for them"
-   "we telephoned all the way round Army, Navy and Air Force to come in ... ready to act as an informal bearer party".

Veness has stated that it was "for certain reasons ... a highly desirable state of affairs" that "the post-mortems had been arranged at relatively short notice". Veness fails to disclose what the "certain reasons" are. The post-mortems are covered in a later chapter.

Patrick Launay is the only witness to suggest "that the speed with which the Princess was repatriated did not shock" – but even that is an admission that the repatriation was conducted with speed. Launay – as did Rees – compares it with Dodi's repatriation, but Dodi's did not require an embalming, a royal flight which travelled to Aberdeen and picked up others along the way, a separate flight carrying embalmers, the special opening of two airports, the organisation of bearer parties, the coordination of official departure and welcoming parties, special police escorts and the closing of roads.

In summary, the evidence shows – Clive, Green, Donnelly, Rees – that the repatriation of Diana was unexpectedly rapid and carried out under extreme time pressure. Ritchie shows that a lot of behind the scenes effort went in to enabling the repatriation to occur.

Back to the question: Who was driving this? Who was it that made the decision that Princess Diana must be returned to the UK that very day – something that was achieved, but under great stress?

Another issue is: Was the person or persons behind this authorised to carry out the actions that were taken?

To answer these questions, I believe that one needs to address another issue – a major event that occurred concurrently with this rapid, forced repatriation of Diana, Princess of Wales.

Post-Death Status Change

Early on Sunday morning – along with a decision to carry out an as-quick-as-possible repatriation – a decision was made to reverse a 28 August 1996 edict, from the Queen, that had removed Princess Diana's royal status.[a]

There are five events, listed below, that took place on 31 August 1997 – events revealing that effectively the dead Diana had been welcomed back into the royal family, a family that she had been unceremoniously ousted from, whilst alive, only 12 months previously.

---

[a] The ousting of Diana from the royal family has been addressed in Part 2. Diana's post-divorce status was also covered earlier in this chapter.

All of these events have been included in the evidence – statement and inquest – as though they were normal for the circumstances. This, however, is not the case.

The elephant in the room is that Princess Diana was no longer a part of the royal family – and had not been for 12 months – at the time of her death. It was therefore not normal for that status to change immediately following Diana's demise.

The reasons why this occurred will become clearer as this chapter progresses.

The five events are:

1) Employment of the royal undertakers, Levertons.

This has already been covered – Anthony Mather called Levertons at about 6.30 a.m., around 3½ hours after the official time of Diana's death.[a]

In their statements, Keith and Clive both said[b]: "We are the funeral directors who have since 1991 been asked by the Lord Chamberlains office to care for members the Royal Family in the event of one of them passing away."[189]

2) Appearance of the royal standard to cover Diana's coffin.

3) Choice of the royal coroner to conduct the inquest.[c]

4) Prince Charles' visit to Paris to repatriate Diana's body.

5) Delivery of Diana's body to St James' Palace.

Royal Standard

Levertons carried the Royal Standard with them on the 1 p.m. flight to Paris.

Clive Leverton, Royal Funeral Director: 13 Jul 04 Statement: **Jury Didn't Hear**:

"The Royal standard for placing on the coffin was now in our possession. The transportation was all arranged, and therefore our work started from when we arrived in France."[190]

Keith Leverton, Royal Funeral Director: 27 Oct 04 Statement: **Jury Didn't Hear**:

"The Royal standard arrived at our office. This was to be placed on the coffin. Clive, David, Bill, and the first call coffin and their equipment went to RAF Northolt."[191]

Keith Moss: 22 Oct 04 Statement: **Jury Didn't Hear**:

---

[a] Diana's official time of death was 4 a.m. in Paris, which was 3 a.m. in the UK.

[b] Keith copied from Clive's statement – see earlier.

[c] The initial plan was for the inquest to be conducted by the royal coroner. In the end the inquest was controlled by Scott Baker, who was not the royal coroner. Light will be shed on what occurred later in this chapter and also in Part 5.

"The Royal Flight was due to arrive at 1700hrs [5 p.m.], and the plane would also bring the coffin, the Royal Standard, a bearer party and representative from the Royal Undertakers. The flight was scheduled to depart at 1900hrs [7 p.m.]."[192]

Clive Leverton, Royal Funeral Director: 22 Nov 2007: 75.24:

Hough: Q. Once you had transferred her into the coffin, she was viewed by the family members and then the coffin was taken back to Villacoublay Airport.

A. Yes. We got out of the room – once the Royal party had been in and left, we fastened the lid. I was in possession of the Royal standard, which I placed on the coffin.

Clive Leverton, Royal Funeral Director: 13 Jul 04 Statement: **Jury Didn't Hear**:

"I had seen the Princess of Wales family arrive but was not present when they viewed her in the open coffin.[a] Once this had been concluded with the help of our French colleagues we placed the wooden and zinc lid on the coffin.... The Royal Standard was placed on top and secured. The French bearer party carried the coffin downstairs to the entrance where I had originally arrived. The coffin was placed in a hearse...."[193]

Patrick Launay, PFG Repatriation Director: 21 Mar 06 Statement: **Jury Didn't Hear**:

"In the hospital, we left the coffin and the equipment (trestles, the British royal standard etc.) in a side room where the Princess of Wales was. We then waited for Prince Charles and the Princess's two sisters to arrive."[194]

Keith Moss: 22 Oct 04 Statement: **Jury Didn't Hear**:

---

[a] There is a minor conflict in the order of events. Clive states: Charles, Sarah and Jane "viewed her in the open coffin". This indicates that Diana's body was placed in the coffin prior to the viewing. Other witnesses disagree with this: Moss – Charles and the sisters "went in to pay their last respects to the Princess of Wales.... After a short while they rejoined the dignitaries in the corridor.... It took around fifteen minutes for the undertakers to transfer the remains into the coffin and for it to be draped in the Royal Standard. The coffin was then escorted from the hospital"; Launay – "Prince Charles ... went in with the two sisters and the priest. They stayed there for perhaps ten minutes or so. I recall that when they came out, Prince Charles ... went to speak to the French VIPs. Meanwhile, we got on with placing the body in the coffin."; Plumet – "[Plumet] looked into the room where the Princess of Wales' body was – she was on a bed and had been dressed". Plumet arrived about an hour after Clive and an hour before Charles. Sarah McCorquodale has never been asked about what occurred in the hospital – see later. Sources: Keith Moss, Witness Statement, 22 October 2004, reproduced in *The Documents* book, p658 (UK Edition); Patrick Launay, Witness Statement, 21 March 2006, reproduced in *The Documents* book, p515 (UK Edition); Jean-Claude Plumet, Witness Statement, 11 November 2005, reproduced in *The Documents* book, p473 (UK Edition).

"It took around fifteen minutes for the undertakers to transfer the remains into the coffin and for it to be draped in the Royal Standard. The coffin was then escorted from the hospital and the cortège departed...."[195]

Michael Jay, British Ambassador to France, 1996-2001, Paris: 31 Aug 97 Diary read out 11 Feb 08: 107.10:

"After ten minutes or so, the coffin, draped in the Royal Standard, leaves the room, followed by Martin Draper[a] in white robes and carried by French pall-bearers."

Michael Jay,: 31 Aug 97 Diary read out 11 Feb 08: 108.2:

"The cortège moves with dignity – through central Paris, the western scruffy suburbs and the road to Villacoublay. The Prince says [it] all seems unreal. Our conversation is a little inconsequential, with silences. He was surprised and pleased by the Standard on the coffin. I was surprised too. I do not know where it came from."

Charles Ritchie, Military Attaché British Embassy, Paris: 12 Feb 08: 146.24:

Burnett: Q. You were one of those who was in the group that, as you say, met the Prince of Wales and the Princess's sisters when they arrived at Villacoublay later on the 31st and you travelled back to the hospital in the vehicles that included the Prince of Wales and the Princess's sisters.

A. That is correct.

Q. I think, Brigadier, it was you, wasn't it, who made the decision that the coffin should be draped with the Royal Standard, given the circumstances and the status of the Princess?

A. That is correct. Because when the Royal Air Force party arrived, they brought with them a Union Jack and a Royal Standard. That was then taken to the hospital, and it was only when they were ready to move the body did they say, "By the way, shall we put the Union Jack on the coffin or the Royal Standard?" Having seen and watched what was happening on television and worldwide and the Embassy besieged by people bringing flowers and wanting to sign books, I had nobody to ask at that particular moment; I said, "To my mind, at this moment in time, the right decision to do is to put on the Royal Standard," and that is how it happened.

Q. Yesterday, Lord Jay told us that it was a gesture that touched the Prince of Wales himself.

A. So I believe, sir.

Colin Tebbutt: 5 Jul 04 Statement: **Jury Didn't Hear:**

---

[a] Father Martin Draper, Anglican Arch-Deacon of France.

"Transport was arranged by Brigadier Richie and the coffin was carried out by French uniformed men. I had been concerned that no one had thought to bring a Royal Standard, but Levertons had brought the flag."[196]

John Burton, Royal Coroner, 1997: 16 Jun 04 Statement: **Jury Didn't Hear**:

"I saw a coffin draped in the Royal Standard with a wreath on top inside the mortuary. I knew that it contained the body of Diana Princess of Wales. I asked the undertakers where the Royal Standard came from and was told that the Lord Chamberlain had provided it."[197]

Comment: There is a huge difference between the full evidence and what the jury heard.

The jury heard just three items of evidence:

- Clive: "I was in possession of the Royal standard, which I placed on the coffin."
- Jay: "[Charles] was surprised and pleased by the Standard on the coffin. I was surprised too. I do not know where it came from."
- Ritchie, quoting himself: "the right decision ... is to put on the Royal Standard".[a]

Some very significant evidence was not heard by the jury:

- Clive: "the Royal standard for placing on the coffin was now in our possession" – in London before leaving
- Keith: "the Royal standard arrived at our office – this was to be placed on the coffin" – in London before leaving
- Moss: "the plane would also bring the coffin, the Royal Standard ... the Royal Undertakers"[b]
- Launay: "we left the ... British royal standard ... in a side room"[c]
- Clive: "the Royal Standard was placed on top [of the coffin] and secured"
- Moss: "the coffin [was] ... draped in the Royal Standard"
- Tebbutt: "Levertons had brought the [Royal Standard]"
- Burton: "the Lord Chamberlain had provided [the Royal Standard]".

I suggest that the general evidence from the other witnesses – Clive, Keith, Moss, Launay, Burton – raises serious doubts about Ritchie's detailed account told to the jury:

---

[a] Clive Leverton was cross-examined on 22 November 2007, whereas Jay and Ritchie were heard on 11 and 12 February 2008, respectively. This 3 month gap would have made it difficult for the jury to compare Clive's evidence with the other accounts.

[b] Moss did not at this stage appear to realise that the royal undertakers and their equipment were set to come on an earlier flight – see earlier.

[c] Launay met Clive, Keith and Green at the airport and travelled with them to the hospital.

- no other witness mentions anything at all about a Union Jack being present
- the Royal Standard is stated by the two key witnesses as being the flag that was intended to be placed on the coffin: Clive – "the Royal standard for placing on the coffin"; Keith – "the Royal standard ... was to be placed on the coffin"
- Ritchie is not placed in the room, at the time of the closing of the coffin, by any witness, other than himself – Ritchie is mentioned by Tebbutt, but only in connection with arranging the transport.

This evidence raises an important question: Why is it that Ritchie was specifically asked about this by Burnett – "it was you ... who made the decision that the coffin should be draped with the Royal Standard" – but Clive, who was also cross-examined, was not asked why the Royal Standard was placed on the coffin?

The evidence, from the witnesses who were more likely to be knowledgeable about the circumstances regarding VIP deaths, was one of surprise that the coffin came from France adorned in the Royal Standard:

- Charles: "[Charles] was surprised and pleased by the [Royal] Standard on the coffin" – to Jay in the car after leaving the hospital
- Jay: "I was surprised too – I do not know where [the Royal Standard] came from"
- Burton: "I knew that [the coffin] contained the body of Diana.... I asked the undertakers where the Royal Standard came from".

Tebbutt conflicts with this view: "I had been concerned that no one had thought to bring a Royal Standard". I suggest that this evidence from Tebbutt is itself surprising. Earlier evidence – in the embalming chapter – indicated that Tebbutt's account may have been influenced by Paget officers. There is a possibility that this view is retrospective, but that is not how Tebbutt has stated it.

Tebbutt was fully aware that Diana had been removed from the royal family a year earlier. I suggest that Tebbutt should have realised it would be unlikely that Diana's coffin would be draped in the Royal Standard – particularly within 15 hours of her death.

The reality is that out of eight witnesses who have provided evidence about the presence of the Royal Standard – Clive, Keith, Burton, Launay, Tebbutt, Ritchie, Jay, Moss – the jury were only allowed to hear one – Ritchie – questioned on the circumstances of how the Royal Standard actually got there.

Given that Ritchie's evidence conflicts seriously with the other witness evidence – Clive, Keith, Burton, Moss, Launay – and no other evidence places Ritchie in the room at the time, one has to wonder exactly how Ritchie came up with the elaborate account he told the jury.

Ritchie's testimony includes:

- a verbatim account of a conversation in Diana's room, at the time of the closing of the coffin
- evidence of the placing of the Royal Standard on the coffin being a spontaneous, last minute decision made by himself
- a statement that the reasons he decided to favour the Royal Standard over the Union Jack were: a) "what was happening on television and worldwide"; b) "the Embassy besieged by people"
- placing himself as the only person who could make the decision: "I had nobody to ask".

There are two pertinent questions:

1) What did the massive reaction by the public to the death of Diana have to do with whether the Union Jack or the Royal Standard was placed on the coffin?

Ritchie should have been asked this. He wasn't.

2) Why didn't Ritchie quickly slip out into the corridor and ask his boss, Michael Jay, which flag should go on the coffin?

The effect of the evidence heard by the jury – primarily from Ritchie (see above) – would have led to a view that the decision to place the Royal Standard on the coffin was last-minute and spontaneous.

This view directly conflicts with the general witness evidence – the use of the Royal Standard was planned well ahead of the time of placement. The evidence of Clive, Keith and Burton shows that the Royal Standard was delivered during the morning to Levertons from the Lord Chamberlain: Keith – "the Royal standard arrived at our office"; Burton: "the Lord Chamberlain had provided [the Royal Standard]".

Other evidence in this chapter – see earlier and later – shows that the placement of the Royal Standard on the coffin was part of an orchestrated plan to bring the dead Diana back into the royal fold.[a]

I suggest that it is no coincidence that the Baker inquest heard a false account of this important event – the false account of Brigadier Charles Ritchie, that it was he who chose the Royal Standard, spontaneously, and at the last minute.[b]

Royal Coroner

It was decided on 31 August 1997 that royal coroner, John Burton, would be conducting the inquest into the death of Princess Diana.[c]

---

[a] The reason this was done will be addressed later.

[b] Burnett described it as a "gesture".

[c] That never actually occurred, because Burton died in December 2004. He resigned from ill health in March 2002, and the inquest didn't take place until October 2007.

17.   There is no acknowledgment of the request by himself in his other capacity but it is clear that he thereafter acted as the coroner of the Royal Household.

c.   A handwritten note, dated 31st August. I have set out below the text as far as possible as it was written by Dr Burton

"Sunday 31 August 1997

Phoned palace -   Lucy Dove -   believed buried Windsor

Assume Household Jurisdiction   ?   Arrive Northholt   Liase
with
myself

speak Levertons. Burial

Burgess informed of Fayed by Surrey Police.   Burial - Brookwood

Problem with time for funeral

If P.M at Fulham   -   between   Heliport and Mosque.

Inspector Rees involved via Leicester.   Problems in France.

Chapman to do P.M.   asked to continue when

Diana arrived.

Diana to arrive later.   Fulham en route to   ? Levertons.

Need for P.M. + embalm

Transfer jurisdiction of Al Fayed at Fulham to Burgess to

allow him to direct P.M before body arrived in Surrey.

Chapman assumes I do P.M today El Fayed. Transfer Jurisdiction West London/Household

See family of Diana.   Now to be funeral at Althorpe.

Body to Lie in St James.   Body in my jurisdiction -

physically - so give Burial order."

Figure 10

Typed version of handwritten notes drawn up by royal coroner, John Burton, dated 31 August 1997.

"Expanded handwritten jottings re 31 August 1997.

Sunday 31 August 1997. Heard news.

Phoned Palace. Lord Chamberlain in difficulty with switchboard. To Phone back.

Contacted Coroners Officer Brown, to arrange mortuary, if necessary.

Phoned Palace - Lucy Dove - told body coming to England.(Position re HRH was not clear. ? family or Royal funeral.

Told thought burial at Windsor. Believed body coming to Northolt.

Levertons dealing with funeral.

Contact Levertons. Told a burial.

As I covered Northolt as West London and Windsor as Household, able to liase with myself.

Burgess informed by Surrey Police that Dodi coming to Brookwood for burial before nightfall. Arrangements for Chapman to do rapid autopsy in Surrey before burial.

Plans changed. Dodi to go to London Mosque then Brookwood. Chapman and Burgess come to Fulham mortuary to do autopsy before service.

As body not yet in Burgess jurisdiction -- s.4 Transfer to provide jurisdiction.

Inspector Rees (Palace liason) contacted by Leicester Police,

He is informed there are problems in France in releasing bodies.

Chapman asked to do Diana autopsy after Dodi at Fulham.

Body of Dodi arrived and was autopsied and removed.

Diana to go to Levertons or to St James's Palace. Asked them to call at Fulham in passing.

Note - Household coroner only assumes jurisdiction when body arrives in a Palace, although the Home Office say he will take jurisdiction from place of funeral. To avoid going to Palace and coming back, s 14 transfer to Household from West London.

Dr Chapman carried out autopsy. Dr Peter Wheeler, Doctor to Princess Diana, present and identified the body.

The position of Diana after divorce and loss of HRH was sensitive.

Coffin had Royal Standard. Thought advisable to follow Home Office guideline and have Household jurisdiction and not seize body for West London.

The family of Diana attended mortuary. Thought the funeral would now be at Althorpe, but the body was to lie at St James's - Not her home – Kensington. However both were in Household jurisdiction.

Burial Order given to Funeral directors at conclusion of autopsy

Figure 11

Typed notes drawn up by royal coroner, John Burton, dated 31 August 1997.

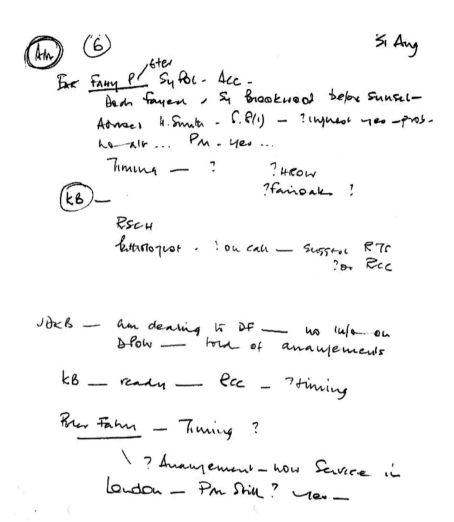

Figure 12

Page 1 of Surrey coroner Michael Burgess'
handwritten notes from 31 August 1997.

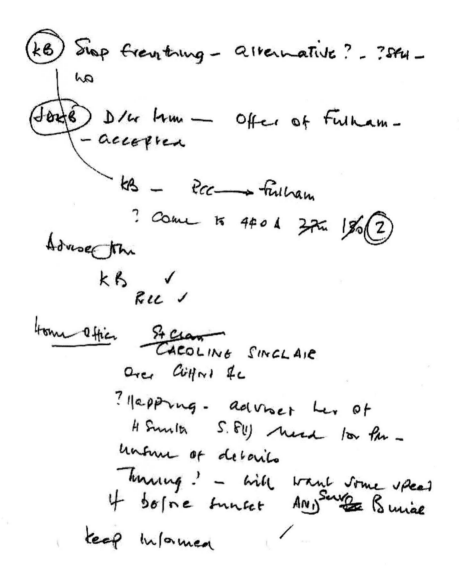

Page 2 of Surrey coroner Michael Burgess' handwritten notes from 31 August 1997. The other three pages of his notes appear in *The Documents* book.

H.M.Coroner for Surrey
re: Dodi Fayed

Aide Manaui ale (handwritten)

Actions - 31 August 1997

Time	Action
Time	Action
0520 approx	Heard radio news of death of D, PoW while travelling in a car with Dodi Fayed (who was also killed)
0900 approx	Teld JDKB - as he Cor of The Queen's Household and likely to be involved with D, PoW, offered whatever help he might want
0945 approx	Tel from Peter Fahy - Sy Pol - DF coming to Surrey - Brookwood burial before sunset ... advised of cor requirements ... re PM etc
1000 approx	Tel KB - Plse arrange for PM at RSCH - discussionas to pathologist ... see if RTS avail if not the RCC
	Tel JDKB and advised him of DF interest and would keep him advised of what transpires/develops
	Tel Peter Fahy (Sy Pol) advised him opf arrangeemnts - plse keep me advised of developments as he hears of them ... no news yet on timings
	Tel call from KB - arrangements in hand ... said he would advise me when timings and arrangements known
	Tel Call from Peter Fahy .. .arrangements now changed ... first a Service in Mosque in London - said still required body to be PMd ... would review and advise him.
	Tel KB - advised him to ease back on arrangements would need to review in light of Service in London
	Tel JDKB Advising him of need to alter arrangements - discussed as to variations - agreed that body to Fulham, PM there and then to Mosque and on to Burial ... no knowledge of times yet ... vartious other tel calls inc JDKB confirmed that mort could be available and that his mortician would attend .... also confirmed that RCC could examine DPoW later
	Tel KB and Peter Fahy - advised them of change of plans ... stand RSCH mortuary down and direct RCC to attend in Fulham
	KB teld MB - arrangements had been altered ... KB to attend at MB's home at 1400 hrs and then go to Fulham together. RCC finding own way there
1230	Tel from John Macnamara - discussed arrangements ... gave me his personal tel no and MB advised him of his mobile no. I advised him of arrangements so far made ... as cor I required a PM and probable inquest to comply with S.8 (CA) and Helen Smith ... would do best to achieve release of body before nightfall as they required but did depend on body arriving in sufficeint time.
	Tel call to and from Caroline Sinclair (HO) - she anxious to know what was happening ... advised her and said that if she wanted would keep her informed. However, as cor I required a PM and probable inquest to comply with S.8 (CA) and Helen Smith ... would do best to achieve release of body before nightfall as they required but did depend on body arriving in sufficeint time.
	In course of day, while attempting to make arrangements, tel calls made to and received from JDKB, Peter Fahy and KB

EE
Printed: 15/06/2004

Figure 14

Page 1 of Michael Burgess' typed-up notes relating to events of 31 August 1997. The second page is reproduced in *The Documents* book.

DIANA INQUEST: THE BRITISH COVER-UP

The body of Diana Princess of Wales was returned to Northolt from France. The death had been notified to me as Coroner of the Queen's Household. It was thought that the funeral might be held at Windsor. This conformed with Home Office Circular 79/1983.

In order to direct a post mortem examination before the body arrived within that jurisdiction, this is a request in writing in accord via section 14 of the Coroners Act 1988, from West London to the Queen's Household.

[signed in handwriting]

John Burton

Figure 15

Undated document raised by John Burton, transferring jurisdiction for the body of Princess Diana to himself, as royal coroner. This action was based on Burton's belief that Diana's "funeral might be held at Windsor" Castle. This document appears to be incomplete or not grammatically correct – it reads: "this is a request in writing in accord via section 14 of the Coroners Act 1988, from West London to the Queen's Household" – the critical missing words are "to transfer jurisdiction", which should appear before "from West London". This document has been reproduced from the 8 January 2007 inquest pre-hearing held by Elizabeth Butler-Sloss – it was not shown to the inquest jury.

John Burton, Royal Coroner, 1997: 16 Jun 04 Statement: **Jury Didn't Hear**:

"Early on the morning of Sunday 31st of August 1997, I was at home when I heard of the news of the death of Diana Princess of Wales and Mr Dodi Al Fayed via the radio.

"Being the coroner for the Royal Household and for the district of West London, which included Heathrow Airport and RAF Northolt, I anticipated that I would be taking jurisdiction should the body of Diana Princess of Wales be repatriated to England.

"I telephoned the switchboard of Buckingham Place and spoke to a person who identified himself as being the Lord Chamberlain. He was unable to assist much further at this stage and it was agreed that I should phone back later.

"I again phoned the Buckingham Palace switchboard and spoke to a young lady who informed that they were experiencing problems, as there were no contingency plans for the death of Diana Princess of Wales. She was able to tell me that Levertons undertakers were dealing and that her body was going to be repatriated back to England later that day via RAF Northolt. The burial was likely to be at Windsor Castle.

"I did not know where the funeral was to take place but I decided that didn't matter because as I previously mentioned I had jurisdiction for RAF Northolt and the body would likely lay in one of the Royal Palaces.

"Having taken the decision that I would be taking jurisdiction I was aware that Diana Princess of Wales had died as a result of being a passenger in a car that had crashed earlier that day in Paris. She had therefore died an unnatural death. I was unaware if a post mortem had taken place in France. I needed to obtain evidence from a Post Mortem and in keeping with the Coroners rules together with my own normal practice I would be ordering a post mortem on the body of Diana Princess of Wales. I knew that I would require a post mortem to be carried out because I had an unnatural death and no evidence from a post mortem.

"Later that morning I spoke to Levertons the undertakers in order to make arrangements for the post Mortem to be carried out at the Hammersmith and Fulham mortuary. I did not give them any other instructions nor was the subject of embalming mentioned. I would have ... assumed that the body transported by air would have been embalmed. Levertons informed me that Diana Princess of Wales was to be buried and not cremated.[a] I believe that I did inform Levertons that I was intending to have a post mortem.

"I phoned one of my coroner's officers Harry Brown and asked him to make arrangements for the post Mortem to be held at the Hammersmith and Fulham mortuary and place the duty home office pathologist on standby.

"Around midday Michael Burgess the coroner for the county of Surrey and also my deputy as the coroner for the Royal Household phoned. He offered me his assistance in relation to matters surrounding Diana Princess of Wales. He informed me that he intended to take jurisdiction over the body of Mr Dodi Al Fayed in the knowledge that he was to be buried at Brookwood cemetery in Surrey. He was arranging a post mortem at Chertsey and had Dr Chapman the home office pathologist on standby.

"We discussed the need to get Mr Dodi Al Fayed buried before nightfall. We agreed that in order to facilitate this and the wishes of Mr Mohamed Al Fayed that the post mortem of Mr Dodi Al Fayed would take place first.

"I received another call from Michael Burgess who informed me that Mr Mohamed Al Fayed wanted a service for his son in the mosque in Regents Park, London and then a burial in Brookwood cemetery, Surrey. We agreed that Dr Chapman should hold both post mortems at the Hammersmith and

---

[a] It is not known how Levertons came by this information.

Fulham mortuary. He later informed me that the French authorities were apparently delaying the release of the body of Mr Dodi Al Fayed, as they were concerned that an investigation was to be carried out in England. This would have delayed the examination and any funeral arrangements. I do not know what the problems were in France or where this information came from.

"That afternoon I attended at the Hammersmith and Fulham Mortuary....

"Michael Burgess arrived at some stage and I handed over to him a note in accordance with Section 14 of the Coroners Act 1988. A hand written document, which transferred the Jurisdiction of the body of Mr Dodi Al Fayed because at that stage the body would be lying within the District of West London and had not yet reached the County of Surrey and given Michael Burgess jurisdiction. This was clearly expedient, as he had made the necessary arrangements and the body would be buried within the County of Surrey....

"I saw a coffin draped in the Royal Standard with a wreath on top inside the mortuary. I knew that it contained the body of Diana Princess of Wales. I asked the undertakers where the Royal Standard came from and was told that the Lord Chamberlain had provided it.

"Colonel Mather from the Lord Chamberlains office was now in attendance with 2 sisters of Diana Princess of Wales at the mortuary. I cannot remember their names. They were taken to the office area where I spoke to them. I explained to them that as the coroner of the Royal Household I had taken jurisdiction over Diana Princess of Wales and was obliged to hold an inquest and order that a post mortem be carried out.

"I had recently seen some conspiracy theories being aired on television in relation to the death of WPC Yvonne Fletcher and was most concerned and warned them that the death of Diana Princess of Wales would attract even more speculation and invention. I therefore would need to be extremely thorough in my inquires. They left shortly after that.

"I believed at this time that Diana Princess of Wales was to be buried at Windsor Castle so I transferred jurisdiction from myself as coroner for the district of West London again to myself as coroner for the Royal Household in writing. This made sense and was expedient....

"I did not take an active part in the post mortem but again assisted in the cleaning of the body and mortuary.

"Once I was happy that all official matters for my purposes were carried out I issued a burial order in accordance with rule 14 of the Coroners rules and released her body back to the undertakers. I was aware that the undertaker needed some time because they had work to carry out in relation to possible further embalming or cosmetics.

"A burial order can only be issued if an inquest is to be held. This was in line with the Helen Smith judgement and rule 14 of the Coroners rules....

"I did not speak to anyone from the Home or Foreign Office that day. Nor did I speak to anybody in the British Embassy or anyone in France. The next working day I did speak to the department in the Home Office that deals with coroner. I cannot remember who I spoke to but did advise them that I had taken jurisdiction of the body of Diana Princess of Wales. A post mortem had taken place and that there would have to be inquest....

"I had no concerns regarding the post mortem but I did have concerns as I have earlier mentioned from my previous experiences of the media speculations and inventions.

"The only notes that I made on the day of the post mortems were the two 'transferral of jurisdiction orders' and a 'burial order'. Having transferred Mr Dodi Al Fayed to Michael Burgess the coroner for Surrey, I was no longer responsible for the documentation in relation to him.

"In mid October 1997, I prepared a document from memory regarding the events that had taken place that day which I handed over to Michael Burgess my successor when I retired. This was an aide memoir and a briefing note for the Home Office. As a coroner I did have to report to The Home Office, as did all other coroners. In a case such as this it would be naïve to believe that they would not be receiving numerous enquiries in relation to the deaths of Diana Princess of Wales and Dodi al Fayed. Part of my duty was to supply them with the facts in accordance with current rules pertaining to rules of coroners, which would have included the fact that inquests would have to be held at some date in the future.

"I was concerned that it should not appear that I was excluding Diana Princess of Wales from my jurisdiction as the Coroner to the Royal Household. There was never any pressure for me to treat Diana Princess of Wales any differently from the way in which I did. I carried out my duties in relation to her in my normal fashion....

"I wish it be recorded that the French Authorities provided me via the Metropolitan Police Service a copy of Judge Stéphan's files and reports that could not be normally disclosed under French law. This disclosure came about after a written request from me to the French authorities via the British Embassy.

"I am very grateful to Judge Stéphan and the French Authorities for their cooperation in providing the Metropolitan Police Service with copies of statements etc....

"I did not receive or know of any instructions from The Home Office in relation to the inspection of wombs in this case....

"The only advice in relation to the deaths of Diana Princess of Wales was in relation to my very first press release regarding her death and the need to hold an inquest. The advice was to keep the press statement short. Under normal circumstances I did not make press releases prior to the opening of an inquest when one is not in possession of all the facts.

"I had a primitive mobile phone in August 1997 but I am certain that I never used one on the day in question. I do not recollect making or receiving any calls other than those mentioned in this statement."[198]

John Burton, Royal Coroner, 1997: 29 Aug 04 Statement: **Jury Didn't Hear**:

"Further to my statement dated 16th of June 2004. I have been asked to clarify issues raised in the statement. In relation to my telephone conversation with the Lord Chamberlain.... I telephoned the single number for Buckingham Palace. It was a manual switchboard type set up. The operator put me through at my request to the Lord Chamberlain's department. The telephone was answered by a man that identified himself as being the Lord Chamberlain. I do not recall what his name was. I explained that I was the Coroner of the Royal household and that if the body of Diana Princess of Wales was repatriated back to the UK a coroner would have to be notified. He was unfamiliar with the working of his telephone system/switchboard and asked me to ring back later. There was no more conversation between us. He was unable to give me any information as to what was happening, the plans of repatriation or any instructions of any kind.

"This conversation lasted a minute or two, no longer. It was very brief....

"I talk of the fact that a burial order can only be issued if an inquest is to be held. In explanation the facts are: In all cases where bodies are repatriated to England where deaths have occurred abroad, if the Coroner has reason to believe that the person died of unnatural causes there must be an inquest. There is no requirement that Post Mortems must be carried out. The requirement for such is at the direction of the coroner. He does not need to order a post mortem. A burial order issued by a coroner can only be issued when an inquest is to be held."[199]

Michael Burgess, Royal Coroner, 2002 to Present: 16 Aug 04 Statement:[a] **Jury Didn't Hear**:

"Question: Please explain how you come to have jurisdiction in relation to the deaths of Diana Princess of Wales and Mr Dodi Fayed?

Answer: I am Her Majesty's Coroner for the County of Surrey and therefore have jurisdiction in relation to the death of Mr Dodi Fayed and in addition I am coroner of the Royal Household and have therefore taken over from my

---

[a] The statement of Michael Burgess was not signed or sworn – this has been addressed in Part 3.

predecessor [John Burton] the jurisdiction in relation to the death of Diana Princess of Wales".[a]

Question: Can you please tell me what happened on Sunday 31st August 1997?

Answer: It was at about 5.20 a.m. that by chance I heard on a radio that Diana Princess of Wales had been killed whilst travelling in a car with Dodi Fayed.

Around 9 a.m. I spoke to Dr John Burton, the then coroner of the Royal Household on the phone regarding the death of Diana Princess of Wales who as the coroner to the Royal Household was likely to take jurisdiction in relation to her death and offered to him as his deputy my assistance if required.

Around 9.45 a.m. I received a call from Peter Fahy the Assistant Chief Constable of Surrey Police. He informed me that the body of Dodi Fayed was being brought back for burial at Brookwood Cemetery before sunset. He asked me if I would become involved. I advised him that due to the case of Helen Smith and Section 8 (1) of the Coroners Act there was a requirement for a post mortem and an inquest, I would be taking jurisdiction of the body of Dodi Fayed. There was a suggestion that the body would be arriving at either Fairoaks Airfield in Surrey or Heathrow Airport. He was unable to assist with the timing of the arrival of the body.

At approximately 10 a.m. I phoned Mr Keith Brown one of my coroner's officers and informed him that I would be taking jurisdiction in relation to the body of Dodi Fayed and asked him to arrange the opening of the mortuary at the Royal Surrey County Hospital and in addition to arrange for a Home Office Pathologist either Dr Richard Shepherd or Dr Robert Chapman to attend and conduct the post mortem on the body of Dodi Fayed. We chose a Forensic Pathologist because they are available out of hours and because we wanted to obtain the best evidence available.

I then telephoned Dr Burton and advised him that I would be taking jurisdiction of the body of Dodi Fayed and was arranging a Post mortem at Guildford.

I then spoke to Keith Brown who confirmed that he had made arrangements for the opening of the mortuary at the Royal Surrey County Hospital and for Dr Chapman to attend in order to conduct the post mortem on the body of Dodi Fayed.

---

[a] Burgess was royal coroner at the time of this interview. He later resigned. The details of the line of succession of royal coroners in this case has been covered in the first Timeline of Events in Part 1 and will be further addressed in Part 5.

I then spoke to ACC Peter Fahy asking him for the estimated time of arrival of the body of Dodi Fayed.

During that telephone call, or later, he told me that there was a change in plans in as much as the body was to go to a service at Regents Park Mosque before burial in Surrey. He asked me if there would still be a post mortem. I told him the answer was 'yes'.

I then spoke to Keith Brown and asked him to stop everything as there was a change of plan and that I was looking for an alternative arrangement for the post mortem.

I then spoke to Dr Burton and discussed the need to alter my arrangements in relation to the post mortem of Dodi Fayed in as much as the body was going to London first. We also discussed the need where possible to accommodate the desires of the family, that the body should be buried in keeping with Muslim traditions before nightfall. Dr Burton offered the facility of the Hammersmith and Fulham mortuary together with the help of his mortuary assistant, which I accepted. Then, or during a later telephone call, Dr Burton asked if he could use the services of Dr Chapman for a post mortem examination on the body of Diana Princess of Wales as and when that was repatriated – the details for this were still unknown. The body of Dodi Fayed would be brought to Hammersmith & Fulham for the post mortem and then onto a London Mosque prior to burial in Surrey.

I then phoned Keith Brown told him of the new arrangements and asked him to redirect Dr Chapman to the Fulham mortuary. In addition I asked him to come to my home at 2 p.m. in order that we could travel together to the mortuary.

I then had a call from Caroline Sinclair from the Home Office. Her position was senior to Mr Clifford my normal contact in the Home Office department that deals with Coroners. She wanted to know what was happening and if there were any problems. I told her that there were no problems and asked her whether she was expecting any. I advised her that because of the case of Helen Smith and section 8 (1) of the Coroners Act, there was a need for a post mortem as I needed to establish the details of the death of Dodi Fayed. As I was concentrating on the arrangements of Dodi Fayed, I believe that she was aware that Dr Burton was dealing with the arrangements for Diana Princess of Wales but did not know of the arrangements. We discussed the timing of arrangements and the need for things to be speeded up as the family wanted the body buried before sunset and that could only happen after the post mortem and the service in a London Mosque. We agreed to keep each other informed.

At some point around about midday, I had a telephone call from Mr John Macnamara....

I telephoned Dr Burton and ACC Peter Fahy and advised them of the situation regarding the repatriation of the body of Dodi Fayed and that the post mortem was being moved to Fulham Mortuary.

Keith Brown came to my home address and we left to go to the mortuary at around 2.15pm....

Around 3.40 pm we arrived at Fulham mortuary. Officers from the Royalty Protection unit were in attendance and had secured the premises. Dr Burton was present as was Robert Thompson a mortuary assistant....

Dr Burton issued me a section 14 transfer of jurisdiction notice, which transferred the jurisdiction from him to me. This was because the body of Dodi Fayed was physically lying within his jurisdiction and as Surrey Coroner, unless there was a S14 transfer, I would not have the requisite jurisdiction to order a post-mortem or, subsequently to authorise the burial....

I left the mortuary with Keith Brown before the body of Dodi Fayed was returned to the coffin in order to prepare a burial order.... This was at 7.15 pm. I believe Keith Brown handed the burial notice to the undertakers.

At 7.25pm Mr Mohamed Al Fayed and his retinue left with the coffin....

I had a discussion with Dr Burton regarding me assisting him with his duties. He declined my offer as he felt it was not necessary.

I was in a side room when I saw various officials arrive with Sarah McCorquodale and Jane Fellowes. They went into a waiting room.

Dr Burton introduced me as the deputy coroner of the Royal Household, to Colonel Mather of the Lord Chamberlains Office, and told him if he had problems he could always speak to me.

Around 8.15pm together with Keith Brown, I left the mortuary and went home. I had no further calls.

The following morning I spoke to Dr Burton regarding the need to make a small press release. I did make an announcement in relation to Dodi Fayed, which was released via Surrey Police....

Question: Why did you take jurisdiction for the coronal procedures in relation to the body of Dodi Fayed?

Answer: Under the Home Office Circular 1983/79, issued after the Helen Smith judgement and appeals, the Home Office advised coroners that where a body was repatriated, having died abroad, it would be expedient for the coroner for the district where the burial or cremation is to take place to assume jurisdiction, although, legally, this can only be done by, as in this case, there was a transfer under s.14.

....Question: Did you receive any instructions from the Home Office?

Answer: No.

Question: Did anyone try and influence you in the way you carried out your duties and responsibilities?

Answer. No.

....Question: Did you make or receive telephone calls from the French Authorities?

Answer. No.

Question: Did you speak to anyone in the Embassy in Paris?

Answer. No.

Question: Did you see the coffin of Diana Princess of Wales?

Answer: No. I left prior to the PM of Diana. I never saw her coffin at all.[a]

.... Question: You are using various documents to assist with your answers. Did you make any original notes?

"Mr Burgess produced to me a copy of a two page document titled 'H.M. Coroner for Surrey. Re Dodi Fayed. Actions 31 August 1997'. He explained to me that this was an 'Aide Memoir' only that had been made sometime after the incident. I took possession of this as my exhibit KCR/ 1.

He also produced to me a copy of a letter written by him to Ms Carolyn Sinclair & Mr Robert Clifford dated 1 September 1997. I took possession of this as my exhibit KCR/ 2.

He also produced to me a copy of his Press Statement in relation to the death of Dodi Fayed together with a copy of a fax message addressed to Surrey Police. I took possession of this as my exhibit KCR/ 3.

He also produced a copy of a letter sent to him by Ms Carolyn Sinclair dated 1 September 1997. I took possession of this as my exhibit KCR/ 4.

He also produced a copy of transfer of jurisdiction notice issued by Dr Burton in respect of Mr Dodi Fayed, dated 31 August 1997. I took possession of this as my exhibit KCR/ 5.

Lastly he produced to me a photocopy of five pages of handwritten notes with the heading 31 Aug. I took possession of this as my exhibit KCR/ 6.[b]

"Question: The last item appears to be copies of your notes made on the day. Is this correct?

Answer: Yes.

Question: How were they made?

Answer: I sometimes kept old headed paper to hand near to the phone at home. I must have grabbed a handful and used it to write notes as I went

---

[a] This appears to be in conflict with earlier comments in this same statement. Burgess stated above: "Around 8.15 p.m. ... I left the mortuary and went home." The general evidence is that Diana's body arrived at Northolt at around 7 p.m. The Property Register document – reproduced later – shows items being removed from Diana's body while at Fulham Mortuary at 7.55 p.m. Burgess also said: "I saw various officials arrive with Sarah McCorquodale and Jane Fellowes" – they arrived around the same time as Princess Diana's body. The evidence indicates that Diana's coffin arrived at Fulham around 40 minutes ahead of Burgess' departure at 8.15 p.m.

[b] None of these 6 exhibits were shown to the jury.

along. The originals are folded in half so that I could put them into my jacket pocket.

Question: When were they made?

Answer: At different times during the day. Sometimes as I was talking and on other occasions a short while later.

Question: Did you use them to make your aid memoir?

Answer: No, I forgot I had them. After the first interview I searched through all my paperwork. Some had been put into a separate file because of a Judicial Review. I found them there.

Question: Did you speak to Robert Clifford on 31 August?

Answer: I regret that I have no specific recollection. As I was then, in 1997, Secretary of the Coroners' Society, I had many telephone contacts with him each week, often several a day when we would discuss particular issues concerning coroners. On 31 August 1997, I did have a number of telephone calls with a number of different people and I may well have spoken to Robert Clifford, in addition to his senior Miss Carolyn Sinclair, amongst others then and on the following day, 1st September. If I did speak to Mr Clifford then I would have told him of the actions which I was taking; on no account would I have accepted any instructions from him as to how I was to conduct my duties. I had no instruction given to me by anyone.

Question: In relation to the letter dated the 1st September from Carolyn Sinclair, can you explain the reference in the last paragraph to 'some issues'?

Answer: "Miss Sinclair appears to have been no more than responding to my faxed letter of 1 September, and to the 2 numbered 'issues' to which I refer in my letter. Reading my letter of 1 September again, I see that I inadvertently referred to s.15 as the statutory provision for transferring jurisdiction rather than s.14 – this was clearly a mistake on my part."[200]

Comment: The issues are:

   1) Who made the decision for Burton to be the coroner with jurisdiction over the body of Diana, Princess Of Wales?

   2) Why was Burton made the coroner with jurisdiction?

   3) Was that decision legal?

The law relating to a coroner's jurisdiction over a body appears to be reasonably straightforward.

The Judiciary of England and Wales states on its website: "The coroner's jurisdiction is territorial – it is the location of the dead body which dictates which coroner has jurisdiction in any particular case."[a201]

---

[a] This is a reflection of Section 8 of the Coroners Act 1988 which refers to "the body of a person ... lying within [the Coroner's] district".

In light of that, Her Majesty's Coroners Eastern District of London website specifically addresses what happens when a body is "brought into the jurisdiction from abroad": "If a body is repatriated to this country it is generally accepted that the Coroner within whose jurisdiction the body will finally lay must be notified. The Coroner will then decide if an inquest is necessary."[202a]

An analysis of the evidence in this case will reveal that expectations of where "the body will finally lay" – the ultimate burial location – was the key factor regarding jurisdiction over Princess Diana's body.

The very first handwritten note that Burton took on 31 August 1997 confirms the importance of burial location: "Phoned palace – Lucy Dove – believed buried Windsor". This note is fleshed out in Burton's typed notes: "Phoned Palace – Lucy Dove – told body coming to England. (Position re HRH was not clear. ? family or Royal funeral. Told thought burial at Windsor. Believed body coming to Northolt. Levertons dealing with funeral."

Burton describes the same call in his statement: "I again phoned the Buckingham Palace switchboard and spoke to a young lady who informed that they were experiencing problems, as there were no contingency plans for the death of Diana Princess of Wales. She was able to tell me that Levertons undertakers were dealing and that her body was going to be repatriated back to England later that day via RAF Northolt. The burial was likely to be at Windsor Castle."

This phone call to Buckingham Palace revealed to Burton:
- there was no specific plan for dealing with the death of Princess Diana[b]
- Levertons were dealing
- repatriation was occurring on the same day through RAF Northolt
- "position re HRH was not clear. ?" – this could relate to a question-mark over Diana's post-death level of seniority within the royal family[c]
- it was not known if the funeral would be "family or Royal"
- "burial was likely to be at Windsor Castle".

It is very significant that of these six points, only one was noted in Burton's original 31 August 1997 handwritten notes – "believed buried Windsor".

The central concern for Burton after hearing about Diana's death was whether or not he would be taking jurisdiction. Lucy Dove from Buckingham Palace conveyed to him that the likely burial site was to be Windsor Castle.[a]

---

[a] This is supported by Home Office Circular 89/1983 – see later.
[b] This has been addressed earlier in the section on Post-Divorce Status.
[c] Some may argue that this could indicate that it was not clear whether Diana was to be treated as a royal. It would seem unlikely that Burton was confused about Diana's new royal status – the note: "believed buried Windsor" indicates that he already knew she was being treated as a royal.

Windsor Castle[b] – as royal land – fell within Burton's jurisdiction as royal coroner. The concerns stated in the phone call – lack of clarity regarding the HRH, possible family funeral – were not as significant as the burial site. This approach fits with the law – shown earlier – that the burial location is the key factor for determining which coroner takes jurisdiction.[c]

Burton next notes: "assume household jurisdiction".[c]

There are some concerns regarding the early actions of John Burton.

There is no explanation of who "Lucy Dove" is, other than what Burton says in his statement: she was a "young lady" on "the Buckingham Palace switchboard".

This raises the question: Why didn't Burton, as royal coroner, ask to speak to someone more senior regarding this important issue – the Lord Chamberlain, David Ogilvy, or Anthony Mather, the Assistant Comptroller?[d]

Burton had already made an earlier phone call to Buckingham Palace – a call about which he has provided conflicting evidence.

This first call is not mentioned in Burton's original notes – this could fit with his later evidence that the call was fruitless.

In his typed notes, Burton writes: "Phoned Palace. Lord Chamberlain in difficulty with switchboard. To phone back."

Burton's statement account: "I telephoned the switchboard of Buckingham Palace and spoke to a person who identified himself as being the Lord Chamberlain. He was unable to assist much further at this stage and it was agreed that I should phone back later."

There are two main conflicts in the evidence:

-   in the notes Burton spoke to the "Lord Chamberlain", whereas in his statement Burton spoke to "a person who identified himself as being the Lord

---

[a] As stated, it is obvious from Burton's earliest notes that the most significant aspect of this conversation was the burial location of Windsor Castle – it is the only point he wrote down. It is possibly significant that by the time Burton gave his 2004 statement he had relegated "the burial was likely to be at Windsor Castle" to be the last of the six items of information. This could be because events show that 7 days later Diana was buried at Althorp – outside of Burton's jurisdiction. After that burial had occurred it was no longer in the interests of the royals to be highlighting the relevance of burial location to coroner jurisdiction. The full significance of this is discussed later.

[b] Windsor Castle is the normal burial site for senior members of the royal family.

[c] There is a question mark following this, but in between is a fairly large gap. Elizabeth Butler-Sloss, who apparently typed these notes up, has said: "I have set out below the text as far as possible" (see document reproduced earlier). This indicates that there may be other word(s) – possibly unreadable – before the question mark.

[d] Both of these people were present at Buckingham Palace on the morning of the crash – see earlier evidence from Mather.

Chamberlain". The Lord Chamberlain in 1997 was David Ogilvy[a] and had been in the role for 13 years, since 1984.[203] Burton had been royal coroner for 11 years, since 1986.[204] Ogilvy was "Lord Chamberlain of the Royal Household"[b] and Burton was "Coroner of the Royal Household".[c] I suggest that it is likely Burton would have known if he was talking to the Lord Chamberlain, and his earliest notes indicate that he did know who he was talking to

-   in the notes Ogilvy was "in difficulty with switchboard", whereas in the statement Ogilvy "was unable to assist much further at this stage".

Two months after giving his statement, Burton was asked to clarify. This time, Burton combines both explanations: "The operator put me through at my request to the Lord Chamberlain's department. The telephone was answered.... I explained that I was the Coroner of the Royal household and that if the body of Diana Princess of Wales was repatriated back to the UK a coroner would have to be notified. He was unfamiliar with the working of his telephone system/switchboard and asked me to ring back later. There was no more conversation between us. He was unable to give me any information as to what was happening, the plans of repatriation or any instructions of any kind."

This August 2004 explanation from Burton reveals that he did go through an operator and a conversation with Ogilvy took place. This raises doubts about Burton's account – in both the typed notes and this same second statement – that Ogilvy was "unfamiliar with the working of his telephone system". Burton had Ogilvy on the line: all Ogilvy had to do was talk into his phone – this does not appear to have anything to do with Ogilvy's level of knowledge of the phone system.[d]

As shown above, Burton's primary concern "at this stage" would have been whether the body of Diana would fall within his jurisdiction. The evidence from the handwritten notes supports this – immediately after finding out from the second Buckingham Palace call that the burial site should be Windsor Castle, Burton wrote "assume household jurisdiction".[e]

---

[a] Also known as Lord Airlie.

[b] The Lord Chamberlain's role is addressed later.

[c] The Royal Household comprises of 1,200 staff: British Monarchy Website, The Royal Household, www.royal.gov.uk

[d] One could suggest that Ogilvy was having trouble transferring Burton to someone else who could assist, but there is nothing in Burton's evidence to support that.

[e] Had the body not fallen within Burton's jurisdiction, after the arrival of Diana's body at RAF Northolt, Burton – who was also coroner for West London (that included Northolt) – would have been able to complete a s14 transfer document assigning jurisdiction to the coroner in charge of the area containing the burial site – i.e. Althorp – and would not have then needed to be involved in the decisions regarding the body, e.g. conduct of the post-mortem.

The evidence indicates that Burton did speak to Ogilvy during this call and I suggest that if Ogilvy had been in a position to tell Burton the likely burial site, he would have.

This appears to place Burton's first call to Buckingham Palace quite early.[a] It appears to be before the 8.30 a.m. arrival of Mather – see earlier. Mather stated that Ogilvy was already there when he arrived.

This early timing fits with Burton's statement account: "Early on the morning of Sunday 31st of August 1997, I was at home when I heard of the news of the death ... via the radio.... I telephoned the switchboard of Buckingham Place...."

Along with Mather's evidence – "when I got into the Palace, the Lord Chamberlain was in" – Burton's account also reveals Ogilvy was at Buckingham Palace early on that Sunday morning.

I suggest that Ogilvy was unable to help as it was Mather – delegated from Comptroller Ross – who had been given the responsibility of organising the repatriation and embalming[b] – see earlier. Ogilvy has never been required to give evidence to any police investigation – it is obvious that he should have been heard from at the inquest, but he wasn't.

When Burton called Buckingham Palace the second time, it appears that Mather still wasn't in – otherwise I suggest Burton would have spoken to Mather – but the information Burton needed was now available, from Lucy Dove.

Dove was able to convey to Burton the plan which had been earlier passed on to Mather by Ross.[c] Levertons had already been called in by Mather – he did this from home, see earlier. It appears that Mather had called Dove at Buckingham Palace to update her, prior to leaving home headed for Buckingham Palace himself. He arrived around 8.30 a.m.

This then places Burton's second call to Buckingham Palace – when he spoke to Dove – prior to 8.30 a.m.

---

[a] Burton fails to produce much information on timing – there may be a reason for this, which will become increasingly apparent.

[b] Not the initial embalming call though – that was made around 3.30 a.m. London time – see Embalming chapter. This issue is discussed again later.

[c] This is supported by evidence from Keith Leverton about what Mather told him around 6.30 a.m. on 31 August 1997: "[Mather] said his thought at the time was that [Diana] would eventually be at St Georges Chapel, Windsor, but beyond that there were no instructions where the burial would be."

The next evidence from Burton shows him deciding a post-mortem will be conducted and phone calls are made – to Levertons[a] and Brown – to organise that.[b]

Burton then addresses the first phone call he received from Michael Burgess, coroner for Surrey and deputy royal coroner at that time.[c]

One of the major themes of Burton's evidence is a dearth of timings. There are no timings in the original "handwritten" notes – that have been typed up by Elizabeth Butler-Sloss[d] - and there are also none in Burton's expanded typed notes. One could suggest that this is not a particularly professional approach for the royal coroner, who was possibly dealing with the most significant death of his career. I suggest that it may be no coincidence that timings have been omitted – for reasons that will become increasingly apparent as this chapter progresses.

Burton's first inclusion of any sense of time in his evidence is in the statement, drawn up in 2004, 7 years after the events.

In that document, Burton uses vague terms like "early on the morning" and "later that morning". Burton's first use of a specific time is regarding the first phone call from Burgess: "Around midday Michael Burgess ... phoned".

In conflict with this, Burgess times his initial phone call to Burton at "around 9 a.m."

The first call that Burgess records in his handwritten notes is from Peter Fahy of Surrey Police.[e] According to Burgess' typed notes and statement, this call – which included the information that Dodi would be buried at Brookwood before sunset[f] – occurred at "around 9.45 a.m. This would place the Fahy call after the first call to Burton, but in the handwritten notes, the first call of the day is from Fahy.

---

[a] The phone call to Levertons has been addressed earlier in connection with prior knowledge of a UK post-mortem.

[b] The post-mortem is dealt with later in the UK Post-Mortems chapter.

[c] Burgess took over from Burton as royal coroner in 2002.

[d] Butler-Sloss was appointed deputy royal coroner between September 2006 and April 2007. On 8 January 2007, Butler-Sloss conducted an inquest pre-hearing, where she reproduced Burton's handwritten notes in a typed format, stating: "I have set below the text as far as possible". There is a possibility that timings have been missed out – but if they were, they have also been omitted from Burton's own expanded typed version that was completed in "mid-October 1997" – see p564, *The Documents* book (UK edition).

[e] There is a time above this which appears to read 6 a.m. – this could not relate to the Fahy call, as John Macnamara, who was responsible for organising the Dodi repatriation, indicates in his statement that he didn't start on it until after 7 a.m. Burgess said that he heard about the death of Diana at "about 5.20 a.m." It is possible that the reference to 6 a.m. refers to that event. Refer to *The Documents* book, p518.

[f] This information would have originated from Macnamara – see previous footnote.

This indicates that the first 9 a.m. call to Burton is not recorded in Burgess' handwritten notes and the call to Burton – listed as "JDKB" – on page 1 of those handwritten notes must be the second call, which Burgess timed in his evidence as 10 a.m.

In his statement, Burton mentions two initial calls from Burgess, the first being at "around midday" – noted above.

There is a 3 hour time difference on the first call between Burgess' evidence – 9 a.m. – and Burton's evidence – midday.

Burton describes the content of the first call:
- Burgess offers assistance regarding Diana
- Dodi is to be buried at Brookwood
- Burgess is taking jurisdiction over Dodi[a]
- Burgess has Chapman on standby for a Chertsey post-mortem
- Dodi's post-mortem "would take place first" – due to the requirement to be buried pre-sunset.

Burgess' account of this first call is completely different. Burgess describes a phone call that is only about Diana – "[I] offered to him as his deputy my assistance if required". There is no mention of Dodi at all.

Burgess goes on to describe the second call – just after 10 a.m.:
- Burgess is now "taking jurisdiction of the body of Dodi"
- Burgess is "arranging a post mortem at Guildford".[b]

There is a real possibility that Burton has merged the two calls into one and placed a later time on it – midday.

Burgess' timing for arriving at the jurisdiction decision on Dodi – 9.45 to 10 a.m. – fits with Macnamara's account that he started work on the arrangements after 7 a.m. Macnamara also says: "During the latter part of the morning I liaised closely with Mr Michael Burgess"[205] – this liaising between Macnamara and Burgess would have occurred after Burgess had taken jurisdiction.

This evidence indicates that Burton's timing of midday for the Burgess call could not be correct.

I suggest that there is a reason why Burton has omitted specific timings of anything earlier, then has placed Burgess' call significantly later than it actually was – midday instead of 9 to 10 a.m. The reason will be revealed as this chapter develops.

Another significant point on timing is that pages 1 to 3 of Burgess' handwritten notes – apart from the "6 a.m." mentioned above – are

---

[a] The jurisdiction decision of Michael Burgess, coroner for Surrey, based on burial at Brookwood cemetery is further evidence that jurisdiction is based on burial site.
[b] Burgess' description of this call in his handwritten notes is somewhat different – this discrepancy is covered below.

completely devoid of any timing information. Then on page 4 there is note of "?3pm"[a][b] and on page 5 events are suddenly subjected to – compared to the earlier pages – microtiming. Times of various events on page 5 are placed at 5.15, 5.25, 7.15 and 7.25 p.m.

Burgess' handwritten document was subjected to close scrutiny in Part 3[c] and it was shown that certain critical parts had been doctored.

I suggest here, with regard to the dearth of timings on pages 1 to 3, that it is possible that times did exist on the original document. During his police interview Burgess confirmed that the 5 pages of notes he handed over were "copies". Burgess said that the originals had been made on "old headed paper" and were "folded in half so that I could put them into my jacket pocket".

Page 1 and 2 of these notes are reproduced earlier[d] – they are copies of what Burgess handed to the British police. They are not on headed paper.

This reveals that the notes Burgess gave to the police are not a full copy of the original notes – the heading is missing. I suggest that it is also possible that timings are missing on pages 1 to 3 – there are 4 specific timings on page 5 and Burgess provided times in his typed-up document (see earlier).

The discussion above showed that the first Burton call listed on page 1 of Burgess' handwritten notes must refer to the second 10 a.m. call, because it comes after the 9.45 a.m. Fahy notification that Dodi was to be buried at Brookwood.

Burgess describes this call: "JDKB[e] – am dealing w[f] DF[g] – no info on DPOW[h] – told of arrangements".

The critical words here are: "no info on DPOW".

Although Burgess provides no timing on this document, his other documents – the typed notes and his statement, discussed above – reveal that the timing is at around 10 a.m. The words "am dealing [with] DF" show that Burgess has already made the jurisdiction decision, and is now notifying Burton of that.

Burgess is also telling us that at around 10 a.m. there was still "no info on DPOW".

There are several reasons why this comment is a concern:

---

[a] The timing of that event had special significance in the discussion relating to the hold-up of Dodi's repatriation – this is covered thoroughly in Part 3.

[b] It is shown in Part 3 that page 4 could have been inserted much later than 31 August 1997.

[c] See pages 636-640 of Part 3 (UK edition).

[d] The full 5 pages are included in *The Documents* book.

[e] John Burton's full initials.

[f] This appears with a "-" above it – short for "with".

[g] Dodi Fayed.

[h] Diana, Princess of Wales.

1) Before this call occurred, Burton had already been given details from Buckingham Palace regarding Diana – repatriation that day; burial at Windsor Castle; Levertons were dealing. As shown earlier, Burton had this "info" before 8.30 a.m.

2) This call has to have occurred after the 9.45 a.m. Fahy call because it includes the information that Burgess is dealing with Dodi. The next record of a call on the Burgess handwritten notes is on page 2 where Burton offers Burgess the use of Fulham Mortuary. Between these two Burton calls, Burgess has two other calls to Brown and one to Fahy.

3) Burgess' handwritten notes are abbreviated and deal only with issues affecting him on the day – i.e. things to do with his jurisdiction: the repatriation and post-mortem of Dodi. This reference to Diana is the only reference to anything outside of Burgess' domain in the whole 5 pages.

4) Burton's record of the call refers mainly to aspects related to Dodi – see earlier – but it does include the comment: "the post mortem of Mr Dodi Al Fayed would take place first". This means that it was already known – at the time of this call – that there was going to be a post-mortem of Diana: Dodi's "would take place first" – ahead of Diana.

The question then is: Why has Burgess included "no info on DPOW" regarding this call, when it couldn't be true?

I suggest that the reason is the same as why Burton has timed the Burgess call at midday. The reason will emerge below.

In Part 3 it shows how Burgess' handwritten notes have been doctored – see earlier. I further suggest that this part of Burgess' notes has also been doctored. It is possible that the original note just read:[a] "JDKB – am dealing [with] DF" and that the remainder of this note "– no info on DPOW – told of arrangements" has been added in later.

There is a major issue here, which I believe British authorities have attempted to cover up.

The issue is: The speed with which the royals took control of events following the death of Princess Diana.

This is a problem for authorities for two reasons:

1) As shown earlier, Diana was no longer a member of the royal family.[b] This means that the royals had no right to be dictating the post-death events relating to Diana's body. These decisions should have been made by her family – or at the very minimum, the family should have been consulted before any actions were taken. The earlier Embalming chapter – and later

---

[a] As discussed earlier, I also believe there could have been a timing, which has been left off on the copy.

[b] See earlier section on Diana's post-divorce status.

parts of this chapter – reveal that this basic step never occurred: Diana's family did not make any of the critical decisions and the family were not consulted before actions were taken.

This raises the inevitable question: Why?

2) The speed of events was so quick – witness the 3.30 a.m.[a] call to the president of Kenyons in the Embalming chapter and the 6 a.m. call to Mather – that it indicates:

a) a concerted effort to get events moving before anyone else – i.e. family and others – had a chance to know about the events or realise what was happening

b) the possibility of prior knowledge of the crash – a plan may have been in place to deal with the aftermath of Diana's death before the crash actually occurred. I am not at this stage suggesting prior knowledge, but I raise it as a possibility.

At the moment, the issue is the early involvement of the royal coroner. In going through this evidence, I am not suggesting that John Burton, the royal coroner in 1997, had prior knowledge of the Paris crash. I believe he did not.

There is substantial evidence though – in Part 3, earlier and later in this volume – that Burton did play a part in the massive cover-up of events that has occurred since 31 August 1997.

The undated s14 jurisdiction transfer document – reproduced near the beginning of this section – includes an important statement: "The death [of Diana] had been notified to me as Coroner of the Queen's Household."

This is in conflict with Burton's notes and statement evidence – there is nothing in those documents to support a specific notification to Burton of the death of Diana. Burton's evidence is that he heard about the death on the radio news and subsequently called Buckingham Palace.

This raises the question of whether Burton received – as did Mather (see earlier) – an early call from Malcolm Ross, David Ogilvy, Robert Fellowes or Anthony Mather. There is no witness evidence of this occurring.

If that did occur, it would have been additional evidence of early royal control – earlier evidence has shown attempts to cover up aspects of that.[bc]

I believe the evidence is revealing that Burton heard about the crash early on the radio – or was notified, or both – and subsequently made the calls to Buckingham Palace – to either rule in or rule out his involvement.

---

[a] UK time.

[b] It is possible that notification to the coroner is a requirement of the law. According to the Third Report of the Shipman Inquiry, Chapter 7, Paragraph 15 under the heading: "The Basis of the Coroner's Jurisdiction": "A coroner can act only if and when a death is reported to him/her.": www.the-shipman-inquiry.org.uk

[c] This chapter has, and will, show a major coordinated effort by the royals to convert the dead Diana back into a royal. It would seem likely that notification to the royal coroner would have been just another required step in that process.

It is possible that Burton was set up to be involved, when he was told that "the burial was likely to be at Windsor Castle". I suggest that the royals – the Queen, Ross, Mather[a] – would have known that the burial wouldn't be at Windsor Castle:

- the Queen – who had a year earlier ousted Diana from the royal family – wouldn't have wanted Diana buried at Windsor Castle
- Diana's family – particularly Earl Spencer[b] – would never allow Diana to be buried at Windsor Castle
- Diana's will may have precluded a burial at Windsor Castle.

Burton was deliberately told Windsor Castle because the law – see earlier – would then require his involvement. Lucy Dove has never been required to supply evidence to any police investigation or the inquest – she should have been.

From the time Burton heard the words "Windsor Castle" he considered his responsibility was to take jurisdiction over Diana. I believe his later actions will show – and have shown – that Burton has taken part in the cover up, but there is nothing in the evidence to directly imply prior knowledge on his part.[c]

It is in this light – the speed of early royal control – that the evidence from Burton and Burgess needs to be viewed.

I suggest that Burgess has later added the comment "no info on DPOW" to the handwritten notes[d] on the 10 a.m. phone call to falsely indicate that Burton still didn't have any details on Diana. The indication from that of

---

[a] See earlier Royal Power Structure.

[b] Spencer's famous eulogy at Diana's funeral revealed a distaste for royal control. Also, once the coffin was at Althorp, Spencer removed the royal standard: "The Royal Standard that had been draped over the coffin was gone, replaced by the white, red, black and gold of the Spencer flag": Paul Burrell, A Royal Duty, 2003, p304.

[c] Having said this, there are arguments that could chip away at Burton's presumed early innocence on this: 1) In Burton's typed notes relating to the Dove phone call, he has noted "family or Royal funeral" but has been "told thought burial at Windsor". Burton probably should have been asking himself: If a family funeral was a possibility, how would it then be possible for a burial at Windsor Castle? 2) As royal coroner, when Burton was told by Dove that "there were no contingency plans for the death of Diana", this should have rung alarm bells.

I believe though that the balance of the evidence falls in Burton's favour – the knowledge of a likely Windsor Castle burial would have been the primary influence on Burton's early actions.

[d] In support of this, there is no mention of the "no info on DPOW" in the typed-up notes. Burgess states that the notes were "made sometime after the incident". I suggest that they would have been typed after the incident, but well before any late manipulation of the handwritten document.

351

course is that there was no unholy rush by the royals to take control of Diana's body – had there been, then by 10 a.m. Burton would have had the information and be organising the post-mortem.

The truth is that by 10 a.m. Burton already had the post-mortem at least half organised.[a]

In a similar vein, I suggest that Burton has manipulated the timings in his evidence. In his statement, Burton has provided vague references to times – see earlier – until the specific remark: "Around midday Michael Burgess ... phoned." This approach effectively leaves the timing of the earlier events – of relevance here, the second phone call to Buckingham Palace[b] – very open.

There are no timings at all in Burton's "expanded" typed-up notes and also none in Butler-Sloss' typed version of Burton's handwritten notes.

This then leaves us in a situation where it is impossible – from Burton's evidence – to have any credible knowledge of when the Lucy Dove call took place.[c] This means that one cannot draw conclusions – from Burton's evidence – on how quickly the royals were taking control of events.

It is particularly significant that when Burton commented in his statement on the notes he had made, he neglected to mention his most important notes – the handwritten ones, dated 31 August 1997: "The only notes that I made on the day of the post mortems were the two 'transferral of jurisdiction orders' and a 'burial order'.... In mid October 1997, I prepared a document from memory regarding the events that had taken place that day which I handed over to Michael Burgess my successor when I retired. This was an aide memoir and a briefing note for the Home Office.[d]"

It is possible that Burton failed to mention the handwritten notes because they may have contained critical timing information, possibly indicating early royal involvement.

Then when the handwritten notes do finally surface – in January 2007 by the hand of then deputy royal coroner, Elizabeth Butler-Sloss – they are no longer handwritten. Butler-Sloss instead types up the notes stating: "A handwritten note, dated August 31st. I have set out below the text as far as possible as it was written by Dr Burton".

Why didn't Butler-Sloss just provide the handwritten document?

I suggest that it is possible there were timings on the original document that may have been left off the Butler-Sloss typed document.

---

[a] This will become clearer in the Post-Mortems chapter.

[b] Where Burton speaks to Lucy Dove and is given the key information regarding the repatriation and burial of Diana.

[c] The earlier calculation of the timing of this call – prior to 8.30 a.m. – is based on the evidence from Anthony Mather.

[d] This is the "expanded" typed notes.

Once again, timings that may have been further proof of early royal control.[a]

There are eight documents that record what took place: Burton's June 2004 statement; Burton's August 2004 statement; Burton's handwritten notes dated 31 August 1997[b]; Burton's expanded typed notes; Burgess' August 2004 statement; Burgess' handwritten notes dated 31 August 1997; Burgess' typed "aide memoir"; Burton's s14 jurisdiction transfer document.[c]

It is very significant that the jury only got to see 2 documents out of 8 – both of Burton's sets of notes. Judge Baker had been given all the other 6 documents[d], but withheld them from his jury. John Burton died four months after his last statement, but it is incomprehensible that Michael Burgess, who superseded him as royal coroner, was not cross-examined at the inquest.

This inquest was investigating the circumstances of the death of Princess Diana, yet the jury never got to see the key evidence that influenced the decision of who would conduct that inquest – the coroner.

There are two reasons why this is significant:

1) Justice. Justice must be done and must be seen to be done.

Because of the estranged relationship between the royal family and Princess Diana during the 1990s – as outlined in Part 2 – if Diana had been assassinated, then some members of the royal family automatically would be seen to be key potential suspects.

This created a situation where an inquest conducted by the royal coroner could be perceived as leaning towards bias in favour of the royal family.

---

[a] In this context – see earlier in the Lord Chamberlain's Office section – the jury did get to hear that Ross phoned Mather at about 6 a.m., but that was it. The next thing they heard was that Mather arrived at Buckingham Palace at 8.30 a.m. and contacted Levertons later. There was absolutely no mention of what Ross said to Mather or that Levertons was immediately notified at 6.30 a.m. The jury did hear later that Clive Leverton was contacted at 6.45 a.m. but with Mather's earlier detailed account indicating a time closer to after 9 a.m., I suggest the jury would have been confused. This issue has already been addressed in the Comment section on the Role of Levertons. The jury also heard nothing of the Kenyons president's involvement – the 4 a.m. (UK time) phone call to Racine – see Embalming chapter and later this chapter.

[b] These have been typed up – the original has never surfaced.

[c] These documents have been reproduced at the beginning of this section on the Royal Coroner.

[d] By Operation Paget.

2) Legality. The inquest must be controlled by a coroner who is legally entitled to conduct it.[a]

The legal basis for the control of the Princess Diana inquest[b] appears to hang on the undated s14 jurisdiction transfer document completed by John Burton – shown earlier.

The basis for the legal involvement of Burton in the case is laid out in that document: "The death had been notified to me as Coroner of the Queen's Household. It was thought that the funeral might be held at Windsor. This conformed with Home Office Circular 79/1983."

Home Office Circular: HC79/1983: **Jury Didn't Hear**:

"Because bodies are usually brought into England and Wales from abroad by air, it will not always be clear whether the death should be reported to the coroner with the relevant airport in his jurisdiction or the coroner for the area in which the remains are to be buried or cremated. Because the relatives will normally live in the latter area, where they are being buried mainly, and the funeral directors collecting the body will usually be based there, it will generally be more convenient for the coroner at the place of disposal to hold the inquest and coroners may wish to notify funeral directors in their area accordingly."[206]

---

[a] This issue of legality is also addressed by Butler-Sloss in the 8 January 2007 inquest pre-hearing. The transcript is on the inquest website – see points 27 to 38. It includes a description by Butler-Sloss of some key points put forward by Michael Mansfield, including this in point 27: "Mr Mansfield questioned whether Dr Burton was told by the Palace that the Princess would be buried within the Royal district. He had not been notified where Princess Diana might be buried nor the part he, as Royal Coroner, was to play. He must have recognised that she was not going to be buried at Windsor. He was told by the family that she would be buried at Althorp [see later] and there must have been a strong assumption that she would be buried there. In that case he should have made the transfer request to the Coroner of Northamptonshire and not to himself as the Coroner of the Queen's Household. On the transfer document there was neither date nor acceptance. The language of his handwritten note was in the past. On the face of it, it appears that Dr Burton made a retrospective authorisation of what had already happened in his transfer request and in doing so he was under a serious misapprehension and misassumption of what was going on. It was not expedient for him to complete the transfer and he was in error in making that decision." The jury were never provided with this transcript.

[b] There were two inquests – one for Diana, one for Dodi – held jointly. For the purposes of this series of books it has been practical to describe the event as one combined inquest. Both inquests were set up by Michael Burgess, who replaced John Burton as royal coroner, in January 2004. Burgess was also coroner for Surrey – the area containing the Brookwood cemetery where Dodi was buried – in 1997. There is no dispute about Burgess' right to conduct the inquest into the death of Dodi Fayed. The issue is whether Burgess, as royal coroner, had the legal entitlement to set up the inquest into the death of Princess Diana.

Comment continued: There is no evidence of Burton having the death notified to him – Burton's evidence is he heard about it on the radio and then called Buckingham Palace. This has been addressed earlier.

Burton states: "It was thought that the funeral might be held at Windsor."

This is based on the early conversation with Lucy Dove – a person who has never been interviewed and wasn't heard at the inquest.

In his statement, Burton relates the circumstances under which he completed the jurisdiction transfer document – at the mortuary, prior to the UK post-mortem of Princess Diana on 31 August 1997: "Colonel Mather ... was now in attendance with 2 sisters of Diana.... They were taken to the office area where I ... explained to them that as the coroner of the Royal Household I had taken jurisdiction over Diana ... and was obliged to hold an inquest and order that a post mortem be carried out.... They left shortly after that. I believed at this time that Diana ... was to be buried at Windsor Castle, so I transferred jurisdiction from myself as coroner for the district of West London again to myself as coroner for the Royal Household in writing.[a] This made sense and was expedient[b]."

It is significant that Burton has omitted from his statement a key aspect of the conversation he had with Diana's sisters, Sarah and Jane. It is included in Burton's original notes and the typed-up notes.

Burton's 31 August 1997 notes read: "See family of Diana. <u>Now to be funeral at Althorpe</u>. Body to lie in St James. Body in my jurisdiction – physically – so give Burial order."

Burton's typed-up notes read: "The position of Diana after divorce and loss of HRH was sensitive. Coffin had Royal Standard. Thought it advisable to follow Home Office guideline[c] and have [Royal] Household jurisdiction and not seize body for West London. The family of Diana attended mortuary.

---

[a] Burton's reasoning was that he was both coroner for West London and royal coroner. Had the burial been at Windsor Castle, then he would have needed to transfer jurisdiction to himself, as royal coroner, because Windsor Castle was on royal land. At that stage, the body was still in West London – at Fulham Mortuary – so to legally conduct the post-mortem, it was required for jurisdiction to be transferred to the coroner who legally should have jurisdiction, the royal coroner, Burton. It will be shown that this act was illegal, because at this stage Burton already knew that the burial location would not be Windsor Castle, but Althorp. To be legal, Burton should have transferred jurisdiction to the coroner for Northamptonshire, the area that contained Althorp.

[b] "Expedient" is an interesting word for Burton to use. Oxford gives 2 definitions: 1: "Convenient and practical although not always fair or right". Or, 2: "Suitable or appropriate."

[c] This is a reference to the "Home Office Circular 79/1983" mentioned in the s14 document. This has been shown above.

355

Thought the funeral would now be at Althorpe, but the body was to lie at St James's – Not her home – Kensington. However both were in Household jurisdiction. Burial order given to Funeral directors at conclusion of autopsy".

The evidence appears to reveal concern on the part of Sarah and Jane regarding the direction of events.

Mather described his role: "I attended Fulham Mortuary on Sunday 31st August 1997 in company with Lady Sarah McCorquodale and Lady Jane Fellowes. I took them to the office area where Dr Burton spoke to them concerning his role and the post mortem examination."[207]

There is a possibility that the two sisters had complained about what was happening – the royal control; an impending post-mortem – to Charles, on their return to the UK from Paris.

Whatever the case, it appears that Mather has been delegated to take care of them. According to the evidence – Burton, Mather[a] – Mather, Sarah and Jane arrive at the mortuary, are delivered to a private area – the office – where Mather hands the sisters over to Burton.

Burton talks to Sarah and Jane, then "they left shortly after that".

It seems that the primary purpose of the Sarah-Jane visit to the mortuary was to talk with Burton.

Sarah and Jane may have been concerned that another post-mortem[b] was about to be held.

Burton appears to immediately describe to them what was going on – Burton had jurisdiction as royal coroner; there would be an inquest and post-mortem.

At some point in this short conversation – omitted from Burton's statement – Sarah and Jane have told Burton that the funeral is to be held at Althorp.

Burton has "recorded" this statement from Sarah and Jane in three different ways:

1) Original document: "now to be funeral at Althorpe"
2) Typed-up document: "thought the funeral would now be at Althorpe"
3) Statement: Completely omitted.

It has undergone an evolution from a definite statement – "now to be" – to a "thought" – to a complete disappearance.

Why?

I suggest that the original document is the closest to the truth: "now to be funeral at Althorpe".

---

[a] Diana's sister, Sarah McCorquodale, was cross-examined at the inquest, but was not asked about this. She should have been.

[b] There had already been one in Paris – see Chapter 1.

It appears that Sarah and Jane had told Burton something like: "There will be no funeral or burial at Windsor Castle – the funeral will be held at Althorp".[a]

What happens next is very critical.

Burton – who earlier had been basing his jurisdiction on burial location, as was the legal requirement (see earlier)[b] – now completely changes his basis for determining which coroner will get jurisdiction:

- Original notes: "Body to lie in St James. Body in my jurisdiction."
- Typed notes: "the body was to lie at St James's – Not her home – Kensington. However both were in Household jurisdiction".[c]

Burton's basis for coroner's jurisdiction has now changed from burial location to the post-autopsy location of St James' Palace.

But then when Burton gives his sworn statement, 6 months before his death, he makes two critical changes to this:

1) Burton deftly omits the Sarah-Jane statement that the funeral will be at Althorp

2) Burton now reverts to his earlier position that his jurisdiction was based on burial location: "I believed at this time that Diana ... was to be buried at Windsor Castle so I transferred jurisdiction ... to myself as coroner for the Royal Household in writing."

In doing this, 1997 royal coroner John Burton, has lied under oath – Burton has falsely stated that he believed Diana "was to be buried at Windsor Castle", when he had already been told by Sarah and Jane that the funeral would be held at Althorp.

The evidence from Burton's original notes – that he was not intending to hand over jurisdiction to the coroner for the area including Althorp[d] – indicates that at some point on 31 August 1997, either:

- Burton had decided that, as royal coroner, he would be taking jurisdiction regardless of the legality of him doing so

---

[a] Keith Leverton's evidence – see earlier – was that Mather told him at 6.30 a.m. "[Diana] would eventually be at St Georges Chapel, Windsor". This shows that earlier than 3½ hours after Diana's official time of death the royals had already decided on her burial location. I suggest that it would have been distressing to Sarah and Jane when they found out these important decisions were being made without consultation.

[b] Burial location was also the basis for Dodi's jurisdiction.

[c] In a strange twist to this, in Burton's typed notes, just a few lines earlier, he has actually invoked the "Home Office guideline" – "thought it advisable to follow Home Office guideline". This is a document (shown earlier) which recommends choosing the coroner based on burial location in cases of repatriation.

[d] This would have been the coroner for Northamptonshire.

- or, Burton had been told – by an authority – that he must take jurisdiction, by whatever means.

I suggest that the latter was the most likely – that Burton was following orders – and it is possible that Burton had been told that there would be no consequences for his actions on the day or for any subsequent false statements that he may need to make.

In summary, the key events relating to coroner's jurisdiction on the day, were:

- Diana's death was "notified to [Burton] as Coroner of the Queen's Household"[a]
- Burton phoned Buckingham Palace before 8.30 a.m. and is told by Lucy Dove that "the burial was likely to be at Windsor Castle"
- Burton made "the decision that I would be taking jurisdiction" based on the Windsor burial location
- at 9.45 a.m. Surrey coroner, Michael Burgess, decides he will "be taking jurisdiction of the body of Dodi Fayed" based on the burial location of Brookwood cemetery being in his area
- at around 8 p.m. Burton tells Diana's sisters, Sarah and Jane, "that as the coroner of the Royal Household I had taken jurisdiction over Diana"
- Sarah and Jane tell Burton that the funeral is to be held at Althorp
- Burton completes a s14 jurisdiction transfer form which states: "It was thought that the funeral might be held at Windsor.... This is a request in writing [to transfer jurisdiction] from West London to the Queen's Household".

This evidence reveals that Burton completed the form to transfer jurisdiction "from West London to the Queen's Household" giving the reason "the funeral might be held at Windsor", even though he knew from talking to family members that the funeral was to be held at Althorp.

Instead of transferring jurisdiction to himself as royal coroner, Burton should have transferred it to the coroner for Northamptonshire.[bc]

---

[a] Burton has never explained how that happened.

[b] This is the area that contains Althorp, where Diana was eventually buried.

[c] In his statement, Burton reveals that he signed another jurisdiction transfer document for Dodi: "Michael Burgess arrived at some stage and I handed over to him a note in accordance with Section 14 of the Coroners Act 1988. A hand written document, which transferred the jurisdiction of the body of Mr Dodi Al Fayed because at that stage the body would be lying within the District of West London and had not yet reached the County of Surrey and given Michael Burgess jurisdiction. This was clearly expedient, as he had made the necessary arrangements and the body would be buried within the County of Surrey." This again reveals that jurisdiction is based on burial location. If Burton had done the same thing with Dodi's jurisdiction as he did with Diana's, he could have claimed jurisdiction of Dodi for himself, as

In completing this transfer to himself, I suggest that royal coroner, John Burton, acted dishonestly and illegally.

An analysis of Burton's jurisdiction-related actions, after he became aware that the funeral was intended to be held at Althorp, is very revealing.

Burton's Actions After Talking to Diana's Sisters						
Action	**Date**	**Legal/ Signed**	**Locations Mentioned**			**Jurisdiction Basis Used**
			Althorp	**Windsor**	**St James' Palace**	
Transfer Document	31 Aug 97[a]	Yes	No	Yes	No	Burial Location
Written Notes	31 Aug 97	No	Yes	No	Yes	Current[b] Location
Typed Notes	Mid-Oct 97	No	Yes	No	Yes	Current Location
Statement	16 Jun 04	Yes	No	Yes	No	Burial Location

The above table reveals that when a document is legal or signed – i.e. a document one could expect to end up in the public arena at an inquest[c] – Burton has not mentioned that he was told by Sarah and Jane that the funeral would be at Althorp.

The table also reveals:

- when Burton mentions Althorp, he doesn't mention Windsor Castle, but does mention St James' Palace and uses the current location – St James' Palace – as the jurisdiction basis

- when Burton doesn't mention Althorp, he instead mentions Windsor Castle, and doesn't mention St James' Palace and then uses the burial location – Windsor Castle – as the jurisdiction basis.

Dodi's body lay in the Fulham Mortuary, which fell within Burton's area of West London.

[a] This document is undated, but Burton claimed in his statement that he completed it after talking to Sarah and Jane, but before the post-mortem: "I believed at this time that Diana ... was to be buried at Windsor Castle so I transferred jurisdiction ... to myself as coroner for the Royal Household in writing."

[b] The body was currently at Fulham, but was about to be transferred to the St James' Palace.

[c] What actually happened was that these two "legal/signed" documents were never seen by the jury, but the other two documents were – see below.

What this means is that Burton was happy to use burial location to determine jurisdiction, only when that location was Windsor Castle. In the cases where he admits to being told about Althorp as burial location, he instead introduces St James' Palace, and then proceeds to change the jurisdiction basis to current location.

The fact that Burton has only used burial location for jurisdiction in the legal or signed documents indicates that he knew, by law, that burial location was the correct basis to use. In those cases he has deftly omitted mention of Althorp and replaced it instead with Windsor Castle – deceitfully, dishonestly and illegally.

In all cases – whether using burial location or current location – Burton has claimed that jurisdiction over the body of Princess Diana was his, as royal coroner.

Just as deceitfully, Scott Baker – Burton's successor as inquest coroner[a] – has only provided two out of the four documents (in the chart) to his jury.

I suggest they have been carefully chosen.

The two documents the jury got to see both say the same thing – that Burton set up the jurisdiction based on current location – not burial location. It would have been impossible for the jury to understand that Burton could have acted illegally without seeing at least one of the other documents – Burton's police statement or the jurisdiction transfer document.

Inquest coroner, Scott Baker, ensured that this never happened.

Burton said in his statement: "I was concerned that it should not appear that I was excluding Diana Princess of Wales from my jurisdiction as the Coroner to the Royal Household. There was never any pressure for me to treat Diana Princess of Wales any differently from the way in which I did. I carried out my duties in relation to her in my normal fashion."

I suggest that the evidence has shown that Burton did not treat Diana's case in a "normal fashion".

Diana was not a royal – and was not buried as a royal – yet Burton treated her as a royal.

Burton has said: "There was never any pressure for me to treat Diana ... any differently from the way in which I did."

I believe that the question is: Was there any pressure to treat Diana in the way he did?

That is the question – but it has not been answered, because Baker's inquest never heard from the people who were in a position to pressure Burton: the Queen; the Lord Steward, Matthew Ridley; the LCO Comptroller, Malcolm Ross; the Lord Chamberlain, David Ogilvy.

---

[a] Baker was never actually appointed to the post of royal coroner. The succession of inquest coroners is addressed in Part 5. Earlier volumes of this series have at times wrongly described Scott Baker as "royal coroner".

The inquest did hear from LCO Assistant Comptroller, Anthony Mather, and Robert Fellowes, the Queen's Private Secretary, but they were not asked anything about the role of or contact with the royal coroner.

Burton says: "I did not speak to anyone from the Home or Foreign Office that day."

Burgess says: "I then had a call from Caroline Sinclair from the Home Office. Her position was senior to Mr Clifford my normal contact.... She wanted to know what was happening and if there were any problems.... I believe that she was aware that Dr Burton was dealing with the arrangements for Diana Princess of Wales but did not know of the arrangements. We discussed the timing of arrangements and the need for things to be speeded up as the family wanted the body buried before sunset and that could only happen after the post mortem and the service in a London Mosque. We agreed to keep each other informed."

The question is: Why have the Home Office, on the day, shown an interest in the arrangements for Dodi, but not Diana?

Sinclair has phoned Burgess, not Burton – even though "she was aware that Dr Burton was dealing with the arrangements for Diana ... but did not know of the arrangements".

I suggest the answer is that the royals were running the repatriation and embalming of Diana – not the Home Office. The Home Office was involved with the arrangements for Dodi – the royals weren't.

This is what the evidence continually points to: early royal control of Princess Diana's dead body. Diana may have been outside of royal control after the 1996 divorce, but she was rapidly reclaimed by the royal family after 3 a.m. on 31 August 1997.

Burton states that he didn't "speak to anyone from the Home or Foreign Office" and he goes on to claim: "Nor did I speak to anybody in the British Embassy or anyone in France."

It's notable that in this disclaimer Burton fails to mention senior royals – family or household. After all, Burton was appointed by the Lord Steward[a] – a person who "receives his appointment from the Sovereign in person".[208] In 1997 the Lord Steward was Matthew Ridley.[b]

It was to Ridley that, according to the Coroners Act 1988[c], Burton was to deliver all of his "inquisitions, depositions and recognizances ... to be filed among the records of [the Lord Steward's] office". The Act also states: "The

---

[a] Coroners Act 1988.
[b] 4th Viscount Ridley.
[c] Section 29.

coroner of the Queen's household shall reside in one of the Queen's palaces or in such other convenient place as may ... be allowed by the Lord Steward".

This indicates a reasonably close connection between the royal coroner and the Lord Steward – between Burton and Ridley.

There is no evidence of where Ridley was located on 31 August 1997. The jury may not have even been aware that such a person existed.

I suggest that because Burton carried out an illegal action on 31 August 1997 – the completion of an illegal jurisdiction transfer form – the royals were able to seize control of Princess Diana's body.[a]

This, in turn, gave the royal coroner the power over the conduct of the post-mortem and any future inquest.

I also suggest that it is no coincidence that that inquest was subsequently delayed for a period of 10 years, until October 2007. By then, the witnesses had to recall events from 10 years ago and the public had lost interest in the outcome – they had decided, after 10 years, that it was time to get it over with, and move on.

This issue will be addressed in Part 5.

Robert Thompson, Fulham Mortuary Manager: 13 Jun 01 Affidavit: **Jury Didn't Hear**:

"[Paragraph] 16. On a more general matter, I have from time to time heard Dr. Burton make comments about the possibility of an inquest. He has obviously been extremely irritated by correspondence received from Mr. Al Fayed's lawyers. I remember on one occasion Dr. Burton walked into the staff room whilst we were discussing Princess Diana and he said something along the lines of, 'I have a good mind to hold the bloody thing (i.e. the inquest) and not tell anyone'. He would also often come into the staff room at the Mortuary and say something along the lines of 'They have been on at me again — here's another fax' (i.e. from Mr. Al Fayed's lawyers).

"[Paragraph]17. I am not sure why Dr. Burton is continuing as Coroner in this case. He is aged 71 and the normal retiring age is 70. He has already stepped down as Coroner for West London. My impression is that he was starting to find the role too demanding; he was beginning to show signs of lack of coherence and sometimes was not entirely rational in his behaviour. As far as I know, he is solely staying on as Coroner for the Royal Household to conduct the inquest into Princess Diana. Unusually, he frequently carries the file relating to Princess Diana's post mortem with him. The usual practice is for the file to be kept in his office."[209]

Robert Thompson: 9 Nov 04 Statement: **Jury Didn't Hear**:

---

[a] Appendix 1 – at the end of this book – reproduces a FOIA (Freedom of Information Act) Centre article exposing a connection between Michael Burgess' resignation as inquest coroner in 2006 and the illegal seizure of jurisdiction by Burton on 31 August 1997.

Note: Thompson was asked by the police to comment on the content in the above affidavit.[a]

"Paragraph 16 ('On a more general matter ...'). Dr Burton's comment 'I have a good mind to halt the bloody thing (ie the inquest) and not tell anyone' is not a quote I made. Since my illness[b] I have had problems remembering things and this quote suggests that I had an extremely good recollection of what was said some four years after it was supposedly said. I wouldn't say I don't recall hearing a comment along those lines as it's the sort of thing Dr Burton might have said but I certainly wouldn't have repeated that myself. I would say that everything else in paragraph 16 is quite possible.

"Paragraph 17 ('I am not sure why ...'). The first two sentences, which refer to Dr Burton's age, are true as the normal age of retirement is seventy. However, I do not recall ever saying that myself and in fact, I am not even sure I knew how old Dr Burton was at that time. I have no recollection of saying anything contained in the next three sentences (from 'He has already stepped down as Coroner for West London ...' to '...wherever he goes.'[c]). This is not the sort of thing I would say. The last sentence of paragraph 17 ('Normally a file would be kept in the Coroner's office') is correct though I don't remember saying this myself."[210]

John Burton, Royal Coroner, 1997: *Daily Telegraph* Interview: 1 Apr 01: **Jury Didn't Hear**:

An inquest into Diana and Dodi's deaths would be "a waste of everyone's time and money. Nobody can be forced to give evidence as a witness and it would serve no purpose. The aim of an inquest is to identify the cause of death but in this case all the evidence was collected in France and any inquest would just be a forum for different people's views."

Daily Telegraph: "The coroner who is due to hold the inquest into the death of Diana, Princess of Wales is campaigning for a change in the law so that the inquiry never takes place.

"Dr John Burton, the coroner for the Royal Household, believes that any inquest into the Princess's death, and that of her companion, Dodi Fayed, would be costly and pointless. He told the *Telegraph* that he has been lobbying Jack Straw, the Home Secretary, for a change in the law that requires an inquest in every case where a body is returned to Britain after a death abroad."[211]

---

[a] The police did not actually show Thompson the affidavit, but an earlier document with similar content – this is discussed below.

[b] Thompson suffered with depression from October 2001. See *The Documents* book, pp600-1

[c] The wording is different here to the affidavit, but the gist of the content appears to be similar.

Comment: The general perception of the public would be that the role of a coroner is to seek the truth about the circumstances regarding a particular death.[a]

The above evidence – from Fulham Mortuary manager, Robert Thompson and the Burton interview – would appear to cast doubt on whether finding the truth was the aim of John Burton, in the case of the deaths of Diana and Dodi.

There are two main quotes that raise real concern:
- heard by Thompson before June 2001: "I have a good mind to hold the bloody [inquest] and not tell anyone"
- said to the *Telegraph* in March 2001[b]: the inquest would be "a waste of everyone's time and money.... It would serve no purpose.... Any inquest would just be a forum for different people's views."

When Thompson was interviewed by Paget officers in 2004, he backed away from the quote in his 2001 affidavit.

There are several points:

1) Thompson's recall of the original quote is recorded in a signed and sworn affidavit on 13 June 2001

2) The police did not show Thompson the sworn affidavit, but instead an earlier unsworn document that was taken during the previous month, May 2001. Thompson said in the police statement: "I have been shown a document headed 'Record of Statement given orally by Robert Thompson to Stuart Benson on 16 May 2001'. I have read this 'Record of Statement' and I do not believe that this was the affidavit I made to the Harrods organisation. I have been asked to comment on this document and the first thing I would say is that I do not know who Stuart Benson is and cannot recall the date of 16th May 2001."[212]

It is quite possible that had the police shown Thompson the sworn affidavit, it may not have been so easy for them to secure a retraction.

3) Paget may have put Thompson under other pressure to achieve this retraction. Operation Paget's interviewing methods are addressed in Part 5.

4) Although Thompson's comments in his November 2004 statement appear to be a retraction, he does make a critical qualification. Although Thompson says "I certainly wouldn't have repeated that myself", he admits: "I wouldn't say I don't recall hearing a comment along those lines as it's the sort of thing Dr Burton might have said".[c]

---

[a] The Coroner's role in this case is specifically addressed in Part 5.

[b] The interview was published on 1 April 2001.

[c] Thompson also states that he has "had problems remembering things" since his depression. In the same statement, Thompson says: "I realised that I was suffering from depression ... in <u>October 2001</u>". In an apparent conflict to this, Thompson goes on to say: "I went to see my GP on <u>19th October 2000</u> and she signed me off with depression." The affidavit was taken in June 2001, so it is difficult to determine

5) Thompson's affidavit account is supported by the *Telegraph* interview – taken just two months earlier than Thompson's testimony.

The Thompson affidavit and the *Telegraph* interview of Burton should be viewed together. Whilst at the mortuary Burton said that he might conduct the inquest without telling anyone. To the *Telegraph* – and therefore the public – Burton has suggested that the inquest <u>shouldn't be held at all</u>: "a waste of everyone's time and money"; "it would serve no purpose".

When this is seen in the light of the events on 31 August 1997 – that Burton illegally set himself up as the jurisdiction coroner, in the face of information from the family that the burial was outside of his jurisdiction – a pattern appears to emerge.

Burton has:

- insisted illegally in 1997 that he be the one to conduct this inquest into the death of Princess Diana
- then delayed the inquest for 4 years[a]
- stayed on "as Coroner for the Royal Household to conduct the inquest into Princess Diana"[bc]
- then stated publicly that to hold the inquest would be "a waste of everyone's time and money" and "would serve no purpose".

Burton had carried out these acts and made these statements in his role as royal coroner, answerable to the Queen.[d] There is little doubt that if the Queen had not been comfortable with Burton's actions or statements, then she would have made that known to him – or to the public.

There is no evidence of that occurring.

Instead what we see is the continuing stamp of royal control over the process – a delay in conducting the inquest, which eventually stretched out (beyond Burton's lifespan) to 10 years.

---

whether it was taken before or during the period of depression. The police should have realised there was a conflict and clarified it with Thompson. That never happened. Thompson was not cross-examined at the inquest and none of his evidence was heard by the jury.

[a] In 2001.

[b] See Thompson above.

[c] Burton was born in 1929 and resigned as coroner for West London at the age of 70, in 2000. Burton didn't resign as royal coroner until March 2002 – due to ill health. He died from prostate cancer on 8 December 2004. Sources: Obituary: John David Keith Burton, BMJ (British Medical Journal) Volume 331, Number 7512, 4 August 2005; FOIA Centre News, Royal Coroner Resigns Diana Inquest After FOIA Revelation Shows He Had No Jurisdiction, 24 July 2006. The FOIA article is reproduced in Appendix 1 of this volume.

[d] See earlier.

Burton showed no intention to act within the law in 1997 – holding illegally onto control over Diana's body – then in 2001, appears to be attempting to sway public opinion away from the legal requirement to conduct any inquest at all.

It appears that Burton – along with other players in this case (see Parts 1 to 3) – had been provided, right from day one, a green light to carry out whatever actions and make whatever statements he deemed necessary, with no threat of accountability hanging over him.

The actions of the various coroners – Burton, Burgess, Butler-Sloss, Baker – will be examined in Part 5. It will be shown that relentless legal pressure has been placed on them over the years by Mohamed Al Fayed. Mohamed obviously got involved in this case because of the death of his son, Dodi.

I suggest at this stage that had Princess Diana died alone (without Dodi) then there is a possibility – based on the actions, statements and attitude of John Burton, acting on behalf of the Queen – that there may have been no inquest at all held into that death.

Repatriation by Charles

On 31 August 1997, Charles – Diana's ex-husband – dashed across from Balmoral to Paris to retrieve Diana's body.

Why?

Decision

There is conflicting evidence on how this decision – a same day repatriation by Charles – was arrived at.

Keith Moss, British Consul General, Paris: 22 Nov 07: 21.3:

Hough: Q. Did you, along with [Stephen Donnelly], make plans relating to the flying in of the Prince of Wales?

A. The actual arrangements for the flight were done by others, not by us.

Q. But you liaised with those who were making those arrangements, did you?

A. Yes.

Stephen Donnelly, British Vice Consul, Paris: 22 Sep 05 Statement read out 17 Dec 07: 126.21:

"I have been asked if I made or received any instruction that day dealing with the repatriation of the Princess of Wales' body. No, I was not involved with the repatriation."

Keith Moss: 22 Oct 04 Statement: **Jury Didn't Hear**:

"At 0555hrs [5.55 a.m.] Mr Chevènement and Sir Michael Jay gave the Press Conference, which I attended. The Doctors explained the Princess of Wales' injuries and what they had done to try to save her life...."

"Back in the hospital, the corridors were cleared. A small team of nurses were instructed to move the Princess of Wales' body from the Intensive Care Unit to the floor above....

"Not long after the Princess of Wales' body had been moved ... [the nurses] mentioned the possibility of long-range cameras being able to take photographs into the room. On my agreement, the nursing staff set up curtains at the windows....

"There followed a lengthy period when I took and made telephone calls in order to assist in arrangements to have the body returned to the United Kingdom. I liaised with the hospital, Balmoral and the Embassy, where an Emergency Unit had been set up.

"Plans began to take shape for an aircraft of the Royal Squadron to attend Paris to accompany His Royal Highness Prince of Wales and the Princess of Wales' two sisters and members of the Prince's Household staff. It was decided that Wing Commander Steve Gunner, one of the Assistant Service Attachés at the British Embassy, was responsible for arranging the Royal Flight.

"The decision came from the UK that HRH Prince Charles and his party would travel out to Paris to accompany the return to Britain, of the Princess's remains. Robin Janvrin, Her Majesty The Queen's Private Secretary or Steven Lamport, the Prince of Wales' Private Secretary would have informed me. The Embassy Incident Control Unit would have liaised with French officials to assure the use of the Villacoublay Military Airport on the outskirts of Paris."[213]

Michael Jay, British Ambassador to France, 1996-2001, Paris: 13 Dec 05 Statement: **Jury Didn't Hear**:

"At approximately 5.30 a.m., I was walking across the grounds of the Pitié Salpêtrière Hospital to a lecture room, which had been converted into a temporary press centre. I was walking in the company of the French Interior Minister, M Jean-Pierre Chevènement, it being intended that both of us should make a statement to the press about the deaths of the Princess of Wales and Mr Dodi Al Fayed."[214]

Michael Jay: 13 Dec 05 Statement: **Jury Didn't Hear**:

"I spent three periods at the Pitié Salpêtrière Hospital on Sunday 31/08/1997.[a] On all three occasions I was accompanied by my wife.

"We first arrived at the Hospital at about 2.20 a.m. on 31/08/1997, being driven there from our residence by Tim Livesey. We were driven home by an Embassy driver some time between 0700 [7.00 a.m.] and 0800.

---

[a] The three visits to the hospital were: 1) 2.20 a.m. to 7 a.m.; 2) Approximately 8.30 to 9.30 a.m.; 3) At 5.40 p.m. accompanying Charles, Sarah and Jane.

"Secondly, at about 0820, we received a telephone call from the French authorities to say that Madame Chirac would be at the Hospital at about 0900. We drove back to the Hospital shortly afterwards....

"After this second visit we drove back to the Embassy probably between 0900 and 1000, where I held a meeting and allocated responsibilities, and where a period of very intense activity ensued."[215]

Michael Jay: 13 Dec 05 Statement: **Jury Didn't Hear**:

"At the time when I left the Hospital after the early press conference, it was still entirely unclear what arrangements would be made for the repatriation of the Princess' body, in particular whether it should take place that day, 31/08/1997, or at a later date. In the course of the early morning however I had discussions with Sir Robin Janvrin, the Queen's Private Secretary, who was at Balmoral, as a result of which we came to the decision that the Princess' body should be repatriated as soon as possible. From that point we aimed at repatriation taking place the same day. This called for a very high degree of organisation, not only having regard for the need to get everybody, including visiting dignitaries, in the right place at the right time, to ensure that the ceremonial was sufficient and dignified, but also the need to comply with the various legal formalities required by the French authorities, which normally take much longer than one day to complete, particularly when that day is a Sunday.

"In all the circumstances, it was quite remarkable that we were able to achieve the repatriation of the Princess' body in an orderly and dignified fashion over such a short time scale. This was due to the outstanding efforts and efficiency of the Embassy staff, but was also in great measure due to the co-operation and support of the French, to whom I paid warm tribute in my telegram sent in the evening of 31/08/1997, in which I said, 'From the President down, the French authorities have dealt with last night's events with extraordinary generosity, efficiency and sensitivity'."[216]

Michael Jay: 13 Dec 05 Statement: **Jury Didn't Hear**:

"As I recollect, my first step, after returning from my second visit to the Hospital at about 0900 [9.00 a.m.] in the morning of 31/08/1997, was to have a meeting with the people available at the Embassy in order to allocate responsibilities. There is so far as I am aware no record of the meeting, and I cannot recall in detail who attended....

"It seemed likely that there would be a visit or visits that day from members of the Royal family or other dignitaries who would most probably use military facilities, and I asked Brigadier Ritchie to make the necessary arrangement with the Paris military airport at Villacoublay, where such visitors would arrive. I also asked Brigadier Ritchie, with the assistance of Wing Commander Gunner, to make all necessary arrangements as the need arose for ceremonial and protocol, with regard to the reception of visitors, the organisation of the cortège should that be necessary, and so forth."[217]

Michael Jay: 13 Dec 05 Statement: **Jury Didn't Hear**:

"I have been asked whether I made any decisions in respect of the repatriation of the Princess' body to the UK. There was never any question but that the Princess' body would be repatriated to the UK for her funeral to take place there. The main matter that fell for decision was when her body should be repatriated. I have already described how the decision was made in the course of my discussions with Sir Robin Janvrin in the morning of 31/08/1997, that her body should be repatriated as soon as possible, and that we immediately started working towards repatriating the body that day. The detailed arrangements, with regard to the visits by French Ministers and others, and the arrangements for the arrival of the two aircraft from England, all flowed from and were determined by that decision. Although I took part in the discussions about the date of repatriation and contributed to the decision, it would not be correct to say that I took the decision that the Princess' body be repatriated that day. Consequential matters such as the composition of the cortège were for the most part left to others, though I may well have been consulted.

"Details of the way in which arrangements were made are moreover set out in my various reports and records, and the Consular Report made by Mr Keith Moss. I will not repeat them here save to emphasise that plans changed and developed during the course of the day."[218]

Michael Jay: 31 Aug 97 Diary read out 11 Feb 08: 103.9:

"At 3.45 [a.m.], Chevènement, absent for a few minutes, returned to ... say, visibly moved, that the Princess was dead. I telephoned Robin Janvrin in Balmoral, the resident clerk and Manila[a]. Tim [Livesey] and Keith Moss busy busy too.... After a short but frustrating delay – because news was leaking out – we went into some sort of hall for a press conference. The hospital surgeon, Chevènement, me and others. Press all over the place.... We go back to the hospital and wait for a bit....

"After the press conference, Chevènement says he would like to pay his respects to the body. I agree. Chevènement, Sylvia and I go in to see the Princess....

"We leave around 7.00 a.m. and drive back to the house for coffee and a shower. Matignon tells me Jospin is flying up from La Rochelle to pay respects. Jean-David Levitte tells me Mme Chirac will be there in half an hour. Sylvia and I dress quickly, for the second time this morning, and drive to the hospital....

"Sylvia, Jean Gueginou, Martin Draper and I squeeze into the Jaguar ... and drive back here. Keith Moss, the Consul General, stayed at the hospital. The

---

[a] British Foreign Secretary, Robin Cook, was in Manila.

Embassy is full. Some people called in by us, some coming in because they wanted to help. The next few hours are incessant phone calls with Robin Janvrin at Balmoral and Nick Archer from the Prince's staff, Jean-David Levitte at the Élysée, the Prefecture and others. Some of the Princess's staff are here by now. I am not sure where they've come from. None of us here knew the Princess was in Paris and nor did the French authorities....

"Chirac comes on the phone to talk about the ceremony at the hospital when the Prince arrives to collect the body – as Balmoral have now decided, rightly, he should, with Sarah McCorquodale and Jane Fellowes coming with him."

Colin Tebbutt: Jul 04 Statement: **Jury Didn't Hear**:

"When we boarded the plane it was about 7 a.m. It was full of members of the Press. Also on the plane was a man I recognised as Superintendent Kingsmill from SO14, who was going to Paris as an advance for His Royal Highness Prince Charles' visit. I remember he was unable to obtain a seat on the flight, and as a consequence had to sit in the pilot's jump seat."[219]

Colin Tebbutt, Diana's Driver and Security: 26 Nov 07: 88.6:

Hough: Q. I think you boarded a plane at about 7 o'clock in the morning.

A. I understand it was 6.30, not 7, but it was early in the morning.

Comment: The key issues relating to the Charles trip are who, when and why.

Who made the decision for Charles to go to Paris? When was that decision made? And why did the trip happen?

Earlier evidence has shown that the repatriation of Diana was very rushed – everything was carried out on the same day. The witness evidence will show that this decision to repatriate on the same day is closely connected to the decision for Charles to be the one doing that repatriation.

Logic would suggest that the decision for a same day repatriation would have been made very early, as it involved so many factors coming together – in the words of British Ambassador, Michael Jay: "this called for a very high degree of organisation".

It is very significant that the evidence of the following 7 key witnesses was not heard at the inquest – the Queen; Robin Janvrin – the Queen's deputy private secretary; Prince Charles; Stephen Lamport – Charles' private secretary; Nick Archer – Charles' staff member; Jane Fellowes – Diana's sister; Catherine Bouron – Jay's private secretary.

The inquest did hear from Sarah McCorquodale, but in an incredible "oversight", she was never asked anything about this trip to Paris.

We are left then to rely on the evidence of Michael Jay and Keith Moss, the British Consul-General.

At the inquest it was suggested by Jonathon Hough – and not denied by Moss – that Stephen Donnelly was involved in organising the repatriation.

Donnelly has said "I was not involved with the repatriation"[a] – and there is no credible evidence that suggests otherwise. Donnelly did state earlier that he was "surprised to find out that both Diana ... and Dodi ... were repatriated" on the same day – he said that "the normal procedure ... [would] take between five to seven days".

There are two aspects to the evidence: 1) the decision itself, and 2) the planning and arrangements to enable the implementation of that decision.

Moss records in his statement:
- "a lengthy period when I took and made telephone calls in order to assist in arrangements to have the body returned"
- "plans began to take shape for an aircraft of the Royal Squadron to attend Paris to accompany ... [the] Prince of Wales and ... [Diana's] two sisters"
- "the decision came from the UK that HRH Prince Charles and his party would travel out to Paris to accompany the return to Britain, of the Princess's remains. Robin Janvrin, Her Majesty The Queen's Private Secretary or Steven Lamport, the Prince of Wales' Private Secretary would have informed me".

Jay states:
- "in the course of the early morning ... I had discussions with Sir Robin Janvrin ... as a result of which we came to the decision that the Princess' body should be repatriated as soon as possible. From that point we aimed at repatriation taking place the same day" – statement
- "the decision was made in the course of my discussions with Sir Robin Janvrin ... that her body should be repatriated as soon as possible, and that we immediately started working towards repatriating the body that day" – statement
- "the detailed arrangements, with regard to the visits by French Ministers and others, and the arrangements for the arrival of the two aircraft from England, all flowed from and were determined by that decision" – statement
- "although I took part in the discussions about the date of repatriation and contributed to the decision, it would not be correct to say that I took the decision that the Princess' body be repatriated that day" – statement
- "it seemed likely that there would be a visit or visits that day from members of the Royal family or other dignitaries who would most probably use military facilities" – statement

---

[a] Hough had Donnelly's statement saying this.

- "the next few hours are incessant phone calls with Robin Janvrin at Balmoral and Nick Archer from the Prince's staff, Jean-David Levitte at the Élysée, the Prefecture and others" – diary, heard at inquest
- "Chirac comes on the phone to talk about the ceremony at the hospital when the Prince arrives to collect the body – as Balmoral have now decided, rightly, he should, with Sarah McCorquodale and Jane Fellowes coming with him" – diary, heard at inquest.[a]

There is substantial conflict – conflict between Jay's diary and statement; conflict between Jay and Moss.

The only evidence the jury heard was from Jay's diary – neither Moss nor Jay's statements were read out and neither of them were cross-examined about this. Combined with the failure to hear any other witnesses – listed above – this indicates a major cover-up of the evidence by Scott Baker.

Moss describes: a) his telephone involvement "in order to assist in arrangements" for repatriation; and b) "plans began to take shape" for the royal flight.

But when Moss talks about the decision – which must have come first, before the arranging – Moss doesn't claim any involvement in that: "the decision came from the UK.... Robin Janvrin ... or Steven Lamport ... would have informed me".

So Moss states "the decision came from the UK" and he would have been notified of that by either Janvrin or Lamport – Moss mentions Janvrin first.

The decision Moss is talking about is "that ... Charles ... would travel out to Paris to accompany the return ... of the Princess's remains". Moss has both events together – Charles' visit to repatriate Diana's body.

In his statement, Jay describes something quite different – Jay talks about "discussions with ... Janvrin" that lead to a mutual "decision ... aimed at repatriation taking place the same day".

A joint decision made by Jay and Janvrin. Just same-day repatriation – no mention of Charles.

Jay later states: "arrangements for the arrival of the two aircraft from England ... flowed from and were determined by that decision" – the earlier decision for same-day repatriation made by Jay and Janvrin.

---

[a] When one considers that the Charles visit must have been one of the major events of the day, it is really very surprising that Jay's diary contains nothing about the initial notification to him that Charles was coming over. There is a possibility that this diary has been doctored, or parts of it have been omitted. The document – or copies of it – have never been made available. The diary also includes the comment: "None of us here knew the Princess was in Paris and nor did the French authorities" – this is revealed, in Part 3 (pp504-7 UK edition) and also in Part 5, to be a false statement.

I suggest that what Jay is saying doesn't make sense – that an arrangement for Charles to dash across the Channel "flowed from" or was "determined by" the same-day repatriation decision made by Jay and Janvrin.

I instead suggest that it is more likely that the decision for Charles to dash over was the initial decision and same-day repatriation would have naturally flown from that.

Jay's diary evidence – the only evidence the jury actually heard – contains none of this information.

Jay talks about hours of "incessant phone calls" with Janvrin, Archer and the French – but no mention of the content of those calls.

A call from Chirac is the first mention of same-day repatriation and Charles coming. The two are merged together – "when the Prince arrives to collect the body" – and the decision-making doesn't involve Jay – "Balmoral have now decided".

The Moss account of the decision almost fits with Jay's diary record:
- Moss: "the decision came from the UK"
- Jay's diary: "Balmoral have now decided"
- Moss: "Charles ... would travel out to Paris to accompany the return ... of the Princess"
- Jay's diary: "when the Prince arrives to collect the body".

Moss states that the decision was conveyed to him by Janvrin or Lamport. In her book, *The Queen & Di*, royal author Ingrid Seward states that "Stephen Lamport [was] in London" at the time. Seward says that "the Prince's assistant private secretary, Nick Archer, ... was staying in [a] house on the [Balmoral] estate".[220]

This fits with Jay's diary account that he talked "with Robin Janvrin at Balmoral and Nick Archer" – he makes no mention of Lamport.[a]

There is much more conflict with Jay's statement evidence: a joint decision of same-day repatriation made between Jay and Janvrin; the decision for Charles to come was a flow-on, "determined by [the same-day repatriation] decision".

What is the true account?

Was the same-day repatriation decision made by Jay and Janvrin – Jay's statement – or was it from the UK – Jay's diary, Moss' statement?

Was the Charles visit decision made later than the same-day repatriation – Jay's statement? Or was it made at the same time – Moss' statement, Jay's diary?

---

[a] This is not to suggest that Moss wouldn't have talked with Lamport. As Charles' private secretary, Lamport – who ranked above Archer – would have been involved in making the arrangements, but Charles' man on the ground in Balmoral was Archer.

As with most issues, the timing is possibly the most critical factor.

Moss describes the 5.55 a.m. press conference, then the move of Diana to the final room, which occurred around 7 a.m. – see earlier.

Moss then mentions the placement of curtains in the room – earlier evidence has shown that occurred around 12 noon. Moss is wrong in placing that "not long after" 7 a.m.[a]

Moss then says: "There followed a lengthy period when I took and made telephone calls in order to assist in arrangements to have the body returned".

As indicated earlier, it is common sense that the organising of arrangements could only occur after the decision had been made and then conveyed. Moss says the "decision came from the UK" and was conveyed to him by Janvrin or Lamport.

When one considers that Moss mentions Janvrin first, that Lamport wasn't in Balmoral – see above, and Moss – who was organising events at the hospital – would have been a key person to notify, it would seem logical that Moss would have been told by Janvrin.

This would fit with Jay, who although he mentions Archer, certainly has more of an emphasis on contact with Janvrin: "I had discussions with Sir Robin Janvrin"; "in the course of my discussions with Sir Robin Janvrin"; "incessant phone calls with Robin Janvrin at Balmoral and Nick Archer".

Moss describes arrangements being organised at some point after 7 a.m. Moss is not specific on the timing of this and gives no information on the timing of when he was told of the decision.

Jay describes the same 5.55 a.m. press conference as Moss – "at approximately 5.30 a.m." Jay was walking towards it.

In his statement, Jay says: "we were driven home ... [from the hospital] some time between 0700 [7.00 a.m.] and 0800". Jay states that at this time "it was still entirely unclear what arrangements would be made for the repatriation ... in particular whether it should take place that day, 31/08/1997, or at a later date".

Then this: "In the course of the early morning however I had discussions with Sir Robin Janvrin" and describes how they arrived at the same-day repatriation decision – see above.

Then "shortly after" 8.20 a.m. "we drove back to the hospital".

Then: "we drove back to the Embassy probably between 0900 [9 a.m.] and 1000, where I held a meeting".

Later in the same statement Jay describes this meeting "at about 0900 [9.00 a.m.] in the morning". Jay goes on: "It seemed likely that there would be a visit or visits that day from members of the Royal family" – so nothing definite here: Jay is showing that he is proactive – he hasn't been told Charles was coming, but "let's think ahead".

---

[a] See Embalming chapter.

So in the same statement Jay has created a scenario where Janvrin and him have already made a decision between them – "in the course of the early morning", apparently between 7 and 8.30 a.m.[a] – that there will be a same-day repatriation. Then, after 9 a.m., Jay holds a meeting "to allocate responsibilities", because "it seemed likely that there would be a visit or visits that day from members of the Royal family or other dignitaries who would most probably use military facilities". He enlists Ritchie and Gunner.

Nothing definite.

That's not how Ritchie described it – see earlier: "We had to do two major matters. The first was to get the French Air Force to open Villacoublay which is the equivalent of RAF Northolt, to open it up, get it fully manned.... We understood that a Hercules was coming in with the coffin. And then a completely separate arrangement[b] was made to welcome Prince Charles and Princess Diana's two sisters and make all the necessary arrangements for them. All the protocol side had to be looked at and even I remember Lady Jay making us all black armbands as at one stage it looked as though we were not going to be able to get the Royal Air Force regiment bearer party and so we telephoned all the way round Army, Navy and Air Force to come in, who were there, ready to act as an informal bearer party".

Jay has stated that after 9 a.m. nothing definite was known about a Charles visit: "it seemed likely ... visit or visits ... members of the Royal family or other dignitaries".

Is this plausible?

Jay presents a completely different scenario in his diary: No mention of a meeting here on returning from the second hospital visit: "The next few hours are incessant phone calls with Robin Janvrin at Balmoral and Nick Archer...."[c] Then at some unknown point Chirac calls to "talk about the ceremony at the hospital when the Prince arrives".

Earlier evidence has shown that Anthony Mather was called at 6 a.m. – 7 a.m. in Paris – to organise the same-day repatriation. By 6.45 a.m. – 7.45 a.m. in Paris – Levertons were in top gear. Clive said: "I did exceed the speed limit". Levertons already knew: "we had no time at all"; "we had to get out to Paris quickly"; "we were required to return her quickly".

---

[a] Allowing for 10 minutes after being notified of Mme Chirac's impending 9 a.m. hospital visit and presuming that Jay is holding these discussions with Janvrin from within the Embassy. Jay certainly places the Janvrin discussions after he left the hospital at 7 a.m. – see above.

[b] A person could argue that Ritchie is suggesting the Charles arrangements came later. Later evidence in this Comment will show that that was not the case.

[c] See full quote earlier.

There are several pieces of evidence that cast serious doubt on Jay's account – described twice in Jay's statement – that after 7 a.m.[a] Janvrin and himself arrived at the same-day repatriation decision:[b]

-    Mather was told about the decision by Ross at 6 a.m. – 7 a.m. in Paris – and was already implementing it when he called Daniel Tassell of Levertons at around 6.20 a.m.[c]

-    Tebbutt reveals that Kingsmill was already boarding the flight from Heathrow to Paris at 6.30 a.m. – 7.30 a.m. in Paris[d]

-    Jay's diary evidence is that the decision was from Balmoral: "Balmoral have now decided"

-    Moss' evidence was: "the decision came from the UK".

Why has Jay lied in his statement, bringing himself into the decision-making process, when this was clearly not the case?

As has been shown in this section on Diana's post-death status change, there were very early efforts for royal control of Diana's body. The Charles visit will be shown to be part of that very coordinated effort.

Jay's 2005 evidence including himself as a decision maker removes any possible suggestion that the decision could have been made by the Queen. This contributes to the post-crash perception that has been created: the Queen was sitting up there in Balmoral in a state of helpless shock, paralysed and unable to make decisions – and decisions being made for her: by Tony Blair, Alastair Campbell, Prince Charles and in this case, Robin Janvrin and Michael Jay.

---

[a] Jay said in his statement: "At the time when I left the hospital after the early press conference, it was still entirely unclear what arrangements would be made for the repatriation of the Princess' body, in particular whether it should take place that day, 31/08/1997, or at a later date." Other evidence reveals the press conference started at 5.55 a.m. and he left the hospital about 7 a.m.

[b] It is possible that the decision was conveyed to Jay after 7 a.m. This would fit with Moss – see earlier – and I suggest it also fits with common sense: the people who needed to know about the decision first were in the UK – people like Kingsmill – see below, Mather and Harding – see later. Those people in the UK had to get things moving – the events in France were not going to happen until later in the day: Charles arrived at Villacoublay about 5 p.m.

[c] Mather said in his statement: "From my recollection an RAF BAe 146 was sent to Aberdeen from RAF Northolt to collect the Prince of Wales. Subsequently Operation Overstudy was requested by me, as this was the most logical method of repatriating Diana, Princess of Wales." This is an indication from Mather that the plane for Charles was organised ahead of Operation Overstudy – calling Levertons. Mather called Levertons around 6.30 a.m., so this would place the implementation of the decision re Charles' involvement – sending the plane – earlier than 6.30 a.m. The original decision for Charles to go would have been made even earlier.

[d] This reveals that Kingsmill must have been notified that he needed to join this flight much earlier than 6.30 a.m. – this is discussed below.

It will be shown that the Queen is the one central person in all the early decisions that were made – the Royal Standard, the royal coroner, the Charles trip, the same-day repatriation, the embalming, and the placement in St James' Palace.[a]

The reality is that these decisions have been and will be shown to have emanated from royal sources and were brought to fruition by people who were answerable to the Queen – these events could not have occurred without the Queen's direct approval.[b]

Jay's evidence that he was involved in the decision-making rules out a direct role by the Queen, but Jay's evidence has already been shown to be false. Michael Jay has lied under oath.

Who made the decision for Charles to repatriate the body the same day?

Well, obviously we are hamstrung by a lack of any proper investigation – by the police and Baker – but the evidence we have from Jay and Moss points to the decision being relayed to them by Janvrin.[c]

Yet it was Charles' trip.

But if the decision had been made by Charles, it is logical that it would have been relayed by Archer – who in Lamport's absence was acting as Charles' private secretary.

That is not what we see. We see a minor role played by Archer – Jay – and Lamport – Moss. But the primary role – revealed by both Jay and Moss – was played by Janvrin.

I suggest that Janvrin was relaying to Moss and Jay a decision made by his direct boss, the Queen: "Charles will be arriving with Sarah and Jane to repatriate Diana's body today".[d]

---

[a] Tony Blair wrote in his 2010 book: "Just before I left for church [at about 9.30 a.m.] I had my first [post-Diana's death] telephone call with [the Queen], in which I expressed my condolences. She was philosophical, anxious for the boys [William and Harry], but also professional and practical. She grasped the enormity of the event, but in her own way. She was not going to be pushed around by it. She could be very queenly in that sense.": Tony Blair, A Journey: My Political Life, p140.

[b] See the royal power structure diagram near the start of this chapter.

[c] At the time Janvrin – in Fellowes' absence – was acting as the Queen's private secretary.

[d] This evidence-based finding raises questions about earlier accounts put forward by royal writers Penny Junor (1998) and Ingrid Seward (2000). They have both stated that the Queen was initially against Charles repatriating Diana's body on a royal flight, until Janvrin challenged her: "What would you rather, Ma'am – that she came back in a Harrods van?" This Junor/Seward account has also been disputed by Buckingham Palace, which stated in 1998 that it was a "grotesque misrepresentation of the truth". Sources: Penny Junor, Charles: Victim or Villain?, 1998, p20; Ingrid

The other area of conflict in Jay's statement was: "the arrangements for the arrival of the two aircraft from England ... flowed from and were determined by that decision[a]".

Tebbutt's evidence is important in this – Tebbutt noted that Kingsmill is already on the plane at Heathrow at 6.30 a.m. "as an advance for ... Charles' visit".

I suggest that for Kingsmill to make that early scheduled international flight he would have needed notification at least as early as 5 a.m.[b] This indicates then that the decision itself – for Charles to repatriate the body that day – would have been made at 4.30 a.m. or even earlier.

This evidence from Tebbutt – not heard by the jury – reveals that the decision for Charles to carry out the repatriation was no later add-on. It was an integral part of the original decision, and was made very early – a decision made at 4.30 a.m. is a decision made about 1½ hours after Diana's official death[c].[de]

Why did the Queen tell Charles to repatriate the body of Diana?

This repatriation trip made by Charles tends to be viewed as a stand-alone event. I believe this is a mistake. The trip took place as an integral part of a coordinated royal response to the death of Diana: the royal undertakers – Levertons – despatched to Paris, the royal standard on the coffin, the royal presence – Charles – for the repatriation, the royal coroner at the post-mortem, laying to rest on royal property – St James' Palace.[f]

Seward, The Queen & Di, 2000, p16; Royal Anger Over Di Book, BBC News, 25 October 1998.

[a] The decision made jointly by Jay and Janvrin that there would be a same-day repatriation.

[b] Kingsmill would have needed to be at the airport by around 6 a.m. I suggest he would have been woken at his home sometime earlier than 5 a.m.

[c] At 3 a.m. UK time.

[d] When Mather recorded the events in his statement he put "an RAF BAe 146 was sent to Aberdeen from RAF Northolt to collect the Prince of Wales" ahead of "I communicated with Keith Leverton over the telephone to his office in Camden". It is possible the Defence Services Secretary, Peter Harding – who Mather said was at Buckingham Palace before 8.30 a.m. – would have been involved in this. Harding's role is dealt with later.

[e] The sheer logistics of what had to happen also dictates a reasonably early decision. Crew had to be organised for a plane to be sent from London to Aberdeen to pick up Charles and his entourage, then Sarah – in Lincolnshire – and Jane – in Norfolk – had to be picked up along the way, before heading to Paris. As Ritchie and Jay pointed out, this was going to be a major exercise – from both the UK and French sides.

[f] In Paris on 30 August 1997 Diana was not a royal. 24 hours later – as she was laid to rest in St James' Palace by the royal undertakers – Diana had been effectively reclaimed as a royal.

All these coordinated events had one central purpose – the reclaiming of the dead Diana as a royal. This enabled full royal control of post-death events: the first embalming[a], the UK post-mortem, the second embalming[b], the funeral and the inquest.

As was revealed in the Royal Coroner section, the Home Office were only interested in the arrangements for Dodi, not Diana. It was hands-off for the civil authorities with regard to Diana – from soon after her moment of death in Paris, Diana was back under royal control.

Sarah and Jane were invited to accompany Charles to Paris. This family presence would also have been coordinated. It provided credibility to Charles' presence: people might have asked questions if Charles – the ex-husband – had gone alone, but with Sarah and Jane walking into the hospital with him, who could criticise that?

The earlier evidence from Mather and Burton[c] indicates that Sarah and Jane were starting to ask questions about what was going on, but the public did not get to hear about that – and neither did the inquest jury 10 years

Repatriation

Keith Moss: 22 Oct 04 Statement: **Jury Heard Part Only**:[e]
"At around 1400hrs [2 p.m.] a meeting was called by the French Foreign Ministry Chief of Protocol, whose name I do not recall. Also in attendance were hospital staff, French Police Officials, Superintendent Kingsmill the then Head of British Royalty Protection and Inspector Ian Von Heinz, who was a member of HRH Prince of Wales' Protection Team. The purpose of this meeting was to make arrangements for the impending visit of HRH Prince of Wales, the security arrangements required and to develop a media strategy. The Royal Flight was due to arrive at 1700hrs, and the plane would also bring the coffin, the Royal Standard, a bearer party and representative from the Royal Undertakers. The flight was scheduled to depart at 1900hrs.
"At around 1700hrs, President Chirac arrived at the hospital with his wife. He was accompanied by an Honour Guard of the Garde Républicaine, the French Foreign Minister Mr Hubert Vedrine, Doctor Kouchner, the French Ambassador from London and Sir Michael and Lady Jay. They were introduced to the hospital staff who had been involved with the Princess of Wales.

---

[a] The royal control aspect of this will be addressed later.
[b] See later.
[c] See earlier section on the Royal Coroner.
[d] The statements of Burton and Mather were not heard at the inquest.
[e] This was very briefly covered on 22 Nov 07: 31.21 to 32.15.

"At around 1740hrs HRH Prince of Wales and the Princess of Wales' two sisters Lady Jane and Lady Sarah arrived at the hospital. They were introduced to President and Mrs Chirac and the accompanying dignitaries.

"They were accompanied upstairs, where they went in to pay their last respects to the Princess of Wales, in the presence of the Venerable Martin Draper.

"After a short while they rejoined the dignitaries in the corridor and were introduced to the medical staff. It took around fifteen minutes for the undertakers to transfer the remains into the coffin and for it to be draped in the Royal Standard. The coffin was then escorted from the hospital and the cortège departed at around 1815hrs. I recorded that the Royal Flight left Villacoublay at 1900hrs."[221]

Michael Jay, British Ambassador to France, 1996-2001, Paris: 31 Aug 97 Diary read out 11 Feb 08: 106.10:

"At 4.00 [p.m.] Sylvia and I drive to Villacoublay to meet the Prince. He is delayed a bit, but we walk to the steps to greet him. He is composed, greeting the greeters almost as normal. Sarah and Jane are upset and disoriented. I drive with the Prince, Sylvia with Sarah and Jane. I tell the Prince what I know about the accident and tell him of last night in the hospital. We pause for a bit, driving into a sunny warm Paris, then talk about France. A lot has changed, the Prince says, since we last met before the elections. He says how often tragedies happen in August, the death of Mountbatten, the Gulf War. I tell him what I think will happen at the hospital, though there is bound to be some improvisation.

"The crowds on either side of the road are huge as we drive into the gates. At the entrance to the building, Chirac and his wife greet the Prince and introduce him to Vedrine, Kouchner and others. Sarah and Jane are introduced too. We go upstairs. The Prince and the sisters go along the corridor to the room with the Princess, Sylvia going with them but staying outside. Martin Draper is with them. I stay in the hallway, talking to Chirac and Vedrine and the Prince's party, including Stephen Lamport. I thank the hospital staff again.

"After ten minutes or so, the Prince and the sisters come out of the room. The Prince is introduced by Chirac to the hospital staff. Sylvia takes Sarah and Jane to a small room set aside for them. They are upset. After ten minutes or so, the coffin, draped in the Royal Standard, leaves the room, followed by Martin Draper in white robes and carried by French pall-bearers. It was taken along the few yards of the corridor, across the hallway where we stood with the Prince, Jane and Sarah, the Chiracs, Vedrine, Kouchner, Jean Gueginou and the hospital staff. It is taken down the stairs and we follow.

"The Prince says thank you to the Paris police in the hall on the ground floor while the coffin is taken down the front steps and past a line of unarmed Gardes Republicaines to be put in the hearse. We follow a minute or two later, standing on the steps for a few seconds before going to our cars. The cortège drives slowly out of the hospital gates and turns right past press and rank on rank of French men, women and children and tourists too. As the hearse – a low-key green van – passes, they clap and wave goodbye.

"The French authorities have cleared the whole route to Villacoublay and the cortège moves with dignity – through central Paris, the western scruffy suburbs and the road to Villacoublay. The Prince says all seems unreal. Our conversation is a little inconsequential, with silences. He was surprised and pleased by the Standard on the coffin. I was surprised too. I do not know where it came from.

"At Villacoublay we stood in line on the tarmac. The RAF bearer party took the coffin from the hearse and in a slow march past a line of French soldiers and into the aircraft's hold. The Prince and the Princess's sisters walk to the plane and we say goodbye. We walk back to the grass verge and I talk to Vedrine. He leaves as the plane takes off. We wait til it's in the air, then drive, still with our motorcycle escort, back to Paris, peeling off left across the river as the cars go on to the Quai."

Colin Tebbutt, Diana's Driver and Security: 26 Nov 07: 96.25:

"His Royal Highness arrived. I was outside the room, he came up and he was totally in control, very calm. I spoke to him. He said I was to go back with the body...."

Colin Tebbutt, Diana's Driver and Security: 5 Jul 04 Statement: **Jury Didn't Hear**:

"Before [the French embalmers] were allowed into the hospital room, Inspector Peter Von-Heinz, the Personal Protection Officer for Prince Charles and his advance, went into the room to look at where the Prince of Wales would be taken. I explained the circumstances to him and he then spoke with the local French Police. He was a fluent French speaker."[222]

Colin Tebbutt, Diana's Driver and Security: 5 Jul 04 Statement: **Jury Didn't Hear**:

"President Jacques Chirac and entourage were shown into the room to pay their respects. Paul Burrell and I went outside the room and His Royal Highness Prince Charles, Lady Sarah McCorquodale and Lady Jane Fellowes arrived along with Sandy Henney the Prince's Press Secretary at that time. We tried to make ourselves discrete but we were unable to get out of the way. His Royal Highness Prince Charles approached me and the two Ladies went straight to Paul Burrell. Prince Charles shook my hand and acknowledged our efforts. He was charming and tremendously controlled. I said, 'We've done our best Sir'. Prince Charles informed me that Paul Burrell and I would be joining them on the plane back to England. The two Ladies then came to me, while Prince Charles then spoke with Paul.

"Prince Charles, Lady Sarah and Lady Jane then went into the room with whom I presume to be Medical Staff.

"Shortly after, the Medical Staff left. Prince Charles came out and said, 'Are there any Priests here Colin?'. Being aware that a French and British Priest were in the room next door, one or both of them went in with the family. They remained in the room approximately twenty minutes. Praying I believe.

"Transport was arranged by Brigadier Richie and the coffin was carried out by French Uniformed men. I had been concerned that no one had thought to bring a Royal Standard, but Levertons had brought the flag.

"When we came out of the Hospital I was standing behind Prince Charles on the steps of the Hospital. The coffin was placed into the Funeral Director's vehicle. I don't know if this was a Levertons car and I do not know who travelled with the coffin.

"The cortège comprised of HRH Prince Charles, President Chirac, other Officials and a motorcycle escort. Paris had come to a standstill. Members of the public were crying and applauding everywhere on route. I was four or five vehicles back with the English Priest as we made our way to the Airport. I do not remember which airport this was, but it looked like a military airport....

"When we reached the airport, Military Officers waiting there took the coffin from the vehicle and placed it into the hold of the airplane. I then boarded the airplane by the back stairs. Also on board were HRH Prince Charles, Lady Jane and Lady Sarah, Paul Burrell, Sandra Henney, and Prince Charles' Personal Protection Officer. I sat in the front of the plane with the crew and Paul Burrell. The Royal Family has a separate area within another part of the airplane.

"I had organised for one of my drivers Paul Mellor to collect Mr Michael Gibbins and convey him to RAF Northolt.

"When we landed at RAF Northolt, there was a line of Officials to greet HRH Prince Charles and to receive the arrival of the coffin. Mr Gibbins was on the end of this line. The coffin was removed from the aircraft by RAF Officers, who placed it into a funeral directors vehicle. There was a separate vehicle for the Family. Mr Gibbins, Paul Burrell and I travelled in the same car, and there was also a Police escort. Prince Charles did not remain with the cortège, and immediately flew on to another destination.

"The journey to the Fulham Mortuary was incredible. People were lining the A40 and there were flowers being thrown at the cortège everywhere we went. No one could have expected this."[223]

Patrick Launay, PFG Repatriation Director: 21 Mar 06 Statement: **Jury Didn't Hear**:

"On the morning of 31 August 1997, I contacted Villacoublay Airport to find out at what time the plane and the coffin were due to arrive. From memory, I left home at around 1300 [1 p.m.] to 1330hrs and I arrived at Villacoublay Airport by 1400hrs....

"At Villacoublay, I met the British funeral directors. I think that there were three of them, but I can only remember the one in charge. I cannot remember his name or the name of the company. We spoke at length, at the airport, during the journey, and at the hospital, about the arrangements and the return. Having taken charge of it at Villacoublay, we remained together for the rest of the afternoon. The coffin was collected from the airport by hearse, but I do not remember how many cars we had. I think that I left my own car at the airport and that we took a PFG car with the British funeral directors in order to get to the hospital.

"I think that we arrived at the hospital between 1530 and 1600 hrs. We took the coffin to the [hospital] wing in order to be able to proceed with the placing of the body in the coffin. As I speak English, I had to assist the British undertakers and later take the coffin back to the airport for its return to England. In the hospital, we left the coffin and the equipment (trestles, the British royal standard etc.) in a side room where the Princess of Wales was. We then waited for Prince Charles and the Princess's two sisters to arrive. I do not remember if they were upstairs before or after I arrived, but I saw Mr and Mrs Chirac; Mr Kouchner, the Minister of Health; Mr Hubert Vedrine, the Foreign Minister; and Mr Massoni, the Prefect of Police, there. The priest who later paid his respects with Prince Charles was also possibly in the room. Mr Jauze and Mr Plumet were there too, I think that they arrived before me.

"I remember speaking to Mr Jauze to decide on the arrangements for the removal of the body from the hospital wing. We then decided that the representative from the British funeral directors would come out at the head of the coffin with me, and the priest at the front, with Mr Jauze remaining at the rear between the coffin and the VIPs....

"When Prince Charles and the two sisters arrived, they spoke to Mr Chirac. I asked the police officer outside the Princess's room to let me into the room in order to check the layout and to ensure that we could let the family in to pay their respects. I went very briefly into the room and it is possible that my British counterpart came with me. The Princess was laid out on a hospital bed. The sheet covered her as far as her neck and the appearance of the body, in my opinion, was acceptable for it to be shown to the family.

"I came out of the room and someone introduced me to Prince Charles. The room was indicated to Prince Charles, who went in with the two sisters and the priest. They stayed there for perhaps ten minutes or so. I recall that when they came out, Prince Charles shook my hand and thanked everyone for their efforts. Prince Charles went to speak to the French VIPs. "Meanwhile, we got on with placing the body in the coffin. I personally was not present when

383

they transferred the body from the bed into the coffin. I do not know who did it, as I was talking with Mr Jauze about the arrangements for removing the coffin from the hospital wing. It is possible that the English representative and his staff were present. I do not remember whether I was present when the coffin was closed.

"I should explain that in France there is a strict requirement for the presence of a police authority (a sworn person) when the coffin is closed and that person draws up a statement. There is no requirement under French law for a representative of the funeral directors to be present. You have shown me this statement from your file at reference UK.58.

"We then did the departure of the coffin from the room to the hearse, followed by the family and the authorities. The Ambassador, Prince Charles and the Princess of Wales's sisters then followed the cortège and left for Villacoublay. I made that journey in the hearse. It is possible that the British representative was with me. Mr Jauze and Mr Plumet did not go to Villacoublay. The cortège had a police escort."[224]

Jean-Claude Plumet, PFG Director of Paris Agencies, Paris: 4 Nov 05 Paget description of Statement: **Jury Didn't Hear**:

"Mr Plumet was asked whether he remembered meeting with British counterparts from Levertons whilst at the hospital. He explained that he remembered seeing a man, but that he could not remember much more. He clarified again that he was not present when the body was placed in the coffin.

"Mr Plumet explained that he was downstairs when HRH the Prince of Wales arrived at the Hospital with the Princess of Wales' sisters. The party went up to the floor where the Princess of Wales was, and there they thanked the Medical staff. They were then shown to the room where the Princess of Wales was. After a little while they came out of the room. Mr Plumet recalls HRH the Prince of Wales kissing Mme Chirac's hand upon meeting her. Mr Plumet explained that the body of the Princess of Wales was placed into the coffin, which had been brought by the British Undertakers Levertons from London. He does not know who placed the body in the coffin, but explains that Mr Launay would probably be able to assist us with this question. The coffin was then taken down to the vehicles waiting outside. He recalls HRH the Prince of Wales and two others getting into a Jaguar motor vehicle. The convoy of vehicles then departed. Mr Plumet believes that Mr Launay accompanied the coffin to Villacoublay airport at around 1700hrs [5 p.m.], while he and Mr Jauze returned to their office."[225]

Gérard Jauze, PFG Branch Director, Paris: 21 Mar 06 Statement: **Jury Didn't Hear**:

"Having left the room where the Princess was, M. Plumet and I waited for the VIPs. We went downstairs and back up again, and went back and forth, but we did not return to the room where the Princess of Wales was. M. Patrick

Launay must have arrived roughly thirty minutes after me. The only other people from PFG at the hospital were the porters, who must have arrived between 1600 [4 p.m.] and 1630hrs, but they remained behind outside until the VIPs had paid their last respects and the coffin was ready to leave.

"I do not remember the order in which the VIPs arrived because at that time everything was happening very quickly. President Chirac, Prince Charles and the Princess's sisters, everything happened very quickly, like a whirlwind. They were received by the Hospital Director and by M. Bernard Kouchner, the Health Minister.

"Prince Charles thanked us, and we waited while they paid their last respects. Once that was done, the coffin was immediately closed and taken to the hearse. The coffin was then transported to Villacoublay airport by our chauffeur, whose name I have forgotten. M. Patrick Launay followed the cortège to ensure that everything went as it should. M. Plumet and I remained at the hospital, and we were able to catch our breath."[226]

Comment:[a] Was it logical that Charles would be the one who would repatriate the dead Diana?

The Charles dash across the Channel was the public face, on the day, of the early royal control of Princess Diana's body. The trip was widely reported in the press – the media were present at the hospital and also for the 7 p.m. landing at RAF Northolt.

Media coverage was very positive – one *Associated Press* report described "Prince Charles … escorting the body of his 'English rose'".[227]

Was this how Princess Diana would have wanted it?

The history of Diana's 16 years of mistreatment at the hands of the royal family is well documented in many books[a] and it is not something I can address in this book.

---

[a] There are some minor conflicts in evidence, but they do not appear to have any significance in the story – they may be a result of memory problems due to the huge delays in providing evidence.
They are:
- Launay recalls Diana's body being covered in a sheet, whereas the general evidence is that the body was dressed by the time he viewed it
- Launay says the body was transferred to the coffin after the viewing by the VIPs, whereas Clive Leverton said the VIPs viewed the body after it was already in the coffin – this has been addressed earlier
- Moss says that Jay arrived with Chirac, whereas Jay – who provides a full account of this – describes going to the airport, meeting the VIPs, and travelling with Charles into the hospital.

Diana herself has described her marital relationship with Charles, following the birth of Harry in 1984 – just three years after their wedding: "Then suddenly as Harry was born it just went bang, our marriage, the whole thing went down the drain.... Something inside me closed off. By then I knew he had gone back to his lady [Camilla] but somehow we'd managed to have Harry."[228]

Princess Diana recorded those words in 1991[b], well before the late-1992 separation and subsequent divorce in 1996.

An analysis of the Diana-Charles relationship – as has been done by other authors[c] – reveals that the marriage had effectively broken down by 1985, but a public face was maintained to avoid the sensitivity of a royal separation or divorce.

By late 1995 – a year before the official divorce – the relationship had sunk so far that Diana believed Charles intended to remove her in a car crash. Diana wrote: "This particular phase of my life is the most dangerous – my husband is planning 'an accident' in my car, brake failure and serious head injury.... I have been battered, bruised and abused mentally by a system for 15 years[d] now.... I am strong inside and maybe that is a problem for my enemies.

"Thank you Charles, for putting me through such hell and for giving me the opportunity to learn from the cruel things you have done to me."[229ef]

Effectively what occurred was that Diana's body was repatriated from France by the very person Diana believed could have planned the crash – her ex-husband Charles.

Charles was a person Diana had indicated was an enemy, who had put her "through such hell".

I suggest that Charles would have been the last person Diana would have wanted to "rescue" her from the French hospital.

When this evidence is seen in the context of the placement of the royal standard, the use of the royal coroner and the transfer to St James' Palace, one begins to realise just how orchestrated these post-death events were. Orchestrated to achieve an end result – the royal control over Diana's body.

---

[a] I point readers to books such as: *Diana: Her True Story – In Her Own Words* by Andrew Morton; *Charles at Fifty* by Anthony Holden and *Princess Diana: The Lamb to the Slaughter* by Joy Jones Daymon.

[b] They were published in 1992.

[c] See earlier footnote.

[d] The courtship started in 1980 and the note was written in 1995. The abuse started during the courtship, but the inexperienced 19 year old Diana believed that things would improve after the wedding.

[e] This note is fully addressed in Part 2, pp281-290.

[f] This note is corroborated in a separate conversation Diana had with her lawyer, Victor Mishcon, in October 1995. This is addressed in Part 2, pp291-7.

The Queen was not able to control Diana while she was alive, but immediately after her death, she took immediate control over her body.

The earlier evidence indicated that the decisions were being made by the Queen, not Charles.[a] Jay gave evidence from his diary: "[Charles] was surprised and pleased by the Standard on the coffin." This is a further indication that Charles may not have even been aware of a wider plan, but was just playing his role, following orders – repatriating the body.

Operation Paget revealed in their report that they interviewed Charles[230], but the transcript of that interview has never been published and was not made available to the jury.[b]

The earlier evidence – Burgess – revealed that the Home Office took no interest, on the day, in the arrangements for Diana – only Dodi. I suggested earlier that this was because the royals had already taken early control.

The family should have been allowed to take control of events. The royals – who were extremely estranged from Diana – could have played a role in events, without taking control. The government could have assisted the family in providing transportation, an escort for Diana's sisters and a Union Jack to cover the coffin, and been more involved in organising the events, including the funeral.

The Queen and royal family should have come down from Balmoral earlier than they did – and they could have done that, with humility.

Instead, what occurred was the Queen actively kept her distance, staying in Balmoral, whilst behind the scenes she took very early total control of the body and events. She kept the royal family at Balmoral, but very soon after Diana's death, despatched Charles to Paris to secure physical royal control over the body.

This move was supported by the early despatching of Kingsmill and also Levertons – the royal undertakers – to Paris, complete with royal standard, to prepare for the arrival of Charles. Levertons topped off their role with a late night-early morning second embalming on royal territory, at St James' Palace.

Meanwhile the royal coroner – who I suggest was acting on instructions – was illegally taking legal control of Diana's body.

---

[a] Tony Blair wrote in 2010: "For Prince Charles, it was really ghastly. He and Camilla were an obvious focus of intense interest and speculation. What could he do? Appear grief-stricken and he would be called a fraud. Appear calm and he would seem cold. It was an impossible situation, his every gesture interpreted or more likely misinterpreted, and people ready to pounce on any slip.": Tony Blair, A Journey: My Political Life, p146.

[b] In the Paget Report "Overview" document, p3, John Stevens confirmed that he had "spoken with" Charles.

This coordinated royal control set the scene for an incredibly blatant travesty of justice – a 10 year delay in the conduct of the inquest, with the legal requirement – should there be a jury – for that jury to be drawn only from members of the Queen's royal household.[a]

Sarah McCorquodale, Diana's Sister: 28 Jan 08: 111.14:

Burnett: Q. Now, I will move forward, if I may, but briefly, to the events of the weekend after you spoke last to your sister. We have heard evidence from others that you and members of the family travelled to Paris before returning to the United Kingdom, and I don't need to ask you any questions at all about what happened in Paris and events surrounding those hours or indeed those one or two days.

Comment: Sarah McCorquodale was a key witness to the rushed Charles trip to Paris – she was the only person from that royal flight to appear at the inquest.[b]

Yet, inquest lawyer Ian Burnett completely bypasses the subject – "I don't need to ask you any questions at all about what happened". And no other lawyers took this subject up with Sarah.

This is typical of the approach taken at Baker's "thorough" inquest – a complete failure to get to the bottom of important issues, and in this case, the lawyer – possibly at the request of the judge – decides to omit the issue altogether from his questioning.

Midnight Embalming at St James' Palace

The final act to complete Princess Diana's 31 August 1997 change of status was to deliver her body to the Chapel Royal at Charles' residence[c] – St James' Palace.

Clive Leverton, Royal Funeral Director: 22 Nov 07: 77.13:

Hough: Q. After that post-mortem examination, you conveyed the coffin back to the Chapel Royal at St James's Palace.

A. Correct.

Q. And I think once the body was there, your staff did carry out a process of embalming or preservation on the body?

A. Yes.

Q. What was the nature of that procedure? Can you help us with that?

A. Well, there had been a thorough post-mortem examination at Fulham and our embalmer, David Green – it was a very difficult situation, it was in the

---

[a] The Coroners Act 1988, s29 (4) states: "The jurors on an inquest held by the coroner of the Queen's household shall consist of officers of that household...."

[b] No evidence at all – cross-examination or statement – was heard from Charles or Jane Fellowes, or anyone else who may have been on that critical flight to Paris.

[c] In 1997 Charles lived in York House and moved to Clarence House after the death of the Queen Mother. Both these residences are a part of St James' Palace.

Chapel Royal – he carried out a thorough embalming. I am not a qualified embalmer, I have to say, so I cannot give you too many technical answers.

Clive Leverton: 13 Jul 04 Statement: **Jury Didn't Hear**:

"We waited here whilst the post mortem examination took place from about 1930 [7.30 p.m.] to 2300 hours. I had not received any information or detail about the post mortem. We received the Princess back in the same coffin and we conveyed her to the Chapel Royal, St James' Palace. Here David carried out embalming, this was under instruction from the Lord Chamberlains office via my brother Keith. Embalming after a post mortem is quite difficult and carrying it out at the chapel was not ideally suited. This embalming process lasted till about 4 a.m. in the morning."[231]

Keith Leverton, Royal Funeral Director: 27 Oct 04 Statement: **Jury Didn't Hear**:

"We waited inside the [Fulham Mortuary] building until the body was released. I then learnt from Mather that Diana, Princess of Wales was to be taken to St James', a Royal Palace, as soon as possible....

"Operation Overstudy concerned the repatriation only, and from the arrival into the UK the Lord Chamberlains office had their own plans for any member of the Royal family's funeral preparations and arrangements. I was aware that these plans involved the requirement for embalming as they would for any other deceased person. We were trusted in carrying out this care once she was released by the coroner."[232]

David Green, Embalmer, UK: 13 Jul 04 Statement: **Jury Didn't Hear**:

"We knew that she was to be taken to Fulham Mortuary for a post mortem and that we would have to wait for further instructions of where and when we were to do this. Upon return to the U.K later that evening I returned to our office at Chalk Farm to await further instructions following this post mortem. At about 11 to 11.30 p.m. I went to the Chapel at St James' Palace to carry out the embalming. Keith and Clive were present along with a police officer that watched the whole procedure. I was unaware of what work had been carried on her out at casualty or in the French hospital operating theatre, however I could see injuries to the chest, and the forehead. There was a major incision from the neck to the pubis, across the chest and the skull from the post mortem. The major organs (viscera) including the uterus and brain, which would normally be removed and replaced into the chest and abdominal cavity, were present in a bag. I removed the bag and placed it into another bag and cavity fluid was poured over the viscera to preserve it. I did not need to nor was asked to note the embalming points on the body enough to give any opinion as to the extent or how well the embalming was done.

"During my procedure I collected body fluids from the chest cavity by using cotton wool. These were disposed of. It took about five hours to carry out the work to my satisfaction."[233a]

Comment: Keith Leverton was the contact who had received instructions from Mather throughout the day – see earlier.

Keith's evidence is: "I then [after the post-mortem] learnt from Mather that Diana ... was to be taken to St James' ... as soon as possible". And this: "I was aware that these [LCO] plans involved the requirement for embalming".

This evidence reveals:

1) Mather was still at Fulham Mortuary at the end of the post-mortem – about 11.30 p.m.[b] Yet there is no mention in Mather's evidence of any involvement in events after taking Sarah and Jane to see Burton at Fulham Mortuary.[c]

This raises the question: Why was it so important for Mather to stay at Fulham until the end of the post-mortem?

2) Even at 11.30 p.m. events were still being rushed – Mather told Keith to take Diana "to St James' ... <u>as soon as possible</u>".

At the conclusion of the post-mortem Diana was in a "safe" environment – a London mortuary. The body was in a situation where it could be refrigerated overnight. Mather could have left instructions for the body to remain at Fulham Mortuary – Mather, Clive, Keith and Green could have all gone home, had a good night's sleep, and continued in the morning.

But that is not what we see happening.

Instead we see Mather obsessed with making sure Diana made it to St James' Palace that night.[d]

Why? Why not leave Diana in Fulham Mortuary overnight?

There are three relevant differences between Fulham Mortuary and St James' Palace:

---

[a] In Green's later September 2004 statement he said: "Other reasons I would not embalm a body would be, if there was no authority to embalm by the family or their representative...." This was the case here, yet Green still went ahead and carried out this embalming. I suggest this was because he was in his role as the royal embalmer and was acting under instruction. Source: David Green, Witness Statement, 17 September 2004, reproduced in *The Documents* book, p507 (UK Edition).

[b] Chapman's post-mortem report shows it ending at 11.20 p.m. – see later.

[c] There is also no mention of Mather's presence in Chapman's post-mortem report – see later – but there is also no mention of Levertons. It may be that Mather waited outside the post-mortem room with the Levertons, for the three hours of the post-mortem.

[d] Mather was very familiar with St James' Palace – he said at the inquest: "75 per cent of my time is in St James' Palace and 25 per cent was in Buckingham Palace": 22 Nov 07: 83.19.

- Fulham Mortuary provides body refrigeration facilities, St James' Palace doesn't
- Fulham Mortuary provides embalming facilities, St James' Palace doesn't
- St James' Palace was royal territory, Fulham Mortuary wasn't.

I suggest that Mather had been given instructions – possibly from the Queen, via Malcolm Ross[a] – that Diana had to be returned to royal property that night. Mather had to stay around to make sure that occurred – and only after that could he go home.[b]

The late-night transfer of Diana's body to the Chapel Royal at St James' Palace – a non-refrigerated area – ensured that a second embalming had to be carried out in the middle of the night. Had Diana been left at Fulham Mortuary overnight, the UK embalming would not have been needed until the next day.

What's more is the embalming was then conducted in the Chapel Royal, a building with no facilities for that – in the words of Clive Leverton: "carrying it out at the chapel was not ideally suited"; and at the inquest: "it was a very difficult situation, it was in the Chapel Royal".[c]

I believe Diana was returned to royal land at St James' Palace that night to help provide early credibility to the claim by John Burton – royal coroner – for jurisdiction over the body.[d]

This is further evidence of a highly coordinated royal operation – each person playing their role, but all these people answerable to the Queen.[e]

Green has stated: "It took about five hours to carry out the [embalming] to my satisfaction". In earlier evidence Green said that he "would have needed three hours to ... carry out a complete [embalming]" in the Paris hospital.

---

[a] Ross started the day at home in Scotland, but Alastair Campbell describes him as the "main man" in a meeting held the next day – Monday, 1 September 1997 – at the Lord Chamberlain's Office in Buckingham Palace: Alastair Campbell, The Blair Years: The Alastair Campbell Diaries, p235.

[b] There is no evidence of Mather's presence after the body arrived at St James' Palace. Green says: "Keith and Clive were present along with a police officer that watched the whole procedure".

[c] I suggest that Levertons could have been very surprised: in the middle of the night, they were forced to whisk Diana away from an ideal situation at Fulham Mortuary – refrigeration, embalming facilities – to a chapel at St James' Palace that was far from ideal, and had no appropriate facilities.

[d] This act didn't give Burton legal jurisdiction, but the fact that Diana was now on royal land may have helped create the perception that the inquest should be conducted by the royal coroner. This subject is covered in the earlier section on the Royal Coroner.

[e] See Royal Structure diagram near the beginning of this chapter.

Why 5 hours in London, but 3 hours in Paris?

There are two possible explanations for this conflict:[a]

1) the difficulty of conducting a St James' Palace embalming may have added to the time required

2) this may be additional evidence that the Paris embalming was substandard[b] – it may take additional time to "repair" a poorly done embalming.

Princess Diana officially died at 4 a.m. on 31 August 1997. Within 25 hours – by 4 a.m. UK time, the following day – Diana's body had been subjected to two post-mortems – one in France, one in the UK – and two embalmings.

Key Royal Household[c] Players

Some members of the Queen's royal household had significant roles in the events that took place.[d]

Robert Fellowes: Queen's Private Secretary

Robert Fellowes, Queen's Private Secretary, 1990-99, UK: 12 Feb 08: 111.12:

Mansfield: Q. Were you on holiday at the time?

A. I was on holiday from early – well somewhere around the first week of August.

Q. Until?

A. The week after the death of the Princess and Mr Al Fayed, and I went back to Balmoral on the following Sunday, I think, after the funeral.

Q. So would it be fair to say that you were not, in fact, therefore, at the Palace or nearby when all of this was happening?

A. I was at the Palace certainly until the end of July.[e]

Alastair Campbell, Tony Blair's Press Secretary: 2011 Published Diary: **Jury Didn't Hear**:

---

[a] Green should have been asked about this at the inquest, but he was never heard and none of this evidence was ever read out.

[b] See previous chapter.

[c] There are around 1,200 members in just the Queen's household, then there are substantial additional numbers in the other households – Philip's, Charles' etc. The players here are people who had a significant known role in the early post-death events. Source: The Royal Household, The Official Website of the British Monarchy, www.royal.gov.uk/TheRoyalHousehold

[d] All of these people appear on the Royal Structure diagram near the beginning of this chapter.

[e] Mansfield's questioning relates to events prior to the crash. The issue of relevance here is the timing of Fellowes' return from holiday.

31 August 1997: "At about 4 [a.m.], I got a flavour of the royal Establishment's approach when Angus[a] and I had a conference call with Robert Fellowes. 'You know about Diana, do you? She's dead.' I said yes. We were sorting when TB[b] should speak to the Queen. It was all very matter-of-fact and practical, though he too, like TB earlier, said 'Those poor boys'."[234]

1 September 1997: "Angus Lapsley and I were called to a meeting at the Lord Chamberlain's Office.... Airlie[c] chaired the meeting, which was also attended by Robert Fellowes, Michael Gibbins from Diana's office, Mark Bolland[d], Penny Russell-Smith[e], Dickie Arbiter[f] and Lt Col Malcolm Ross, who sat to the Lord Chamberlain's left and appeared to be the main man. I was asked to sit opposite the LC[g], with Fellowes to his right. It took some time to get going as they took ages to link a conference call to Robin Janvrin and Stephen Lamport at Balmoral."[235]

"At the second palace meeting[h], Anji[i] came too and we went to the meeting where Malcolm Ross briefed the relevant departments on thinking so far. He said the 'People's Princess' was the main theme and it would be a People's Funeral. He emphasised the role of [Diana's] charities, said they wanted a proper ethnic mix.... Fellowes struck me as a kind person, but one who had worked out this [funeral] had to be different, and had to be successful, and he had no qualms about letting us take the lead where that might help make it happen."[236]

Comment: At the inquest Fellowes said that he returned from holiday "the week after the death of the Princess and Mr Al Fayed, and I went back to Balmoral on the following Sunday, I think, after the funeral".

In saying this, Fellowes has indicated under oath that he returned to work on the Sunday following the funeral, 7 September 1997.

Tony Blair's press secretary, Alastair Campbell – in his diarised book, *The Blair Years* – has revealed that Fellowes was talking with him on the phone as early as 4 a.m. on 31 August 1997, just one hour after the official time of Diana's death. Campbell also shows that Fellowes was heavily

---

[a] Angus Lapsley, Private Secretary, Home Affairs, Downing Street.
[b] TB = Tony Blair.
[c] Lord Chamberlain.
[d] Charles' deputy private secretary.
[e] Queen's Communications and Press Secretary.
[f] Media Manager for the Royal Family.
[g] LC = Lord Chamberlain.
[h] At Buckingham Palace later on the same day, 1 September 1997.
[i] Anji Hunter, Presentation and Planning, Downing Street.

involved in the organisational meetings ahead of the Diana funeral, which occurred on 6 September 1997.[a]

Campbell's revelations indicate that Fellowes lied under oath to the jury at the inquest. Fellowes has said that he was on holiday until September 7, when Campbell's diary has instead shown that he was busily involved in organising Diana's funeral on behalf of the Queen.

The consequence of Fellowes' false statement was that he was not questioned at the inquest on any of the early post-crash events that have been covered in this chapter. When one realises that Fellowes was one of only two royal witnesses heard, from a pool of 11 key royal witnesses of these events – the Queen, Charles, Fellowes, Janvrin, Lamport, Archer, Ogilvy, Mather, Ross, Ridley, Burton – the lie regarding Fellowes' involvement becomes very significant.

Fellowes' role is of particular importance because: a) as private secretary he would have been receiving direct instructions from the Queen; b) Fellowes was Diana's brother-in-law; c) Fellowes was one of three people Princess Diana feared – see Part 2;[237] and d) Raine[b] gave evidence that Fellowes was instrumental in preventing Jane from having contact with Diana – see Part 2.[238]

Campbell's account is that there was a conference call with Fellowes at 4 a.m. on 31 August 1997. There were three participants – including Lapsley – but Campbell indicates the call was initiated by Fellowes: "'You know about Diana, do you? She's dead.' I said yes." Campbell describes Fellowes' tone as "very matter-of-fact and practical" – even though he has just discovered that his sister-in-law is dead.

Campbell reveals that Fellowes was involved in events right from just after the death.[c]

---

[a] In addition to the above quotes from Campbell, there are other references to Fellowes' involvement in the pre-funeral events up to page 143 of his book.

[b] Diana's step-mother.

[c] There is evidence from at least two early newspaper reports that place Robert Fellowes in the group that visited with Charles to the Paris hospital on 31 August 1997: *The Independent* on 1 September 1997: "About 5.40 [p.m.] local time [the crowds] saw a grave-faced Prince Charles arrive, accompanied by Diana's two sisters, Lady Sarah McCorquodale and Lady Jane Fellowes, together with her husband Robert, the principal private secretary to the Queen...."; *The Mirror* on 1 September 1997: "Looking tired and drawn, Charles visited the eight-storey casualty ward where medics fought to keep the princess alive. Lady Jane, 40, and Lady Sarah, 41, looked tearful and deeply distressed. Lady Jane's husband Sir Robert Fellowes, the Queen's private secretary, was also present." There is no witness evidence that supports this and there is no record of Fellowes leaving the flight at RAF Northolt on arrival in the UK. That would indicate that Fellowes would have stayed on the plane and returned to Aberdeen with Charles. I suggest this is unlikely, as Fellowes was placed by Campbell in London the following day – see above. Sources: Louise Jury,

Fellowes has said that he was "in Norfolk" at the time of the crash.[239a] The evidence from Campbell then reveals that Fellowes was present at two Buckingham Palace meetings on the following day, Monday 1 September 1997.

The record reveals a picture of a man – Robert Fellowes – who is on holiday up to the death of his sister-in-law, then immediately following the death, is on the phone to senior government officials talking in a manner described as "very matter-of-fact and practical". Later that day, or very early the following morning, Fellowes travels from Norfolk to London and is very quickly at the centre of negotiations and planning for the funeral. Then, immediately following the funeral – "the following Sunday" – Fellowes reports for duty at Balmoral, in the far north of Scotland.

There appears to be no period of shock or mourning at the violent loss of Fellowes' sister-in-law, Diana.

Why did Fellowes indicate to the jury that he returned to work on 7 September 1997, when the evidence shows he was working from within an hour of Diana's death?

I suggest that Fellowes attempted – and succeeded – to distance himself from early involvement in the post-crash events. It is because the royals do not want public awareness of the role that they played in achieving early post-death control over the "unroyal" body of Princess Diana.

This is a theme of this chapter – a general distancing of the royals from this early control, that did occur.

On this issue, both of the royal witnesses who were heard at the inquest – Mather[b] and Fellowes – have lied.

Campbell presents a situation where the Blair government was having an input into the planning of the funeral – "Fellowes ... had worked out this [funeral] had to be different, and had to be successful, and he had no qualms about letting us take the lead where that might help make it happen". It should be noted though, that out of the 11 people Campbell lists as present in

---

The Tragedy: Prince Paid His Last Respects ... Then the Coffin Lid Was Closed, The Independent, 1 September 1997; Anton Antonowicz, Home to a Nation in Mourning: Charles Brings Diana Back, The Mirror, 1 September 1997.

[a] This has never been specifically corroborated by any other witness. Paget said: "This information has been confirmed to Operation Paget officers.": Paget Report, p622. There is other evidence that suggests Fellowes may have been at the British Embassy late on 30 August 1997 – this is dealt with in the Part 5 chapter on the British Embassy.

[b] See earlier.

the initial meeting, 8 are from the royal household, 2 are government –
Campbell and Lapsley – and Gibbins[a] alone represented Diana.

I suggest that by the time the meetings on the funeral started – on Monday
September 1 – the main issue that concerned the Queen – royal control of
Diana's body – had already been sorted out (see earlier). I believe that the
issues relating to the conduct of the funeral, although still important, were of
lesser concern to the royals – and royal control of that was not deemed so
essential.[b]

Malcolm Ross: LCO[c] Comptroller

According to the Queen's official website: "Despite its name, the Lord
Chamberlain's Office [LCO] is as independent of the Lord Chamberlain as
the other Departments. It is headed by the Comptroller."[240]

The general evidence shows that the 1997 LCO Comptroller, Malcolm
Ross – who has never been interviewed by any police investigation and was
not heard from at the inquest – played a key role in the early post-death
events:

-   Ross called Mather at 6.00 a.m. – Mather: "[Ross] contacted me at
0600 hours [6.00 a.m.] at my home, as a result of which I went straight to
Buckingham Palace"

-   Ross made contact with Diana's family – Mather: "I understand that
Sir Malcolm Ross and Dr Burton were involved in communicating with the
Princess of Wales' family"[d]

-   Ross was the "main man" at the first September 1 meeting to organise
Diana's funeral – Campbell: "Ross, who sat to the Lord Chamberlain's left
and appeared to be the main man"

-   Ross appeared to control the second September 1 meeting to organise
the funeral – Campbell: "Ross briefed the relevant departments on thinking
so far. He said the 'People's Princess' was the main theme and it would be a
People's Funeral. He emphasised the role of [Diana's] charities, said they
wanted a proper ethnic mix."

It is amazing that in consideration of Ross' important role, his name was
only heard once in the entire 6 months of the inquest.[e]

---

[a] Also, it has already been shown that Gibbins was putting royal interests ahead of
Diana's in not communicating with her family – see earlier.

[b] For example, the freedom of speech allowed to Earl Spencer during the funeral
service.

[c] Lord Chamberlain's Office.

[d] Earlier evidence has shown that Burton's family contact occurred with Sarah and
Jane at the Fulham Mortuary ahead of the post-mortem. The contact between Ross
and the family is discussed below.

[e] This was in connection with the 6 a.m. phone call – see Mather's evidence near the
beginning of this chapter.

Mather has stated that as a result of Ross' 6 a.m. call "I went straight to Buckingham Palace". Earlier evidence has shown – Clive and Keith Leverton – that prior to leaving home Mather called Levertons.

Keith stated: "[Mather] instructed that we utilise Operation Overstudy to return her body to the United Kingdom". The earlier Speed of Repatriation section has already shown that after the Mather-Keith phone call at around 6.30 a.m., Levertons was aware that Diana had to be repatriated that day – "we were required to return her quickly". Clive stated: "we had to be at the airport by 1 [p.m.]"

This evidence reveals that Ross – who was Mather's direct boss – had, at 6 a.m., given Mather clear instructions that the repatriation had to be completed that day. It was Mather's job to work out the details and pass on the instructions to the right people.

Concurrent to the actions of Levertons, Mather also stated: "an RAF BAe 146 was sent to Aberdeen from RAF Northolt to collect the Prince of Wales".

The earlier evidence of Diana's driver Colin Tebbutt was that at 6.30 a.m. at Heathrow he boarded a Paris-bound plane in which he saw "Superintendent Kingsmill from SO14, who was going to Paris as an advance for ... Prince Charles' visit". It has earlier been suggested that for Kingsmill to be on that 6.30 a.m. British Airways flight to Paris, he would have needed notification by 5 a.m. at the latest.

Evidence in the Embalming chapter and later in this chapter reveals that the president of Kenyons, a subsidiary of PFG, was notified before 4 a.m.[a] that PFG's services would be required as a result of the death of Princess Diana.

The Kenyons' president was in London and following that early notification he, at 4 a.m., called Hervé Racine, the president of PFG in France, setting in train a series of phone calls that led to PFG conducting the French side of Diana's repatriation and BJL – a company connected to PFG – carrying out the French embalming.

The question is: Who was it that called the Kenyons president at sometime around 3.30 a.m. on 31 August 1997?

Jean-Claude Plumet, PFG Director of Paris Agencies, Paris: 4 Nov 05 Paget description of Statement: **Jury Didn't Hear**:

"Mr Plumet has since been made aware that Mr Chapillon had himself been informed of the incident by telephone by Mr Racine. Mr Racine is believed to have been at his home in Paris, and had in turn been telephoned by the company President of the United Kingdom based affiliate; but he does not recall his name, the company name or the location of their offices."[241]

---

[a] UK time.

Gérard Jauze, PFG Branch Director, Paris: 21 Mar 06 Statement: **Jury Didn't Hear**:

"According to what M. Jean-Claude Plumet tells me, the director of the Paris agencies of PFG, M. Hervé Racine, was contacted by the British subsidiary of PFG, who are called Kenyons. In 1997, PFG and Kenyon belonged to Service Corporation International (SCI), an American company."[242]

Patrick Launay, PFG Repatriation Director: 21 Mar 06 Statement: **Jury Didn't Hear**:

"You[a] tell me that Mr Chapillon was informed by Mr Racine, the President of PFG, who in turn had been informed by Mr Gerald Pullins, the Director of SCI Europe. I do not however have any recollection of that sequence of events."[243]

Patrick Launay, PFG Repatriation Director: 21 Mar 06 Statement: **Jury Didn't Hear**:

"We dealt with the repatriations through the English funeral directors that called us, normally Kenyons and Tony Rowland."[244]

Alan Puxley, Vice-President Operations, Kenyon International: 16 Jun 04 Statement: **Jury Didn't Hear**:

"Kenyon's International was previously known as Kenyon Emergency Services and was owned originally by the Kenyon family who also owned J.H Kenyon Funeral Directors. For many years J.H Kenyon conducted funerals for the Royal Family. However this I understand was until the early 1990's...."[245]

Anthony Mather, Asst Comptroller, Lord Chamberlain's Office: 23 Aug 05 Statement: **Jury Didn't Hear**:

"In August 1991 Levertons & Sons Ltd often known as Levertons of Camden became the undertakers to the Royal Family. They took over this role from J.H Kenyon, known as Kenyon's."[246]

Clive Leverton, Royal Funeral Director: 13 Jul 04 Statement: **Jury Didn't Hear**:

"We are the funeral directors who have since 1991 been asked by the Lord Chamberlains office to care for members [of] the Royal Family in the event of one of them passing away. We took on this from another company of undertakers called J.H Kenyon."[247]

Keith Leverton, Royal Funeral Director: 27 Oct 04 Statement: **Jury Didn't Hear**:

"We are the funeral directors who have since 1991 been asked by the Lord Chamberlains office to care for members the Royal Family in the event of one of them passing away. We took on this from another company of undertakers called J.H Kenyon."[248]

---

[a] Operation Paget, who were conducting this interview.

Comment: Plumet states that Racine was "telephoned by the company President of the United Kingdom based [PFG] affiliate; but he does not recall his name [or] the company name".

Jauze indicates that Plumet did recall the company name: "According to what M. Jean-Claude Plumet tells me, the director of the Paris agencies of PFG, M. Hervé Racine, was contacted by the British subsidiary of PFG, who are called Kenyons".

The key point gained by examining these statements – Plumet, Jauze – is that Racine was called by the president (Plumet) of Kenyons (Jauze), a subsidiary of PFG (Jauze).

According to Launay, Paget identified the name of the individual making this call as Jerald Pullins – "had been informed by Mr Gerald Pullins, the Director of SCI Europe". This is supported in the diagram constructed by Operation Paget – see near beginning of Embalming chapter – "Jerald Pullins: Former European Managing Director". Paget have never revealed how they identified the caller as Jerald Pullins.

There is a critical conflict here.

Between Jauze and Plumet, their evidence is that the unnamed president of Kenyons made the call. Paget has stated – through Launay – that Jerald Pullins "Director of SCI Europe" made the call.

Some background information: In the early 1990s Kenyons was acquired by PFG, then in 1995, PFG – including Kenyons – was sold to SCI.[249]

Jerald Pullins was appointed Executive Vice-President of SCI's European operations in 1994[a], and on 14 August 1997 – just two weeks before the Paris crash – it was announced that he had been promoted to Executive Vice-President International Operations.[250b]

By 1997 Kenyons was a part of the French company PFG, which was in turn a part of the US company SCI.

The Plumet-Jauze evidence indicates that the call to Racine was made by the president of Kenyons – not the Executive Vice-President International Operations for SCI, Jerald Pullins.

---

[a] Earlier, Pullins was part-founder of the Sentinel Group which merged with SCI in 1991.: SCI Announces the Appointment of Jerald L. Pullins as Executive Vice-President International, PR Newswire, 14 August 1997, www.prnewswire.com/news-releases

[b] This helps explain why Paget describe Pullins' position as "former European Managing Director" in the Paget Report. At the time of the phone call Pullins had been just two weeks in his new role.

It is significant that Paget have never disclosed how they arrived at the conclusion this call was placed by Pullins, when the "available"[a] witness evidence suggests otherwise.

Puxley, Mather, Clive and Keith all concur that up until 1991 J.H. Kenyon was the official royal funeral director – that role was then taken over by Levertons. Puxley and Mather reveal that J.H. Kenyon and Kenyons are one and the same.

The above evidence shows that in 1997 Kenyons – the company that was the royal funeral directors up to 1991 – had been a subsidiary of PFG since the early 1990s.[bc] Earlier evidence has shown that in 1997 BJL – the embalming company – was also partly owned by PFG.

At the time of the 1997 crash, Malcolm Ross had already been LCO Comptroller for 6 years and prior to that had been Assistant Comptroller since 1987.[251] Malcolm Ross' work in the LCO included organising royal funerals.[252]

By 1997, all up Ross had 10 years of experience in royal funeral planning and organisation.

Ross' assistant, Anthony Mather, revealed in his statement that the organisation of funerals is an ongoing process. In relation to the Queen's upcoming funeral he said: "Since my official retirement in 1999 I am still involved at the Palace with the Lord Chamberlain's office in respect of the planning and overall co-ordination for the state funeral of the Queen."[d]

During the first 4 years of Ross' time in the LCO – from 1987 to 1991 – he would have needed a working relationship with Kenyons, in their role as royal funeral directors.

I suggest that it is logical that Malcolm Ross may have been reasonably familiar with the 1997 president of Kenyons as a result of his work in those earlier years.

---

[a] None of this evidence was available to the jury and it was only made public for the first time when *The Documents* book was published in 2010.

[b] There is some conflict in the research on the precise timing of PFG's acquisition of Kenyons. *Private Client Adviser* magazine indicates that it occurred after 1990, whereas Clifton Bryant, in his exhaustive book on *Death and Dying* states it was in 1989. Sources: The British Funeral Service, *Private Client Adviser* Magazine, Volume 5 Issue 2, January 2000; Clifton Bryant, *Handbook of Death and Dying*, Sage, 2003, Vol. 1, p615.

[c] I suggest the possibility that in 1991 the Queen withdrew from Kenyons the role of royal funeral directors as a result of it being acquired by the French company, PFG.

[d] Mather also referred to constant ongoing work on Operation Overstudy: "I was involved in the operational plan named 'Operation Overstudy' from 1991 until 1999. During that time I was involved in updating and reviewing it on a regular basis in conjunction with the RAF.": Anthony Mather, Witness Statement, 23 August 2005, reproduced in *The Documents* book, p661 (UK Edition)

This evidence – which has been altered by Paget and was suppressed at the inquest – reveals a link between Malcolm Ross, Kenyons and PFG.

Earlier evidence in this book, from French embalmer Huguette Amarger, revealed that the British had ordered the embalming – "the British wanted it to be a woman to take care of giving the treatment"[a].

The evidence in this chapter has already shown that it was the British royals who took early control over Diana's body, therefore it is likely that this 4 a.m. phone call from the president of Kenyons to Racine was triggered by an even earlier call from someone within the royal family or household.

It is logical that this earlier call – probably around 3.30 a.m. – must have been made by someone with a) the knowledge of who to ring to initiate the French side of the repatriation and embalming of Princess Diana, and b) a familiarity with the person called, given the early[b] timing.

This evidence points to Malcolm Ross making the 3.30 a.m. call:

- as head of the LCO Ross has direct contact with the Queen, so could have received an early instruction
- Ross would have been familiar with staff from Kenyons, due to his work between 1987 and 1991
- Ross would have been aware that Kenyons was now run by a French company – that takeover occurred around the same time the Queen replaced Kenyons with Levertons
- by 1997 Ross had 10 years of knowledge regarding royal funeral organisation and would have accumulated contacts within the industry
- earlier evidence has revealed Ross was busy on the phone to Mather early that same morning.

Operation Paget has covered up Kenyons' involvement in the events in two ways:

1) They told Launay that the call to Racine was made by Pullins, when they do not appear to have any credible source for that. Jauze told them the call came from Kenyons.

Launay and Jauze were both interviewed on the same day – 21 March 2006.

If Launay was interviewed first, why didn't Paget challenge Jauze when he comes up with someone different than Pullins as the source of the call?

If Jauze was interviewed first, why have Paget then told Launay a different story than what they had just heard from Jauze?

---

[a] The evidence in the Embalming chapter reveals the detail showing this statement was connected to the initial embalming order – timing is the key factor.
[b] Early in the day – 3.30 a.m.

401

2) In the Paget Report diagram[a], Pullins has been shown as the source of the call, even though they had credible evidence from Jauze – received 9 months ahead of the report's publication – showing the call came from Kenyons.

Paget appear to have avoided the use of the "Kenyons" word because it is known in the UK that Kenyons had been the royal funeral directors.[b] An early morning call from the president of Kenyons to Hervé Racine in France is a further indication of royal involvement in the earliest critical events following the death of Princess Diana.

The evidence from both Anthony Mather and Alastair Campbell reveals that Malcolm Ross was playing a key role in the events.

Campbell also reveals something more. When Campbell describes the second meeting on 1 September 1997 – the first official day of funeral planning – he describes Ross relaying decisions that have already been made:

- "the 'People's Princess' was the main theme"
- "it would be a People's Funeral"
- "emphasised the role of [Diana's] charities ... they wanted a proper ethnic mix".

There are two points here:

1) as Comptroller and Head of the LCO Department, Ross was directly answerable to the Queen.[c] I suggest that Ross would not have been able to make clearly defined statements of this nature unless the Queen had already approved these measures

2) the decisions that Ross was outlining to the September 1 meeting – listed above – all occurred on the day of the funeral: it was the People's

---

[a] Reproduced near the beginning of the Embalming chapter.

[b] The involvement of Operation Paget in this cover-up will come as no surprise to people who have read the 2007 book *Cover-Up of a Royal Murder: Hundreds of Errors in the Paget Report.*

[c] Mather says in his statement: "The Lord Chamberlains office took instructions from the Prince of Wales' and the Queen's private secretaries." The context of this is in reference to the events on 31 August 1997. There is no evidence supporting that account – the official Monarchy website reveals that the LCO is a completely separate department in a similar way that the Lord Chamberlain is: "The Lord Chamberlain's Office [LCO] is as independent of the Lord Chamberlain as the other Departments". There is no mention of the LCO Comptroller being answerable to or taking instructions from private secretaries. Sources: Anthony Mather, Witness Statement, 23 August 2005, reproduced in *The Documents* book, p662 (UK Edition); The Lord Chamberlain's Office, The Official Website of the British Monarchy, www.royal.gov.uk/TheRoyalHousehold

Funeral, with Diana recognised as the 'People's Princess' and the charities were emphasised with a "proper" ethnic mix.[a]

This evidence reveals a Queen who was making or approving early decisions – not a person who was languishing up in Balmoral in a state of shocked, paralysed indecision, as has been portrayed by media and the entertainment industry.

I suggest the following scenario, which includes some speculation, but is also based on the available evidence:

Following the 3 a.m.[b] death of Princess Diana the following early decisions were made by the Queen:

1) that Diana's body should be subjected to embalming (by a female) – to cover for any possible pregnancy, ahead of a British post-mortem. Effectively, this required a French embalming, because it would not have been possible to carry out an embalming in the UK, when it was known a post-mortem would be taking place[c]

2) that Diana's body should be repatriated as soon as possible, following the embalming – the earlier events happen, the less debate is attracted to them

3) that the repatriation should be seen to be carried out by Charles

4) that the coffin of Diana would be covered with the royal standard

5) that the royal coroner must take jurisdiction over Diana's body on its arrival in the UK – this would eventually lead to an inquest controlled by the royal coroner.

For the Queen's decisions to be carried out, it clearly required early action in France – to facilitate a rapid embalming and repatriation. This led to a phone call by Malcolm Ross to the president of Kenyons at around 3.30 a.m. – to order the French embalming and French side of the repatriation.

Evidence – from Amarger and Tebbutt – in the Repatriation Issues chapter[d] will show that just minutes before the French embalming took place, Charles' bodyguard, Peter Von-Heinz, entered Diana's room with an advance. They applied sticky tape to the window blinds to absolutely ensure there could be no media knowledge of what was about to take place.

Royal involvement in embalming decisions is supported by the evidence from Levertons:

---

[a] Princess Diana's funeral, on 6 September 1997, was attended by over a million people and was watched by 2.5 billion people around the world: Diana's Funeral Watched by Millions, BBC News, 6 September 1997.

[b] UK time.

[c] It will be shown in the Post-Mortem chapter that embalming does seriously impact on post-mortem test results.

[d] See the section on Presence of British Police.

- "we wouldn't have embalmed [Diana] ... without authority from the Lord Chamberlain" – Green
- "any instructions to carry out ... embalming would come from the Lord Chamberlain" – Green
- "had [embalming] been requested or ordered then we would have to of taken instructions from the Lord Chamberlain's office"[253] – Clive
- "had [embalming] been required or requested by any one I would have referred the question back to Mather" – Keith
- "the Lord Chamberlain's office had their own plans.... I was aware that these plans involved the requirement for embalming as they would for any other deceased person" – Keith.[a]

Malcolm Ross, as LCO Comptroller, was the man in the position to receive and carry out the Queen's instructions regarding repatriation and embalming:
- it was Ross' responsibility to plan and organise royal funerals
- Mather's evidence shows Ross was on the phone to him at 6 a.m.
- Campbell's diary reveals that Ross took control of the funeral organisation, right from the first meeting on September 1 – Ross "appeared to be the main man".[b]

I suggest that by 1997 – after 10 years in the LCO department – Malcolm Ross would have had enough knowledge or connections in the funeral industry to have known who to call in the event of a required repatriation or French embalming. If Ross didn't know to call the Kenyons president, he would have had the contacts to point him in the right direction.

I believe that at around 3.30 a.m. on 31 August 1997, just 30 minutes or so after the official death of Princess Diana, it was Malcolm Ross who picked up the phone to call the president of Kenyons, in order to fulfil instructions from his direct boss, Queen Elizabeth.

Ross' phone records should have been checked as part of the investigation – what instead happened is that Ross has never been interviewed.

Mather has said: "I understand that Sir Malcolm Ross ... [was] involved in communicating with the Princess of Wales' family".

There is no specific evidence of the nature of Ross' contact with the family, but other evidence indicates – see earlier – it would have been to organise Sarah and Jane's presence on the Charles' plane to Paris.

---

[a] This involvement of the LCO in embalming decisions is also shown in earlier evidence relating to the events straight after the UK post-mortem. Levertons were instructed around midnight to move Diana's body to St James' Palace, where a second embalming took place immediately.

[b] Mather's evidence – see earlier – was that Ross was at home in Scotland on the Sunday morning. At some stage – either later on August 31 or early on September 1 – Ross must have travelled to London to be present for the next day's meetings at Buckingham Palace.

Common sense would suggest there also would have been contact with Diana's family throughout the week to organise their role in the Saturday funeral. This contact could have been carried out by Ross as LCO Comptroller.

There is no evidence though of the family being consulted regarding the general funeral organisation. There was no one from the family present at the two funeral coordination meetings described by Campbell on 1 September 1997 – see earlier.[a]

Campbell states in his 2011 book regarding the first September 1 meeting: "When they were talking about the procession, the Lord Chamberlain said it would be important to consult the Queen and Charles. Fellowes added 'And her family.' The Lord Chamberlain coughed and said yes, in that order.... Janvrin was clear you could not do [the walk behind the coffin] without Charles Spencer. We agreed he should be kept informed of all these discussions. Nothing could be agreed finally without the family."[254]

Despite this apparent agreement there is no evidence that anyone from Diana's family was "informed of all these discussions". Campbell does though refer to Charles Spencer's presence at a funeral rehearsal on Friday 6 September 1997.[255]

At the inquest Mather should have been asked to explain Ross' role "in communicating with the Princess of Wales' family" – that never occurred.

Anthony Mather: LCO[b] Assistant Comptroller

Anthony Mather was called by his direct boss, Malcolm Ross, at around 6 a.m. on 31 August 1997 – see earlier.

Mather's statement evidence is: "I went straight to Buckingham Palace arriving at 0830 hours.... Operation Overstudy was requested by me, as this was the most logical method of repatriating Diana, Princess of Wales".

There are two relevant factors here:
1) Mather times the set-up of Operation Overstudy after his 8.30 a.m. arrival at Buckingham Palace
2) Mather states: "Operation Overstudy was requested by me".

The earlier evidence from Clive and Keith Leverton reveals that Operation Overstudy was not set up after 8.30 a.m., but rather at around 6.40 a.m., when Mather requested Levertons to repatriate Diana.

---

[a] There is a possibility that Michael Gibbins – who Campbell says was present – passed on details to the family. Gibbins gave earlier evidence though that he was unable to contact the family on the issue of embalming – see Embalming chapter.
[b] Lord Chamberlain's Office.

At the inquest Mather – with the help of inquest lawyer, Jonathon Hough – maintained this false account, that Levertons was called after Mather arrived at Buckingham Palace – after 8.30 a.m.

When Hough asked Mather about his role in the "organisation of the repatriation", Mather replied: "We started operation – or I started Operation Overstudy".

I suggest it is no coincidence that Mather has commenced his answer with "we" then realised what he had said, and corrected himself: "I started Operation Overstudy". The correction matches with Mather's statement account: "Operation Overstudy was requested by me".

The Mather evidence that Overstudy was requested and started by him after 8.30 a.m. shifts the decision-making away from an early involvement from Balmoral. This is a theme of this chapter – early decisions made at Balmoral, but a concerted cover-up that shifts decision making to a later time frame and away from Balmoral.

The earlier evidence indicates that at 6 a.m. Ross would have told Mather that Operation Overstudy was to be engaged – this led to Mather calling Levertons straightaway and then heading to Buckingham Palace.

The reality is that Diana was no longer a member of the royal family (see earlier) and if Diana was going to be welcomed back into the royal fold – which is what occurred – the decision to do that could only be made by the Queen – not by Anthony Mather.

It was the Queen who withdrew Diana's royal rights in August 1996[a] and only the Queen could make the decision to reinstate those rights to the dead Diana.

It is significant that Alastair Campbell, despite providing a full list of those present at the first September 1 funeral organisation meeting, makes no mention of Anthony Mather. Mather does not figure at all in Campbell's diary of the events.

This is a further indication that Mather was not a major player and certainly not a decision-maker. Mather was following orders conveyed to him from Malcolm Ross.[b]

In light of that, it is critical that Mather was cross-examined at the inquest, but the two people upline from him – Ross and the Queen – were not heard from: they were not cross-examined and neither of them has been interviewed by any police investigation.

How is it possible to establish the full truth of what occurred – and why it occurred – without interviewing the most important witnesses?

---

[a] It was shown earlier that the specific funeral plan for Princess Diana had been removed prior to her death.

[b] Mather followed his orders well – 3 months later he was awarded the CVO – see earlier footnote.

A study of the Timeline of Events near the front of this book, reveals that the arrival of Mather at Buckingham Palace – at 9.30 a.m. Paris time – occurs about 15 minutes ahead of two other key events in Paris:

1) Moss' call to Plumet to officially request PFG's services. It is possible that Mather was asked to organise this, to help cover up the fact that PFG's services had already been solicited through other – royal – channels much earlier in the day.

2) Hauffman's second call to Amarger giving specific instructions. It is possible that Monceau was waiting on confirmed instructions from Mather before Amarger was given her final instructions.

David Ogilvy[a]: Lord Chamberlain

The precise role of David Ogilvy on 31 August 1997 is difficult to define.

Anthony Mather reveals[b] that Ogilvy did have a role: "When I got into the Palace, the Lord Chamberlain was in, as was the defence services secretary[c]. We each took our particular roles and got on with our jobs."

Mather wasn't asked what "our jobs" were in relation to Ogilvy or the Defence Services Secretary. Ogilvy was not heard from at the inquest and has never been interviewed by any police investigation.

By 1997 Ogilvy must have been well versed in royal affairs, as he had been Lord Chamberlain for 13 years.[256d]

As was shown earlier, the Lord Chamberlain is a completely separate department to the Lord Chamberlain's Office (Ross and Mather) – "despite its name".[e]

According to the Queen's website the role of Lord Chamberlain is very important: "The Lord Chamberlain is <u>the senior official</u> of the Royal Household. His role is to oversee the conduct and general business of the

---

[a] Also known as Lord Airlie.

[b] At the inquest.

[c] The Defence Services Secretary is dealt with later.

[d] Ogilvy left that post on 31 December 1997, just 4 months after these events: Lord Chamberlain, Wikipedia, http://en.wikipedia.org/wiki

[e] This evidence from the Official Website of The British Monarchy actually conflicts with the evidence from the royal funeral directors. Clive Leverton: "The Lord Chamberlain is amongst other things, directly responsible to the Monarch who entrusts funeral arrangements to him, his comptroller, and then assistant comptroller." Keith Leverton: "The Lord Chamberlain is amongst other things, directly responsible to the Monarch who deputises down funeral arrangements to him, his comptroller, and then the assistant comptroller." According to the royal website the Lord Chamberlain's Office is responsible for funerals – there is nothing at all in the section on the Lord Chamberlain about any involvement with funerals.

Royal Household and to be a source and focal point for important matters which have implications for the Household as a whole." In what could be seen as a contradiction to this, the website entry continues: "His role is non-executive and his post is part-time."[257]

One can see from this chapter that the Queen saw the death of Diana as the "business of the Royal Household" – so it is perfectly understandable that Ogilvy was on duty at Buckingham Palace early on that Sunday morning.

What do we know about what Ogilvy did during this critical period? There are several clues:

1) Ogilvy took royal coroner, John Burton's first call to Buckingham Palace. Burton presented two conflicting accounts of this call – "Lord Chamberlain in difficulty with switchboard"; "He was unable to assist much further at this stage".[a]

2) Ogilvy despatched the Royal Standard to Levertons on the morning of the crash: Keith – "the Royal standard arrived at our office"; Burton: "the Lord Chamberlain had provided it".[b]

3) At around 7 p.m. at RAF Northolt, while waiting for the return of Diana's body, Ogilvy negotiated with Tony Blair and Alastair Campbell: **Alastair Campbell**, Tony Blair's Press Secretary: 2011 Published Diary: **Jury Didn't Hear**:

31 August 1997: "I had a catch-up meeting with Angus [Lapsley] at Number 10[c] and then we left for RAF Northolt, to be greeted by an extraordinary array of Establishment figures.... The Lord Chamberlain (Lord Airlie) arrived in his enormous Rolls-Royce. He had quite the shiniest toecaps I'd ever seen, impressive white hair. The mood was a bit edgy. I sensed the concerns they all had about where it was heading. TB[d] arrived with George Robertson[e], and again I was struck by how, in this company, they emanated a sense of being very different. Yet in these circumstances they knew that they maybe lacked the skills to navigate through. The LC[f] said as much.... I was hovering near TB as he chatted to the Lord Chamberlain and they called me over. The LC was clear that this was an extraordinary situation and they would find it useful if we could be involved in the discussions about this. TB volunteered me for the next few days and said we would do whatever they asked of us."[258]

Comment: Ogilvy – as with the department heads – was answerable directly to the Queen.

---

[a] This evidence has been dealt with in the earlier section on the Royal Coroner.

[b] This has been covered earlier in the section on Diana's Post-Death Status Change.

[c] Downing St – Prime Minister Tony Blair's residence. Blair was away at his Sedgefield constituency.

[d] Tony Blair.

[e] Secretary of State for Defence.

[f] Lord Chamberlain.

I suggest that it is common sense that Ogilvy – who is seen here requesting the government's help in organising the funeral – would not be doing this unless he had been given approval – or orders – to do so, by his boss, the Queen.[ab]

4) Ogilvy chaired the first September 1 funeral planning meeting: Campbell – "Airlie chaired the meeting".[c]

Peter Harding: Defence Services Secretary

As with Ogilvy, Mather noted that Peter Harding was already at Buckingham Palace when he arrived: "When I got into the Palace, the Lord Chamberlain was in, as was the defence services secretary. We each took our particular roles and got on with our jobs."

And as with Ogilvy, no lawyer at the inquest asked Mather what Harding's job was. The Defence Services Secretary (DSS) is also missing from the official royal website.

According to Wikipedia, the Defence Services Secretary – a role filled by Harding between 1994 and 1998 – "is responsible for liaison between the Sovereign and the British Armed Forces. He has an office at Buckingham Palace and an office at the Ministry of Defence in the Main Building, Whitehall."[259]

---

[a] The movie *The Queen* suggests that at this point there were discussions between Blair and Charles. There is nothing in the Blair or Campbell books to substantiate that. According to Campbell the discussions were with Ogilvy. Campbell describes Charles at RAF Northolt: "He looked sad, and not surprisingly was finding the never-ending small talk difficult.": Alastair Campbell, The Blair Years, 2007, page 234
[b] On Thursday September 4, in his book Campbell shows Ogilvy passing on information directly from the Queen: "LC ... said she [the Queen] was keen to discuss it all with the Prime Minister." This was in reference to a plan conveyed to Campbell during a conference with Balmoral: "Today [Thursday] and tomorrow [Friday] members of the [royal] family would start to visit the Chapel Royal. The Duke of Edinburgh has suggested that they go to church this evening before the boys [William and Harry] head south. The Prince of Wales comes down tomorrow and visits Kensington Palace, Buckingham Palace and the chapel. The Queen and Queen Mother would come back and also visit the chapel royal and the Queen would do a broadcast." The indication from Ogilvy to Campbell that the Queen "was keen to discuss" all this "with the Prime Minister" is also a direct contradiction to *The Queen* movie. That movie shows the Queen unwilling to discuss anything with Blair and grudgingly taking his phone calls. Source: Alastair Campbell, The Blair Years, 2007, page 241.
[c] According to Campbell's 2007 book – pp235-243 – Ogilvy went on to be present at all of the subsequent meetings through that week and was involved in the organisation for the funeral.

It is notable that early on 31 August 1997 Harding was at Buckingham Palace. This is in keeping with the evidence in this chapter that it was the royals who took early control of the post-death events.

What was Peter Harding doing in his office at Buckingham Palace before 8.30 a.m. on Sunday 31 August 1997?

The Wikipedia site goes on to say: "Unless his [the DSS] assistance is specifically invited he does not ... concern himself ... with royal travel."[260]

Unless there is some secret aspect to this, it would seem that the very reason Harding was working would have been to organise the royal travel – the Charles flight and also possibly the Leverton flight.[a]

This evidence would then suggest that Harding was "specifically invited" on that historic morning.

Who would have made that invitation?

Wikipedia: "The Defence Services Secretary is answerable to the Sovereign's Private Secretary"[261] – Robert Fellowes, who – see earlier – was at work from at least 4 a.m.

Once again, the line of authority points to the Queen – the Queen to Fellowes to Harding.

Matthew Ridley: Lord Steward

Matthew Ridley – or Lord Steward – has not been mentioned in any evidence related to this case.

Ridley, who was Lord Steward from 1989 to 2001[262], has been included here because of legislation – the Coroners Act 1988 – that reveals a critical connection between the Lord Steward, who is answerable directly to the Queen[b], and the royal coroner.

The important role of the royal coroner in securing illegal jurisdiction over Diana's body on 31 August 1997 has already been thoroughly covered.

According to the Coroners Act 1988, s29: "Coroner of the Queen's Household":

- "the coroner of the Queen's household shall continue to be appointed by the Lord Steward"
- "the coroner of the Queen's household shall make his declaration of office before the Lord Steward"

---

[a] Harding's background was in the RAF. He joined the RAF in 1952 but was forced to resign in 1994 after revelations of an affair with Bienvenida Buck, the wife of Anthony Buck, an MP in the Major government. Harding was removed from the Air Force list but was promptly reemployed by the Queen as Defence Services Secretary.: Peter Harding, Wikipedia, http://en.wikipedia.org/wiki

[b] "The Lord Steward receives his appointment from the Sovereign in person and ... is the first dignitary of the [royal] court".: Lord Steward, Wikipedia, http://en.wikipedia.org/wiki

- "all inquisitions, depositions and recognizances shall be delivered to the Lord Steward of the Queen's household to be filed among the records of his office"
- "the coroner of the Queen's household shall reside in one of the Queen's palaces or in such other convenient place as may from time to time be allowed by the Lord Steward".

It is not known where Ridley was on 31 August 1997.

Matthew Ridley has never been interviewed by any police investigation and was not heard from at the inquest. The inquest jury was never even told of the existence of the Lord Steward's office.

In light of the illegal actions of the royal coroner, John Burton – as have been outlined earlier in this chapter – evidence from Ridley should have been taken.

Why wasn't it?

Conclusion

On 28 August 1996 Queen Elizabeth removed the HRH status of Princess Diana and effectively ousted her from the royal family, as a part of the divorce settlement between Diana and Charles.

Princess Diana was removed from the royal family by the Queen and it is common sense that only the Queen had the power to reverse that decision, and reinstate her.

The evidence in this chapter shows that immediately following Diana's death, that is precisely what occurred – the dead Diana was reinstated as a member of the royal family, by the Queen.

Early on the morning of 31 August 1997 critical decisions were being made at Balmoral:
- a decision to repatriate Diana's body on that day
- a decision for Charles to travel to Paris, accompanied by Diana's sisters, to carry out that repatriation
- a decision to cover Diana's coffin with the royal standard
- a decision to deploy royalty protection officers to the Fulham Mortuary – see later[a]
- a decision to state the burial of Diana would be at Windsor Castle – this led to the royal coroner illegally taking jurisdiction of Diana's body
- a decision to ensure that Diana's dead body was returned to royal land – at St James' Palace – as soon as possible.

The key people who were entrusted with ensuring that these decisions were carried out – Malcolm Ross, Anthony Mather, John Burton, Prince

---

[a] This is covered in the Police Presence section of the UK Post-Mortems chapter.

Charles, Peter Harding, David Ogilvy – were all directly or indirectly answerable to Queen Elizabeth.

This evidence leads to the inescapable conclusion that in the hours following the death of Princess Diana, the Queen of England was not in a state of inactive, paralysed shock – as has tended to be portrayed by both the media and entertainment industries over the years.

The question is: Why did the Queen move so quickly and definitely to reinstate Diana as a royal, and thereby ensure her control over the dead Diana's body?

There are three key aspects to this:

1) The speed[a] – and level of orchestrated coordination – with which these events occurred, raises the possibility of prior knowledge of the crash on the part of the Queen. In saying this, prior knowledge is not necessarily an indication of direct involvement in the assassination plot. However, it could indicate knowledge that an assassination was going to or had taken place – i.e. knowledge that this crash was no accident.[b]

2) This control of the body resulted in royal control of any future inquest into the death of Princess Diana, even though she was not a member of the royal family at the time of her death.

3) The royal coroner was able to take control of the UK post-mortem conducted at Fulham Mortuary at 8.21 p.m. that night – Burton was able to influence events at the mortuary. This issue is covered in the later chapters on the Post-Mortem and Pregnancy (Part 5).

This control gave the royal coroner – acting on behalf of the Queen – the ability to delay the conduct of the inquest by 10 years. There was also the perception that any future inquest jury would be made up of members of the royal household.[cab]

---

[a] I suggest that getting things done quickly in these circumstances gives other people less time to ask questions or suggest alternatives. Before anyone knew much at all, Diana was already back in the UK and "safely" on royal property – having undergone two embalmings and two post-mortems.

[b] Campbell relates an incident in his book that occurred at CHOGM (Commonwealth Heads of Government Meeting) in Edinburgh, on 25 October 1997 – just 7 weeks after the Diana funeral. This event indicates the Queen very quickly wanted to move on past the death of Diana: "Fellowes said I ought to meet the Queen. He took me to where she was listening to a gaggle of Heads, and as she turned from them, Fellowes said to her how much help I had been to them in the week after Diana's death. She looked deeply unimpressed, nodded a little and then said 'Do you always travel with the Prime Minister?' I said yes, usually, and that was about it.": Alastair Campbell, The Blair Years, 2007, page 256.

[c] Coroners Act 1988, s29(4): "The jurors on an inquest held by the coroner of the Queen's household shall consist of officers of that household....".

I suggest that points 1 and 2 are connected – the knowledge that this death was as assassination led to the decision that royal control had to be asserted to ensure that the inquest would be delayed, or even not occur at all.

After a 10 year delay, the public interest in the inquest had dissipated so markedly that many people just wanted it over with, at any cost – the sentiment well before the start of the inquest being: "let Diana rest in peace" and "it is time to move on".

Witness evidence also is notably less reliable after a lengthy time lapse between the event and the taking of testimony.

Both of these points: the delay in the inquest – "justice delayed is justice denied" – and the unreliability of 10 year old witness evidence, have assisted in muddying the waters and making it more difficult for the truth to become known.[c]

I suggest that on the morning of 31 August 1997 the key issue for the Queen was to have her royal coroner claim jurisdiction over the body of Diana – it was that action alone that enabled control over decisions regarding the inquest and post-mortem. And I suggest the key problem facing the Queen was that Diana was not a royal and any action by the royal coroner to claim jurisdiction would be illegal.

So the Queen faced an early morning quandary on 31 August 1997 – the need to have coroner's control over Diana's body, but the reality that any actions to claim that control would be illegal.

I suggest that it was this quandary that led to the other actions on the day: use of the royal undertakers and the royal standard, Charles conducting the repatriation, delivery of the body to St James' Palace – all these actions created an environment where the dead Diana was being seen by the public to be treated as a royal again.[d]

---

[a] This never actually occurred. Elizabeth Butler-Sloss, who was deputy royal coroner, stated in the January 2007 pre-inquest hearing: "I shall not summons a jury of officers of the Queen's Household."

[b] In the end, the inquest, starting in 2007, was not conducted by the royal coroner. This issue of the succession of coroners is addressed in Part 5. I suggest here that in 1997 this would have been a factor that led to the Queen wanting the royal coroner's jurisdiction over Diana's body.

[c] There are other factors of course, not least of which was a corrupt judge. These issues that plagued the inquest will be addressed in more detail in Part 5. The issue being addressed here is how the Queen would have viewed the situation on the morning of 31 August 1997 and the result of actions that she initiated.

[d] I suggest that many people felt good about this at the time – that Diana had been welcomed back into the royal fold, after years of ongoing friction.

More important to the Queen, these other actions enabled the royal coroner's manoeuvre to take jurisdiction appear normal and acceptable, in the circumstances – even though it was actually illegal.

Statements made by royal coroner John Burton in 2001 – see earlier: an inquest "would serve no purpose" – indicate that there may have been a plan not to hold any inquest at all. This will be addressed again in Part 5 – evidence will show that the inquest was only held after concerted legal action from Mohamed Al Fayed and Paul Burrell's late 2003 release of the "Burrell Note" written by Diana.[a]

Subsequent to the 31 August 1997 actions directed by the Queen, there has been a huge cover-up of the evidence.

There has been a major failure by both police investigations – France and the UK – and the Baker inquest, to obtain evidence from key royal figures, both family and household. Other relevant non-royal witnesses were also not heard from at the inquest, and those few who were, were not asked the questions that could have led to an understanding of what actually occurred.

The evidence in this chapter revealed that the key decisions were made from Balmoral, yet it is beyond belief that Scott Baker conducted this inquest without any evidence from one person who was at Balmoral on the night-morning of 30-31 August 1997.

Not the Queen, not Philip, not Charles, not Janvrin, not Archer – no one who was at Balmoral was heard from.

Instead, when Balmoral came up at the inquest, witnesses were able to say words like: "I do not go to Balmoral as a matter of course" – Miles Hunt-Davis[263bc]; "I was on holiday from ... around the first week of August.... I went back to Balmoral ... after the funeral" – Robert Fellowes[d].

The point here is that Scott Baker was conducting an inquest into the death of a prominent British citizen, Diana, Princess of Wales. Substantial evidence pointing to murder was heard – see Part 1 – and among the prime suspects are senior British royals: the Queen, Philip, Charles – see Part 2. At the time of the death, these suspects were at Balmoral, yet no one who was present at Balmoral – including the three suspects – was heard from at the inquest.[e]

---

[a] The Burrell Note predicted a car crash – see Part 2.

[b] Philip's private secretary.

[c] There would have been an assistant private secretary who took Hunt-Davis' place, but this person's identity has never been disclosed.

[d] See earlier.

[e] These people at Balmoral have also never been interviewed by the police. There was apparently a short interview of Charles by John Stevens but the content of it has never been divulged.

Regarding the early royal control, there were at least 18 other witnesses that were not heard from: Jane Fellowes, Sarah McCorquodale[a], Robert Fellowes[b], John Burton[c], Michael Burgess, Keith Leverton, David Green, Bill Fry, Stephen Lamport, Stephen Donnelly[d], Robert Thompson, Patrick Launay, Jean-Claude Plumet, Gérard Jauze, Malcolm Ross, David Ogilvy, Peter Harding, Matthew Ridley and Jerald Pullins.

On top of that major "oversight", of the 67 items of witness evidence in this chapter, only 22 were heard by the jury. Again we are confronted with a key aspect of this case where the jury only heard part of the story – only the part that inquest judge Scott Baker allowed to be heard.

In other words, the evidence again points to a massive travesty of justice – a blindfolded jury with arms tied behind its back.

What occurred after Princess Diana's death was that the events, including her funeral, were organised by the very people she had come to despise – the royal household "men in grey suits". The theme from the evidence – both police statement and inquest cross-examination – was that this was perfectly natural, that the royals would take post-death control of the events.

The elephant in the room is that Princess Diana was no longer a member of the royal family. Diana's family should have been enabled to take control and the decisions should have been made by them. This is not what occurred.

---

[a] Sarah was cross-examined at the inquest but was not asked anything about the critical post-death events on 31 August 1997.

[b] Fellowes was cross-examined at the inquest but was not asked anything about the critical post-death events on 31 August 1997.

[c] Burton died before the inquest but his witness statement should have been read out – it wasn't.

[d] Donnelly's statement was read out, but he was never cross-examined – he should have been.

4   Repatriation Issues[a]

The repatriation of Princess Diana to the United Kingdom was conducted under extreme time pressure – see previous chapter.

Documentation

There was very little documentation.

Clive Leverton, Royal Funeral Director: 13 Jul 04 Statement: **Jury Didn't Hear**:

"For members of the royal family there is an operational plan for Royal Air Force involvement, and our part in it, to repatriate the body when death occurs away from London and which requires their transportation....

"We do not have any company documents or standard procedures concerning arrangements for repatriation or embalming concerning the Royal family, we get on with the task based upon our experience, knowledge and instructions at the time."[264]

Keith Leverton, Royal Funeral Director: 27 Oct 04 Statement: **Jury Didn't Hear**:

"I called [Mather] from my home.... He instructed that we utilise Operation Overstudy to return her body to the United Kingdom.... There were no other written procedures that we had to comply with. We undertook the task based upon our experience."[265]

Anthony Mather, Asst Comptroller, Lord Chamberlain's Office: 23 Aug 05 Statement: **Jury Didn't Hear**:

"Operation Overstudy is a Royal Air Force plan to repatriate any member of the Royal Family following their death abroad, back to the United Kingdom.

---

[a] Repatriation has already been covered in Chapter 3. This chapter deals with issues not already addressed.

I was involved in the operational plan named 'Operation Overstudy' from 1991 until 1999. During that time I was involved in updating and reviewing it on a regular basis in conjunction with the RAF."[266]

Comment: There appears to be a conflict in the evidence:

-   Clive: "we do not have any company documents or standard procedures concerning arrangements for repatriation or embalming concerning the Royal family"

-   Clive: "for members of the royal family there is an operational plan"

-   Mather: "Operation Overstudy is a ... plan to repatriate any member of the Royal Family".

The evidence from Mather is that Operation Overstudy is a repatriation plan that he "was involved in updating and reviewing ... on a regular basis ... from 1991 until 1999". According to Keith, that is the plan that Mather "instructed that we utilise".

Clive concurs that "there is an operational plan ... and our part in it, to repatriate the body". But Clive also indicates that there is no "standard procedures ... for repatriation ... we get on with the task based upon our experience, knowledge and instructions at the time".

Keith also states: "We undertook the task based upon our experience."

There is a big difference between having "an operational plan" and having no "standard procedures ... concerning the Royal family" – Clive, who was cross-examined at the inquest, should have been asked about this, but wasn't.

Clive Leverton, Royal Funeral Director: 13 Jul 04 Statement: **Jury Didn't Hear**:

"There was nothing, nor anyone that dictated what paperwork such as Cause of Death Certificate, F.F.I or Airwaybill was completed or was to be taken with the deceased. I presumed someone else was dealing [with it]. We did not receive these papers. I believe this was because of whom the deceased was, the requirement for all concerned to carry out a professional and very fast repatriation. Therefore the family needs and the return flight timing subjected all normal protocols and procedures to things such as the viewing and prompt transportation."[267]

Clive Leverton, Royal Funeral Director: 13 Jul 04 Statement: **Jury Didn't Hear**:

"When we receive a coffin into the U.K we would usually receive a full Death or Cause of Death Certificate, translated and verified by the British Consulate, a Certificate of Embalming, an F.F.I (Freedom from Infection Certificate) and an Airwaybill. This paperwork would normally be required for coffins coming into the UK to enable repatriation to be allowed. However our staff or myself received none of this paperwork at the time of the repatriation of Diana Princess of Wales, nor any since."[268]

David Green, Embalmer, UK: 17 Sep 04 Statement: **Jury Didn't Hear**:
"In the case of Diana, Princess of Wales we followed the instructions [from] the Lord Chamberlains office. She was repatriated on a private flight, and ... therefore the rules of hermetically sealing of the coffin and embalming with the appropriate certificate did not apply."[269]

Gérard Jauze, PFG Branch Director, Paris: 21 Mar 06 Statement: **Jury Didn't Hear**:
"You ask me if I remember receiving any documents confirming the authorisation to close the coffin and which authorise the transportation of the body to the airport. I did not receive any.

"You ask me if it would have been normal to have received these documents. Under normal circumstances, yes. However, this was an exceptional case, with representatives from the British Embassy, the Prefecture of Police and the President of France. That was a guarantee to proceed."[270]

Patrick Launay, PFG Repatriation Director: 21 Mar 06 Statement: **Jury Didn't Hear**:
"I asked Mr Jauze for the documents relating to the repatriation. I was provided with the burial certificate [TN: Fr. permis d'inhumer], issued by the Deputy Public Prosecutor, Mme Maude Coujard. I produce a copy of this document as my exhibit PL11. I do not remember who gave me this document. It is possible that it was Mr Jauze or Mr Plumet. This document certifies that the Public Prosecutor has no objections to the body being returned to the family and allows for the funeral arrangements to be made. It also allows for the repatriation of the body. I think that the original of the burial certificate accompanied the coffin back to the United Kingdom. It is likely that I gave it to the English funeral directors.

"Normally you have to have authority for the transportation of the body issued by the Prefecture of Police and also a death certificate issued by the Town Hall [TN: Fr. Mairie] of the place of death. However, given the speed of the repatriation, the fact that it was a Sunday (with all government offices closed) and the presence of the Prefect at the time of departure, it was taken as read that all the documents would be regularised the following day, which was the case. Under normal circumstances, for a person other than a VIP, the body would not be transported until the Monday. However, on that day all the French authorities required for the repatriation of the body were present at the hospital.

"You have shown me two documents in your statement folder, reference OD137 (Folder 27) FCO Docs: 'Complete copy of the death certificate' and 'Mortuary Pass'. You have also shown me a document marked D 100 (UK58), the official record of the placing of the body in the coffin. These are the documents I just mentioned to you[a], which are necessary for the repatriation of a body and which must be presented at the airport before the body leaves French soil and also at the country of destination. Documents OD137, as you can see, were completed later."[271]

Alan Puxley, Vice-President Operations, Kenyon International: 16 Jun 04
Statement: **Jury Didn't Hear**:

"Repatriation normally requires the following documents. A Certificate of Death, an Embalming Certificate, a declaration that the remains are contained in a container suitable for international Transportation. Also required is a copy of the deceased Passport, or a Laisse Passer, which is a Mortuary passport. Sometimes a Freedom from Infection certificate known as a F.F.I is also required. Any document should be translated for the funeral director into the language of the destination country.

"For a British subject, then once the Embassy have been notified of death they enter the fact in a register kept at the embassy. They often provide a bone-fide translation of the documents received by the funeral director repatriating. The correct translation and the right details are very important on these documents. Embassies then issue a Consular or Mortuary Certificate, which is officially stamped. This also forms part of the documents accompanying the deceased. Additionally accompanying the body may be a funeral directors certificate stating the coffin contains the deceased and their clothing, listed personal effects etc. Finally an 'Airwaybill' (one word). The airwaybill is needed because anything flown as cargo requires it in all cases to track it.

"There is great importance for the funeral director to identify the documents with the body and ensure they are present and accurate. It is also important to identify and know who initially took the deceased into their custody, such as a mortuary technician, police officer, coroner's officer or another funeral director. Sometimes a coroner's officer is appointed, such as a police officer, or funeral director to ensure that the repatriation is carried out smoothly. They would remain with the deceased to the destination. The documents should remain with the coffin.

"Once the deceased has arrived in the U.K there would be a requirement for these documents to be taken to the Registrar of Births, Deaths and Marriages to issue a Certificate of no liability to register the death for burials if the coroner does not wish to assume jurisdiction. This would be because the burial certificate in the country of origin, had already registered the death.

---

[a] The documents that Launay had "just mentioned" included: "authority for the transportation of the body issued by the Prefecture of Police". This document – which is referenced as UK57 (see below) – is not among the documents Launay has described being shown.

"However if the coroner is involved then a Coroners order for burial is issued. Funeral directors work to the laws and regulations in the country concerned, and once the body is in the country of destination those laws and regulations apply. There is little if no overlap and there are no international agreements to ensure uniformity between countries."[272]

Comment: Alan Puxley, who is very experienced[a], has outlined what documents are required during a repatriation:

- a death certificate
- an embalming certificate
- a transportation declaration regarding the suitability of the coffin
- "the deceased Passport, or a Laisse Passer, which is a Mortuary passport"
- "a Freedom from Infection certificate known as a F.F.I."
- "Consular or Mortuary Certificate"
- "a funeral directors certificate"
- an airwaybill
- "a Coroners order for burial"[b].

In addition Patrick Launay mentions the need for:

- the burial certificate
- police authority for transportation.

Paget showed the following documents to Launay:

- death certificate
- mortuary pass
- "record of the placing of the body in the coffin".[c]

Clive Leverton – in evidence not heard by the jury – has stated: "our staff or myself received none of this paperwork".

Clive gives two completely different explanations for Levertons not having any documentation:

1) "I presumed someone else was dealing [with it]"
2) "the requirement for all concerned to carry out a professional and very fast repatriation".

The first explanation – "someone else was dealing" – appears to presume that there was paperwork, but Levertons just didn't get to see any.

The second – professionalism and speed – raises a very important question: How do you achieve a "professional" repatriation without any documentation?

----

[a] In his statement Puxley said: "For 25 years I was General Manager at Will Case and Partners ... who are registered funeral directors". He also stated that he had worked at Kenyons since 2001.

[b] Burton has stated that this was completed – see previous chapter. It was not available to the inquest jury.

[c] These same three documents were also shown by Paget to Jean Monceau – see Embalming chapter.

David Green, who comments on the lack of an embalming certificate, says it was because "[Diana] was repatriated on a private flight".

Launay said: "I asked Mr Jauze for the documents relating to the repatriation". Launay was apparently only given the one document – the burial certificate – possibly from "Mr Jauze or Mr Plumet". Launay then says: "it is likely that I gave it to the English funeral directors". But Clive – as discussed above – said: "There was nothing.... We did not receive these papers".

Launay also stated: "I produce a copy of this [burial certificate] as my exhibit PL11". What did Paget do with this critical document – it never appeared at the inquest?[a]

Launay – without explaining how Jauze reacted when he "asked ... for the documents relating to the repatriation" – then comes up with explanations for the lack of documentation:

- "the speed of the repatriation"
- "it was a Sunday (with all government offices closed)"
- "the presence of the Prefect [of police] at the time of departure".[bc]

Launay has come up with different reasons than Clive or Green for the paperwork breakdown – except he agrees with Clive on speed.

We now have 6 reasons – from 3 people – for there being no documents: someone else dealing; speed; to be professional; a private flight; it was Sunday; the Prefect was there.

Launay next states under oath: "it was taken as read that all the documents would be regularised the following day, which was the case".

If this "was the case" – the documents were "regularised" on Monday, 1 September 1997 – then: Where are they?

There are three possibilities:

1) there was no completion of documents on – not just the Monday – on any day

2) there was completion, but Paget have not tried to get – or have had withheld from them – the documents

3) there was completion and Paget have the documents, but have suppressed them.

Effectively, in the repatriation of Diana, Princess of Wales, there are 7 out of 12 documents missing: embalming certificate; coffin transportation

---

[a] Issues regarding the burial certificate have already been dealt with in the Embalming chapter.

[b] This was also a theme of the Embalming chapter – the Prefect was present so the law didn't apply.

[c] Launay later states: "All the French authorities required for the repatriation of the body were present at the hospital".

declaration; FFI; Consular certificate; funeral directors certificate; airwaybill; coroner's burial order.

Operation Paget – from the statements of Plumet, Jauze[a], Launay and Monceau – have 5 of the documents[b]: the burial certificate, death certificate, police authority, mortuary pass and the coffin placement record.[c] There are concerns with regard to the police authority document – these are addressed below.

Only one document out of the 12 was seen by the jury investigating the death – the death certificate.

This evidence raises a critical question: Why is it that this documentation would exist for a normal citizen, but it doesn't exist for Princess Diana?[d]

Clive stated: "This paperwork would normally be required ... to enable repatriation to be allowed."

Why wasn't Clive Leverton asked about this missing documentation at the inquest?

The evidence from the previous chapter has shown that the repatriation was controlled by the royals, and that they took illegal control of Diana's body. The evidence above now reveals that the royals presided over and controlled an illegal repatriation – a repatriation that was not carried out within the law.

I suggest that there is a connection between this illegal repatriation and the illegal claim to jurisdiction over the body. The evidence points to the royals being obsessed with taking control of Diana's body as quickly as possible and this approach led to a complete failure to abide by the law in their conduct of the repatriation.

Colin Tebbutt, Diana's Driver and Security: 5 Jul 04 Statement: **Jury Didn't Hear**:

"I have been asked specifically whether I ever took control of any paperwork relating to the Princess of Wales that day. I can say that I did not see or take possession of any papers relating to the Princess of Wales. I am aware that Superintendent Kingsmill and others were involved in writing and signing of documents, however I do not believe that Mr Kingsmill returned to the UK with the body, and I can only assume that paperwork would have been handed to the family."[273]

---

[a] See Jauze and Plumet statements below.

[b] This is not divulged in the Paget Report – it comes from the leaked documents, published in *The Documents* book.

[c] Even though Clive Leverton stated that he never saw the death certificate, there is no record of Paget showing him that document after that – even though they showed the death certificate and other documents to Launay and Monceau. This may be because Clive was interviewed in 2004, whereas Monceau and Launay were interviewed later in the investigation – Monceau in late 2005 and Launay in 2006.

[d] There was also a lack of documentation for the embalming – see earlier.

Comment: Colin Tebbutt has stated under oath that he saw "Superintendent Kingsmill and others were involved in writing and signing of documents".

Kingsmill, head of royalty protection, was in Paris on behalf of Prince Charles.[a] It is obvious that Kingsmill should have been cross-examined at the inquest regarding his role in the events. This never occurred – no evidence was heard from him and Kingsmill also has never been interviewed by any police investigation.

No documents with Kingsmill's signature on have ever surfaced.

Police Authority

Jean-Claude Plumet has provided an account stating that a police authority allowing transportation was completed by a police "Commissaire" at the hospital on 31 August 1997.

Jean-Claude Plumet, PFG Director of Paris Agencies, Paris: 4 Nov 05 Paget description of Statement: **Jury Didn't Hear**:

"Around the same time [before 10.00 a.m.] a male 'Commissaire de Police' also telephoned him a number of times at his office. Mr Plumet does not recall the name of this 'Commissaire', but he appeared to be in charge and appeared to have been appointed to liaise directly with PFG.

"For the comprehension of the reader, and upon clarification by Mr Plumet, the rank of 'Commissaire' in the French Police, is equivalent to the rank of Commander in the Metropolitan Police Service. Because on Sunday the Town Hall and the Police Administration Offices were closed, Mr Plumet asked the 'Commissaire' to produce a statement declaring that he authorised Mr Plumet to have the body moved to the United Kingdom. In Mr Plumet's opinion, this 'Commissaire' would have probably also given authority to embalm, and would also have dealt with all the issues surrounding the body of Dodi Al Fayed.

"Because on Sunday the Town Hall and the Police Administration Offices were closed, Mr Plumet had to contact Mme Celadon at the 'Operations Mortuaires de la Prefecture de Police', which translates as the Police Administration Offices for Funeral Issues, on Monday 1st September 1997. This was in order that the relevant documentation could be 'regularised', that is, to have it completed retrospectively."[274]

Jean-Claude Plumet: 4 Nov 05 Paget description of Statement: **Jury Didn't Hear**:

"[Plumet] then recalls travelling to the Pitié Salpêtrière hospital, nearby, in company of Mr Jauze. The hospital was closed off, and Mr Plumet explained

---

[a] See earlier Keith Moss statement.

423

that he had to contact the 'Commissaire' for the doors to be opened to them and for them to be allowed in....

"It was around this time, before the arrival of HRH the Prince of Wales, that the 'Commissaire' gave Mr Plumet the paperwork he required, namely a Police statement allowing him to proceed with the necessary arrangements to have the Princess of Wales returned to the United Kingdom. Mr Plumet was shown document D99 from the French Dossier in this investigation, otherwise registered as document UK57 in the Operation Paget Office Manager system, and confirms that this is the Police statement, a copy of which was provided to him, allowing him to proceed. Document UK57 is in fact a Police statement signed by Police Commandant Jean-Claude Mulès. Despite further discussions with Mr Plumet it still remains unclear whether Commandant Mulès was the 'Commissaire' that Mr Plumet dealt with, or simply representing the 'Commissaire'. The statement is signed by Mr Mulès "P/O le Commissaire Divisionaire" which is an abbreviation of "Pour Ordre le Commissaire Divisionaire", which in turn translates as "pp Operational Command Unit Commander.

"Mr Plumet clarifies that upon his arrival at the hospital, he asked to see the 'Commissaire'. He explains that he and Mr Jauze then went up onto the floor where the Princess of Wales body was....

"Other than himself and Mr Jauze, Mr Patrick Launay of PFG was also at the hospital and was making all the necessary arrangements, but Mr Plumet does not recall if he arrived there before or after him.

"Mr Plumet's role at the hospital was to supervise, delegate, and ensure the transfer of the body. Mr Launay was in charge of transport and staff issues. Mr Jauze did not have any role, other than being on hand if further assistance was needed....

"Mr Plumet believes that Mr Launay accompanied the coffin to Villacoublay airport at around 1700hrs, while he and Mr Jauze returned to their office."[275]

Gérard Jauze, PFG Branch Director, Paris: 21 Mar 06 Statement: **Jury Didn't Hear**:

"Having left the IML, Mr Plumet and I drove to the Pitié Salpêtrière hospital. Mr Plumet says that from memory, it was hard to get into the hospital because of the press, the public and the police. However, my recollection is different. We had to go to the hospital as representatives of PFG, as PFG had been entrusted with her repatriation.

"From memory, with the exception of the embalmers, I think that we were the only representatives from PFG at the hospital to arrive before the coffin. I remember that there were lots of people at the hospital. Together with Mr Plumet, I went upstairs to where the body of the Princess of Wales was....

"After that day, M. Plumet has said to me that he had met a French police officer to whom he spoke that morning, but I do not even remember that episode."[276]

Gérard Jauze, PFG Branch Director, Paris: 21 Mar 06 Statement: **Jury Didn't Hear**:
"You have shown me a copy of document UK57, page D99 of the French judicial dossier. I have never seen that document, but M. Plumet should have seen it. It allows for a funeral following a violent death and enables authority to be obtained for transportation."[277]

Comment: Jean-Claude Plumet has given evidence regarding an unnamed police Commissaire.

Plumet states that this Commissaire gave him – at the hospital – "a Police statement allowing him to proceed with the necessary arrangements to have the Princess of Wales returned to the United Kingdom".

Plumet's account is:
- before 10.00 a.m. "a male 'Commissaire de Police' ... telephoned him a number of times at his office"
- "Plumet asked the 'Commissaire' to produce a statement declaring that he authorised Mr Plumet to have the body moved to the United Kingdom"
- "the hospital was closed off, and Mr Plumet ... had to contact the 'Commissaire' for the doors to be opened ... for them to be allowed in"
- "upon [Plumet's] arrival at the hospital, he asked to see the 'Commissaire'"
- at the hospital "the 'Commissaire' gave Mr Plumet ... a Police statement allowing him to proceed ... to have the Princess of Wales returned to the United Kingdom"
- Plumet "confirms that [UK57] is the Police statement" that allowed repatriation
- UK57 is signed by Mulès. "Plumet ... remains unclear whether Commandant Mulès was the 'Commissaire' that Mr Plumet dealt with, or simply representing the 'Commissaire'"
- "Mr Plumet had to contact Mme Celadon ... on Monday 1st September 1997 ... in order that the relevant documentation could be 'regularised'".

There are several concerns relating to Plumet's evidence:

1) There were other people who should have seen this UK57 document on the day – Jauze, Launay, Clive – but none of them actually saw it.
- Jauze: "I have never seen that document [UK57]"
- Launay: "I asked Mr Jauze for the documents relating to the repatriation. I was provided with the burial certificate.... Normally you have to have authority for the transportation of the body issued by the Prefecture of Police.... It was taken as read that all the documents would be regularised the following day, which was the case."
- Clive: "our staff or myself received none of this paperwork at the time of the repatriation of Diana Princess of Wales, nor any since".

This raises the question: If Plumet received this document from the Commissaire on the day, what did he do with it?

2) Even though Jauze was with Plumet, he has a different account of events, with no recall at all of any dealings with a Commissaire.

a) Jauze says: "Mr Plumet says that from memory, it was hard to get into the hospital because of the press, the public and the police. However, my recollection is different. We had to go to the hospital as representatives of PFG, as PFG had been entrusted with her repatriation."

Jauze has been told – presumably by Plumet – that the reason it was hard to get in to the hospital was "the press, the public and the police". Plumet's account to the UK police was that "the hospital was closed off".

Plumet then said he "had to contact the 'Commissaire' for the doors to be opened" but Jauze indicates that there was no problem because they were there "as representatives of PFG".

I suggest that Jauze's account is common sense: Plumet and Jauze were there as the funeral directors "entrusted with [Diana's] repatriation" – it would be logical that they would have access to the hospital, without needing to contact a Commissaire. One would think that, had Plumet and Jauze been shut out of the hospital, then Jauze – as a funeral director for Diana – would have remembered that.

b) Plumet: "Mr Plumet clarifies that upon his arrival at the hospital, he asked to see the 'Commissaire'. He explains that he and Mr Jauze then went up onto the floor where the Princess of Wales body was."

Jauze: "I remember that there were lots of people at the hospital. Together with Mr Plumet, I went upstairs to where the body of the Princess of Wales was".

Plumet says "he asked to see the 'Commissaire'" before "he and Mr Jauze ... went up onto the floor where the ... body was". Jauze makes no mention of the Commissaire – "with Mr Plumet, I went upstairs to ... the body".

c) Plumet: "the 'Commissaire' gave Mr Plumet ... a Police statement allowing him to proceed" and "[UK57] is [that] Police statement".

Jauze: "I have never seen that document [UK57], but M. Plumet should have seen it".

Jauze recorded the movements of Plumet and himself: "Having left the room where the Princess was, M. Plumet and I waited for the VIPs. We went downstairs and back up again, and went back and forth, but we did not return to the room where the Princess of Wales was.... Prince Charles thanked us, and we waited while they paid their last respects.... The coffin was ... transported to Villacoublay airport.... M. Plumet and I remained at the hospital, and we were able to catch our breath."

In summary, Plumet describes three events at the hospital relating to the Commissaire: "the hospital was closed off" and he "had to contact the 'Commissaire' for the doors to be opened"; "upon his arrival ... he asked to see the 'Commissaire'"; "the 'Commissaire' gave Mr Plumet ... a Police statement [UK57] allowing him to proceed" with the repatriation.[a]

Jauze, who was with Plumet, has no recall of any of the three events, no recall of a Commissaire at all and no recall of the hospital being "closed off".[b]

The evidence from Jauze indicates that the two, Plumet and Jauze, stayed together at the hospital and he has recorded their movements – there is no mention of any interaction with a Commissaire.

In contrast, Plumet's evidence includes minimal references to his movements, outside of the visit to Diana's room – see above. Plumet instead describes the interaction with the Commissaire – "the 'Commissaire' gave Mr Plumet the paperwork he required" – and their roles at the hospital – see above. Later Plumet says "he was downstairs when HRH the Prince of Wales arrived" and he finishes up: "[Plumet] and Mr Jauze returned to their office".

3) Plumet said: "This 'Commissaire' ... appeared to have been appointed to liaise directly with PFG".

Yet there is no evidence from either Jauze or Launay[a] – both key PFG employees – confirming the Commissaire's existence.

---

[a] Plumet's account appears to be that the Commissaire gave him the UK57 document straight after the arrival of Jauze and himself at the hospital. There are difficulties in Plumet's evidence because it is not first-hand, but instead a Paget description of what he said. After describing the handover of the UK57 document, Paget says: "Mr Plumet clarifies that upon his arrival at the hospital, he asked to see the 'Commissaire'. He explains that he and Mr Jauze then went up onto the floor where the Princess of Wales body was." Plumet's account is that earlier in the day he requested the Commissaire to organise the document: Over the phone before 10 a.m. "Plumet asked the 'Commissaire' to produce a statement declaring that he authorised Mr Plumet to have the body moved to the United Kingdom". It's logical that Plumet would then seek out the document straight after his relatively late arrival – at 4.50 p.m., held up by events at the IML (see Part 3). This would have involved meeting up with the Commissaire straight after arrival and receiving the document. The evidence from both Jauze and Plumet is that they visited Diana's room together – Plumet indicates that happened after the Commissaire interaction. Jauze recalls visiting the room straightaway – this is common sense because they were the funeral directors and viewing the body would be a priority. Jauze has no recall of interaction with the Commissaire after arriving at the hospital and prior to viewing the body. In fact, Jauze has no recall at all of the Commissaire.
[b] Gérard Jauze has said: "After that day, M. Plumet has said to me that he had met a French police officer to whom he spoke that morning, but I do not ... remember that episode." Plumet appears to have raised the matter after the event – "after that day" – but Jauze doesn't say how long after, but he does say: "I do not ... remember that episode".

4) Plumet indicates that the "police statement" was the only document required for repatriation – "the paperwork he required, namely a Police statement allowing him to proceed with the" repatriation – yet the general evidence is that there were 11 French documents required – see earlier.

In contrast, earlier in his statement, Plumet had said he "had to contact Mme Celadon ... on Monday 1st September 1997. This was in order that the relevant documentation could be_'regularised', that is, to have it completed retrospectively."

Plumet doesn't tell us which documents were "regularised".[b] There are only 5 documents – see above – known to exist: the burial certificate, death certificate, police authority, mortuary pass and the coffin placement record.

We know from the general evidence that the burial certificate and death certificate were both raised on 31 August 1997. It is Plumet's later assertion that the police authority was also completed on the day – courtesy of the Commissaire.

That leaves just two documents – the mortuary pass and the coffin placement record.

I suggest that when one considers that Diana never went near a mortuary in France – see Chapters 1 to 3 – it may be that the existence of a "mortuary pass" is possibly dubious.

Whichever way, it would seem that the police authority enabling repatriation would be the document that one would really be seeking to "regularise", had it not been completed before the body left.[c] It will be

---

[a] Launay was actually a key person in the repatriation. In his statement Launay said: "In 1997, I was in charge of a regional office that I had established called PFGTI (Pompes Funèbres Générales Transports Internationaux), which deals with the importation and exportation of bodies...." In contrast, Plumet's role in PFG was not specifically dedicated to repatriations – Plumet's statement: "In 1997 Mr Plumet's responsibilities centred primarily on a 'commercial role', management and administration of personnel." Launay's evidence shows that he asked Jauze for the documents. This would have been because he was the PFG representative that stayed with the UK team – Clive, Green and Fry – and Launay would have been the person who would pass the documents on to them. His evidence though is that no documents – bar the burial certificate – existed. Sources: Patrick Launay, Witness Statement, 21 March 2006, reproduced in *The Documents* book, p510 (UK Edition); Jean-Claude Plumet, Witness Statement, 4 November 2005, reproduced in *The Documents* book, p469 (UK Edition)

[b] In this context, Mme Celadon is another person who has never been interviewed in any of the investigations.

[c] Launay said in his statement: "In France there is a strict requirement for the presence of a police authority (a sworn person) when the coffin is closed and that person draws up a statement." It appears that this document was also "regularised", but there is less emphasis on it in the general evidence. Source: Patrick Launay,

suggested below that when the complete available evidence is analysed, it would appear that the police authority was not completed on 31 August 1997, but instead was one – maybe the only one – of the key documents "regularised" after the event.

5) Plumet describes being "telephoned ... a number of times at his office" by the Commissaire, before 10 a.m.[a]

Plumet describes the content of these calls:

- "Plumet asked the 'Commissaire' to produce a statement" required for repatriation
- "in Mr Plumet's opinion, this 'Commissaire' would have probably also given authority to embalm"
- the Commissaire "would also have dealt with all the issues surrounding the body of Dodi Al Fayed".

Of the three points above, Plumet is only definite about his request for the "police statement" required for repatriation.

The other two points are more vague: "would have probably" authorised embalming and "would also have" dealt with Dodi.

There is substantial evidence relating to the embalming[b], but there is no claim – outside of this passing reference by Plumet – of any involvement in the authorisation by a police Commissaire.

There is also a considerable amount of evidence regarding Dodi's repatriation – particularly the very significant stoppage at the IML in the afternoon[c] – but again, no evidence of any involvement from a police Commissaire, other than this passing reference from Plumet.

6) Plumet's evidence is that the Commissaire "telephoned ... a number of times" in the morning, then when he and Jauze arrived at the hospital he had to contact the 'Commissaire' for the doors to be opened", then once in the hospital "he asked to see the 'Commissaire'" and "the 'Commissaire' gave ... [him the] Police statement [UK57]".

Yet, even with all that interaction, when Paget shows Plumet the UK57 document, which is signed by Jean-Claude Mulès, Plumet "still remains

---

Witness Statement, 21 March 2006, reproduced in *The Documents* book, p516 (UK Edition)

[a] Plumet's account of being called "a number of times" is reminiscent of Claude Roulet's assertions of repeated phone calls outside Chez Benoît – Part 1 – and at the IML – Part 3. As with Roulet, it will be shown below that again there is nothing to corroborate Plumet's evidence on this.

[b] See Chapter 2.

[c] See Part 3. When a problem cropped up the Head of the Judicial Police, Patrick Riou, got involved – not a Commissaire.

unclear whether Commandant Mulès was the 'Commissaire' that [he] dealt with".[a]

Paget officers DS Adrian Grater and DS Philip Easton interviewed Plumet in November 2005[278], then 8 months later, in July 2006, these very same officers – Easton and Grater – interviewed Jean-Claude Mulès. During his interview Mulès was not asked about any interaction with Plumet.

The question is: Why is it that Easton and Grater – who took the Plumet evidence – didn't ask Mulès: a) whether he was in communication with Plumet on 31 August 1997; and b) the following questions regarding form UK57, which was signed by him?

Mulès should have been shown the document UK57 and asked:
-   Was he present at the La Pitié Salpêtrière Hospital in the afternoon of 31 August 1997?
-   Did he hand the UK57 document to Plumet at the hospital on 31 August 1997?
-   If not, then when was UK57 completed?

At the inquest Scott Baker was in possession of both Plumet and Mulès' Paget statements, yet these statements were not read out to the jury. Also, Mulès was cross-examined at the inquest, yet was not asked about Plumet or UK57. Plumet was not cross-examined at the inquest – this meant that the jury heard no evidence at all from him and in fact were never told that he existed.

Why is this? The repatriation of Diana is central to this case – as the previous chapter has shown – yet critical questions that could have helped clear up issues regarding its legality, have not been asked by the British police or by the inquest lawyers.

The reality is that earlier in the day Mulès had been appointed by the Director of the Judicial Police, Patrick Riou, to run the Brigade Criminelle investigation into the crash.[b] I suggest that Mulès' role of being the on-the-ground Commander of the crash investigation could have precluded him from being directly involved on the day in the repatriation of Princess Diana, which at that stage would have been, at most, a peripheral issue.

There is actually no evidence that places Mulès at the hospital on the afternoon of 31 August 1997 and the fact that he signed UK57 is in itself an indication that the document was drawn up after the repatriation and it did

---

[a] In light of this, it is notable that Plumet was able to remember the name of "Mme Celadon at the 'Operations Mortuaires de la Prefecture de Police'", who played a far lesser role in the events than the Commissaire.

[b] See Part 3, section headed "Role of the Brigade Criminelle" and inquest transcripts: 5 Feb 08: 33.6 and 62.25.

not accompany the body, as was legally required.[a] This is supported by the earlier evidence from Clive Leverton – there was no documentation with Diana's body: "our staff or myself received none of this paperwork at the time of the repatriation".

I suggest that Mulès' role would not have included phoning a funeral director "a number of times" and also would not have included visiting the hospital in the late afternoon.

Plumet has indicated that the Commissaire phone calls were made before 10 a.m., yet Mulès was present at the Henri Paul autopsy from 8.20 a.m. until its conclusion at 10 a.m.[b]

The only evidence that indicates Mulès' role in the repatriation on the day comes from Plumet and Mulès' signature on the UK57 document. The evidence in this section however indicates that the UK57 document was not completed ahead of the repatriation – but rather was retrospective – and Plumet has lied about the involvement of an unnamed Commissaire, in order to "legalise" a repatriation that was conducted illegally.

7) Plumet's evidence is not in the form of a sworn or signed statement, at his request. This is a concern which has already been addressed in the Embalming chapter.

It is noteworthy that Operation Paget showed document UK57 to Plumet and Jauze, but failed to show it to Launay[c] or Clive[d] – even though both of them were involved in the repatriation, and had expressed concerns about the lack of documentation.

Form UK57 should have accompanied the body with Levertons, but the evidence is that Levertons never saw it. Even if the document was raised after the event – which the evidence suggests is the case – one would have expected a copy to have gone to Levertons, but the evidence from Clive is that no documentation had been received since the repatriation.

This indicates again that the document was raised later in order to achieve legality in France, with maybe little or no thought going to the situation in the UK.[e]

---

[a] The earlier general evidence showed that Prefect of Police, Philippe Massoni, was at the hospital prior to the repatriation. Massoni would have been on hand if a document had been there to sign, but it is not his signature that is on the document.
[b] See Part 3. Also inquest document: INQ0041596.
[c] Launay was interviewed on the same day as Jauze, 21 March 2006.
[d] Clive was interviewed in 2004, possibly before Paget came by the UK57 document. There is however no evidence that Clive was ever shown the document, even before his inquest cross-examination in 2007.
[e] The evidence from Plumet and Jauze showed that the document UK57 was "D99 from the French Dossier". D99 is a 31 August 1997 reference number, but I suggest

In summary, the police authorisation prior to repatriation is an important document towards enabling the repatriation to be legal – had it been completed at the time. It appears that Plumet has lied about the existence of this Commissaire – he has introduced evidence of phone calls prior to 10 a.m., where he requested the form from the Commissaire in order to support his later evidence that the Commissaire gave him the completed form at the hospital.

There is no evidence – outside of Plumet – that this document handover occurred. I instead suggest that Plumet's evidence – both, of the early phone calls and the document handover – is fictional.[a]

Plumet has possibly been requested to present this account, to provide "legality" to what was an illegal repatriation of Diana, Princess of Wales, completed under immense time pressure from the royals.

The royal world appears to be one of strict protocols and systems. One would expect thorough documentation – all the i's dotted, and all the t's crossed.

But that is not what we see here: When it came to their illegal repatriation of Princess Diana, the documentation is either non-existent or a shambolic mess.

Out of 12 documents required, the jury at the inquest into Diana's death got to see just one.

Why is this?

French Involvement

There is conflicting evidence on the degree of French involvement in the repatriation of Princess Diana.

Patrick Riou, Head of the Judicial Police, Paris: Statement 16 Nov 06 read out 21 Nov 07: 54.16:

"The arrangements for the repatriation of the bodies were subject to discussions between the Prefect of Police and the British authorities."

Philippe Massoni, Prefect of Police, Paris: British Statement: 14 Nov 06 read out 21 Nov 07: 60.9:

"The arrangements for the transfer of the body were the result of a decision between our two governments. It was my responsibility to implement it."

Martine Monteil, Head of Brigade Criminelle: 15 Nov 06 Statement: **Jury Didn't Hear**:

---

that the evidence in Part 3 has already shown that document numbers were changed and refiled where "necessary" during the French investigation. In the Plumet-Jauze descriptions of this document, there is no mention of the date. It is obvious that this document should have been shown at the inquest, but that never happened.

[a] Earlier evidence in the Embalming chapter has shown that Plumet would also have been aware that the embalming was conducted illegally.

Question: "What was your role in the repatriation of the Princess of Wales and of Dodi Al Fayed?

Answer: "The police dealt with registering the deaths with the registrars of births, deaths and marriages at the Town Hall for the 13th arrondissement and the British Embassy with regard to the Princess of Wales and with the Town Hall of the 8th arrondissement in respect of Dodi Al Fayed. It was the British authorities that took the necessary decisions for the repatriation of the Princess's body. Mr Al Fayed took care of the repatriation of his son's body. It is not up to the Judicial Police to deal with the arrangements in respect of the repatriation of bodies." [279]

Maud Coujard, Deputy Public Prosecutor, Paris: 20 Nov 07: 16.9:

Burnett: Q. Did you have any further involvement with the treatment of the bodies or their subsequent repatriation to the United Kingdom?

A. Well, I had no decision to make in that regard, but I must have been made aware that the bodies were going to be repatriated to the United Kingdom.

Anthony Mather, Asst Comptroller, Lord Chamberlain's Office: 22 Nov 07: 86.16:

Hough: Q. Did you yourself, at any stage, communicate with any officials in France about the repatriation or about the arrangements for the body?

A. None, none whatsoever.

Comment: The evidence from the French witnesses is:

-   Riou: "the repatriation ... [was] subject to discussions between the Prefect of Police [Massoni] and the British authorities"

-   Massoni: "arrangements for [repatriation] were the result of a decision between our two governments. It was my responsibility to implement it"

-   Monteil: "it was the British authorities that took the necessary decisions for the repatriation of the Princess's body"

-   Coujard: "I had no decision to make in that regard".

Prefect of Police, Philippe Massoni, was certainly present when Diana was removed from the hospital – see earlier evidence: Launay, Jauze. Massoni has stated that it was his "responsibility to implement" the repatriation. That may be, but the general evidence is that he had virtually nothing to do with it on the day – it was carried out by PFG and Levertons.[a] Massoni's closest involvement in the implementation appears to have been the supply of a police escort and clearing the route between the hospital and the airport – see earlier. The key involvement by the French police that could have helped make the repatriation legal – the completion of the appropriate

---

[a] Earlier evidence has shown that both PFG and Levertons were instructed by the royals, not the French police.

paperwork to accompany the body – does not appear to have occurred – see earlier.[a]

Riou says the decisions were made from "discussions between the Prefect of Police [Massoni] and the British authorities". Massoni conflicts with this: it was a "decision between our two governments". Monteil says: "it was the British authorities that took the necessary decisions".

So from three police chiefs – Police, Judicial Police, Brigade Criminelle – we have three completely different assertions as to who made the repatriation decisions.

We already know from earlier evidence that none of these is right and the decisions were made from Balmoral. Monteil was the closest – "the British authorities" – but her account was not heard at the inquest.

Hermetic Sealing[b]

Princess Diana's coffin was not hermetically sealed and there is conflicting evidence on why this didn't happen.

Clive Leverton, Royal Funeral Director: 22 Nov 07: 70.6:
Hough: Q. Did you consider it necessary to seal the coffin using its hermetic seal function?
A. We did not consider it necessary. We were under extreme pressure time-wise and we knew that the – sorry, can you say that again, please?
Q. Did you have to seal the coffin hermetically?
A. No, we did not consider it necessary.

Clive Leverton: 13 Jul 04 Statement: **Jury Didn't Hear**:
"Hermetically sealing means placing the lid on the coffin, either metal soldering or use of a plastic sealant all around the gap.
"Specific to the Diana Princess of Wales coffin, it was not considered necessary to seal in this way; the zinc lid and the wooden lid were placed on top it was then secured by several screws."[280]

David Green, Embalmer, UK: 13 Jul 04 Statement: **Jury Didn't Hear**:
"I also took a toolbox with other items used for other aspects of funeral directing such as sealing the coffin. The Princess of Wales coffin was not hermetically sealed because it was a private flight and no procedure such as those for commercial flights was required. Nothing or no one dictated that this must be done, and there was no leakage that made it necessary."[281]

David Green: 17 Sep 04 Statement: **Jury Didn't Hear**:
"She was repatriated on a private flight, and ... therefore the rules of hermetically sealing of the coffin and embalming with the appropriate certificate did not apply."[282]

---

[a] Plumet provided evidence of the involvement of a police Commissaire, but other evidence indicates this never actually occurred.
[b] Hermetic sealing of a coffin makes it airtight.

Comment: Three main reasons have been put forward for not hermetically sealing Diana's coffin:
- Clive: "we were under extreme pressure time-wise"[a]
- Green: "it was a private flight"
- Green: "there was no leakage".

Role of Stephen Donnelly

There is conflicting evidence regarding British Vice-Consul Stephen Donnelly's role in the repatriation.

Keith Moss, British Consul General, Paris: 22 Nov 07: 20.6:

Hough: Q. We have heard that you were liaising with everybody at the British end and you also had connection with various French officials and that you were extremely busy. Were you involved with the arrangements for the repatriation of the body and for the start of the arrangements leading to the funeral?

A. Yes.

Q. In that role, did you have to liaise with Stephen Donnelly?

A. Yes, I did.

Q. What was his role?

A. Steven Donnelly was, and I think still is, a senior Vice-Consul, a locally engaged Vice-Consul, ie not a Foreign Office member of staff but a locally engaged British national who has been working in the Consulate for many years and was the head of the protection section that I described earlier, ie the section responsible for the road accidents, the deaths, the prisoners, the football hooligans and so on. So he was the most experienced member of staff for that type of issue. I knew he was at home and so I telephoned him.

Q. Did you, along with him, make plans relating to the flying in of the Prince of Wales?

A. The actual arrangements for the flight were done by others, not by us.

Q. But you liaised with those who were making those arrangements, did you?

A. Yes.

Q. Was it you or Mr Donnelly who contacted the French undertakers, PFG?

A. I think it was Steven Donnelly.

Q. Did he also contact Levertons, the Royal undertakers?

A. I am not sure.

Q. Did you have any contact with them?

A. I did during the day, but I cannot recall asking for them to be sent out.

Keith Moss: 22 Oct 04 Statement: **Jury Didn't Hear**:

---

[a] The issue of time pressure has been covered in the Royal Control chapter.

435

"Throughout the day, I had tasked Steven Donnelly to liaise with the Undertakers in France, PFG and the Royal Undertakers in the UK, Levertons. I would have asked him for guidance from time to time, with regards to detailed procedures around the repatriation of the body and whether any specific permissions were required."[283]

Stephen Donnelly, British Vice Consul, Paris: 22 Sep 05 Statement read out 17 Dec 07: 126.21:

"I have been asked if I made or received any instruction that day dealing with the repatriation of the Princess of Wales' body. No, I was not involved with the repatriation."

Jean-Claude Plumet, PFG Director of Paris Agencies, Paris: 4 Nov 05 Paget description of Statement: **Jury Didn't Hear**:

"You ask me if I know or if I knew Mr Steven Donnelly from the British Consulate in Paris. No."[284]

Patrick Launay, PFG Repatriation Director: 21 Mar 06 Statement: **Jury Didn't Hear**:

"You ask me if I remember getting a call from Mr Steven Donnelly of the British Consulate on Sunday 31 August 1997. I knew Mr Donnelly well, but I do not remember such a call. It is possible that there was contact, but I have no recollection of it."[285]

Gérard Jauze, PFG Branch Director, Paris: 21 Mar 06 Statement: **Jury Didn't Hear**:

"You ask me if I remember speaking to the British Consul General in Paris, Mr Keith Moss. I do not remember. I do not know if he would have wanted to speak to us, but I cannot tell you, I'm not sure.

"You ask me if I remember speaking to any English people. Once again, I do not remember."[286]

Comment: In his 2004 statement Keith Moss said: "I had tasked Steven Donnelly to liaise with ... PFG and ... Levertons".

This account is disputed by all three parties – Donnelly, PFG and Levertons.

Stephen Donnelly has said straight out: "No, I was not involved with the repatriation."

Plumet and Launay both have no recall of any contact with Donnelly on the day and Jauze cannot "remember speaking to any English people".

The general evidence from Clive, Keith and Green was that they were only in contact with Anthony Mather of the Lord Chamberlain's Office – see earlier.

It is significant that the repatriation evidence was scattered throughout the inquest – this made the jury's job very difficult. Moss was cross-examined on 22 November 2007, but the statement of Donnelly – who wasn't cross-examined – was held back until December 17. Ambassador Jay wasn't heard from until February the following year. In the 3½ weeks between Moss and

Donnelly's evidence the jury heard a considerable amount of witness testimony on other subjects – it would have been very unlikely that that jury would ever have been in a position to compare Moss and Donnelly's evidence side-by-side.

As for the evidence of Plumet, Jauze and Launay, the jury never heard any evidence at all from any of them, and would not have even been aware of their existence.

Clive was cross-examined on the same day as Moss – 22 November 2007 – but he was not asked about this subject.

Moss' false account of Donnelly's involvement in the repatriation dilutes the overwhelming evidence – see Chapter 3 – that there was complete royal control over events on the day. A picture is instead painted of Moss and Donnelly liaising with both lots of funeral directors.

The reality is that PFG received early instructions from the royals and Levertons were given instructions directly from the Lord Chamberlain's Office.

Presence of British Police

British police were present at the hospital.

Huguette Amarger, French Embalmer: 8 Mar 05 Statement read out 22 Nov 07: 94.2:

"Before I could start my [embalming] work, I was put out by seeing the Scotland Yard police officers putting black sticky tape over the blinds lowered over the windows....

Question: How do you know they were English police officers?

Answer: That was what everyone was saying, and I heard them speaking French with a British accent, saying that they had to protect themselves from journalists in the trees with infrared cameras."

Colin Tebbutt: 5 Jul 04 Statement: **Jury Didn't Hear**:

"At that point the Funeral Directors[a] immediately went into a side room and got dressed in what appeared to be protective clothing.

"Before they were allowed into the Hospital room, Inspector Peter Von-Heinz, the Personal Protection Officer for Prince Charles and his advance, went into the room to look at where the Prince of Wales would be taken. I explained the circumstances to him and he then spoke with the local French Police. He was a fluent French speaker.

---

[a] These are embalmers. Tebbutt referred to them as "funeral directors" in error – see Embalming chapter.

"The Hospital Funeral Directors were wearing gowns and facemasks.... The Funeral Directors went into the room and were joined by two female nurses...."[287]

Comment: Huguette Amarger, who carried out the French embalming, recalled "Scotland Yard police officers putting black sticky tape over the blinds" just before she started work.

Tebbutt also describes events just before the embalming: "Before [the embalmers] were allowed into the hospital room, Inspector Peter Von-Heinz, the Personal Protection Officer for Prince Charles and his advance, went into [Diana's] room". Tebbutt adds that Von-Heinz "was a fluent French speaker".

Tebbutt and Amarger both witnessed the presence of French-speaking Scotland Yard officers in Diana's room just before the embalming commenced.

Tebbutt states that the reason Von-Heinz and the "advance" officer entered the room was "to look at where the Prince of Wales would be taken".

That may be one of the reasons, but the question is: Why did Tebbutt say that these police officers went in "before [the embalmers] were allowed into the hospital room"?

It appears that at the time Amarger saw them they were "putting black sticky tape over the blinds". The officers told Amarger that "they had to protect themselves from journalists".

This event occurred at around 12.30 p.m. – about 5 hours ahead of when Charles was due to arrive.

Earlier evidence has shown that male police officers were not allowed in the room during the embalming – this makes it unlikely that these men were taking action to "protect themselves".

Why did these officers enter the room and apply the sticky tape just before the embalming?

I suggest that the purpose of the black sticky tape – a separate incident to the earlier blankets that had been set up[a] – was to absolutely ensure there could be no media footage or photos of anything to do with the embalming.

This is further evidence of royal involvement in the embalming process – Von-Heinz being a Charles bodyguard. This evidence reveals an awareness that a critical event was about to take place. Before the embalmers were allowed to proceed, Von-Heinz and the advance entered the room to secure it from any possible media intrusion – this is after steps had already been taken by Tebbutt and others to put blankets up for the same purpose.

Colin Tebbutt: 5 Jul 04 Statement: **Jury Didn't Hear**:

---

[a] See Embalming chapter.

"Superintendent Kingsmill arrived at the Hospital in company of a French Police Officer and the Princess of Wales' personal belongings that had been taken from the crash site...."[288]

Keith Moss: 22 Oct 04 Statement: **Jury Didn't Hear**:

"At around 1400hrs [2 p.m.] a meeting was called by the French Foreign Ministry Chief of Protocol, whose name I do not recall. Also in attendance were hospital staff, French Police Officials, Superintendent Kingsmill the then Head of British Royalty Protection and Inspector Ian Von Heinz, who was a member of HRH Prince of Wales' Protection Team. The purpose of this meeting was to make arrangements for the impending visit of HRH Prince of Wales, the security arrangements required and to develop a media strategy."[289]

Comment: In his evidence Tebbutt places the arrival of Kingsmill to the hospital after the embalming – which concluded around 1.30 p.m.[a]

Moss places Kingsmill in the 2 p.m. meeting.

This is further evidence that the embalming was completed before 2 p.m. – the embalming occurred before the arrival of Kingsmill, who was at the hospital for the 2 p.m. meeting.[b]

Use of British Embalmers[c]

Clive Leverton was accompanied by two embalmers – David Green and Bill Fry – when he headed to Paris.

The question here is: Why were two British embalmers sent to Paris?

The evidence from the Levertons is that they received no instructions with regard to embalming:

-   Clive: "never received any instruction to embalm her" – confirmed at inquest
-   Clive: "we were not told to go out embalm and return her, we were given no instructions as to how to prepare her" – statement
-   Clive: "I ... did not discuss preparation care ... with the family" – statement
-   Clive: "I did not receive instructions from the police, the coroner nor the coroners' officer at all concerning preservation care" – statement
-   Clive: "no specific instructions were given" – statement
-   Clive: "I did not ... receive any instructions from [Mather]" – statement

---

[a] See Embalming chapter.
[b] The timing of the embalming is discussed at length in the Embalming chapter.
[c] Much of the witness evidence referred to in this section is from the Role of Levertons section in the Royal Control chapter.

- Keith: "there was nothing else ... instructed during this [initial] conversation [with Mather]"
- Keith: "the question of embalming never cropped up with the Lord Chamberlains office, or anyone else"
- Keith: "we were not given any specific instructions of how to prepare in any way Diana's ... body"
- Keith: "I ... did not discuss preparation care ... with any family member"
- Keith: "I had no communication with or instruction from the British Police or the Coroner's office"
- Keith: "there were no instructions from the Lord Chamberlains office for me to pass onto Clive"
- Green: "I was given no instruction what to do before we left for France".

All up, Clive and Keith gave 11 denials of instructions in their statement evidence. I suggest that in itself could be odd – do they "protest too much"?

Clive gave statement evidence on some of the detail of Operation Overstudy: "For members of the royal family there is an operational plan.... It refers to the undertaker (myself or Keith) two assistants, the repatriation coffin, and equipment such as for embalming, being flown to the destination in one air force aircraft...."

The key words in Clive's account are "two assistants" – not two embalmers, but two assistants.[a] So why is it that in the case of Diana, Princess of Wales, this was changed to two embalmers?

The above evidence – the 11 denials – would suggest that, if there were no instructions, then Clive and Keith must have come up with this themselves. And that is precisely what Clive – who was the only Levertons representative cross-examined – testified:

Horwell: "The decision to take embalmers with you to Paris was yours and yours alone?" Clive: "Yes and my brother's; ours."

At the inquest, Clive provided unsolicited evidence on the process of enlisting the embalmers, Green and Fry.

Clive was asked by inquest lawyer, Jonathon Hough: "Was another embalmer involved called Bill Fry?" This was a simple "yes/no" question.

Clive's answer was: "Yes, in the event, I had to try to get hold of Bill because it was a bank holiday Sunday in August. David Green was camping on a farm in Dorset and we were having a hell of a job to get hold [of] him and getting him back to London, so I had to get hold of another embalmer in case I could not get hold of David."

---

[a] At the inquest Clive changed this to: "myself or my brother, who is now retired, two others, one of whom would be an embalmer and a third person".

Clive states here that Bill Fry was only called in because "we were having a hell of a job to get hold [of Green] and getting him back to London".

This appears to conflict with both Keith and Clive's police statements:

Keith: "I contacted Clive by telephone and informed him what I had been told by Mather. We agreed to meet at our office at Camden as soon as possible. I phoned David Green our embalmer and Clive contacted Bill Fry the other embalmer. I arrived at our office later that morning and met with Clive. We agreed that I would remain in London and he would go to Paris..... Clive, David, Bill, and the first call coffin and their equipment went to RAF Northolt."

Clive: "I had received a call [from Keith] at about 0645 a.m. on the Sunday morning whilst I was in Cheltenham. So I then travelled to my house in Crouch End, a 1 and ½ hour journey, and from there went to our office in Camden. I met up with Keith and Daniel at about 1000 a.m.... We had real trouble getting David back to the office from Dorset or Hampshire where he was at the time. He arrived just before we were due to leave the office. Bill was given a police escort part of the way from his home to our office."

This evidence shows that straight after Keith had been called by Mather at about 6.30 a.m., he called Clive. They "agreed to meet at [their] office at Camden as soon as possible" and Keith then "phoned David Green ... and Clive contacted Bill Fry". Clive then started driving from Cheltenham to his home in Crouch End and on to the meeting in Camden.

There is no delay between contacting Green and Fry – as was indicated in Clive's inquest account. It seems in fact that to minimise any delay, they split the job: "I phoned David Green our embalmer and Clive contacted Bill Fry".

Green states: "On Sunday the 31st August 1997 I was away in Hampshire when Keith Leverton contacted me. He informed me that Diana Princess of Wales had died in Paris and I should return to our office in Camden immediately. This I did and met up with Clive Leverton and Bill Fry whom I was to travel with on the RAF flight. I believe they used Bill as a backup in case I couldn't return in time for the 1 p.m. flight out. Bill however did come with us to assist in any case; he is also a qualified embalmer. I took with me a large case containing all the items required for embalming which I keep ready for use at any time."

Green's account indicates that he was told that Bill was a backup, but this is not reflected in the statements of Keith and Clive, who were in charge. There is also no indication of a delay in Green's evidence – contrary to what was suggested in Clive's inquest account. Green's account indicates that the Levertons called two embalmers – so they would have Fry if Green didn't make it.

There are several other points to consider:

441

1) They were not catching a commercial flight. Even though there was a 1 p.m. deadline, this flight could have been delayed – say 30 minutes or so – until everyone was on board. There was already a scheduled two hour gap in France, between the time the Leverton team arrived at the hospital – 3.40 p.m. – and the time Charles arrived – 5.40 p.m.

2) Clive's evidence was that Operation Overstudy required three people – see above – one of which was Clive or Keith, as the other would remain in London to control events at that end. There is no indication in any of the evidence – Clive, Keith, Green statements; Clive cross-examination – of who the third person would have been if only one embalmer had arrived.

3) Green carried the embalming equipment – "I took with me a large case containing all the items required for embalming". This equipment would have been used if they had needed to conduct an embalming in Paris.

4) Had it become necessary, I suggest that Mather would have organised a helicopter to get Green to RAF Northolt. Clive describes Fry being "given a police escort" – this is an indication that substantial resources were available, to make sure these embalmers got to the 1 p.m. flight.

5) The statement evidence – shown below – on why the embalmers were taken shows Keith and Clive both referring to Green and Fry as though the taking of both was necessary[a] - e.g. Clive: "The reason I took David and Bill was because...."

I suggest that it was decided before 6.30 a.m. that two embalmers were required for the flight to Paris. Soon after 6.45 a.m. Keith contacted Green and Clive contacted Fry – Clive and Keith statements.

In volunteered inquest testimony Clive changed his account, even indicating that they couldn't get hold of Green: "we were having a hell of a job to get hold [of] him ... I had to get hold of another embalmer in case I could not get hold of David". Just in case that wasn't clear, later in his testimony Clive volunteered this again: "As I said, I had trouble getting hold of David Green".[b]

There is nothing in any of the three statements – Clive, Keith, Green – to support this claim that Levertons had trouble "to get hold" of Green. The closest to it is Clive: "we had real trouble getting David back to the office" – but there is nothing in his statement to suggest that Fry was only called in because of that difficulty.

It is possibly significant that at the inquest Clive said "I had trouble getting hold of David Green", when both statements – Clive and Keith – reveal that it was not Clive who called Green – it was his brother, Keith.

---

[a] The reason why it was necessary is addressed later.
[b] The question this time was: "Can you explain why you took those [embalmers], despite having no specific instructions to embalm?" Clive: "I just used my common sense, basically. As I said, I had trouble getting hold of David Green. That is why I contacted Bill Fry, who kindly came down. They were the two chaps."

The question becomes: Why were two British embalmers required for the trip to Paris?

The witness evidence is:

Keith: "David Green and Bill Fry were to go to Paris with Clive to assist him and fulfil the role of embalmers only if it was required. Clive took them because we didn't know if embalming had been carried out or not, nor whether any was necessary. By taking the embalmers we would be prepared."

Clive: "We used [Bill Fry] as a backup in these circumstances[a].... The reason I took David and Bill was because if the deceased required embalming they would carry it out for me" – statement

Clive: "I took David and Bill because I didn't know what embalming if any, had been carried out, nor whether any was necessary at all. By taking the embalmers we would be prepared and able to carry out embalming if necessary in Paris" – statement

Clive at inquest: Asked: "Can you explain why you took those [embalmers], despite having no specific instructions to embalm?" Clive: "I just used my common sense, basically."

So we have:

- Keith: "to assist [Clive] and fulfil the role of embalmers only if it was required"
- Clive: "if the deceased required embalming they would carry it out for me"
- Clive: "we would be ... able to carry out embalming if necessary in Paris".

This evidence reveals that these two embalmers, complete with equipment[b], were taken over to Paris with the specific intention of carrying out an embalming on Princess Diana, if required.[c]

Earlier evidence has already shown Green maintaining that he couldn't have done an embalming had it been required: "Had I been told to start any embalming and to carry out a complete job it would not have been possible because of the time limitation. I would have needed three hours to do this." Evidence of the scheduling – a 1 p.m. departure from London to arrive at the Paris hospital around 3.45 p.m., with Charles arriving two hours later –

---

[a] The context here is Fry as a backup in assisting Green in Paris, if an embalming was required. This is not connected to Green's use of the word "backup" – see above. The full text is in the Role of Levertons section of the Royal Control chapter.

[b] See Green's evidence above.

[c] Green said in his statement: "I was there to embalm the Princess": David Green, Witness Statement, 13 July 2004, reproduced in *The Documents* book, p503 (UK Edition)

reveals it was known before the Levertons team left that there would not be enough time for a full embalming.

We have also seen evidence that Levertons knew there was going to be a post-mortem on Diana's body in London that evening – Burton told them about this before their 1 p.m. departure for Paris: "Later that morning I spoke to Levertons ... in order to make arrangements for the post mortem". It will be shown later that embalming significantly affects post-mortem test results.

This evidence reveals:

a) there was not enough time to do a "complete" embalming

b) a determination to conduct an embalming – "if required" – even though it was already known a post-mortem was to occur later that day.

This then shows that these embalmers – Green and Fry – were rushed[a] over to Paris with a clear determination to conduct an incomplete embalming if it was required.

I suggest that this situation – conducting an incomplete embalming; knowingly embalming ahead of a post-mortem – could not have occurred without instructions. In other words, Green and Fry were placed in this situation as a result of instructions – directly from Mather, but ultimately from higher up: Malcolm Ross and above him, Queen Elizabeth.

This evidence points to a very definite resolve by the royals to have an embalming carried out. Earlier evidence has revealed that the French were instructed to conduct an embalming. I suggest that British embalmers were sent over as a backup plan – if for some reason Monceau and Amarger had been prevented from carrying out their work, then Levertons were arriving before 4 p.m. with instructions to make sure an embalming would occur.

Green's evidence is that there was not enough time for a full embalming. The French evidence showed that a full embalming never occurred even when there was enough time.

The general evidence indicates that a full embalming was not required – the main event that successfully occurred during the French embalming was the complete removal of all urine from Princess Diana's body. All other work done appears to have been incomplete and poorly done.

I suggest that the instructions for the British would have been the same – had they been needed: the complete removal of urine and a superficial embalming that would have been "fixed up" with a full embalming later that night at St James' Palace.

The British embalmers may never have actually received those specific instructions, because by the time they got there the job had been done. Levertons may have just been told to take the embalmers and await further instructions – information on a "need to know" basis.

---

[a] See earlier evidence on the speed of Diana's repatriation.

I believe the evidence shows that Clive and Keith Leverton have lied repeatedly by saying they received no instructions regarding embalming – see earlier.

Two embalmers arrived at the Paris hospital, ready to work, if required.

I suggest Fry was sent to assist Green – Green: "Bill however did come with us to assist"; Clive: "we used [Bill Fry] as a backup".

Had anything gone wrong with the timing, having a backup embalmer on hand may have become extremely important.

The sending of two embalmers and only one funeral director reflects the importance the royals were placing on the embalming process. Princess Diana was to be returned to the UK that day, but it was even more important that she was "properly" embalmed before that took place.

Jean Monceau, BJL Director and Embalmer, Paris: 18 Oct 05 Statement: **Jury Didn't Hear**:

"On that day, I was told that Prince Charles was coming to Paris and that he was bringing with him some British embalmers. This led me to believe that he wanted the Princess to be embalmed."[290]

Gérard Jauze, PFG Branch Director, Paris: 21 Mar 06 Statement: **Jury Didn't Hear**:

"I remember earlier in the day someone saying or being informed that someone was meant to be coming from the UK to do the embalming."[291]

Patrick Launay, PFG Repatriation Director: 21 Mar 06 Statement: **Jury Didn't Hear**:

"At about 1130hrs [11.30 a.m.], Mr Plumet informed me that a plane carrying the coffin from England would be arriving at Villacoublay, a military airport. He told me that I should take charge of meeting the coffin at Villacoublay and for its transfer to the Pitié Salpêtrière Hospital....

"On the morning of 31 August 1997, I contacted Villacoublay Airport to find out at what time the plane and the coffin were due to arrive....

"At Villacoublay, I met the British funeral directors. I think that there were three of them, but I can only remember the one in charge. I cannot remember his name or the name of the company. We spoke at length, at the airport, during the journey, and at the hospital, about the arrangements and the return. Having taken charge of it at Villacoublay, we remained together for the rest of the afternoon. The coffin was collected from the airport by hearse....

"In the hospital, we left the coffin and the equipment (trestles, the British royal standard etc.) in a side room where the Princess of Wales was."[292]

Jean-Claude Plumet, PFG Director of Paris Agencies, Paris: 4 Nov 05 Paget description of Statement: **Jury Didn't Hear**:

"Mr Plumet explained that the body of the Princess of Wales was placed into the coffin, which had been brought by the British Undertakers Levertons from London."[293]

Anthony Mather, Asst Comptroller, Lord Chamberlain's Office: 22 Nov 07: 86.16:

Q. Did you yourself, at any stage, communicate with any officials in France about the repatriation or about the arrangements for the body?

A. None, none whatsoever.

At 87.23: "From the Lord Chamberlain's office, we had no communications with France."

Comment: The evidence from Monceau and Jauze reveals French knowledge on the day that British embalmer(s) were coming.

This raises the question: Who told them?

The evidence from Levertons was that they only communicated with Mather – see earlier. Mather has categorically stated: "we had no communications with France".

Launay reveals that the flight information needed to meet the British plane came from Plumet at around 11.30 a.m. In light of that, it is notable:

- that Plumet completely avoids mentioning anything about this in his statement – Plumet's sole comment is that "British undertakers" had brought over the coffin

- that Launay also makes no mention of British embalmers at all – Launay is told by Plumet that the plane was "carrying the coffin from England".[a] Launay mentions leaving "the equipment (trestles, the British royal standard etc.) in a side room" – yet fails to mention it included embalming equipment.[b]

After Launay meets the plane, from then on he describes all three men – Clive, Green, Fry – as "British funeral directors", even though he "spoke at length" with them and "remained together [with them] for the rest of the afternoon".

---

[a] This conversation is omitted from Plumet's unsworn account.

[b] The evidence from Clive and Green reveals that the embalming equipment was brought into the hospital. Clive: "Bill and David went with our equipment and the coffin into the hospital via a more discreet entrance"; Green: "My kit and the coffin were taken upon our arrival to the upstairs room where the Princess lay". This was supported by Monceau at the inquest: "they came with their equipment to embalm the body of the Princess": 20 Nov 07: 80.9. Sources: Clive Leverton, Witness Statement, 13 July 2004, reproduced in *The Documents* book, p492 (UK Edition); David Green, Witness Statement, 13 July 2004, reproduced in *The Documents* book, p503 (UK Edition).

I suggest this is a remarkable error by Patrick Launay – spending the afternoon with two embalmers, but describing them as funeral directors[a] – when one considers that he has had many years of experience in the funeral industry.

Jauze's account is not just that an embalmer was coming over, but that this person was "coming ... to do the embalming".

The general evidence reveals that Jean-Claude Plumet was the central figure in the PFG actions on the day – he had an involvement in the French embalming; he had prior knowledge of the Charles visit[b]; he organised both Jauze and Launay's activities on the day[c] – and it was he who told Launay to meet the Levertons plane.

Earlier evidence has shown that Jauze basically spent the afternoon with Plumet. I believe it is likely that the knowledge Jauze had of British embalmers coming over, came from Plumet.

It is possibly significant that both Plumet and Launay completely avoided mention of British embalmers in their statements. This, despite the indication from the evidence that Plumet had been told of their impending visit and Launay had clearly spent the afternoon with these embalmers.

Who was it that told Plumet the embalmers were coming?

Mather has denied any contact with the French, but then Mather has already been shown to be a liar. I suggest Mather is the most likely person to have been in contact at an operational level during the day with Plumet or Monceau, or both.

It is difficult to know why the French needed to be told that British embalmers were coming, unless it was to encourage Monceau into action – Monceau did say: "This [knowledge] led me to believe that [Charles] wanted the Princess to be embalmed."

---

[a] Tebbutt made a similar error regarding the French embalmers – see Embalming chapter – but Tebbutt is not himself a funeral director.

[b] Launay said: "I was also told that Prince Charles would be coming to the hospital to pay his respects, but that that would be later, and that he would be coming in another aircraft to Villacoublay and that the British ambassador would be meeting him. Mr Plumet did not say how he found out about this.": Patrick Launay, Witness Statement, 21 March 2006, reproduced in *The Documents* book, p511 (UK Edition).

[c] Launay's statement: "In this case my instructions came from Mr Plumet, who was the person in charge on an operational level for the two repatriations": Patrick Launay, Witness Statement, 21 March 2006, reproduced in *The Documents* book, p512 (UK Edition)

5 UK Post-Mortems[a]

Coroner: To Professor Robert Chapman: 26 Nov 07: 56.13: "Long experience, I dare say, shows that if you do not follow a rigorous procedure with samples and their transmission and labelling, et cetera, that difficulties are likely to arise."

---

[a] Although two post-mortems were conducted – Princess Diana and Dodi Fayed – the primary focus in this chapter is on the Diana post-mortem because Dodi's has less significance to the central issues of the case.

The royal flight from Paris carrying Princess Diana's body, Diana's sisters Sarah and Jane and Prince Charles, landed at RAF Northolt at around 7 p.m. local time. Just 13 minutes later – at 7.13 p.m. – Charles reboarded the flight to head back to Aberdeen and Balmoral.

Sarah and Jane accompanied Diana's body in the cortège which headed to the Fulham Mortuary. The route and the footbridges down the A40 were lined with people and flowers were tossed over the cars. Vehicles on both sides of the motorway stopped to honour the passing princess.

After arriving at the mortuary, the second post-mortem[a] of Diana, Princess of Wales commenced at 8.21 p.m. It was conducted by Professor Robert Chapman.

Was It Legally Required?

There is conflict over whether a post-mortem was required by law.
Coroners Act 1988, s20 (1): **Jury Didn't Hear**:
"The coroner may, at any time after he has decided to hold an inquest[b], request any legally qualified medical practitioner to make a post-mortem examination of the body...."
John Burton, Royal Coroner, 1997: 16 Jun 04 Statement: **Jury Didn't Hear**:
"I would often require a second post mortem examination be carried out in England, even if I was aware that a post mortem examination had already taken place in the country where the death occurred."[294]
John Burton: 16 Jun 04 Statement: **Jury Didn't Hear**:
"Having taken the decision that I would be taking jurisdiction I was aware that Diana ... had ... died an unnatural death. I was unaware if a post mortem had taken place in France. I needed to obtain evidence from a Post Mortem and in keeping with the Coroners rules together with my own normal practice I would be ordering a post mortem on the body of Diana Princess of Wales. I knew that I would require a post mortem to be carried out because I had an unnatural death and no evidence from a post mortem."[295]
John Burton: 29 Aug 04 Statement: **Jury Didn't Hear**:
"In all cases where bodies are repatriated to England where deaths have occurred abroad, if the Coroner has reason to believe that the person died of unnatural causes there must be an inquest. There is no requirement that Post Mortems must be carried out. The requirement for such is at the direction of the coroner. He does not need to order a post mortem." [296]

---

[a] The first had been conducted earlier in the day in Paris by Professor Dominique Lecomte – see Chapter 1.
[b] In this case an inquest was required by law – see earlier Royal Control chapter.

Michael Burgess, Royal Coroner, 2002 to Present:[a] 16 Aug 04 Statement: **Jury Didn't Hear**:

"Around 9.45 a.m. I received a call from Peter Fahy the Assistant Chief Constable of Surrey Police. He informed me that the body of Dodi Fayed was being brought back.... He asked me if I would become involved. I advised him that due to the case of Helen Smith and Section 8 (1) of the Coroners Act there was a requirement for a post mortem and an inquest, I would be taking jurisdiction of the body of Dodi Fayed....

"I ... spoke [again] to ACC Peter Fahy.... He told me that there was a change in plans.... He asked me if there would still be a post mortem. I told him the answer was 'yes'....

"I ... had a call from Caroline Sinclair from the Home Office.... I advised her that because of the case of Helen Smith and section 8 (1) of the Coroners Act, there was a need for a post mortem as I needed to establish the details of the death of Dodi Fayed....

"I had a telephone call from Mr John Macnamara, the head of security at Harrods.... He was concerned about a post mortem examination being carried out on the body of Dodi Fayed.... I told him that the coroner had duties because of section 8 (1) of the Coroners Act. I explained to him the necessity for a post mortem....

"I received a [later] call from John Macnamara.... I told him that my duties were laid down in the Coroners Act and that if the body came back I had no alternative but to have a post mortem. I noted the concerns of Mr AL Fayed but I had no alternative....

"At Fulham mortuary ... I met Mr Mohamed Al Fayed who ... did not want a post mortem carried out. I explained that it was essential because the injuries and condition of the body had to be recorded. I told Mr Al Fayed that the pathologist would only do what was necessary to achieve his goals as a professional."[297]

Michael Burgess: 16 Aug 04 Statement: **Jury Didn't Hear**:

Question: "Why did you hold a PM?"

Answer: "Although a post-mortem examination may not be required in every inquest case, if there was or could be in the future any doubt about the injuries that resulted in the death, then a post-mortem examination should be made with all the injuries and the state of the body carefully noted by the independent pathologist employed to make the examination."[298]

Comment: The law – in the Coroners Act 1988 – states that whether a post-mortem is conducted is at the discretion of the coroner – it is not legally required.

---

[a] In 1997 Michael Burgess was Surrey Coroner and also Deputy Royal Coroner. In 2002 he was promoted to the position of Royal Coroner, after John Burton resigned due to failing health.

Yet, that is not what we see in the statements made by the coroners – Burton and Burgess – both on the day and in their later statements.

The coroners have said:

- Burton: "in keeping with the Coroners rules ... I would be ordering a post mortem" – Jun 04 statement
- Burton: "there is no requirement that post mortems must be carried out" – Aug 04 statement
- Burgess: "due to the case of Helen Smith and Section 8 (1) of the Coroners Act there was a requirement for a post mortem" – to Fahy, in statement
- Burgess: "because of the case of Helen Smith and section 8 (1) of the Coroners Act, there was a need for a post mortem" – to Sinclair, in statement
- Burgess: "the coroner had duties because of section 8 (1) of the Coroners Act ... the necessity for a post mortem" – to Macnamara, in statement
- Burgess: "my duties were laid down in the Coroners Act and ... I had no alternative but to have a post mortem" – to Macnamara, in statement
- Burgess: "a post mortem ... was essential because the injuries and condition of the body had to be recorded" – to Mohamed, in statement
- Burgess: "a post-mortem examination may not be required in every inquest case, if there was or could be in the future any doubt ... then a post-mortem examination should be made" – statement.

There is a pattern here.

In the evidence relating to the decision made on the day, both coroners claim that a post-mortem was legally required, but when challenged on this by the police – 7 years after the event – they both back off: Burton – "there is no requirement"; Burgess: - "a post-mortem ... may not be required".

It is significant that when claiming a legal requirement, each coroner has used a different legal basis.

Burton said it's in "the Coroners Rules", but then neglects to quote the rule, or say which rule or which year the ruling was made.[a]

Burgess makes no mention of Coroners Rules. Burgess instead gives two reasons for the requirement of a post-mortem: a) Helen Smith; b) Section 8 (1) of the Coroners Act.[b]

Burgess has quoted the Coroners Act 1988 s8 (1), but this section does not relate to the holding of a post-mortem. The Act states: "When a coroner is

---

[a] In Burton's hand-written notes, there is a short note: "Need for P.M. + embalm" – see reproduction in Royal Control chapter. This issue is addressed in the Conclusion section of this chapter.

[b] When talking to Mohamed at the mortuary, Burgess doesn't provide a legal basis for his actions, instead simply stating: "a post mortem ... was essential because the injuries and condition of the body had to be recorded".

informed that the body ... is lying within his district and ... has died ... an unnatural death ... then ... the coroner shall as soon as practicable <u>hold an inquest</u> into the death...." [a]

The word "post-mortem", or similar, does not appear in section 8 (1) of the Act, because it is not related to post-mortems, but instead to the holding of an inquest.

Burgess also drew on the case of Helen Smith. Helen Smith was a 23 year old UK nurse who died in unusual circumstances in Saudi Arabia on 20 May 1979. The evidence relating to the Helen Smith case reveals that the West Yorkshire Coroner, Philip Gill, declined to hold an inquest, declaring instead that it did not fall within the jurisdiction of an English coroner's court. Helen's father, Ron Smith, was able to succeed in having that ruling overturned.[299]

The point here is that the issue with the Helen Smith case was again the holding of an inquest – not the post-mortem, as has been suggested by Michael Burgess.[b]

John Burton has referred to a part of the Coroners Rules that doesn't exist, to support his decision that he "needed to obtain evidence from a post-mortem". Burton himself indicates the rule doesn't exist, when in a statement just two months later, he says: "There is no requirement that post-mortems must be carried out" and "[The Coroner] does not need to order a post mortem".

Michael Burgess invoked the Coroners Act four times and the case of Helen Smith twice, to state that "there was a requirement for a post mortem". Burgess, in his role as coroner, must have been aware of the law in this area, and that both s8 (1) and Helen Smith relate to the holding of an inquest, not a post-mortem.

This evidence reveals that two coroners – John Burton re Diana and Michael Burgess re Dodi – lied on 31 August 1997 in their assertions that post-mortems were legally required in the UK for Diana and Dodi.[c]

The truth is revealed in the Coroners Act 1988, s20 (1) where it states: "The coroner <u>may</u> ... request any legally qualified medical practitioner to make a post-mortem examination".

Legally, the holding of a post-mortem is at the coroner's discretion.

The question is: Why did both these coroners lie on the same day – 31 August 1997 – about this critically important issue?

---

[a] This section of the Act actually reveals that Burton broke the law by not holding the Diana inquest "as soon as practicable". This issue is addressed in Part 5.

[b] There has been no shortage of post-mortems in the Helen Smith case – according to Wikipedia, 6 took place over a period of 30 years, from 1979 to 2009, when Helen Smith was finally laid to rest.

[c] There is no evidence of Burton conveying this reasoning to anyone else on 31 August 1997, but he has stated later under oath that that was his rationale on the day.

The answer will become clearer as this chapter progresses.

One could argue that a post-mortem should have been held in this case because of Princess Diana's prominent position, and therefore an implicit need to remove any possible questions that could arise in the future.[a]

I agree that that is a valid proposition, but that is not the reasoning that was used by Burton and Burgess on the day. The basis for their decision was a fictional Coroners Rule, and misrepresentation of case law and an Act of Parliament.

It is also relevant that Dominique Lecomte had already conducted a post-mortem earlier in the day.[b] Burton mentions instances where "a post mortem examination had already taken place in the country where the death occurred". Later in the same statement – when outlining his reason for conducting the post-mortem – Burton says: "I was unaware if a post mortem had taken place in France".

The evidence of Burton and Burgess was not heard and the issue of legal requirement for a post-mortem was not addressed at the London inquest.

Why?

Scotland Yard Meeting: 4.15 p.m.

A meeting attended by several British police officers was conducted ahead of the post-mortems of Diana and Dodi.

Jeffrey Rees, Head of Early Crash Investigations, British Police: 17 Dec 2007: 81.15:

Mansfield: Q. You had asked for certain officers to be appointed?

A. Yes.

Q. Were you aware of any meeting at New Scotland Yard with regard to these officers?

A. No, sir.

Q. I just wanted to ask you – and I know you have been asked about this before – but one of the officers, Mr Stoneham, was already there at the post mortem when you got there.

A. I do not recall if he arrived before or after me.

Philip Stoneham, Detective Sergeant, British Police: 18 Dec 07: 2.13:

Hilliard: Q. I think you were present at the post-mortem examinations that took place on 31st August 1997 at the Fulham Mortuary. Is that right?

A. Yes, I was.

---

[a] Seven years later Burgess alluded to this in his August 2004 statement – "if there was or could be in the future any doubt about the injuries that resulted in the death".

[b] See Chapter 1.

Q. As far as documentation is concerned, did you actually make any notes at the time?

A. No, sir.

Q. Shortly thereafter, did you make some notes in a pocket book?

A. I had a – the time that I spent as a crime scene coordinator/laboratory liaison sergeant, I always had a notebook of what I did day-to-day. Very much of my work was from a pager, to make contact with whoever paged me, so I made the note when I received a pager message and the time that that came through and what the instructions were. That is the note that I have made.

Q. So you have that original note. When would that have been made?

A. The note in the book, I only have a copy. I do not have the original note anymore. I do not know where it has gone.[a] That would have been – the pager message would have been at 2.30 on that day, to make contact with the Metropolitan Police contact desk who would have passed the message to me, and the instructions were to attend a room at New Scotland Yard at 4.15 on that day.

Q. So those notes would have been made obviously sometime after 2.30 on the 31st?

A. Yes.

Q. All right. Are those the only notes that you have that you made that day?

A. Those are the only notes that I have.

Q. Then, moving a long way on, 1st November 2004, do you remember you were seen by two police officers – is that right – who were just asking for your account of these events on that day?

A. Yes, that is right.

Q. One of those officers took notes at the time and those notes have been typed up?

A. They have been transcribed.

Q. Do you have a copy of those with you there?

A. Yes.

Q. You have made two witness statements, is this right?

A. Yes.

Q. The first was on 31st March 2005.

A. That is correct.

Q. The second was on 21st March 2006.

A. Yes.

Q. You have copies of all of those with you?

---

[a] This raises the issue of what is in the part of the notes – which appear below – that hasn't been photocopied. This appears to be a case of disappearing evidence – it is obvious that the original notes existed at the time of the photocopying, so what then happened to the original? Paget officers should have been asked about this.

A. I have.

....Q. You have told us that at half past 2 or so – is this right – on the afternoon of 31st August, you had a call telling you to go to New Scotland Yard?

A. Yes, I did.

.... Q. Now as far as the call is concerned – I am looking at the notes of the meeting with you on 1st November 2004 – that says that you received a call from Superintendent Rees....

A. Yes, indeed.

Q. Is that as you remember it?

A. I actually don't remember who called me or who I spoke to. What I do know is that whoever had called me, I would have received the pager message because that is how the on-call system worked for out of hours and weekends.

Q. But it looks as if, doesn't it, at 1st November 2004, you thought that the contact was from Mr Rees?

A. It may well have been. It also may well have been from him via a contact desk at New Scotland Yard. I am not really sure. I really don't remember.

Q. Right. Who was present at the meeting at New Scotland Yard?

A. I believe that certainly Inspector Sharp and Sergeant Wall. I know that my notes of the – the notes of the meeting and 1st November suggest that Superintendent Rees was there. I am really not sure whether he was or he was not or whether I saw him at the mortuary.

Q. But it looks as if, as at 1st November 2004, your recollection was that he was there.

A. My recollection was that he was there, yes.

Q. What was discussed at that meeting?

A. Again, my memory is a little hazy, but it – from the statements that I have made, I think that it was no more than to tell me that we were going to go to Fulham Mortuary to deal with two post mortems.[a]

Q. Looking again towards the bottom of the first page of the notes of the meeting with you on 1st November of 2004, there is reference there to a "special post mortem". Do you see that?

A. Yes.

Q. What did you understand by a "special post-mortem examination"?

---

[a] This initial response from Stoneham does not appear to make a lot of sense. If the reason for this meeting was "no more than to tell me that we were going to go to Fulham Mortuary to deal with two post mortems", then one could wonder: Why wasn't Stoneham just told over the phone to go straight to Fulham Mortuary? The fact that this meeting was called on the Sunday afternoon, indicates there was more to it than what Stoneham has said here.

A. Special post mortems, for the time that I spent doing this work, was that police personnel would be present and a forensic pathologist would conduct the post mortem, as against a routine post mortem where no police personnel were present, and they would have been conducted by the mortuary technician and a pathologist, not necessarily a forensic pathologist. Those are the two distinct differences and those are the only two that I know of.

Q. Was a decision made at that meeting, the 4.15 one at New Scotland Yard, about the post mortems to be special ones?

A. I have no idea.

Q. If you look towards the bottom of that page, there is a passage that says this, in the last paragraph, at the beginning of it: "It was decided that a special post mortem was to be carried out on both bodies. I do not know who actually made the decision and I played no part in this myself, but it was decided that they would be specials because there was a police investigation into their deaths and also because of the sensitivity surrounding the examinations. A special post mortem is carried out by a forensic pathologist and usually takes place where the death is a suspicious one." Do you see that?

A. Yes, that is right.

At 11.7: Mansfield: Q. Appreciating that you get a call, you now don't remember whether it was directly from Superintendent Rees or indirectly, via the call desk, as it were?

A. Well, my – the papers I have in front of me, there is the transcription saying that Superintendent Rees called me. My notebook, for which I have a copy, shows that on 31st August at 2.30 [p.m.], I received a call from contact desk, and I would say that – and it was normal for an officer to call the contact desk, to call the lab sergeant –

Q. To get you there?

A. To get me there or to get me to call them. So it would have been the contact desk that would have called me, and whether or not I rang Superintendent Rees or rang them back, I cannot remember.

Q. No, I understand. It is a long time ago. However, it is the next stage: you go to New Scotland Yard and Superintendent Rees is there.

A. He may have been. He may not have been.

Q. Why do you have a question mark over his presence?

A. Simply because I do not remember whether I met three people or two people. It is as simple as that.

Q. When the notes were taken of an interview with you by the Paget officers in November 2004, did you have your notes with you[a], the ones you have there?

A. These notes? No. It was purely from memory.

Q. But it would be fair to say from the notes that the officers took of the

---

[a] A copy of those notes, written on 31 August 1997, appears below.

interview with you then, that there was in fact, according to the notes, no question from you about whether there were two or three people, was there? If you read it, it says: "Present at that briefing were Graham Sharpe[a], Dick Wall ... and Superintendent Rees." Then somebody says "Anyone else present?"

A. That was my recollection in 2004, yes.

Q. Has anyone told you before coming here today that, in fact, Superintendent Rees does not admit that he went to New Scotland Yard first?

A. No.

Q. So, you are unaware of that difference of recollection?

A. I am.

.... Q. If you look at your ... statement in March 2006....: "In my time as a lab sergeant, I was only ever called upon to attend post-mortem examinations when the examination to be conducted was a 'special' one." Is that right?

A. That is right.

Q. "In this particular case, I attended New Scotland Yard for a briefing at approximately 4.15 ... and was instructed to attend Fulham Mortuary in my role as laboratory sergeant." It says here: "At no time did anybody tell me that I was going to be attending two 'special' post mortems. It was purely an assumption on my part, bearing in mind my previous involvement ..." Then the sentence: "The only people present at this briefing were Dennis Sharp, Dick Wall and myself." The one name that is omitted from this one is Rees again. Do you see that?

A. Yes.

Q. Not "I am not sure how many", but it was a very categoric statement omitting Rees; "The only people present ..."

A. Yes.

Q. But Mr Rees, you think, probably was present?

A. Well, the second – the 21st March statement was 18 months on from the meeting I had on 1st November 2004. I did not have the benefit of these notes, I was never given a copy of these notes, and both were purely from memory.

Q. I accept that.

A. In fact, almost two years on from that, I actually could not tell you who was or who was not there.

Q. I just want to ask you about the one in 2006. Do you remember who came to see you about the one in 2006 and why they were taking another statement from you? Did they say why they wanted another one?

A. I remember who came to see me. I have no idea why they came to see me.

---

[a] Other evidence reveals this person to be Dennis Sharp.

Q. Who was it who came to see you in March 2006?

A. I think it was a Sergeant Head and a Sergeant Grater, I think.

Q. Right. Now, just going back to the notes in 2006[a]. If you look at the document to your left there where you deal with – having dealt with who was present: "There was not a great deal of time to have an in-depth briefing, so really it was just to inform us that Diana, Princess of Wales and Dodi Al Fayed had been killed in a road accident in France, that their bodies were being flown into Northolt Airport and that they would be going to Fulham Mortuary where the post mortems would take place. To [your] knowledge, nothing was recorded regarding this briefing." That is that paragraph. Then it begins as was read out.... "It was decided that a special post mortem was to be carried out." Do you see that?

A. Which paragraph?[b]

Q. The bottom paragraph, "It was decided ..."

A. Yes.

Q. So the impression that you are giving in November 2004, would you agree, is that a decision either had been taken or was taken while you were there and that is how you knew that it was a special post mortem? Do you follow?

A. I follow what you are saying.

Q. In other words, quite different to the statement in March 2006, where it says "at no time did anybody tell me that I was going to be attending ..." Do you follow?

A. Yes, I do indeed follow.

Q. I am wondering how this difference came about.

A. As I tried to explain, there is a gap of 18 months. I did not have the benefit of the transcribed notes of the meeting on 1st November until after I made this statement and I do not recall, now, which one it is.

Q. ... Was November 2004 the first time that you had been asked to recollect?

A. Yes.

Q. So the chances are that that is more likely to be a better recollection than ones that come two years later.

A. It would – I could not disagree with you.

Q. No. One other aspect, looking at that bottom paragraph, that was in your recollection in 2004: "It was decided that they would be specials [that is special post mortems] because there was a police investigation into their deaths." That was your understanding?

---

[a] I believe this should read "2004" not "2006".

[b] Stoneham is asking "Which paragraph?" when only about 20 minutes earlier Hilliard had already quoted the exact same lines from the same statement. Mansfield's quoting from the paragraph is at 18.8 and Hilliard's is at 7.17 in the transcripts. At this stage Stoneham had been on the witness stand for less than half an hour.

A. That would have been my recollection at the time –

Q. And of course –

A. – but I would not have known what kind of police investigation that was going to be.

Q. ... So it looks as though, from this note of your recollection, that you either were informed or were present when a decision was taken that they would be specials because of a police investigation?

A. And, indeed, a special post mortem with police personnel present would have made it a police investigation, regardless of any other investigation that would have been before or after.

Q. Exactly.

A. The fact that police personnel were going to be at the post mortem is in itself, however small, an investigation. So it may have been that to which I was referring. I have no idea.

Coroner: So by your definition of "special", once you are at the post mortem, you are a police presence and therefore it is special?

A. Yes.

Q. And the officers who asked you to go would realise that, wouldn't they?

A. If I did not play any part in taking that decision, one assumes they had made that decision before I arrived.

At 29.4: Horwell: Q. And you have been asked about a reference in your note, "It was decided that they would be specials because there was a police investigation ...", there was of course, at that very moment, a police investigation in France into their deaths.

A. Indeed, yes.

John Burton, Royal Coroner, 1997: 16 Jun 04 Statement: **Jury Didn't Hear**:

"I cannot remember in what order they arrived at the mortuary but I was aware of the arrival of Detective Superintendent Jeffrey Rees and team, including a forensic laboratory liaison officer (FLO) and Metropolitan Police Service photographic officer. I had no prior knowledge of their attendance. I had met D/Supt Rees a few weeks earlier. I had not made the decision for these people to attend. In fact I did not have that authority as a coroner to do so....

"I recognised D/Supt Rees and knew him to be a police Palace liaison officer. I was not surprised that somebody from the Metropolitan Police Service had decided to call him. I would not be responsible for directing the way that he carried out his duties."[300]

Michael Burgess, Royal Coroner, 2002 to Present: 16 Aug 04 Statement:[a]
Jury Didn't Hear:
"Detective Superintendent Jeff Rees arrived at the mortuary. He had apparently been flown in by helicopter from Leicester. He introduced himself to me and told me that he had been appointed as the Senior Investigating Officer."[301]

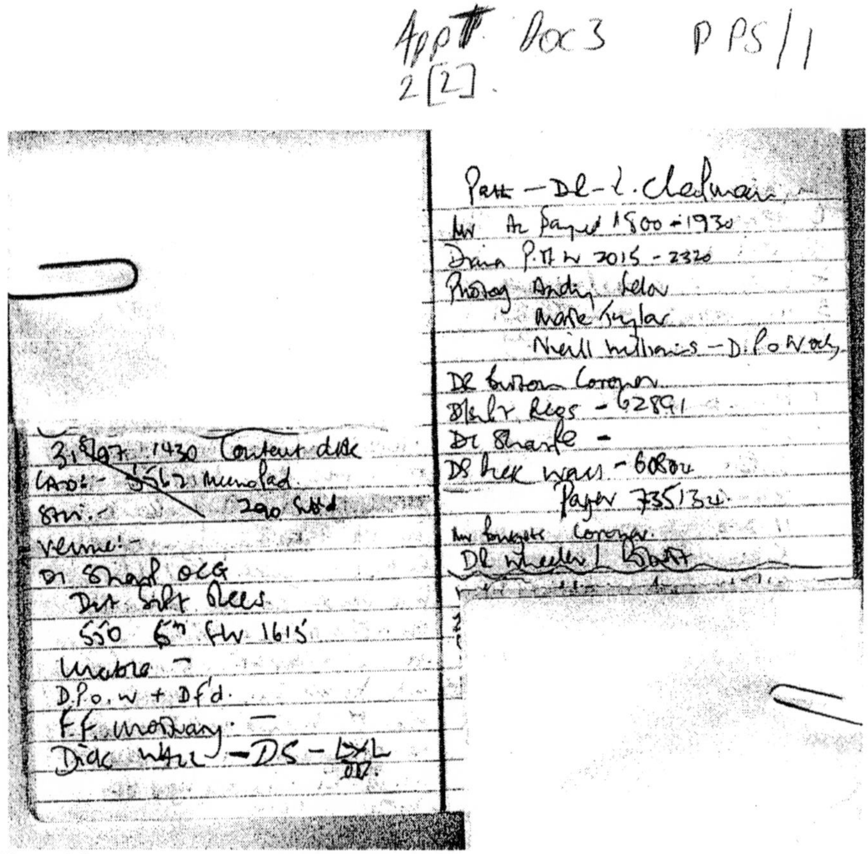
Appt Doc 3 PPS/1
2[2].

31/8/97 1430 Contact desk
Venue:-
Det Supt Rees
SSO 5th Flr 1615
D.P.o.w + Dfd.
F.F. mortuary. -
Dick Wall - DS -

Path - Dr R. Chapman
Mr Al Fayed 1800 - 1930
Diana P.M. 2015 - 2320
Photog Andy Fellow
Mark Taylor
Neill Williams - D.Po W
Dr Burton Coroner
Dr Sharpe -
Mr Burgess Coroner

Figure 16

Notes made by Philip Stoneham on 31 August 1997 reveal that Sharp, Rees and Wall were present at the 4.15 p.m. (1615) meeting at Scotland Yard. These notes were never shown to the inquest jury.

[a] The statement of Michael Burgess was not sworn or signed – this has been addressed in Part 3.

Comment: There is conflicting evidence over whether Jeffrey Rees attended this pre-post-mortem New Scotland Yard meeting, held at 4.15 p.m. on 31 August 1997.

The evidence is:

- 31 August 1997 – Stoneham brief handwritten notes indicating the presence of Rees
- 16 June 2004 – Burton statement: "I was aware of the arrival of Detective Superintendent Jeffrey Rees and team" at Fulham Mortuary
- 16 August 2004 – Burgess statement: "[Rees] had apparently been flown in [to Fulham] by helicopter from Leicester"
- 1 November 2004 – meeting notes showing Stoneham included Rees in the list of meeting attendees
- 21 March 2006 – Stoneham attendee list that omits mention of Rees
- 17 December 2007 – Rees denies that he was even aware of the meeting
- 18 December 2007 – Stoneham inquest evidence: "[Rees] may have been. [Rees] may not have been" present.

Philip Stoneham's evidence has changed.

On the day of the meeting Stoneham wrote notes – shown above – which indicate he received a call or pager message at 2.30 p.m.

In November 2004 Stoneham stated that he had "received a call from Superintendent Rees".

At the inquest Stoneham said he was requested "to make contact with the Metropolitan Police contact desk who would have passed the message to me, and the instructions were to attend a room at New Scotland Yard at 4.15 [p.m.] on that day". Under cross-examination, Stoneham added: "It may well have been [a contact from Rees]. It also may well have been from him via a contact desk at New Scotland Yard."

The balance of this evidence indicates that it was Jeffrey Rees who at 2.30 p.m. asked Philip Stoneham to attend the 4.15 p.m. Scotland Yard meeting.

In the 31 August 1997 notebook document Stoneham appears to have listed the people present at the meeting: "DI Sharp OCG[a]; Det Supt Rees ... Dick Wall".

This is then confirmed in the notes to the 1 November 2004 meeting where Stoneham said: "Present at that briefing were Graham Sharpe, Dick Wall ... and Superintendent Rees."

Then when Stoneham is revisited by Paget officers 16 months later, in March 2006, his evidence has changed: "The only people[a] present at this briefing were Dennis Sharp, Dick Wall and myself."

---

[a] Organised Crime Group. The nature of this organisation is addressed in Part 5.

21 months later, at the inquest, Stoneham has switched again: "[Rees] may have been. [Rees] may not have been" present.

Jeffrey Rees has not just denied attending this meeting, but in his inquest evidence he confirmed to Michael Mansfield that he was not even "aware of any meeting at New Scotland Yard". This was despite the fact that Rees admitted he "had asked for certain officers to be appointed" to the case, who in turn attended the meeting.

It's incredible that at the inquest, Rees was not confronted with Stoneham's evidence – particularly Stoneham's 31 August 1997 notebook entry.

Both coroners – Burton and Burgess – made specific reference to Rees' arrival at the Fulham Mortuary, that evening.

Burton says: "I was aware of the arrival of Detective Superintendent Jeffrey Rees, and team", but qualifies that with: "I cannot remember in what order they arrived" – apparently suggesting they may not have all arrived at the same time.

Burgess stated that Rees "had apparently been flown in [to Fulham] by helicopter from Leicester".

Both of these accounts appear to provide separate support for Rees' evidence that he wasn't at the meeting: Burton indicates the police didn't all attend the mortuary from the same place, arriving at the same time; Burgess indicating that if Rees came from Leicester, then he didn't come from a London meeting.

Rees, Burton and Burgess have all been shown – in Part 3 or earlier in this volume – to be liars.

The hard evidence on this issue comes from the Stoneham notebook entry – not shown to the jury – made on the day of the meeting. This note reveals Rees' presence and it is supported by Stoneham – the only other officer cross-examined who was present at the meeting – in his November 2004 account.

The fact that Stoneham's evidence has switched since – an outright denial in 2006, evasive answers at the inquest – may be a reflection of pressure from outside influences. Stoneham was visited three times by police ahead of the inquest – in November 2004, March 2005, and March 2006. This could be a reflection of intense concern over Stoneham's evidence.[b]

---

[a] The use of the word "only" indicates that there has been a suggestion that there were others present, e.g. Rees. Despite this, Stoneham insists at the inquest that in 2006 he was talking "purely from memory". When one views this in the light of Stoneham's 1997 notes and 2004 evidence, it seems possible that in 2006 he is saying what he has been told, or asked, to say.

[b] The Paget Report stated: "[Stoneham] received a call on Sunday 31 August 1997 to attend New Scotland Yard and meet with DI Sharp. There he was advised of two post-mortem examinations that were to take place later that day at Hammersmith and

Why has Stoneham's account changed?

How is it that Stoneham can consistently remember the presence of Sharp and Wall, but when it comes to Rees – who was in charge – his "memory is a little hazy"[a]: "I am really not sure whether he was or he was not".

When Mansfield asks Stoneham: "Why do you have a question mark over [Rees'] presence?" Stoneham replies: "I do not remember whether I met three people or two people. It is as simple as that."

But it is not as simple as that. It is not 3 or 2 – it is Rees or no Rees. It is not a question of numbers – it is the identities present that is the issue.

It is the presence of Jeffrey Rees – the person who asked Stoneham to the meeting; the person who appears in Stoneham's notebook on the day; the person who in November 2004 Stoneham says was there – that Stoneham is evasive about in his inquest evidence.

Why does Rees not want to be placed at the 4.15 p.m. meeting?

In Part 3 it was clearly shown that Rees lied at the inquest about his early involvement in events. The evidence reveals that prior to 2.30 p.m. Rees made a call to Burton regarding a French hold-up in "releasing bodies".[b] This call eventually led to a hold-up by Dominique Lecomte in the movement of Dodi Fayed's body.

The Stoneham notes on the day – and his November 2004 account – indicate that Rees also called him at around 2.30 p.m. to organise the 4.15 p.m. meeting. Rees later attended that meeting with Stoneham, Wall and Sharp.[c]

Rees appears to have denied knowledge of the Scotland Yard meeting, as it helps "strengthen" his case that he was not the one who called Burton before 2.30 p.m.[d] It is an attempt to distance himself from early involvement

---

Fulham mortuary.": Paget Report, p637. This is part of a third person representation of what Stoneham said and Paget fail to give it a date. It appears to be a manipulation of the evidence by Paget – indicating that the meeting was just between Sharp and Stoneham when they already had Stoneham's original notepad entry (reproduced earlier) showing that Rees and Wall were also present.

[a] Stoneham specifically states this in connection to what was discussed at the meeting, but uses the word "again", indicating his hazy memory also related to the presence of Rees. The evasiveness of his inquest evidence certainly supports that view.

[b] Referring to the bodies of Diana and Dodi.

[c] It appears logical that Rees, who could have been travelling by helicopter – Burgess – had time to leave Leicester sometime after 2.30 p.m. and be at Scotland Yard before 4.15 p.m.

[d] This was despite the fact that Rees' name appears in Burton's handwritten and typed notes – see Part 3.

in events. This may not just be about protecting Rees' position[a] – it has been shown in Part 3 that royal coroner, Michael Burgess, has also lied about the Rees-Burton phone call.

It is obvious that Rees should have been asked at the inquest about the Stoneham evidence. Not only did this not happen, but the inquest also never got to hear any evidence at all from the other two witnesses, Dennis Sharp and Richard Wall.

The jury also were not shown any of the following documents: Stoneham's notebook copy, the November 2004 notes, Stoneham's 2005 and 2006 statements.

Why is this?

The statements of both Wall and Sharp – excerpts of which appear later – also indicate an unwillingness to admit to being at the 4.15 p.m. meeting:

-   Sharp: "[Sharp] made his way to Hammersmith and Fulham Mortuary but did not recall if he attended New Scotland Yard prior to that"

-   Wall: "he travelled directly to the mortuary".

Why is it that Rees, Sharp and Wall have all either denied or "forgotten" about a critical pre-post-mortem meeting, even though there is hard documentary evidence from Stoneham's notebook that places all three there?

The answer to this should emerge as this chapter progresses.

Special Post-Mortems

There is conflicting evidence over: a) whether the post-mortem of Princess Diana was "special", and b) what constitutes a special post-mortem.
Dr Robert Chapman, Pathologist, UK: 26 Nov 07: 24.14:
Hilliard: Q. I want to ask you, please, about special and, if the opposite of that is "ordinary", ordinary post-mortem examinations. All right? First of all, were either of these post mortems ever given any particular designation?
A. No.
Q. You just carried on and got on with it?
A. Yes.
Q. But in some circumstances, can you be asked to carry out what is called a "special post-mortem examination"?
A. Yes.
Q. If you are asked to do that, what will you then do differently from a not special one?
A. You would first of all expect that this examination is going to take place at a convenient time for everybody to attend. There will be a greater attendance of persons in the mortuary and indeed around the body. The body will be photographed. There will be police officers present to witness the examination, to see the injuries, and exhibits will be taken by the police for

---

[a] Rees retired from the police force in 2000: 17 Dec 07: 27.3.

further analysis.

Q. Right. Now you say that this was not designated either special or not special, but those things did happen here, didn't they, in these particular post-mortem examinations?

A. Certainly. Yes, there were, as we have said, a number of people present and photographs were made and so on, yes.

Q. Given the identity of those concerned, did any of those features and the fact that you were taking samples and so on – did any of that surprise you?

A. No.

Q. Had you received any formal briefing before either or both of the post-mortem examinations took place?

A. No.

At 32.6: Mansfield: Q. I want to ask you about the difference between a special post mortem and an ordinary one, and perhaps to do it this way. If this had just been a road traffic accident in which the Princess of Wales was a passenger and had died and you conducted the post mortem, what ordinarily would you do? In other words, how would it differ, if it differs at all, from the post mortem that took place here, in terms of your examination?

A. I am not sure I follow the question.

Q. Well –

A. Can you rephrase that?

Q. Yes. Leave out the Princess of Wales.

A. Yes.

Q. You have a passenger in a car and you are conducting a post mortem.

A. Right. If one is dealing with that sort of situation, someone who has died in this sort of situation, abroad, one would carry out an examination. It would not normally be carried out at the weekend or out of hours; it would probably be carried out in a mortuary on a sort of normal operating morning within a mortuary when there were a number of other cases, probably, also being examined. It would involve myself and a mortuary assistant, but would not normally involve photography, the attendance of police officers, exhibits officers.

Q. Sorry, not exhibits officers?

A. No. It would not normally involve exhibits officers.

Q. So does that follow that you would not be taking samples, or you would, but it would not involve an exhibits officer?

A. I would be taking samples for toxicology where appropriate.

Q. Well, where would they be appropriate and when would they be appropriate?

A. They would be appropriate if one is concerned about the toxicological status of the individual and it is quite normal to take those in a road traffic accident.

Q. Could you explain what the normal ones would be?

A. One would try to take blood, urine, vitreous humour, perhaps liver and stomach contents.

Q. Anything else in the "normal", if I can put it, road traffic passenger case?

A. I cannot think of anything else.

Q. Now, in relation therefore to these cases, both of them, the real difference appears to be – one is that you took a sample of hair in both cases, is that right?

A. Yes.

Q. Was that because you were asked to?

A. I think it would have emerged from a discussion between myself and police officers present and – well, the crime scene manager.

Q. I will have to come back to that in a moment. So that is one of the differences. The other major difference in terms of the circumstances, beside obviously being at a weekend, is that you did have the presence of very senior police officers and exhibits officers and at least two photographers.

A. Yes.

Q. Now as a result of that, did you in fact therefore treat this not as an ordinary but as, in fact, a special examination?

A. Yes.

Q. Did you note that, that it was special?

A. I do not think I formally noted it anywhere, no.

At 65.23: Hilliard: Q. Dr Chapman, you were asked about a special examination. Can I just read to you? I will do it slowly. It is section 20, subsection 4 of the Coroners Act of 1998[a] which governs it, so we might as well know what we are listening to: "Special examination in relation to a body means a special examination by way of analysis, test or otherwise of such parts or contents of the body or such other substances or things as ought, in the opinion of the Coroner, to be submitted to analyses, tests or other examination with a view to ascertaining how the deceased came by his death." So, that is what special examination means.

A. Yes.

Q. Taking parts and samples and so on for testing for that purpose; yes?

A. That is the definition that you have read, yes.

Dr Robert Chapman, Pathologist, UK: 24 Feb 05 Statement: **Jury Didn't Hear**:

"I would regard the [Diana post-mortem] investigation of 31/8/97 as a special examination...."[302b]

---

[a] This should be "1988".

[b] This appears in Chapman's statement under the heading: "DIANA, PRINCESS OF WALES: POSTMORTEM EXAMINATION".

Michael Burgess, Royal Coroner, 2002 to Present: 16 Aug 04 Statement:
Jury Didn't Hear:
Question: "Was [Dodi's] PM[b] a normal one?"
Answer: "The pathologist was authorised by me, to make the examination.
He was given the usual instructions to make an examination. Through my
officer he was told that the deceased was understood to have been the rear
seat passenger in a car and was the victim of a road traffic crash in Paris. It is
understood that he had died from his injuries."
Question: "Did you request a special PM?"
Answer: "I did not request any special examination, and had no reason to
believe at that time that one might be necessary. I had no knowledge of any
particular Police involvement until we arrived at the mortuary. Police officers
do quite frequently attend post-mortem examinations, especially of road
traffic casualties because they can assist the pathologist in relating specific
injuries to possible scenarios."
Question: "What is the difference between a normal and a special PM?"
Answer. "Theoretically none. However, the coroner may, in certain cases,
pay the pathologist an enhanced fee for making an examination that is
unusually complex or difficult. Further in certain circumstances, a police
force that is making inquiries or investigating the death may ask the
pathologist to perform additional services and give advice to it concerning
the injuries and possible causes, and also advise as to whether injuries are
consistent with certain possible scenarios. Such examinations are made by
duly Home Office accredited forensic pathologists and the police pay an
additional fee to them for the extra advice and services rendered."
....Question: "Did you give any special instructions to Dr Chapman?"
Answer. "I did not give any instructions to Pathologists other than please
carry out the normal procedure."[303]
John Burton, Royal Coroner, 1997: 16 Jun 04 Statement: **Jury Didn't
Hear**:
"Both post mortems were conducted in the normal fashion but were made
special by the police and the methods taken by the police to secure evidence.
It was the police that authorised the taking of the photographs. I was happy
with the method and timing of when the photographs were taken. Where the
police are involved in an investigation the coroner cooperates and the
investigations are conducted at the same time. Sometimes samples are taken
by the pathologists for both the police and also the coroner....

---

[a] The full text of what Chapman said on this in his statement appears in the following
Decision Process section.
[b] Post-Mortem.

"Clinical pregnancy tests are not carried out on dead bodies. I have never known one being carried out at a post mortem. There were no unusual events during the post mortems. From all the various information I gleaned on the day I had no reason to treat the death of Diana Princess of Wales as being suspicious.

"The injuries that I saw on the body of Diana Princess of Wales were consistent with having been involved in a car crash. The post mortem revealed nothing inconsistent with a car crash."[304]

Robert Thompson, Fulham Mortuary Manager: 13 Jun 01 Affidavit: **Jury Didn't Hear**:

"A routine post mortem does not usually involve photography nor very extensive sample taking; but most importantly, there is no police involvement. Police are normally only present, and photography and extensive sample taking involved, in situations where the death is suspicious. In the case of both Dodi Al Fayed and Princess Diana, police were present throughout and the post mortems received the fullest possible treatment, (i.e. the type of treatment normally reserved for suspicious deaths). Photographs were taken by the police photographer, all under very close supervision. There was also present a laboratory liaison officer, Detective Sergeant Stoneham. In the case of a suspicious death the laboratory liaison officer is there to receive the samples and specimens taken from the body and deliver them to the Metropolitan Police Forensic Science Laboratory, Lambeth."[305]

Robert Thompson: 9 Nov 04 Statement: **Jury Didn't Hear**:

"At that time Mr Burton was the Coroner for West London and he used to attend most of the forensic post mortems, which are carried out in all cases where the death was suspicious. On the day in question, I believe the original intention was to have a different pathologist carry out each of the post mortem examinations. As Dodi Al Fayed was a resident of Surrey, the Surrey Coroner, Mr Burgess, would have chosen a pathologist to carry out the post mortem on his body. The pathologist contacted for this examination was Dr Chapman and he had arrived punctually at the mortuary. I believe that Harry Brown, who was making all the arrangements, tried to contact Dr Iain West (who is now deceased) with a view to him carrying out the post mortem examination on Princess Diana's body. However Dr West was, I think, out of the country at the time so it was logical that as Dr Chapman was already at the mortuary he would carry out the post mortem examinations on both bodies....

"I would just like to explain that in the case of a criminal/forensic post mortem it is the police exhibits officer who takes the samples but it was a different situation in the cases of the Princess and Dodi Al Fayed. Any samples stored at the mortuary prior to being sent to the laboratory would have been kept in the mortuary fridge.... I do not actually recall being handed the samples following the post mortems of Diana, Princess of Wales and Dodi Al Fayed but I'm sure they would have been given to me."[306]

Robert Thompson: 13 Jun 01 Affidavit: **Jury Didn't Hear**:

"Dr. Burton then turned up during the course of the afternoon. I understood from him that he had tried to get a pathologist from Guys Hospital to come in to carry out the post mortem on the Princess but failed."[307]

Jeffrey Rees, Head of Early Crash Investigations, British Police: 17 Dec 07: 81.4:

Mansfield: Q. Had you ever been to [a post-mortem] before?

....A. Yes.

Q. A special one?

A. I think every post mortem I ever attended was a special one.

Q. Yes. So before you went on this one, did you appreciate that that is what this one would be?

A. Yes.

Comment: The evidence comes from six witnesses – Chapman, Burton, Burgess, Thompson, Rees, Stoneham – who all attended the post-mortems.[a] Of these, only three were heard at the inquest: Chapman, Rees, Stoneham. The jury heard no evidence from Burton, Burgess and Thompson.

Were the post-mortems of Princess Diana and Dodi Fayed special?

-   Chapman: "these post mortems [were not] given any particular designation" – answer to Hilliard question

-   Chapman: "this was not designated either special or not special" – confirmed to Hilliard

-   Chapman: this was treated "not as an ordinary but as, in fact, a special examination" – confirmed to Mansfield

-   Chapman: "I would regard the [Diana post-mortem] investigation of 31/8/97 as a special examination" – statement

-   Stoneham: "it was decided that a special post mortem was to be carried out on both bodies" – notes, 1 November 2004

-   Stoneham: "at no time did anybody tell me that I was going to be attending two 'special' post mortems – it was purely an assumption on my part" – statement, 21 March 2006

-   Stoneham: "I have no idea" if "a decision [was] made at that meeting[b] ... about the post mortems to be special ones" – reply to Hilliard at the inquest

---

[a] Burgess only attended Dodi's: "I left prior to the PM of Diana. I never saw her coffin at all.": Michael Burgess, Witness Statement, 16 August 2004, reproduced in *The Documents* book, p540 (UK Edition).

[b] The Scotland Yard meeting at 4.15 p.m. on 31 August 1997 – see earlier.

- Stoneham: "I was only ever called upon to attend post-mortem examinations when ... [it] was a 'special' one" – statement, 21 March 2006
- Burgess: "I ... had no reason to believe at that time[a] that [a special post-mortem] might be necessary"
- Burton: "both post mortems were conducted in the normal fashion but were made special by the police.... I had no reason to treat the death of Diana ... as being suspicious"
- Thompson: "police were present throughout and the post mortems received the fullest possible treatment, (i.e. the type of treatment normally reserved for suspicious deaths)" – affidavit, 13 June 2001
- Thompson: "in the case of a criminal/forensic post mortem it is the police exhibits officer who takes the samples but it was a different situation in the cases of the Princess and Dodi Al Fayed" – statement, 9 November 2004
- Rees: "every post mortem I ever attended was a special one".
What then makes a post-mortem special?
- Coroners Act 1988: "taking parts and samples and so on for testing for [the] purpose" of determining cause of death – paraphrased by Hilliard, confirmed by Chapman
- Chapman: "a convenient time"; "greater attendance of persons"; "the body will be photographed"; "police officers present"; "exhibits will be taken by the police for further analysis" – inquest
- Stoneham: "police personnel would be present"; "a forensic pathologist would conduct the post mortem" – inquest
- Stoneham: "a special post mortem is carried out by a forensic pathologist and usually takes place where the death is a suspicious one" – meeting notes, 1 November 2004
- Stoneham: "once you are at the post mortem, you are a police presence and therefore it is special" – confirmed to Baker at inquest
- Burgess: "the coroner may ... pay the pathologist an enhanced fee for making an examination that is unusually complex or difficult"; "a police force ... may ask the pathologist to perform additional services and give advice"; "police pay an additional fee to [the pathologist] for the extra advice and services"
- Burton: "both post mortems were ... made special by the police and the methods taken by the police to secure evidence. It was the police that authorised the taking of the photographs.... Sometimes samples are taken by the pathologists for both the police and also the coroner"
- Thompson: "a routine post mortem does not usually involve photography nor very extensive sample taking ... there is no police involvement" – affidavit, 13 June 2001

---

[a] At the time of the post-mortem of Dodi.

- Thompson: "in the case of a suspicious death the laboratory liaison officer is there to receive the samples and specimens ... and deliver them to the Metropolitan Police Forensic Science Laboratory, Lambeth" – affidavit, 13 June 2001.

A special post-mortem is legally defined in s20 of the Coroners Act 1988: "analysis, test or otherwise of such parts or contents of the body or such other substances or things ... with a view to ascertaining how the deceased came by his death".

In layman's terms: analysis and/or the taking of samples for testing to assist in determining the cause of death. I suggest that this "analysis" could also include the taking of photographs.

A post-mortem, by definition, is: "an examination of a dead body to establish the cause of death".[a]

So, all post-mortems – special or normal – examine the body to determine cause of death. According to the legislation – the Coroners Act – a special post-mortem is different because it involves analysis, with the taking of samples for testing, to help establish that cause of death.

The majority of the witness accounts – Chapman, Stoneham, Burton and Thompson –appear to support this. Chapman, Burton and Thompson mention photographs and samples. Stoneham includes the presence of a forensic pathologist.

The evidence of Burgess is possibly the most confusing – he suggests that the pathologist receives extra payments from both the police and the coroner. Burgess mentions "additional services" but fails to define what those are.

None of the witnesses specifically refer to the purpose of this analysis and testing – to help determine the cause of death.

Scott Baker – who as inquest judge, was in a position that could influence the jury – attempted to define a special post-mortem quite differently:
To Stoneham: "By your definition of 'special', once you are at the post mortem, you are a police presence and therefore it is special?" To which Stoneham agreed.

Clearly, this evidence is false – the above evidence shows that a special post-mortem is an analysis, including samples and photos being taken, with a view to determining the cause of death. The police may attend, but their presence does not legally define the post-mortem as special.

The question that should have been asked at the inquest – but wasn't – is: If special post-mortems were carried out in the cases of Princess Diana and Dodi Fayed[b], then why was this?

---

[a] Oxford Dictionary.

[b] It will be shown that these post-mortems were special.

Were special post-mortems conducted?

Robert Chapman has given conflicting evidence:

- confirmed to Hilliard, the post-mortems were "not designated either special or not special"
- confirmed to Mansfield, it was "in fact, a special examination"
- statement, "I would regard the [Diana post-mortem] ... as a special examination".

This contradictory evidence is from the pathologist who conducted both post-mortems.

Chapman makes no mention of the post-mortems being special in his official post-mortem report – see later.[a] Chapman told Mansfield: "I do not think I formally noted [that it was special] anywhere". That is not true. On 24 February 2005 Chapman submitted a formal statement to Operation Paget in which he noted that he regarded the post-mortem of Princess Diana "as a special examination".[b]

Burgess fails to declare that the post-mortem was special: "I did not request any special examination, and had no reason to believe at that time that one might be necessary".

Burton says the post-mortems "were made special by the police".

Stoneham consistently testified that the post-mortems were special – he only ever attended special post-mortems.[c]

Rees concurs with this: "every post mortem I ever attended was a special one".

Thompson doesn't use the word "special", but describes the characteristics of a special post-mortem: "the post mortems received the fullest possible treatment".

The evidence is confusing.

The performing pathologist, Robert Chapman, is the most important witness, but his evidence is conflicting – both "not designated" and "special".

Rees and Stoneham – who both attended – say they were special.

Burgess, despite being asked, fails to say. He says he "did not request" a special.

Burton says they were special.

---

[a] The relevant part of Chapman's post-mortem report appears in *The Documents* book, p573.

[b] In a later comment in the same statement, under the heading, "DODI AL FAYED: POSTMORTEM EXAMINATION", Chapman wrote: "I make the same comments with regard to the status of this examination as I have with regard to that of Diana, Princess of Wales.": Robert Chapman, Witness Statement, 24 February 2005, reproduced in *The Documents* book, p589 (UK Edition)

[c] Stoneham gave conflicting evidence on how the post-mortems became special – this is addressed below.

Thompson describes special post-mortems, without using the word.

It is fair to conclude that – although there is some conflict – the balance of the witness evidence shows the post-mortems were both special.

Post-Mortems on Passengers

Should the bodies of Princess Diana and Dodi Fayed have been subjected to special post-mortems?

Diana and Dodi died as a result of being passengers in a car crash. Earlier French evidence in chapter 1 has shown that a post-mortem is irrelevant for a passenger:

-   Eva Steiner: "usually, there is no post mortem for the passengers because it is completely irrelevant"
-   Martine Monteil: "it is not usual to carry out a post mortem on the passengers because in most cases it is not relevant".

Earlier evidence in this chapter has shown that an inquest in the UK was required, but a post-mortem was not.

Yet, what we see in the evidence is the coroners, Burgess and Burton, both requiring a post-mortem on false grounds – see earlier.

David Veness, MPS Assistant Commissioner Specialist Operations, told the inquest: "At the post-mortem [of Diana and Dodi] ... all appropriate samples and forensic exhibits should be properly collated and recorded" – see later.

The question is: Why would you have "appropriate samples and forensic exhibits" to take from a victim who was a passenger in a car crash?

Michael Mansfield asked Robert Chapman what happens when "you have a passenger in a car". Chapman replied – among other points – that: a) "one would carry out an examination"; b) "I would be taking samples for toxicology where appropriate".

Mansfield then asked the obvious question: "When would [taking samples] be appropriate?" And Chapman replied: "If one is concerned about the toxicological status of the individual". Then Chapman adds an amazing comment, which passed unchallenged: "It is quite normal to take those [samples] in a road traffic accident." [a]

There are two questions:

-   Under what circumstances would a pathologist be "concerned about the toxicological status of " a dead passenger in a car crash?
-   Why does Chapman consider it normal to take samples from dead passengers who were in a car crash?

---

[a] Chapman doesn't specifically include the word "passenger" in this sentence, but the context of this interchange is dealing with passengers in a car crash.

I suggest that it is common sense that in general the toxicological status of a passenger would have no significance in a car crash. I also suggest that it would be unusual to conduct a post-mortem on a car crash passenger, and it would be particularly unusual to have a special post-mortem.

The issues that are being raised here were not addressed during Scott Baker's "thorough" inquest.[a]

Decision Process

How did these post-mortems – on the bodies of two passengers in a car crash – become special?

Coroners Act 1988, s20 (1): **Jury Didn't Hear**:
"The coroner may, at any time after he has decided to hold an inquest, request any legally qualified medical practitioner to make a post-mortem examination of the body or a special examination of the body or both such examinations."

Dr Robert Chapman, Pathologist, UK: 24 Feb 05 Statement: **Jury Didn't Hear**:
"Medico-legal postmortems, whether in cases of suspicious death or not, are requested by the Coroner via the Coroner's Officer. At weekends ... there is an on-call system run by the partnership and previously by the departments in which I have worked.
"Postmortem examinations involve a briefing of the circumstances surrounding the case usually given by a coroner's officer and a police officer if appropriate."[308]

Dr Robert Chapman, Pathologist, UK: 24 Feb 05 Statement: **Jury Didn't Hear**:
"The decision as to whether an examination is regarded as a "special" examination is taken by HM coroner although a pathologist can advise on the basis of circumstances and initial findings if he/she feels that an "ordinary" examination should be proceeded with as a "special". My understanding is that a Coroner can request a pathologist of particular experience such as a forensic pathologist to carry out an examination on the grounds that the death is suspicious or carries the likelihood of additional legal proceedings based on the pathological findings and police investigation. Such a case would usually involve the attendance of police officers at the examination, the taking of photographs and other exhibits to further the investigation and

---

[a] The evidence in Part 3 indicated that there was an awareness by Rees – passed on to the coroners – at around 2.30 p.m. that the deaths were being treated in France as suspicious. That information could have been a flow on result of Riou's earlier ticking YES for medico-legal issue in the death certificate. It is possible that information of that nature could have triggered a decision to conduct a special post-mortem.

would take place at a time convenient to all these parties and separate from any other "routine" examinations.

"I would regard the investigation of 31/8/97 as a special examination because of the attendance of the various police officers present and the taking of exhibits and photographs by the police as well as the unique circumstances which attended this examination with respect to the identity of the deceased and the circumstances of her death. I did not discuss the nature of the examination with the Coroner, except to confirm with him that I would carry out a full dissection of the body. Whether this examination was to be called a special or ordinary examination appeared irrelevant when a large number of personnel were gathered and it was clear that only a thorough and complete examination would suffice. I personally supervised the process, the photography and carried out all of the removal of organs and subsequent dissection. Mr. Thompson would have incised the scalp and sawn the skull. I obtained all of the exhibits and toxicology samples.

"An ordinary postmortem examination is usually carried out in the absence of any police officers, photography or exhibit collection in cases in which there are no suspicious circumstances or a requirement for additional police investigation. Such examinations are usually grouped together within the mortuary and carried out during set sessions and there is usually a greater involvement of technical staff in the preparation of the bodies for the pathologist.

"I did not receive any formal briefing prior to my examinations."[309]

Michael Burgess, Royal Coroner, 2002 to Present: 16 Aug 04 Statement: **Jury Didn't Hear:**[a]

"Around 9 a.m. I spoke to Dr John Burton, the then coroner of the Royal Household on the phone regarding the death of Diana Princess of Wales....

"At approximately 10 a.m. I phoned Mr Keith Brown one of my coroner's officers and ... asked him to arrange the opening of the mortuary at the Royal Surrey County Hospital and in addition to arrange for a Home Office Pathologist either Dr Richard Shepherd or Dr Robert Chapman to attend and conduct the post mortem on the body of Dodi Fayed. We chose a forensic pathologist because they are available out of hours and because we wanted to obtain the best evidence available.

"I then telephoned Dr Burton and advised him that I ... was arranging a post mortem at Guildford.

---

[a] The evidence shown here from Burgess and Burton is abridged. A fuller version appears in the Royal Control chapter. The complete statements are included in *The Documents* book, pp533-569.

"I then spoke to Keith Brown who confirmed that he had made arrangements for the opening of the mortuary at the Royal Surrey County Hospital and for Dr Chapman to attend in order to conduct the post mortem on the body of Dodi Fayed.

"I then spoke to ACC Peter Fahy.... During that telephone call, or later, he told me that there was a change in plans in as much as the body was to go to a service at Regents Park Mosque before burial in Surrey....

"I then spoke to Keith Brown and asked him to stop everything as there was a change of plan and that I was looking for an alternative arrangement for the post mortem.

"I then spoke to Dr Burton.... Dr Burton offered the facility of the Hammersmith and Fulham mortuary together with the help of his mortuary assistant, which I accepted. Then, or during a later telephone call, Dr Burton asked if he could use the services of Dr Chapman for a post mortem examination on the body of Diana....

"I then phoned Keith Brown ... and asked him to redirect Dr Chapman to the Fulham mortuary."[310]

Michael Burgess: 16 Aug 04 Statement: **Jury Didn't Hear**:
Question: "Did anyone try and influence you in the way you carried out your duties and responsibilities?"
Answer: "No."
Question: "Did you give any special instructions to Dr Chapman?"
Answer: "I did not give any instructions to pathologists other than please carry out the normal procedure".
Question: "Did anyone give you instructions regarding the post mortems?"
Answer: "None".
.... Question: "Did anyone attempt to influence your decisions on the day of the PM?"
Answer: "No. Save for Mr Macnamara being anxious that the Post mortem should be both kept to a minimum and that it should not delay the burial, and of Mr M Al Fayed, saying to me that he didn't want his son's body subject to a PM."[311]

John Burton, Royal Coroner, 1997: 16 Jun 04 Statement: **Jury Didn't Hear**:
"I would take each case on its own merits and would decide if I required a post mortem to be carried out. I would be the person that instructed the pathologist to undertake the post mortem."[312]

John Burton: 16 Jun 04 Statement: **Jury Didn't Hear**:
"I phoned one of my coroner's officers Harry Brown and asked him to make arrangements for the post mortem to be held at the Hammersmith and Fulham mortuary and place the duty home office pathologist on standby.

"Around midday Michael Burgess ... phoned.... He was arranging a post mortem at Chertsey and had Dr Chapman the home office pathologist on standby. We discussed the need to get Mr Dodi Al Fayed buried before nightfall. We agreed that in order to facilitate this and the wishes of Mr Mohamed Al Fayed that the post mortem of Mr Dodi Al Fayed would take place first.

"I received another call from Michael Burgess who informed me that Mr Mohamed Al Fayed wanted a service for his son in the mosque in Regents Park, London and then a burial in Brookwood cemetery, Surrey. We agreed that Dr Chapman should hold both post mortems at the Hammersmith and Fulham mortuary. "[313]

Dr Robert Chapman, Pathologist, UK: 26 Nov 07: 2.21:

Hilliard: Q. What role were you playing that weekend in your capacity as a forensic pathologist?

A. It was my what we call "on-call weekend"; in other words, I was liable to be called for any examinations that needed doing over that weekend.

Q. Is that entirely, as it were, at random, the way you happened to come to be on call?

A. There is a rota for that sort of thing.

Q. So to perform any examinations that would be needed that weekend on behalf of who? How does it happen?

A. On behalf of the coroner and the police.

Q. When you say "the coroner", which coroner would that be?

A. That would include a number of coroners covering the Metropolitan area of London and Surrey.

Q. What was the first contact that you had in relation to these particular post-mortem examinations?

A. My recollection is that I was rung up by a coroner's officer, Mr Keith Brown, who was talking to me on behalf of Mr Burgess, who is the coroner for Surrey.

Q. So Mr Keith Brown, coroner's officer on behalf of Mr Burgess, the coroner for Surrey, contacts you and asking, what, if you will carry out an examination?

A. Yes.

Q. In respect of whom?

A. In respect of Mr Al Fayed.

Q. Did you learn where that was to take place?

A. I was told eventually that the examination would be taking place at the Hammersmith and Fulham Public Mortuary.

Q. Initially, was anything said about conducting an examination in respect of the Princess of Wales?

A. Not at that stage, no.

Q. So did you make your way to the Hammersmith and Fulham Mortuary?

A. Yes.

Q. The examination in respect of Mr Al Fayed began, according to your report, at 6 o'clock. By that time, had anything been said about the post-mortem examination in respect of the Princess of Wales?

A. Yes.

Q. How did that come about?

A. I think that fairly soon after my arrival at the mortuary, I was met by Dr Burton.... He indicated to me that the body of Princess Diana would be arriving some time later that day and that it would be practical if I could carry out that examination, when I had finished the examination of Mr Al Fayed.

Dr Robert Chapman, Pathologist, UK: 24 Feb 05 Statement: **Jury Didn't Hear**:

"I was on–call during the weekend of 30/31 August 1997 for any postmortem examinations which required performing on behalf of the Coroner for Surrey as well as some other London areas. I was contacted by a Coroner's Officer, Keith Brown, on behalf of Mr. M Burgess requesting I attend to carry out a postmortem examination on the body of Mr. Al Fayed. I do not recall whether I was spoken to directly by Mr. Burgess at this stage. I was subsequently informed that the examination would take place at the Hammersmith and Fulham Public Mortuary at Fulham because of the plans for a service in central London for Mr. Al Fayed.

"I was not asked to carry out a postmortem examination on Diana, Princess of Wales until I arrived at Fulham Mortuary. I was then asked directly by Dr Burton to undertake this task following the examination of Mr. Al Fayed....

"The decision to carry both examinations at Fulham was taken by the two Coroners involved and did not involve me."[314]

Robert Thompson, Fulham Mortuary Manager: 13 Jun 01 Affidavit: **Jury Didn't Hear**:

"Sometime during the morning of Sunday 31 August, I was told that Princess Diana had been killed in a car crash in Paris. Obviously, like everyone else, I was shocked but also remember thinking that it was quite likely I would soon get a call regarding this. I think this conversation took place about 11.00 a.m. Only a few minutes later, my pager went off. It was from Harry Brown, the Coroner's Officer, asking me to telephone. I called him and he told me something along the lines that the job (i.e. Princess Diana's and Dodi's post mortems) would be coming to our mortuary. It was clear from the conversation that there was no desperate rush as the bodies would not be arriving back till much later in the day, but I decided to go in fairly early in the afternoon in order to get things ready."[315]

Robert Thompson: 9 Nov 04 Statement: **Jury Didn't Hear**:

"I had stayed overnight on the Saturday (30th August 1997) in North West London with my lady friend and it wasn't until I got up on the Sunday morning that I heard about the deaths of Diana, Princess of Wales and Dodi

Al Fayed. I remember saying to my lady friend something like "You wait, my pager will go off in a minute" and, sure enough, it did almost straight after I had said it. The pager displayed a telephone number which I would have contacted. I subsequently spoke to Harry Brown, one of the Coroner's Officers, who told me that the post mortems would be carried out at Hammersmith and Fulham mortuary. I then went to the mortuary, arriving around 10am or 11am. There were a lot of people hanging around in the car park and in particular several men in dark suits who at the time I assumed were police officers from Royalty Protection or something like that. I was later told that they were from the Diplomatic Protection Squad as well as from Royalty Protection."[316]

John Macnamara, Al Fayed Director of Security: 14 Feb 08: 79.12:
Burnett: Q. Did you then immediately become involved in the no doubt very difficult and distressing practical arrangements that had to be made in the hours that followed?
A. Yes. I went to Harrods very early in the morning and began the arrangements, firstly for the repatriation of Dodi's body and the reception of Dodi's body and also to secure a burial site at Brookwood Cemetery.
....Q. At some stage, did you become aware that there was at least the likelihood – which in due course it became obvious was the need – for a post-mortem examination in England?
A. Well, yes. I knew that once the body came back to England, there would have to be a post mortem.
....Q. Did you have contact with the Surrey coroner into whose jurisdiction the plan was that Dodi's body would in due course come because that is where he was to be buried?
A. Yes, I had several conversations with Mr Burgess, yes.
....Q. Did you meet him during the course of the day or was all the contact by telephone?
A. It was all by telephone. I did not meet Mr Burgess until I went to the mortuary late that afternoon.

John Macnamara: 3 Jul 06 Statement: **Jury Didn't Hear**:
"I went to Harrods shortly after 7 a.m. I spent most of the day arranging for the repatriation and burial of Dodi Al Fayed's body.... It was intended to bury Dodi before sunset in accordance with Islamic religion. A suitable burial plot was secured at Brookwood Cemetery near Guildford, Surrey.
"During the latter part of the morning I liaised closely with Mr Michael Burgess, Coroner for Surrey.... I also liaised closely with Commander Michael Messinger....
"During conversations with Michael Burgess I explained that if at all possible the burial should be effected before sunset. I was of course aware that there

had to be a full post mortem. Michael Burgess told me that he had agreed with Dr Burton ... that Dodi's post mortem could be conducted at Fulham mortuary. This certainly assisted in the planned arrangements whereby Dodi's body would be taken to Regent's Park mosque for blessing before being taken to Brookwood Cemetery for burial."[317]

Keith Brown, Surrey Coroner's Officer: 5 May 05 Statement read out 11 Mar 08: 211.20:

"On Sunday 31st August 1997, I was the 'on-call' Coroner's Officer for the Guildford and Waverley areas of Surrey. I was at home and due to the news coverage I was aware of the deaths of Diana, Princess of Wales and Mr Dodi Al Fayed in Paris earlier that morning.

"Mr Burgess then phoned me to say that ... the post mortem would be ... held at Fulham Mortuary."

Comment: The issues are:

1)   At what point was it decided that the post-mortems would be special?
2)   Who made that decision?

Burton and Burgess provided earlier evidence:

- Burton said: "both post mortems were ... made special by the police".
- Burgess denied involvement: "I did not request any special examination".

Is Burton's claim – that the police made the post-mortems special – supported by any other evidence?

Stoneham provided conflicting evidence: In November 2004 he said that "it was decided that a special post mortem was to be carried out". 18 months later Stoneham says the opposite: "At no time did anybody tell me that I was going to be attending two 'special' post mortems". Then at the inquest: "I have no idea" if a decision on specials was made at that Scotland Yard meeting.

So Stoneham appears to have three positions on three occasions: "it was decided"; I wasn't told; "I have no idea".

Stoneham's November 2004 account – which is his earliest evidence – should be studied more closely.

Mansfield's reading of the 2004 document shows that there is a paragraph dealing with the meeting – "There was not a great deal of time to have an in-depth briefing.... To [your[a]] knowledge, nothing was recorded regarding this briefing." Then Mansfield says: "That is that paragraph. Then it begins as was read out....[b] 'It was decided....'"

This reveals that there are two separate paragraphs.

---

[a] Stoneham's. Mansfield is reading from the document – he appears to have replaced "my" with "your".

[b] These dots show there are missing – but irrelevant – words. These words are from Mansfield: "I do not want to keep repeating what was read out except this:": 18 Dec 07: 18.3.

In the second paragraph Stoneham says "it was decided...", but he also says: "I do not know who actually made the decision and I played no part in this myself".

When one considers that Stoneham was present at the meeting, his evidence – "I played no part in this" – raises the possibility that the decision was made prior to the commencement of the meeting. This could be supported by Stoneham's inquest suggestion: "One assumes they had made that decision before I arrived".

Jeffrey Rees has never been asked about this and the other two officers present at this meeting – Wall and Sharp – were not heard from at the inquest.[a]

In summary, Stoneham's November 2004 evidence reveals that:

a) there was a decision to make the post-mortems special – "it was decided"

b) that decision was made prior to the 4.15 p.m. meeting – "I played no part in this"

c) Stoneham does "not know who ... made the decision".

Michael Burgess reveals that an early decision – "approximately 10 a.m." – was made to ask either Richard Shepherd[b] or Robert Chapman to conduct Dodi's post-mortem.

Burton's account is quite different: Burton asked Harry Brown to "place the duty home office pathologist on standby".

Burgess stated he wanted Shepherd or Chapman – forensic pathologists – for Dodi; Burton just asked for the duty pathologist for Diana.

Are both these accounts true? Is it possible that specific forensic pathologists could be chosen for Dodi, but when it comes to Diana, Burton is happy to go with the duty pathologist?

Both of the pathologists requested by Burgess – Chapman and Shepherd – are forensic pathologists. Stoneham stated earlier that "a special post mortem is carried out by a forensic pathologist".[c] What occurred in the end was that

---

[a] Wall and Sharp did provide police statements which have never been made public. Small third person excerpts appear in the Paget Report – these are visited later in this chapter.

[b] Shepherd later became both the Paget and inquest's expert pathologist.

[c] I suggest this is also common sense. A special post-mortem requires analysis and the taking of samples – see earlier. The definition of "forensic" is: "relating to the use of scientific methods to investigate crime": Oxford. So if a forensic pathologist is skilled in using scientific methods – e.g. sampling and analysis – then it is logical they would be used to conduct a special post-mortem. A description of the practical activities of a forensic pathologist appears in the next footnote.

both post-mortems were special and were conducted by Robert Chapman, a forensic pathologist.[a]

This evidence raises the possibility that at the time Burgess phoned Keith Brown to arrange for Chapman or Shepherd, the decision had already been made to conduct special post-mortems.

Burgess says: "we chose a forensic pathologist" and "we wanted to obtain..." This indicates that he did not make the decision to employ a forensic pathologist on his own.

The question then is: Who is Burgess referring to when he says "we"?

According to Burgess' account, he spoke to Burton "around 9 a.m." – approximately an hour before he requests Brown to arrange Shepherd or Chapman for the post-mortem.

The fact that Burgess has used the word "we" – maybe inadvertently – indicates that the two coroners had already discussed the need for a forensic pathologist during their 9 a.m. phone conversation.[b]

This evidence raises serious doubts about Burton's account: "I phoned ... Harry Brown and asked him to ... place the duty home office pathologist on standby."[c]

These doubts are added to with the statement account from Robert Thompson, the Fulham mortuary manager: "Harry Brown ... tried to contact Dr Iain West ... with a view to him carrying out the post mortem examination on Princess Diana's body. However Dr West was ... out of the country...."[d]

---

[a] "Forensic pathologists perform medico-legal post-mortem examinations on behalf of Coroners.": Dr Richard Jones and Professor Richard Shepherd, The Role of the Forensic Pathologist, Victorian Institute of Forensic Medicine, June 2010. "Forensic pathology is ... concerned with the investigation of deaths where there are medico-legal implications, for example, suspected homicides, death in custody and other complex medico-legal cases. Much of the day-to-day work of forensic pathology is performing autopsies, for example in the case of stabbing, shooting or head injury, which are common methods of homicide in the United Kingdom. These autopsies are usually carried out under the authority of the coroner in England and Wales, with police present.": Prof Helen Whitwell, Forensic Pathology, The Royal College of Pathologists, www.rcpath.org

[b] It could be argued that when Burgess uses "we", he is referring to input from Keith Brown. This view could be supported by Burgess' typed document – reproduced in the Royal Control chapter – where he writes about the Brown call: "discussion as to pathologist ... see if RTS available...." It will later be suggested that the typed document was raised after the decision had been made to create evidence pointing to an early Surrey post-mortem. The evidence relating to this will emerge throughout this section.

[c] There is nothing in Burton's handwritten or typed notes about asking for the duty pathologist.

[d] Thompson said in his June 2001 affidavit: "I understood from [Burton] that he had tried to get a pathologist from Guys Hospital to come in to carry out the post mortem

Burton has said he asked Harry Brown for the duty pathologist. Harry Brown has never been interviewed. Thompson says Harry Brown "tried to contact Dr Iain West" who was abroad.

There are two points here:
-   if Iain West was "out of the country", that means that he couldn't have been the duty pathologist
-   Iain West was – like Chapman – a forensic pathologist.[318]

Burton has also stated that in the same conversation he asked Harry Brown "to make arrangements for the post mortem [of Diana] to be held at the Hammersmith and Fulham mortuary".

Again, Harry Brown has never been interviewed, but Robert Thompson has.

Thompson has said in his sworn police statement, that before 10 a.m. he was contacted by Harry Brown "who told me that the post mortems would be carried out at Hammersmith and Fulham mortuary".[a]

There is a major conflict here – both Burton and Burgess state that initially the arrangement was for Dodi's post-mortem to be held at Guildford (Burgess) or Chertsey (Burton)[b] and for Diana's to be held at Fulham. Thompson has said that before 10 a.m. he was contacted to open up the Fulham Mortuary for both post-mortems.

Burton's account is that when he spoke with Burgess "around midday", Burgess "was arranging a post mortem at Chertsey". Then in another call – sometime after midday – the plans have been changed: "We agreed that Dr Chapman should hold both post mortems at the Hammersmith and Fulham mortuary".

Burgess has stated that "at approximately 10 a.m. I ... asked [Keith Brown] to arrange the opening of the mortuary at the Royal Surrey County Hospital". Burgess "then telephoned Dr Burton and advised him".

Next: "Keith Brown [then] confirmed that he had made [the] arrangements".

---

on the Princess but failed." This also appears to be a reference to Iain West who was the Head of the Forensic Medicine Department at Guys Hospital from 1994 to 1998. West died in July 2001. Source: Bill Hunt, Iain West – Obituary, The Independent, 28 July 2001

[a] In the 2001 affidavit Thompson timed this at "about 11.00 a.m." Thompson's statement appears to provide a fuller order of events – he describes staying the night "with my lady friend"; "I got up on the Sunday morning"; "I heard about the deaths"; "my pager" went off "almost straight after".

[b] This location conflict between Burgess and Burton will be addressed later.

Then during a call to Fahy – "during that telephone call, or later" – Burgess learns of "a change in plans" – the post-mortem venue may need to be changed.

Burgess "then spoke to Keith Brown and asked him to stop everything". Burgess next calls Burton: "Burton offered the ... Fulham mortuary ... which I accepted. Then, or during a later telephone call, Dr Burton asked if he could use the services of Dr Chapman".

The main difference between Burton and Burgess' accounts is the timing – Burton places Burgess' first contact with him at "around midday". Burgess places it "at approximately 10 a.m." These timing issues have already been addressed at length in the Royal Control chapter.

Otherwise, the Burton and Burgess accounts basically concur. There is a possibility of collusion in the Burton-Burgess evidence – this serious issue is addressed later in this section.

The major problem with the Burton-Burgess account is that it is not supported by any other witnesses, or by the Coroners Act 1988.

In his statement, Robert Chapman, the post-mortems pathologist declares: "I was contacted by ... Keith Brown ... requesting I attend to carry out a postmortem examination on the body of Mr. Al Fayed.... I was subsequently informed that the examination would take place at the ... Fulham [mortuary]".

John Macnamara "spent most of the day arranging for the repatriation and burial of Dodi Al Fayed's body". He stated to the UK police: "Michael Burgess told me that he had agreed with Dr Burton ... that Dodi's post mortem could be conducted at Fulham mortuary."

Keith Brown, who was the Surrey coroner's officer, has stated: "Mr Burgess then phoned me to say that ... the post mortem [of Dodi] would be ... held at Fulham Mortuary."

Chapman – the pathologist; Macnamara – working for Mohamed; Brown – working directly for Burgess. All three are key witnesses, but none make any mention of an earlier arrangement for a post-mortem in Surrey.

Chapman initially describes being asked to carry out the post-mortem. He is then "subsequently informed" of the venue – Fulham. At the inquest Chapman was specifically asked: "Did you learn where that [post-mortem] was to take place?" Chapman replied: "I was told eventually ... Fulham Public Mortuary." Chapman has replaced "subsequently" with "eventually", but nevertheless has made no mention of any other venue in either account – statement or inquest.

Macnamara has simply stated: "Michael Burgess told me that he had agreed with Dr Burton ... that Dodi's post mortem could be conducted at Fulham mortuary." Macnamara was not asked about this at the inquest.[a]

---

[a] After being asked a specific question regarding a possible early arrangement for a post-mortem at the Royal Surrey County Hospital, Macnamara has stated to me:

Keith Brown was not cross-examined at the inquest, but his police statement – which was read out – is clear: Brown was told by Burgess that "the post mortem [for Dodi] would be ... held at Fulham Mortuary".

There were two other critical witnesses – Harry Brown, Burton's officer; Peter Fahy, Burgess' contact at Surrey police – but neither of these people have been interviewed by any investigation and they also were not heard from at the inquest.

Burton's evidence was: "I phoned ... Harry Brown and asked him to ... place the duty home office pathologist on standby." Later, when Dodi's post-mortem was changed to Fulham: "We[a] agreed that Dr Chapman should hold both post mortems".

Up to that point, Burton's evidence has detailed the phone calls that were made to organise the post-mortems: "I phoned ... Harry Brown"; "Michael Burgess ... phoned"; "I received another call from Michael Burgess".

Yet after the decision is made "that Dr Chapman should hold both post mortems at ... Fulham", there is no mention of the subsequent call – that would have been needed – to Harry Brown to ask him to: a) notify Thompson that Dodi's post-mortem will also be at Fulham[b]; b) notify Thompson that Dodi's body will be arriving much earlier than Diana's is expected to[c]; and c) notify the duty pathologist – who had earlier been arranged to conduct Diana's post-mortem – that his/her services would no longer be required.

Harry Brown's evidence has not been heard, but there is nothing in Thompson's affidavit or statement to indicate any change in plans. Thompson's evidence is that the initial plan was for both post-mortems to be conducted at Fulham Mortuary. Thompson describes one phone call with Harry Brown – "I then went to the mortuary".

The duty pathologist that Burton asked Brown earlier in the day to organise for Diana's post-mortem has never been named. There is no evidence of this unnamed pathologist being asked to do Diana's post-mortem and there is no evidence of the arrangement with him/her being cancelled.

I suggest that may be because Burton did not ask for the duty pathologist – and that the initial plan was to use a forensic pathologist for Diana's post-mortem: "we chose a forensic pathologist" (Burgess). Thompson has named the forensic pathologist that Burton initially sought: "Harry Brown ... tried to contact Dr Iain West ... with a view to him carrying out the post mortem

---

"There was never any mention [on 31 August 1997] of Royal Surrey County Hospital.": Email correspondence, John Macnamara, 19 November 2010.
[a] Burgess and Burton.
[b] There will be two post-mortems to prepare for, not just one.
[c] As it turned out, Dodi's body was held up in France – see Part 3 – but still arrived at Fulham Mortuary 2½ hours earlier than Diana's.

examination on Princess Diana's body. However Dr West was ... out of the country...."

Burton and Burgess both describe the decision to use Chapman for both post-mortems: Burgess – "Burton asked if he could use the services of Dr Chapman"; Burton – "we agreed that Dr Chapman should hold both post mortems".

Yet the evidence is that Chapman is not told of this decision until after his arrival at Fulham Mortuary: Chapman – "I was not asked to carry out a post-mortem ... on Diana ... until I arrived at Fulham".[a] It is possible this delay in telling Chapman was for security reasons – limiting knowledge of what was happening, or planned, i.e. the "normal" policy of providing information on a "need-to-know" basis.[bc]

There is conflicting evidence between Burton and Burgess over the location of the initial venue for the Dodi post-mortem:
-   Burgess: "I ... asked [Keith Brown] to arrange the opening of the mortuary at the Royal Surrey County Hospital"
-   Burgess: "I ... advised [Burton] that I ... was arranging a post mortem at Guildford"
-   Burton: "[Burgess] was arranging a post mortem at Chertsey".

Burgess has said the "Royal Surrey County Hospital" (RSCH) and "Guildford" – the RSCH is in Guildford.

Burton has indicated that Burgess told him "Chertsey".

Chertsey and Guildford – although both in Surrey – are completely different places, about 25 km apart.[d]

There has never been any explanation for this conflict.

Outside of Burton-Burgess, the general evidence is that there was only one mortuary and one pathologist organised: Fulham and Chapman – Thompson, Macnamara, Keith Brown, Chapman.[a]

---

[a] Burton doesn't mention notifying Chapman in his statement, but it is in both sets of his notes: Handwritten – "Chapman to do P.M. ... asked to continue when Diana arrived"; Typed – "Chapman asked to do Diana autopsy after Dodi at Fulham".

[b] This is discussed in Part 5 with reference to the intelligence agencies. Burton was working on behalf of the Queen – see earlier – and there is every reason to believe that on that day, 31 August 1997, information would have been provided only as needed.

[c] Thompson says: "it was logical that as Dr Chapman was already at the mortuary he would carry out the post mortem examinations on both bodies". This evidence could be read to indicate that the decision for Chapman to conduct the Diana post-mortem was last-minute, at the mortuary. Other evidence from Burton and Burgess – see above – shows that this decision was made earlier in the day.

[d] Brookwood Cemetery – where Dodi was buried – is about 17 km from Chertsey and about 13 km from Guildford.

Why did Burton and Burgess put forward evidence of an earlier plan for two mortuaries – RSCH[b] and Fulham – and two pathologists – "unnamed" and Chapman?

Royal coroner, John Burton, seems to have been very determined to distance himself from being the one responsible for making the post-mortem of Princess Diana special:

- Burton appears to falsely state that he asked Harry Brown to "place the duty home office pathologist on standby" – Harry Brown has never been asked for his evidence regarding this

- according to Burton, Chapman – a forensic pathologist – only becomes the pathologist for Diana's post-mortem after an unrelated change to the arrangements for Dodi's post-mortem. Otherwise, Diana's post-mortem would have been conducted by the unnamed "duty pathologist"

- Burton appears to falsely state: "both post mortems were ... made special by the police".[c]

It has already been shown that Philip Stoneham's evidence indicated the decision to carry out special post-mortems was made prior to the start of the 4.15 p.m. Scotland Yard meeting. The above evidence reveals that the special post-mortem decision could have been made by the two coroners when they chose to have the post-mortems conducted by a forensic pathologist.

There is other important evidence to consider:

1) The Coroners Act indicates that it is the coroner who is legally permitted to request the pathologist to conduct a special post-mortem. s20 (1) of the 1988 Act states: "The coroner may ... request ... a special examination of the body...."[d]

2) Robert Chapman has stated: "The decision as to whether an examination is regarded as a 'special' examination is taken by HM coroner."

The coroner is the person who is legally responsible for the holding of an inquest.[e] The general evidence is that it is the coroner – not the police – who has the legal power to request a post-mortem, as a part of obtaining the evidence towards the inquest. And it is the coroner who has the power to make that post-mortem "special".

---

[a] The failure by the police to ever interview Harry Brown and Peter Fahy only adds to the expectation that their evidence also would have conflicted with Burton and Burgess.

[b] Royal Surrey County Hospital. Burton doesn't actually name the other mortuary. The evidence on this is dealt with shortly.

[c] The reasons this statement is false are addressed below.

[d] The full text has been shown earlier.

[e] By definition, the coroner is "an official who holds inquests into violent, sudden or suspicious deaths": Oxford.

487

3) The timing issue with Burton's evidence – addressed in the Royal Control chapter – also becomes a factor in this subject. Burton indicates that it is towards midday[a] when he phoned Harry Brown to arrange a post-mortem for Diana at Fulham Mortuary.

Thompson's detailed statement account is that he arrived at Fulham "around 10 a.m. or 11 a.m." – he therefore was probably called by Harry Brown before 10 a.m.

Macnamara says in his police statement that he started work at Harrods "shortly after 7 a.m." and then "liaised closely with Mr Michael Burgess ... during the latter part of the morning". Macnamara has confirmed to me that he "was told by Michael Burgess about 10 a.m. ... that the [Dodi Fayed] post-mortem would be conducted at Fulham mortuary".[319]

Macnamara has said at the inquest that he "had several conversations with Mr Burgess" and I suggest that it is logical that information on the post-mortem venue would have been of major importance to both himself and Mohamed Al Fayed.[b] It is quite possible that that issue could have been a part of their initial conversation.[c]

In summary, the evidence of both Thompson and Macnamara conflicts with Burton's account. Thompson and Macnamara indicate that the decision to use Fulham Mortuary was made before 10 a.m. Statement evidence from Thompson describes seeing, on his arrival at Fulham, "several men in dark suits who ... I assumed were police officers from Royalty Protection or something like that". This indicates notification to Balmoral of Fulham Mortuary as the post-mortem venue earlier than 10 a.m.[d]

4) Chapman has stated: "I did not discuss the nature of the [Diana] examination with the Coroner, except to confirm with him that I would carry

---

[a] Burton only gives scant references to timing. The call to Harry Brown appears in Burton's statement between a call to Levertons "later that morning' and a call from Burgess "around midday".

[b] Given the religious importance to Mohamed of Dodi being buried before sunset – see earlier.

[c] In his statement Burgess decribes Fulham Mortuary being mentioned in his initial conversation with Macnamara. Burgess however times this call "at some point around about midday". It has however been shown at length in Part 3, how Burgess lied about the communications between himself and Macnamara on the day, including the issue of timing. There is no reason to doubt Macnamara's claim that he started at 7 a.m. on the Sunday morning – the circumstances were very pressing: Macnamara had the responsibility of ensuring that Dodi was buried before sunset. Given these circumstances, I suggest that it is unlikely that Macnamara – a former MPS Detective Chief Superintendent – would leave it 5 hours (till midday) before making contact with the key person whose cooperation was critical to ensuring Dodi could be buried on time, Michael Burgess.

[d] The presence of Royalty Protection is addressed in the Police Presence section – see later.

out a full dissection of the body." He continues: "A large number of personnel were gathered and it was clear that only a thorough and complete examination would suffice. I personally supervised the process.... I obtained all of the exhibits and toxicology samples." Then later this: "I did not receive any formal briefing prior to my examinations."

In making these statements, Chapman appears to be suggesting that he himself made the examinations special – "I did not receive any formal briefing prior to my examinations" and "I did not discuss the nature of the examination with the Coroner".

Chapman appears to outline his reasoning behind this: "A large number of personnel were gathered and it was clear that only a thorough and complete examination would suffice." Chapman seems to be indicating that the catalyst for "a thorough and complete examination" is the "number of personnel" who are in the room.[a]

In a possible conflict, Chapman has said: "The decision as to whether an examination is regarded as a 'special' examination is taken by HM coroner although a pathologist can advise...." And on the night, Chapman said he did "confirm with [Burton] that I would carry out a full dissection of the body."

When Chapman outlined that it is the coroner who makes "the decision as to whether an examination is ... a 'special'", he is basically reflecting the law as it is found in the Coroners Act – see point 1 above. This would then appear to make Chapman's extraordinary admission – "I did not discuss the nature of the examination with the Coroner" – a possible admission of a knowing breach of the law.

This post-mortem of Princess Diana was possibly one of the most significant jobs Chapman had ever undertaken – it seems unbelievable that he would take on that responsibility without consulting the royal coroner, who was present in the mortuary.

Chapman expects us to believe that "after my arrival at the mortuary, I was met by Dr Burton.... [who] indicated to me that ... it would be practical if I could carry out that examination" of Princess Diana's body, yet Chapman: a) does not receive any instructions on the procedure, and b) doesn't ask for any instructions on the procedure.

I suggest that there is a possibility that Robert Chapman has been asked to distance the royal coroner, John Burton, from direct involvement in making Diana's post-mortem special. Evidence later in this chapter will reveal that Chapman is an unreliable witness.

---

[a] I suggest that this type of reasoning is not far removed from the way some of the decisions were made in the French investigation – see Part 3.

The Burgess-Burton evidence includes references to an original plan to carry out a Surrey post-mortem on Dodi Fayed's body. The reality is that this evidence finds no support in the known evidence from any of the other witnesses – Chapman, Keith Brown, Macnamara, Thompson: see earlier.

There appear to be three possibilities:

a) The Burton-Burgess account is true, but all the other witnesses have forgotten that there was a plan to hold a post-mortem for Dodi in Surrey

b) There was an initial plan for a Surrey post-mortem, but it was changed to Fulham much earlier than Burton-Burgess have indicated. This could mean the plan was only of minor significance and that is the reason it is not mentioned by the other witnesses

c) Burton and Burgess have created the Surrey post-mortem plan to assist in distancing Burton – and therefore also his Balmoral instructors – from responsibility in calling for a special post-mortem to be conducted on Princess Diana's body.

I suggest that possibility a) is extremely unlikely. There are 3 witnesses – Chapman, Keith Brown, Macnamara – who should have recalled this important event in their evidence, but fail to. Macnamara has since been specifically asked about a Surrey post-mortem and has specifically denied knowledge of it – see earlier footnote. On top of that, Thompson's evidence indicates that both post-mortems were requested for Fulham at the same time.[a] And then, there are the two other witnesses who have apparently never been asked – Harry Brown and Peter Fahy.

If either b) or c) are true, then that is evidence of possible collusion between Burton and Burgess and provision by both of a false and misleading account of their evidence.

Is there any credible evidence that Burton and Burgess may have colluded in their evidence?

Burton's statement was taken on 16 June 2004, just six months before he died. Burgess, on the other hand, was interviewed three times – 15 June 2004; 30 July 2004; 16 August 2004 – before anything was committed to the record, on 18 August 2004. Even then, Burgess refused to provide the police with an official, sworn or signed statement.[320] It may not be a coincidence that Burgess' first interview was one day before Burton's – this raises the possibility that Burton was provided with Burgess' initial account prior to

---

[a] If Dodi's post-mortem had initially been organised for Surrey, then one would have expected Thompson to receive two phone calls – one for Diana's post-mortem and a later one – after the plan change – for Dodi's. This would have been a significant issue for Thompson because it would have meant that the Fulham Mortuary had to be ready for action at least 2 to 3 hours earlier than when Diana's body was expected to arrive.

completing his own statement. Likewise, Burgess may have been provided with Burton's final account before his later interviews.[a]

If there was collusion between Burton and Burgess – with the possible assistance of Paget – on this issue of the Dodi post-mortem, it is not the first time in this series of books that such a possibility has been raised. The evidence in Part 3 regarding the Burton and Burgess accounts of events relating to the body transfer hold-up indicated that, at the least, these two witnesses had compared notes ahead of giving evidence.[321]

There are mentions of a Surrey post-mortem plan for Dodi's body in the notes – handwritten, Burgess; typed, Burton and Burgess. It may however be significant that any possibility of such a plan is completely missing from Burton's handwritten notes from the day.

Burton's handwritten notes – over the three relevant lines – read:
"Burgess informed of Fayed by Surrey police. Burial – Brookwood
"Problem with time for funeral
"If P.M at Fulham – between Heliport and Mosque." [b]

It's a different story when we look at a copy of the typed notes that Burton says he prepared "in mid October 1997 ... from memory regarding the events that had taken place that day which I handed over to Michael Burgess my successor when I retired."

Those notes read:
"Burgess informed by Surrey Police that Dodi coming to Brookwood for burial before nightfall. Arrangements for Chapman to do rapid autopsy in Surrey before burial.
"Plans changed. Dodi to go to London Mosque then Brookwood. Chapman and Burgess come to Fulham mortuary to do autopsy before service."[c]

Burgess provided Paget with "a photocopy of five pages of handwritten notes with the heading 31 Aug".[322de] These notes have been subjected to

---

[a] The methods used by Operation Paget in conducting interviews and taking statements are addressed in Part 5. Earlier evidence in this volume has indicated that Keith Leverton was able to copy portions of Clive Leverton's Paget statement.

[b] It could be significant that Burton denied the existence of these notes when he made his 2004 statement. Burton said: "The only notes that I made on the day of the post mortems were the two 'transferral of jurisdiction orders' and a 'burial order'". This issue has been addressed earlier in the Royal Control chapter.

[c] Both Burton's handwritten and typed notes appear at the start of the Royal Coroner section of the Royal Control chapter.

[d] The first two pages of these notes appear at the start of the Royal Coroner section of the Royal Control chapter.

[e] It is possibly significant that Burgess has never shown Paget the originals of these notes. This is addressed in Part 3.

intense scrutiny in the Body Transfer section of Part 3 and it has been shown there that parts of them may have been doctored.

On the first page, Burgess has written:

"KB

"RSCH

"Pathologist: on call – suggest RTS
                                    ? or RCC"

Further down the page:

"KB – ready – RCC - ?timing"

Then:

"Peter Fahy – Timing?

? Arrangement – now service in London – PM still? Yes – "

Then on the next page:

"KB Stop everything – alternative? – ?SFW – No

"JDKB [Unknown] - Offer of Fulham –

" – accepted

"KB – RCC → Fulham" [a]

Burgess provided a copy of typed notes that he said "was an 'Aide Memoir' only, and had been made sometime after the incident".

Those notes read:

"1000 approx Tel KB – Plse arrange for PM at RSCH – discussion as to pathologist ... see if RTS avail if not [then] RCC"

Further down the page:

"Tel Call from Peter Fahy ... arrangements now changed ... first a Service in Mosque in London – said still required body to be PMed ... would review and advise him.

"Tel KB – advised him to ease back on arrangements would need to review in light of Service in London

"Tel JDKB Advising him of need to alter arrangements – discussed as to variations – agreed that body to Fulham, PM there and then to Mosque and on to Burial ... no knowledge of times yet ... various other tel calls inc JDKB confirmed that mort could be available and that his mortician would attend .... also confirmed that RCC could examine DPoW later[b]

---

[a] Burgess used several abbreviations: KB = Keith Brown; RSCH = Royal Surrey County Hospital; RTS = Richard Shepherd; RCC = Robert Charles Chapman; PM = Post-Mortem; JDKB = John David Keith Burton.

[b] Chapman has stated: "I was not asked to carry out a postmortem examination on Diana ... until I arrived at Fulham Mortuary" – police statement. This was also confirmed at the inquest: "Fairly soon after my arrival at the mortuary ... [Burton] indicated to me ... that it would be practical if I could carry out that examination" of Princess Diana. Burton said: "We agreed that Dr Chapman should hold both post mortems at the Hammersmith and Fulham mortuary." Burgess said: "Dr Burton asked if he could use the services of Dr Chapman for a post mortem examination on

"Tel KB and Peter Fahy – advised them of change of plans ... stand RSCH mortuary down and direct RCC to attend in Fulham"[a]

There are several points regarding <u>Burton's handwritten notes</u>:

1) An analysis of these notes is made difficult because they cannot be viewed in their original handwritten form – they have been typed up by Elizabeth Butler-Sloss.[b]

2) As stated above, there is no mention of a Surrey post-mortem for Dodi.

3) Burton does appear to confirm that Chapman was enlisted by Burgess – "Chapman to do P.M. ... asked to continue when Diana arrived." This fits with Chapman's account – see earlier.

4) The three lines quoted above – from "Burgess" through to "Mosque" – appear to be closely connected.

Burton has used "full stops" in his notes, but there is no full stop between "Burial – Brookwood" and "Heliport and Mosque".

These three lines relate to the arrangements for Dodi. To paraphrase what appear to be just three points shown: a) the burial is at Brookwood; b) there is a problem with the funeral time; c) part of the solution could be having the post-mortem[c] at Fulham, because it is between the heliport and the mosque.

Points regarding <u>Burton's typed notes</u>:

1) Burton introduces the possibility of a "rapid autopsy" for Dodi. There is evidence from Burgess of "Macnamara being anxious that the post mortem should be both kept to a minimum and that it should not delay the burial", but this reference is the only admission from anyone, including Burton himself and Burgess, that a quick post-mortem for Dodi was actually planned.[d]

2) Burton outlines the initial conversation with Burgess, including the Surrey post-mortem, then shows the plan change to a Fulham post-mortem

3) Throughout these notes the word "autopsy" appears 4 times and there is no use of the word "post-mortem".[e] In contrast, Burton used "PM" – standing for "post-mortem" – 5 times in his handwritten notes, with no use of

---

the body of Diana." This evidence indicates that Burton and Burgess made a decision during the day, for Chapman to conduct the Diana post-mortem, without actually consulting Chapman.

[a] Abbreviations: 1000 = 10 a.m.; Tel = Telephone; DPoW = Diana, Princess of Wales. Other abbreviations have been explained in the previous footnote relating to the Burgess handwritten notes.

[b] See earlier in Royal Control chapter.

[c] There is a possibility this is both post-mortems – Diana's post-mortem venue may not have been locked in at this stage.

[d] Dodi's post-mortem took about 1¼ hours, whereas Diana's took 3 hours. This is addressed later.

[e] The word "autopsied" appears once as well.

the word "autopsy". Likewise, in Burton's police statements[a], he used the word "post-mortem(s)" 48 times – with no usage of the word "autopsy".

There is a further issue in Burton's statement account. Describing his initial conversation – before the plan change – with Burgess, Burton says: "We agreed that in order to facilitate this and the wishes of Mr Mohamed Al Fayed that the post mortem of Mr Dodi Al Fayed would <u>take place first</u>."

This appears in the same conversation that Burton describes: Burgess "was arranging a post mortem at Chertsey[b]". Burton's statement account is that prior to this conversation with Burgess, he had already made arrangements for the Diana post-mortem to be held at Fulham Mortuary.

Burton's statement evidence then is that at the stage of this first Burgess conversation[c], there were two completely separate post-mortems being organised – Diana at Fulham, Dodi at Chertsey. This means that the two post-mortems could in theory[d] have been held concurrently – it would not have mattered because the initial plan was to have:

- two different venues – Fulham (Diana) and Chertsey (Dodi)
- two different pathologists – unnamed "duty" (Diana)[e] and Chapman (Dodi)
- two different coroners – Burton (Diana) and Burgess (Dodi).

In light of that, Burton's statement – "we agreed that ... the post mortem of Mr Dodi Al Fayed would take place first" – does not actually fit. This would only fit if the decision had already been made – at the time of this initial Burgess-Burton phone call – that the two post-mortems were to be held at the same venue: Fulham Mortuary.

There are also issues with <u>Burgess' handwritten and typed notes</u>:

1) There is a possibility that Burgess' handwritten notes have been doctored to include "evidence" of an earlier plan for a post-mortem of Dodi in Surrey. This cannot be proven, but it is informed speculation based on the inescapable fact that there are four other witnesses who – if there had been such a plan – would have had to be privy to it, yet it does not appear in their evidence.[f]

---

[a] Burton's statements run to 15 pages of *The Documents* book.

[b] Chertsey is in Surrey. Burton's mention of Chertsey as a post-mortem venue for Dodi has been addressed earlier.

[c] This is the first conversation described by Burton – Burgess mentions an additional earlier conversation in his statement.

[d] In practice, Diana's body was due to arrive in the UK a lot later than Dodi's.

[e] See earlier.

[f] This has been dealt with earlier. The witnesses are Keith Brown, John Macnamara, Robert Chapman and Robert Thompson. There are also two other witnesses who have never been interviewed, but should have been had the police – or Scott Baker – been interested in establishing exactly what occurred. The only witnesses who have

In this light, it is particularly significant that:

- Burgess failed to provide the originals of his notes – handwritten and typed – to Operation Paget [a]
- Burgess failed to provide a sworn or signed statement to Paget, he was not cross-examined at the inquest and the jury were also prevented from hearing his statement – in essence, the inquest jury heard no evidence at all from Michael Burgess
- Scott Baker had both sets of Burgess' notes, but also failed to make those available to his jury.

Looking closer at the handwritten Burgess notes:[b]

a) There is a possibility that the first "KB" entry on page 1 has been doctored. This is the only place in the 5 page document[c] that a person's initials – "KB" – are shown, with nothing written directly beside it.[d] There is a possibility that something has been removed and "RSCH"[e] has been inserted later.

b) At the bottom of page 1, the diagonal line coming down from "Peter Fahy" and the writing adjacent and below it – "? Arrangement – now service in London – PM still? Yes – " – may have been inserted later.

c) At the top of page 2, the writing – "KB Stop everything – alternative? – ?SFW – No

JDKB [Unknown] – Offer of Fulham – – accepted" – and the long curved downward diagonal line, could all have been inserted later.

2) Besides not showing the original documents to Paget, Burgess said that his typed notes were "made sometime after the incident". Burgess – who is saying this in 2004 – provides no inkling whatsoever as to when this typed document may have been put together.

---

provided evidence on this earlier plan are the two coroners – Burton, who is now dead, and Burgess, whose evidence was not heard at the inquest.

[a] See earlier : Paget received "a photocopy of five pages of handwritten notes" and "a copy of a two page document" – the typed notes.

[b] The relevant pages are pages 1 and 2 – they have both been reproduced in the Royal Coroner section of the Royal Control chapter.

[c] The complete document is reproduced in *The Documents* book, pp545-550.

[d] It could be argued that this is because the "KB" has been placed too close vertically to the "?Fairoaks!" entry (on the right hand side) – so the author, Burgess, has dropped a line to write "RSCH". I believe this is possible, but the balance of the evidence – see earlier – is that there was never an intention to hold a post-mortem in Surrey.

[e] Royal Surrey County Hospital.

I suggest that at the time Burgess produced this typed document, it had been decided to change the evidence to support an early Surrey post-mortem for Dodi.

Suspicious Deaths

The question is: Did a perception of the deaths being suspicious contribute to the decision to make the post-mortems special?

The evidence of Stoneham and Thompson:

- Stoneham: "a special post mortem ... usually takes place where the death is a suspicious one"

- Thompson: "police are normally only present, and photography and extensive sample taking involved, in situations where the death is suspicious" – affidavit, 13 June 2001

- Thompson: "the post mortems received the fullest possible treatment, (i.e. the type of treatment normally reserved for suspicious deaths)" – affidavit, 13 June 2001

- Thompson: "there was also present a laboratory liaison officer, Detective Sergeant Stoneham – in the case of a suspicious death the laboratory liaison officer is there to receive the samples and specimens" – affidavit, 13 June 2001

- Thompson: "in the case of a criminal/forensic post mortem it is the police exhibits officer who takes the samples but it was a different situation in the cases of the Princess and Dodi" [a] – statement, 9 November 2004

This evidence reveals the link between a special post-mortem and a suspicious death – if a death is suspicious, then a special post-mortem can be called for.

Is this what occurred in the case of Princess Diana?

Thompson has provided conflicting evidence. In his 2001 affidavit Thompson has stated: "the post mortems received ... the type of treatment normally reserved for suspicious deaths". But three years later in Thompson's police statement he indicated that "the police exhibits officer" – Philip Stoneham – didn't take the samples, as he would have in "a criminal/forensic post mortem".

Just a few sentences later in Thompson's statement he admits: "I do not actually recall being handed the samples following the post mortems". The chain of custody regarding Diana's samples is a critical issue and it is covered later in this chapter.

Thompson has stated that he believes Stoneham didn't take the samples, but he also has no recall of taking them himself. Later evidence will reveal

---

[a] The issue of what happened to Princess Diana's samples is very important – see later.

that these samples from Diana were switched – it will be shown that the true samples eventually came under the control of the police.

This evidence could suggest that Thompson's earlier affidavit account may be more accurate on this issue, than his later police statement.

There is certainly evidence that on the 31 August 1997 there was a view that the deaths of Princess Diana and Dodi Fayed were suspicious:

- there is the evidence – shown in Chapter 1 – that soon after Princess Diana's death Professor Bruno Riou completed a death certificate by marking the Medico-Legal Issues box

- there is also evidence – shown in Part 3 – that Jeffrey Rees had made a phone call prior to 2.30 p.m., stating that "the deaths were suspicious and therefore the body would be delayed" in France.[a] Rees distanced himself from any involvement in that, but it was revealed in Part 3 that Rees had lied under oath – as he did when he denied his presence at the 4.15 p.m. Scotland Yard meeting (see earlier).

The earlier evidence has indicated that the decision to conduct a special post-mortem was made by the coroners. On the day, John Burton – the senior and royal coroner – was working on behalf of the Queen in Balmoral.[b] I suggest that the analysis and taking of samples that occurred would have been under orders given to Burton from Balmoral, possibly via the Lord Steward or Buckingham Palace.

The above evidence – from Stoneham and Thompson – reveals that a special post-mortem is generally called when the deaths are viewed as suspicious, but it does not necessarily follow that because a special post-mortem is called that the deaths are viewed as suspicious. In other words, a special post-mortem is not always because the death is suspicious.

Having said that, the evidence in these volumes has revealed that the deaths were suspicious and that there was an assassination. This volume has shown that the early post-death decisions were being made from Balmoral. These early actions may indicate an early knowledge by the royals – on 31 August 1997 – that the deaths were suspicious.

Coroner's Role

There is conflicting evidence on the role royal coroner, John Burton, played in the post-mortem of Princess Diana.

Jeffrey Rees, Head of Early Crash Investigations, British Police: 17 Dec 07: 100.23:

---

[a] This is from testimony provided by John Macnamara regarding a call from Burgess, who had in turn been phoned by Burton, and originally Rees. This is a complex subject which is dealt with thoroughly in Part 3.

[b] See Royal Control chapter.

Horwell: Q. You have been asked about the post-mortem examinations. We have heard already – and can I ask you to confirm – that both coroners were present at these post-mortem examinations.

A. Yes.[a]

Q. And whatever they would have wanted to have occurred would have occurred, is that right, in terms of work done by the pathologist or samples taken from the respective bodies?

A. I assume so because obviously they are very senior people.

Q. If a coroner issues instructions or orders at a post-mortem examination, you would expect them to be carried out?

A. Yes, sir, although I have to say, I have never seen a coroner present at a post-mortem examination before. Again, this was a situation without precedent.[b]

Q. Yes, so yet another instance of this being a unique event, the first time in your experience that a coroner had been present at a post-mortem examination?

A. Yes, sir.

Q. Just to revisit what I was asking you: if a coroner in these circumstances had given any instruction or order, you would have expected it to be carried out without fail?

A. Yes.

John Burton, Royal Coroner, 1997: 16 Jun 04 Statement: **Jury Didn't Hear**:

"As a coroner I would normally be dealing with approximately 2,500 deaths/ post mortems a year. As the coroner for Heathrow I was involved in the inquest of numerous bodies that were repatriated to England. I attended a lot of these post mortems. During a post mortem the pathologist is in charge and is normally assisted by one or more mortuary assistants. Although I directed that a post mortem be ... carried out I was not in charge of the mortuary or any of the staff.

---

[a] The evidence – post-mortem reports and the coroners' statements – shows that both Burton and Burgess were at Dodi's post-mortem, but only Burton was at Diana's.

[b] Evidence below shows that Rees appears to have lied when he said: "I have never seen a coroner present at a post-mortem examination before". Rees "supports" this evidence by saying: "this was a situation without precedent". It was a recurring theme through Rees' cross-examinations to justify his evidence by saying there was no precedent: "this was a situation without precedent for the Metropolitan Police": 32.4; "we have to remember that this was a situation without precedent for the Metropolitan Police": 79.1; "this was a situation without precedent for us": 85.6; "this was a situation without precedent": 101.14. It is interesting that Rees has used exactly the same words each time – "this was a situation without precedent" – as though this aspect of his evidence had been rehearsed ahead of his appearance.

"There have been many occasions where I have assisted at post mortems. Most of these were out of hours and were mainly suspicious deaths.... Quite often having called people out during the middle of the night I would assist in the cleansing of bodies [at] the mortuary. I would sometimes make notes at the dictation of the pathologist and would hold the photographer's second or remote flashlight to assist him. On numerous occasions I gave people a lift home.

"This was not the normal case with Robert Thompson. He was the mortuary superintendent at the Hammersmith and Fulham Mortuary. He was very good at his job and didn't normally require any assistance and had his own transport to get home....

"The undertakers arrived with the coffin holding the body of Mr Dodi Al Fayed.... I was acting as the gofer and in order to open the coffin I went to my car to get some tools that I always carried for that purpose. On my return we unscrewed the lid of the coffin. Inside ... a plastic seal had been used to seal tight the channel to the lid. I then went to collect more tools on my return the coffin had been opened by the undertakers. I know they used my screwdriver to open the seal on the coffin....

"I assisted in the removal of the body from the coffin... I took no active part in this post mortem apart from my cleaning duties....

"When the post mortem had finished I cleaned the body and then went and spoke to the undertakers to make sure that we were doing all we could to comply with needs of the Muslim faith. I explained that I had cleaned the body and they requested clean linen in which the body could be buried. I obtained clean linen and assisted in the dressing of the body....

"I did not take an active part in the [Diana] post mortem but again assisted in the cleaning of the body and mortuary.

"Once I was happy that all official matters for my purposes were carried out I issued a burial order in accordance with rule 14 of the Coroners rules and released her body back to the undertakers."[323]

Robert Thompson, Fulham Mortuary Manager: 9 Nov 04 Statement: **Jury Didn't Hear**:

"At that time Mr Burton was the Coroner for West London and he used to attend most of the forensic post mortems, which are carried out in all cases where the death was suspicious.

"Dr Burton had been the Coroner from the time I had first started working at Fulham mortuary and was still the Coroner when I left. He had his office within the Coroner's Court and although we weren't close socially, we did work closely together. He was hardworking and good to work with. We got on very well. He was present during both post mortems and for a good while

499

after. He made sure that all the important points of the post mortem were covered and was very much involved in proceedings."[324]

Dr Robert Chapman, Pathologist, UK: 24 Feb 05 Statement: **Jury Didn't Hear**:

"I had known Dr John Burton since 1988 as West London Coroner. I would have frequent contact with him during inquests and at some of the postmortem examinations."[325]

Comment: There are three different witnesses who have spoken about Burton's role – Burton, Rees, Thompson – and there are three completely conflicting accounts.

But first: Do coroners normally attend post-mortems?

The evidence is:

- Rees: "I have never seen a coroner present at a post-mortem examination before"

- Burton: "there have been many occasions where I have assisted at post mortems"

- Thompson: "Burton ... used to attend most of the forensic post mortems"

- Chapman: "I would have ... contact with [Burton] ... at some of the postmortem examinations".

Rees was actually asked a different question: Horwell, the MPS lawyer, wanted to know whether anything Burton or Burgess "would have wanted to have occurred would have occurred" during the post-mortems. Initially Rees – who was very evasive through most of his inquest cross-examinations[a] - says "I assume so". Rees – who was there at both post-mortems – comes across as reluctant to confirm the coroner's power.

Horwell then re-asks the question, using different words. This time Rees answers "yes ... although" and then volunteers: "I have never seen a coroner present at a post-mortem examination before".

Maybe Horwell is surprised by that response, because he next asks Rees to confirm that it is the first time he has seen "a coroner ... present at a post-mortem examination". Rees confirms, and then Horwell asks his original question for the third time: Would Rees "have expected [a coroner's instructions] to be carried out without fail"? This time Rees simply replies: "Yes."

Both Burton and Thompson say the opposite to Rees: they state that coroner Burton did attend post-mortems, and not just one or two – Burton: on "many occasions"; Thompson: he attended "most of the forensic post mortems". Chapman supports Burton and Thompson: "I would have ... contact with [Burton] ... at some of the postmortem examinations".

---

[a] It has been shown in Part 3 that Rees lied under oath at the inquest.

I suggest that the account of Burton, Thompson and Chapman is common sense. The coroner is required, under the Coroners Act 1988 s8, to in certain circumstances "as soon as practicable hold an inquest". By definition, the purpose of an inquest is to determine the cause of death. The purpose of a post-mortem is also to determine cause of death – see earlier. In many cases a post-mortem is called – under the law[a] – by the coroner, to assist in his or her search for the cause of death.

Therefore I suggest it is logical to expect that the coroner – who is required to seek out the cause of death – would attend a post-mortem that he has called.

I further suggest that Jeffrey Rees – who David Veness, Assistant Commissioner at Scotland Yard, has described as "the best officer that I could find available" – has lied to the inquest when he said: "I have never seen a coroner present at a post-mortem examination before".

Rees' evidence on this raises two questions:

1) Why did Rees state that he had "never seen a coroner present at a post-mortem examination before"?

2) Why was Rees so reluctant to admit that if the coroner gave instructions "you would expect them to be carried out"?[b]

One of the themes of evidence in this book has been that there was a concerted effort to distance the royal coroner from any significant involvement in the critical events that were occurring on 31 August 1997.

Rees' evidence appears to be a part of that, as is the evidence from Burton himself – see below.

When Rees said that he had "never seen a coroner present at a post-mortem examination before", he appears to be downplaying the general role of a coroner in a post-mortem – in fact, he completely negates the role: if a coroner doesn't attend a post-mortem at all then effectively he has no hands-on role.

Likewise, Horwell had to ask Rees the same question – regarding a coroner's instructions being carried out at the post-mortems – three times, because Rees realised an unqualified affirmative answer acknowledged the real power of the coroner. This information means that the royal coroner, the Queen's representative at Diana's post-mortem, had the power to influence the events that took place.

---

[a] s20 of the Coroners Act 1988.

[b] Horwell had to ask this question three times before he got an unqualified answer – see above.

I suggest that this is opposite to the message that the Establishment wanted the jury to hear – the general evidence has shown that there has been a major effort to distance the royal coroner from the events that took place.

Burton has acknowledged that he had attended post-mortems on "many occasions" and has provided evidence on his role at a post-mortem, and also specifically at the post-mortems of Diana and Dodi.

Burton, on his general role at post-mortems:
-   "I would assist in the cleansing of bodies"
-   "I would sometimes make notes at the dictation of the pathologist"
-   "I ... would hold the photographer's second or remote flashlight to assist him"
-   "I gave people a lift home".

Burton, on his role at Dodi's post-mortem:
-   "I was acting as the gofer"
-   "I went to my car to get some tools ... in order to open the coffin" and "I ... went to collect more tools"
-   "we unscrewed the lid of the coffin"
-   "I assisted in the removal of the body from the coffin"
-   "I cleaned the body"
-   "I obtained clean linen"
-   "I ... assisted in the dressing of the body".

Burton, on his role at Diana's post-mortem:
-   "I ... assisted in the cleaning of the body and mortuary"
-   "I issued a burial order".

For each case – other post-mortems; Dodi's post-mortem; Diana's post-mortem – Burton has given additional evidence that appears to further limit his role:
-   Other post-mortems: "although I directed that a post mortem [was] to be carried out I was not in charge of the mortuary or any of the staff"
-   Dodi's post-mortem: "I took no active part in this post mortem apart from my cleaning duties"
-   Diana's post-mortem: "I did not take an active part in the [Diana] post mortem".

Burton – as earlier evidence has shown – was present on the night primarily because of his involvement in the Princess Diana post-mortem. Yet his evidence appears to show him playing a lesser role in Diana's post-mortem than he had in Dodi's, or in other post-mortems that he has described.

I suggest that all of the duties Burton has described himself doing are jobs that one would expect to be carried out by mortuary assistants – not the coroner.[a]

Fulham mortuary manager, Robert Thompson, has stated: "[Burton] made sure that all the important points of the [Diana] post mortem[b] were covered and was very much involved in proceedings".

So we have two witnesses on Burton's role at the Diana post-mortem:
- Burton: "I took no active part in this [Diana] post mortem"
- Thompson: Burton "was very much involved in proceedings".

It appears that someone is lying – both statements cannot be true.

There are several points:

1) Pathologist, Robert Chapman, has stated: "At the direct request of Dr Burton I also retained a small sample of the injured area of the heart...."[c] This appears to be evidence of involvement by Burton in the post-mortem proceedings.

2) Robert Thompson, as mortuary manager, does not appear to have a motive for lying – he seems to have related events as he saw them on the day. Royal coroner, John Burton, on the other hand, has already been shown in this volume to have illegally taken jurisdiction over Diana's body and there have been instances of him providing false and misleading evidence.

3) Burton wrote in his original notes: "Transfer jurisdiction of Al Fayed at Fulham to Burgess <u>to allow him to direct P.M.</u> before body arrived in Surrey."

---

[a] Only two other witnesses gave evidence on this – Thompson and Burgess. Burgess appeared to support Burton's account, regarding his role at Dodi's post-mortem: "Dr Burton ... was acting as an assistant technician". In contrast, Thompson – who was present for both post-mortems – doesn't provide any support for Burton's claim that he was involved in cleaning bodies. Thompson said: "Once the post mortem examinations got underway it was mainly me who assisted Dr Chapman though I was assisted by Nigel Munns.... Once the examinations were finished, it was my responsibility to reconstitute the bodies and clean them.... I recall Nigel Munns helping me move the bodies, as physically that was the one thing I couldn't do alone." Sources: Michael Burgess, Witness Statement, 16 August 2004, reproduced in *The Documents* book, p540 (UK Edition); Robert Thompson, Witness Statement, 9 November 2004, reproduced in *The Documents* book, pp602-3 (UK Edition).
[b] Thompson states that Burton "was present during both post mortems", but I suggest he is referring here to the Diana post-mortem, which was Burton's primary responsibility. Although Burton was present during Dodi's post-mortem, the presiding coroner was Surrey coroner, Michael Burgess – see earlier.
[c] This appears under the heading: "DIANA, PRINCESS OF WALES: POSTMORTEM EXAMINATION: ... Histology" in Robert Chapman, Witness Statement, 24 February 2005, reproduced in *The Documents* book, p588 (UK Edition).

This indicates that Burton on 31 August 1997 believed Burgess would "direct" Dodi's post-mortem. "Direct" means supervise, control or manage[326] – active involvement. This may be written evidence from Burton that he believed the coroner's role was active.

4) This post-mortem of Princess Diana would have to be one of the most significant of John Burton's career. I suggest that it is logical that as a part of Burton's primary role to establish cause of death, he could have been involved in the proceedings. Chapman's evidence in point 1) would seem to support that.

It appears that Burton's claim that he "took no active part in this [Diana] post mortem" may be further evidence of a concerted effort to distance the royal coroner from any significant involvement in the events of 31 August 1997.

Conclusion

The overall evidence on the lead-up to the post-mortems is a little patchy, primarily because the testimony of some of the key witnesses has been withheld.

The jury got to hear from Robert Chapman who was cross-examined on 26 November 2007, and Jeffrey Rees and Philip Stoneham on 17 and 18 December, and then John Macnamara two months later on 14 February 2008. Keith Brown's short statement was read out the following month, on 11 March 2008, but two other statements from him were not read out.[a]

The jury did not hear any evidence at all from the most significant witnesses on pre-post-mortem events, coroners John Burton and Michael Burgess. There was also nothing heard from other key witnesses: Robert Thompson, Harry Brown, Dennis Sharp, Richard Wall, Peter Fahy. For any hope of the full truth being established, these five witnesses, Michael Burgess and Keith Brown should all have been subjected to full cross-examinations. The statement of John Burton – who died in 2004 – should have been read out. None of this occurred.

The inquest jury had access to a copy of Burton's handwritten[b] and typed notes[c], but were prevented from seeing Burgess' handwritten and typed notes.

---

[a] Keith Brown made three police statements altogether: 5 May 2005, 14 February 2006, 22 March 2006. The jury only heard the initial 5 May 2005 statement. See footnote on p625 of *The Documents* book (UK edition).

[b] They had a copy of these notes that had been typed up by Butler-Sloss. It has been reproduced in the Royal Control chapter of this book.

[c] The fact that the terminology is different in this document – use of the word "autopsy" when Burton otherwise used the word "post-mortem" (see earlier) – raises a possible question mark over the authenticity of this typed document.

The general evidence reveals that the post-mortems of Princess Diana and Dodi Fayed were "special". The Coroners Act 1988 defines a special post-mortem – paraphrased at the inquest – as "taking parts and samples and so on for testing for [the] purpose" of determining cause of death.[a]

The elephant in the room is: Why was it necessary to conduct a post-mortem involving the taking of samples from the bodies of two passengers in a car crash?[b]

This was an issue that was raised in connection with the post-mortems that were conducted on Diana and Dodi's bodies by Dominique Lecomte – see chapter 1 – and the same issue applies to these UK post-mortems on the same bodies.

Later in this chapter it will be revealed that the evidence shows Princess Diana's samples were switched with another person's – the official toxicology was conducted on samples that did not belong to Princess Diana.

A truer and fuller picture of what actually occurred will emerge as this chapter progresses.

What seems clear at this stage is that there has been a major concerted attempt to cover-up events that took place in the UK on 31 August 1997, during the lead up to the post-mortems:

- the withholding of key witness evidence from the inquest jury, preventing them from being able to ascertain what occurred

- evidence shows the decision to conduct special post-mortems was made by Burton and Burgess early in the day – not late in the day by the police[c]

- Burton falsely stated that he asked for the duty pathologist[d]

- false evidence from Burton and Burgess indicated a separate post-mortem for Dodi had been arranged in Surrey

---

[a] The full definition under the Act has been shown earlier.

[b] Burgess' evidence appears to reveal that Surrey police officer, Peter Fahy, was not necessarily expecting a post-mortem to be conducted on Dodi Fayed's body. Burgess' handwritten notes for the initial call from Fahy read: "PM – Yes" and for a later call "PM Still? Yes". In his statement Burgess said: "Fahy ... asked me if there would still be a post mortem. I told him the answer was 'yes'". Fahy has never been interviewed by any police investigation and was not heard from at the inquest.

[c] There is more evidence on this in the following Police Presence section.

[d] In summary, the evidence on choice of pathologist is quite simple. Both coroners sought a forensic pathologist to conduct their post-mortem: a) Burgess sought Chapman or Shepherd; b) Burton sought Iain West; c) Burgess got Chapman; d) Burton didn't get West; e) Burton and Burgess decided Chapman should do both post-mortems; f) Burton doesn't tell Chapman he wants him to do Diana's post-mortem until after Chapman had arrived at the Fulham Mortuary.

- there is possible evidence of collusion in the testimony of Burton and Burgess
- there is evidence of attempts by Rees and Burton to understate the role of the coroner in post-mortems, and in particular, the post-mortem of Princess Diana.

Overall, the evidence in this section reveals a cover-up directed at suppressing evidence of the significance of the royal coroner's role – in both the lead-up to the post-mortem and during the post-mortem itself. This is a continuation of the theme that has already emerged during the earlier Royal Control chapter.

Earlier evidence has shown that on the day, the royal coroner was making decisions on behalf of the Queen, who was in Balmoral.

It appears that this effort to understate John Burton's role has had the effect of neutralising any role that Balmoral played in the events. If it can be shown that events were being driven from sources other than the royal coroner, then that basically takes influence from the Queen out of the equation. I suggest at this stage that it is not a good look for the Queen to be linked to early post-crash events, especially in connection to the handling of Diana's body – which within 25 hours of death had been subjected to two post-mortems and two embalmings.

When one considers that at the time of her death Princess Diana was not a royal, this evidence revealing early post-death actions from Balmoral is really quite amazing.

A fuller understanding of the significance of these actions will become clearer throughout this chapter.

Police Presence

A significant number of British police attended the post-mortems of Princess Diana and Dodi Fayed – both inside and outside the building.

There is conflicting evidence on why they were present.

David Veness, MPS Asst Commissioner Specialist Operations, UK: 15 Jan 08: 47.11:

Hilliard: Q. You then mention in your statement the question of forensic issues. Can you just help us with what they were and how they arose?

A. In the course of the day, I think, around the midday period, it became apparent that both bodies would be returning to the jurisdiction within the United Kingdom and arrangements were being made to conduct a post-mortem.

Q. When you say "forensic issues" in your witness statement, what do you mean by those, just so we understand?

A. That there should be appropriate arrangements made at the post-mortem in order that all appropriate samples and forensic exhibits should be properly collated and recorded.

Q. Right. As a result of appreciating the need for that, what did you do?

A. I asked my staff officer to contact an investigating officer within the command in order to address the forensic aspects and to attend the post-mortems. That officer was Superintendent Jeffrey Rees.

At 91.16: Mansfield: Q. If this is a car accident, you don't really need the OCG involved, do you?

A. There was – I think [Mulvehill[a]] was forming a view about what might have been necessary in the very near future, in the imminent hours and days ahead. They could not see a role at that stage.

....Q. [Rees] had a long-standing lunch appointment and then he got a pager message, essentially from you.

A. Yes.

Q. You felt it was so imperative that he be involved, the very man who knew a great deal about Mohamed Al Fayed and the allegations, you sent a helicopter to get him, didn't you?[b]

A. Yes.... On that Sunday, as events were moving forward with some rapidity in that the post-mortems had been arranged at relatively short notice, which for certain reasons that appeared to be a highly desirable state of affairs, and that the bodies were returning to the United Kingdom, there was a need to move with expedition in order to have an able officer in order to conduct –

Q. Conduct what?

A. In order to conduct – assist to conduct the post-mortems.

Q. How?

A. There is a need for a very experienced officer in order to marshal the various exhibits, to arrange for the attendance of the key technical specialists, including exhibit officers, to ensure that the optimum forensic samples are recovered subject to the directions of the pathologist.

Q. This was a car accident, albeit involving some very well known people. You had on hand a very experienced pathologist, Dr Chapman; you had a very experienced exhibits officer who had done this many times before, Mr Stoneham. You knew that?

A. Yes, indeed.

Q. You had, in fact, the makings of a team that could swing into action without sending a helicopter for Mr Rees, didn't you?

A. No. My judgment was that we needed to initiate what potentially would be very significant post mortems with the assistance of the best officer that I could find available in the notice to hand.

---

[a] Commander Mulvehill was head of the OCG.

[b] The issue of employing Jeffrey Rees on 31 August 1997 to head the investigation is addressed in Part 5.

At 99.19: Q. Plainly access to the coroners is relatively straightforward from your point of view because you have got an officer who goes down to the post mortem – in fact more than one, three go; a minimum of three are there[a] – and if you wanted to contact the coroner at any time since you are setting up really at the behest of the coroner, it's not a problem, is it?

A. No. This was a straightforward support to the coroner.

David Veness: Paget Description of Statement: **Jury Didn't Hear**:

"He stated that on Sunday 31 August 1997 discussions were held within the MPS regarding possible forensic issues following the repatriation of the bodies of the Princess of Wales and Dodi Al Fayed that might require a police response.

"DCI Heard was the senior officer on call but when Sir David Veness became aware that DCI Heard was travelling to Canada the next day on OCG business, he appointed Detective Superintendent Rees to manage the police response."[327]

Jeffrey Rees, Head of Early Crash Investigations, British Police: 17 Dec 07: 31.9:

Hilliard: Q. Perhaps as is the way of these things, no sooner had you got into your lunch than you got a pager message – is that right?

A. That is correct, sir.

Q. – to contact somebody called the "staff officer" to Assistant Commissioner Veness. By "staff officer" is meant an officer who assists him day-to-day?

A. An assistant effectively.

Q. All right. What were you told once you had contacted the staff officer?

A. I was told that the bodies of Princess Diana and Dodi Fayed were going to be flown back later that day. They were likely to be arriving at Fulham Mortuary around about 5 o'clock that day, and Mr Veness said I had to do whatever had to be done from the police point of view at the mortuary.

Q. Right. You had to do whatever had to be done from the police point of view as regards the bodies. What kind of things did you envisage that might involve?

A. Sir, I think this was a situation without precedent for the Metropolitan Police and clearly it needed somebody in authority to represent the Metropolitan Police's interests and that responsibility fell to me. So, as a matter of course, I ensured that the people who would normally attend a post mortem attended. So that is a photographer[b], exhibits officer, laboratory liaison. But obviously I had a host of other considerations as well: security –

---

[a] There were actually 7 people from the police present in the post-mortem room – see later.

[b] All up, there were three photographers – see later. Neal Williams took photos at Diana's post-mortem, Andrew Selous took photos at Dodi's and Mark Taylor assisted at both post-mortems.

the eyes of the world were on the Metropolitan Police that day, so I had to think of what security we had around the mortuary; that kind of thing.

Q. Now you spoke to the staff officer, but I think not to Mr Veness at that stage, is that right?

A. That is correct, sir.

Q. At the end of the telephone call, did you make arrangements – and I am going to the top of your [statement] page 4 – to get back to London?

A. I did.

Q. I think you had been told that Detective Inspector Sharp would also be attending the mortuary, is that right, in the conversation?

A. That is correct.

Q. As well as making immediate arrangements for you to get back to London, did you confirm with Mr Sharp that he would be liaising with the Coroner's officer for Fulham?

A. Yes, sir.

Q. So that the Coroner would be aware of your attendance at the mortuary?

A. Yes.

Q. Did you make sure that Inspector Sharp appointed an experienced officer to act as exhibits officer?

A. I did.

Q. That he arranged the attendance of a detective sergeant from the Forensic Science Laboratory?

A. Yes, sir.[a]

Q. And also Metropolitan Police photographers?

A. Yes, sir.

Q. Along the lines of the things that you were just telling us about?[b]

A. Indeed.

Q. You, I think, got to Fulham Mortuary sometime between half past 4 and 5 o'clock in the afternoon of 31st August 1997.[c] Is that right?

A. That is correct.

Q. We have already heard about the people who were present, but just to bring it back to mind[a] ... and three photographers from the photographic

---

[a] This was Philip Stoneham. The evidence from Stoneham was that he was contacted by Rees or the Scotland Yard contact desk. There was no mention of a call from Sharp in Stoneham's testimony.

[b] This appears to be a reference to: "I ensured that the people who would normally attend a post mortem attended" – see above.

[c] Rees attended the 4.15 p.m. meeting at Scotland Yard, which would suggest that he would not have arrived at Fulham until after 5 p.m. He was travelling by helicopter – see earlier. There is no independent evidence of Rees' arrival time at Fulham mortuary.

department of the Metropolitan Police?

A. Yes.

At 70.17: Mansfield: Q. What did you think might have come back?

A. Obviously at some stage the bodies would be returning to the United Kingdom, there would have to be further post-mortem examinations[b] and so forth. Then it was possible that we might become involved, but I do not think – well I know that we did not envisage the bodies returning so quickly to the United Kingdom.

Q. No, and even if they did, it would involve your group?

A. Well, no, we were the natural people, I think, to take charge in that kind of situation at the mortuary.

At 101.24: Horwell: Q. Was your primary concern that although these events were unprecedented and the events at this mortuary somewhat unique, you wanted this to be conducted as if it was a road traffic accident post mortem?

A. I had an open mind sir. I wanted everything done properly.

Q. But in addition you have said that you erred on the side of caution.

A. That is right.

Q. The reasons for that being the unprecedented and unique nature of these events?

A. Yes.

Jeffrey Rees: Paget Description of Statement: **Jury Didn't Hear**:

"Detective Superintendent Rees stated that although he was not on-call that weekend he was at that time the Acting Detective Chief Superintendent ... of the OCG.... He telephoned Commander Niall Mulvehill, his line manager. They assessed that short-term implications for the OCG were unlikely at that stage.

"It was some time later that day that Detective Superintendent Rees received a pager message to contact AC David Veness's staff officer. Detective Superintendent Rees cannot now recall the name of that officer. As the bodies were to be repatriated that day he was informed that AC Veness wished him to take over responsibility from DCI Heard and for him to do whatever was necessary from the police point of view concerning the post-mortem examination of the bodies of the Princess of Wales and Dodi Al Fayed....

"The earliest documentation relating to this is in a policy file document timed at 9 a.m. on Monday 1 September 1997 titled *'Operation Paris'* (Unregistered Docket 678/2000/DO)....

"This document ... stated that the OCG's role in this case was specifically to gather evidence and facts on behalf of the Coroners....

---

[a] The listing of those present is shown below.

[b] This indicates knowledge by Rees that post-mortems had already occurred in France. This has been addressed in Chapter 1.

"In a report dated 22 January 1998 ... he reported that he had been additionally directed by the two Coroners to monitor the French investigations on their behalf."[328]

Jeffrey Rees: Paget Description of Statement:[a] **Jury Didn't Hear**:

"He stated that he was instructed by Sir David Veness, through his Staff Officer, to do whatever was necessary from the police point of view concerning the post-mortem examinations of the bodies of the Princess of Wales and Dodi Al Fayed. He understood this to mean taking the steps normally taken by the police at a post-mortem examination; for example ensuring the taking of appropriate samples by the pathologist and the laboratory Sergeant, and ensuring the taking of necessary photographs and exhibits.

"He also understood the instruction to mean that he should represent the police interest as the circumstances required and he should attend the post-mortem examinations. He was informed that DI Dennis Sharp would be attending the mortuary on the Sunday afternoon and ensured that he made the Coroner for West London, Dr John Burton (also the Coroner of the Queen's Household), aware that police would be attending the post-mortem examinations.

"In his statement Detective Superintendent Rees explained why he asked for police resources at the examinations: 'Concerning the resources identified, I asked for these to be available as I did not know what to expect at the post mortem examinations, so I decided to err on the side of caution.... DI Sharpe, who was my deputy, was responsible for arranging the attendance at the examinations of the laboratory sergeant and the exhibits officer."[329]

Peter Heard, DCI, MPS Organised Crime Group: Paget Description of Statement: **Jury Didn't Hear**:

"DCI Heard was at home at around midday on Sunday 31 August 1997 when he received a telephone call or a pager message to contact New Scotland Yard. He was unable to recall with whom he made contact. He was ... told that he should make any arrangements that needed to be made from a police perspective in relation to the post-mortem examination later that day. His instructions only concerned the Princess of Wales. He was given no instructions regarding Dodi Al Fayed....

"As to why the MPS attended the post-mortem examination of the Princess of Wales on Sunday 31 August 1997, DCI Heard stated that when he was notified that there was to be an examination later that day and that he was

---

[a] Operation Paget has never explained why they show only short excerpts from the statements of Rees, Heard, Wall and Sharp and mostly in the third person – not verbatim evidence.

asked to attend, it came as no surprise to him whatsoever. Nobody ever suggested to him that he would be attending as an investigator dealing with a criminal investigation. On reflection, he concluded that the reason for police attendance at the post-mortem examinations that day was simply due to the identity of the personalities involved and nothing else."[330a]

Dennis Sharp, DI, MPS Organised Crime Group: Paget Description of Statement: **Jury Didn't Hear**:

"Shortly after learning of the deaths of the Princess of Wales and Dodi Al Fayed he received a telephone call from DCI Heard, his line manager at the time. He was told to attend Hammersmith and Fulham mortuary that afternoon for the post-mortem examination of the Princess of Wales, but he no longer recalls if he was told anything about Dodi Al Fayed....

"He made his way to Hammersmith and Fulham mortuary but did not recall if he attended New Scotland Yard prior to that....

"Asked about the MPS presence at the post-mortem examinations, he stated that they attended solely because it was the Princess of Wales who had died. The OCG were involved as their unit had sole responsibility for dealing with all issues concerning the Royal Family. They would be the obvious and only appropriate unit to attend. "[331]

Richard Wall, DS, MPS Organised Crime Group: Paget Description of Statement: **Jury Didn't Hear**:

"He was telephoned by DI Sharp and instructed to attend the examinations. He cannot recall if Detective Superintendent Rees gave any directives regarding the samples to be taken.

"He travelled directly to the mortuary. As to why the MPS attended the post-mortem examinations and whether the MPS were carrying out any 'criminal investigation' into their deaths at that stage, he states that as far as he was concerned the officers were in attendance purely because of the status of the person involved. He stated that the Princess of Wales had died in a car crash overseas and that the MPS were not carrying out any sort of criminal investigation whatsoever. Had there been any suggestion that their deaths were suspicious, then Detective Superintendent Rees would have told him about it, he was certain."[332]

Neal Williams, Police Photographer: 1 Sep 97 Statement: **Jury Didn't Hear**:

"On the 31st August 1997, at Fulham Public Mortuary, I took thirty-six (36) photographs of Diana, Princess of Wales. The nine (9) exposed rolls of film, I placed in an Exhibit Bag, Serial Number B2119741, which I sealed. I then

---

[a] Heard was taken off the case later that day as "he was heavily committed to a highly sensitive and complex investigation that was due to take him to Canada on Tuesday 2 September 1997": Paget Report, p627. This issue regarding choice of officers will be addressed in Part 5.

took this Exhibit to the Photographic Branch Headquarters at 2-1 6 Amelia Street, Walworth, London, SE17 3PY, where at 23.50 hours [11.50 p.m.], I handed the Exhibit to Acting Higher Photographic Officer Catherine Brown. At 01.00 hours, on the 1st September 1997, I received from Acting Higher Photographic Officer Catherine Brown, nine (9) rolls of processed photographic negatives. I then selected photographic negatives for printing and at 01.40 hours, I handed these to Photographic Officer Steven Field. At 03.15 hours from Photographic Officer Steven Field, I received the resulting photographic prints. These photographic prints I now submit, in an indexed album, as Exhibit NW/614/S0/97. The unretouched negatives and spare duplicate negatives, plus two (2) photographic albums produced from the selected negatives were handed to Senior Photographic Officer Isted, at 04.00 hours on the 1st September 1997."[333]

Keith Brown, Surrey Coroner's Officer: Paget Description of Statement:[a]
Jury Didn't Hear:
"It did not strike him as unusual to see police officers at the examination, in fact he expected it. Had the examinations been conducted in Surrey[b] (as opposed to West London) they would almost certainly have had police officers present. In his opinion MPS officers were present on this particular occasion simply because of the people involved, not for any other reason. He was certainly not aware that they were conducting any sort of 'official investigation' at that time."[334]

Dr Robert Chapman, Pathologist, UK: 26 Nov 07: 14.18:
Hilliard: Q. If you can just help us with who was present and what their role or occupation was.
A. Again[c], Detective Superintendent Rees, the senior police officer; a Metropolitan Police photographer, Mr Williams; again, Detective Sergeant Wall, as exhibits officer; a Detective Inspector Sharp; Detective Sergeant Stoneham again as crime scene manager; Dr Burton, Her Majesty's Coroner; Mark Taylor as assistant photographer; Nigel Munns, he has the title

---

[a] A statement from Keith Brown was read out to the inquest on 11 March 2008, but it did not include this evidence, which was sourced from the Paget Report. The Paget Report – on page 639 – appears to quote from two statements: "Statement 143 and 143A". The question is: Why was only one of these statements from Keith Brown read out to the inquest jury?

[b] Brown mentions this because he was Coroner's Officer for Surrey. There is nothing in Brown's evidence to suggest there was ever a plan to hold Dodi's post-mortem in Surrey – see earlier.

[c] Chapman is saying "again" because earlier he had stated who was present at Dodi's post-mortem.

principal services officer within the mortuary service; and Robert Thompson, mortuary assistant.

At 36.14: Mansfield: Q. Did you know Mr Rees before?

A. No.

Q. Did he say where he was from?

A. I do not recall.

.... Q. Why was he there?

A. Well, I did not think it was particularly unusual that a senior Metropolitan Police officer would be present in an examination of this type.

.... Q. I am going to suggest to you that if you had asked, you would have discovered that he was a very senior officer in the international and organised crime group. Did you know that?

A. No.

Q. I mean, if he had said that is where he was from, would you have asked "What does this post mortem have to do with the international and organised crime group"?

A. I think I would have found it certainly worthy of a comment or a question.

Q. Yes. So does it appear that he actually perhaps did not tell you that is where he was from?

A. I cannot answer. I think I – I think if he had told me that, I would recall it frankly.

Q. What they are concerned with, that group, is kidnapping, overseas murders and that sort of category of crime. Did you know that?

A. No, not in that detail at all.

....Horwell: Sir, can I just raise this? The title "organised crime group" [OCG] is an unusual one. The layman probably has not heard of it before. One of the duties of the organised crime group is to investigate crimes that put the security of members of the Royal Family at risk.[a] That is an important part of their duties, in my submission, and should not be forgotten during the course of this cross-examination of Dr Chapman.

....Q. There is another officer called Detective Inspector Sharp. You had not met him before?

A. Again, not that I recall.

Q. Did you know what he was doing there?

A. No, other than being a Metropolitan Police officer.

Q. Do you normally allow police officers, however senior, just to be there without finding out exactly why they are there?

A. I am normally satisfied that if they are present, they do have a function,

---

[a] The role of the OCG is addressed in Part 5. By 2010, the OCG appears to have been renamed the "Serious and Organised Crime Command". On the MPS website their activities are listed – there is however no mention of security involving the royal family.: Metropolitan Police Service, Specialist Crime, Serious and Organised Crime, www.met.police.uk/scd

and that it is not really my place to examine them on that.

Q. No, no, I appreciate that. What was the function that these two officers said they were playing?

A. They were witnesses or observers.

Q. To what?

A. To the examination.

Q. On behalf of?

A. Well, as police officers.

Q. You have Detective Sergeant Stoneham, well known to you. He is there essentially on behalf of police officers. You have a coroner's officer there.

A. On behalf of the coroner, yes.

Q. I mean, did these two officers appear to do anything; that is Sharp and Rees?

A. I was really rather busy.

.... Q. You see, the other person who was there – in fact, if it was royalty that was concerned here – although she was not a member of the Royal Family, but leave that aside – there was a royal protection officer there, wasn't there, SO14?

A. I do not know.

Q. His name was Michael Walker.

A. He does not appear on my –

Q. No, he does not. But according to other evidence which we may hear in fact today, he was there at the mortuary.

A. Well, he may have been at the mortuary. The mortuary is, of course, as you are aware, a large place. There is an office and corridors and so on.[a]

Q. Just returning to the two officers who did, at one stage or another – were you introduced to DI Sharp between these two post mortems?

A. I cannot remember.

Q. Well, did, on any occasion, either of these two officers say that they were investigating or they were there in order to consider investigating any crime against a member of the Royal Family?

A. I would have certainly remembered that had they told me.

Q. Yes.

A. So they did not.

Q. One of the particular functions which my learned friend kindly raised, they never mentioned?

A. No.

Q. Does this all come as a bit of a surprise to you, to discover two very senior

---

[a] Evidence from Colin Tebbutt regarding the presence of Michael Walker appears later.

officers who have these apparent roles not disclosing the squad from which they come?

A. I do not think it comes as a great surprise. I do not think that I would regard them as trying to conceal any purpose of being present. I was quite happy they were there. They were obviously senior police officers. I was happy they were present as witnesses to what I was doing and I left it at that.

Q. As far as you can remember ... did either of those officers appear to be taking any notes?

A. Not that I can remember, no.

At 62.10: Horwell: Q. You have said that had these have been ordinary people, the post-mortem examinations would not have taken place until the following day.

A. Well, at some point in the following week probably.

Q.... And that you would not have expected police officers or photographers to have been present?

A. No.

Q. Now, the Princess of Wales, of course, was anything other than an ordinary person and were you, in any sense, surprised to see the police present at both of these post-mortem examinations?

A. Not at all.

Q. There were not only police officers present at the examinations themselves, but there were police officers present outside the mortuary, guarding it, controlling it, from those who were present as spectators. Is that right?

A. Yes.

Q. Now, it has been suggested, perhaps, that the presence of certainly certain police officers was sinister. Did any of the police officers present during either of these two examinations stop you from doing anything that you wanted to do, Dr Chapman?

A. No.

Comment: Who makes the decision to notify the police about an upcoming post-mortem?

Earlier evidence has shown that the post-mortems were called by the coroners – Burton and Burgess.

Veness says: "around the midday period, it became apparent that ... arrangements were being made to conduct a post-mortem".

How did that become apparent? Veness has never been asked.

There is no admission in any of the evidence that the police were told about a post-mortem by the coroner or the coroner's office. The closest we get to it is from Michael Mansfield – who is not a witness – to Veness: "you are setting up really at the behest of the coroner".

I suggest that this is common sense. The coroner sets up the post-mortem. The coroner decides who should be invited. How do people – specifically, the police – know there is a post-mortem happening, unless they are notified by the coroner or his office?

Any communication notifying the police of the Princess Diana post-mortem is missing from the evidence. It is not mentioned by John Burton, who would logically have been the person to do the notifying – Burton has listed his calls made on the day (see earlier), but has failed to include any call to the police.[a] It is also not mentioned by Veness or Rees.

Instead Burton has stated: "I had no prior knowledge of [the police] attendance.... I had not made the decision for these people to attend. In fact I did not have that authority as a coroner to do so."[b]

So Burton has stated: a) "I had no prior knowledge"; b) "I had not made the decision"; and c) "I did not have that authority".

This begs the question: If Burton, as royal coroner, "did not have that authority" to advise the police, then who did? [c]

Burton's "I had no prior knowledge of [the police] attendance" is directly in conflict with Rees' account. Rees confirmed to Hilliard that he made sure "Sharp ... would be liaising with the Coroner's officer for Fulham ... so that the Coroner [Burton] would be aware of [the police] attendance at the mortuary".

The general evidence shows that there were police present inside and outside of the Fulham Mortuary. Initially we will deal with the police who

---

[a] There is evidence of contact during the day between Rees and Burton in Burton's notes. The handwritten notes read: "Inspector Rees involved via Leicester. Problems in France." The typed notes read: "Inspector Rees (Palace liaison) contacted by Leicester Police, He is informed there are problems in France in releasing bodies." There is no mention of this contact in Burton's statement. This issue has been addressed at length in Part 3.

[b] In support, Burgess has said: "I had no knowledge of any particular police involvement until we arrived at the mortuary". Burgess also said: "So far as the Metropolitan Police is concerned, I had no contact with them until I arrived at Fulham [mortuary] and then I told them what I was proposing to do." (See p540 *The Documents* book). Burgess did qualify these statements with: "Police officers do quite frequently attend post-mortem examinations...." He appears to have used his words carefully – no knowledge of "particular police involvement". Burgess' own coroner's officer, Keith Brown, comes across as more forthright: "He expected [a police presence]. Had the examinations been conducted in Surrey ... [there] would almost certainly have had police officers present".

[c] Rees said in his statement: "In a report dated 22 January 1998 ... [Rees] reported that he had been additionally directed by the two Coroners to monitor the French investigations on their behalf.": Paget Report, p632. This indicates that the coroners had the power to "direct" the police.

were inside – present in the room during the post-mortems of Princess Diana and Dodi Fayed.

These police were:[335]

Detective Superintendent Jeffrey Rees – Senior Investigating Officer (SIO) OCG

Detective Inspector Dennis Sharp – Coordinator OCG[a]

Detective Sergeant Philip Stoneham – Laboratory Liaison Officer/Crime Scene Manager

Detective Sergeant Richard Wall – Exhibits Officer

Neal Williams – MPS Photographer

Andrew Selous – MPS Photographer[b]

Mark Taylor - MPS Assistant Photographer.

There is conflicting evidence on why these seven men were present at the examinations.

The reasons given are:
- Veness: "to marshal the various exhibits"
- Veness: "to ensure that the optimum forensic samples are recovered"
- Veness: "a straightforward support to the coroner"[c]
- Rees: "to do whatever had to be done from the police point of view"
- Rees: "to represent the Metropolitan Police's interests"
- Rees: "to gather evidence and facts on behalf of the Coroners"
- Rees: "taking the steps normally taken by the police at a post-mortem"
- Rees: "ensuring the taking of appropriate samples by the pathologist and the laboratory sergeant"
- Rees: "ensuring the taking of necessary photographs and exhibits"
- Rees: "represent the police interest as the circumstances required"
- Heard: "make any arrangements that needed to be made from a police perspective" for Diana's post-mortem
- Heard: "due to the identity of the personalities involved and nothing else"
- Sharp: "they attended solely because it was the Princess of Wales"
- Wall: "purely because of the status of the person involved"
- Keith Brown: "simply because of the people involved, not for any other reason"
- Stoneham: "there was a police investigation into their deaths"
- Stoneham: "because of the sensitivity surrounding the examinations"

---

[a] Sharp is only listed as present in Diana's post-mortem – not Dodi's. This is discussed below.

[b] Neal Williams took photos of Princess Diana's post-mortem and Andrew Selous took photos of Dodi Fayed's.

[c] Chapman gave evidence that Wall took notes during the post-mortem: 26 Nov 07: 35.24.

- Chapman: "there will be police officers present to witness the examination"
- Chapman: "to see the injuries"
- Chapman: "exhibits will be taken by the police for further analysis"[a]
- Chapman: "they were witnesses or observers ... to the examination"[336]
- Burton: "the police ... authorised the taking of the photographs"
- Burgess: "police officers ... assist the pathologist in relating specific injuries to possible scenarios"
- Thompson: "photographs were taken by the police photographer"
- Thompson: "the laboratory liaison officer is there to receive the samples and specimens"[b].

During cross-examination the pathologist, Robert Chapman, showed initial reluctance to answer questions relating to the reasons for police presence.

Mansfield asked: "Why was [Rees] there?" Chapman dodged the question: "Well, I did not think it was particularly unusual that a senior ... officer would be present in an examination of this type." [c]

Later Mansfield asked: "Did you know what [Sharp] was doing there?" Chapman: "No, other than being a Metropolitan Police officer."

The above listed evidence, coming from 11 witnesses, comprises a considerable variety – and conflict – over reasons for the police presence.

There are several important points relating to the presence of the British police at the post-mortems:

1) Four of the witnesses – Heard, Sharp, Wall, Brown – insisted that the only reason police attended was "because it was the Princess of Wales".

There is however substantial evidence of police involvement in the collection of samples and taking of photos – see earlier and later.

There are two questions:

---

[a] Chapman was describing a special post-mortem. Straight after this Hilliard asked Chapman if "those things [police officers present to witness the examination, to see the injuries, and exhibits will be taken by the police for further analysis] did happen here ... in these particular post-mortem examinations" and Chapman replied "Certainly". Chapman later admitted to Mansfield that these post-mortems were special – see earlier.

[b] Issues regarding samples taken are dealt with more thoroughly later in this chapter.

[c] In his 2005 statement Chapman methodically went through his prior knowledge of and interaction with the various key individuals who attended the post-mortems: Mohamed Al Fayed (attended the mortuary only), Robert Thompson, John Burton, Michael Burgess, Philip Stoneham, Richard Wall, Nigel Munns. It is notable that Jeffrey Rees is missing from this list. See *The Documents* book, pp581-2.

-    Why are the police taking samples and photos if they are only there because of the status of the person involved?

-    Why did the police attend the post-mortem of Dodi Fayed – also taking samples and photos – if they were only there to attend the post-mortem of Princess Diana?

2) Of the remaining seven witnesses, four – Veness, Rees, Chapman, Thompson – have included the taking of samples as a reason for the police presence.

Philip Stoneham does not specifically include sample taking as a reason, but his evidence – see later – directly addresses the sample-taking aspect of the post-mortem.

The two remaining witnesses are the two coroners, Burton and Burgess.

Burton refers only briefly to the taking of samples in his statement: "Photographs and samples were taken at the direction of Dr Chapman and the FLO."[337] Burton explained earlier in his statement that the FLO was the "forensic laboratory liaison officer" and part of the police team present.[a] The FLO was Philip Stoneham – see earlier.

In 12 pages of statements[b] Burgess appears to avoid the subject of sample-taking altogether. Burgess stated: There were "2 or 3 police officers [present], one taking notes and one with a camera, taking photographs at the direction of the pathologist. There may have been others present but if so I cannot recall who they were or what they were doing."[338]

Later evidence will reveal that the sample-taking process in these post-mortems was extremely significant to determining what took place. The fact that Burgess has not mentioned it at all and Burton has only just briefly referred to it, could be a further indication that these two coroners compared notes before giving their final accounts. This possibility has been addressed earlier in this volume.

The failure of the coroners to adequately address the subject of sample-taking may not be a coincidence. The possible reason for avoiding this issue will emerge as this chapter develops.

3) Jeffrey Rees has stated that he understood the Veness instruction – "to do whatever was necessary from the police point of view concerning the post-mortem examinations" – meant "that he should represent the police interest as the circumstances required".

The jury never heard this[c], but it should have been read out, and Rees should have been asked: What was the "police interest" in the post-mortems of Princess Diana and Dodi Fayed – both passengers in a car crash?

---

[a] See p559 of *The Documents* book.

[b] In *The Documents* book.

[c] It was in Rees' police statement.

4) Three witnesses – Rees, Burton, Thompson – mention photo-taking as a reason for the police presence.

Neal Williams, the police photographer at the Diana post-mortem, states: "I took thirty-six (36) photographs of Diana, Princess of Wales". The post-mortem finished at 11.20 p.m., but Williams says that he didn't wait until the next day before getting them developed. By 1 a.m. Williams had the negatives and "at 03.15 [a.m.] ... I received the resulting photographic prints". Williams puts these photos into "an indexed album" and at 4 a.m., precisely 23 hours after Diana's official time of death, the album – and other albums of negatives – "were handed to Senior Photographic Officer Isted".

Isted has never been interviewed and was not heard from at the inquest.

Again, two questions:
- Why the rush?
- What do the police want with these 36 photos of a person who was a passenger in a car crash?

5) There is conflict over which post-mortems Sharp attended.

The Paget Report states: "[Sharp] attended both post-mortem examinations.... He arrived at the mortuary before the arrival of the bodies."[339]

Dennis Sharp's name is however missing from the list of people present at Dodi's post-mortem – drawn up by Robert Chapman, based on notes taken on the night.[340] This was confirmed by Chapman – Mansfield asked Chapman: "In relation to the [post-mortem] on Dodi, there was a police officer who must have turned up later or, if he was there, did not participate. Detective Inspector Sharp is present on the second [post-mortem list] but not on the first." Chapman confirmed: "That is correct."[341]

There has never been any explanation for this conflict. No evidence from Sharp was heard at the inquest.

There is a possibility that Sharp was only asked to attend the Diana post-mortem. Sharp's statement reads: "[Sharp] was told to attend ... the post-mortem examination of the Princess of Wales, but he no longer recalls if he was told anything about Dodi Al Fayed".

Later evidence will show that there is conflicting testimony between the police officers present over pre-post-mortem communication regarding the procedure to be used for taking samples. It may be that Sharp changed his evidence to falsely place himself "at the mortuary before the arrival of the bodies", so that he was in a position to testify about the sampling controversy – which he did (see later).

The documentary evidence from Chapman's 5 September 1997 post-mortem attendance list – based on 31 August 1997 notes and confirmed at the inquest – should take precedence over the Paget third person account of

Sharp's statement – made at least 7 years after the event, and not tested or heard at the inquest.

This evidence indicates that Sharp only attended the Diana post-mortem, not Dodi's.[a]

6) Peter Heard stated: "[Heard's] instructions only concerned the Princess of Wales. He was given no instructions regarding Dodi Al Fayed."

The general evidence reveals that the police were fully involved with both post-mortem examinations – including the taking of samples and photographs. Heard appears to have been contacted earlier than Rees. It is possible that the initial MPS focus was on Diana's post-mortem, but it may have soon been realised that if they focused only on Diana and not Dodi, then that could raise awkward questions.

Robert Thompson, Fulham Mortuary Manager: 13 Jun 01 Affidavit: **Jury Didn't Hear**:

"When I got to the mortuary, there were already a few men in suits who said that they wanted to check the whole building for security. Then gradually more people began to turn up, particularly police, some uniformed some not. I was told that there were people there from two separate police protection groups. I am not exactly sure what these groups were but I was given to understand that they were the Royalty Protection Group and the Diplomatic Protection Group."[342]

Robert Thompson: 9 Nov 04 Statement: **Jury Didn't Hear**:

"I then went to the mortuary, arriving around 10 a.m. or 11 a.m. There were a lot of people hanging around in the car park and in particular several men in dark suits who at the time I assumed were police officers from Royalty Protection or something like that. I was later told that they were from the Diplomatic Protection Squad as well as from Royalty Protection. They wanted to know all the exits and entrances to the building and were very interested in how the mortuary building could be overlooked from surrounding buildings."[343]

Jeffrey Rees, Head of Early Crash Investigations, British Police: 17 Dec 07: 34.19:

Hilliard: Q. I think the Coroner's officer was also at the mortuary.

A. He was.

Q. Then, in plain clothes, a number of royalty protection department officers – is that right?

A. Yes.

Q. – most of whom, I think, you thought had flown down from Balmoral where members of the Royal Family were?

A. Yes.

---

[a] This evidence could be significant in the debate over the sample procedures – see later.

Q. And the Coroner's officer and those royalty protection department officers remained outside, as you call it, the body examination area?

A. That is correct.

Colin Tebbutt, Diana's Driver and Security: 26 Nov 07: 98.6:

Hough: Q. When you got into the private area, did you see any policemen you recognised?

A. Yes, there was one SO14 officer.

Q. Who was that?

A. Michael Walker.

Q. Do you know why he was there?

A. I think he was there to provide police coverage during the night, sir.

Q. As far as you were aware, did he go into the room to see the post-mortem examination?

A. I am not aware of that, sir.

Colin Tebbutt: 5 Jul 04 Statement: **Jury Didn't Hear**:

"After a while, Paul Mellor drove Lady Sarah Fellowes[a] back to Lincolnshire; and I went home. Only one Police Officer Michael Walker of SO14 remained at the Mortuary."[344]

Anthony Mather, Asst Comptroller, Lord Chamberlain's Office: 22 Nov 07: 86.25:

Hough: Q. I think that you did, however, attend the Fulham mortuary with the Princess of Wales' two sisters.

A. I did.

Q. That was later on the Sunday, wasn't it? Now I think you also had communications with the Metropolitan Police about certain aspects of the arrangements. What were they handling?

A. At that stage, we were plotting the route from RAF Northolt back to the mortuary and the special escort group and anything that the police advised on a security level.

Anthony Mather: 23 Aug 05 Statement: **Jury Didn't Hear**:

"The other people that I would have communicated with were the Metropolitan Police Service although I cannot now recall whom this was with. This would have been concerning the security, transport and ceremonial aspects of the journey from RAF Northolt to the Fulham mortuary, subsequently for the removal of the coffin to St James's Palace, thence to Kensington Palace, and the funeral arrangements themselves."[345]

Comment: Anthony Mather describes contact with the police to organise "security".

---

[a] This should probably be "McCorquodale".

The evidence from Robert Thompson is that there was a security presence at Fulham Mortuary before he arrived "around 10 a.m. or 11 a.m." These people were "in dark suits" and Thompson "assumed [they] were police officers from Royalty Protection or something like that". In his affidavit, Thompson continues: "Gradually more people began to turn up, particularly police, some uniformed some not". He was later told "that they were the Royalty Protection Group and the Diplomatic Protection Group".

Jeffrey Rees confirmed to Hilliard that there were "in plain clothes, a number of royalty protection department officers ... most of whom ... had flown down from Balmoral".

This evidence, from Thompson and Rees, indicates that the "several men in dark suits" – in plain clothes – who Thompson saw, when he first arrived at around 10.30 a.m. and "assumed were police officers from Royalty Protection", were from Balmoral.

This appears to be further evidence of early control of events from the royals at Balmoral. While early plans were being made for Diana's embalming in the Paris hospital, the employment of Operation Overstudy, Charles' mission to Paris, and Burton's illegal jurisdiction over Diana's body, preparations were in place for a team of Royalty Protection officers to be despatched from Balmoral, headed to the Fulham Mortuary.

Earlier evidence has shown that royal coroner, John Burton, could not have made the decision to conduct a post-mortem on Princess Diana, until he had first decided to claim jurisdiction over her body. Evidence in the Royal Control chapter shows that Burton called Buckingham Palace at around 8 a.m. on 31 August 1997, and spoke with Lucy Dove who told him that Diana's "burial was likely to be at Windsor Castle". Burton said that it was on the basis of that information, that he went ahead and claimed jurisdiction over the body.

It could only have been after that point – sometime after 8 a.m. – that Burton decided to have a post-mortem on Diana's body.

There is no known evidence from anyone that reveals how Balmoral came by that information – that Burton was conducting a post-mortem.

The evidence from Rees, that "plain clothes ... royalty protection department officers" – seen by Thompson outside Fulham Mortuary at about 10.30 a.m. – "had flown down from Balmoral", raises two possibilities:

a) that the royals were conveyed Burton's post-mortem decision immediately after he made it, then reacted very quickly, assembling the royalty protection team, organising a plane and despatching them to London in time for them to be present at the mortuary by 10.30 a.m.

b) that the post-mortem decision was made earlier at Balmoral and was conveyed to Burton during the morning.

Evidence in the Royal Control chapter has already shown that events on the morning of 31 August 1997 were being driven by the Queen at Balmoral.

In the light of that, I suggest that b) is the most likely possibility and that the decision to conduct the post-mortems of Princess Diana and Dodi Fayed was made in Balmoral.

Colin Tebbutt says that when he left "only one police officer, Michael Walker of SO14, remained at the mortuary". This appears to conflict with Anthony Mather, who stated he communicated with the MPS about "the removal of the coffin to St James's Palace" – which took place following the post-mortems (see earlier).

Tebbutt describes himself leaving around the same time as Sarah McCorquodale. Earlier evidence revealed that McCorquodale appears to have left prior to the commencement of the post-mortem – Fellowes and McCorquodale "left shortly after" talking to Burton.

There is no evidence from any other witness on this subject – either to corroborate or contradict Tebbutt's account.

If the primary purpose of the police presence – outside of the main room – was to provide security for the post-mortems, it seems strange that only one officer remained before the Diana post-mortem commenced.

The general evidence indicates that Tebbutt is incorrect on either: a) his time of departure, or b) his recollection on the degree of police presence when he departed.

Sampling Issues

There are major issues relating to the samples taken in the Princess Diana post-mortem – they raise serious concerns about what actually took place at the Fulham Mortuary on the evening of Sunday, 31 August 1997.

Pre-Post-Mortem Instruction

There is conflicting evidence on whether the police were given instructions on which samples to request to be taken.

Philip Stoneham, Detective Sergeant, British Police: 18 Dec 07: 8.22:

Hilliard: Q. Now as far as what kind of samples were taken at the post-mortem examinations, do you remember anything said to you about that by anyone?

A. From the 1st November notes, I have made mention that Superintendent Rees said that samples would be taken relating to road traffic accident. I actually have no recollection now of any of that conversation.

Q. No, but it looks as if you must have done on 1st November 2004.

A. Yes, indeed.

Q. The passage in the note there reads: "Superintendent Rees told us that he had been given a directive that the only samples to be taken at the post-mortem examinations of both Diana, Princess of Wales and Dodi Al Fayed

would be those taken at any routine road traffic accident post mortem."
A. Yes, that is correct.
At 21.5: Mansfield: Q. You were told at the mortuary, is this right ... by the time you had got there, Mr Rees was saying, "Well, actually we are going to treat it as road traffic"?
A. These notes and statements suggest that, yes.
Q. Now if you go back to your statement in 2005, is there any reference there to being told, by Rees, about any directive?
A. No, I do not think there is, no.
Q. So it is only in the later statement in 2006 that it reappears, it having been in the notes in 2004, that "Rees told me that he had received a directive that the only samples to be taken ..." Now, can you help about this? The sampling that in fact took place, was it ordinary sampling or special sampling? Do you appreciate the difference I am putting to you? Do you remember in fact what happened?
A. I do not remember what happened. I do not remember what samples were taken.
Q. What would be the samples that would normally be taken on a special?
A. The standard post mortem samples for a special post mortem start from the head and really go from head to toe.
Q. Head to toe. I appreciate again there is a time lapse. If you need to look at the notes – you were asked this question in November 2004..... Do you see, it says: "In a normal special post mortem, the standard samples are head hair, mouth swabs, pubic hair, finger nails, blood for DNA, blood for toxicology, urine or vitreous humour if no urine is present, liver and stomach contents."
A. That is right, yes.
Q. Did that happen in this case or you can't ... ?
A. I do not know. I do not know.
Q. Those are the samples that have to be taken if it is the normal special post mortem. Where do the samples in a normal special post mortem go?
A. Forensic science laboratory.
Q. Forensic science. Not a hospital?
A. No.
Q. Did you play any part in the decision-making about where the samples would go in this particular case? If you cannot remember, I will leave it.
A. I really cannot remember. I mean I have read my statements so I know there is reference to the samples, whatever they were, went to Charing Cross Hospital, but I do not know what part I played.
At 27.9: Horwell: Q. You have only been concerned with special post mortems?
A. That is right.
Q. You have used the word "directive". You are not suggesting that actual word was used by Mr Rees at any time, are you?

A. No, I do not think so. I think it was my choice of word rather than sort of a diktat, if you like.

Philip Stoneham: Paget Description of Statement: **Jury Heard Part Only**:

"When he arrived at the mortuary he met Detective Superintendent Rees for the first time. Detective Superintendent Rees told him that he had received a directive that the only samples to be taken during the post-mortem examinations of the Princess of Wales and Dodi Al Fayed were to be ones routinely taken during any post-mortem examination following a road traffic accident. DS Stoneham stated that he did not know who gave Detective Superintendent Rees this directive."[346]

Jeffrey Rees, Head of Early Crash Investigations, British Police: Paget Description of Statement: **Jury Didn't Hear**:

"Detective Superintendent Rees for his part did not recollect receiving or giving such a directive [to Stoneham], he stated 'err on the side of caution' in taking samples rather than relating it to a traffic accident."[347]

Jeffrey Rees: 17 Dec 07: 37.7:

Hilliard: Q. You also noted that you don't remember asking Dr Chapman to carry out any particular tests in respect of either body. Is that right?

A. That is correct.

Q. Is that the kind of thing that you might ever do?

A. Yes. I discussed the situation with Dr Chapman and what I said was, "Obviously all the samples that would normally be taken in a road traffic accident should be taken, but, in addition, we should take anything else which might just become relevant". I was thinking in particular of head hair, stomach contents and anything like that.

Q. That was what you said to him, but had you been given any instruction by anybody else as to what samples and exhibits should be taken? Had anybody given you instructions about that?

A. No, sir.

At 81.25: Mansfield: Q. Do you remember talking to [Mr Stoneham]?

A. Not really, no.

Q. About samples?

A. There was a general discussion, not specifically with him but with the officers there and with the pathologist about samples.

....Q. He says that you told him that you had received a directive that the only samples to be taken during the post-mortem examinations of Diana, Princess of Wales and Dodi Al Fayed were to be ones routinely taken during any road traffic accident post mortem.

A. That is not correct.

Q. I mean, could you have said something that he misunderstood?

A. I do not think so because I was never given any instruction like that and it would be so exceptional. I cannot conceive of a situation where I could be given that kind of instruction.

Q. Well, unless there was a concern by somebody back at the Yard that at this stage matters are contained within certain limits?

A. I was not given that instruction or anything like it.

At 101.19: Horwell: Q. Just to revisit what I was asking you: if a coroner in these circumstances had given any instruction or order, you would have expected it to be carried out without fail?

A. Yes.

Q. Was your primary concern that although these events were unprecedented and the events at this mortuary somewhat unique, you wanted this to be conducted as if it was a road traffic accident post mortem?

A. I had an open mind sir. I wanted everything done properly.

Q. But in addition you have said that you erred on the side of caution.

A. That is right.

Q. The reasons for that being the unprecedented and unique nature of these events?

A. Yes.

Q. The situation has been envisaged that Veness brings you in to be part of a cover-up, to restrict the samples taken at the post-mortem examination as part of that cover-up. Did you restrict the number of samples taken at this post-mortem examination?

A. Absolutely not. Quite the reverse.

Q. To err on the side of caution –

A. Yes.

Q. – you asked for additional samples to be taken?

A. Yes.

Q. The only discussion that you can remember as to how either the post mortem or the samples should be treated was that there was a discussion as to whether the police or the pathologist would have control of the samples?

A. Yes.

Q. And the conclusion was that as this was being treated as a road traffic accident and you had no reason to treat it otherwise, the normal road traffic accident procedure would follow, which was that the pathologist would take care of the samples, but himself using extra special care because of the identity of the bodies involved?

A. Yes, and I was making sure that we could retrieve the situation if we needed to revert to the procedures that I was more used to.

Jeffrey Rees: Paget Description of Statement: **Jury Didn't Hear**:

"Detective Superintendent Rees stated that while at the post-mortem examinations he did not recall asking the pathologist, Dr Robert Chapman, to take any specific samples from either the body of the Princess of Wales or Dodi Al Fayed. The view he expressed to Dr Chapman was that they should err on the side of caution and take any samples that could possibly be required in the future."[348]

Dennis Sharp, DI, MPS Organised Crime Group: Paget Description of Statement: **Jury Didn't Hear**:

"Before the examinations took place, he did not recall being given any directive by Detective Superintendent Rees or overhearing him giving any directive to other officers regarding the sampling that was to take place at both examinations."[349]

Richard Wall, DS, MPS Organised Crime Group: Paget Description of Statement: **Jury Didn't Hear**:

"He cannot recall if Detective Superintendent Rees gave any directives regarding the samples to be taken."[350]

Dr Robert Chapman, Pathologist, UK: 26 Nov 2007: 34.21:

Mansfield: Q. Before the first [post-mortem] began, which was on Dodi Al Fayed, you spoke, did you, to a number of police officers?

A. I would have had conversations in the normal course of events with those present. That would include police officers, yes.

At 40.4: Q. When you had a discussion at the beginning, what was the nature of the discussion with at least Mr Rees, if not Mr Sharp?

A. I cannot recall the details of that. I do not recall any specific details or specific conversations with either of them.

At 42.2: Q. Did either of those officers [Rees and Sharp] say directly to you that only the normal samples should be taken; "normal" meaning the ones that you normally take in a road traffic case should be taken in this case.

A. I do not recall either of those two officers directly telling me about sampling.

Q. Did they tell Mr Stoneham, who you knew, something to that effect?

A. I think they probably did. I think there was a discussion with myself and DS Stoneham and we decided those would be the samples to take.

Q. You think they probably did. I do not want you to guess. Is that because you have a recollection that the officer, Stoneham, told you that he had been told by one of those officers that you should only take the normal samples?

A. No.

Q. So when you say that probably happened, what are you relying on?

A. I am relying on what I would expect to normally happen during an examination or before an examination, where there is some discussion, perhaps between officers and the pathologist, as to what would be appropriate to take.

Q. Why do the officers who do not normally attend a road traffic – as we may consider in this case, why would officers like that have a need to tell Mr Stoneham only to take the normal samples? There would not be any need, would there?

A. I think that all I can say to that is that Mr Stoneham would naturally look up to those officers as senior officers. He would expect, perhaps, some guidance on what to take.

Q. What, on road traffic?

A. This is a road traffic of a very eminent person/persons, and I think with them present, he would expect some guidance or some discussion with them, perhaps. Again, I have no direct recollection of this and I do not know whether that happened.

Comment: Philip Stoneham, the police laboratory liaison officer, has stated in 2004: "Superintendent Rees told us that he had been given a directive that the only samples to be taken ... would be those taken at any routine road traffic accident post mortem."

There is no mention of this in Stoneham's 2005 account, then it reappears in 2006.

At the 2007 inquest, Stoneham says: "I actually have no recollection now of any of that conversation".

Stoneham's testimony has been categorically denied by Jeffrey Rees:

- "I was never given any instruction like that"
- "I was not given that instruction or anything like it".

Other police present have not denied it, but have said:

- Sharp: "he did not recall being given any directive by Detective Superintendent Rees or overhearing him giving any directive to other officers regarding the sampling"
- Wall: "he cannot recall if Detective Superintendent Rees gave any directives regarding the samples to be taken".

It may be significant that both Sharp and Wall have said they do not recall Rees himself giving a directive. They do not appear to be directly addressing Stoneham's account: "Superintendent Rees told us that <u>he had been given</u> a directive".

In short, we have Rees outrightly denying Stoneham's evidence and his colleagues, Sharp and Wall, both saying they have no recall.

In 1997 Rees, Sharp and Wall were all members of the OCG, whereas Stoneham was not – he was a detective sergeant in the MPS, operating as a laboratory liaison officer. It may be that Sharp and Wall – as OCG colleagues of Rees – are not prepared to, or have been told not to, give evidence contradicting Rees' account.

At the inquest, Stoneham's account was initially supported by the pathologist, Robert Chapman. Chapman confirmed to Mansfield: "I think [Rees or Sharp] probably did" tell Stoneham "that only the normal samples ... that you normally take in a road traffic case should be taken in this case".

Chapman went on: "I think there was a discussion with myself and DS Stoneham and we decided those would be the samples to take."[a]

When Chapman is placed under pressure from Mansfield – "I do not want you to guess" – he partially backs away from this position: "I am relying on what I would expect to normally happen". Chapman supported his account: "I think with [senior officers, Rees and Sharp] present, [Stoneham] would expect some guidance or some discussion with them" on what samples to take.

There are similarities between the evidence relating to this directive to Rees and the evidence of the 4.15 p.m. Scotland Yard meeting – see earlier:
- the main evidence comes from Stoneham
- Rees outrightly denied knowledge of the meeting
- Sharp "did not recall" a meeting and Wall ignored it in his evidence[b]
- Stoneham's main evidence comes in his 2004 account
- in his 2005 statement Stoneham fails to address the two key issues – Rees' presence and knowledge of a special post-mortem[c]
- in his 2006 statement Stoneham then addresses the two key issues.

There is a possibility that Stoneham was lent on by police – particularly in 2005 – to produce evidence that fell closer into line with the position taken by Jeffrey Rees.

Effectively the position on the directive to Rees is that Stoneham and Rees directly conflict, Sharp and Wall don't recall, and Chapman has provided some support for Stoneham – "I am relying on what I would expect to normally happen".[d]

As usual, only one account can be true – Stoneham and Rees cannot both be correct.

---

[a] When Chapman says, "we decided those would be the samples to take", he is referring to samples "you normally take in a road traffic case". Chapman's assertion that there was agreement to limit the samples to a normal road traffic situation, conflicts with Rees' account that he told Chapman "in addition, we should take anything else which might just become relevant".

[b] Paget have only provided third person excerpts of the Sharp and Wall statements in the Paget report. There is a possibility that Wall did not ignore the issue and Paget have not included what he may have said. No evidence from Wall was heard at the inquest.

[c] This can be seen in the inquest transcript: 18 Dec 07: 15.12.

[d] There is an apparent conflict between Chapman and Rees on whether Rees spoke to Chapman directly on samples. Chapman says: "I do not recall either of those two officers [Rees or Sharp] directly telling me about sampling." Rees says: "I discussed the situation with Dr Chapman and what I said was, 'Obviously all the samples that would normally be taken in a road traffic accident should be taken, but, in addition, we should take anything else which might just become relevant'."

Who is lying?

Rees has already been shown to be a liar – in Part 3 and earlier in this volume. In contrast, Stoneham does not appear to have any reason to give a false account.

There are two relevant questions:

1) Why would Jeffrey Rees lie about an instruction to do with sampling at these post-mortems of Princess Diana and Dodi Fayed?

2) Why would Rees, on the day, be given a directive to restrict samples to "those taken at any routine road traffic accident post mortem"?

I suggest that the two questions are closely connected.

Although it has not been expressly stated, there is a possibility that Rees' directive came from superior officers. Stoneham said in his statement: "He did not know who gave Detective Superintendent Rees this directive".[a] Police lawyer, Richard Horwell, indicated the directive may have come from Veness – "Veness brings [Rees] in to ... restrict the samples taken at the post-mortem examination"[b] – although he does not state how he knows this.

It is significant that Veness – although cross-examined at the inquest – was not asked about this directive, by Horwell or any other lawyer present.

As there is no evidence, any statement on the reasons for this directive can only be speculation.

Up to that point – the period immediately prior to the post-mortems – the post-death decisions had been made by the royals – see earlier. This directive appears to be the first attempt by the MPS to have an influence on events related to the handling of the bodies.

This may have been a decision by a senior figure in the MPS to try and influence the post-mortems, particularly Princess Diana's. It could have been a reaction from the MPS against the royal control of events. Possibly there was a fear that the royals may push for a very invasive post-mortem with extensive testing – as could happen in a special post-mortem (see earlier). Such a fear could lead to a directive to Rees – the senior officer present – to try and ensure the samples were limited to "those taken at any routine road traffic accident post mortem".

I suggest that a cautionary directive of this nature could be made on the day, but also with a view to possible future public knowledge of the procedures carried out during the post-mortems.

Dr Robert Chapman, Pathologist, UK: 24 Feb 05 Statement: **Jury Didn't Hear**:

"The senior officer, Det. Supt. Rees would liaise with D.I. Sharp and D.S. Stoneham in advising on the seizure of exhibits. D.S. Stoneham helped with

---

[a] Not heard by the jury.

[b] Horwell is not suggesting this is correct – the context shows that he is quoting what he believes is alleged.

the retrieval of toxicology samples and the hair sample and I would expect him to advise or guide the exhibits officer in the correct packaging and labelling of the same.... The exhibits officer, D.S. Wall was responsible for receiving and documenting the various exhibits taken during the examination as well as the packaging."[351]

Comment: Chapman indicates here that the police had a role in determining which samples would be taken: "Rees would liaise with ... Sharp and ... Stoneham in advising on the seizure of exhibits".

Effect of Embalming

There is conflict over the degree of impact an embalming will have on samples taken during a later post-mortem.

Dr Robert Chapman, Pathologist, UK: 26 Nov 07: 26.5:

Hilliard: Q. What sort of experience have you got of conducting post-mortem examinations where the body has been embalmed?

A. Quite extensive experience.

Q. And in general terms, what are the effects of that? How does it impact on the tasks that you have to perform?

A. It both – one can say it both helps and hinders. It helps in the sense that it can preserve body tissues in a reasonable state if there is going to be a delay between the death and the examination taking place, but the technical procedures involved can cause damage to the organs of the body. The procedure becomes more unpleasant because of the nature of the chemicals used and there are artefacts produced because of the use of those chemicals.

Q. By an "artefact", you mean, sorry?

A. I mean a technical change in the body's appearance. As a result of the effect of the chemicals, there will be colour changes to the organs; for example, maybe blood clots are produced in places where there were not before death.

Q. So it might give you the impression of something that had not actually been the case?

A. Yes. Unless one is experienced at looking at embalmed bodies, one could be misled.

Q. Then, as far as the taking of samples is concerned, if a body has been embalmed, does that mean you have to go about things in a particular way or from particular locations?

A. This is a difficulty. The embalming procedure will – depending upon how complete it is – it will affect the body fluids. It certainly affects blood and perhaps urine and, to a lesser extent, the eye fluid, because of the use of chemicals, which will make toxicology difficult or indeed sometimes impossible.

Q. Is this right, that you did not take samples from near to obvious sites of embalming fluid installation?

A. One would try and avoid an obvious site of damage or an installation point from a fluid, but one was really trying to get a sample from the leg veins, which is a standard practice in any case.

Q. Right.

A. There may be only very small quantities of fluid available in any case.

At 45.17: Mansfield: Q. Was there any discussion [during a meeting in London including Dominique Lecomte in June 1998[a]] about embalming?

A. Yes, I think there was.

Q. Right. Can I deal with that? Do you remember what the thrust of that discussion was?

A. I think the point that I would have made is that the embalming had been thorough in the sense that most of the body tissues had been affected by the embalming, that there had been damage related to the use of cannulae or trocars with installation of embalming fluids, and that this had impinged upon, slightly at least, the area of injury to the heart of Princess Diana.

.... Q. Now, the embalming in this case was a full embalmment, was it not, as far as you could tell?

A. Yes.

Q. Which meant that the blood that you took from any part of the body was likely to be contaminated?

A. Yes.

Q. Of course, the reason I ask is in relation to blood tests that can on occasion be done in relation to pregnancy.

A. Yes.

Q. But in your view, even the blood that you took was likely to have been contaminated?

A. Yes.

Dr Robert Chapman: 24 Feb 05 Statement: **Jury Didn't Hear**:

"I do have a very wide experience of the examination of embalmed bodies because of the requirement to carry out postmortem examinations on cases referred to the Coroner involving deaths abroad. Embalming makes the examination more difficult because it fixes or hardens the tissues and involves the use of unpleasant, irritant and potentially dangerous chemicals. It often creates artifacts such as damage to the skin and organs from the introduction of trocars or needles for the instillation of the embalming fluids. There will be incisions in the skin placed to identify blood vessels for the same purpose.

"Embalming points were identified on the body of Diana, Princess of Wales by the locations of the sites used and the postmortem nature of the

---

[a] This meeting with Lecomte is addressed later.

incisions.... No samples were obtained by me near to obvious sites of embalming fluid installation but the body was fully embalmed....

"All of the available blood was contaminated or even largely replaced by the embalming fluid making any sample rather unreliable for toxicology testing."[352]

Dr Robert Chapman: 24 Feb 05 Statement: **Jury Didn't Hear**:
"The sample of blood was taken from the iliac vessels within the pelvis although I have no direct record or recollection of this. These are in direct continuity with the femoral vessels within the thigh and fluid is 'milked' up from these vessels in the leg. Samples would not have been taken from heart, neck, body cavity or arm veins in view of the likelihood of contamination of these areas with body fluids. Only a small quantity of fluid was obtainable from these blood vessels as a result of the nature of the injury suffered by the deceased and the subsequent embalming. It is highly likely that embalming fluid had contaminated this sample."[353]

John Burton, Royal Coroner, 1997: 16 Jun 04 Statement: **Jury Didn't Hear**:
"There was a discussion [during the post-mortem] regarding the obtaining of toxicology samples when a body had been embalmed and a desire to find a fluid that had not been contaminated by the embalming fluid."[354]

David Green, Embalmer, UK: 13 Jul 04 Statement: **Jury Didn't Hear**:
"Embalming in the case of a sudden death in the U.K before a post mortem is unusual because any incisions, fluids removed or added could destroy evidence as to the cause of death.

"I have been asked by the officer taking this statement if in my experience and opinion that if embalming was to take place when a foetus was in a uterus what effect might the fluid have.

"Embalming fluid is a preservative and therefore any visible foetus would be preserved and I cannot see that it would remove it. I am unable to give any opinion on the effect of embalming fluid on body samples removed."[355]

David Green, Embalmer, UK: 17 Sep 04 Statement: **Jury Didn't Hear**:
"However in my experience had I known that there was going to be a post mortem examination on any deceased person then any incisions or removal of fluids would change the state of the body and therefore it would not be the same as it was at the time of death."[356]

Alan Puxley, Vice-President Operations, Kenyon International: 16 Jun 04 Statement: **Jury Didn't Hear**:
"Ideally a body known to require an autopsy would not be embalmed, however in my experience most pathologists would have at some time carried out autopsies on embalmed bodies."[357]

René Deguisne, BJL Assistant General Manager: 9 May 05 Statement: **Jury Didn't Hear**:

"Question: Did Hygeco know that an autopsy was going to be carried out on the body either in France or in Great Britain?

Answer: No.

Question: If you had been informed of that would it have changed anything in the embalming treatment?

Answer: I think that we would simply not have carried out that treatment, but since we had the agreement of the Criminal Investigation Police, through Mrs Monteil[a], we assumed that there would not be an autopsy.

....Question: In general, not in the particular case of the Princess of Wales, if a body which has to be repatriated to the United Kingdom where you are aware that an autopsy will be performed on it, do you carry out treatment if you are requested?

Answer: Yes, but I have never come across that scenario; I have never been aware of the fact there was going to be an autopsy on the other side of the Channel on a body for which our services have been requested."[358]

Jean-Claude Plumet, PFG Director of Paris Agencies, Paris: 4 Nov 05 Paget description of Statement: **Jury Didn't Hear**:

"When asked whether it was ever brought to his attention that the Princess of Wales would be subject to a post-mortem on her return to the United Kingdom, Mr Plumet replied that it had not. He clarifies that if he had been told of this, he would have asked the 'Commissaire' what he should do next, and what he should do about the embalming."[359]

Jean Monceau, BJL Director and Embalmer, Paris: 18 Oct 05 Statement: **Jury Didn't Hear**:

"You have asked me whether, if I had known that the Princess of Wales was going to undergo an autopsy prior to carrying out the embalming, I would have done anything different. No, because the embalming does not affect the autopsy. In France, we often carry out autopsies after embalming and the experts recognise the puncture points. This is why we leave a flask of fluid with the body.[b] However, in France, if for a medico-legal reason for a

---

[a] This issue has been addressed earlier in the Embalming chapter.

[b] Monceau said in his statement: "You have asked me how many flasks of embalming fluid were placed in the coffin. From memory it was one. That is enough for the chemist to determine the level of autolysis." This is in conflict with Clive Leverton's account: "David made me aware some time ago that he was given two phials of the embalming fluid, labelled Bottle 1 and 2, used by the French embalmer for the Princess of Wales." This is supported by David Green's statement: "The French embalmers ... handed me two phials of samples of the fluid they had used.": Jean Monceau, Witness Statement, 18 October 2005, reproduced in *The Documents* book, p418 (UK Edition); Clive Leverton, Witness Statement, 13 July 2004,

medico-legal autopsy, the body would be taken to the Medico-Legal Institute and it would be impossible to carry out embalming."[360]

Maud Coujard, Deputy Public Prosecutor: 15 Nov 06 Statement: **Jury Didn't Hear**:

"Question: If you had known that the Princess of Wales would be [the] subject of [a] post mortem on her return to the United Kingdom, how would this have changed the decisions and authorisation to conduct embalming in France?

Answer: I cannot reply to this questions nine years after."[361a]

Comment: The witness evidence is:

- Chapman: confirmed to Mansfield: "the blood that [I] took was likely to have been contaminated" – inquest
- Chapman: "all of the available blood was contaminated or even largely replaced by the embalming fluid making any sample rather unreliable for toxicology testing" – statement[b]
- Green: "any incisions, fluids removed or added could destroy evidence as to the cause of death"
- Green: "any incisions or removal of fluids would change the state of the body and therefore it would not be the same as it was at the time of death"
- Green: "I am unable to give any opinion on the effect of embalming fluid on body samples removed"
- Puxley: "ideally a body known to require an autopsy would not be embalmed"
- Deguisne: "we would simply not have carried out that [embalming] treatment" had "Hygeco [known] that an autopsy was going to be carried out"
- Plumet: "if he had been told of [a future post-mortem] he would have asked the 'Commissaire' what he ... should do about the embalming"
- Monceau: "the embalming does not affect the autopsy"
- Coujard: "I cannot reply to this questions".

---

reproduced in *The Documents* book, p494 (UK Edition); David Green, Witness Statement, 13 July 2004, reproduced in *The Documents* book, p503 (UK Edition).

[a] The police did not ask if Coujard knew there would be a post-mortem – they appear to have just presumed that she didn't. Coujard avoided answering. At the inquest, the following year, Coujard was asked if she knew – see earlier section on Prior Knowledge in the Embalming chapter.

[b] Chapman makes no mention of the effect of embalming contamination in his September 1997 post-mortem report, although he does describe the presence of embalming incisions and other signs that there had been an embalming.

In light of the situation regarding possible pregnancy or poisoning, it is probable that the most significant aspect of the Diana post-mortem was the samples taken and any ensuing test results.

The question then is: Are the results from toxicology tests conducted on the post-mortem samples affected by an embalming?

To Hilliard, Chapman spoke generally: "It ... will make toxicology difficult or indeed sometimes impossible".

Mansfield asked the specific question: "Even the blood that you took was likely to have been contaminated?" Chapman answered: "Yes." [a]

Chapman's statement – which the jury never heard – was more forthright: "all of the available blood was contaminated or even largely replaced by the embalming fluid making any sample rather unreliable for toxicology testing".

There are two issues here:
1) Does embalming affect post-mortem toxicology results?
2) How effective or complete was the French embalming of Princess Diana?

It is Chapman's evidence that the embalming was thorough – "all of the available blood was contaminated or even largely replaced". There is substantial evidence in the earlier Level and Quality section of the Embalming chapter that indicates this embalming was not thorough or complete.

Chapman's account – that embalming affects post-mortem test results – is supported by the general evidence of other witnesses: Green[b], Puxley, Deguisne, Plumet. These four witnesses all suggest that if a post-mortem was to be held, then that would raise a question mark over carrying out an earlier embalming. That evidence in turn indicates that an embalming could have an effect on results from any future post-mortem. The evidence of all four of these witnesses was not heard at the inquest.

---

[a] Later evidence will show that there was no embalming fluid in the blood tested. It would be fanciful to suggest that Chapman, as the performing pathologist, would be unaware of Diana's toxicology results from Paterson, and I suggest that he would also have been aware that the inquest jury were not privy to those results. Robert Thompson stated on p3 of his 2001 affidavit: "Arrangements had been made for the samples and specimens to go to the Pathology Laboratory at Charing Cross Hospital (Dr. Sue Paterson). I do not usually see the report when it comes back as the results usually go direct to the pathologist [in this case, Chapman] via the Coroner's office."
[b] Green states that "any incisions or removal of fluids would change the state of the body and therefore it would not be the same as it was at the time of death", but then says: "I am unable to give any opinion on the effect of embalming fluid on body samples removed". It would seem logical that if the state of the fluids in the body has been changed by the embalming, then any samples – e.g. blood, urine – removed would be affected. It is not known why Green, an embalmer, refused to specifically comment on this. None of Green's evidence was heard at the inquest.

The odd witness out is Jean Monceau, the embalmer – he states: "the embalming does not affect the autopsy". Monceau's account is not supported by any other witness and he has been shown, in the Embalming chapter of this volume, to be a liar.

In summary, the situation is that:

a) a post-mortem's results are affected by an embalming

b) it is known that the embalming of Princess Diana was of poor quality and was not thorough – see Embalming chapter

c) it is therefore not known how much effect the embalming would have had on the results from Princess Diana's post-mortem

d) Robert Chapman has stated that "the embalming in this case was a full embalmment"[a] and "all of the available blood was contaminated or even largely replaced by the embalming fluid".

It appears that Robert Chapman has lied in his descriptions of this embalming. This has to be viewed in the light of the Embalming chapter evidence, where this subject of the extent of the embalming has been thoroughly addressed.

The reason why Chapman has lied about this issue will become clearer as this chapter progresses.

Dr Susan Paterson, Toxicologist, UK: 28 Sep 04 Statement[b]: **Jury**

---

[a] Confirmed to Mansfield.

[b] This excerpt comes from a statement Paterson made to Paget in September 2004 – 7 years after her toxicology testing on Princess Diana's samples was actually carried out. Paterson's original 1997 report is referred to in the 2004 statement: "I produce the Toxicology Report for case No. 676/97 which was supplied to HM Coroner as exhibit SP/1." I have never been able to sight the original report, but I raise the question: Why has Paterson produced a 2004 statement for Paget when it appears to be a replica of what should have been already written up in her 1997 toxicology report? The answer may lie in a short "note" that appears on page 2, towards the end of Paterson's Paget statement: "Dr Chapman later requested analysis for carboxyhaemoglobin. As there was very limited preserved blood remaining, after consultation with Dr Chapman, it was decided to not carry out this analysis. This decision was to be revised if analysis of preserved blood from Male (Fulham 31897), Lab No. 677/97 [Dodi Fayed], showed a significant amount for carboxyhaemoglobin to be present." This is relevant to the evidence of Robert Chapman included in the section on 1st autopsy samples "Quantity Received" in Part 3 (p93). The evidence from Chapman indicates that he was referring to a sample of Henri Paul's blood in Paterson's possession, whereas Paterson's statement indicates it was a sample of Princess Diana's blood. There are two important points: 1) Diana didn't stop breathing until over 1½ hours after the crash, so there would not appear to be any relevance in testing her blood as a comparison for the carbon monoxide level in Henri Paul's blood. Because Dodi died on impact – as did Henri Paul – Dodi's blood

Didn't Hear:

"As the body had been embalmed, both preserved blood and vitreous humor were screened for drugs and ethanol. Vitreous humor is contained within the eye and is protected from contamination by embalming fluid. There was no evidence to show that the blood had been contaminated with embalming fluid." [362]

Dr Susan Paterson: 11 Jul 06 Notes from Telephone Call to Royal London Hospital: **Jury Didn't Hear**:

"What is a possible explanation for this as the embalming and preserved blood were added to and taken from the femoral area?...

"I can only conclude that the blood submitted for analysis had not been contaminated with embalming fluid.

"(Had the embalming been successful? I think this is a question for the pathologist.)....

"Even eye fluid can become contaminated during the embalming process.... From my limited experience with embalming cases if the samples have been contaminated with embalming fluid then a huge amount of methanol or ethanol would be detected during the analysis for ethanol....

"We now know that the embalming fluid contained: 'a solution of conserving product containing formaldehyde, phenol, methanol, glycerol and amaranth, mixed in the farm of arterial fluid which itself is diluted in the order of 2500 cc of water to 300 cc of solution. A draining, anti-coagulant product is added to this mixture'....[a]

"Looking at the results for unknown female for analysis for ethanol; the analysis of vitreous shows no evidence of either methanol or ethanol; the

---

would have been far more relevant to test for carbon monoxide. 2) Why has Paterson compiled this statement 7 years after the crash, when all it does is repeat the testing she carried out on Diana's samples on 1 September 1997 – all information which should have already been in her report written up on that day? The only difference appears to be the "note" quoted above in this footnote. Paterson's statement certainly raises the possibility that the blood sample Chapman was referring to belonged to Princess Diana and not Henri Paul, as indicated in Part 3. This issue will be revisited in the final volume.

[a] This was taken directly from Monceau's statement given to Paget – see p417 of *The Documents* book (UK edition). Paterson appears to have been provided this by Paget. On 7 April 2005 – over a year earlier than this phone call by Paterson – Operation Paget took control of the 2 sample bottles of embalming fluid supplied on 31 August 1997 by the French embalmers (see Clive Leverton's 7 April 2005 statement on pp495-6 of *The Documents* book). The question is: Why didn't Paget pass on these bottles – or a part of them – to Susan Paterson? That would have put her in a position where: a) she would have been able to confirm whether the information from Monceau on the make up of the embalming fluid was consistent; and more importantly, b) she would have been able to check if any of that fluid was in the samples "from Diana" that she had analysed.

analysis of blood has what could possibly he a small amount of methanol (but it is more likely a system peak) but it is far less than I would expect if the blood had been contaminated with embalming fluid."[363]

Prof Robert Forrest, Expert Inquest Toxicologist, UK: 17 July 06 Report to Paget:[ab]

"Dr Paterson ... has sent me the Gas Chromatography tracing from the blood and vitreous humour analysis on the Deceased Female.[c] The vitreous tracing is absolutely clean. The blood tracing does show a peak that could reflect the presence of methanol. The peak is relatively small. Normally, in an embalmed body where methanol is used in the embalming fluid one sees a much larger peak. This raises the issue of how thorough the embalming before the post-mortem actually was."[364d]

Comment: Susan Paterson conducted the toxicology testing on the samples submitted to her following the post-mortem of Princess Diana.

Paterson's evidence – not shown to the jury – was that the blood sample tested "had not been contaminated with embalming fluid".

There appear to be only four possibilities:

1) the embalming conducted by the French[e] was so inadequate that the blood sample taken from Princess Diana's body contained no embalming fluid

2) the blood sample submitted to Paterson for testing did not come from Princess Diana's body

3) Paterson's testing has given a false result

4) Susan Paterson has given a false account in her toxicology report.

---

[a] Just 6 days after Paterson's above phone call.

[b] Although this document was available to the jury, it was not read from at the inquest and it is unlikely they would have understood what it meant, as they were not given any evidence from Paterson – including the toxicology report. The jury may not have even realised this related to Princess Diana, because it is a paragraph tacked on to the end of a report that otherwise completely relates to Henri Paul's autopsies and toxicology.

[c] It is interesting that Forrest describes the analysis on the readings from "the deceased female" rather than referring to Princess Diana. Was he aware that this analysis did not refer to Princess Diana, but rather samples from another deceased female?

[d] In this same document Forrest states: "Dr Paterson wants me to review her file. I totally agree with her that another toxicologist should review her file in advance of the Inquest and I am prepared to do it." It appears at that stage that it was intended for the Paterson toxicology report to be available at the inquest. The question then is: Who later decided that it wouldn't be made available to the inquest jury? See INQ0001800 on the inquest website.

[e] See earlier Embalming chapter.

There is no evidence to suggest that Paterson has lied and there is no apparent reason for Paterson to lie. The fact that Paterson has taken notes from her communication with the Royal London Hospital indicates that she was genuinely concerned about the results from the case, and was possibly seeking an explanation for the contradictory results.[a]

Paterson states at the beginning of her toxicology report: "I am ... head of the Toxicology Unit at Imperial College London.... I am a registered forensic practitioner and have over 25 years experience in the analysis of drugs and ethanol in post mortem body fluids and in the interpretation of the results."

There is no reason to suggest that Paterson – who holds a respected office – is incompetent and she has provided an account of her testing methods in her toxicology report and signed statement.

Having said this, it is an incredible "oversight" that: a) Paterson was not cross-examined at the Baker inquest; b) Paterson's Toxicology Report on Princess Diana was withheld from the inquest jury; c) Paterson's police statement relating to the Diana post-mortem test results was withheld from the inquest jury.

Forrest has introduced the possibility that the blood test result "raises the issue of how thorough the embalming before the post-mortem actually was".[b]

Is it possible that Diana's body could have been embalmed without contaminating a later blood sample?

Huguette Amarger, the woman who conducted the embalming of Diana, stated: "I injected about 10 litres of formalin, that is, one two-and-a-half litre jar into each artery which goes to remake the blood circuit. I then massaged each limb in order to move the product along and push out the blood which goes out towards the suction jar." And this: "I made incisions at four points, in the two carotid arteries[c] and the two femoral arteries. Separately, I injected the formalin-based liquid into each of the arteries with a cannula."

Jean Monceau, Amarger's boss, also described the process: "We injected the right femoral in the direction of the leg. Then we proceed with the extraction from the external left femoral and inject the left leg."

---

[a] There is a possibility that Paterson communicated with Chapman to ask him about the absence of embalming fluid in the samples. It is obvious that Paterson should have been cross-examined at that inquest – but wasn't. The jury never even saw any of her reports.

[b] Forrest's assessment is also less definite than Paterson's – "the [ethanol] peak is relatively small", compared to Paterson's "far less than I would expect". Forrest has been shown in Part 3 to be an unreliable witness. It may be that when Forrest is confronted with evidence indicating the blood tested does not belong to Diana, he decides to question the thoroughness of the embalming instead. Other evidence in this chapter will show that there are several indications – other than the lack of embalming fluid – that the samples tested were not from Diana's body.

[c] The two main arteries carrying blood to the head and neck.

Amazingly, there is nothing in Chapman's post-mortem report to show the source of the Diana blood sample[a], but in his 2005 statement he did state: "the sample of blood was taken from the iliac vessels within the pelvis" – "these are in direct continuity with the femoral vessels within the thigh". Chapman though continues: "I have no direct record or recollection of this" – that the "blood was taken from the iliac vessels".

At the inquest, Chapman said: "One would try and avoid an obvious site of damage or an installation point from a fluid, but one was really trying to get a sample from the leg veins, which is a standard practice in any case."

Paterson's evidence supports Chapman's account: she said, in her 2006 telephone notes, that the Chapman blood sample was "taken from the femoral area".[b]

Both Amarger and Monceau specifically stated that the femoral area was injected with formaldehyde. According to Amarger the femoral arteries were two of only four artery points injected – so even with a poor quality embalming, one could expect the femoral area to be one of the first areas to be contaminated.

There is substantial evidence that the French embalming was incomplete and poorly executed[c], but no witness has suggested that formaldehyde was not put into the blood system.[d]

There are witness accounts of the smell of formaldehyde around the time of the embalming and also during the post-mortem:

- Tebbutt: "upon our return the room [where Diana was] smelt of chemicals and it was an awful smell – a mortuary type smell I recognised from the post-mortems I had been to as a police officer"
- Burton: "I could see and smell that the body of Diana Princess of Wales had clearly been embalmed"
- Thompson: "I could smell formaldehyde on the Princess".[365]

---

[a] When one considers the controversy over the source of blood samples in the French autopsies of Henri Paul, this certainly raises a concern over procedures in the UK. As this chapter develops other concerns over UK post-mortem procedures in the case of Princess Diana will develop.

[b] Paterson doesn't declare where this came from – Chapman is a likely source.

[c] See the Embalming chapter.

[d] The closest to anyone suggesting that is Robert Thompson: "The embalmers had obviously not bothered embalming the whole of her body, just bits and it seemed as though it had been done in a hurry.... I could see that some organs were still red, whereas they should have been green had the embalming fluid taken its full effect." Thompson doesn't say which specific areas of the body had been embalmed – "just bits". He mentions a lack of embalming fluid around internal organs that are unrelated to the femoral area.

This evidence indicates that it is likely that the femoral blood sample taken by Robert Chapman from Princess Diana's body could have been contaminated with embalming fluid.

The blood sample tested by Susan Paterson in the days following the Diana post-mortem, had "no evidence to show that the blood had been contaminated with embalming fluid".

In light of the above evidence, this then raises the possibility that the blood tested by Susan Paterson may not have belonged to Princess Diana.

Additional evidence, later in this chapter, will show that the samples picked up from Fulham Mortuary by an employee of the Toxicology Unit at Imperial College, London, on 1 September 1997 – and later toxicology tested by Susan Paterson – did not belong to Diana, Princess of Wales.

Alcohol[a]

Robert Thompson stated that there was a presence of alcohol in Princess Diana's stomach.

Robert Thompson, Fulham Mortuary Manager: 9 Nov 04 Statement: **Jury Didn't Hear**:

"Although I could smell formaldehyde on the Princess, when her stomach was opened I smelt what I believe was alcohol, not formaldehyde. When I noticed this, I was standing very close to Dr Chapman and, thus, very close to the body of Diana, Princess of Wales. The smell caused me to step back a pace and although Dr Chapman did not say anything, he reacted in such a way as to cause me to believe that he had experienced something that he was not expecting. I must stress, however, that there was no comment made about this between Dr Chapman and myself. I have been present at enough post mortems to know what people smell like when they have been drinking prior to death. It is not so much the alcohol that you smell but rather the effects it has on the body, which causes the contents of the stomach to smell strongly of alcohol. Embalming fluid also contains ethanol but the smell of embalming fluid in a body is completely different to that of alcohol." [366]

Robert Thompson: 9 Nov 04 Statement: **Jury Didn't Hear**:
"I know what I smelt during the post mortem of Diana, Princess of Wales and I cannot change that fact."[367b]

---

[a] Aspects of the evidence on this subject have also been addressed in the Procedure section of the Embalming chapter.

[b] This statement was made in reference to the smell from Diana's stomach. The full text can be viewed in *The Documents* book.

Robert Thompson, Fulham Mortuary Manager: 13 Jun 01 Affidavit: **Jury Didn't Hear**:

"With regard to the [post] mortem conducted on Princess Diana, when her stomach was opened up there were signs of a recent meal and an extremely strong smell of alcohol. Indeed, it was so strong that it forced me to step back a pace. All the other people in the post mortem room (other than Dr. Chapman) such as the police officers present were all towards the outside of the room, but I saw even some of those clearly react to the smell. Such a smell is not abnormal. Someone who has consumed a fair amount of alcohol shortly before death will give off precisely the same sort of smell when the stomach is opened."[368]

Dr Robert Chapman, Pathologist, UK: 26 Nov 07: 28.4:

Hilliard: Q. Did you open the Princess of Wales' stomach?

A. Yes.

Q. When that happened, do you remember there being – because I think, you know, that somebody says there was. I want to know whether you were aware of a smell of alcohol at all....

A. No, I was not aware of any smell of alcohol from the stomach.

Q. Is it possible that opening the stomach may result in a release of the odour of the embalming fluid?

A. Yes, yes, it is.

Dr Robert Chapman:[a] 31 Aug 97 Post-Mortem Exhibits Notes: **Jury Didn't Hear**:

"Cannula damage related to lesser curve of stomach & the related overlying inferior surface of the left side of the liver

"Large quantity of fluid and part-digested food matter

"RC/2[b]   Stomach Contents"[369]

Dr Robert Chapman: 10 Sep 97 Statement: **Jury Didn't Hear**:

"Postmortem wide bore needle damage was also noted to the lesser curve of the stomach and the immediately related overlying inferior surface of the left side of the liver. The stomach contained a large quantity of fluid and partly digested food matter."[370]

Dr Robert Chapman: 24 Feb 05 Statement: **Jury Didn't Hear**:

"I cannot recall the exact nature of the smell of the [embalming] fluid. Embalming fluids vary in their constituents but formaldehyde, methanol and ethanol may be present. It would not be possible to mistake the smell of

---

[a] These notes were dictated by Robert Chapman and written up by Richard Wall – see earlier.

[b] "RC/2" is the alpha-numeric code for the sample of stomach contents taken. This is addressed later.

embalming fluid for pure ethanol (alcohol) if one has any experience of embalmed bodies....

"I did not notice anything unusual or surprising when opening the stomach. I did not experience any odour of alcohol (ethanol) when opening the stomach although it is possible there was a release of embalming fluid which has a distinct odour. I do not recall anyone noticing or remarking on a smell of alcohol from the body. The stomach had been punctured by the embalming trocars and probably contained a significant quantity of fluid as a result.

"I found no evidence of the consumption of alcohol. The absence of ethanol detected in blood or vitreous humor (fluid) means that there was no evidence of either the consumption of alcohol or the presence of ethanol in the embalming fluid. Vitreous fluid is generally better protected from the effects of decomposition and embalming but even this may be affected by a thorough embalming process. Vitreous fluid would probably not have been taken in 1997 had an uncontaminated sample of urine been available, although it is now increasingly recognised as a useful sample in general toxicology....

"It was not possible to see what the stomach contents contained other than being food matter. This suggests a degree of digestion of the material. The material did not smell of alcohol."[371]

Comment: The question is: Was the smell from Diana's stomach alcohol or embalming fluid?

We have evidence from only two witnesses, Robert Chapman and Robert Thompson.

Thompson – who was not heard at the inquest – has said:
- "I smelt what I believe was alcohol, not formaldehyde"
- "the smell caused me to step back a pace"
- "Chapman ... reacted in such a way as to cause me to believe that he had experienced something that he was not expecting"
- "the smell of embalming fluid in a body is completely different to that of alcohol"
- "there were signs of a recent meal and an extremely strong smell of alcohol"
- "I saw even some of those [who were towards the outside of the room] clearly react to the smell"
- "someone who has consumed a fair amount of alcohol shortly before death will give off precisely the same sort of smell".

Chapman has said:
- "I was not aware of any smell of alcohol from the stomach"
- "it would not be possible to mistake the smell of embalming fluid for pure ethanol (alcohol) if one has any experience of embalmed bodies"
- "I did not notice anything unusual or surprising when opening the stomach"

- "I did not experience any odour of alcohol (ethanol) when opening the stomach"
- "I do not recall anyone noticing or remarking on a smell of alcohol from the body"
- "I found no evidence of the consumption of alcohol"
- "the material [in the stomach] did not smell of alcohol".

There are two witnesses – both there on the night; both with over ten years of experience in the conduct of post-mortems[a] – but two very conflicting accounts.

There appears to be just one aspect that Robert Thompson and Robert Chapman agree on, and that is that the difference in smell between embalming fluid and alcohol is considerable, and unmistakeable. Thompson says: "the smell of embalming fluid in a body is completely different to that of alcohol"; Chapman says: "it would not be possible to mistake the smell of embalming fluid for pure ethanol (alcohol)".

Two eye-witnesses, both very experienced with post-mortems and embalmed bodies[b], both agreeing the smells are completely different – but both with opposing accounts:

- Thompson: "there [was] ... an extremely strong smell of alcohol"; Chapman: "I did not experience any odour of alcohol"
- Thompson: "Chapman ... experienced something that he was not expecting"; Chapman: "I did not notice anything unusual or surprising"
- Thompson: "I saw even some of those [who were towards the outside of the room] clearly react"; Chapman: "I do not recall anyone noticing ... a smell of alcohol".

Thompson and Chapman can't both be right – someone appears to be lying. There were 8 other witnesses in the room – Rees, Stoneham, Wall, Sharp, Williams, Burton, Taylor, Munns – yet none of them have ever been asked about this.

---

[a] Chapman began his pathology training in 1982: "Following qualification in 1982 as a doctor I spent a number of years in training as a pathologist." So, by 1997 Chapman had about 15 years experience. Thompson stated: "I was employed in the mortuary business for fifteen years. I started at Southwark in 1986" – so by 1997 Thompson had 11 years experience in mortuaries. Sources: Robert Chapman, Witness Statement, 24 February 2005, reproduced in *The Documents* book, p579 (UK Edition); Robert Thompson, Witness Statement, 9 November 2004, reproduced in *The Documents* book, p600 (UK Edition).
[b] Chapman: "I do have a very wide experience of the examination of embalmed bodies"; Thompson: "During my profession within the mortuary business I experienced many embalmed bodies".

Rees and Stoneham were cross-examined at the inquest, but this critical issue was not addressed.

The inquest briefly heard Robert Chapman's account, but the jury never heard anything from Robert Thompson.[a]

When inquest lawyer, Nicholas Hilliard, brought up the issue with Chapman, he appears to become awkward in deliberately avoiding the mention of Thompson's name – "when that happened, do you remember there being – because I think, you know, that somebody says there was". That "somebody" of course is Robert Thompson, but Hilliard doesn't even quote anything of what Thompson has said. Chapman knows what Hilliard is talking about, but the jury – who are the ones meant to be deciding on the significance of the evidence – are not let in on the secret.

Then to close the issue, Hilliard introduces embalming fluid and Chapman confirms – "yes, yes, it is" – that it is "possible that opening the stomach may result in a release of the odour of the embalming fluid".

So the jury are left thinking that embalming fluid was smelt after Diana's stomach was opened – and completely unaware that this is a significant issue of major contention: it is linked to the evidence that Princess Diana's samples may have been switched prior to being toxicology tested (see later).

If Thompson is correct – that there was alcohol in Diana's stomach – then Diana would have been drinking alcoholic beverages on the night, before the crash.

Rene Delorm, Dodi's Butler: 1998 Book: **Jury Didn't Hear**:
Describing events at Dodi Fayed's Paris apartment before Diana and Dodi left for the Ritz Hotel at 9.30 p.m. on 30 August 1997:
"Dodi appeared and said, 'Rene, would you put some music on? Julio Iglesias, please.' As I fiddled with the CD player in the living room, the princess emerged ... asking for her customary half glass of wine. Dodi sipped a little bit of vodka and the two of them sat listening to the music.... Ten minutes later, I bought caviar....
"At about twenty past nine, I went back to the living room for my last check on them before they left for dinner....
"A few minutes later, they were in the foyer, preparing to leave for the restaurant."[372]

---

[a] The inquest did hear that Thompson existed – 26 Nov 07: 5.22 – but not that he had been interviewed by the police.

The wineglass bearing Diana's lipstick imprint and fingerprints. She had sipped from this glass just before leaving the apartment on the night of the accident. Several days after the tragedy, while sitting despondently on the living room couch, I noticed the glass hidden among the crystal decanters on the coffee table. (*Sunday Mirror*)

Figure 17

The wine glass used by Princess Diana prior to departing from Dodi's apartment at 9.30 p.m. on 30 August 1997 – just 3 hours before the crash that took the lives of her and Dodi. This photo is reproduced from Rene Delorm's 1998 book: *Diana & Dodi: A Love Story*, opposite p161,

Rene Delorm: 5 Dec 07: 179.23:

Hough: Q. You say in your [1998] book that at some time that evening, when the Princess was not around, Mr Al Fayed spoke to you and asked for you to have some champagne on ice. Do you recall that?

A. Absolutely.

.... Q. What did he say?

A. Yes, I was in the kitchen. It is in between my quarters and the apartment. I always leave open the door. He came to the kitchen and he waved at me. I went toward him. He took a look at the other side of the apartment to make sure that the Princess was not close by and he said, "Rene, have some champagne ready because when we come back, I am going to propose to the Princess".[a]

Thomas Sancton and Scott MacLeod, *Time* Magazine journalists: 1998 Book *Death of a Princess: An Investigation*: **Jury Didn't Hear**:

Describing events immediately after Diana and Dodi's arrival at the Ritz Hotel at 9.50 p.m. on 30 August 1997:

"The couple headed down the main corridor ... and entered the hotel's two star restaurant, L'Espadon. Diana ordered scrambled eggs with mushrooms and asparagus for a starter, sole with vegetables tempura as a main dish. Dodi chose a grilled turbot and a bottle of Taittinger champagne."[373]

Frank Klein, President, Ritz, Paris: 15 Dec 10 Email Correspondence to Author: **Jury Didn't Hear**:

"At [Diana and Dodi's] dinner at the Ritz, no champagne was served but a bottle of Pouilly Fumé (white wine)."[374]

Dr Susan Paterson, Toxicologist, UK: 28 Sep 04 Statement: **Jury Didn't Hear**:[b]

"Male (Fulham 31897) (deceased) Lab No. 677/97....

"The amount of ethanol present in preserved blood and vitreous humor was measured.... The blood was found to contain seventy eight milligrammes of ethanol per one hundred millilitres of blood (78 mg/100mL) and the vitreous contained eighty two milligrammes of ethanol per one hundred millilitres of vitreous humor (82 mg/100mL)....

"The preserved blood contained 78 mg/100ml ethanol. The vitreous humor contained 82 mg/100ml ethanol....

---

[a] The words from Dodi in Delorm's book are: "Make sure we have champagne on ice when we come back from dinner. I'm going to propose to her tonight.": Rene Delorm, Barry Fox & Nadine Taylor, *Diana & Dodi: A Love Story*, p158.

[b] The jury were verbally told the basic test results during the cross-examination of Chapman – 26 Nov 07: 12.4 – but were not provided with any evidence from Paterson.

"In the average male, assuming all the ethanol had been absorbed and absorbed before any elimination had taken place, assuming the stomach contents was empty and that the ethanol was consumed in one go, a blood concentration of 78 mg/100ml is equivalent to consuming about two and a half glasses of wine or about two pints of beer."[375]

Dr Susan Paterson, Toxicologist, UK: 28 Sep 04 Statement: **Jury Didn't Hear**:

"Female (Fulham 31897) (deceased) Lab No. 676/97....

"The amount of ethanol present in preserved blood and vitreous humor was measured.... Ethanol was not detected in either the preserved blood or vitreous humor."[376]

Comment: Was Princess Diana drinking alcohol on the night of 30 August 1997?

The evidence from Rene Delorm, Dodi's butler at his apartment on the night, is that at some point towards 9 p.m.[a], Diana asked "for her customary half glass of wine" and "Dodi sipped a little bit of vodka".

Delorm reproduced a photo of that final apartment wine glass that Diana drank from – shown above – and wrote in the caption: Diana "had sipped from this glass just before leaving the apartment on the night of the accident."

The general evidence – see Part 1 – is that the couple left Dodi's apartment at around 9.30 p.m. and the Ritz CCTV records their arrival at the hotel at 9.50 p.m.

This evidence reveals that Princess Diana drank half a glass of wine until sometime just before 9.30 p.m. on 30 August 1997.

Delorm also states that Dodi was contemplating celebrating their – Diana and Dodi's – engagement[b] later that night, with champagne: "Rene, have some champagne ready [for] when we come back...."

In their 1998 book, Thomas Sancton and Scott MacLeod stated that once at the Ritz – at around 10 p.m. – Dodi ordered "a bottle of Taittinger

---

[a] Diana and Dodi left the Ritz Hotel at 7.01 p.m. and arrived at Dodi's apartment at around 7.15 p.m. – see Part 1. That was a difficult arrival, including a clash between security and paparazzi. After recovering inside, Delorm describes the couple unpacking and organising their luggage. Delorm says Diana "then took a long bath", while Dodi showered. It was after dressing and getting ready for going out to dinner that they settled down for the drink that Delorm describes. The couple then left the apartment at around 9.30 p.m. Source: Rene Delorm, Barry Fox & Nadine Taylor, *Diana & Dodi: A Love Story*, pp 157-160.

[b] The issue of Engagement is covered in Part 2.

champagne".[a] In a December 2010 email, Frank Klein, the Ritz president, said that there was "no champagne ... but a bottle of Pouilly Fumé[b] (white wine)" was served.[cd]

There is no evidence of any order for non-alcoholic drinks and it is logical to presume that the bottle of white wine would have been shared between the two – Diana and Dodi.

Toxicologist Susan Paterson's statement reveals that Dodi's "preserved blood contained 78 mg/100ml ethanol" – or alcohol – and that this basically "is equivalent to consuming about two and a half glasses of wine". This finding supports Klein's account.

Delorm's evidence showed Diana and Dodi drinking pre-dinner alcoholic beverages together in the apartment before departing for the Ritz, and there is no reason to suggest that they would not have continued drinking together during their dinner at the hotel.

The above evidence indicates that Princess Diana did consume alcohol on the night, possibly drinking until around midnight[e] – but there is not enough available information to determine precisely how much alcohol Diana consumed. There is every reason to believe that the bottle of white wine would have been shared between the couple during the two hour period[f] they were in the Imperial Suite.

Any metabolism of alcohol Diana had consumed would have stopped occurring when she ceased breathing at 2.12 a.m. – see Part 2.

The effect of this evidence is three-fold:

-    it gives possible credibility to Robert Thompson's account – "I smelt what I believe was alcohol" after Diana's stomach was opened

-    it raises the possibility that Robert Chapman lied when he said: "I was not aware of any smell of alcohol from the stomach"

---

[a] The general evidence – including from Ritz CCTV footage – is that Diana and Dodi first went to the restaurant, but then moved themselves upstairs to the Imperial Suite at 10.02 p.m. According to Sancton and MacLeod the order for the meals and accompanying wine was made while they were still in the restaurant – i.e. between 9.50 and 10.02 p.m. Sources: Timeline Summary, Key Events of 30th - 31st August 1997, p5 on Inquest Website; Thomas Sancton and Scott MacLeod, Death of a Princess: An Investigation, p134.

[b] White wine produced from Sauvignon grapes grown at Pouilly-sur-Loire in the Burgundy region of central France.

[c] In a separate email – on 13 December 2010 – Klein confirmed that the MacLeod-Sancton description of the meals was correct.

[d] Klein's evidence fits with Delorm's account that Dodi told him to keep champagne on ice for their later return.

[e] The evidence in Part 1 – based on Ritz CCTV footage – shows that Dodi and Diana emerged from the Imperial Suite at 12.06 a.m. on 31 August 1997, prior to their departure in the Mercedes S280.

[f] From 10.02 p.m. to 12.06 a.m.

- in conjunction with other evidence – earlier and later – it casts doubt over the toxicology test result for Princess Diana: "ethanol[a] was not detected in either the preserved blood or vitreous humor".[b]

It could be significant that in the post-mortem document, handwritten at the time – reproduced later in this chapter – it reads "large quantity of fluid" in the stomach: it does not specify the type of fluid.

In contrast, written earlier in the same document: "considerable embalming fluid in abdomen" – so there, the type of fluid is specified.

Then in the first typed post-mortem report – undated, but duplicated in Robert Chapman's 10 September 1997 statement – Chapman states: "the stomach contained a large quantity of fluid". Again, Chapman has failed to specify the nature of the fluid. In this same document Chapman also stated: "considerable embalming fluid was present within the chest cavity".[377c]

So on September 10 Chapman has specified the type of fluid in the chest cavity – embalming – but again hasn't specified the type of fluid in the stomach.

Then in his next statement – eight years later on 24 February 2005, but just 3 months after Thompson's police statement[d] – Chapman specifies for the first time the type of fluid found in Diana's stomach: "when opening the stomach ... it is possible there was a release of embalming fluid".

Ensuring there was no misunderstanding in this 2005 statement, Chapman emphasised his account on the alcohol issue: "I did not experience any odour of alcohol"; "I found no evidence of the consumption of alcohol"; "the material [in the stomach] did not smell of alcohol".

I suggest that it is no coincidence that Chapman's statement was retaken three months after Thompson's account, and that Chapman's account was then modified.

---

[a] Alcohol.

[b] Later evidence will show that the blood and vitreous humour tested did not come from Princess Diana's body.

[c] The presence of fluid in the chest cavity is not mentioned in the handwritten report – reproduced later. Instead it includes the presence of embalming fluid in the abdomen, which is not mentioned in the September 10 report. It is difficult to understand why this conflict occurred and it is something that Chapman should have been asked about at the inquest. The chest cavity is a completely different area to the abdomen – the chest is the upper section of the trunk, whereas the abdomen is the lower section. In Chapman's 2005 statement – which was not a full post-mortem report, but instead addressed specific issues – there is no mention of the chest cavity or abdomen, other than Chapman's comments on the stomach issue which are dealt with in this section.

[d] Taken on 9 November 2004.

Robert Chapman has and will be shown to have lied on other issues, whereas Robert Thompson does not appear to have any reason to lie.

Why would Chapman lie by denying there was alcohol in Diana's stomach?

The answer to this may be linked to the later evidence showing that the alcohol testing – which revealed no alcohol present – may have been conducted on samples from a different body – not Princess Diana's.

Earlier evidence has shown that the royals – in the form of the royal coroner – were controlling events leading up to the post-mortems. There is a possibility that Chapman had been instructed to ensure that the post-mortem produced nothing that could cause controversy – e.g. confirmation of pregnancy, evidence of poisoning.[a]

I suggest that there would have been considerable surprise – as Thompson has stated – when Diana's stomach was opened to a strong smell of alcohol. Earlier evidence has shown that Chapman was dictating notes to Richard Wall, but with Thompson and others present he would not have been in a position to declare verbally that there was embalming fluid in the stomach, when it was obvious to Thompson – and maybe others – that the smell was from alcohol.

To get around this, Chapman appears to have simply stated to Wall that there was fluid in the stomach, without specifying the nature of that fluid.

Then in late 2004, Robert Thompson gave clear evidence that the smell from the stomach was alcohol.

I suggest that it was then decided that Chapman's evidence had to be retaken with a change to specify that the smell was from embalming fluid.

By that time, over 7 years after the events, it became simply Thompson's word against Chapman's.[b] But at the inquest, things took an even more sinister line, when Scott Baker ensured that the voice of Robert Thompson was not heard.

Instead, between Hilliard and Chapman, all the jury heard was that there must have been embalming fluid in Diana's stomach – see earlier – and that the toxicology testing resulted in no alcohol being detected.

Dr Susan Paterson, Toxicologist, UK: 28 Sep 04 Statement: **Jury Didn't Hear**:

"Female (Fulham 31897) (deceased) Lab No. 676/97....

"The stomach contents were screened for salicylate and paracetamol using colourimetric techniques. Neither was detected.

---

[a] This could also be linked to the reason for switching Diana's samples – this is addressed later.

[b] The Paget Report included parts of Thompson's statement – on pages 641-2 – but effectively negated any possible significance it could have by burying it between Chapman's testimony and Paterson's toxicology results.

"The preserved blood, stomach contents and vitreous humor were screened for common basic drugs using gas chromatography with a nitrogen specific detector. No drugs were detected."[378]

Comment: Robert Chapman has provided conflicting accounts on the contents of Diana's stomach:

-   10 September 1997 statement: "the stomach contained a large quantity of fluid and partly digested food matter"

-   24 February 2005 statement: "the stomach had been punctured by the embalming trocars and probably contained a significant quantity of fluid as a result"

-   24 February 2005 statement: "it was not possible to see what the stomach contents contained other than being food matter".

In the initial statement – 10 September, 10 days after the post-mortem – Chapman makes a definite observation: "the stomach contained a large quantity of fluid", yet as stated above, fails to identify the type of fluid.

By 2005 Chapman has changed his account, now identifying the fluid – "the stomach ... probably contained a significant quantity of [embalming] fluid" – but a less definite statement: "probably". This appeared under the heading: "Alcohol".

Later in the 2005 statement – under the heading "Samples" – Chapman now indicates that anything other than food matter could not be identified: "it was not possible to see what the stomach contents contained other than being food matter".

This evidence raises inevitable questions:

-   If the fluid in Diana's stomach could not be identified, why didn't Chapman state that fact, in first, the dictation to Wall on the night; and second, in his post-mortem report[a]?

-   If Chapman couldn't identify the fluid in the stomach, why didn't he ask the toxicologist, Susan Paterson, to test for ethanol, methanol or other substances that could have assisted with the identification?

In an amazing twist, instead of getting the stomach contents tested for alcohol or embalming fluid, Chapman uses Paterson's other test results – on blood and vitreous humour – to back up his insistence that there was no alcohol in the stomach.

Chapman states in 2005: "I found no evidence of the consumption of alcohol. The absence of ethanol detected in blood or vitreous humor (fluid) means that there was no evidence of either the consumption of alcohol or the presence of ethanol in the embalming fluid."

Why didn't Chapman just get the stomach contents tested?[a]

---

[a] The post-mortem report was replicated in the 10 September 1997 police statement.

Chapman is not saying that there is no embalming fluid – just "that there was no evidence of ... <u>the presence of ethanol in</u> the embalming fluid".[b]

This is in direct conflict with Paterson's earlier conclusions: "if the samples have been contaminated with embalming fluid then a huge amount of methanol or ethanol would be detected", and this: "I can only conclude that the blood submitted for analysis had not been contaminated with embalming fluid."

I suggest that the reason Chapman didn't ask Paterson – either on the following day or later – to test the stomach contents for alcohol or embalming fluid is because the stomach contents sample that Paterson had been given would have returned the same result as it did for blood and vitreous humour. That is, a negative result – no alcohol, but uncomfortably for Chapman and Burton, no embalming fluid.

I suggest that this is because – and this will be shown later – the samples which Paterson was given to test did not belong to Princess Diana. The stomach contents sample that Paterson tested is not a sample of the contents in the stomach that caused Thompson to declare: "there were signs of ... an extremely strong smell of alcohol".

Robert Thompson, Fulham Mortuary Manager: 13 Jun 01 Affidavit: **Jury Didn't Hear**:

"What is particularly surprising is that I was subsequently told by Detective Sergeant Stoneham that when the test results came back, the blood allegedly showed negative for alcohol. Detective Sergeant Stoneham expressed extreme surprise at this finding. I also find this unbelievable and it led me to the conclusion that the blood sample had either been corrupted, or a false statement made."[379]

Robert Thompson: 9 Nov 04 Statement: **Jury Didn't Hear**:

"I was very surprised when I subsequently found out that no alcohol had been found in the Princess's body....

"I was aware that there was no alcohol present in the blood of Diana, Princess of Wales and I was either told this or overheard it being said by Stoneham."[380]

Comment: Fulham mortuary manager, Robert Thompson, has stated – in his 2001 affidavit that was provided to Scott Baker before the inquest –

---

[a] It is possibly significant that Chapman took a sample of the stomach contents. Later evidence will show that with Dodi's post-mortem – conducted ahead of Diana's – no stomach contents sample was taken.

[b] Monceau stated: "We inject a solution of conserving product containing formaldehyde, phenol, <u>methanol</u>, glycerol and amaranth" – see footnote in Embalming chapter. Paterson said: "Looking at the results for unknown female for analysis for ethanol; the analysis of vitreous shows no evidence of either methanol or ethanol".

"Stoneham expressed extreme surprise at this finding" that "the blood allegedly showed negative for alcohol".

This highlights again major deficiencies in Baker's conduct of the 2008 inquest.

The question is: Why wasn't Philip Stoneham asked about Thompson's comment during his cross-examination?

Stoneham has never been questioned about either the alcohol in Diana's stomach or his reaction on learning that the alcohol results were negative.

Robert Thompson is a witness who has expressed serious reservations about these events – "it led me to the conclusion that the blood sample [of Princess Diana] had either been corrupted, or a false statement made" [a] – yet the inquest jury heard no evidence from him: no cross-examination and no statement read out.

Why is this?

Record-Keeping and Chain of Custody

"Chain of custody" is simply about being able to track the movements of the samples taken from Princess Diana. This primarily involves straightforward record-keeping.

It will be shown that in the case of Princess Diana's samples, there are serious deficiencies in the record-keeping – both general post-mortem related records and the sample recording. There are also issues regarding the movement of samples.

These major problems have been completely ignored in the police investigations and at the Baker inquest into the deaths of Princess Diana and Dodi Fayed.

There are parallels that can be drawn with the chain of custody issues that surrounded the Henri Paul [b] samples in France. On some very important points, the UK record-keeping of Princess Diana's post-mortem and samples

---

[a] In an earlier oral statement – on 16 May 2001 – Thompson is recorded by Stuart Benson as saying: "I find this inconceivable and it does lead me to the conclusion that there has been a deliberate attempt to cover up a potentially embarrassing situation." Thompson was confronted with this in 2004 by the British police and replied: "I can see how it would have covered up such a situation but I definitely would not have said that. I know what I smelt during the post mortem of Diana, Princess of Wales and I cannot change that fact.": Record of Statement Given Orally by Robert Thompson to Stuart Benson on 16 May 2001, p2; Robert Thompson, Witness Statement, 9 November 2004, reproduced in *The Documents* book, p610 (UK Edition).
[b] The driver of the crashed Mercedes S280. This is addressed in Part 3.

was more deficient than what occurred in the case of Henri Paul – this will become clear as this section develops.

It is significant that up to now this important issue has been ignored in all the investigations.

UK POST-MORTEMS

Samples section of Dodi Fayed's post-mortem report:

The following exhibits were obtained and handed to DS Wall, Exhibits Officer:

RC/1   Plucked head hair

RC/2   Brown material from mouth

RC/3   Blood preserved

RC/4   Liver sample

RC/5   Vitreous humour

Exhibits RC/3, RC/4 and RC/5 were labelled Male Fulham 31/8 and handed to Robert Thompson for storage. I understand that they were subsequently supplied to the Toxicology Unit of Imperial College of Science, Technology & Medicine for analysis.

Figure 18

Samples section of Princess Diana's post-mortem report:

The following exhibits were obtained:

RC/1   Plucked head hair

RC/2   Stomach contents

RC/3   Preserved blood

RC/4   Section of liver

RC/5   Vitreous humour

Exhibit RC/1 was handed to Detective Sergeant Wall. Exhibits RC/2 to RC/5 were handed to Robert Thompson for storage. I understand these were subsequently analysed by the Forensic Toxicology Unit of the Imperial College of Science, Technology & Medicine, London W6.

Figure 19

The figures on the previous page are reproductions of the samples section of Robert Chapman's official post-mortem reports on firstly, Dodi Fayed, and secondly, Princess Diana. A comparison between the two figures reveals flaws that are indicative of sloppy record-keeping by the pathologist, Robert Chapman – in what must have been two of the most significant post-mortems of his career. The main differences are: 1) Dodi's heading includes the detail of who the samples were initially handed to – "DS Wall, Exhibits Officer". That is missing from the heading in Diana's report; 2) Dodi's reveals labelling information – "RC/3, RC/4 and RC/5 were labelled Male Fulham 31/8". That is completely missing from Diana's. Dodi's also has no information on the labelling of RC/1 and RC/2; 3) Diana's states that "RC/1 was handed to Detective Sergeant Wall". The destination of RC/1 and RC/2 is completely missing from Dodi's – later evidence will show that RC/1 and RC/2 from Dodi's post-mortem were taken by Wall. Other evidence in this section reveals that the deficiencies regarding record-keeping of the post-mortems of Princess Diana and Dodi Fayed went far deeper than general sloppiness.

POST MORTEM EXHIBITS
(PATHOLOGISTS COPY)

Name of Victim: THE PRINCESS OF WALES

P.M. at (Venue) FULHAM

Pathologist: DR ROBERT CHAPMAN

Photographer: H.P.O. N WILLIAM

S.I.O. Det SUPT G. REES

On Date / Time 31/8/97 2015

Exhibits Officer D/S WALL

Scene Co-ordinator:- D/I SHARP.
Lab Sergeant D/S P. STONEHART

DR PETER JOAN WHEELER (0171) 245 4333) DR BURTON ~~~~~~~

Exhibit No.	Exhibit
	OTHERS PRESENT
	MR MARK TAYLOR — ASST./ PHOTOGRAPHER
	MR NIGEL MUNNS — PRINCIPAL SERVICES OFFICER
	MR ROBERT THOMPSON — LAB /ASSISTANT
	2015 Dr Wheeler To make formal identification of Diana Princess of Wales — Not made on first night
	2021 Dr Wheeler formally identifies Diana The Princess of Wales
	2025 Dr Wheeler leaves.
RC/1	Plucked head hair
	BRAIN 1640 GRAMS
	SKULL IS INTACT. MINOR S.A.H. BRAIN SWOLLEN
	BRUISING UNGUT RELATED TO EMBALMING TRACTS.
	CRYSTALS & COTTON WOOL LEFT IN UNGUT TRACTS
	CONSIDERABLE EMBALMING FLUID IN ABDOMEN
	BRUISING LOWER RIBS - LEFT SIDE.
	ANT~~~~~~~
	THOR. PASSAGE THROUGH THE FOURTH SPACE,
	THROUGH THE BREAST BONE & FIFTH SPACE
	ON RIGHT.
	CHEST ORGANS PARTIALLY FIXED
	PARTIALLY FIXED BLOOD CLOT LINED CHEST.
	DIAPHRAM APPEARS INTACT.
	CANNULA DAMAGE RELATED TO LESSER CURVE
	OF STOMACH & THE RELATED OVERLYING
	INFERIOR SURFACE OF THE LEFT SIDE OF THE
	LIVER.
'	LARGE QUANTITY OF FLUID & PART DIGESTED
	FOOD MATTER

Exhibit No.	Exhibit 2
RC/2	STOMACH CONTENTS APPENDIX PRESENT. BRUISING TO HEPATIC FLX & TRANSVERSE MESO COLON. SPLEEN INTACT. FRESH BRUISING RELATED TO LEFT KIDNEY & AORTA. BRUISING TO THE RIGHT LEAFLET ON DIAPHRAM, OVER RIGHT SIDE OF LIVER. FRACTURE OF RIGHT FIRST RIB. POST. SECOND RIB SAME PLACE. THIRD RIB - NINE RIB POSTERIALLY ON THE RIGHT SIDE WITH PERFORATION OF THE PLEURAL LININGS LEFT RIBS/ONE FRACTURED POST TO LAT. BLADDER EMPTY. UTERUS & OVERIES NORMAL. INJURY TO SIDE OF RIGHT HIP. PASSES UPWARDS TOWARDS THE FRONT - APPROX 11CMS.
RC/3	PRESERVED BLOOD RIGHT CLAVICLE DISLOCATED. CONSIDERABLE BRUISING AROUND RIGTH SHOULDER JOINT BRUISING4 LACERATION TO INNER ASPECT OF UPPER LIP 1.5CMS. HEART SAC OPON — MULTIBLE CANULATION HOLES. (12) IN THE RIGHT AITRIUM & RELATED HEART SAC BLUISH SUTURE MATERIAL PRESENT IN WHAT APPERS TO BE PULMINARY ARTERY RIGHT LUNG SHOWS CONSIDERABLE PATCHY BRUISING4 THREE PUNCTURE HOLES (EMBALMING) IN POSTERIOR RIGHT LOWER LOBE LEFT LOWER LOBE SHOWS NUMEROUS SIMILER AREAS OF DAMAGE. THERE IS 4 SINGLE VISIBLE PUNCTURE IN THE LEFT UPPER LOBE RELATED TO THE FISS.

Exhibit No.	Exhibit 3
	BRUISING TO AORTA — FIVE MORE CANULAR MARKS TO BASE OF AORTA. DAMAGE TO A PULMANARY VEIN PARTIALLY CLOSED BY BLUE STITCHES. LASERATION 3CMS IN LENGTH THE TEAR INVOLVES ALSO THE UPPER LEFT AITRIUM — MINOR CALC OF THE MITRAL VALVE. HEART 340 GRMS. MINOR ENDO CARDIAL HAEM. CANULAR DAMAGE TO LOWER GULLET. BROWNISH SOFT MATERIAL IN THE AIRWAYS MARKED BRUISING OF BOTH LUNGS THROUGH OUT. LEFT LUNG 360 GRMS RIGHT LUNG 530 GRMS CONTUSION LEFT OCCIPITAL LATERIAL SURFACE & SAH OVER FRONTAL AND P.A.R. REGIONS OF BRAIN. MORE MINOR SAH. RIGHT SIDE. PARA SAG. CONTUSIONS FRONTAL BOTH SIDES DEEP CONTUSION LEFT OCC. NO STONES IN GALL BLADDER LIVER 1750 GRMS.
RC/4	SECTION OF LIVER. SPLEEN 80 GRMS RIGHT KIDNEY 160 GRMS LEFT KIDNEY 170 GRMS PANCREOUS NORMAL. BRUISING RELATED TO BOTH KIDNEYS & DIAPHRAM. COMPLETE 2320.

Figure 20

Three page handwritten "Post Mortem Exhibits" Form, comprising of notes dictated by Robert Chapman to Richard Wall during the post-mortem of Princess Diana at Fulham Mortuary on 31 August 1997. The inquest jury were not shown this critical document. The information in it raises important issues which are addressed in the next Comment.

App P. Doc 1 402

Form 66

METROPOLITAN POLICE
Property concerned in crime/transfer/misc.

Serial No: 50/97.

Station code: O.C.G .... Other refs. (crime bk., etc.): CONFI/ TO SUPT REES.

	Time	Date	Where found:
Found	6m-1130m	31/8/97	
Deposited	0 950 ·	1/9/97	

List property
Property retained by prisoner and property retained by police
(see instructions for completing Form 57)
Entries to be signed by depositor and countersigned by Station Officer

Name and address of finder:

D/S WALL

Name and address of depositor (if not finder):

D/S WALL.

A) PLUCKED HEAD HAIR FROM:
A FEMALE (A1484982)
A) PLUCKED HEAD HAIR FROM
A MALE (A1776301)
A) BROWN MATERIAL FROM MALE'S
MOUTH. (B2119764)

Each entry in 1, 2, 3 below MUST be signed & dated

1. Circumstances of finding:

Confidential Enqy to Det Supt Rees

2. Enquiries made:
(inc. initial enqs. by officer depositing at sub-divn. station)

Confidential.

.... continued over

3. Result:

Invest. Officer: Sign:

Name/Rank/No. D/S WALL.

Station Officer: Sign:

Name/Rank/No.

Property cleared	
Date	Signature

The ...THREE... non-bulky items of property marked ...A: sealed with:		The .... non-bulky items of property marked .... sealed with:		The .... non-bulky items of property marked .... sealed with:	
Seal No. D 4099479		Seal No.		Seal No.	
Bk. 105 No.	Date 1/9/97	Bk. 105 No.	Date	Bk. 105 No.	Date
Signed		Signed		Signed	
Re-seal No.	Bk 105 No. 3691	Re-seal No.	Bk 105 No.	Re-seal No.	Bk 105 No.
Sgd/Date		Sgd/Date		Sgd/Date	
Reason		Reason		Reason	
Central Store/Date		Central Store/Date		Central Store/Date	
Sgd/Property Off.		Sgd/Property Off.		Sgd/Property Off.	

Figure 21

> Above and previous page show police documentation for the depositing into storage of samples from the post-mortems of Princess Diana and Dodi Fayed. Samples taken and deposited by Richard Wall at 9.50 a.m. on 1 September 1997 were RC/1 from Diana and RC/1 and RC/2 from Dodi. The samples were deposited on behalf of the OCG with the notation "confidential enquiry to Det Supt Rees".

Dr Robert Chapman, Pathologist, UK: 26 Nov 07: 14.4:
Hilliard: Q. So the Princess of Wales, was her body identified to you by somebody called Dr Wheeler?
A. Yes.
Q. Who was he?
A. My understanding is that he was a physician to her.
....Q. Now he identified the body to you, is this right, at 21 minutes past 8?
A. Yes.
Q. So that we understand, would it be almost immediately after that that you began the post-mortem examination?
A. It would be, yes.
Q.... If you can just help us with who was present and what their role or occupation was.
A. Again, Detective Superintendent Rees, the senior police officer; a Metropolitan Police photographer, Mr Williams; again, Detective Sergeant Wall, as exhibits officer; a Detective Inspector Sharp; Detective Sergeant Stoneham again as crime scene manager; Dr Burton, Her Majesty's Coroner; Mark Taylor as assistant photographer; Nigel Munns, he has the title principal services officer within the mortuary service; and Robert Thompson,

mortuary assistant.[a]

At 22.10: Q. In [Diana's] case, were exhibits taken, RC1 to 5?

A. Yes, they were.

Q. And RC1, plucked head hair; RC2, stomach contents; RC3, preserved blood; RC4, section of liver; and RC5, the vitreous humour again. Is that right?

A. Yes.

Q. And RC1, the plucked head hair, that I think was given to Detective Sergeant Wall, is that right?

A. Yes.

Q. And RC2 to 5, those were given to Mr Thompson for storage, is that right?

A. Yes.

Q. Did you understand that certainly the blood and the vitreous humour were examined again for alcohol?

A. Yes.

Q. I think the position is this, there was no alcohol in either; none.

A. No alcohol was found in either the blood or the vitreous humour samples.

At 52.18: Mansfield: Q. The samples that were being taken from [Diana], did you know at that stage where they were going or was there discussion about where they were going to go?

A. At the time they were actually taken from the body, no. The normal procedure is once one has completed the examination, discussion will then take place, normally with the crime scene manager, as to where those samples will be directed, where they will be sent and analysed.

Q. Who determines where they are going to go normally?

A. It is a joint decision between the pathologist and the police officers present, particularly the crime scene manager.

Q. In this –

A. Sorry, there may also be input from any coroner's officer present.

Q. What happened on this occasion?

A. Again, I do not recall exactly. I would expect there to have been some discussion with DS Stoneham.

Q. And the result?

A. The result was that they would stay within the mortuary complex, within a fridge, prior to them being transported in what we might call the "coroner's system" up to a laboratory used by the coroner for analysis.

---

[a] Chapman appears to understate Thompson's role. The Paget Report describes Thompson as "mortuary manager at Hammersmith and Fulham mortuary in 1997", p641. Burton said Thompson was "the mortuary superintendent" – see earlier. Thompson stated: "in 1994 I went to Hammersmith and Fulham where I became Mortuary Manager" – see *The Documents* book, p600.

At 55.4: Keen: Q. If you turn to page 7 of 13 [of the 24 February 2005 statement] , there is a heading, "Samples".

A. Yes.

Q. You say there: "DS Stoneham was responsible for the supply of containers with appropriate preservatives as is usual in an examination in which police exhibits are being taken. I do not know if he or one of his colleagues brought the containers to the mortuary. Both the blood and vitreous samples were placed in appropriate containers with preservative. DS Wall received and packaged the exhibits and signed them. I also signed them as my exhibits."

A. Yes.

Q. Is that a reflection of standard practice in order to identify the samples that you are taking?

A. It is.

Q. Is this a stage in what is sometimes referred to as the "chain of custody of samples"?

A. Yes.

Q. So that we know that from the point when you take the samples from a body to the point at which they arrive in a laboratory for toxicological examination, you are examining and handling the same material?

A. Yes.

Q. I think you go on to say ... that some of the samples were then passed to Robert Thompson for retention prior to transportation to the laboratory. "There is a courier system for the transportation of such samples and I would expect the samples to be appropriately refrigerated and stored prior to transportation."

A. Yes.

Coroner: Long experience, I dare say, shows that if you do not follow a rigorous procedure with samples and their transmission and labelling, et cetera, that difficulties are likely to arise.

A. Exactly so.

Q. Thank you. I am obliged, sir. In other words, you are not just doing this as a matter of procedure, it has a very clear and obvious practical underpinning, namely the need to ensure that there is a degree of certainty about the identification of samples?

A. Yes.

Dr Robert Chapman: 10 Sep 97 Statement: **Jury Heard Part Only**:[a]
"On 31/08/97 at 20.21hrs [8.21 p.m.] within the Hammersmith & Fulham Public Mortuary, Townmead Road, London SW6, Dr Peter John Wheeler identified to me the body of: <u>Diana - Princess of Wales</u>.

---

[a] Underlining in this excerpt is by Robert Chapman.

"At the request of Dr J D K Burton, H M Corner, I performed a postmortem examination. Photographs were taken under my direction....

"The following exhibits were obtained:

RC/1	Plucked head hair
RC/2	Stomach contents
RC/3	Preserved blood
RC/4	Section of liver
RC/5	Vitreous humour

"Exhibit RC/1 was handed to Detective Sergeant Wall. Exhibits RC/2 to RC/5 were handed to Robert Thompson for storage. I understand these were subsequently analysed by the Forensic Toxicology Unit of the Imperial College of Science, Technology & Medicine, London W6.

"Further Investigations

"Small samples of the major organs were retained for later histological study."[381]

Dr Robert Chapman, Pathologist, UK: 24 Feb 05 Statement: **Jury Heard Part Only**:

"D.S. Stoneham was responsible for the supply of containers with appropriate preservatives as is usual in an examination in which police exhibits are being taken. I do not know if he or one of his colleagues brought the containers to the mortuary. Both the blood and vitreous samples were placed in appropriate containers with preservative. D.S. Wall received and packaged the exhibits and signed them. I also signed them as my exhibits. I do not recall if D.S. Wall wrote the notes for me.

"Head hair is a normal sample taken during a postmortem of this type. Head hair may be useful in matching similar material deposited at a scene, on a weapon or in/on a vehicle. During the early stages of an investigation samples may be taken which later appear irrelevant with the benefit of hindsight.

"It was decided that the samples intended for toxicology analysis were to be sent to the Toxicology Unit at Charing Cross Hospital and this may be the reason that D.S. Wall did not formally receive them. Once the samples have been taken there would normally be a discussion as to the appropriate destination of those samples between police and coroner or coroner's officer. If the outcome of the postmortem and other available information indicates that charges are unlikely to be brought against anyone by the police it is common practice to send samples to the laboratory which is used to dealing with the coroner's samples from that mortuary. The reason for this is that the turnaround time for such analysis is usually more rapid than from the laboratories used by the police (Forensic Science Service). I would not have any direct control of this decision although had I felt strongly that the decision was inappropriate I would have said so at the time. The samples were then passed to Robert Thompson for retention prior to transportation to the laboratory. There is a courier system for the transportation of such samples and I would expect the samples to be appropriately refrigerated and stored prior to transportation. I do not have responsibility for the samples once they have been obtained and handed to a police officer or an appropriate mortuary staff member....

"The continuity of the samples is the responsibility of the police once they are received from the body. If the samples are to be left for local analysis the responsibility for them passes to the mortuary staff prior to collection and transportation....

"Small samples of the major organs (brain, lungs, liver, kidney, spleen, adrenal, heart) were retained for microscopic study. The purpose of this is to exclude any disease process not visible to the naked eye and to study any injury in more detail. The retention of such samples is standard practice in a complete postmortem examination. In a healthy woman it is unlikely such study would contribute much to the investigation but the samples were examined and found to show no significant natural abnormalities. The samples are in the form of wax blocks and glass slides and are stored in a histopathology laboratory within a hospital. No unprocessed tissue has been retained.

"At the direct request of Dr Burton I also retained a small sample of the injured area of the heart to include the area of the back of the left atrium and the attempted surgical repair. The retention of this sample allowed a more in-depth analysis of the injury following the postmortem. The sample is stored in the tissue retention area of St Georges Hospital histopathology department.

"It is usual to attempt toxicology analysis on samples obtained from people dying from non-natural causes on behalf of the Coroner and Police. Samples of stomach contents, blood, liver and vitreous were retained for this purpose."[382]

Richard Wall, DS, MPS Organised Crime Group: 19 Oct 04 Statement: **Jury Didn't Hear**:

"Further to my statement provided to Operation Paget on the 29th June 2004 I have been asked to comment further on the evening of Sunday 31st August 1997, when I attended Fulham mortuary to perform the role of Exhibits Officer at the post mortem examinations of Diana, Princess of Wales and Dodi Al-Fayed. In my previous statement the post mortem examination of Dodi Al-Fayed took place first, between 6pm and 7.30pm followed by the examination of the Princess of Wales between 8.15 p.m. and 9.20 p.m.[a]

---

[a] This appears to be a mistake. Wall wrote on the Exhibits document – see earlier – that the post-mortem of Diana finished at 2320 or 11.20 p.m.

"In my previous statement I said from recollection I don't recall taking any of the physical exhibits from either post mortem away from Fulham mortuary, and had no dealings with them.

"I have been shown by DC Emeny a copy of a Metropolitan Police Book 66 Property concerned crime record, reference 402, bearing my name and signatures.[a] This concerns the following exhibits that I received from Dr Chapman at the aforementioned post mortem examinations.

"It refers to, Plucked head hair from a female seal number (A1484982) produced as Dr Chapman's exhibit RC/1, Plucked head hair from a male seal number (A1776301) also produced as Dr Chapman's exhibit RC/1,and Brown material from male's mouth seal number (B2119764).[b]

"During the post mortem examination I completed two exhibit books for each of the deceased, which I have been shown today by DC Emeny exhibits TJS/2 and TJS/3.[c] These record the fact that the aforementioned exhibits were placed in a locked safe on the fifth floor at New Scotland Yard at 0030 hours [12.30 a.m.] on the 1st September 1997.

"The copy of a Metropolitan Police Book 66 Property concerned crime record, reference 402, shows that at 0950 hours [9.50 a.m.] the same day, 1st September 1997, I deposited these exhibits in a sealed bag number D4099479, in the Metropolitan Police OCG (Organised Crime Group) store, New Scotland Yard. They were recorded in the Book 105, entry reference number 3691."[383]

Toby Smith, DC, MPS Paget Officer: 26 Jun 06 Statement: **Jury Didn't Hear**:

"On 9 March 2004 I was on duty in plain clothes in Room 589 at New Scotland Yard engaged on duties relating to Operation Paget in company with Detective Chief Inspector Mark Hodges.

"From 'one (1) brown envelope marked '66 /' sealed with tape and Police Evidence Bag D4099479' DCI Hodges removed the following packaged items:

---

[a] This document is reproduced above.

[b] The earlier Exhibits document for Diana reveals that Chapman found "Brownish soft material in [her] airways". Although Chapman was apparently unable to identify what it was, he failed to take a sample for analysis. Chapman did take a sample of the "brown material" he found in Dodi's mouth, but instead of sending it to the Imperial College for analysis, he handed it to the police. There is no evidence of this sample ever being subjected to testing. It seems odd that Chapman, an experienced forensic pathologist, was unable to identify the brown material present in both bodies. But it may be even stranger that he didn't then have the material from either body analysed by Susan Paterson at the Imperial College.

[c] An excerpt of TJS/3 a Property Register record of the movement of Princess Diana's samples is reproduced later. I have never seen TJS/2 but it appears to be a similar record for Dodi Fayed's samples.

"Plucked head hair (D. Al-Fayed) sealed in Police Evidence Bag A1776301 Exhibit RC/l

"Brown material from mouth (Mr Al-Fayed) sealed in Police Evidence Bag B2119764 Exhibit RC/2

"Plucked head hair (Diana, Princess of Wales) sealed in Police Evidence Bag A1484982 Exhibit RC/1.

"In order to avoid the potential for future confusion arising from the presence of two items bearing the exhibit identification mark 'RC/l', I designated the 'Plucked head hair (Diana, Princess of Wales) sealed in Police Evidence Bag A1484982 Exhibit RC/1' as 'Exhibit RC/la'"[384]

Robert Thompson, Fulham Mortuary Manager: 9 Nov 04 Statement:
Jury Didn't Hear:

"The sample containers used during post mortems are provided by either the police or the laboratory. It would have been Phil Stoneham's job to take the samples from Dr Chapman; it is not something that I would do as Mortuary Manager....

"I wasn't involved in the identification of the bodies as this was done outside the post mortem room. The body of Dodi Al Fayed had been transported by helicopter and hearse.... Mohamed Al Fayed came with his son's body. I filled out the Mortuary Register, which provides details of the person bringing each body into the mortuary. I remember that I initially filled out his name as 'Dodi Al Fayed' and subsequently had to change it to his correct, full much longer name. It is also mortuary procedure to fill out a form recording the clothing, valuables, etc. found with the body. This form then goes off to Council Records....

"The body of Diana, Princess of Wales was transported to the mortuary by the undertakers....

"I cannot recall being in possession of any post mortem samples from Dodi Al Fayed's body though I do remember having samples from Diana, Princess of Wales. I would just like to explain that in the case of a criminal/forensic post mortem it is the police exhibits officer who takes the samples but it was a different situation in the cases of the Princess and Dodi Al Fayed. Any samples stored at the mortuary prior to being sent to the laboratory would have been kept in the mortuary fridge. It was very difficult to store bodies in the lower rung so we would use it for samples instead. During the time I worked at Hammersmith and Fulham Mortuary it was common practice for samples to be sent to Charing Cross hospital for analysis.

"I do not actually recall being handed the samples following the post mortems of Diana, Princess of Wales and Dodi Al Fayed but I'm sure they would have been given to me. I would not have signed any exhibit label, as this is not one of the roles carried out by a Mortuary Manager. I do, however, remember that the day after the post mortems I dispatched the samples taken from the Princess to the lab at Charing Cross hospital.

"At the mortuary we had started a register of samples but I cannot say whether this book was up and running at the time the post mortem examinations of Diana, Princess of Wales and Dodi Al Fayed. I particularly remember the samples going to Charing Cross hospital because they sent someone on a pedal bike to collect them. I assumed he was one of their lab technicians but I refused to let him take the samples as I felt they should be transported by vehicle, as that would have been more secure and therefore a lot safer. He left the mortuary empty handed but returned later that day in a car, which I believe was a taxi. I recall giving him the samples taken at the Princess's post mortem examination but I do not recall giving him any of the samples from Dodi Al Fayed. I may well have done but just cannot remember now.

"The samples had been stored in the mortuary fridge, as was the norm at a temperature of around four degrees centigrade. The fridge itself is not locked but it is situated within the mortuary area, which is kept secure. I do not know whose decision it was to send the samples to the lab at Charing Cross but, as I have said, this was the usual course of action at that time.

"As is the case during all post mortems, it is the pathologist who takes the samples. This was also the case with Diana, Princess of Wales and Dodi Al Fayed. I recall the bodies left the mortuary that night after each of the post mortem examinations. I was never involved in any briefing or debriefing after the post mortems of Diana, Princess of Wales and Dodi Al Fayed." [385]

Robert Thompson, Fulham Mortuary Manager: 13 Jun 01 Affidavit: **Jury Didn't Hear**:

"There was also present a laboratory liaison officer, Detective Sergeant Stoneham. In the case of a suspicious death the laboratory liaison officer is there to receive the samples and specimens taken from the body and deliver them to the Metropolitan Police Forensic Science Laboratory, Lambeth....

"Although, as mentioned, Detective Sergeant Stoneham was present for the purpose of receiving and delivering samples to the Metropolitan Police Laboratory, which is the norm, Dr. Burton had made special arrangements to have the specimens taken from Princess Diana removed to Charing Cross Hospital and had also arranged for an entirely separate courier to come and collect those specimens on the following day (i.e. Monday). The specimens were stored in the mortuary refrigerator overnight. Detective Sergeant Stoneham performed his customary role in that he received the specimens from the pathologist and labelled them. They were then refrigerated at the mortuary, but I cannot now recall who did this or on whose instructions. When the courier arrived the following day all the specimens were eventually handed to him. However, he had in fact come on a bicycle and I refused to hand them to him or allow him to carry them back to the hospital until he had arranged an acceptable form of transport. He therefore organised for a taxi to collect him. What is particularly surprising is that I was subsequently told by Detective Sergeant Stoneham that when the test results came back, the blood allegedly showed negative for alcohol. Detective Sergeant Stoneham expressed extreme surprise at this finding. I also find this unbelievable and it lead me to the conclusion that the blood sample had either been corrupted, or a false statement made....

"During the course of the post mortem, a number of specimens and samples are taken. These are then sent off to a separate laboratory for testing and reports to be produced. In the case of Dodi Al Fayed and Princess Diana, arrangements had been made for the samples and specimens to go to the Pathology Laboratory at Charing Cross Hospital (Dr. Sue Paterson). I do not usually see the report when it comes back as the results usually go direct to the Pathologist via the Coroner's office. Apart from the alcohol issue, I do not recall hearing anything else of any particular importance regarding the test results.

"Princess Diana's post mortem took about 4 hours and the body was released at about midnight."[386]

Dr Susan Paterson, Toxicologist, UK: 28 Sep 04 Statement: **Jury Didn't Hear**:

"Female (Fulham 31897) (deceased) Lab No. 676/97....

"On 1st September 1997, one of the toxicologists, Neil McLachlan-Troup went to Fulham mortuary and was handed, by a member of the mortuary staff, samples relating to a Female (Fulham 31897). He brought the samples directly to the Toxicology Unit where they were assigned the unique case number 676/97

"Each sample was individually sealed in a police evidence bag. The samples included: -

Exhibit RC/2 labelled: Stomach contents, A Female, Fulham Mortuary, 31/8/97, Dr R Chapman

Exhibit RC/3 labelled: Blood preserved, A Female, Fulham Mortuary, 31/8/97, Dr R Chapman

Exhibit RC/4 labelled: Liver section, A Female, Fulham Mortuary, 31/8/97, Dr Chapman

Exhibit RC/5 labelled: Vitreous humor, A Female, Fulham Mortuary, 31/8/97, Dr Chapman

"Dr R. Chapman, on behalf of HM Coroner, requested that I analyse the samples for ethanol and drugs. I was informed that the deceased had received multiple injuries."[387]

Dr Robert Chapman: 5 Sep 97 Statement: **Jury Heard Part Only**:[a]
"The following exhibits were obtained and handed to DS Wall, Exhibits Officer:
RC/1   Plucked head hair
RC/2   Brown material from mouth
RC/3   Blood preserved
RC/4   Liver sample
RC/5   Vitreous humour
"Exhibits RC/3, RC/4 and RC/5 were labelled Male Fulham 31/8 and handed to Robert Thompson for storage. I understand that they were subsequently supplied to the Toxicology Unit of Imperial College of Science, Technology & Medicine for analysis.
"Small samples of the major organs were retained for later histological study."[388]

Dr Susan Paterson, Toxicologist, UK: 28 Sep 04 Statement: **Jury Didn't Hear**:
"Male (Fulham 31897) (deceased) Lab No. 677/97....
"On 1st September 1997, one of the toxicologists, Neil McLachlan-Troup went to Fulham mortuary and was handed, by a member of the mortuary staff, samples relating to a Male (Fulham 31897). He brought the samples directly to the Toxicology Unit where they were assigned the unique case number 677/97
"Each sample was individually sealed in a police evidence bag. The samples included:-
Exhibit RC/3 labelled: Blood preserved, A Male, Fulham Mortuary, 31/8/97, Dr R Chapman
Exhibit RC/4 labelled: Liver sample, A Male, Fulham Mortuary, 31/8/97, Dr Chapman
Exhibit RC/5 labelled: Vitreous humor, A Male, Fulham Mortuary, 31/8/97, Dr Chapman
"Dr R. Chapman, on behalf of HM Coroner, requested that I analyse the samples for ethanol and drugs."[389]

Philip Stoneham, Detective Sergeant, British Police: 18 Dec 07: 21.18:
Mansfield: Q. The sampling that in fact took place, was it ordinary sampling or special sampling? Do you appreciate the difference I am putting to you? Do you remember in fact what happened?
A. I do not remember what happened. I do not remember what samples were taken.
Q. What would be the samples that would normally be taken on a special [post-mortem]?
A. The standard post mortem samples for a special post mortem start from

---

[a] Underlining in this excerpt is by Robert Chapman.

the head and really go from head to toe.

Q. Head to toe. I appreciate again there is a time lapse. If you need to look at the notes – you were asked this question in November 2004.....

A. Yes, I see.

Q. Do you see, it says: "In a normal special post mortem, the standard samples are head hair, mouth swabs, pubic hair, finger nails, blood for DNA, blood for toxicology, urine or vitreous humour if no urine is present, liver and stomach contents." [a]

A. That is right, yes.

Q. Did that happen in this case or you can't ... ?

A. I do not know. I do not know.

Q. Those are the samples that have to be taken if it is the normal special post mortem. Where do the samples in a normal special post mortem go?

A. Forensic science laboratory.

Q. Forensic science. Not a hospital?

A. No.

Q. Did you play any part in the decision-making about where the samples would go in this particular case? If you cannot remember, I will leave it.

A. I really cannot remember. I mean I have read my statements so I know there is reference to the samples, whatever they were, went to Charing Cross Hospital, but I do not know what part I played.

Q. No, I understand. Thank you very much.

At 27.16: Horwell: Q. What we have heard is evidence that there came a stage in these post-mortem examinations when there was a discussion as to where the samples should go. If this had been a suspicious death post mortem, the samples would have been kept under the control of the Metropolitan Police?

A. Indeed.

Q. But because this was not a suspicious death post mortem, because it was a road traffic accident post mortem, the contrary view was also expressed, that

---

[a] It seems odd that Stoneham – who was still a police officer in 2007 (18 Dec 07: 2.10) – knew specifically what samples were taken in a special post-mortem in 2004, but when asked at the inquest three years later, simply answers "head to toe". Stoneham's evidence – see earlier – was that he only attended special post-mortems and as laboratory liaison manager was involved with the taking of samples. Thompson said in his statement: "Detective Sergeant Stoneham performed his customary role in that he received the specimens from the pathologist and labelled them." Mansfield generously excuses Stoneham: "I appreciate again there is a time lapse." But this is not a specific issue of remembering what occurred – for a person in Stoneham's position this was a general question central to the nature of his every day job.

in such cases the samples are kept under the control of the pathologist. Do you remember a discussion of this nature?

A. I am sorry, I do not remember. I really do not remember.

Q. The evidence that we have heard is that it was decided eventually that, because this was a road traffic accident, the samples would not be kept under the control of the Metropolitan Police, but would be kept under the control of the pathologist and would be sent to a hospital. Do you remember any of that?

A. I do not remember. I have to take your word for it.

Q. May it be that it is that discussion that you have remembered over all of these years, rather than any other about how this post mortem was to be treated?

A. That may well be right, too, yes. That may well be the case, yes.[a]

Philip Stoneham: Paget Description of Statement: **Jury Didn't Hear**:

"[Stoneham] received a call on Sunday 31 August 1997 to attend New Scotland Yard and meet with DI Sharp. There he was advised of two post-mortem examinations that were to take place later that day at Hammersmith and Fulham mortuary. He attended the post-mortem examinations of Dodi Al Fayed and the Princess of Wales and witnessed DS Wall (exhibits officer) packaging and labelling exhibits that were handed to him by the pathologist, Dr Chapman."[390]

Jeffrey Rees, Head of Early Crash Investigations, British Police: 17 Dec 07:37.7:

Hilliard: Q. You ... noted that you don't remember asking Dr Chapman to carry out any particular tests in respect of either body. Is that right?

A. That is correct.

Q. Is that the kind of thing that you might ever do?

A. Yes. I discussed the situation with Dr Chapman and what I said was, "Obviously all the samples that would normally be taken in a road traffic accident should be taken, but, in addition, we should take anything else which might just become relevant". I was thinking in particular of head hair,

---

[a] Horwell then moved on to the next topic. This was a very strange period of cross-examination. Richard Horwell, who is the police lawyer, asks Stoneham: "Do you remember a discussion of this nature?" – that "the samples [would be] kept under the control of the pathologist". Stoneham replies: "I am sorry, I do not remember. I really do not remember." Horwell, evidently not happy with this response, rewords and asks the question again: "Do you remember any of that?" Stoneham again: "I do not remember. I have to take your word for it." Horwell then takes a very strange – and apparently manipulative – angle: "May it be that it is that discussion that you have remembered over all of these years, rather than any other about how this post mortem was to be treated?" Horwell is referring to a discussion that Stoneham has told him twice that he can't remember. But Stoneham's reply is even stranger: "That may well be right, too, yes. That may well be the case, yes."

stomach contents and anything like that.

....Q. Now we have heard about the samples and exhibits that were taken. Was there some discussion as to where those samples and exhibits should be examined?

A. There was.

Q. What was the effect of the discussion?

A. I discussed with Dr Chapman what the normal process would be in a road traffic accident, and in a road traffic accident, samples would normally be examined at the pathologist's hospital, whereas in a murder or suspicious death, the samples would go to the police laboratory, to a different laboratory. So because the findings were consistent with a road traffic accident, after discussions we decided that the route of the samples should be the normal one in a road traffic accident, but I was concerned that if anything should later emerge, we could retrieve the situation. So the continuity of the exhibits would be maintained and there would be no loss of evidence in any way.

Q. Right.

A. I might say I was also concerned about security because – for example, the Princess's head hair, I was very concerned that anything like that could fall into the wrong hands and Dr Chapman assured me that the system would be tight.

Q. So the upshot was that examinations would be carried out by scientists at his hospital?

A. Yes.

Q. You had raised those particular concerns and you had been given assurances about them?

A. Correct.

RCC:SC.39/97

The Forensic Medicine Unit
St George's Hospital Medical School
Cranmer Terrace
London SW17 0RE

Telephone: 0181 725 0015/0016
Fax: 0181 725 0017
e mail: r.shepherd@sghms.ac.uk

On 31/08/97 at 20.21hrs within the Hammersmith & Fulham Public Mortuary, Townmead Road, London SW6, Dr Peter John Wheeler identified to me the body of:

Diana - Princess of Wales

At the request of Dr J D K Burton, H M Coroner, I performed a postmortem examination. Photographs were taken under my direction.

Those present:

Detective Superintendent G Rees
Mr N Williams - Photographer
Detective Sergeant Wall - Exhibits Officer
Detective Inspector Sharp
Detective Sergeant P Stoneham
Dr J Burton - H M Coroner
Mark Taylor - Assistant Photographer
Nigel Munns - Principal Services Officer
Robert Thompson - Mortuary Assistant

EXTERNAL EXAMINATION

The body was that of a young white woman, 5ft 10½ins (1.79m) in height and of slim build. The body was clothed in a black dress and black shoes. Elasticated bandages had been applied over the upper chest, the right upper arm and the groins and perineal regions.

There were the following features related to embalming and cosmetic postmortem processes:

1. Two short, fine incisions on each side of the base of the neck placed almost vertically along the long axis of the body. These had been closed with fine sutures and some form of adhesive sealant.

Signature: .... Signature of Witness: ....

Figure 22

First page of official post-mortem report for Diana, Princess of Wales, drawn up by Robert Chapman. Although this report shows no date at all in the document, it is the only official post-mortem documentation to include a reference number: "RCC:SC:39/97" – see top left-hand corner. It is possible that "39" could be a date – September 3 – but as the document is undated, this cannot be confirmed. This document was not shown to the inquest jury.

UK POST-MORTEMS

PM No.	DATE RECEIVED	PM DATE	PATHOLOGIST	DELIVERY	MORTUARY
661/97	28·8·97	21·8·97	WEST	ALLWAYS	FULHAM
662	"	22·8·97	"	"	"
663	"	26·8·97	PATEL	"	"
664	"	27·8·97	"	"	"
565	"	28·8·97	BOWEN	"	HORNSEY
666	"	27·8·97	"	"	"
667	"	"	"	"	"
668	"	26·8·97	CROMPTON	"	NPH
669	"	"	"	"	"
670	"	"	"	"	"
671	"	"	CHAPMAN	"	UXBRIDGE
672	"	27·8·97	"	"	"
673	29·08·97	29·08·97	MCKENZIE	POST	HARROW
674	"	26·8·93	KINSEY	COURIER	LOWESTOFT
675	"	23·8·97	RIMMER	POST	BEDFORD
676	1·9·97	31·8·97	CHAPMAN	PICK-UP Ng	FULHAM
677	"	"	"	"	"
678	1·9·97	1·9·97	JADER	HACKON FOXCOX	
679	"	"	"	COURIER	"

On this and the next page are the records of samples received at the
Toxicology Unit at Imperial College London around the time of the Paris
crash. The rows of data on the next page are an extension of the rows on this
page. The form shows the receipt of samples on 1 September 1997 for
"Unknown Female 31897" and "Unknown Male 31897", alleged to belong
to Princess Diana and Dodi Fayed. If you look closely at the entries on the
next page, you will notice there is extra unidentifiable writing just above
the second "unknown" word – it appears that some lettering may have been
covered over, before this document was copied. This form, drawn up by the
Toxicology Lab, is the first evidence of the samples from the post-mortems
being assigned unique numbers – "676/97" and "677/97". This document
was not shown to the jury at the inquest into the deaths.

NAME	ALC	DRUGS	CO	other	COMMENT
▓▓▓▓▓▓▓	✓	✓			
▓▓▓▓▓▓▓	✓	✓			
▓▓▓▓▓▓▓	✓	✓			
▓▓▓▓▓▓▓	✓				
▓▓▓▓▓▓▓	✓	✓			UDAS
▓▓▓▓▓▓▓		✓			
▓▓▓▓▓▓▓		✓			
▓▓▓▓▓▓▓	✓	✓			
▓▓▓▓▓▓▓	✓				
▓▓▓▓▓▓▓	✓				
▓▓▓▓▓▓▓	✓	✓			
▓▓▓▓▓▓▓	✓				
▓▓▓▓▓▓▓	✓	✓			UDAS
▓▓▓▓▓▓▓	✓	✓		MORPH	
▓▓▓▓▓▓▓	✓	✓		SOLVENT	UDAS
UNKNOWN FEMALE 31897	✓	✓			
UNKNOWN MALE 36797	✓	✓			
▓▓▓▓▓▓▓	✓	✓	✓		
▓▓▓▓▓▓▓	✓	✓		UDAS	
▓▓▓▓▓▓▓	✓	✓		Amphet.	

Figure 23

cry OD/634

From Copy file
Ros Chapman

Apx 741004

$\partial \rightarrow$ file.   Pathologist: ...... R. Chapman.

FORENSIC POSTMORTEM HISTOLOGY

SURNAME UNIDENTIFIED FEMALE (WHITE)		FORENSIC REF: F/O91/97		
Forename:		PM No:		PM Date: 31/8/97
Sex: Male/Female Age: _____		Day Cut: 9/8/97		Date Out:

Tissue

SPECIAL STAIN	BLOCK(S)

Total No of Blocks:
12

Slides please.

Figure 24

> The two page document on this and the previous page – sourced
> from within the Paget investigation files – appears to be a request
> for post-mortem related histological slides for various parts of
> Diana's body. The potential significance of this document –
> which was not shown to the inquest jury – is addressed below.

Comment: It could be significant that both the coroners – Burgess and
Burton – failed to address the critical issues involving the samples in their
statements. This is despite the fact they called for the post-mortems and were
present throughout the procedures.[a]

Burgess doesn't mention samples at all – even when he is asked, "What is
the difference between a normal and a special PM?"[b] Earlier evidence has
shown that the samples taken is a key factor in that.[c]

Burton makes only a few quick references to the sampling, without
addressing any of the critical issues:
- "photographs and samples were taken at the direction of Dr Chapman and
the FLO"[391]
- "sometimes samples are taken by the pathologists for both the police and
also the coroner" – see earlier

---

[a] Burton was present at both and Burgess was present for Dodi's only.

[b] Burgess' answer to this has been shown in the earlier section on Special Post-
Mortems.

[c] The closest Burgess comes to mentioning samples is in his evidence of a meeting
held with Dominique Lecomte in 1998. Burgess said: "Dr Chapman offered to show
[Lecomte] histology slides that he kept at his office".: See *The Documents* book,
p543.

- "there was a discussion regarding the obtaining of toxicology samples when a body had been embalmed"[392]
- "Dr Chapman ... referred to samples taken" during the 1998 meeting with Dominique Lecomte.[393]

As mentioned earlier, there are serious deficiencies, problems and issues related to the general record-keeping and chain of custody of the samples in the Princess Diana post-mortem.[a]

The issues are:

1) When the bodies of Princess Diana and Dodi Fayed were delivered to the Fulham Mortuary[b], neither of them were assigned body numbers.

This is the best possible start, if one was interested in covering up post-mortem related documents – if there is no body number then there is no central reference point to put at the top of documents related to the body.

And that is exactly what we see – there is a general lack of reference numbers or reference codes on the key mortuary documents relating to Princess Diana's post-mortem.

The jury were not shown any of these documents, so they would not have been in a position to see that Diana, Princess of Wales was not allocated a Fulham Mortuary body number.

Even Henri Paul was assigned a body number – 2147 – on his arrival at the Paris IML (see Part 3).

Robert Thompson has not said anything regarding the receipt of Diana's body, but said the following about Dodi's: "Mohamed Al Fayed came with his son's body. I filled out the Mortuary Register, which provides details of the person bringing each body into the mortuary. I remember that I initially filled out his name as 'Dodi Al Fayed'.... It is also mortuary procedure to fill out a form recording the clothing, valuables, etc. found with the body. This form then goes off to Council Records."

This evidence appears to indicate that an entry is made in the mortuary register on receipt of a body – it details "the person bringing each body in" and also the name belonging to the body.

There is no mention of a unique body number being assigned to the incoming bodies of Princess Diana and Dodi Fayed at the Fulham Mortuary.

2) The official post-mortem report[c] is undated. It has a reference code in the top left-hand corner – RCC:SC.39/97.

---

[a] In some cases there are also problems with the Dodi Fayed post-mortem – where that is specifically the case, it will be pointed out. The main focus here is on the post-mortem of Princess Diana.

[b] They arrived separately – Dodi at about 5.25 p.m. and Diana around 8.00 p.m.

[c] The first page of this report has been reproduced above.

This same code appears at the top of each page of the 10 page document. It is not known what this code depicts, but it could be that RCC stands for Robert Charles Chapman, the pathologist; SC could be the initials of the person who typed the report; 39/97 could simply be a shortened form of the date of typing the document – if it was typed on 3 September 1997.

The last page of this document is signed Dr R. C. Chapman.

This entire document – but without the reference code RCC:SC.39/97 – was reproduced to make the 10 September 1997 witness statement by Robert Chapman to the British police.[a]

3) The inquest jury was provided with no documentation at all in connection with the post-mortems of Princess Diana and Dodi Fayed.[b]

4) The "Post Mortem Exhibits" form for "The Princess of Wales" – written up at the time by Richard Wall and reproduced earlier in this chapter – shows just four exhibits, or samples, being taken from the body:

RC/1 – Plucked head hair – p1
RC/2 – Stomach Contents – p2
RC/3 – Preserved Blood – p2
RC/4 – Section of Liver – p3

Pathologist Robert Chapman's post-mortem report – provided to the British police just 10 days later – shows a different picture:
"The following exhibits were obtained:

RC/1   Plucked head hair
RC/2   Stomach contents
RC/3   Preserved blood
RC/4   Section of liver
RC/5   Vitreous humour

".... Small samples of the major organs were retained for later histological study."

Then eight years later, in February 2005, Chapman outlines to the police the specifics of the "small samples of the major organs": "brain, lungs, liver, kidney, spleen, adrenal, heart were retained for microscopic study". Then Chapman added: "I also retained a small sample of the injured area of the heart".

So there are major conflicts between the original document – dictated by Chapman to Wall during the post-mortem – and the two later statements by Chapman:

- 31 August 1997 document: just 4 samples taken – RC/1 to RC/4 – no vitreous humour and no organ samples other than liver

---

[a] The witness statement is double-spaced so, although containing the same words, runs to 16 pages compared to just 10 pages of the original document.
[b] This also includes no documentation related to the toxicological testing of the samples taken.

-   10 September 1997 statement: 5 main samples taken – RC/1 to RC/5 – includes vitreous humour – "small samples of the major organs" taken

-   24 February 2005 statement: 5 main samples taken – described as "head hair" and "stomach contents, blood, liver and vitreous" – 8 other samples taken – "brain, lungs, liver, kidney, spleen, adrenal, heart" and "a small sample of the injured area of the heart".

On the night there were just 4 samples taken; 10 days later there are 5 listed samples plus other "samples of the major organs"; by 2005 there are 13 samples altogether.

The three page 31 August 1997 "Post Mortem Exhibits" form – reproduced earlier – is significant because:

-   it is a detailed account of what occurred

-   it should be the most accurate account because it was dictated and written as the time the post-mortem was occurring

-   it appears to be very complete – it shows a starting time of "31/8/97 2015" or 8.15 p.m., identification at "2021" or 8.21 p.m. and the first sample – head hair – taken after Dr Wheeler, the identifier, leaves at 2025, or 8.25 p.m. Then the form finishes with the post-mortem "complete" at "2320" or 11.20 p.m.

-   it is named the "Post Mortem Exhibits" form – so if any document is going to tell us which exhibits – samples – were taken during the post-mortem then this should be it.

Why is there such a conflict in the critical post-mortem documentation?

Why is there no vitreous humour sample taken on the night, but there is one in Chapman's signed statement ten days later?[a]

Why are there only 4 samples taken in the form completed at the time, but 13 samples showing in Chapman's 2005 statement?

Why was Scott Baker's inquest jury not shown any of this post-mortem documentation?

Unrecorded Samples

The completion time of 11.20 p.m. on the Exhibits document appears

---

[a] Some might argue that Chapman took the vitreous humour – eye fluid – from Diana's body after the 11.20 p.m. conclusion of the post-mortem. Chapman's evidence, however, is quite specific: "Both the blood and vitreous samples were placed in appropriate containers with preservative. D.S. Wall received and packaged the exhibits and signed them. I also signed them as my exhibits."

to basically fit with other more general earlier evidence.[a] Clive Leverton stated: "We waited here whilst the post mortem examination took place from about 1930 [7.30 p.m.] to 2300 hours." David Green said: "At about 11 to 11.30 p.m. I went to the Chapel at St James' Palace to carry out the embalming."

The evidence roughly fits – Diana's body was transported to St James' Palace after 11.20 p.m.[b] and the embalming would have begun soon after that. The timing doesn't appear to give Chapman much room to secretly take an additional 9 samples from the body after the completion of the post-mortem.

The February 2005 list of organ samples almost fits with the list on the second page of the two page document – reproduced earlier – headed "Forensic Postmortem Histology". The handwritten list from that form – which was sourced from within the Operation Paget files – reads: "brain, lungs, liver, kid[c], spleen, adrenal, heart".[d] That list is in exactly the same order as Chapman stated to the police in February 2005.[e] But in the 2005 account Chapman in addition mentions "a small sample of the injured area of the heart" – this sample is not included in the Histology form.

The question is: Does this Histology form relate to samples taken from Princess Diana's body?

There are several relevant points:

a) Under "Surname" the Histology form reads "Unidentified Female (Fulham)". This is different to all other known forms:
- the original Exhibits form reads "The Princess of Wales"
- the initial post-mortem report reads "Diana – Princess of Wales"
- the Imperial College toxicology receipt form reads "Unknown Female 31897"
- the official Toxicology Report reads "Female (Fulham 31897)".[f]

It will be shown later that the samples referred to in the receipt form and the Toxicology Report do not belong to Princess Diana.

There are only two known post-mortem documents that relate to Princess Diana – the Exhibits form and the initial undated report – and

---

[a] Earlier relevant evidence on the timing is in the UK Embalming section in the Royal Control chapter.

[b] See earlier.

[c] Probably short for "kidney".

[d] Some of the words in that document are difficult to read, but this appears to be what it says.

[e] Chapman said: "Small samples of the major organs (brain, lungs, liver, kidney, spleen, adrenal, heart) were retained for microscopic study."

[f] The Toxicology Report is reproduced in *The Documents* book, p613.

both refer to her by name, including her title "Princess of Wales".

b) The Histology form appears to show reference numbers: "F/091/97"; "APX 741004"; "OD/634". The reference numbers on the other forms are:

- Exhibits form – no reference numbers
- Post-Mortem report – RCC:SC.39/97 – this is not repeated on the 10 September 1997 statement that shows the same report
- Imperial College receipt – 676
- Toxicology Report – 676/97.

Although there are three different numbers on the Histology form, none of them tie in to any other form.

The official post-mortem documentation is notable for its lack of reference numbers and the failure to assign unique numbers to the bodies of Princess Diana and Dodi Fayed – yet this Histology form presents us with three previously unknown reference numbers. There is no apparent explanation for this.

c) The "Day Cut" reads "9/8/97" yet Diana's body didn't arrive at the mortuary until 31/8/97. The "PM Date" matches Diana's – "31/8/97".

d) The samples listed on page 2 of the Histology form are not numbered, whereas the actual samples taken during the post-mortem were immediately allocated numbers – RC/1 to RC/4.

Maybe the most significant factor is that this Histology form shows samples that were not listed as taken in the initial post-mortem document.

It therefore raises the obvious question: When did Robert Chapman take these samples? [a]

When referring to the 7 "samples of the major organs", Chapman states that they "are stored in a histopathology laboratory <u>within a hospital</u>" – this appears to be very vague, coming from a forensic pathologist. Why doesn't Chapman name the hospital?[b]

In the very next paragraph, when referring to the "sample of the injured area of the heart", Chapman does specifically name that location – "the sample is stored in the tissue retention area of St Georges Hospital histopathology department".

Why did the 7 organ samples go to "a histopathology laboratory within a hospital", while the "sample of the injured area" goes to the "St

---

[a] This will be addressed later.

[b] A Paget form discussed below indicates that these samples are "retained by the Forensic Pathology Alliance". Chapman may have been aware of this.

Georges Hospital histopathology department"? Both are histopathology laboratories, but apparently in different hospitals.

At the inquest there was no mention at all of the 8 organ samples listed in Chapman's February 2005 statement.[a]

Chapman said in the statement: "The [7 organ] samples were examined and found to show no significant natural abnormalities."

When did this examination of the samples occur? Where is the report that would have been completed at the time?

Chapman also says: "The retention of such samples is standard practice in a complete postmortem examination."

I then ask: Is it also "standard practice" to: a) not list these samples in the official exhibits[b]; b) not allocate numbers to these samples; c) make no official record of these samples; d) not advise the inquest jury investigating the death about their existence.

Chapman's earlier evidence was: "I think ... we decided those [normal samples taken in a road traffic case] would be the samples to take".

Mansfield asked Chapman about what would constitute normal sampling for a road traffic accident:

Mansfield: "Could you explain what the normal ones would be?"

Chapman: "One would try to take blood, urine, vitreous humour, perhaps liver and stomach contents."[cd]

Mansfield: "Anything else in the 'normal' ... road traffic passenger case?"

Chapman: "I cannot think of anything else."

Absolutely no mention from Chapman of taking the organ samples he claimed in his statements that he took – even though Mansfield gave

---

[a] There was a reference to the taking of "small samples of the major organs" in the case of Dodi Fayed, but not Princess Diana: 26 Nov 07: 10.14. This was also included in Chapman's 5 September 1997 statement regarding the post-mortem of Dodi Fayed.: Robert Chapman, Witness Statement, 5 September 1997, p12

[b] The heading of the Post-Mortem Exhibits form states that it is the "Pathologists [sic] Copy". If this is Chapman's copy, how is it that he has taken additional organ samples and not listed them at the end of the document?

[c] This is in conflict with Rees who stated: "I discussed the situation with Dr Chapman and what I said was,'Obviously all the samples that would normally be taken in a road traffic accident should be taken, but, in addition, we should take anything else which might just become relevant'. I was thinking in particular of head hair, stomach contents and anything like that." Chapman has included "stomach contents" as a road traffic sample, whereas Rees has indicated it was taken as an extra sample.

[d] Chapman has included vitreous humour in this list but he said in his 2005 statement: "Vitreous fluid would probably not have been taken in 1997 had an uncontaminated sample of urine been available". This conflict is addressed later.

him the extra opportunity to say so: "Anything else in the 'normal' ... road traffic passenger case?"

In the light of Chapman's above account that "we decided those [normal samples taken in a road traffic case] would be the samples to take", this appears to be a major oversight.

Michael Burgess, recounting a meeting in June 1998 with Dominique Lecomte, stated: "I believe that Dr Chapman offered to show [Lecomte] histology slides that he kept at his office but did not know how this was going to happen or if this offer was followed up".[394]

When taken with the Histology form – reproduced above – this is other evidence that these histology slides did exist.[a]

Chapman also said in his 5 September 1997 statement regarding Dodi Fayed's post-mortem: "Small samples of the major organs were retained for later histological study."[b]

In addition, there is a mention of the existence of histology samples from Princess Diana in an Operation Paget document entitled "Biological Samples", which is reproduced later in this chapter.[c]

The undated[d] document states that "these samples are retained by the Forensic Pathology Alliance".[e] It also states: "A note in respect of [these histology samples] is ... contained within [Chapman's] file (Sensitive document 6). Slides were made up at the time but these have not been located and it is thought likely they have been destroyed. There are 12 wax blocks and a single fragment of wet tissue preserved in formalin."

The mention of "12 wax blocks" appears to fit with the "12" in the "Total No. of Blocks" box on the earlier Histology form. The Paget document however says there is "no reference" number, whereas the Histology form had three reference numbers – see earlier.

If these samples are being kept by the Forensic Pathology Alliance – a division of LGC Forensics – then that could explain Chapman's earlier

---

[a] Page 1 of the Histology document reads "Slides please" in handwriting in the bottom left hand corner.

[b] At the inquest Chapman confirmed that he took "small samples of the major organs" from Dodi's body: 26 Nov 07: 10.14. As stated earlier there was no mention of this at the inquest with regard to Diana's post-mortem.

[c] The form also lists a similar batch of samples being held from Dodi Fayed.

[d] Other evidence discussed later in the chapter indicates that the document could not have been created before December 2006.

[e] The Forensic Pathology Alliance was set up by LGC Forensics in late 2006 and was announced to the public on 11 December 2006 – three days before the publishing of the Paget Report. Source: Two Firsts for LGC Forensics, 11 December 2006, www.lgc.co.uk/news

reticence to name the "hospital" involved. LGC carried out extensive work relating to this case, on behalf of Operation Paget. This would fit with later evidence which will show an attempt – particularly at the inquest – to suppress public knowledge that samples from Diana and Dodi had been passed on to the British police.

Did these samples originate from Princess Diana's body?

There would appear to be just two possibilities:

1) Chapman has secretly taken 7 or 8[a] extra samples from Princess Diana's major organs, without providing any proper recording of what he did, and also no reporting on the testing conducted on these samples

2) Chapman didn't take these extra samples from Princess Diana's body, but instead has used samples from another body for histology testing and has pretended the samples were from Diana's body – again, without providing proper recording or reporting.

Whichever is the case, Robert Chapman, the forensic pathologist who conducted the post-mortems, does not come up smelling of roses.

Robert Thompson, Fulham Mortuary Manager: 9 Nov 04 Statement: **Jury Didn't Hear**:

"My next job is to open the skull so that the pathologist can remove the brain for examination.... I think it was at this stage that it really hit home to me that the Princess of Wales was dead. It must have shown on my face because I remember Dr Chapman asking if I was alright. I pulled myself together and said I was fine. All I wanted to do was to carry out my role professionally and properly. At the end of the post mortem, it is my responsibility to return the organs to the body, sew the body up, wash it down again and dry it in order to ensure that the body leaves the mortuary in as good a condition as possible."[395]

Robert Thompson: 9 Nov 04 Statement: **Jury Didn't Hear**:

"Whilst Dr Chapman was examining the organs on the dissecting bench I would have been carrying out my own work away from him so if he had said anything then I would not necessarily have heard him[b].... I just remember Dr Chapman taking the bowl of organs to the dissecting table for examination and then returning to the body to remove the uterus, which he then took over to the dissecting table. I don't know whether the uterus was returned to the body or retained for further examination."[396]

David Green, Embalmer, UK: 13 Jul 04 Statement: **Jury Didn't Hear**:

"The major organs (viscera) including the uterus and brain, which would normally be removed and replaced into the chest and abdominal cavity, were

---

[a] 7 histology samples and one heart sample of the injured area – see earlier.

[b] Thompson is referring here to a comment Chapman made about pregnancy – that issue is covered in Part 5.

present in a bag. I removed the bag and placed it into another bag and cavity fluid was poured over the viscera to preserve it."[397]

Comment: There appears to be a conflict between Thompson and Green.

Thompson states: "It is my responsibility to return the organs to the body [and] sew the body up".

Green states: "The major organs ... were present in a bag."

Most of Thompson's testimony was written down in chronological order. His reference to Chapman removing "the brain for examination" is near the start of his description of the post-mortem. This fits with the Exhibits document where it shows the weighing of the brain – "brain 1690 grams" – as one of the initial actions by Chapman.

The second quote (above) from Thompson – "Dr Chapman was examining the organs on the dissecting bench" – comes much later in his statement.[a]

Thompson's reference to the "return [of] the organs to the body ... at the end of the post mortem" is well out of chronological order. There is a possibility that Thompson is referring here to his general job responsibility – and not necessarily describing what specifically took place in the Diana post-mortem.[b]

There is however another possibility.

If Green's recall is correct – and I suggest there is no reason to doubt what Green says – then Thompson does not appear to have fulfilled his "responsibility to return the organs to the body".

Green stated: "The major organs ... would normally be removed and replaced into the chest and abdominal cavity". Instead Green found them "in a bag". Green is clearly indicating that normal practice – replacing the organs into the body – was not followed in the case of Princess Diana.

This raises the possibility that Thompson has indicated that the organs were returned to the body, when in actual fact he may recall that he failed to do that. In other words, an important part of Thompson's job was to "return the organs to the body" and he may not want to admit that it wasn't carried out at the conclusion of this important post-mortem.

Why would Thompson fail to "return the organs to [Diana's] body"?

Earlier evidence has shown that Thompson was not calling the shots – the people making the decisions here were Burton, Chapman or Rees.

---

[a] Thompson describes "Dr Chapman taking the bowl of organs to the dissecting table for examination". This appears to fit with the latter part of the Exhibits document, where Wall has described or recorded weights for the lungs, liver, kidneys and pancreas, all in fairly close succession.
[b] Thompson states later: "I don't know whether the uterus was returned to the body", but doesn't comment on any other specific organs.

This evidence raises the possibility that while Thompson was fulfilling his function to "sew the body up, wash it down again and dry it" – after the 11.20 p.m. post-mortem conclusion – Chapman could have been busily taking his 8 unrecorded samples from the major organs of Princess Diana. By the time Chapman has completed this, the organs can no longer be returned to Diana's body, so they are put "in a bag".[ab]

The evidence relating to these 8 unrecorded samples should be viewed in the context of evidence – yet to be dealt with – showing what occurred with the 4 recorded samples showing on the Exhibits document.

Did the 8 unrecorded samples belong to Princess Diana?

In summary, there is clear evidence that 8 unrecorded samples exist.

There were two possibilities mentioned above – the samples are Diana's or they aren't Diana's.

There is evidence – shown earlier – that suggests the Histology form may not relate to Princess Diana's samples: different names and reference numbers; the "day cut" date; no sample numbers.

There are three significant points though that do indicate the 8 unrecorded samples could belong to Diana:

1) The circumstantial evidence shown above reveals that Chapman did appear to have opportunity to take these samples after the conclusion of the post-mortem

2) It seems unlikely that Chapman – or anyone else – would have a motive to pretend that these 8 samples belong to Diana, when they actually didn't.

3) The listing of histology samples from Princess Diana in the Operation Paget "Biological Samples" document – reproduced later.

Sample Movements

The earlier evidence shows that there were only four samples – RC/1 to RC/4 – taken from Princess Diana's body throughout the post-mortem.

---

[a] Another factor in this would have been the time pressure being exerted by the royals. Mather was hovering outside the post-mortem room and was waiting to have Diana's body rushed to St James' Palace – royal territory – where a subsequent embalming was to take place. See Royal Control chapter.

[b] Thompson said in his statement: "It is usual to obtain internal samples as soon as possible after opening the body in order to avoid other fluids escaping which would contaminate the sample you are trying to obtain." This evidence indicates that if Chapman left the taking of these organ samples to after the conclusion of the post-mortem, then there may have been a risk of contamination. This raises the possibility that at the time Chapman was particularly intent on taking these samples secretly. This is supported by Chapman's failure to make any mention of them in the 31 August 1997 Exhibits report. Source: Robert Thompson, Witness Statement, 9 November 2004, p5.

There is conflicting witness evidence over what then happened to those samples:[a]

- Chapman: "[the samples] would stay within the mortuary complex, within a fridge, prior to them being transported ... up to a laboratory used by the coroner for analysis" – at inquest
- Chapman: "Exhibit RC/1 was handed to Detective Sergeant Wall. Exhibits RC/2 to RC/5 were handed to Robert Thompson for storage. I understand these were subsequently analysed by the Forensic Toxicology Unit of the Imperial College" – 10 Sep 97 statement
- Chapman: "D.S. Wall was responsible for receiving and documenting the various exhibits taken during the examination as well as the packaging" – 24 Feb 05 statement
- Chapman: "It was decided that the samples intended for toxicology analysis were to be sent to the Toxicology Unit at Charing Cross Hospital and this may be the reason that D.S. Wall did not formally receive them[bc].... The samples were then passed to Robert Thompson for retention prior to transportation to the laboratory" – 24 Feb 05 statement
- Wall: "I don't recall taking any of the physical exhibits from either post mortem away from Fulham mortuary, and had no dealings with them" – 29 Jun 04 statement[d]

---

[a] In general the witnesses refer to the movement of 5 samples – RC/1 to RC/5 – but there is no evidence in the Exhibits document of RC/5 – recorded in Chapman's 10 September 1997 statement – being taken.

[b] It will be shown that the samples tested for toxicology by the Imperial College did not belong to Princess Diana. There is a possibility that those samples do not have Wall's signature on them – Susan Paterson, the toxicologist, makes no comment about signatures in her description of the sample labels. Problems with the labelling are addressed later.

[c] There is an apparent conflict here. Earlier in the same statement – see above – Chapman said: "D.S. Wall was responsible for receiving". In further conflict, Thompson said: "Stoneham was present for the purpose of receiving". This could "fit" with Chapman's additional observation in the same statement (see earlier): "I would expect [Stoneham] to advise or guide the exhibits officer [Wall] in the correct packaging and labelling". And also this: "Stoneham was responsible for the supply of containers with appropriate preservatives". Stoneham said that he "witnessed DS Wall (exhibits officer) packaging and labelling exhibits that were handed to him". It seems possible that both Stoneham and Wall were involved with the samples, but it is Wall that wrote up the Exhibits document and the Property Register – reproduced later – showing a listing of the samples.

[d] This is from Wall's October 2004 statement, where he restated what he had said in the earlier June 2004 statement. I have never sighted Wall's June 2004 statement.

- Wall: "the following exhibits that I received from Dr Chapman ... Plucked head hair from a female seal number (A1484982) produced as Dr Chapman's exhibit RC/1.... The aforementioned exhibits were placed in a locked safe on the fifth floor at New Scotland Yard at 0030 hours [12.30 a.m.] on the 1st September 1997.... At 0950 hours [9.50 a.m.] ... I deposited these exhibits in a sealed bag number D4099479, in the Metropolitan Police OCG (Organised Crime Group) store, New Scotland Yard" – 19 Oct 04 statement
- Thompson: "Detective Sergeant Stoneham performed his customary role in that he received the specimens from the pathologist and labelled them. They were then refrigerated at the mortuary, but I cannot now recall who did this or on whose instructions" – 13 Jun 01 affidavit
- Thompson: "Although, as mentioned, Detective Sergeant Stoneham was present for the purpose of receiving and delivering samples to the Metropolitan Police Laboratory, which is the norm, Dr. Burton had made special arrangements to have the specimens taken from Princess Diana removed to Charing Cross Hospital and had also arranged for an entirely separate courier to come and collect those specimens on the following day. The specimens were stored in the mortuary refrigerator overnight.... When the courier arrived the following day all the specimens were eventually handed to him" – 13 Jun 01 affidavit
- Thompson: "I do remember having samples from Diana" – 9 Nov 04 statement
- Thompson: "I do not actually recall being handed the samples following the post mortems of Diana ... and Dodi ... but I'm sure they would have been given to me.... The day after the post mortems I dispatched the samples taken from the Princess to the lab at Charing Cross hospital" – 9 Nov 04 statement
- Thompson: "Charing Cross hospital ... sent someone ... to collect them..... I recall giving him the samples taken at the Princess's post mortem examination but I do not recall giving him any of the samples from Dodi Al Fayed. I may well have done but just cannot remember now" – 9 Nov 04 statement
- Stoneham: "He ... witnessed DS Wall (exhibits officer) packaging and labelling exhibits that were handed to him by ... Chapman" – statement
- Stoneham: "I have read my statements so I know there is reference to the samples ... went to Charing Cross Hospital" – at inquest
- Rees: "in a road traffic accident, samples would normally be examined at the pathologist's hospital.... We decided that the route of the samples should be the normal one in a road traffic accident" – at inquest
- Rees: "the Princess's head hair ... Dr Chapman assured me that the system would be tight.... Examinations would be carried out by scientists at [Chapman's] hospital" – confirmed to Hilliard at inquest

- Paterson: "On 1st September 1997 ... Neil McLachlan-Troup went to Fulham mortuary and was handed ... samples relating to a Female (Fulham 31897). He brought the samples directly to the Toxicology Unit where they were assigned the unique case number 676/97.... The samples included ... Exhibit RC/2 ... RC/3 ... RC/4 ... RC/5" – 28 Sep 04 statement

According to the Exhibits document, the samples taken were:

RC/1 – Plucked head hair

RC/2 – Stomach Contents

RC/3 – Preserved Blood

RC/4 – Section of Liver

According to Susan Paterson, the samples received at Charing Cross Hospital were:

RC/2 – Stomach contents

RC/3 – Blood preserved

RC/4 – Liver section

RC/5 - Vitreous humor

There are three key differences between the samples taken from Diana's body – according to Wall – and the samples received – according to Paterson.

1) RC/1 was taken but not received at the Imperial College

2) RC/5 was not taken, but was received

3) the wording is different: RC/3 – "Preserved Blood" was taken, but "Blood preserved" was received; RC/4 – "Section of Liver" was taken, but "Liver section" was received.

POST MORTEM EXHIBITS
(PATHOLOGISTS COPY)

Name of Victim: MR EMAD EL-DIN MOHAMED   Pathologist: Dr ROBERT CHAPTAN
ABDEL MONEIM AL FAYED

P.M. at (Venue): FULHAM. DOB 17-4-55 GMPT   Photographer: MR ANDREW SCEUS

S.I.O. Der SUPT G REES.

On Date / Time 31-8-97 1800

Scene Co-ordinator:-
Lab Sergeant D/S P. STONEHAM.

Exhibits Officer D/S WALL

CROWN CORONER DR BURTON   SURREY CORONER DR BURGESS.

Exhibit No.	Exhibit
	ALSO ATTENDING:-
	1) MR KEITH BROWN - SURREY CORONERS OFFICER
	2) MR ROBERT THOMPSON - LAB/ASSISTANT
	3) MR MARK TAYLOR - ASST/PHOTOGRAPHER
	4) MR NIGEL MUNNS - PRINCIPLE SERVICES MANAGER.
RC/1	PLUCKED HEAD HAIR.
RC/2	Brown material from mouth
RC/3	"Blood" preserved
RC/4	Mater one. liver sample. Both kidneys are 200 GRM.
RC/5	Po Deep bruising around left kidney. Viterus Humour
	1930 Hours complete

Figure 25

Excerpts showing the samples taken on the original Exhibits
form for Dodi Fayed's post-mortem, written up at the time
by Richard Wall. The handwriting is the same as appears on
Diana's post-mortem Exhibits form – see earlier.

Post-Mortem Sample Descriptions on Key Documents			
Sample No	Exhibits Form	Post-Mortem Report	Toxicology Statement[a]
Princess Diana			
RC/1	Plucked Head Hair	Plucked head hair	NA
RC/2	Stomach Contents	Stomach contents	Stomach contents
RC/3	Preserved Blood	Preserved blood	Blood preserved
RC/4	Section of Liver	Section of liver	Liver section
RC/5	NA[b]	Vitreous humour	Vitreous humour
Dodi Fayed			
RC/1	Plucked Head Hair	Plucked head hair	NA
RC/2	Brown material from mouth	Brown material from mouth	NA
RC/3	Blood preserved	Blood preserved	Blood preserved
RC/4	Liver sample	Liver sample	Liver sample
RC/5	Vitreous Humour	Vitreous humour	Vitreous humour

The above table compares the sample descriptions.

The first two columns – the Exhibits form and the Post-Mortem report – show the descriptions written for the samples while they were still at Fulham Mortuary.

The Exhibits forms – dictated by Chapman to Wall – were handwritten close to the same time as the labels have been affixed to the sample containers.

The Post-Mortem reports – compiled by Chapman in early September[a] – officially list the sample descriptions.

---

[a] "NA" in this column means the sample was not sent to the Imperial College for toxicology testing.
[b] According to the original Exhibits form Vitreous Humour was not taken from Princess Diana – see earlier.

The Toxicology statements – compiled for the police by Paterson in 2004 – show the official record of the sample descriptions at the time they were received by the Toxicology Unit of the Imperial College on 1 September 1997.

The table shows that in every case but one – Diana's RC/5 sample[b] – the sample descriptions between the Exhibits form and the Post-Mortem report are identical, both for Diana and Dodi.

The key revelation from the table comes when the sample descriptions from the mortuary are directly compared to the descriptions of what the sample labels read as they were received by the Toxicology Unit the following day.

The samples from Dodi Fayed that were received by the Toxicology Unit – RC/3, RC/4, RC/5 – have descriptions which are identical to those placed on the samples in the Fulham Mortuary.

This is not the case with two of the sample label descriptions relating to Princess Diana: RC/3 and RC/4.

The evidence indicates that when RC/3 was taken from Diana's body, it was labelled "Preserved Blood", but the sample that arrived at the Toxicology Unit of the Imperial College the following day[c] was labelled "Blood preserved". Likewise, RC/4 was labelled "Section of Liver" but the sample label that arrived at the Toxicology Unit was labelled "Liver section".

As was pointed out at length by the experts, recorded in Part 3, the entire pathology-toxicology process has to be extremely precise, so that the results can be relied on. Absolute accuracy is required in order to maintain confidence in the chain of custody of the samples.

The fact that the sample labels on these two samples were different on their arrival at the Imperial College is further evidence indicating that the samples that were picked up by Neil McLachlan-Troup, an Imperial College toxicologist[d], did not belong to Princess Diana.

Richard Wall, DS, MPS Organised Crime Group: 19 Oct 04 Statement: **Jury Didn't Hear**:

"Further to my statement provided to Operation Paget on the 29th June 2004[e] I have been asked to comment further on the evening of Sunday 31st August 1997....

---

[a] Dodi's was presented to police in a statement on September 5 and Diana's on September 10.

[b] It has been shown earlier that there was no record of a vitreous humour sample (RC/5) being taken from Princess Diana's body prior to the completion of the post-mortem at 11.20 p.m.

[c] 1 September 1997.

[d] As stated by Susan Paterson – see earlier.

[e] I have not been provided with a copy of this earlier statement – it has been quoted from earlier in this book by using third person excerpts from the Paget Report.

"I have been informed by DC Emeny that the post mortem exhibits for both the deceased, bear my signature on the exhibit bag labels. These exhibits (Male) exhibit RC/3 labelled: Blood preserved, RC/4 labelled: Liver sample, RC/5 labelled: Vitreous humor, and (Female) exhibit RC/2 labelled: Stomach contents, RC/3 labelled: Blood preserved, RC/4 labelled: Liver section, and RC/5 labelled: Vitreous humor, were obtained by Dr Chapman in my presence, I signed the labels and entered the details in the exhibit books. I am informed by DC Emeny that Dr Chapman has stated they were stored by Robert Thompson the Mortuary Assistant at Fulham Mortuary. I agree that this would be correct.

"I have also been shown by DC Emeny two copies of the Post Mortems exhibits (Pathologists copy) reference OD 19, concerning each of the deceased. Dr Chapman dictated the details to me after each of the examinations and I recorded them on these documents."[398]

Comment: The above statement was given by Richard Wall on 19 October 2004, four months after his original statement, which has never been made available.

A closer read reveals that the first and third paragraphs reflect the evidence of Richard Wall. The second paragraph appears to be Richard Wall restating what he has been told to say: "I have been informed by DC Emeny"; "I am informed by DC Emeny".

This 2004 account contradicts the Diana post-mortem labelling information that was stated in the 31 August 1997 Exhibits report (Wall) and the early September 1997 Post-Mortem report (Chapman) – "RC/3 labelled: Blood preserved, RC/4 labelled: Liver section" instead of RC/3 Preserved blood and RC/4 Section of liver. This new account matches the label descriptions given by Paterson on 28 September 2004.

The timing seems to be very significant. On 28 September 2004 Susan Paterson produced a statement that revealed the labels on two samples, blood and liver, read differently to the sample labels disclosed in the evidence from 1997 – the Exhibits document and the Post-Mortem report.

Just 21 days following Paterson's statement to Paget, Wall is then reinterviewed by Paget and told to make a statement detailing the labelling of the samples. But instead of Wall being allowed to actually see the sample labels before making this statement, he instead appears to have been told what the sample labels say, by his interviewer, DC Emeny – "I have been informed by DC Emeny".

This evidence indicates that the emergence of the 28 September 2004 Paterson statement created a problem for the police – the labels on the toxicology samples read differently to those put on the samples taken from Princess Diana on the night following the crash.

The police were faced with either changing the Paterson account or the Wall-Chapman account in order to get a "match". It seems that they were able to get a new statement out of Wall that was qualified with the words, "I have been informed by DC Emeny".

Other than the above Wall statement, the only witnesses who have specifically given evidence on what occurred with the samples at the mortuary are pathologist, Robert Chapman, and mortuary manager, Robert Thompson.

Chapman has stated in 1997: "Exhibits RC/2 to RC/5[a] were handed to Robert Thompson for storage", and in 2005: "The samples were then passed to Robert Thompson for retention".

Thompson appears to have difficulty with his recall – "I do remember having samples from Diana"; "I do not actually recall being handed the samples".

The only thing Thompson can definitely recall is his next day handover of Diana's samples: "I recall giving [the man from Charing Cross Hospital] the samples taken at the Princess's post mortem examination".

Thompson has no recall of receiving the samples for Diana or Dodi and also has no recall of handing over Dodi's samples to the Charing Cross man: "I do not recall giving him any of the samples from Dodi Al Fayed".

By the end of this chapter the evidence will be conclusive that the samples tested at the Imperial College did not come from the body of Princess Diana.

Given that, how then did this come about? How did the Imperial College receive samples belonging to someone other than Princess Diana – even when Robert Thompson thought that he was handing over the correct samples?

The general evidence – particularly Paterson's phone call to the Royal London Hospital (see earlier) – indicates that toxicologist, Susan Paterson, also sincerely believed at the time that the samples being tested belonged to Princess Diana.

There would appear to be two main possibilities:

1) at the post-mortem Diana's samples were handed to Robert Thompson who put them in the mortuary fridge

2) at the post-mortem Diana's samples were not handed to Robert Thompson.

In his affidavit Thompson stated that "Stoneham was present for the purpose of receiving and delivering samples to the Metropolitan Police Laboratory, which is the norm".

Stoneham has said that he "witnessed DS Wall (exhibits officer) packaging and labelling exhibits that were handed to him by ... Chapman".

---

[a] The evidence regarding what happened with RC/1 will be addressed later.

Chapman said in his 1997 post-mortem report that "exhibit RC/1 was handed to Detective Sergeant Wall".[a]

Wall has provided two opposing accounts – in June 2004 he stated: "I don't recall taking any of the physical exhibits ... away from Fulham mortuary, and had no dealings with them"; in October 2004 Wall was shown "crime record, reference 402, bearing my name and signatures" which referred to "Plucked head hair from a female seal number (A1484982) ... Dr Chapman's exhibit RC/1".

Other witness accounts appear to conflict with Chapman's post-mortem report account – Thompson, Rees and Stoneham do not differentiate between sample numbers:

- Thompson: "all the specimens were eventually handed to [the courier]"
- Stoneham: "the samples ... went to Charing Cross Hospital"
- Rees: "the route of the samples should be the normal one in a road traffic accident".[b]

Chapman himself also provided conflicting evidence in 2005: "It was decided that the samples intended for toxicology analysis were to be sent to ... Charing Cross Hospital and this may be the reason that D.S. Wall did not formally receive [the samples].... The samples were then passed to Robert Thompson...."

In support of Chapman's post-mortem report, Susan Paterson has never recorded the receipt of RC/1. It will be shown that Paterson never received any of Princess Diana's samples – instead there has been a major cover-up to make it look as though the samples Paterson tested belonged to Diana. The evidence will show that Paterson received the samples from another body – RC/2 to RC/5 – that fitted with the samples shown on Chapman's post-mortem report.[c]

Paget officer, Toby Smith, stated that in March 2004 he sighted a sample he described as: "Plucked head hair (Diana, Princess of Wales) sealed in Police Evidence Bag A1484982 Exhibit RC/1." The reference number, A1484982, matched Wall's account. Smith said that at that stage the sample number was altered to "RC/1a".

In 2006 forensic biologist, Roy Green, was employed by Operation Paget to carry out testing on blood found in the carpet on the back floor of the Mercedes S280.[d] Green wrote in a subsequent police statement: "On 30

---

[a] That was confirmed by Chapman at the inquest: 26 Nov 07: 22.17.

[b] Rees went a step further regarding RC/1 at the inquest – this is addressed below.

[c] The report read: "Exhibits RC/2 to RC/5 ... were subsequently analysed by the Forensic Toxicology Unit of the Imperial College".

[d] This issue is addressed in the Pregnancy chapter in Part 5.

March 2006 the following item was received at the LGC Forensics laboratory, Culham from DS Gary Head of the Metropolitan Police Service in connection with this case: RC.1a Plucked Head Hair from Princess Diana."[399] Green went on to explain that the hair was used for a control DNA test against the blood found in the Mercedes – there was a match.[a]

This evidence, in support of Smith's account, indicates that the police had control of or access to sample RC/1 and had delivered that sample to Roy Green, under the new name "RC.1a".

Jeffrey Rees stated at the inquest: "I might say I was also concerned about security [at the hospital] because – for example, the Princess's head hair, I was very concerned that anything like that could fall into the wrong hands and Dr Chapman assured me that the system would be tight."[b]

In saying this, Rees has specifically said that the very sample – RC/1, the head hair – which other evidence (Chapman, Wall[c], Green, Paterson[d], the "Property Concerned in Crime" document[e]) indicates was taken by the police, was instead sent to the hospital.[f]

Stoneham's evidence – "the samples ... went to Charing Cross Hospital" – supported Rees, and it may be that the police did not want it known that they had a sample of Diana's hair. It sounds much more palatable for the jury – and the public – that all samples went to the Charing Cross Hospital – and that is what they heard from the police witnesses.

---

[a] Green wrote: "A full STR (DNA) profile was obtained from the largest bloodstain. The STR profile obtained matched that obtained from the sample of head hairs (RC.la) from Princess Diana so the blood tested from the carpet could have come from her. If the blood was not from her then it must have come from another person, who by chance has the same STR profile as Princess Diana.": Roy Green, Witness Statement, 23 November 2006, page 3.

[b] Chapman indicated, in his 2005 statement, that he had no responsibility for the samples after the post-mortem was complete: "The continuity of the samples is the responsibility of the police once they are received from the body. If the samples are to be left for local analysis the responsibility for them passes to the mortuary staff prior to collection and transportation". The fact that Rees and Chapman have addressed these issues in their evidence raises the possibility that they are aware that there was tampering with the samples after Diana's post-mortem.

[c] Wall's second account based on documents presented to him.

[d] Paterson never actually tested Diana's samples, but her evidence indirectly shows that RC/1 wasn't stored at the mortuary overnight – thus, by implication, it could have been taken by the police.

[e] Reproduced earlier.

[f] The cross-examination dialogue immediately following this confirms that Rees is talking about security at the hospital: Hilliard: "So the upshot was that examinations would be carried out by scientists at his hospital?" Rees: "Yes." Hilliard: "You had raised those particular concerns and you had been given assurances about them?" Rees: "Correct."

The jury heard conflicting evidence from Chapman:
- "RC1, the plucked head hair ... was given to Detective Sergeant Wall" – confirmed to Hilliard
- "[the samples] would stay within the mortuary complex, within a fridge, prior to them being transported ... up to a laboratory used by the coroner for analysis".

Regarding RC/1, this conflicted directly with his official post-mortem report – "Exhibit RC/1 was handed to Detective Sergeant Wall" – which the jury never saw. Chapman also contradicted his early evidence in his 2005 statement, categorically stating: "D.S. Wall did not formally receive [the samples]".

The Rees-Stoneham account also finds support with Thompson. However, Thompson actually makes no specific reference to the Princess Diana hair sample in any of his evidence.[a] Earlier evidence revealed that Thompson had difficulty with his recall about the samples and there is a possibility that he simply overlooked hair or thought the hair went with "the courier". There does not appear to be any reason for Thompson to deliberately lie about this.

In summary, the evidence from the "Property Concerned in Crime" document; Chapman – in his post-mortem report written up within days of the post-mortem; Wall; Smith; Green; and indirectly, Paterson, indicates that RC/1 was collected by the police and did not accompany the other samples into overnight storage at the Fulham Mortuary. There are other witnesses – Munns, Burton – who should have been asked about this, and certainly Wall and Thompson should have both been subjected to cross-examination at the inquest. None of this ever occurred.

The general evidence – Chapman, Thompson, Wall, Stoneham, Rees, Paterson[b] – is that the samples – RC/2 to RC/5 – did not go to the police, but went into overnight storage at the Fulham Mortuary .

There is however other documentary evidence, dealt with below, that appears to indicate that there were two sets of samples – RC/2 to RC/5 – one set received by the Imperial College, and a completely separate set that went elsewhere.

---

[a] Thompson makes only one general reference to "hair" in his statement: "Any external samples such as nails and hair are then taken before the body is washed down.": Robert Thompson, Witness Statement, 9 November 2004, reproduced in *The Documents* book, p604 (UK Edition).

[b] Again, Paterson's evidence is indirect – see earlier.

DIANA INQUEST: THE BRITISH COVER-UP

Your Reference: 676 & 677/97
Our Reference: OP Paget

Date: 16th August 2004

METROPOLITAN POLICE SERVICE

Dr Susan Paterson PhD
Imperial College of Science Technology and Medicine
St Dunstans Road
London
W6 8RP.

DC Jim Emeny
Room 589
Victoria Block
New Scotland Yard
Broadway,
SW1 H OBG

Dear Dr Paterson,

With reference to our telephone conversation on 10th August 2004 concerning samples in your possession I would be grateful if you could undertake to sign this document in the interests of retaining and preserving evidence.

These samples concern the Coroners inquest into the deaths of :-

Diana Princess of Wales   Female (Fulham 31897)
                                   Lab No. 676/97 Report
                                   date 4.09.97

3odi AL FAYED   Male (Fulham 31897)
                                   Lab No. 677/97 Report
                                   date 4.09.97

The aforementioned samples submitted from these cases are in my possession and will not be destroyed unless notification is received in writing from one of the following persons:

Michael Burgess Coroner of the Queen's Household-&- H.M. Coroner for Surrey.

The head of the enquiry:
Sir John Stevens, Commissioner of the Metropolis, or
an officer acting on his behalf.

Signed ....   - - - - - - - - - Dr Paterson Phd

Witness .... DC Emeny, Operation Paget

Figure 26

An August 2004 letter from Operation Paget to toxicologist, Susan Paterson, reveals that 7 years after the crash the samples belonging to Princess Diana and Dodi Fayed were being held at the Imperial College – not Scotland Yard. There has never been any evidence to indicate that the samples delivered to the Imperial College on 1 September 1997 have ever been moved from there. This letter was not shown to the Baker inquest jury.

Biological Samples

Document / Exhibit number	Description	Comments
RC/1 (now RC/1A)	Plucked head hair of Diana, Princess of Wales	Originally there were approximately 80 hairs of which 20 with roots were selected for DNA profiling,, the root end 1.5cm were cut from these and submitted for profiling. These will have been used in analysis although it is likely that the extract may still remain. The rest of these 20 hairs still remain as do the 60 not selected for profiling some of which would still be suitable for further testing. The hair is retained by LGC Forensics.
RC/2	Stomach contents of Diana, Princess of Wales	The stomach contents originally consisted of 429 grms of material of which 15 grams was divided into aliquots and used by Dr Cowan in his tests. There still remains 419 grms of the main sample which has been retained by LGC Forensics. Note It is unknown at this time what Dr Cowan has remaining of the aliquot samples he used in his tests. (Enquiries are in hand)
RC/3	Preserved blood of Diana, Princess of Wales	This is retained by Operation Paget
RC/4	Section of liver of Diana, Princess of Wales	This is retained by Operation Paget
RC/5	Vitreous Humour of Diana, Princess of Wales	Nothing left of this sample. The empty container retained by Operation Paget
GRH/181	Section of carpet marked 'ARD' from Mercedes 688 LTV 75	The carpet is still largely intact, a portion of the non-blood stained area was cut away and used for control purposes most of these pieces still exist. There are still dried bloodstains on the carpet available for testing if required. The main stain that featured in the tests carried out by LGC Forensics has some parts cut out (these still exist) but there are also parts of the main stain that were not cut out and are therefore available for testing. The carpets and parts of the carpet are still Retained by LGC Forensics Note It is unknown what remains of the samples

		that were generated from the work on the carpet that were passed to Dr Cowan and used in his tests. Enquiries are in hand to establish this. LGC Forensic also retain the Vergote samples (19 year old blood stains from a pregnant woman that were obtained from Ghent University Belgium). It is unknown what Dr Cowan has remaining of the samples he was passed that came from these Vergote samples. Enquiries are in hand.
No reference	Histology Diana, Princess of Wales	The histology samples taken are detailed in Dr Robert Chapman' statement Operation Paget reference S13B . A note in respect of this is also contained within his file (Sensitive document 6) Slides were made up at the time but these have not been located and it is thought likely they have been destroyed. There are 12 wax blocks and a single fragment of wet tissue preserved in formalin. These samples are retained by the Forensic Pathology Alliance. It is likely that the wax blocks and the wet tissue sample represent tall histology taken at the time (aside from the slides that are no longer available). This cannot be confirmed without making up new slides. No request has been made by Operation Paget for this be done.
DGT/1 (Originally part of DD/09032005/1 until split see below)	Blood sample of Henri PAUL taken by Dr CAMPANA on 04/09/1997	There was estimated to be 3-4 ml in this sample of blood. Two sub samples of 10ul were taken from the main sample meaning that there still remains 3-4 mls. This is retained by Forensic Alliance.
DD/09032005/1	This a sample of spinal cord from Henri PAUL by Professor Lecomte on 9th September 1997 (Note : Exhibit originally also included blood sample Henri Paul until	This sample is retained by David Tadd Forensic Directorate, MPS.

	split. See entry above)	
RC/1	Plucked head hair from Emad El-Din Mohamed Abdul Monein Al Fayed	Held by Operation Paget
RC/2	Brown material from the mouth of Emad El-Din Mohamed Abdul Monein Al Fayed	Held by Operation Paget
RC/3	Blood preserved, Emad El-Din Mohamed Abdul Monein Al Fayed	Held by Operation Paget
RC/4	Liver sample from Emad El-Din Mohamed Abdul Monein Al Fayed	Held by Operation Paget
RC/5	Vitreous Humour from Emad El-Din Mohamed Abdul Monein Al Fayed	Held by Operation Paget
No Reference	Histology of Emad El-Din Mohamed Abdul Monein Al Fayed	The histology samples taken are detailed in Dr Robert Chapman' statement Operation Paget reference S13B . A note in respect of this is also contained within his file (Sensitive document 7)

Slides were made up at the time but these have not been located and it is thought likely they have been destroyed.

There are 11 wax blocks. These samples are retained by the Forensic Pathology Alliance.

It is likely that the wax blocks and the wet tissue sample represent tall histology taken at the time (aside from the slides that are no longer available). This cannot be confirmed without making up new slides. No request has been made by Operation Paget for this be done. |

Figure 27

607

The preceding undated three page table from within Operation Paget's files, lists "Biological Samples" held by Paget. This form is documentary evidence of separate samples for both Princess Diana and Dodi Fayed held under the control of the British police. Significant points related to this table are discussed below. Although this document is undated, it does make mention of the "Forensic Pathology Alliance" (FPA). The FPA was set up in December 2006 and a press statement announcing its formation was made on 11 December 2006, just 3 days before the publication of the Paget Report. This would appear to place the timing of this document at some point after 11 December 2006. This listing of samples was not shown to the jury at the inquest and there was no inquest evidence indicating that any samples – other than RC/1 – from Princess Diana were ever held by the British police. The histology samples have been dealt with earlier in this chapter. The blood sample belonging to Henri Paul has already been addressed in Part 3 and the evidence regarding the Mercedes S280 carpet is covered in Part 5. The DNA profiling on the Diana hair sample is connected with the analysis of the blood on the Mercedes' carpet.

Dr Alexander Allan, Forensic Scientist, LGC Forensics: 12 Dec 06 Statement: **Jury Didn't Hear**:
"On the 13th July 2006, 1 received the following item at the laboratory from the Metropolitan Police Service, SCDI (2), Jubilee House, Putney:
*RC/2 (bag No. D4204860) Stomach Contents
*Also described as RCS/2 on Submission Form
"I have been asked to provide aliquots (samples) of stomach contents for Professor David Cowan of the Drug Control Centre, King's College, London....
"The item was labelled, 'A Female, Fulham Mortuary, 31 8 97, Stomach Contents, Dr R Chapman'.
"The stomach contents were received frozen and defrosted overnight on the 13th/14th July 2006. They consisted of 429 grams of food and a clear/colourless liquid with the appearance of water. Two aliquots each of 2 millilitres of the supernatant liquid were removed and stored frozen. The stomach contents were refrozen. On the 2nd August 2006 the stomach contents were defrosted again and a further two aliquots of the resulting slurry were taken on the 3rd August 2006, this time of approximately 5 millilitres each.
"I transferred all four aliquots to the police on the 9th August for transmission to Professor Cowan's laboratory."[400]
Dr Susan Paterson, Toxicologist, UK: 28 Sep 04 Statement: **Jury Didn't Hear**:
"Re: Female (Fulham 31897) (deceased) Lab No. 676/97....

"The approximate quantities of each sample remaining from this case are:-

Exhibit RC/2, Stomach contents, approximately 200 mL

Exhibit RC/3, Blood preserved, approximately 1-2 mL

Exhibit RC/4, Liver section, the complete sample of 15-20 g

Exhibit RC/5, Vitreous humor, no sample remains."[401]

Comment: The main issue with the Biological Samples document – reproduced above – is: Does it list samples from Princess Diana that are completely different to the samples that were subjected to toxicology testing by Susan Paterson on 1 September 1997?

There are several relevant points:

1) The 16 August 2004 letter from Jim Emeny to Susan Paterson – reproduced above – refers to the samples listed for "Lab No 676/97 Report dated 4.09.97". This appears to be a reference to Paterson's Toxicology Report dated 04.09.97[a], which records tests on samples of stomach contents, vitreous humour and blood.[b]

Emeny's letter indicates that the samples were "in [Paterson's] possession" in August 2004 – 7 years after the post-mortems. There has never been any evidence to indicate any movement of the samples – both from Diana and Dodi – away from the Imperial College Toxicology Unit.

In contrast, the Biological Samples document states that RC/2 "has been retained by LGC Forensics" and RC/3, RC/4 and RC/5 are "retained by Operation Paget".[cd]

2) The sample descriptions for RC/3 – "Preserved blood" – and RC/4[e] – "Section of liver" – match the descriptions on the 31 August 1997 Exhibits

---

[a] Reproduced in *The Documents* book, p613 (UK edition).

[b] The liver sample is not included, but this seems to be because Paterson didn't conduct any tests on it: See Paterson's 28 September 2004 statement, reproduced in *The Documents* book, pp614-6 (UK edition).

[c] This document also makes no attempt to distinguish between RC/1 – which earlier evidence shows was taken by the police on the night – and the other samples, RC/2 to RC/5, which earlier evidence revealed went into storage at Fulham Mortuary on the night.

[d] There is no mention in the document of the samples having previously been anywhere else. When discussing the Stomach Contents quantity (addressed below) the word used is "originally" – as though the sample had always been within police control.

[e] RC/2 and RC/5 are not mentioned here because RC/5 is not included in the Exhibits document – see earlier – and there is no conflict in the description of RC/2, probably because there is only one normal way to describe "Stomach Contents". RC/1 is also not included because it was not received by the Imperial College.

document, but do not match the descriptions showing in Susan Paterson's Toxicology report.[a]

3)   The above statement from Alexander Allan reveals that he received RC/2 "from the Metropolitan Police Service" on 13 July 2006.

Allan appears to include a precise description of the sample label for "stomach contents", RC/2, as toxicologist, Susan Paterson, also did in her Toxicology report.

The two descriptions should be compared:

-   Allan: "The item was labelled, 'A Female, Fulham Mortuary, 31 8 97, Stomach Contents, Dr R Chapman'."

-   Paterson: "Exhibit RC/2 labelled: Stomach contents, A Female, Fulham Mortuary, 31/8/97, Dr R Chapman".

These two sample descriptions vary in two main respects:

a)   Allan's description places "Stomach Contents" fourth, whereas Paterson's shows "Stomach contents" as the first item on the label[b]

b)   Allan's date is written "31 8 97" – with spaces between the numbers – whereas Paterson's reads "31/8/97", with slashes between the numbers.

4)   There appears to be a conflict in the size of the stomach contents sample.

Paterson stated: "The approximate quantities ... are: Exhibit RC/2, Stomach contents, approximately 200 mL".

According to the Biological Samples report: "The stomach contents originally consisted of 429 grms of material of which 15 grams was divided into aliquots[c] and used by Dr Cowan in his tests. There still remains 419 grms of the main sample".

Dr Alexander Allan, who set up the aliquots for the Cowan analysis[d], confirmed that "the stomach contents ... consisted of 429 grams of food and a clear/colourless liquid". Allan describes taking "two aliquots each of 2 millilitres of the ... liquid". Later "a further two aliquots of the resulting slurry were taken ... of approximately 5 millilitres each."

This evidence reveals that the stomach contents consisted of two parts – food matter and liquid. The food matter was 429 grams to start with, Allan took two subsamples of 5 ml each – so 10 ml combined – and then after that, according to Paget, "there still remains 419 [grams] of the main sample".

---

[a] These were: RC/3 – "Blood preserved"; RC/4 – "Liver section" – see earlier Table.
[b] Allan also shows "Contents" with a Capital "C", whereas Paterson has it with a small "c".
[c] Samples or sub-samples.
[d] Cowan was looking for a substance relating to contraceptives. This is addressed in the Pregnancy chapter of Part 5.

This then indicates that 10 ml of the food matter is the equivalent of 10 grams of the same matter.[a]

More significantly, it also means that the original weight according to Paget – and confirmed by Allan – of 429 grams, is the equivalent of approximately 429 ml.

This evidence then shows that the 429 gram sample of stomach contents, now "retained by LGC Forensics", is over twice the size of the 200 ml sample tested by Susan Paterson at the Imperial College.

5) The sample of Vitreous Humour held by Operation Paget is an "empty container".

The Exhibits document revealed that no vitreous humour was taken from Princess Diana's body – see earlier.

There is a possibility that this container never contained any vitreous humour – it may have been created afterwards to match the later evidence in Chapman's post-mortem report – that vitreous humour was taken.

Paterson has stated that "no sample remains" from the vitreous humour she carried out tests on.

I suggest that it is a coincidence that there is nothing in both RC/5 sample containers – the one held by the Imperial College and the one "retained by Operation Paget".

The above five points all contribute to the accumulating evidence that on 1 September 1997 Susan Paterson was supplied with samples that did not belong to Princess Diana.

---

[a] This fits with information from internet cooking sites: On average "1 oz = 28.35 gms = 29.57 ml": Measurement Conversion Table, www.recipedelights.com. The heaviest common food ingredient is table salt which weighs 300g per cup – by comparison, a cup of chopped fruits and vegetables weighs just 150g. The same size cup measures to 240ml of the same ingredients.: The Metric Kitchen, www.jsward.com/cooking/conversion

Entry Number	Description of Property	Witness Ref. Number	Court Exhibit Number	Where Found	Found By	Time and Date Found
MW/1	FOUR PHOTOGRAPHS & ONE CHAIN.			ON PERSON OF THE PRINCESS OF WALES B21197504.	PC 1004R. WALTON	31-8-9 1955
RC/1	PLUCKED HEAD HAIR.			ON PERSON OF THE PRINCESS OF WALES A14849782.	DR CHAPMAN	31-8-9. 2137.
RC/2	STOMACH CONTENTS			ON PERSON THE PRINCESS WALES. D47204860	DR CHAPMAN	31-8-9. 2215.

MIR??

UK POST-MORTEMS

Deposited		Movement of Property			Referred to By:	Statement Number	Disposal of Property
Time, Date, Officer	Where Stored	Time/Date Out, Purpose Officer	Date Returned				
31-8-97 2.0000		31-8-97 2.005. RESTORATION.	31-8-97.				RESTORED TO PC WALKER. L. WALKER 80/F.
1-9-97. 0030.	LOCKED SAFE FIFTH FLOOR.	RETAINED BY DR CHAPMAN					

Entry Number	Description of Property	Witness Ref. Number	Court Exhibit Number	Where Found	Found By	Time and Date Found
RC/3	PRESERVED BLOOD			ON PERSON PRINCESS OF WALES B211 97748	DR CHAPMAN	31-8-97 2130
RC/4	LIVER SECTION			ON PERSON OF PRINCESS OF WALES B2119750	DR CHAPMAN	31-8-97 0522
RC/5	VITREOUS HUMOUR			ON PERSON OF PRINCESS OF WALES A177 6303	DR CHAPMA	31-8-9 2119

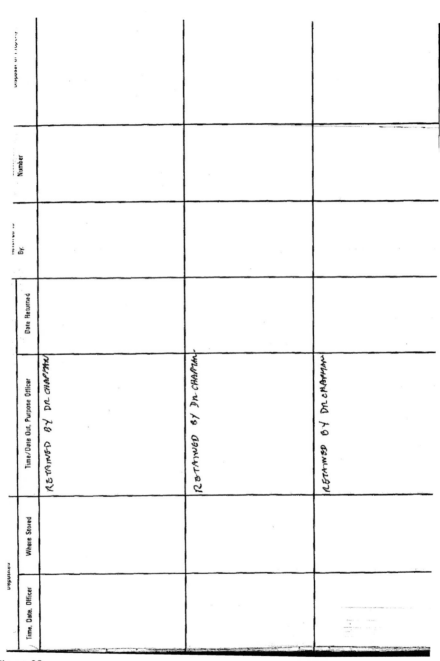

Figure 28

On the preceding four pages are the first two pages of the "Major Incident Property Register" for "Diana Princess of Wales (P.M. Exhibits & Clothing" as at 8 March 2004 – just a couple of months after Operation Paget was set up. Other pages of the register and a fuller explanation of it appear in Chapter 9 of *The Documents* book. Each entry in the register has 14 columns – 7 columns on the first page and 7 columns on the second page. The pages shown here cover 5 samples from Princess Diana's post-mortem – RC/1 to RC/5. Issues raised by these register entries are discussed below. Page 1 also shows an entry "MW/1" which is "Four photographs & one chain" found on the "person" of Diana by PC Walker at 7.55 p.m. – just 20 minutes before the commencement of the post-mortem. The register entry shows that this item was "restored to" and signed for by the same PC Walker ten minutes later, at 8.05 p.m. The question is: Why were these personal items handed over to PC Walker when Diana's two sisters – Jane and Sarah – were in the mortuary building prior to the commencement of the post-mortem (see earlier). Evidence from this same property register reveals that other personal items from Princess Diana have been stored at the MPS Lambeth FSS Lab, rather than being returned to her family – see *The Documents* book and Part 5. There is no mention in the post-mortem documents of the presence of a PC Walker, but Colin Tebbutt provided earlier testimony that a royalty protection officer, Michael Walker, was at the mortuary on the night. It appears that the reference MW/1 stands for "Michael Walker 1". Michael Walker has never been asked what he did with the four photographs and chain belonging to Princess Diana that were "restored" to him at 8.05 p.m. on 31 August 1997 at the Fulham Mortuary.

[a] The preceding excerpts from the British Police's Property Register for Princess Diana seem to have been written up on the night of 31 August 1997. The handwriting appears to belong to Richard Wall, matching the writing on the Exhibits document.

---

[a] MW/1 – the first item on the Property Register and discussed in the preceding caption – includes a "chain" which appears to fit with an account by Paul Burrell in his book *A Royal Duty*. Burrell describes a visit to Diana's Kensington Palace apartment on the morning after her death: "My eyes found what I had gone searching for: the rosary beads given to her by Mother Teresa, draped around a miniature marble statue of Jesus Christ.... I picked up the rosary beads and slipped them into my pocket." Then later Burrell describes what happened in Diana's room at the Paris hospital: "I took Mother Teresa's ivory rosary beads out of my pocket and gave them to the nurse. "Can you please place these in the princess's hand? Thank you.": Paul Burrell, A Royal Duty, pp 286,289. Mother Teresa died on 5 September 1997, just 5 days after Princess Diana. Their final meeting was in the Bronx, New York on 18 June 1997.

There are conflicts between the Exhibits document and the Property Register – these are discussed in the Comment section below.

Wall has said (see below) that he completed the Property Register – TJS/3[a] – "during the post mortem examination", and then "Chapman dictated the details to me after each of the examinations", while Wall recorded those details in the Exhibits documents.

The truth appears to be the reverse – the Exhibits document was written up during the post-mortem, while the Property Register may have been completed later.

Richard Wall, DS, MPS Organised Crime Group: 19 Oct 04 Statement: **Jury Didn't Hear**:

"During the post mortem examination I completed two exhibit books[b] for each of the deceased, which I have been shown today by DC Emeny exhibits TJS/2 and TJS/3. These record the fact that the aforementioned exhibits were placed in a locked safe on the fifth floor at New Scotland Yard at 0030 hours [12.30 a.m.] on the 1st September 1997....

"I have also been shown by DC Emeny two copies of the Post Mortems exhibits (Pathologists copy) ... concerning each of the deceased. Dr Chapman dictated the details to me after each of the examinations and I recorded them on these documents." [402]

Dr Robert Chapman, Pathologist, UK: 24 Feb 05 Statement: **Jury Didn't Hear**:

"The examinations of 31/8/97 were recorded by means of notes made by me on a booklet containing body diagrams and by dictation to a police officer. No dictation of findings to a dictaphone was made....

"The [Exhibits] documents shown to me and said to have been completed by D.S. Wall was dictated by me during the postmortem examinations. They record the personnel present at the examination and the internal findings of the examinations as well as the exhibits obtained." [403]

Robert Thompson, Fulham Mortuary Manager: 9 Nov 04 Statement: **Jury Didn't Hear**:

"I don't remember Dr Chapman speaking into a dictaphone but from previous experience of working with him, that was often what he did. There may have been someone taking notes but again, I can't say for sure." [404]

John Burton, Royal Coroner, 1997: 16 Jun 04 Statement: **Jury Didn't Hear**:

---

[a] See *The Documents* book, p665 (UK edition). The first two pages of TJS/3 are reproduced above. Later pages – relating to items of Diana's clothing – have been reproduced in *The Documents* book.

[b] Wall is referring to the Property Register document – this shouldn't be confused with the Exhibits document which is a completely different report.

"There have been many occasions where I have assisted at post mortems.... I would sometimes make notes at the dictation of the pathologist and would hold the photographer's second or remote flashlight to assist him." [405]

Comment: There is a conflict between the accounts of Richard Wall and Robert Chapman:

- Wall: "Dr Chapman dictated the details to me after each of the examinations and I recorded them on these documents"

- Chapman: "the [Exhibits] documents ... [were] dictated by me during the postmortem examinations".

Wall states that the Exhibits document was completed "after" the postmortem examination, whereas Chapman has said it was "during" it.

The testimony from Burton and Thompson, although not explicit, appears to support Chapman's account – Burton seems to indicate that during postmortems he "would hold the photographer's ... flashlight" and also "make notes at the dictation of the pathologist"; Thompson simply states that "there may have been someone taking notes", indicating by the context that he is referring to the period during the post-mortem.

I also suggest that it is common sense that the Exhibits document would be completed at the same time as the post-mortem was carried out. If Wall's account was correct – that "Dr Chapman dictated the details to me after each of the examinations" – then it indicates that Chapman would be relying on his memory after the event. Clearly, that would compromise accuracy – and there is no logical reason why Chapman would do that.

The balance of the evidence is that the Exhibits document would have been completed by Wall during the post-mortem procedure and it appears that Wall has lied in stating that "Chapman dictated the details ... after each of the examinations".

Wall has also stated that the Property Register – TJS/3 – was completed "during the post mortem examination".

There is no other witness on the timing of the completion of the Property Register – so Wall's account is neither confirmed nor denied. However, the fact that there are three major conflicts – dealt with below – between the content of the Property Register, compared to the Exhibits document, indicates that the two documents would not have been completed at the same time.

Since the evidence above reveals that the Exhibits document was completed throughout the post-mortem examination itself, it would appear likely that the Property Register regarding samples RC/1 to RC/5 was filled out later. This will become clearer – as will the possible reasons why Wall has reversed[a] the timing of each document's completion – as the conflicts between the two documents are examined.

---

[a] Or, been instructed to reverse.

The conflicts are:

1) A difference in the timing of sample collection.

Column 7 of the Property Register shows the "Time and Date Found". It reveals the following timings for the collection of each sample:

RC/1 – 2137 – 9.37 p.m.
RC/2 – 2215 – 10.15 p.m.
RC/3 – 2130 – 9.30 p.m.
RC/4 – 2230 – 10.30 p.m.
RC/5 – 2119 – 9.19 p.m.

All these 5 times fall within the timespan of the post-mortem given in the Exhibits document – 8.15 to 11.20 p.m. – but they indicate the samples were taken in a different order.

The order from the Property Register is:

RC/5, RC/3, RC/1, RC/2, RC/4

As opposed to the Exhibits document:

RC/1, RC/2, RC/3, RC/4.

The Property Register shows the vitreous humour sample being taken first. There are three problems with this:

a) according to the Exhibits document there was no vitreous humour sample taken

b) how could the vitreous humour sample be labelled RC/5 if it was taken first – at that stage (9.19 p.m.) no one could have known how many samples would be taken. It is logical that the first sample taken would be labelled RC/1 – as done in the Exhibits document – not RC/5

c) Chapman said in 2005: "Vitreous [humour] fluid would probably not have been taken in 1997 had an uncontaminated sample of urine been available".

There was no urine in Diana's bladder[a], but if vitreous humour was taken first, at 9.19 p.m. – as recorded in the Property Register – that would have been earlier than the opening of the bladder.[b]

2) The Property Register shows a vitreous humour sample – RC/5 – being taken, but there is no record of this in the Exhibits document.

3) The sample of the liver – RC/4 – is recorded as "Liver Section" in the Property Register, but as "Section of Liver" in the Exhibits document.

I suggest that the reason it shows as "Section of Liver" in the Exhibits document is because Wall was recording the words exactly as dictated. The fact that this very same phrase "Section of Liver" appears in the 2006

---

[a] It was completely removed during the French embalming – see earlier chapter on the Embalming.

[b] This occurs nearly half way down the second page of the Exhibits document, where it reads "Bladder Empty".

Biological Samples document[a] supports the conclusion that the sample was labelled "Section of Liver".

There is no clear explanation for why Wall has listed this sample in the Property Register as "Liver Section" instead of "Section of Liver" as the sample label would have read.[b]

It is possible that if Wall completed the Property Register later, he may have simply written down "Liver Section" without copying it precisely from the sample label.[c]

Whatever the case, as stated above, the three conflicts taken together – timing, vitreous humour, liver description – indicate that the two documents – Exhibits and Property Register – were completed at different times. The evidence strongly shows that the Exhibits document was filled out during the post-mortem. This then indicates that the Property Register was completed at some point after the post-mortem.

This timing is the opposite to what Wall said in his statement.

Wall should have been asked about the discrepancies in the documentation, at the inquest. As it turned out, he was never even heard from – not cross-examined and nor was his statement read out.

Why would Wall lie – or be told to lie – about this in 2004?

I suggest it is to undermine the importance of the Exhibits document – the very document that was completed in real time during the post-mortem procedure and at the time of the procurement and labelling of samples, as a part of that procedure. The Exhibits document is crucial in revealing that the samples tested by Susan Paterson were not the same samples taken from Diana's body at the post-mortem – see earlier.

Wall's 2004 testimony is that the Exhibits document was written up later – if that were true, it would undermine the importance of that document. But that is not true.

The Property Register shows that RC/1 was put into a locked safe on the 5th floor at 12.30 a.m. on 1 September 1997. Wall reveals in his statement that this was the "fifth floor at New Scotland Yard". The fact the police took that sample is confirmed in the MPS "Property Concerned in Crime" document, reproduced earlier.

---

[a] Reproduced earlier.

[b] Some could argue that Wall was copying the labels from the samples that were later picked up and tested by the Imperial College – that liver sample read "Liver Section" and there was a vitreous humour sample. But if that was the case, then Wall has written the wrong description in the Property Register for the blood sample – he wrote "Preserved Blood", whereas the sample Paterson received read "Blood Preserved".

[c] There is a possibility that Wall filled out the Property Register at the time of the sample manipulation after the post-mortem – see later. If that occurred, then it could be that Wall got confused over sample labels.

The Property Register goes on to show that RC/2 to RC/5 were – as at 8 March 2004[a] – "retained by Dr Chapman". The late 2006 Biological Samples document showed that by that time – over two years later – RC/3, RC/4 and RC/5 were "retained by Operation Paget" and RC/2 was by then "retained by LGC Forensics".

This evidence appears to indicate that after the post-mortem Robert Chapman took possession of Princess Diana's RC/2 to RC/5 samples and still had control of them in 2004. At some point between 2004 and 2006 they were handed over to Operation Paget.

Meanwhile – as earlier evidence has shown – a completely separate set of samples belonging to a different person, was picked up by the Imperial College and tested, under the false belief that they belonged to Princess Diana.

Vitreous Humour

Was a vitreous humour sample taken from Princess Diana's body during the Fulham post-mortem late on 31 August 1997?

John Burton, Royal Coroner, 1997: 16 Jun 04 Statement: **Jury Didn't Hear**:

"There was a discussion regarding the obtaining of toxicology samples when a body had been embalmed and a desire to find a fluid that had not been contaminated by the embalming fluid."[406]

John Burton: 29 Aug 04 Statement: **Jury Didn't Hear**:

"In [my earlier statement] the discussion mentioned. It was between Dr Chapman and the Lab liaison officer. They were discussing the need for uncontaminated samples and that they would need to obtain 'Vitreous Samples'. I was not part of this discussion but I was by reason of my previous experiences content that these samples were required. I cannot remember any more details of this discussion."[407]

Dr Robert Chapman, Pathologist, UK: 24 Feb 05 Statement: **Jury Didn't Hear**:

"Vitreous fluid is generally better protected from the effects of decomposition and embalming but even this may be affected by a thorough embalming process. Vitreous fluid would probably not have been taken in 1997 had an uncontaminated sample of urine been available, although it is now increasingly recognised as a useful sample in general toxicology.....
"Both the blood and vitreous samples were placed in appropriate containers with preservative."[408]

---

[a] p665 of *The Documents* book shows the document that appears to hand over the Property Register to Operation Paget on 8 to 9 March 2004.

Dr Robert Chapman, Pathologist, UK: 26 Nov 07: 27.5:
Hilliard: Q. As far as the taking of samples is concerned, if a body has been embalmed, does that mean you have to go about things in a particular way or from particular locations?
A. This is a difficulty. The embalming procedure will – depending upon how complete it is – it will affect the body fluids. It certainly affects blood and perhaps urine and, to a lesser extent, the eye fluid, because of the use of chemicals, which will make toxicology difficult or indeed sometimes impossible.
Q. Is this right, that you did not take samples from near to obvious sites of embalming fluid installation?
A. One would try and avoid an obvious site of damage or an installation point from a fluid, but one was really trying to get a sample from the leg veins, which is a standard practice in any case.
Q. Right.
A. There may be only very small quantities of fluid available in any case.
At 33.19: Mansfield: Q. Could you explain what the normal [samples taken in a road accident post-mortem] would be?
A. One would try to take blood, urine, vitreous humour, perhaps liver and stomach contents.[a]
Philip Stoneham, Detective Sergeant, British Police: 18 Dec 07: 22.5:
Mansfield: Q. If you need to look at the notes – you were asked this question in November 2004..... Do you see, it says: "In a normal special post mortem, the standard samples are head hair, mouth swabs, pubic hair, finger nails, blood for DNA, blood for toxicology, urine or vitreous humour if no urine is present, liver and stomach contents."
A. That is right, yes.
Q. Did that happen in this case or you can't ... ?
A. I do not know. I do not know.
Comment: The strongest evidence of which samples were taken comes from the handwritten Exhibits document that was written up during the post-mortem procedure – it shows no record of a vitreous humour sample.

---

[a] This has been included here for completeness. The context – shown earlier – reveals that Chapman is providing a contemporary (2007) answer to Mansfield's question, by including vitreous humour. It is Chapman's 2005 evidence: "Vitreous fluid would probably not have been taken in 1997 had an uncontaminated sample of urine been available, although it is now increasingly recognised as a useful sample in general toxicology." In other words, vitreous humour would be taken as a matter of course in 2007, but in 1997 it would only be taken in the absence of urine.

Other documentary evidence, completed at a later time – the Property Register, the Biological Samples table[a] – conflicts with this, indicating there was a vitreous humour sample.

It is really impossible to discount the significance of the Exhibits document – it is the only documentary record of what happened there and then, in the post-mortem room. The general evidence has revealed that there was a manipulation of samples that occurred between the close of the post-mortem and the pickup of the samples the following day by the Imperial College toxicologist.

Given that the samples themselves were manipulated and switched, it also becomes possible that the documentation was as well.[b]

Setting aside the documentary evidence for the moment, an analysis of the witness evidence on vitreous humour also reveals conflicts.

There are three witnesses on this – Burton, Chapman and Stoneham.

When Stoneham was asked by Mansfield if, among other things, vitreous humour was taken in place of urine[c], Stoneham replied: "I do not know. I do not know".

Both Burton and Chapman indicate in their evidence that vitreous humour was taken, but then they provide conflicting reasons for why it was taken.

In his first statement, Burton suggested that they were looking for "a fluid that had not been contaminated by the embalming fluid".

It could be significant that Burton makes no comment in that June 2004 statement[d] on; a) what sort of fluid this was; or b) whether any fluid was successfully found and taken.

Two months later, it appears that Burton was queried by Paget on this. This time Burton provides more information – "they were discussing the need for uncontaminated samples and that they would need to obtain 'Vitreous Samples'" – but he distances himself with: "I was not part of this discussion" and "I cannot remember any more details of this discussion".

Burton also does not state that the vitreous sample was taken.

Burton's evidence is that:
a) there was a discussion between Chapman and Stoneham
b) "they would need to obtain 'Vitreous Samples'"

---

[a] The Toxicology Report is not included here because it is clear that the vitreous humour sample in that document belonged to a different body than Princess Diana's.
[b] The way this may have occurred has already been addressed – it could be that the vitreous humour container was empty, as is described in the Biological Samples document.
[c] There was no urine – see earlier.
[d] This is Burton's primary account of what occurred.

c) the reason for the vitreous sample was "to find a fluid that had not been contaminated by the embalming fluid"

d) "I was ... content that these samples were required".

Neither Chapman nor Stoneham have ever confirmed that this discussion ever took place.[a] They should have been asked at the inquest, but that never occurred – but then, the jury also never heard any of Burton's evidence.

Chapman is the sole witness who states that a vitreous humour sample was taken from Princess Diana. He does not state it in the Exhibits document – dictated on the night – but in his 10 September 1997 post-mortem report: "RC/5 Vitreous humour".

Chapman has given general evidence – not specifically related to the Diana post-mortem – on the effect of embalming fluid on vitreous humour:

- statement: "vitreous fluid is generally better protected from the effects of ... embalming but ... may be affected by a thorough embalming process"[b]

- at inquest: "the embalming procedure ... will affect ... to a lesser extent, the eye fluid".

When it came to Chapman's evidence on what occurred during the post-mortem of Diana, he did not indicate that the presence of embalming fluid was the reason for taking vitreous humour.

Instead Chapman's evidence was: "Vitreous fluid would probably not have been taken in 1997 had an uncontaminated sample of urine been available".

At the inquest Hilliard went on to specifically ask about what occurred during Diana's post-mortem: "Is this right, that you did not take samples from near to obvious sites of embalming fluid installation?"

Hilliard is not only talking about blood – he is talking "samples".[c] This was Chapman's opportunity to say something like: "Well, actually, we did the best we could to get an uncontaminated sample – we took vitreous humour".

But that is not what Chapman said – instead we hear: "one was really trying to get a sample from the leg veins".

In summary, there is no record in the original document – the Exhibits form – of a vitreous humour sample being taken from Diana's body.

The first document to reveal the existence of a vitreous humour sample is the Property Register, but there are indications that samples were manipulated and tampered with after the conclusion of the post-mortem.[d]

---

[a] There was evidence of a discussion on the destination of samples – see earlier.

[b] Chapman described the French embalming of Princess Diana as thorough – see earlier.

[c] This is confirmed by the context – see above.

[d] Later in this chapter there is a possible scenario, suggesting what could have occurred.

Chapman is the only witness who has specifically claimed that a sample of vitreous humour was taken during the post-mortem – but he didn't dictate this on the night.[a] Chapman's earliest dated account of this is in his 10 September 1997 police statement[b] - made 10 days after the post-mortem.

Burton has also indicated that there was an intention to take a vitreous humour sample – "they would need to obtain 'Vitreous Samples'" – but there is a significant conflict with Chapman on the reason for doing so.

Burton's reason is "to find a fluid that had not been contaminated by the embalming", whereas Chapman's is because there was no "uncontaminated sample of urine ... available".

I suggest that the strongest evidence is from the original Exhibits document which shows no vitreous sample was taken.

For that document to be brought into question, there would need to be overwhelming contradictory evidence – I suggest that there is not.

The contradictory witness evidence comes primarily from Chapman and to a lesser extent, Burton – both of these individuals have already been shown in these volumes to be liars.

Chapman has never admitted that RC/5 (vitreous humour) doesn't appear on the Exhibits document. And no one else has either.

It may be significant that the Exhibits document was withheld from the inquest jury, as was all the evidence from John Burton, the royal coroner on the night of the post-mortem.

The balance of the evidence suggests a vitreous humour sample was not taken. This contributes to the understanding that the samples tested by Susan Paterson – which included vitreous humour – did not belong to Princess Diana.

Earlier evidence has shown that Chapman appeared to take a number of organ samples without disclosing them on the Exhibits report. It could be argued that he did a similar thing with the vitreous humour.

There are two critical differences with the vitreous humour, that indicate that is not the case:

1) the earlier evidence showed that the organs were physically removed from the body and were not returned to be with the body until after the post-mortem – Chapman could have secretly taken organ samples, without even Thompson being aware of that. In the case of vitreous humour, which is eye fluid, the sample would have had to have been taken directly from the body

---

[a] The point here is: Why hasn't Chapman said "Look, the Exhibits document is wrong – it doesn't show RC/5 being taken, but, believe me, it was."?

[b] A copy of the undated post-mortem report.

2) the additional organ samples were never given official sample numbers, whereas the vitreous humour was – RC/5.

Sample Identification

Paget Officer, Toby Smith, stated in 2006: "In order to avoid the potential for future confusion arising from the presence of two items bearing the exhibit identification mark 'RC/l', I designated the 'Plucked head hair (Diana, Princess of Wales) sealed in Police Evidence Bag A1484982 Exhibit RC/1' as 'Exhibit RC/la'".[a]

Smith's account shows:
a) that the seal number "A1484982" is a "Police Evidence Bag" number[b]
b) that there are apparently no other distinguishing reference numbers on the samples.

This evidence reveals that there was a major problem with the sample references – so significant was this issue that the police decided to alter the sample number "to avoid the potential for future confusion".

The general evidence – the Exhibits statement, Chapman, Paterson – indicates that the sample numbers are allocated based on the initials of the pathologist: "RC" stands for Robert Chapman. This was also heard at the inquest when Chapman confirmed to Hilliard that the samples taken "run through from RC1, so Robert Chapman 1, to RC5, Robert Chapman 5".[409c]

The police Property Register – reproduced earlier – appears to quote seal numbers for samples RC/1 to RC/5 in the "Where Found" column.

There are however no "seal numbers" – as the police quoted – in any of the other evidence relating to samples RC/2 to RC/5, the samples stored at the mortuary and the samples tested by Paterson. Paterson does state that "each sample was individually sealed in a police evidence bag", but she fails to quote any numbers to support this.

Either: a) there were seal numbers on the police bags and Paterson didn't quote them; or b) there were no seal numbers on RC/2 to RC/5.

In Richard Wall's 19 October 2004 statement a seal number is quoted for RC/1 – which matched the Property Register and the number quoted by Smith – but when samples RC/2 to RC/5 are addressed, no seal numbers are quoted.

---

[a] This was confirmed by Roy Green who said that he received a sample "RC.1a".
[b] Wall quoted the same seal number – A1484982 – in his statement. He also referred to similar seal numbers for the two samples from Dodi Fayed that were taken by police on the night of the post-mortem – "plucked head hair from a male seal number (A1776301) ... and brown material from male's mouth seal number (B2119764)".
[c] This was in reference to Dodi's samples, but it is obvious that the same referencing applied with Diana's.

Whichever way – whether there were seal numbers or not – this evidence highlights a major deficiency in the recording or labelling regarding the post-mortem samples of Princess Diana and Dodi Fayed.

If seal numbers existed then why weren't they used by either Chapman – in his post-mortem report[a] – or Paterson – in her toxicology report.

The only reference numbers are the RC numbers.

Because there were also no body numbers assigned by the Fulham Mortuary to Diana and Dodi – see earlier – a situation was created where the only distinguishing factor between the blood samples was the stated gender:

- Diana's: "Exhibit RC/3 labelled: Blood preserved, <u>A Female</u>, Fulham Mortuary, 31/8/97, Dr R Chapman"

- Dodi's: "Exhibit RC/3 labelled: Blood preserved, <u>A Male</u>, Fulham Mortuary, 31/8/97, Dr R Chapman".

Exactly the same reference number – RC/3 – same product, same mortuary, same date, same pathologist, different gender.

This is comparing Diana's samples with Dodi's.

What if there had been a post-mortem conducted by Robert Chapman for another female on the same day at Fulham Mortuary? If there had been, then it seems the samples could potentially have been identically labelled to Diana's.

These samples do not appear to have any unique referencing number on them.

You don't need to be a forensic pathologist to realise that this is a recipe for potential confusion – "the potential for future confusion", as stated by Smith.

Confusion could occur even if people had the best of intentions.

If people didn't have the best of intentions, then there is a situation here where the system is easier to manipulate because of the deficient labelling and the weak chain of custody – see earlier.

Robert Thompson said in his statement: "At the mortuary we had started a register of samples but I cannot say whether this book was up and running at the time".

This raises the question: Why didn't the police – if they were interested in finding out what occurred with these samples – check the Fulham Mortuary archives?

There is no evidence at all of the British police following up on this.

---

[a] The police evidence – Wall, Smith – reveals there was definitely a seal number on RC/1. One could ask why Chapman didn't quote that in his post-mortem report. If there were no seal numbers for RC/2 to RC/4 then it would have looked suspicious just showing the one seal number – for RC/1 – on the post-mortem report and no seal numbers for the other samples.

The fact that both Chapman and Paterson failed to quote seal reference numbers in key documents[a] – see above – raises a further critical question: Why didn't they?

This question will be addressed later.

The accumulation of evidence has and will show that the "female" samples tested by Susan Paterson on 1 September 1997 did not come from the body of Princess Diana.

That then means that something occurred between the post-mortem late on 31 August 1997 and the testing the following day. Somehow the RC/2, RC/3 and RC/4 samples that were taken during the post-mortem went to a different destination – eventually coming under the control of the British police[b] – and samples from another body were picked up by the Imperial College in their place.

Having said this, the evidence – the Biological Samples report; the Toxicology report – also indicates that RC/3, RC/4 and RC/5 samples from Dodi Fayed ended up in the hands of both the Imperial College and the British police.

Although the focus on the night was on the samples from Diana, it is clear from the evidence that similar events occurred regarding Dodi's body. For example, earlier evidence has shown that an early decision was made to conduct the post-mortem for Diana, but a decision was also made to conduct a post-mortem for Dodi.

It seems that whatever occurred with Diana, similar decisions were made regarding Dodi. If it was decided that the police needed Diana's samples then Dodi's also were acquired by the police – see the Biological Samples report; if it was decided that samples of major organs would be taken from Diana, then a decision was also made to take these samples from Dodi – see the Biological Samples report.

I suggest that this duplication of events for Dodi occurred to avoid any unnecessary suspicion – if it could be perceived that Diana's body was being treated differently to Dodi's then that may have led certain observers – at the time or later – to ask why.[c]

The question now is: What did occur to the samples of Diana and Dodi after the 31 August 1997 post-mortems at the Fulham mortuary?

There appear to be three main possible destinations for Diana's samples: a) the Imperial College, b) the British police, or c) Robert Chapman.

---

[a] Both documents – the post-mortem report and the toxicology report – were not seen by the inquest jury.

[b] See Biological Samples form reproduced earlier.

[c] Chapter 1 reveals that in a similar way, Dominique Lecomte conducted autopsies on both Diana and Dodi's bodies – even though Riou had only raised concerns about the nature of Diana's death.

The Imperial College conducted toxicology testing on samples that were purported to be Diana's.

The Biological Samples report – reproduced earlier – shows that the police had control over samples that they claimed were Diana's.

The Property Register – reproduced earlier – shows samples RC/2 to RC/5 from Diana's body were "retained by Dr Chapman".

There has already been significant evidence showing that the samples tested by Susan Paterson at the Imperial College did not come from Diana's body.[a]

It has also been shown earlier that there appear to be possible cover-ups of evidence in two critical areas relating to the movement of the samples:

a) RC/1 – head hair – was taken by the police

b) Chapman took 7 histology organ samples that were not recorded but ended up at LGC Forensics and within the control of the police.

The inquest heard nothing about point b) and conflicting accounts on point a).

One of the themes in this chapter has been the covering up of evidence regarding the police role. At the inquest both Stoneham and Rees were evasive about events related to the post-mortems and particularly failed to provide evidence on sample movements. The other police present – Wall, Sharp, Williams, Taylor[b] – were not heard from at all.[c]

The cover-up of information, the accumulation of evidence indicating Diana's samples were not tested by Paterson, the treatment of RC/1, the Property Register and the Biological Samples report all combine to indicate that the main samples – RC/2, RC/3 and RC/4 – did not go to the Imperial College for testing.

They instead appear to have been "retained by Dr Chapman" – Property Register – and later transferred to Operation Paget – Biological Samples report.

The question is: How did this occur?

Effectively, the evidence has revealed that there were four lots of samples that came from Princess Diana:

1) RC/1 which was "placed in a locked safe on the fifth floor at New Scotland Yard at 0030 hours [12.30 a.m.][d] on the 1st September 1997" – Wall statement

---

[a] This evidence is listed in the Conclusion section of this chapter.

[b] Taylor has never been interviewed by the police.

[c] Andrew Selous also took photos at Dodi's post-mortem and has never been interviewed and wasn't heard from at the inquest.: Robert Chapman, Witness Statement, 5 September 1997, p1.

[d] Just 1 hour and 10 minutes after the completion of the post-mortem at 11.20 p.m.

2) RC/2, RC/3, RC/4 which all ended up under the control of the police[a] – Biological Samples report

3) 7 major organ samples – brain, lungs, liver, kidney, spleen, adrenal, heart – which ended up with the Forensic Pathology Alliance – Biological Samples report

4) A "sample of the injured area of the heart" which "is stored in the tissue retention area of St Georges Hospital histopathology department" – Chapman 2005 statement.

The inquest jury were led to believe that there was just two lots of samples – RC/1 "given to Detective Sergeant Wall" and RC/2 to RC/5 "given to Mr Thompson for storage".

The jury were given no further information on sample movement – nothing on what happened after the samples were "given to Mr Thompson for storage" and nothing on who conducted the toxicology testing.

The truth is that:

a) there were 12 samples taken[b], not the 5 the jury were told

b) the samples were treated in the above 4 ways, none of which were told to the jury

c) none of Diana's samples were tested at the Imperial College.

There is possibly a key conflict between the evidence of Chapman and Thompson about the initial treatment of the recorded samples:

- Chapman: "exhibits RC/2 to RC/5 were handed to Robert Thompson for storage" – Post-Mortem report and 10 September 1997 statement

- Chapman: "the samples were then passed to Robert Thompson for retention" – 24 February 2005 statement

- Thompson: "I do not actually recall being handed the samples following the post mortems of Diana ... and Dodi ... but I'm sure they would have been given to me" – 9 November 2004 statement

- Thompson: "Detective Sergeant Stoneham ... received the specimens from the pathologist and labelled them. They were then refrigerated at the mortuary, but I cannot now recall who did this or on whose instructions" – 13 June 2001 affidavit.

Chapman's evidence is the samples were handed to Thompson. Thompson actually has no recall of this – he instead remembers Stoneham receiving and labelling the samples and "they were then refrigerated at the mortuary", but Thompson can't recall doing that himself.

Thompson also has recall of Burton making "special arrangements" for the samples. He said in his affidavit: "Dr. Burton had made special arrangements to have the specimens taken from Princess Diana removed to

---

[a] RC/2 was eventually "retained by LGC Forensics" after Cowan's testing in 2006.
[b] 4 recorded samples (not including vitreous humour), 7 organ samples and one sample from the injured heart-related area.

Charing Cross Hospital and had also arranged for an entirely separate courier to come and collect those specimens on the following day."

Although Thompson's recall appears at times to be patchy, his evidence – given the reality that Chapman has lied about some events and the chain of custody is so poor – does raise the possibility that the Diana and Dodi samples were not actually passed to Thompson at the post-mortems.

There were others present who could have taken custody of the samples – for example, Nigel Munns, who was Thompson's boss; Richard Wall, who took RC/1 – see earlier; Philip Stoneham, who Thompson said handled the samples[a] – see above; or even Jeffrey Rees, who has played a significant role in the cover-up[b].

There appear to be three main possibilities regarding the recorded samples, RC/2 to RC/4: either, a) the police – possibly Rees or Stoneham – took the samples away straight after the post-mortem; b) Chapman took the samples away; or, c) the samples were initially refrigerated at the Fulham Mortuary.

The witness evidence is:

- Chapman: "[the samples] would stay within the mortuary complex, within a fridge, prior to them being transported ... for analysis" – at inquest

- Thompson: "Stoneham ... received the specimens from the pathologist and labelled them. They were then refrigerated at the mortuary, but I cannot now recall who did this or on whose instructions" – 13 Jun 01 affidavit

- Thompson: "the specimens were stored in the mortuary refrigerator overnight" – 13 Jun 01 affidavit.

Chapman and Thompson both concur that the samples went into a fridge at the mortuary, but Thompson says "I cannot now recall who did this". Thompson earlier stated: "I do not actually recall being handed the samples".

There is a possibility that Thompson is basing his refrigeration evidence from what he knows occurred the following day: "I do, however, remember that the day after the post mortems I dispatched the samples.... I particularly remember the samples going to Charing Cross hospital because they sent someone on a pedal bike to collect them.... I recall giving him the samples taken at the Princess's post mortem examination...."

I suggest that it is logical for Thompson to presume that because he removed the samples from the fridge the following day – 1 September 1997 – then they were the same samples taken from Diana's body and apparently placed in the fridge late the previous night.

---

[a] Thompson appears to be referring to Diana's samples. Stoneham was not present at Dodi's post-mortem – see earlier.
[b] See Parts 3 and 5 and earlier in this volume.

But it appears that is not the case.

Earlier evidence has shown that the samples Thompson removed from the fridge on 1 September 1997 – RC/2 to RC/5 according to Paterson's statement – were not the same samples taken from Diana's body – RC/2 to RC/4, according to the Exhibits form.

RC/2, RC/3 and RC/4 are the same sample numbers – but so were Dodi's – and as has been shown earlier there were no unique sample numbers quoted.

Robert Thompson has indicated his own concern about the integrity of the sample process in two main ways:

1) Thompson voiced doubts over the negative alcohol finding in Diana's samples: "When the test results came back, the blood allegedly showed negative for alcohol. Detective Sergeant Stoneham expressed extreme surprise at this finding. I also find this unbelievable and it led me to the conclusion that the blood sample had either been corrupted, or a false statement made" – 2001 affidavit

Thompson only appears to have been made aware of the blood being tested. This is possibly because he knew that there was no vitreous humour sample taken – see Exhibits form. Thompson may have been even more concerned, had he seen the Paterson toxicology report where evidence is given of an alcohol test on vitreous humour attributed to Princess Diana – "ethanol [alcohol] was not detected in either the preserved blood or vitreous humor".

2) Thompson provided evidence on the Fulham Mortuary security:

Robert Thompson, Fulham Mortuary Manager: 9 Nov 04 Statement: **Jury Didn't Hear**:

"Once Dr Chapman had finished his examinations I probably stayed an hour and a half just to clean up. I thought that a police officer was put outside the mortuary gate until quite late in the evening but it was I who locked the mortuary up.

"The mortuary building is alarmed so the mortuary room and therefore the fridge are secured. Should the alarm have been activated, the police station at Fulham would have been notified. I was the main keyholder but Nigel Munns also had a key and one of my deputies may have too. When I left the mortuary that night I was happy that everything was safe and secure. I cannot say whether any police officers were still outside the mortuary when I locked up.

"I returned to the mortuary the following morning – Monday 1st September 1997 – and I can say that no police officers were present then. Although I was not the first person at the mortuary, the other people present would not have had access to the post mortem room and it was I who unlocked it." [410]

Comment: Just the fact that Thompson has addressed the mortuary security in his statement indicates that it could have been an issue either to him or the police interviewing him.

The discussion on what occurred to the samples following the post-mortem continues after the section on Nigel Munns.

Records of Samples Taken from Princess Diana's Body at Fulham Mortuary on 31 August 1997				
Sample No	Description	Police Seal No	Time Taken[a]	Retained By[b]
RC/1	Plucked Head Hair	A1484982[c]	9.37 p.m.	Police
RC/2	Stomach Contents	D4204860[d]	10.15 p.m.	Chapman
RC/3	Preserved Blood	B2119748[e]	9.30 p.m.	Chapman
RC/4	Section of Liver[f]	B2119750	10.30 p.m.	Chapman
RC/5[g]	Vitreous Humour	A1776303[h]	9.19 p.m.	Chapman

[a] This is from the Property Register – it does not match the order of samples on the Exhibits document. This issue has been discussed earlier.

[b] On 31 August 1997 as per the Property Register.

[c] This same number is in Richard Wall's statement – see earlier – but he has copied it from the Property Register.

[d] This number is corroborated in the 2006 statement by Dr Alexander Allan – see earlier.

[e] This number – and the number for the liver sample, B2119750 – are in a similar sequence to the number quoted by Wall for Dodi's RC/2 sample – B2119764. It is possibly strange that even though Diana's post-mortem was conducted after Dodi's, the seal numbers are earlier in the sequence.

[f] Showing as "Liver Section" in Property Register – discussed above.

[g] The evidence – primarily the Exhibits document – indicates that this sample was not taken but an empty container was later created to match the samples – from another body – tested at the Imperial College. There is no evidence that any tests were done on this "sample" and it was confirmed as empty in the 2006 Biological Samples document.

[h] This number is in the same sequence as the seal number that Wall quoted for Dodi's RC/1 sample – A1776301. This indicates that the empty vitreous humour container was created on 31 August 1997.

Role of Nigel Munns

Nigel Munns was the only person present at the post-mortems who didn't have an official role to play.

Dr Robert Chapman, Pathologist, UK: 26 Nov 07: 4.22:

Hilliard: Q.[a] Can you help us please as to who was present when you carried out that examination [of Dodi Fayed]?

....A. Nigel Munns, who I would regard as Mr Thompson's boss effectively. A more senior technical person.

At 14.18: Q. If you can just help us with who was present and what their role or occupation was [at Diana's post-mortem].

A.... Nigel Munns, he has the title principal services officer within the mortuary service.

Dr Robert Chapman, Pathologist, UK: 10 Sep 97 Statement

"Those present:[b].... Nigel Munns - Principal Services Officer".[c]

Dr Robert Chapman, Pathologist, UK: 24 Feb 05 Statement: **Jury Didn't Hear**:

"I had probably met Nigel Munns occasionally when I was present at the Fulham Mortuary but had no direct professional contact with him....

"The role of Nigel Munns was not explained to me but he provided support to Robert Thompson in readying the mortuary for operation....

"I do not recall whether Nigel Munns was present [during Dodi's post-mortem][d]."[411]

John Burton, Royal Coroner, 1997: 16 Jun 04 Statement: **Jury Didn't Hear**:

"At some stage Nigel Munns arrived. He worked in environmental services. He would also give assistance where required. I am not certain what his official role was."[412]

Robert Thompson: 9 Nov 04 Statement: **Jury Didn't Hear**:

"On my arrival at the mortuary I started getting everything ready. I was working alone because one of my deputies was on leave and the other was heavily pregnant so she couldn't work in the mortuary itself. Instead, she

---

[a] This appears on the inquest website as "A" for Answer, but it is clearly Hilliard asking a question of Chapman.

[b] Underlining by Chapman.

[c] This was in the statement on Diana's post-mortem. Munns was also listed as present in Chapman's report of Dodi's post-mortem.: Robert Chapman, Witness Statement, 5 September 1997, pp1-2.

[d] This is an interesting comment from Chapman because he wrote the post-mortem report – which was given to the police on 5 September 1997 – stating that Munns was present. At the start of the 24 February 2005 statement Chapman had already said that his evidence was "further to my statements dated 10th and 5th September 1997" – see *The Documents* book, p578.

stayed outside the room and carried out a support role, making tea and coffee etc. Therefore, once the post mortem examinations got underway it was mainly me who assisted Dr Chapman though I was assisted by Nigel Munns. This was not a problem as I was quite capable of carrying out the role alone....

"From memory the people present at the mortuary on that Sunday were ... Nigel Munns my line manager....

"I recall Nigel Munns helping me move the bodies, as physically that was the one thing I couldn't do alone....

"I was the main keyholder but Nigel Munns also had a key and one of my deputies may have too."[413]

Comment: There are three witnesses – Thompson, Burton and Chapman – but no one is able to state why Munns was present:

- Burton: "I am not certain what [Munns'] official role was"
- Chapman: "the role of Nigel Munns was not explained to me".

Thompson has stated what Munns did – "I was assisted by Nigel Munns" – but then immediately qualifies that with: "I was quite capable of carrying out the role alone".[a] Later Thompson says that "Nigel Munns [helped] me move the bodies", but earlier evidence has shown that there were enough people present – including 6 police officers – to assist with that.

One could argue that Munns had come in to replace Thompson's pregnant assistant, who "couldn't work in the mortuary itself". There are a couple of problems with that: firstly, that she clearly was there, so she wasn't replaced – "she ... carried out a support role"; secondly, Thompson doesn't make any suggestion that Munns was requested to come in.

Thompson's evidence was that Burton oversaw a lot of post-mortems at Fulham – "Mr Burton ... used to attend most of the forensic post mortems"; "[Burton] had his office within the Coroner's Court".

That account – added to the earlier knowledge that it was Burton who called the post-mortem – gives added significance to Burton's remark: "I am not certain what [Munns'] official role was".

If Burton didn't know why Munns was there, then who did? Chapman says he didn't – "the role of Nigel Munns was not explained to me".

Munns' position at the Fulham mortuary has been variously described:

- Chapman: "Mr Thompson's boss effectively – a more senior technical person" – inquest
- Chapman: "principal services officer within the mortuary service" – inquest

---

[a] Burton's general evidence supported this: "Robert Thompson ... was very good at his job and didn't normally require any assistance".

- Burton: "[Munns] worked in environmental services"
- Thompson: "my line manager".

The general evidence indicates that Munns – as Thompson's boss (Chapman, Thompson); as "principal services officer" (Chapman post-mortem report[a]) – would have been familiar with the workings and procedures of the Fulham Mortuary.

In contrast, Burton has stated that Munns "worked in environmental services". When seen in the context of the later scenario on what may have occurred[b], it could be that Burton has provided this misinformation to distance Munns from any possible role regarding the post-mortem samples.

It is obviously significant that Nigel Munns has never been interviewed by any police investigation and was also not heard from at the inquest.

Possible Scenario

How did the samples from another body undergo toxicology testing at the Imperial College, while the samples from Princess Diana ended up under the control of the British police?

The following is a possible scenario, based on the evidence but also involving some speculation.

Thompson revealed in his police statement: "Once Dr Chapman had finished his examinations I probably stayed an hour and a half just to clean up". This indicates that Thompson would have left the mortuary sometime around 1 a.m. – approximately 1½ hours after the conclusion of the post-mortem, at 11.20 p.m.[c]

Coroner, John Burton has stated: "I believe I left the mortuary sometime after 10 p.m. that night."[414]

Other evidence from Burton indicates that he was there after the conclusion of the post-mortems: "When the post mortem [of Dodi] had finished I cleaned the body.... I obtained clean linen and assisted in the dressing of the body.... I did not take an active part in the [Diana] post mortem but again assisted in the cleaning of the body and mortuary."

Thompson, however, makes no mention of Burton assisting: "I probably stayed an hour and a half just to clean up".

Wall has already indicated that he "placed [RC/1] in a locked safe ... at New Scotland Yard at 0030 hours [12.30 a.m.] on the 1st September 1997".

Other key people – Chapman, Rees, Stoneham – have made no mention of their movements after the 11.20 p.m. conclusion of the post-mortem.

If the samples were tampered with after the post-mortem – and the earlier evidence indicates they were – then Thompson's "hour and a half just to

---

[a] Provided to the police in Chapman's 10 September 1997 statement.
[b] See below.
[c] See the earlier Exhibits report.

clean up" would have provided other players a window of opportunity to act – ahead of the final lock-up of the mortuary for the night.

The end result of the sample manipulation appears to have been:[a]

a) RC/2, RC/3, RC/4, RC/5 samples, purported to be Diana's but belonging to someone else[b], held in the mortuary fridge and picked up the next day by Thompson, who gave them to Neil McLachlan-Troup from the Imperial College Toxicology Unit

b) RC/2, RC/3, RC/4 samples taken from Diana's body, are passed on to Chapman[c] and later – probably in 2004 – passed onto Operation Paget

c) RC/3, RC/4, RC/5 samples taken from Dodi's body were either: i) split into two sub-samples each, with one staying in the fridge to be given to the Imperial College along with a) above, and the other being taken by Chapman; or ii) a similar treatment to Diana's – samples purporting to be Dodi's, but belonging to someone else, are held in the fridge to go to the Imperial College, while Dodi's true samples are taken by Chapman, and later passed on to Paget.[d]

The question then is: How could the above be achieved?

I suggest that at least three people, and possibly four, would need to be involved:

1) a person with an in-house knowledge of Fulham Mortuary procedures, including sample labelling, familiarity with the usage of the fridge – e.g. where samples are placed, samples being stored from other bodies, post-mortems conducted on other bodies

2) a person with a lot of experience or knowledge in the handling and making up of samples

---

[a] In addition, 7 unrecorded organ samples were possibly taken away by Chapman or the police, but they would not have been the subject of tampering. Also, an eighth additional unrecorded sample of the injured area may have been taken by Chapman and passed onto St Georges Hospital – see earlier.

[b] There is a possibility that the samples from the other person were split – half kept for the normal analysis and half used to replace Diana's samples. The remaining sample sizes shown in the toxicology report appear to be quite small: earlier evidence has shown that the stomach contents were 200 ml, about half the size of the true Paget-held sample, 429 gms; blood was just 1-2 ml; the vitreous humour was all used up in the toxicology testing.

[c] At some stage an empty RC/5 (Vitreous Humour) appears to have been added to these – see earlier Biological Samples document.

[d] Only DNA testing on the samples for Dodi held at the Imperial College could establish whether the samples actually came from Dodi's body. Without going into detail, the BAC reading of 0.78 g/L – found by Susan Paterson – could be quite high for the amount of alcohol Dodi appears to have consumed on the night, after allowing for metabolism prior to the crash.

3) a member of the police force able to organise the required police seals and also senior enough to be able to make decisions and handle the responsibility of their part in what took place

4) a person representing the interests of the royal family – earlier evidence has shown royal involvement in the main decisions on the day and there is no reason to suggest that this would have been any different.

It is possible that 1) and 2) could have been the same person – if that was the case, then I believe only three people would have been needed.

Were there people present at the Fulham Mortuary that meet the above criteria?

I stress that what appears above and below is a possible scenario only and there is no "smoking gun" type evidence to show that what is stated here definitely occurred. The evidence presented in this chapter indicates that a manipulation of the samples did occur and this scenario is a possible explanation for how this could have logistically taken place.

I believe the following questions demand answers:

-   Could Nigel Munns have provided the needed knowledge of the workings inside the Fulham Mortuary?

-   Robert Chapman has already been shown to have taken unrecorded samples. Could he also have been involved in making sure the samples were correctly handled to achieve the required outcome?

-   Jeffrey Rees was a very senior police officer – could he have acted on behalf of the MPS, providing seals[a] and support?

-   Did John Burton act as the Queen's representative? I suggest that the instruction for an action of this nature – manipulation of the samples taken – would have come from a very high level in the royal family.[b] Burton would not necessarily have needed to be present at the scene of this crime.[c]

Why was it decided that the "official" toxicology testing of Princess Diana's samples was to be carried out on samples from a different body?

Once again, any answer to this can only be given with speculation, based on the available evidence.

The evidence in this book has shown that the key decisions relating to the treatment of Princess Diana's body on the day – 31 August 1997 – were being made from Balmoral. There is no evidence to suggest that process suddenly stopped when Diana's body arrived at the Fulham Mortuary – and, in fact, there were two senior representatives of the Queen present at the mortuary: John Burton and Anthony Mather.

---

[a] Seal numbers are quoted in the Property Register – reproduced earlier.

[b] See the discussion below on why such action would have been taken.

[c] Earlier evidence has shown that Anthony Mather – from the Lord Chamberlain's Office – was also at the Fulham Mortuary. There is a possibility that he could have played a role in these events, acting on instructions.

Events occurred very quickly on the day – as stated earlier, within 25 hours of her death, Princess Diana has undergone two post-mortems and two embalmings.

I suggest that the decision to switch the samples – made from Balmoral – could have been either from a knowledge – or a fear – of what tests on the samples would reveal.

By preventing the samples from reaching the hands of the official toxicologist – Susan Paterson – in one fell swoop it took away the potential for test results from the samples to cause any "scandal" or embarrassment for the royal family.

Earlier evidence – in Part 2 – has indicated that Diana may have been pregnant at the time of the crash, and this could have become known after her arrival at the La Pitié Hospital.[a] There is also a possibility that a harmful substance had been administered to Diana during the five minute stoppage outside the hospital gates.[b]

Discovery – as a result of the toxicology testing – of either of these possibilities would have been against the interests of the British Establishment.

Even if neither of these possibilities – pregnancy or poisoning – were known at the time of the second post-mortem, I suggest that the fear of such a possibility may have been enough for the Queen to order the samples to be switched.

Elimination of the possibility – by switching the samples – took away the potential for blame, scandal or embarrassment to the royal family.

I suggest that Dodi's samples were also manipulated – either by switching or splitting[c] - in order to ensure that the treatment of both Diana and Dodi was similar. As suggested earlier, special treatment of Diana's body or samples could have raised unwanted concerns, either at the time or later on.

Transportation of Samples: 1 September 1997

The samples were not transported to the toxicology laboratory using the normal system.

Dr Robert Chapman, Pathologist, UK: 24 Feb 05 Statement read out 26 Nov 07: 56.8:

"There is a courier system for the transportation of such samples and I would expect the samples to be appropriately refrigerated and stored prior to transportation."

---

[a] The issue of Pregnancy will be readdressed in Part 5.

[b] The 5 minute stoppage is dealt with at length in Part 2.

[c] See above.

Robert Thompson, Fulham Mortuary Manager: 13 Jun 01 Affidavit: **Jury Didn't Hear**:

"Although ... Detective Sergeant Stoneham was present for the purpose of receiving and delivering samples to the Metropolitan Police Laboratory, which is the norm, Dr. Burton had made special arrangements to have the specimens taken from Princess Diana removed to Charing Cross Hospital and had also arranged for an entirely separate courier to come and collect those specimens on the following day (i.e. Monday)....

"In the case of Dodi Al Fayed and Princess Diana, arrangements had been made for the samples and specimens to go to the Pathology Laboratory at Charing Cross Hospital (Dr. Sue Paterson)."[415]

Dr Susan Paterson, Toxicologist, UK: 28 Sep 04 Statement: **Jury Didn't Hear**:

"On 1st September 1997, one of the toxicologists, Neil McLachlan-Troup went to Fulham mortuary and was handed, by a member of the mortuary staff, samples relating to a Female (Fulham 31897). He brought the samples directly to the Toxicology Unit where they were assigned the unique case number 676/97."[416]

Dr Susan Paterson, Toxicologist, UK: 28 Sep 04 Statement: **Jury Didn't Hear**:

"On 1st September 1997, one of the toxicologists, Neil McLachlan-Troup went to Fulham mortuary and was handed, by a member of the mortuary staff, samples relating to a Male (Fulham 31897). He brought the samples directly to the Toxicology Unit where they were assigned the unique case number 677/97."[417]

Robert Thompson, Fulham Mortuary Manager: 9 Nov 04 Statement: **Jury Didn't Hear**:

"During the time I worked at Hammersmith and Fulham Mortuary it was common practice for samples to be sent to Charing Cross hospital for analysis....

"I do ... remember that the day after the post mortems I dispatched the samples taken from the Princess to the lab at Charing Cross hospital....

"I particularly remember the samples going to Charing Cross hospital because they sent someone on a pedal bike to collect them. I assumed he was one of their lab technicians but I refused to let him take the samples as I felt they should be transported by vehicle, as that would have been more secure and therefore a lot safer. He left the mortuary empty handed but returned later that day in a car, which I believe was a taxi. I recall giving him the samples taken at the Princess's post mortem examination but I do not recall giving him any of the samples from Dodi Al Fayed. I may well have done but just cannot remember now....[a]

"I do not know whose decision it was to send the samples to the lab at Charing Cross but, as I have said, this was the usual course of action at that time....

"I do not know whether it was Dr Burton or Dr Chapman who had made the arrangements for the samples to be taken to Charing Cross hospital."[418]

Robert Thompson, Fulham Mortuary Manager: 13 Jun 01 Affidavit: **Jury Didn't Hear**:

"When the courier arrived the following day all the specimens were eventually handed to him. However, he had in fact come on a bicycle and I refused to hand them to him or allow him to carry them back to the hospital until he had arranged an acceptable form of transport. He therefore organised for a taxi to collect him."[419]

Comment: Chapman stated that "there is a courier system for the transportation of such samples" – and that was the sum total of what the jury heard on the subject of transportation.[b]

Paterson – without providing details – reveals that the normal "courier system" that Chapman refers to was not used in this case: instead, "one of the toxicologists, Neil McLachlan-Troup" picked up the samples.

Thompson has given some conflicting evidence on exactly what occurred, but in his most extensive account in 2004 he confirms that he thought it was a laboratory employee – "I assumed he was one of their lab technicians" – who picked up the samples. Thompson stated that he was "on a pedal bike"[c] and

---

[a] Although Thompson has said, "I do not recall giving him any of the samples from Dodi Al Fayed", the evidence from Paterson indicates that both lots of samples were picked up by the same person: "Neil McLachlan-Troup went to Fulham mortuary and was handed, by a member of the mortuary staff, samples" – in both statements. Thompson has never provided an alternative to Paterson's account and there is no reason to doubt her evidence.

[b] If you go back to the fuller transcript – earlier in this chapter or on the inquest website – you will notice that it is immediately after this that Baker chimes in with his amazing statement: "Long experience, I dare say, shows that if you do not follow a rigorous procedure with samples and their transmission ... that difficulties are likely to arise." The jury would have been left thinking that the "rigorous procedure" was followed, when the witness evidence shows otherwise.

[c] The distance between the Charing Cross Hospital and Fulham Mortuary is approximately 3 to 4 km.

Thompson "refused to let him take the samples" until he "returned later that day in a car, which I believe was a taxi".[a]

Thompson's 2001 account was: "Dr. Burton had made special arrangements to have the specimens ... removed to Charing Cross Hospital and had also arranged for an entirely separate courier ... on the following day".

In his 2004 statement – possibly under police pressure – Thompson backed away from the first part of his earlier account: "I do not know whose decision it was to send the samples to the lab at Charing Cross but, as I have said, this was the usual course of action at that time".

The context of the 2001 testimony was that "Burton had made special arrangements" in light of the fact that "Stoneham was present" and he would normally deliver the "samples to the Metropolitan Police Laboratory".[bc]

The evidence in the previous section indicates that the true samples did eventually go to the MPS, but I believe Thompson was not aware of that.

In 2004 Thompson never commented on his earlier testimony that Burton "had also arranged for an entirely separate courier".

It is common sense that it would not be the normal procedure for the Imperial College to send a toxicologist to pick up samples from the mortuary – as Paterson has stated occurred in this case. Even though Thompson was apparently aware the pickup was done by an Imperial College employee, he did not think it would be a toxicologist – "I assumed he was one of their lab technicians".

This evidence indicates that a decision must have been made to alter the normal procedure – "a courier system for the transportation" (Chapman) – and that appears to be what Thompson has recalled in his 2001 account.

Thompson says that Burton "had also arranged for an entirely separate courier". The evidence from Paterson indicates that this was the use of an Imperial College toxicologist – Neil McLachlan-Troup.

It is difficult to understand why Burton did this, but it is something the police should have asked him when they took his statement.

They didn't, and neither have they specifically asked Thompson to elaborate on the account in his affidavit.

---

[a] In 2001 Thompson's story was similar except that he described the samples being picked up by a "courier". Paterson has confirmed that it was a lab employee – see above.

[b] The general earlier evidence was that in cases where the police were involved the samples would go to the police, but in other cases they would go to a laboratory such as the Imperial College (a part of Charing Cross Hospital).

[c] It fits with the general evidence that Burton would be calling the shots on these issues. Earlier evidence has shown that the royals – or their representatives – were making the decisions and giving the orders on that day, 31 August 1997.

Outside Phone Contact

Gerald Posner testified about an alleged phone call to Chapman during the post-mortem of Princess Diana.

Gerald Posner, Investigative Writer, USA: 28 Feb 08: 176.1:

Burnett: Q. [Police statement] "The source from the NSA also told me ... that a call was made from the British Home Secretary's office to the room where the autopsy was being performed on Diana, Princess of Wales. That call supposedly interrupted the autopsy, and ordered the omission of any reference to pregnancy in the final report. I do not know why or how this source was in possession of this information and I do not know which specific department or person in the Home Office it is alleged that this call came from. The Press Office at the British Embassy in Washington dismissed out of hand any suggestion that such a call happened." You remember that, do you?

A. I do indeed.

Q. Seeing from the way in which you put it in statement, it would seem that that was something the source volunteered to you without giving you any colour at all about how he or she had obtained that information?

A. That is absolutely correct. As a matter of fact, you are very astute at picking up the difference in my language when I talk about some of the caveats built into that statement. That information came unsolicited, it was given at the end of – what I remember is it being given at the end of the interview and I am convinced, based upon my faith in this source, that that is what they were told..... That source believes this to be right but I pass it along just as that, what he reported. I cannot confirm that beyond that statement.

Q. Mr Posner, we have heard a great deal of evidence about the treatment of the Princess's body after her death, both in France and in England. I shall simply leave that and move on.

At 190.1: Horwell: Q. Were you yourself concerned at the accuracy of that information?

A. Well, if I had been concerned about the accuracy of the information, I would not have published it. My – I get essentially a veto power as they have on the UN Security Council. So if I do not think what you have told me is credible, it does not get into a story. There are things I leave out all the time that would get a bigger headline that I just don't think are right. However, one of the things about this – and I go through this process.... Has he had a difficulty with a member of the Home Office or British MI6 so that now he is going to have a telephone call taking place during the all-critical autopsy? You ask yourself this as a journalist. You try to feel it out. You get a feel for the person, as to whether they are being accurate. In this case, I was convinced I was not being told something for an ulterior motive. I was being told something that this individual believed to be absolutely accurate, that they were in a position to know this. And if I may say so, something critical here: all the things that I have reported on from this source can be proven or disproven by much better evidence and that is the documentary evidence. Either that telephone took place or did not take place. I do not know the testimony you have received but there were doctors in that room. If they all say there was no such call, then this source received this information incorrectly. The material about French intelligence is available from their own files. They can release that to debunk it or not. So there is more credible evidence here that can settle these issues.

Q. Mr Posner ... as you would imagine, the pathologist who performed the autopsy on Diana, Dr Chapman, he has been called before this jury and there is absolutely no question of his being told to falsify or fake his autopsy report, do you understand?

A. I do. And never having spoken to the doctor, I must say that, based upon sworn testimony, that I must say that without any hesitation, I must assume that he is being absolutely accurate, factual and correct.

Q. Thank you.

Comment: Earlier evidence from Gerald Posner regarding the movements of Henri Paul, has been dealt with in Part 1.[a]

It could be significant that NSA have suggested that such a call came from the Home Office – earlier evidence from Burgess[b] indicated that the Home office was not taking an interest in the post-mortem of Princess Diana. Instead the evidence has been that events were under the control of the royal family at Balmoral.

I suggest that it is illogical that such a call – to order "the omission of any reference to pregnancy in the final report" – would interrupt the post-mortem. Either it would be made before the post-mortem, after the post-mortem, or would be made to Burton. There is no other evidence to suggest that Chapman would have been taking phone calls during the post-mortem.

Horwell tells Posner that "Dr Chapman ... has been called before this jury" – but Chapman was not asked about phone calls during the post-mortem.[c]

Jeffrey Rees, Head of Early Crash Investigations, British Police: 17 Dec 07: 36.21:

Hilliard: Q. I am turning, Mr Rees, to ... your January statement.... There you indicate that you made and received a number of telephone calls during the

---

[a] See the section on an alleged meeting between Henri Paul and the DGSE during his three hour disappearance: pp196-9 Part 1.

[b] See Royal Control chapter.

[c] I am not suggesting that Chapman would have had a call – I am just pointing out that he wasn't asked about this specific subject.

post-mortem examinations.

A. Yes.

Comment: Rees should have been asked about the nature of the calls, but wasn't.

Head Injury[a]

There is conflicting evidence on the nature or extent of the injury to Princess Diana's head.

The following witness evidence runs in chronological order – from those who first saw Diana immediately following the crash right through to Chapman's evidence based on his knowledge from the post-mortem he conducted.

Clifford Gooroovadoo, Pedestrian Eye-Witness: 31 Aug 97 2.30 a.m. Statement read out 12 Mar 08: 79.6:

"The woman was in a very bad way, she was bleeding profusely from the face and she did not speak."

Sébastien Dorzée, Police Lieutenant: 31 Aug 97 Statement read out 28 Nov 07: 43.9:

"The female seated in the rear ... appeared to me to be in the best shape of all of them. However, blood was coming out of her mouth and nose. You could see a deep wound to her forehead...."

Sébastien Dorzée, 26 Sep 97 Statement read out 28 Nov 07: 51.23:

"One of the fire officers asked me to look after the Princess and to keep her awake when she fell asleep. In addition, blood had begun to appear on the right side of her face, from the nose or the mouth."

Dr Frédéric Mailliez, Passing Emergency Doctor: 13 Nov 07: 15.22:

Burnett: Q. Whilst you were tending to the princess, were you able to make a diagnosis of the injuries she had sustained?

A. Not really. I was just suspecting a brain damage or a chest damage because of my assessment and because of the high-energy accident.

At 23.22: Mansfield: Q. Because of evidence that we have heard – I am not going to describe it in public – but there was a serious injury on Diana's forehead, was there not?

A. I do not remember any serious injury on her forehead. I just remember a few drops of blood, but I would not say a serious injury.

Philippe Boyer, Paris Fire Service: 14 Nov 07: 9.13:

---

[a] This section should be viewed in the light of the evidence in the Pre-Hospital Medical Treatment chapter in Part 2.

Hough: Q. What injuries or trauma did you note?

A. Well, she had trauma on the right shoulder because her arm was trapped in between the two front seats, but that was the only visible injury.

Q. Did you see any trauma in the region of her forehead?

A. No, there was no blood at that time.

Tom Treasure, Inquest Expert Cardio-Thoracic Surgeon: 19 Nov 07: 89.23:

A. She was very definitely alive when first encountered and the head injury aspect, of a scale of 15, she scored 14. In spite of this terrible accident, there was only one point that she dropped. It is a rather crude scale, but it is very robust and it does sort those with brain damage, who need a special sort of attention, from those where the brain is not the immediate anxiety.

Coroner: Is this the Glasgow –

A. Glasgow coma scale, yes. Thank you. 14 out of 15 is very good. The only point she dropped, I think, is she could open her eyes, she was moving, she was responding, but the answers – she was speaking, but the answers were not coherent. That drops you a point. Other than that, it is crude. It does not say that she was in a position to do *The Times* crossword at that moment, but it is a scale of prediction of head injury and it was very favourable.

Dr Jean-Marc Martino, Diana's Ambulance Doctor: 15 Nov 07: 32.22:

Mansfield: "The doctor from SAMU who attended at about 12.40 [a.m.] made this assessment.... This is what he assessed: 'Because of what happened at the scene, that is to say a high-speed accident, the technical wherewithal capable of operating in thoracic, cardiac and abdominal regions was needed.'"

Dr Jean-Marc Martino: 24 Jan 08: 119.15:

Hough: Q. At 00.43 [12.43 a.m.] on the SAMU transcript, there is a further report made by your ambulance to an auxiliary at the SAMU ward.... Do you see a reference there to "Two dead, a front seat passenger having hit the windscreen and a rear passenger with an arm injury"?

A. Yes.

Q. Was that report made by you?

A. Yes, that's correct.

Q. Was that an accurate account of what was then known?

A. Yes, that was my initial assessment, my first sight, my first report.

Dr Marc Lejay, Medical Dispatcher: 29 Nov 07: 9.7:

Hough: Q. Do you see there a call recorded at 00.43 and 20 seconds?

A. Yes.

....Q. Can I just read that report to you.... ".... Rear passenger, would seem an arm, the right arm, completely turned backwards. We are trying to sedate and initial treatment. Over."

A. That is true. That is what I can read.

At 40.21: Hough: Q. I am just going to read you what Dr Martino said about his initial assessment.... This is what he said to Professor Lecomte and

Professor Lienhart [in February 1998]. He said: "She herself had a facial injury, frontal according to the journey log, and was trapped with her right arm bent to the rear, at first glance possibly with a fracture in the upper third. However, she may have had all sorts of other internal injuries, abdominal or thoracic, which might decompensate at any time."

A. That is possible. I don't have that type of information in front of me and I do not have any recollection of that.

Dr Jean-Marc Martino: 31 Aug 97 SAMU Ambulance Report:
"Female ... rear passenger not wearing a seatbelt and projected forward. Right frontal trauma. Right arm bent to the rear   alert upon our arrival. "Initial Cause: Glasgow 14.... removed from vehicle.
"Findings: upper ⅓ of right humerus fractured affecting vasculo-nervous package, fracture to right wrist. Thoracic trauma with sub-cutaneous emphysema, wound to right leg with cutaneo-muscular damage from the iliac crest to the mid ⅓ of the right leg."[420]

Dr Arnaud Derossi, Medical Dispatcher at Crash Scene: 11 Dec 07: 13.13:
Hough: Q. Can we now run through briefly the report that you did give at 20 past 1.... I think you told him that she had "obvious cranial trauma and was showing agitation and confusion".

A. Yes.

Dr Jean-Marc Martino, Diana's Ambulance Doctor: 24 Jan 08: 124.24:
Hough: Q. Now, at 01.19, Dr Derossi made a detailed situation report.... He said that she had cranial trauma, agitation and confusion?

A. Yes.

Q. And he and Dr Lejay agreed that it was a case for the neurosurgical unit at the Pitié Salpêtrière?

A. That's what we see on the report.

Dr Marc Lejay, Medical Dispatcher: 29 Nov 07: 15.4:
Hough: Q. [Derossi] ... told you that she had cranial trauma, that is head injury; yes?

A. That is true.

Dr Marc Lejay: 31 Aug 97 Deployment Report:
"0120 hrs: Fuller report from Doctor Derossi ... 1 female patient aged about 40 – cranial trauma, fracture of the humerus, state of haemorrhagic shock...."[421]

Bruno Riou, Senior Duty Anaesthetist, La Pitié: 15 Nov 07: 9.20:
Hilliard: Q. What was her condition on arrival?

A. Well, very bad because a filling operation had been done. Catecholamines had been administered and despite that, her blood pressure was extremely low and she showed signs of neurological suffering with bilateral ... that is, the dilation of the eyes. Though in this situation it is always very difficult to distinguish between what is actually the consequence of the neurological suffering or the effect of the catecholamines. I had been informed that a cardiac arrest had happened. That is what the physician told me when he arrived.

Prof Dominique Lecomte, Pathologist and Head of IML, Paris: 31 Aug 97 Forensic Report on Princess Diana: **Jury Didn't Hear**:

"I noted ... a sutured[a] wound at the right pararedian[b] forehead, plus an abrasion of the upper lip; a linear echymotic[c] abrasion to the right of the neck".[d]

Huguette Amarger, BJL Embalmer: 8 Mar 05 Statement: **Jury Didn't Hear**:

"Question: In what condition was the Princess's body when it was presented to you?

Answer: She was unrecognizable, like any person killed in a road accident, at least by comparison with what I knew of her in the magazines. She had a wound on her right shoulder, I think, and another on her right hip, and a lot of bruises on the legs, as well as on the face."[422]

David Green, Embalmer, UK: 13 Jul 04 Statement: **Jury Didn't Hear**:

"The Princess lay in a bed. I saw that she was in a black dress.... There was [a] small cut to her forehead that had been concealed with makeup and her hair brushed down over it."[423]

John Burton, Royal Coroner, 1997: 16 Jun 04 Statement: **Jury Didn't Hear**:

"I could see and smell that the body of Diana Princess of Wales had clearly been embalmed.... Her body was dressed in simple black clothing.... Her face was heavily made up."[424]

Post-Mortem Exhibits: 31 Aug 97 Report: **Jury Didn't Hear**:

"Brain 1690 grams[eabc]

---

[a] Stitched up.

[b] This probably should read "paramedian" which means: "situated adjacent to the midline": Merriam-Webster.

[c] Bruising.

[d] This document was reproduced in chapter 1.

[e] Chapman makes no comment on any possible significance of this. 1690 grams is unusually heavy for a female post-mortem brain weight. Female brains are generally around 100 grams lighter than male brains. There are two studies that reveal female brain weights: 1) A British study of brain weights in suicide – 43 females who died from natural causes had an average brain weight of 1184 grams (the maximum weight – from both male and females – was 1420 grams). The only methods of death that gave a maximum weight (for male or female) in the region of 1690 were hanging – 1780 – and car exhaust – 1698 grams. The average female weight from hangings was 1309 grams and there were no females who died from car exhaust – the average

male weight from car exhaust was 1409 grams. Deaths from trauma showed much lower maximum brain weights: "jumping from height" was maximum (male or female) of 1398 grams and "run over by train" was 1359 grams maximum brain weight. The most common form of suicide carried out by females was "overdose" (with 35 cases studied) – the average female brain weight for "overdose" was 1305 grams with a maximum (male or female) of 1558 grams.: Emad Salib & George Tadros, Brain Weight in Suicide: An Exploratory Study, British Journal of Psychiatry, 2000, No. 177, pp257-261. 2) A Canadian study on intelligence and brain size – 38 right-handed females had an average brain weight of 1278 grams, and 20 left-handed or ambi-dextrous females had an average of 1218 grams. This study also quoted average brain weights from earlier studies with a higher sample population: a 1964 study by Pakkenburg & Voigt with a total (both male and female) sample size of 1,090 bodies returned an average female brain weight of 1280 grams; a 1978 study by Dekaban & Sadowsky with a total (both male and female) sample size of 972 bodies returned an average female brain weight of 1255 grams.: S.F. Witelson, H. Beresh & D.L. Kigar, Intelligence and Brain Size in 100 Post-Mortem Brains: Sex, Lateralization and Age Factors, Guarantors of Brain, Oxford Journals, 2006, No. 129, pp386-398.

[a] Embalming can increase the brain weight by around 8%.: Salib & Tadross – see previous footnote. Huguette Amarger, who conducted the embalming and later described the process to the British police – see chapter 2 – made no mention of embalming the brain area, but if fluid was inserted into veins then it could have a possible impact on brain weight. In Chapman's post-mortem report he describes the presence of embalming marks in the area of the neck: "Two short, fine incisions on each side of the base of the neck" and "Some packing cotton wool had been left within the soft tissues of the neck along the embalming tracks." If 8% is taken from the post-mortem weight for Diana's brain, we arrive at a weight of 1554 grams. This is still extremely high for a female's post-mortem brain weight. Earlier evidence has shown that the embalming was poorly conducted and only partial – the impact of this embalming on the brain area may have been substantially less than 8%. Source: Robert Chapman, Witness Statement, 10 September 1997, pp2,10.

[b] According to Salib & Tadross – see earlier footnote – "the weight of the brain is approximately 1.4% of that of the body". This can not be accurately calculated in the present case, because in another flaw in this post-mortem, Chapman failed to record Diana's body weight. Earlier evidence in the embalming chapter indicated that Diana's weight – based on her known height – could have been around 69 kg. If this was correct, it would suggest that her brain weight – at 1.4% – should have been around 966 grams. This is significantly less than the 1690 grams recorded by Chapman.

[c] The research conducted by Salib and Tadros – quoted in the earlier footnote – revealed that the highest brain weight range from suicide victims came from hangings – the maximum was 1780 grams (males and females are not separated). Separate research conducted by Dr Dean Hawley has shown that there are some similarities between the effects of hanging and death by strangulation. When seen in

"Skull is intact. Minor S.A.H.[a] Brain swollen
"Bruising [[b]] related to embalming tracks.[c]"
Post-Mortem Exhibits: 31 Aug 97 Report: **Jury Didn't Hear**:[d]
"Contusion[e] left occipital[f] laterial surface & SAH over frontal and P.A.R.[g]
regions of brain
"More minor S.A.H. right side
"Para Sag[h] contusions frontal both sides
"Deep contusion left occ[i]."[j]
Dr Robert Chapman, Pathologist, UK: 10 Sep 97 Post-Mortem report: **Jury Didn't Hear**:[k]
"There were the following marks of injury:[l]
HEAD & NECK

---

the light of other evidence, this raises the possibility that Diana may have been subjected to strangulation in the ambulance during the five minutes stoppage outside the hospital gates – covered in Part 2. In summary, the evidence that could point to this is: 1) the high unexplained brain weight of 1690 grams; 2) bruising on the neck reported by both Lecomte and Chapman in their post-mortem reports – excerpts from both of these reports are included in the current section; 3) Bruno Riou's completion of the death certificate as a suspicious death – see chapter 1 of this volume; 4) witness reports of a "rocking" ambulance during the 5 minute stoppage outside the hospital – see Part 2.: Source: Dr Dean Hawley, Death by Strangulation, www.markwynn.com

[a] SAH = subarachnoid haemorrhage. In short, this is bleeding in and around the brain. The significance of this is discussed below.

[b] Difficult to read – appears to be "knecit".

[c] This line appears immediately following "brain swollen", but it does not appear to relate to the brain. The next area addressed is the abdomen. See complete Exhibits form which has been reproduced earlier.

[d] This excerpt has been shown separately because it appears towards the end of the Exhibits report, whereas the above excerpt appeared close to the start. This separation of information could be significant and is discussed in the Comment below.

[e] Bruising.

[f] The occipital lobe is the area at the back of the brain.

[g] PAR appears to stand for the parietal lobe which is the middle area of the brain – sitting between the frontal and occipital lobes.

[h] Para Sag appears to stand for "parasagittal". The sagittal plane vertically splits the body into left and right. Parasagittal is "sitting alongside or adjacent to the sagittal plane".: Sources: Medical Dictionary on MedTerms website, www.medterms.com; Merriam-Webster, www.mereriam-webster.com

[i] Occipital lobe.

[j] Exhibits report is reproduced in full earlier.

[k] All underlining in this report is by Robert Chapman.

[l] This external detail does not appear in the Exhibits document, but probably comes from the photos taken.

1. A full-thickness lacerated injury located 3cms above the inner end of the right eyebrow and comprising two almost straight lacerations at right angles to one another with one disposed vertically and the other placed almost horizontally. Each of these was 3cms in length and there was a little faint bruising associated with the lower margin of the horizontal component measuring 3 x 2cms. The wound showed fine greyish suture material closing the injury.

2. Faint bruise 1.5cms in diameter above and outside the outer end of the right eyebrow.

3. Bruise 1cm in diameter immediately lateral and below the outer end of the right eyebrow.

4. Bruise 1cm in diameter immediately below the previous injury on the upper right cheek.

5. An abrasion located 1cm below the inner corner of the right eye, 0.3cms in diameter.

6. Bruise to the bridge of the nose 1.2cms in diameter with a tiny central abrasion.

7. A superficial abrasion to the upper left nostril area, 0.8cms in length.

8. Two minor abrasions to the right upper lip immediately lateral to the philtrum, in total 1.5cms in diameter.

9. A reddish slightly curved bruise on the right side of the neck below the right angle of the jaw 5.5cms in length.

10. Two closely related rounded bruises immediately anterior and above the previous injury on the upper part of the right side of the neck each 0.7cms in diameter.

11. A bruise 1cm below the jaw-line on the left upper neck 2 x 1cm....

"INTERNAL EXAMINATION

HEAD & NECK

Scalp & Skull:

There was bruising to the scalp deep to the externally visible injuries to the right side of the forehead and, additionally, over the right parietal scalp. A patch of bruising was also present to the right occipital scalp reaching to the midline posteriorly.

The skull was of normal thickness. No fractures were present.

There was no evidence of fracture of the nose or mandible.

Brain:

There was no evidence of extra-dural or subdural haemorrhage. The brain coverings appeared healthy. The brain was generally swollen. Patches of contusion were noted to the lateral aspect of the left occipital lobe. There was marked subarachnoid haemorrhage over the cerebral cortices within the frontal and parietal regions on the left side. More minor patchy subarachnoid haemorrhage was noted over the right cerebral cortex. Serial frontal sections of the brain showed para-sagittal deep cerebral contusions within the frontal lobes bilaterally. No other focal abnormalities were noted. The ventricles appeared healthy. The cerebral vessels were of normal anatomical course, thin-walled and patent....

"CONCLUSIONS

.... There were signs of a significant head injury. There was bruising and laceration to the right forehead and evidence of bleeding over the surface of the brain with contusion of the left occipital lobe and within small areas of both frontal lobes."[425]

Dr Robert Chapman, Pathologist, UK: 26 Nov 2007: 16.10:

Hilliard: Q. Again, Doctor, I am not going to go through every detail of this. If anybody wants more details, they can ask you about them. Did you find also – I am going to summarise this – bruises and abrasions to the head, the face and the neck?

A. I did.

Q. Just in particular, did you find a laceration in the area of the right eyebrow?

A. Yes, I did.

Q. Can you just explain the size and location of that? This is the only one I want to ask you about.

A. This was a lacerating injury, a blunt splitting sort of injury to the right forehead, above the inner end of the right eyebrow, so on me, up here (indicating), comprising two almost straight lacerations at right angles to one another, one vertical and one almost horizontal, and each of these was 3 centimetres long.

Q. All right.

At **18.2**: Q. Then ... the internal examination, did you find that the brain was generally swollen and that there had been some bleeding in the area of the brain as well?

A. That is correct, yes.

Q. Again, is that the kind of thing that you find in a car crash?

A. Yes, it is.

At **24.5**: Q. Then you say that there were signs of a significant head injury. Is that the one that you have told us about?

A. Yes, well she had a number of marks on the skin surface, on the outside and she had some evidence of bleeding in and around the brain.

At **65.2**: Horwell: Q. In terms of injuries to her head, she had obvious external and internal head injuries. Is that right?

A. Yes.

Q. As you might expect from somebody who had died in the course of a car crash?

A. Yes.

Robert Thompson, Fulham Mortuary Manager: 13 Jun 01 Affidavit: **Jury Didn't Hear**:

"It was surprising that there was no visible sign of any internal head injury. Signs of such an injury are extremely common in a car crash."[426]

Comment: There is a substantial amount of evidence showing witness perceptions of the injuries to Diana.

In summary, the evidence is:

- Gooroovadoo: "she was bleeding profusely from the face"
- Dorzée: "blood was coming out of her mouth and nose. You could see a deep wound to her forehead" – 31 August 1997 statement
- Dorzée: "blood had begun to appear on the right side of her face, from the nose or the mouth" – 26 September 1997 statement
- Mailliez: "I do not remember any serious injury on her forehead. I just remember a few drops of blood" – at inquest
- Boyer: "No [there was no trauma in the region of her forehead], there was no blood at that time" – response to Hough
- Treasure: "the head injury aspect, of a scale of 15, she scored 14.... 14 out of 15 is very good ... she was speaking, but the answers were not coherent.... it is a scale of prediction of head injury and it was very favourable"
- Martino: "the right arm, completely turned backwards" – 12.43 a.m. 31 August 1997
- Martino: "she herself had a facial injury, frontal according to the journey log" – February 1998
- Derossi: "obvious cranial trauma and was showing agitation and confusion" – 1.20 a.m. 31 August 1997
- Lejay: "cranial trauma, fracture of the humerus, state of haemorrhagic shock" – based on Derossi's 1.20 a.m. report
- Lecomte: "a sutured wound at the right [paramedian] forehead, plus an abrasion of the upper lip"
- Green: "there was [a] small cut to her forehead"
- Chapman: "there were signs of a significant head injury" – 10 September 1997 post-mortem report conclusion
- Chapman: "she had a number of marks on the skin surface, on the outside and she had some evidence of bleeding in and around the brain" – inquest
- Thompson: "there was no visible sign of any internal head injury".

There were 10 witnesses who described the condition of Princess Diana in the Mercedes S280 during the 17 minutes following the crash, prior to the arrival of the SAMU ambulance carrying Dr Jean-Marc Martino. They were paparazzi, Romuald Rat, Christian Martinez and David Odekerken; pedestrian bystanders, Abdelatif Redjil and Clifford Gooroovadoo; police officers, Lino Gagliardone and Sébastien Dorzée; fire department medics, Xavier Gourmelon and Philippe Boyer; and passing emergency doctor, Frédéric Mailliez.[a]

Of these 10 people, only two – Gooroovadoo and Dorzée – made specific mention of any head injury. It may be significant that the other 8 witnesses did not apparently consider any head injury serious enough to mention in their evidence.

Two of these witnesses were specifically asked about this at the inquest – both had medical experience and both replied negatively – Mailliez: "a few drops of blood"; Boyer: "no blood at that time".

The two witnesses who described head injuries in their testimony – Gooroovadoo and Dorzée – were not cross-examined at Baker's "thorough" inquest.

Gooroovadoo has said that Diana "was bleeding profusely from the face". This same witness also said that "she did not speak", but there is a considerable amount of witness evidence declaring that Diana was speaking while she was in the back of the Mercedes.[b]

There is a possibility that Gooroovadoo has exaggerated his account.

Dorzée described "blood ... coming out of her mouth and nose" and modified this under 4 weeks later to "blood ... from the nose or the mouth".

Lecomte noted during her autopsy of Diana: "an abrasion of the upper lip" and this was later supported by Chapman's post-mortem report: "two minor abrasions to the right upper lip".

There is a possibility that the blood described by Gooroovadoo and Dorzée was a result of the upper lip abrasion(s) noted by Lecomte and Chapman.

Mailliez – who is a qualified emergency doctor – remembered it as "a few drops of blood" and by the time the fire brigade medics arrived, Boyer stated: "there was no blood at that time".

Out of those first 10 witness accounts, only Dorzée commented on the forehead injury – "a deep wound to her forehead".[c]

Dr Martino arrived in the SAMU ambulance at 12.40 a.m. The ambulance report reveals that Diana was initially evaluated with a "Glasgow 14" rating.[d] The inquest cardio-thoracic expert, Tom Treasure, said that was out "of a

---

[a] The full evidence from these witnesses is in Chapter 9A of Part 2.

[b] This is thoroughly covered in Part 2.

[c] The existence of a forehead wound is supported by other witness evidence – see above and below.

[d] The Glasgow scale is discussed in more detail in Part 2.

scale of 15" and "14 out of 15 is very good.... It is a scale of prediction of head injury and it was very favourable".

The earliest report from Martino describing Diana's injuries was at 12.43 a.m. – three minutes after his ambulance arrived – "an arm, the right arm, completely turned backwards". No mention of any head injury.

Martino changed this account in his February 1998 evidence: "his initial assessment ... 'She herself had a facial injury, frontal according to the journey log[a]'." The SAMU medical dispatcher on the night, Marc Lejay, stated: "I do not have any recollection of that".

The first page of the ambulance report – made available to the jury[b] – also does not support Martino's 1998 account. The key excerpt, shown above[c] under the heading "Findings", after "removed from vehicle", lists 4 separate injuries – right humerus[d], right wrist, thoracic trauma, right leg. Again, no mention of any head injury.[e]

Dr Arnaud Derossi, who was assisting Martino in the ambulance, provided the next injury report to Lejay, at 1.20 a.m. At that time Derossi made two critical departures from the injury assessment showing in the "findings" section of the ambulance report:

1) Derossi stated that Diana had "obvious cranial trauma"
2) Derossi stated twice: "nothing to report for the thorax"[f]

The general evidence from Part 2 reveals that Princess Diana had a life-threatening thoracic injury that had resulted from the car crash. The possible reasons why Derossi stated there was "nothing to report for the thorax" have been covered extensively in Part 2. Effectively, Derossi removed any possible concerns the receiving hospital would have of a thoracic injury and replaced them with "obvious cranial trauma".

In a significant twist[g], a table on page 2[a] of the ambulance report[b] – not shown to the jury – directly conflicts with the "findings" on page 1[c]. The

---

[a] No one has ever seen the "journey log" that Martino is referring to.

[b] The jury were only given the first page.

[c] The full page has been reproduced in Part 2 and the other pages of the report appear in *The Documents* book, pp328-330 (UK edition).

[d] Upper arm bone.

[e] In an amazing twist, page 2 of the ambulance report – reproduced on p328 of *The Documents* book – reveals a completely different picture to this. This is addressed below.

[f] This is dealt with at length in Part 2.

[g] When Part 2 was written I only had knowledge of page 1 of the ambulance report – the same as what the jury had. The other pages – reproduced in *The Documents* book – were provided to me just prior to the publication of Part 3.

table is headed "Trauma" and provides boxes to be marked with a cross under headings related to various key parts of the body. Just three boxes have been marked with an "x" on that document: Cranial – Wound[d]; Rt. Arm – Closed Fracture; Rt. Leg – Wound. The column headed "THX"[e] has been left blank.

So on page 1 of the Ambulance Report we have: right humerus, right wrist, thoracic trauma, right leg. On the next page thoracic trauma has gone and it has been replaced by "cranial wound".[f]

These Ambulance Report pages are not headed or numbered – see earlier footnote – and there is a possibility that the hospital were not given every page. A close look at page 1 of the report reveals that the ambulance left the hospital at 4.11 a.m.[g] and returned to the base at 4.17 a.m. That is information that could not have been completed until several hours after Diana's admission.

If the hospital were only provided with pages 2 to 4 of the Ambulance Report on admission, then the injury information – head injury and no thoracic trauma – would have matched what Derossi had officially told the base at 1.20 a.m.[h], 46 minutes before arriving at the hospital.

The weight of evidence covered in Part 2 indicated that Derossi had lied at 1.20 a.m., when he told the base that there was "nothing to report for the thorax" and it appears that lie was continued on the second page table of the Ambulance Report.

The next witness to describe the forehead injury was Dominique Lecomte, during her post-mortem operation – "I noted ... a sutured wound at the right [paramedian] forehead". It is significant that although Lecomte carried out a post-mortem – she determined cause of death[i] – she appears to find no evidence of brain injury.

---

[a] The Ambulance Report pages – of which there are four in total – are not numbered or headed. I have described them with page numbers to help distinguish them from each other. When the jury were just given page 1, they had no means of knowing that there were any other pages.

[b] Reproduced on p328 of *The Documents* book (UK edition).

[c] Quoted above.

[d] Boxes on the left hand side of the table distinguish between different types of injuries to the respective body part – e.g. wound, fracture.

[e] Short for "Thorax".

[f] On the table on page 2 of the report the "x" in the box for "rt. arm – closed fracture" appears to account for both the fracture of the right humerus and the right wrist, described on page 1.

[g] This has been addressed in Part 2.

[h] There were no other injury reports after 1.20 a.m. – see Part 2.

[i] See chapter 1.

Colin Tebbutt saw Diana ahead of the embalming – he stated that there "appeared to be lacerations to the right hand side of her face". At the inquest Tebbutt said there was "not a lot of damage to her face".[ab]

Huguette Amarger, the French embalmer – who, as with Tebbutt, saw Diana prior to the embalming, described her as "unrecognizable". Amarger made no specific comment on the forehead wound, but there were "a lot of bruises ... on the face".

David Green, the British embalmer, observed after his 3.40 p.m. arrival at the hospital: "there was [a] small cut to her forehead".

The final evidence on Princess Diana's head injury comes from just two witnesses who had key roles at the UK post-mortem later that night – Robert Chapman, the pathologist and Robert Thompson, the mortuary manager.

There is a clear conflict – Thompson has stated that "there was no visible sign of any internal head injury", while Chapman has said "there were signs of a significant head injury" and "she had some evidence of bleeding in and around the brain".

Chapman and Thompson do agree on one thing – that one could expect an internal head injury from a car crash: Thompson – "signs of [an internal head] injury are extremely common in a car crash"; Chapman: "obvious external and internal head injuries ... [is what] you might expect from somebody who had died in the course of a car crash"[c] – confirmed to Horwell.

As noted earlier, both Chapman and Thompson had extensive experience of post-mortems. This means that one of them appears to be lying – either Diana had internal head injury or she didn't.

The earliest documentary evidence from the post-mortem was the Exhibits document, completed at the time by Wall, from Chapman's dictation.

The Exhibits document[d] reveals Chapman initially describing, in his dictation to Wall, the existence of "minor SAH" and later "SAH over frontal and [parietal] regions" and "more minor SAH right side".

SAH stands for subarachnoid haemorrhage – bleeding in and around the brain. That is clearly a reference to the presence of internal brain injury.

There are two significant points to note from a close scrutiny of the Exhibits document:

---

[a] Michael Gibbins, who was in London but receiving updates from Tebbutt, said in his police statement that "there was damage to one side of her face".

[b] Paul Burrell, Diana's butler, was with Tebbutt when they viewed the body. Burrell said in his 2003 book: "What I witnessed before me was indescribable, and it is not appropriate to explain further.": Paul Burrell, A Royal Duty, 2003, p288.

[c] One point to note is that Diana didn't die in the car crash – see Part 2.

[d] Reproduced in full earlier.

1) Chapman's main use of abbreviations is in his description of the brain.

An analysis of abbreviations or shortened words used by Chapman throughout the Exhibits document reveals that there are 14 abbreviations used, and of those 6 relate directly to his descriptions of the brain area – that is 43%.

In contrast, the body text of the Exhibits document runs to 89 lines. Of those just 8, or 9%, are devoted to the area of the brain.

The question is: Why has Chapman used the abbreviation SAH three times, when he could just as easily have simply said "bleeding"?

There was an audience of 8 people[a] in the post-mortem room when Chapman dictated the Exhibits document[b], yet I suggest that it is possible that very few of them understood what "SAH" stood for.[c]

After reading through the three page handwritten Exhibits document, it strikes me that it is reasonably easy for the layman to follow – except when it comes to Chapman's descriptions of the brain area. That area is effectively made unintelligible by the use of abbreviations – SAH, PAR, Para Sag and Occ.[d]

2) Chapman's descriptions of the brain appear in two completely different parts of the Exhibits document.

The brain was the first organ weighed and described by Chapman – in two lines "Brain 1690 grams. Skull is intact. Minor S.A.H. Brain swollen".

And that appears to be the end of the brain description – but it's not.

Chapman returns to the brain towards the end of the document – this time he adds another 6 lines of description and his account also appears to change.

The SAH is no longer "minor" – Chapman now describes "SAH over frontal and [parietal] regions". Chapman also adds contusions, or bruising, not previously described – "contusion left occipital laterial surface"; "contusions frontal both sides"; then "deep contusion left [occipital]".

Chapman's late description appears to be far more serious than his initial one – bleeding no longer minor and deep bruising.

The question is: What is it that led Chapman to redo the brain description towards the conclusion of the post-mortem? [e]

---

[a] See earlier.

[b] Chapman stated in 2005: "The internal findings were dictated by me in such a way as to be audible in the room".: Robert Chapman, Witness Statement, 24 February 2005, reproduced in *The Documents* book, p582 (UK Edition)

[c] The fact that Wall has put dots between the letters of PAR and SAH (the first time) indicates that he wasn't aware that PAR stood for just one word, "parietal", or SAH stood for two words, subarachnoid haemorrhage.

[d] These abbreviations have all been explained in earlier footnotes.

[e] Chapman doesn't do this with any other organ and also doesn't do it with any organ described in the Exhibits document for Dodi's post-mortem.

The evidence relating to the reports from the Paris ambulance – extensively covered in Part 2 – reveals that signs of thoracic trauma were found very early by the SAMU doctor, Jean-Marc Martino. This critical information was withheld from the SAMU base and therefore was not conveyed to the receiving hospital. Instead Dr Arnaud Derossi – who was working with Martino – told Dr Marc Lejay at the base that Diana had "obvious cranial trauma and was showing agitation and confusion". It was agreed that "it was a case for the neurosurgical unit at the Pitié Salpêtrière".[a]

After the SAMU ambulance arrived at the scene, 17 minutes after the crash, Princess Diana had a Glasgow coma rating of 14 out of 15 – inquest expert, Tom Treasure, said: it was a "prediction of head injury and it was very favourable".

The only external evidence of head injury appears to have been the cut on Diana's forehead, which has been variously described in the witness evidence:
- Dorzée: "a deep wound to her forehead"
- Lecomte: "a sutured wound at the right [paramedian] forehead"
- Green: "there was [a] small cut to her forehead"
- Chapman: "a full-thickness lacerated injury ... 3cms above the ... right eyebrow and comprising two almost straight lacerations ... 3cms in length".

The general evidence – including the omission of the cut from most witness descriptions – indicates that this wound was not particularly significant. Earlier evidence has shown that the blood some witnesses described appeared to have come from "two minor abrasions to the right upper lip", noted during the post-mortems of Chapman and Lecomte.[b]

It appears to be significant that there is absolutely no mention of a head or cranial injury in any of the witness or documentary[c] evidence from the hospital. This indicates that Princess Diana was not suffering from a significant head injury during the time she was treated at La Pitié Hospital.

Later in the morning, after her death, Diana was subjected to a post-mortem examination by Dominique Lecomte.[d] In her report, Lecomte makes no mention of any significant head injury, internal or external – just the reference to the forehead and lip injuries detailed above.

In the afternoon Green described the wound as a "small cut to her forehead".

---

[a] La Pitié Salpêtrière Hospital was the receiving hospital for Princess Diana – see Part 2.
[b] Lecomte only noted one.
[c] The jury was not shown any of the documentary evidence from the hospital – it appears in *The Documents* book, pp343-390
[d] See chapter 1.

Pathologist Robert Chapman makes no mention of the forehead wound during his post-mortem dictation – his only description of it is in the later post-mortem report: "a full-thickness lacerated injury ... comprising two almost straight lacerations ... 3cms in length".

Chapman does though describe internal brain injuries – discussed above – in his dictation, written up in the Exhibits report.

Robert Thompson, who was also heavily involved in the post-mortem operation, completely disagrees: "there was no visible sign of any internal head injury".

Robert Chapman concludes his assessment in the 10 September 1997 post-mortem report: "there were signs of a significant head injury". Chapman then appears to make a connection between the internal brain injury and the cut on the forehead: "There was bruising and laceration to the right forehead and evidence of bleeding over the surface of the brain with contusion of the left occipital lobe and within small areas of both frontal lobes." [a]

In summary, there are just three sources of evidence claiming there was a serious head injury:

1) Derossi's 1.20 a.m. phone call to the base – Diana had "obvious cranial trauma"

2) the 2nd page of the Ambulance Report – box marked "x" for "Cranial – Wound"

3) Chapman's post-mortem report conclusion – based on the Exhibits document – "there were signs of a significant head injury".[b]

The reality is that there are major problems with all three of these items of evidence.

The account from Derossi's call conflicts with the "findings" showing on the first page of the Ambulance Report, where there are four specific injuries noted, but there is no mention of a head injury. It has already been shown in Part 2 that Derossi lied during his 1.20 a.m. phone call to the base – he stated twice that there was "nothing to report for the thorax" and instead replaced the thorax trauma with "obvious cranial trauma".[c]

The marked box on the 2nd page of the Ambulance Report – "Cranial – Wound" – conflicts directly with the first page of the same report, which has

---

[a] There was no mention of any internal or external head or brain injury in Chapman's 2005 statement. There may be no significance in that, because that statement was not a post-mortem report, but instead a statement about events and factors relevant to the post-mortems.
[b] Chapman reiterated this at the inquest: "she had obvious external and internal head injuries" – confirmed to Horwell.
[c] Martino and Derossi removed an outcome that one would expect from a high speed car crash – thoracic trauma – and replaced it with another outcome that one would expect – head trauma.

no cranial or head injury listed under "findings". The inquest jury had access to the first page, but not the second page.

Robert Chapman's conclusion of "a significant head injury" is directly contrary to Robert Thompson's, "there was no visible sign of any internal head injury".

Again, why has Robert Chapman made two apparently conflicting descriptions of the brain injury during the dictation of the one Post-Mortem Exhibits report? Why does "minor SAH" or bleeding, become simply "SAH" in the course of the same document?

The following is a scenario based on the available evidence.

I suggest that the evidence indicates that the "obvious cranial trauma" account was created inside the ambulance[a] to replace the true threat to Diana's life, the thoracic trauma.[b] The timing appears to have been after the "findings" section on the first page of the Ambulance Report had already been completed[c], but prior to filling out the table on the second page – and also prior to Derossi's 1.20 a.m. phone call to the base.

After the 1.20 a.m. phone call and the completion of page 2, it then became imperative that there would be a finding in the post-mortem to support the ambulance evidence – i.e. a finding of serious head trauma and brain damage in addition to the inescapable thoracic injury.[d]

Otherwise questions would be raised – like, why did Derossi say "obvious cranial trauma" if there was nothing to support that?

This is where Chapman came in.

Earlier evidence has shown that the people calling the shots during the day were up in Balmoral. John Burton, as royal coroner, represented the Queen and it was he who had called for the post-mortem, even though he had no legal jurisdiction over Diana's body.

I suggest that Burton had been made aware of the importance of a finding of significant head injury in the post-mortem. Burton would have needed to convey that information to Chapman ahead of the post-mortem and there is earlier evidence that the two – Chapman and Burton – did converse prior to the commencement of the post-mortem.[e]

---

[a] It was pointed out in Part 2 that Derossi and Martino may have also been receiving instructions or guidance from other people outside of the ambulance.

[b] There is substantial evidence to support this, in Part 2.

[c] After Diana's transfer into the ambulance, which was at 1.06 a.m., where she was examined by Martino – see Part 2.

[d] The thoracic injury was inescapable because that was the cause of death, which is what a post-mortem is meant to find.

[e] Chapman: "I was then asked directly by Dr Burton to undertake [the Diana post-mortem] following the examination of Mr. Al Fayed".

Chapman may have been reluctant to go along with this – at least initially, he may not have wanted to lie during his post-mortem of Princess Diana. I suggest that is why Chapman made so much use of abbreviations during his brain descriptions.

After the commencement of the post-mortem, Chapman studied the brain first up.[a] That's when he dictated to Wall: "Minor SAH. Brain swollen".

That may not have been enough for Burton[b] – he needed something to substantiate "obvious cranial trauma". It is possible that Burton – who Thompson described as "very much involved in proceedings"[c] – asked Chapman to "elaborate" on this towards the conclusion of the post-mortem.

That is when Chapman added six extra lines to his brain description and changed the evidence from "minor SAH" to "SAH".[d]

Role of Dominique Lecomte

In 1998 French pathologist, Dominique Lecomte, requested copies of reports on the post-mortems conducted by Robert Chapman.

Dr Robert Chapman, Pathologist, UK: 26 Nov 07: 43.17:

Mansfield: Q. You had a further meeting once the autopsies were over in 1998 at New Scotland Yard, didn't you?

A. Yes.

Q. And the same officer, Mr Rees, was present, wasn't he?

A. Yes.

Q. So that it is clear, it is in June 1998, isn't it?

A. It was certainly in 1998, although I do not have a record of the exact date.

Q. No, don't worry. The purpose of that meeting was what?

A. The purpose of that meeting was to meet pathologists from France and to hand them details of the injuries, post-mortem reports.

Q. Which you did?

A. Which I did.

Q. Were you given any reason why they wanted your results?

A. The reason would be that they would require –

Q. Sorry, did they give – not what they would. I know it may be a small distinction. Were you given any reason as to why they wanted your results?

A. I am sure it would have been told.

---

[a] In Dodi's post-mortem, Chapman didn't look at the brain until just over half way through.

[b] As a coroner with a lot of post-mortem experience – see earlier – I believe Burton would have understood what SAH was, but "minor" might not have been sufficient for him.

[c] Burton himself said: "I took no active part in this [Diana] post mortem".

[d] There is a further possibility that internal brain injury has been emphasised by Chapman to help create a false perception that Diana's situation was hopeless, even without the thoracic issues.

Q. Do you have a record of the meeting?

A. No.

Q. Anywhere?

A. No.

Q. Any reason for that?

A. No. I regard it as a meeting with professional colleagues to hand them reports.

Q. Was one of the persons present – or at least two of them, were they French pathologists?

A. Yes.

Q. Was one of them Professor Lecomte?

A. Yes.

Q. So the results of your examination were given to her?

A. Yes.

Q. And any further discussion between the two of you, that is you and Professor Lecomte?

A. Yes, she wanted to know in more detail the exact location of the injury to Princess Diana on the heart. She wanted to know really more details about that injury.

Q. Yes, that is one area. Any other area that you can recall?

A. She wanted to have some discussion about Dodi, about the injuries to him –

Q. Yes.

A. – but I do not recall any other areas we discussed in that meeting.

Q. In that meeting, nothing was discussed about pregnancy?

A. No.

Jeffrey Rees, Head of Early Crash Investigations, British Police: 17 Dec 07: 56.9:

Hilliard: Q. Just so that we have an idea of the sort of thing that you were doing, we heard about a meeting that took place between Dr Chapman and the French pathologist and, is this right, the two coroners?

A. Yes.

Q. Were you present at that meeting?

A. I was.

John Burton, Royal Coroner, 1997: 16 Jun 04 Statement: **Jury Didn't Hear**:

"I attended a meeting at New Scotland Yard in June 1998. The meeting I believe was called following a request from Professor Lecomte. Present were, Michael Burgess, D/Supt Rees, Dr Chapman Professor Lecomte, her assistant, one or more interpreters and myself....

"I did not take copies of the post mortem report in relation to Diana Princess of Wales to this meeting. The only reports I saw were in English and to my knowledge have never been translated into French. As far as I was aware neither, professor Lecomte or her assistant could speak English.

"Dr Chapman introduced his findings, post mortem photographs and referred to samples taken. Professor Lecomte made written notes throughout the meeting.

"I did not keep notes of this meeting.

"She did not request at the time copies of the post mortem reports or other material in relation to the evidence gained at the post mortems. Had Judge Stéphan or any representative of his made a similar request for such material I would have supplied it to them. I would however have requested that any such material should be treated with extreme confidentiality as I have duty of care to relatives of the deceased to ensure the confidentiality of such intimate material. Post mortem reports should only be used for official purposes and because of the intimate nature of these documents, I would not want to see them being used in the public arena."[427]

Michael Burgess, Royal Coroner, 2002 to Present: 16 Aug 04 Statement: **Jury Didn't Hear**:

Question: "Please describe the events surrounding the meeting with Professor Lecomte in June 1998.

Answer: "Present were Professor Lecomte, her assistant, D/Supt Rees, Dr Burton, Dr Chapman, an interpreter and myself. There may have been another MPS officer there – but if so, I am not sure who it was.

"After the introductions, Professor Lecomte explained that she had to run the medical enquiry in France, which would be entirely separate to the judicial enquiry and when complete she would be feeding her conclusions into the judicial enquiry....

"I believe Dr Chapman or I gave her a copy of [Dodi's] post mortem report presumably in English....

"The conversation ... moved onto matters in relation to Diana Princess of Wales. I sat in, but did not participate. There was a long discussion regarding the injury to her left pulmonary vein.

"I do not recall if Diana Princess of Wales report was given to Professor Lecomte. She was shown some photographs by Dr Chapman. I do not know if Professor Lecomte kept the reports. I presume that she was given the toxicology reports. I believe that Dr Chapman offered to show her histology slides that he kept at his office but did not know how this was going to happen or if this offer was followed up....

....Question: "Did anything unusual occur during this meeting?

Answer: "No. Professor Lecomte seemed to be a skilled professional and was talking with her English equivalent, Dr Chapman."[428a]

Comment: There is a striking similarity in the answers from Burgess and Burton on the issue of who attended this London meeting.

The following exact same words have been used by both: "Present were"; "D/Supt Rees"; "Dr Chapman"; "Professor Lecomte"; "her assistant"; "and myself".[b]

Burgess – whose evidence was unsworn and unsigned[c] – was interviewed three times altogether – the first time was on 15 June 2004, just one day ahead of Burton's statement.[429]

The alignment of their evidence – use of the same words – indicates that Burton may have been provided with a copy of Burgess' first interview before he made his statement.

This is an issue that came up earlier in this volume and in Part 3.

As indicated by John Burton, Dominique Lecomte's trip to London in June 1998 appears to have been for research into the medical treatment of Princess Diana – part of fulfilling an assignment[d] given to her and Dr Lienhart in February 1998, by Judge Stéphan.

There does not appear to be anything particularly sinister about the London meeting, but it is a concern that the resulting Lecomte-Lienhart report – given to Stéphan in November 1998[430] – has never been made public.

Conclusion

The evidence has highlighted several basic deficiencies in the recording methods employed by the Fulham Mortuary and the forensic pathologist, Robert Chapman:

- the bodies of Princess Diana and Dodi Fayed were not assigned body numbers
- post-mortem samples were only referenced by the pathologist's initials, e.g. RC/2
- there were no unique identifying numbers or names on the sample labels received by the toxicologist

---

[a] A fuller account of Burgess' evidence on this can be viewed in *The Documents* book, pp542-3 (UK edition).

[b] Generally there are variations in descriptions, even when it comes to people's names. For example, Professor Lecomte could be "Dominique Lecomte" or "Prof Lecomte" or "Professor Dominique Lecomte".

[c] See earlier and Part 3.

[d] The assignment was to "review and report on all medical aspects of the treatment provided to the Princess of Wales". This is covered in Part 2.

- although the toxicologist received samples in sealed police bags there do not appear to have been any associated seal reference numbers on the bags
- no source was shown on the blood sample label or in the post-mortem report
- the pathologist's official post-mortem report was undated
- there was a sample – vitreous humour – later recorded as taken, that did not appear in the official Exhibits report written up during the post-mortem
- there were 8 samples of major organs taken for which no records were made by the pathologist, or anyone else
- there are no photos of any of the sample bottles or labels.

The result of these serious deficiencies means that in the case of Princess Diana the chain of custody that is required to protect the integrity of the samples is virtually non-existent – I believe worse than that of Henri Paul's.[a]

Robert Chapman is a very experienced forensic pathologist. So, why is it that he conducted this post-mortem of Princess Diana – possibly the most significant of his career – in such a careless fashion?

Why is it that again we are studying a subject about which the 2008 inquest jury heard only paltry levels of evidence?

The documentary evidence reproduced in this chapter and in the UK Post-Mortems chapter of *The Documents* book reveals 21 important documents that were in the hands of Scott Baker, but withheld from the eyes of his jury.

What post-mortem related documentary evidence did the jury get to see? Virtually nothing.

The closest the jury got to it was the two pages of John Burton's notes about the events of that day – reproduced earlier in this book.

When it came to witness evidence, the only people the jury got to hear from were Robert Chapman, Jeffrey Rees and Philip Stoneham.

Both Chapman and Rees have lied in their inquest evidence and Stoneham was evasive, at best.

Nothing from John Burton[b], Michael Burgess, Robert Thompson, Keith Brown, Harry Brown, Nigel Munns, Richard Wall, Dennis Sharp, Michael Walker, Neal Williams and Mark Taylor – no statements read out and no cross-examination from any of these people.

Possibly the most significant question here is: Why was the inquest jury prevented from seeing the post-mortem and toxicology reports of the people whose deaths they were supposed to be investigating – Princess Diana and Dodi Fayed?

---

[a] The chain of custody for Henri Paul is addressed in Part 3.
[b] Burton's notes – mentioned above – were available to the jury but there was no witness evidence from him.

What is the point in holding a post-mortem – which is to determine cause of death – if the inquest jury – which is also determining cause of death – are not allowed to view the reports from it?

Why was all this evidence withheld?

It appears to be because the evidence reveals information Baker did not want the jury to be aware of – particularly the discovery that Princess Diana's samples were tampered with.

A close analysis of all the available evidence – most of which the jury had no access to – highlights several key factors that indicate the toxicology testing was carried out on samples that did not come from the body of Princess Diana:

-   the body had been embalmed, but there was no embalming fluid detected in the tested samples
-   Diana had consumed alcohol, but there was no alcohol in the tested samples
-   Chapman's apparent lies denying the presence of alcohol in the stomach[a]
-   there was no vitreous humour sample taken during the post-mortem, yet a vitreous humour sample was tested
-   the Property Register reveals that the samples were "retained by Dr Chapman" with no record of them going to the toxicologist
-   the Biological Samples report reveals that in late 2006 Operation Paget had the samples from Diana[b]
-   the stomach contents sample recorded in the Biological Samples report is twice the size of the sample officially tested by the toxicologist
-   the sample labels received by Paterson – for both blood and liver – read differently to the descriptions in the post-mortem documentation
-   the stomach contents sample label received by Allan reads differently to the sample received by Paterson
-   there are no police seal numbers or unique reference numbers quoted in the official post-mortem and toxicology reports, but there were seal numbers in the police Property Register and also quoted on the samples officially taken by the police
-   the samples held at the Imperial College have never been subjected to DNA testing.

---

[a] Chapman appears to have stated in 2005 that there was no alcohol to support the negative alcohol result from the phony toxicology test – see earlier section on Alcohol.
[b] There is no evidence of the tested samples being removed from the Imperial College. This perception is supported by the 2004 letter from Paget to Susan Paterson – reproduced earlier.

Evidence early in this chapter revealed that a post-mortem was not required, but it may be that if a post-mortem had not been held then people would have asked why it wasn't.[a]

For whatever reason, the post-mortems were held, but then in the case of Diana, the samples were switched ahead of toxicological testing.

So, the public perception is that the post-mortem samples were tested and the results were made public in the Paget Report[b] and at the inquest[c].

There are two main problems with this public perception:

1) the toxicology results were based on tested samples that came from a body other than Princess Diana's

2) the full results were not provided – neither the Paget Report nor the inquest revealed that there was no evidence of embalming fluid in the tested samples.

We end up with a situation where no one can accuse the authorities of not doing a post-mortem – in other words, "no stone left unturned"[d] – but any information from the post-mortem has been effectively neutralised because:

a) the jury investigating the death were not allowed to see the post-mortem report

b) the jury were not allowed to see the toxicology report

c) the toxicology report was dealing with samples from another body anyway.

Diana's samples may have been switched out of knowledge or fear of what the samples might have revealed – possible pregnancy or possibly a harmful substance administered in the ambulance.

The inquest jury was left with the false impression that the samples were completely contaminated because the embalming was thorough.

The toxicology report reveals that the samples were devoid of embalming fluid – but the jury did not hear that.

There are two actions that should be carried out:

1) The samples held by Operation Paget and LGC Forensics should be subjected to extensive toxicological testing.

2) The samples held at the Imperial College should be subjected to DNA testing.[e]

---

[a] It was shown early in the chapter that both Burton and Burgess pretended in their early evidence that a post-mortem was required, but backed away from this later.

[b] The Paget Report covered Paterson's toxicology results – including selective excerpts from her report – on pages 642-3.

[c] The results were briefly addressed during the cross-examination of Robert Chapman on 26 November 2007: Dodi at 12.4 and Diana at 23.1.

[d] These volumes have revealed that there were actually many stones left unturned, but we are talking about the public perception here.

[e] It would appear to be no coincidence that when the authorities wanted to conduct a DNA test to verify the blood on the Mercedes carpet, they did it with RC/1 – the hair

Only then can the truth of what has occurred be more fully established.

---

sample retained by the police – and did not use the samples that were held at the Imperial College. I suggest that had they used any of the Imperial College samples, there would have been no match – but instead many red faces.

6   Conclusion

Within 25 hours of Princess Diana's official time of death, her body had undergone two post-mortems – France and the UK – and two embalmings – France and the UK.

This knowledge raises the inevitable question: If this crash was just the accident that the police from France and the UK have both concluded it was, then Princess Diana died as a passenger in a traffic accident.

Why then was she subjected to two post-mortems and two embalmings in such a short period?

Some might argue that the issues addressed in this volume are not central to the case.

The inquest was supposed to be the official investigation into the deaths of Princess Diana and Dodi Fayed.

What can be more central to the investigation of a person's death, than the post-mortem report and the associated toxicology report?

What can be more central than a quick autopsy – that has been falsely made out to be an external examination – conducted just 1½ hours after the official time of death?

What can be more central than an early embalming conducted ahead of the official post-mortem?

What can be more central than a sudden change of status that occurs at the very point of a person's death?

This volume has again revealed an immense cover-up of the evidence on all of these central issues – a cover-up that started on 31 August 1997 and has continued right through to the close of the inquest in April 2008.

It has been shown that events moved very quickly after the death of Princess Diana.

It has also been shown that those critical events were being driven from the residence of Queen Elizabeth, who was holidaying at Balmoral, in the north of Scotland.

Post-death events were controlled directly by the royals – both family and household.

The question is: Why?

This volume has raised questions that are crying out for answers:

Why did Dr Bruno Riou indicate that the death of Diana was suspicious when he completed the death certificate?

Why was Lecomte's examination of Diana portrayed as being external, when the evidence indicates it was a post-mortem where samples were taken?

Why was an embalming ordered from the UK very soon after Diana's death?

Why was the most successful part of the French embalming the removal of urine from Diana's bladder?

Why did the Queen reinstate Princess Diana as a member of the royal family immediately following her death?

Why did the royal coroner – John Burton – take illegal jurisdiction over Diana's body following its arrival in the UK?

Why did the post-mortem samples sent to the Imperial College for toxicology testing come from a body other than Princess Diana's?

These are all questions that should have been answered by the London inquest into the deaths of Princess Diana and Dodi Fayed.

The stunning truth – revealed in this volume – is that the inquest jury were provided with so little evidence on these issues, that they would not have even been in a position to ask the questions, let alone receive any answers.

Appendix 1

Freedom of Information Article

The following article can be found on the FOIA website:
www.foiacentre.com/news-diana-060724.html

FOIA Centre

News

Homepage | News | Contacts

FOIA and "open-access" laws

UK bodies subject to FOIA

FOIA around the world

How we can help

Prices

Notes to prices

How to place your order

Order form

Royal coroner resigns Diana inquest after FOIA revelation shows he had no jurisdiction

24.07.06 Look out for updates on this subject

Coroner Michael Burgess resigned from the inquest into the death of Diana, princess of Wales, hours after the government admitted that he had no jurisdiction.

He was carrying out the inquest in his role as "coroner for the Queen's household" after his predecessor, the late Dr John Burton, had assumed responsibility for the Diana inquest on a false basis.

The department for constitutional affairs (DCA) finally admitted, following a request under the freedom of information act (FOIA) for material relating to the choice of coroner, that Burton made a mistake when he assumed this responsibility.

The false claim of jurisdiction for the coroner for the Queen's household is crucial because it enables, exceptionally, the jury to be made up entirely of royal staff members. The prospect of such a jury raised questions about the independence of the inquest.

Mystery; royal coroner conduct Diana inquest on false basis

The official reason given for Burgess's resignation on Friday was his "heavy and constant" workload as the coroner for Surrey.

In his role as Surrey coroner, Burgess was conducting a separate inquest into the death of Dodi Al Fayed, who was buried in his district after dying with Diana in the infamous road crash in Paris in 1997. Burgess also resigned from conducting that inquest on Friday.

He is understood to have complained privately about pressure over his conduct of the two inquests from royal aides, the government and Dodi's father, Mohamed.

Some six months after receiving the FOIA request, and after granting itself ten extensions to the 20-day statutory limit to supply the material sought, the DCA finally released its reply on Friday making the admission that the royal coroner was carrying out the Diana inquest on a false basis.

Hours later, Burgess announced his resignation from both inquests.

In its reply, the DCA's head of current coroner policy, Judith Bernstein, says: "The body of Diana, Princess of Wales, was repatriated in the course of the early evening of August 31, 1997 to RAF Northolt in the district of the then West London coroner, the late Dr John Burton.

"Dr Burton arranged for a post-mortem examin-ation to be held at the public mortuary within his West London district at Fulham. The body of Diana, Princess of Wales, was taken after the post-mortem examination to lie in the Chapel Royal, St James's Palace within the jurisdiction of the coroner for the Queen's household.

"At that time, Dr Burton understood the body of Diana, Princess of Wales, would be buried in Windsor Castle or its grounds which are also part of the district for the coroner of the Queen's household.

"However, there is no evidence to support Dr Burton's understanding, and as Dr Burton is no longer alive, there is no way of clarifying his reasoning on this point. Dr Burton therefore transferred jurisdiction to himself... in his capacity as coroner of the Queen's household."

Bernstein adds that Burton, who died in 2004, retired as West London coroner in 2000, but remained as royal coroner until 2002. Burgess, who was already Surrey coroner, took over the role as royal coroner.

The DCA also released a home office circular to coroners from 1983, which sets out the procedure that determines which coroner has jurisdiction for a British citizen who dies a violent, unnatural or sudden death abroad.

It makes clear that the choice of coroner depends on either the body's point of entry into the UK or where it "lies".

This suggests that Burton, or his successor, as coroner for the district containing RAF Northolt had a duty to carry out the Diana inquest. In the current circumstances, where this has not happened, the inquest should be carried out by the coroner whose district includes the Althorp estate, where Diana was buried.

The established procedure has flexibility to allow, for example, an inquest to be carried out in the district where the body lies, instead of the point of entry into the UK, to enable it be conducted near where the relatives live. Alternatively, if more than one Briton has died in the same incident, a joint inquest can be carried out in the district where the bodies entered the UK.

Newspapers often wrongly assume that the royal coroner has responsibility because Diana was a member of the royal family. This is wrong because, first, she was no longer a member of the royal family at the time of her death and, second, even if she were, it is not in itself a relevant factor in determining which coroner has jurisdiction.

The royal coroner might, however, have respons-ibility to conduct an inquest where a body lies in his "district", such as in Windsor Castle, which would generally apply to members of the royal family.

Burgess opened the Diana and Dodi inquests in 2004 and adjourned them to a date to be fixed.

Friday's resignation of Burgess from those inq-uests comes a month before he was due to receive the report of an investigation by the metropolitan police into Diana's death.

The inquest was expected to be held next year, but may be further delayed as a replacement coroner is found.

Burgess has suggested that the lord chancellor appoint a "senior judicial figure", such as a retired high court judge, to become his deputy in order to conduct the inquests, although this would also not be in line with the established procedure for selecting a coroner.

Another version of this article first appeared in the Daily Express.

Figure 29

Evidence, Maps, Diagrams & Photos

Bibliography

Books

Andersen, C., (1998). *The Day Diana Died.* New York: William Morrow & Co Inc.

Blair, T., (2010), *A Journey: My Political Life*, USA, Alfred A. Knopf

Bryant, Clifton, (2003), *Handbook of Death and Dying*, Sage, Vol. 1

Burrell, P., (2003), *A Royal Duty*, Australia: Penguin Books

Campbell, A., (2007), *The Blair Years*, London, UK: Hutchinson

————, (2011), *The Alastair Campbell Diaries: Volume 2: Power and the People: 1997-1999*, Hutchinson

Delorm, R., Fox, B., & Taylor, N. (1998). *Diana & Dodi: A Love Story.* Los Angeles, USA: Tallfellow Press.

Junor, P., (1998), *Charles: Victim or Villain?*, HarperCollins

Holden, A., (1998), *Charles at Fifty*, Random House

Morgan, J., (2007), *Cover-up of a Royal Murder: Hundreds of Errors in the Paget Report*, USA: Amazon

————, (2009), *Diana Inquest: The Untold Story*, USA, Amazon

————, (2009), *Diana Inquest: How & Why Did Diana Die?*, USA, Amazon

————, (2010), *Diana Inquest: The French Cover-Up*, UK, Lightning Source

————, Editor, (2010), *Diana Inquest: The Documents the Jury Never Saw*, UK, Lightning Source

Morton, A., (1997), *Diana: Her True Story – In Her Own Words*, Australia: Harper Collins

Sancton, T., & MacLeod, S. (1998). Death of a Princess: An Investigation. London, UK: Weidenfeld & Nicolson

Seward, I., (2000), *The Queen & Di*, HarperCollins

Wharfe, K., with Jobson, R., (2002), *Diana: Closely Guarded Secret*, London, UK, Michael O'Mara Books Limited

Websites

BBC News · http://news.bbc.co.uk

British Monarchy · www.royal.gov.uk

Coroners Eastern District of London · www.walthamforest.gov.uk

Conseil de la Concurrence · www.afif.asso.fr/francais/conseils

Embalming · www.embalming.net

Federal Climate Complex: Temperatures
http://www7.ncdc.noaa.gov/CDO/cdodata.cmd

Freedom of Information — www.foiacentre.com

Funeral Ideas.com — http://funeralideas.com

Grave Matters — http://grave-matters.blogspot.com

Green Funeral and Burial — www.greenyour.com

Greensprings Natural Cemetery Preserve — http://naturalburial.org

Home Funeral.info — http://homefuneral.info/archives/6

Judiciary of England and Wales — www.judiciary.gov.uk

Last Rights of Central Pennsylvania — www.lastrights.info/faq.htm

Measurement Conversion Table — www.recipedelights.com

The Metric Kitchen — www.jsward.com/cooking/conversion

MPS — www.met.police.uk

MPS Paget Report — www.met.police.uk/news/operation_paget_report.htm

Neyagawa City Funerals — www.city.neyagawa.osaka.jp/sankakakugo.htm

Official Inquest — www.scottbaker-inquests.gov.uk

Optimum Weight Calculations — www.healthchecksystems.com

Shalom Funeral Service — www.shalomfuneral.com

Shipman Inquiry — www.the-shipman-inquiry.org.uk

Sunrise and Sunset Times — www.timeanddate.com

White Pages Paris — www.pagesjaunes.fr/pagesblanches

Wikipedia — http://en.wikipedia.org/wiki/

Newspapers & Periodicals

Alderson, Andrew, Coroner Seeks New Law to Forgo Diana Inquest, *Daily Telegraph*, April 1 2001

Antonowicz, Anton, Home to a Nation in Mourning: Charles Brings Diana Back, *The Mirror*, 1 September 1997

Associated Press, Nightmare Ending to a British Fairy Tale Death of a Princess, *Cincinnati Post*, 1 September 1997

The British Funeral Service, *Private Client Adviser Magazine*, Volume 5 Issue 2, January 2000

Hunt, Bill, Iain West – Obituary, *The Independent*, 28 July 2001

Johnson, Christy, Custer-Glenn Funeral Home Gives Green Option, *The-Daily-Record.com*, 23 November 2008

Jury, Louise, The Tragedy: Prince Paid His Last Respects ... Then the Coffin Lid Was Closed, *The Independent*, 1 September 1997

Obituary: John David Keith Burton, *British Medical Journal*, Volume 331, Number 7512, 4 August 2005

Palmer, Richard, Diana is Still Loved ... But Her Palace Postcards are Banned, *Daily Express*, May 8 2007

Royal Coroner Resigns Diana Inquest After FOIA Revelation Shows He Had No Jurisdiction, *FOIA Centre News*, 24 July 2006

Press Releases

Buckingham Palace, Divorce: Status and Role of the Princess of Wales, PR Newswire Europe Ltd, 28 August 1996

SCI Announces the Appointment of Jerald L. Pullins as Executive Vice-President International, PR Newswire, 14 August 1997

Two Firsts for LGC Forensics, 11 December 2006, www.lgc.co.uk/news

Media Documentaries, Interviews and Transcripts

Channel 5, *Diana: The Night She Died,* Psychology News, 2003

History Channel, *Princess Diana*, A & E Television Networks, 2004

Expert Reports & Articles

Hawley, Dr Dean, *Death by Strangulation*, www.markwynn.com

Jones, Dr Richard, & Shepherd, Professor Richard, *The Role of the Forensic Pathologist*, Victorian Institute of Forensic Medicine, June 2010

Salib, Emad & Tadros, George, *Brain Weight in Suicide: An Exploratory Study, British Journal of Psychiatry*, 2000, No. 177, pp257-261

Whitwell, Prof Helen, *Forensic Pathology*, The Royal College of Pathologists, www.rcpath.org

Witelson, S.F., Beresh, H. & Kigar, D.L., *Intelligence and Brain Size in 100 Post-Mortem Brains: Sex, Lateralization and Age Factors, Guarantors of Brain,* Oxford Journals, 2006, No. 129, pp386-398

Documents from Operation Paget Investigation File

Allan, Alexander, Witness Statement, 12 December 2006

Amarger, Huguette, Witness Statement, 8 March 2005

Burgess, Michael, Witness Statement, 16 August 2004

Burton, John, Witness Statement, 16 June 2004

————, Witness Statement, 29 August 2004

Chapman, Robert & Wall, Richard, Post Mortem Exhibits Report: The Princess of Wales, 31 August 1997

————, Post Mortem Exhibits Report: Mr Emad El-Din Mohamed Abdel Moneim Al Fayed, 31 August 1997

Chapman, Robert, Witness Statement, 5 September 1997

————, Witness Statement, 10 September 1997

————, Witness Statement, 24 February 2005

Coujard, Maud, Witness Statement, 15 November 2006

Deguisne, René, Witness Statement, 9 May 2005
Easton, Philip, Witness Statement, 19 July 2005
———, Witness Statement, 24 October 2005
———, Witness Statement, 14 November 2005
Flecha de Lima, Lucia, Witness Statement, 1 September 2004
Green, David, Witness Statement, 13 July 2004
———, Witness Statement, 17 September 2004
Green, Roy, Witness Statement, 23 November 2006
Jauze, Gérard, Witness Statement, 21 March 2006
Jay, Michael, Witness Statement, 13 December 2005
Launay, Patrick, Witness Statement, 21 March 2006
Lecomte, Prof Dominique, Witness Statement, Paris, 9 March 2005
Leverton, Clive, Witness Statement, 13 July 2004
Leverton, Keith, Witness Statement, 27 October 2004
Macnamara, John, Witness Statement, 3 July 2006
Messinger, Michael, Witness Statement, 21 March 2006
Mather, Anthony, Witness Statement, 23 August 2005
Monceau, Jean, Email to Philip Easton, 19 September 2005
———, Witness Statement, 18 October 2005
Monteil, Martine, Email Reply sent to DS Easton, 19 July 2005
———, Witness Statement, 15 November 2006
Moss, Keith, Witness Statement, 22 October 2004
Mulès, Jean-Claude, Witness Statement, 19 July 2006
Paterson, Susan, Witness Statement: Female Lab No: 676/97, 28 September 2004
———, Witness Statement: Male Lab No: 677/97, 28 September 2004
———, Notes from Telephone Conversation with Royal London Hospital, 11 July 2006
Pavie, Alain, Witness Statement, 9 March 2005
Puxley, Alan, Witness Statement, 16 June 2004
Plumet, Jean-Claude, Witness Statement, 4 November 2005
Riou, Bruno, Witness Statement, 7 March 2006
Shepherd, Richard, Report for Operation Paget, 16 July 2007
Smith, Toby, Witness Statement, 26 June 2006
Steiner, Eva, Witness Statement, 29 September 2006
Tebbutt, Colin, Witness Statement, 5 July 2004
Thompson, Robert, Record of Statement Given Orally to Stuart Benson on 16 May 2001
———, Affidavit, 13 June 2001
———, Witness Statement, 9 November 2004

Wall, Richard, Witness Statement, 19 October 2004
Wheeler, Peter, Witness Statement, 28 June 2006
Williams, Neal, Witness Statement, 1 September 1997

Documents from French Investigation Files

Lecomte, Dominique, Supplementary Expert's Report, 6 November 1997
————, Witness Statement, D1155, Rogatory Commission issued by Judge Bellancourt, Court of Versailles, 31 May 2006
Stéphan, Hervé, Ruling to Commission an Expert, Paris Regional Court, PPD No 972453009, 20 October 1997

Correspondence

Klein, Frank, Email to John Morgan, 13 December 2010
————, Email to John Morgan, 15 December 2010
Macnamara, John, Email to John Morgan, 19 November 2010

Reference Works

Medical Dictionary on MedTerms website: www.medterms.com
Merriam-Webster: www.mereriam-webster.com
Soanes, C., & Hawker, S., (2005), Editors, *Compact Oxford English Dictionary of Current English*, UK, Oxford University Press

Legislation

UK: Coroners Act 1988

Index

E

M

N

O

S

U

V

Author Information

John Morgan was born in Rotorua, New Zealand in 1957, and has lived in Australia for the last 23 years. He and his wife currently reside in Redcliffe, on the shores of Moreton Bay, near Brisbane.

John is an investigative writer with a diploma in journalism from the Australian College of Journalism. He completed his first book titled *Flying Free* in 2005 – about life inside a fundamentalist cult. Information regarding that book can be viewed on the internet at: www.flyingfree.zoomshare.com

In his earlier life John was an accountant for various organisations in Auckland and Sydney. Later during the 1990s, he became a retailer operating a shop on Sydney's northern beaches. Since the 1980s John travelled widely throughout the Pacific, Asia and the Middle East.

He retired in 2003 at the age of 46, after being diagnosed with a severe neurological illness called multiple system atrophy. After a year or two of coming to terms with that devastating turn of events, he eventually found that the forced retirement created an opportunity to fulfil a lifelong ambition to write.

Following the death of Diana, Princess of Wales in 1997, John developed an interest in the events that had led to the Paris crash. Since 2005 he carried out extensive full-time research into those events and studied the official British police report after it was published in late 2006. John subsequently completed a book on that subject in September 2007 – it was titled *Cover-up of a Royal Murder: Hundreds of Errors in the Paget Report.*

Throughout 2008 John Morgan continued his investigations into the crash and closely followed the British inquest into the deaths of Princess Diana and Dodi Fayed. That research resulted in the publishing of the initial volume of work on the inquest entitled *Diana Inquest: The Untold Story* – Part 1: *The Final Journey.* Six months later, during 2009, that work was followed up with the second volume *Diana Inquest: How & Why Did Diana Die?* The third volume, entitled *Diana Inquest; The French Cover-Up* was published early in 2010.

Those books have now been added to with this current fourth volume. John can be contacted at: shining.bright@optusnet.com.au

Notes

[1] Alastair Campbell, The Blair Years: The Alastair Campbell Diaries, 2007, page 232

[2] Prof Bruno Riou, Witness Statement, 7 March 2006, page 2

[3] The Operation Paget Inquiry Report into the Allegation of Conspiracy to Murder Diana, Princess of Wales and Emad El-Din Mohamed Abdel Moneim Fayed, December 14 2006, page 535

[4] Maud Coujard, Witness Statement, 15 November 2006, page 4

[5] Martine Monteil, Witness Statement, 15 November 2006, reproduced in Diana Inquest: The Documents the Jury Never Saw, 2010, p58 (UK Edition)

[6] Martine Monteil, Witness Statement, 15 November 2006, reproduced in Diana Inquest: The Documents the Jury Never Saw, 2010, p57 (UK Edition)

[7] Dominique Lecomte, Witness Statement, Operation Paget, Paris, 9 March 2005, pages 1 to 3

[8] Dominique Lecomte, Witness Statement, 31 May 2006, reproduced in Diana Inquest: The Documents the Jury Never Saw, 2010, p151 (UK Edition)

[9] Eva Steiner, Witness Statement, 29 September 2006, reproduced in Diana Inquest: The Documents the Jury Never Saw, 2010, p466 (UK Edition)

[10] Robert Chapman, Witness Statement, 24 February 2005, reproduced in Diana Inquest: The Documents the Jury Never Saw, 2010, p584 (UK Edition)

[11] Alain Pavie, Witness Statement, 9 March 2005, reproduced in Diana Inquest: The Documents the Jury Never Saw, 2010, p389 (UK Edition)

[12] Jean Monceau, Witness Statement, 18 October 2005, page 12

[13] Prof Bruno Riou, Witness Statement, 7 March 2006, page 3

[14] Dr Peter Wheeler, Witness Statement, 28 June 2006, page 1

[15] Herve Stephan, Ruling to Commission an Expert, Paris Regional Court, PPD No 972453009, 20 October 1997

[16] Dominique Lecomte, Supplementary Expert's Report, 6 November 1997, pages 1 and 2

[17] Dr Richard Shepherd, Operation Paget, 16 July 2007. Although this document is dated in July 2007 – seven months after the conclusion of Operation Paget – Shepherd described work he conducted for Operation Paget on the 6th and 8th of December 2006, just a week prior to the publication of the Paget Report on 14 December 2006.

[18] Paul Burrell, A Royal Duty, 2003, pages 291-2

[19] The Operation Paget Inquiry Report into the Allegation of Conspiracy to Murder Diana, Princess of Wales and Emad El-Din Mohamed Abdel Moneim Fayed, December 14 2006, page 545

[20] Michael Messinger, Witness Statement, 21 March 2006, page 1

[21] Jean-Claude Mulès, Paget Description of Witness Statement, 19 July 2006, page 3

[22] Martine Monteil, Email Reply sent to DS Easton (in response to undated letter from "Lord Stevens of Kirkwhelpington"), 19 July 2005

[23] Martine Monteil, Witness Statement, 15 November 2006, page 4

[24] Dr Richard Shepherd, Operation Paget, 16 July 2007

[25] 15 Nov 07: 2.2

[26] Alain Pavie, Witness Statement, 9 March 2005, reproduced in Diana Inquest: The Documents the Jury Never Saw, 2010, p387 (UK Edition)

[27] Prof Bruno Riou, Witness Statement, 7 March 2006, page 3

[28] Sunrise and Sunset for France – Paris – August 1997, www.timeanddate.com

[29] Federal Climate Complex: Global Surface Summary of Day Data: Paris – Orly – Station No:071490, Maximum Temperature 31 August 1997, NNDC Climate Data Online, NOAA Satellite and Information Service, http://www7.ncdc.noaa.gov/CDO/cdodata.cmd

[30] Colin Tebbutt, Witness Statement, 5 July 2004, reproduced in Diana Inquest: The Documents the Jury Never Saw, 2010, pp439-441 (UK Edition)

[31] Alan Puxley, Witness Statement, 16 June 2004, reproduced in Diana Inquest: The Documents the Jury Never Saw, 2010, p460 (UK Edition)

[32] The Operation Paget Inquiry Report into the Allegation of Conspiracy to Murder Diana, Princess of Wales and Emad El-Din Mohamed Abdel Moneim Fayed, December 14 2006, page 539

[33] Colin Tebbutt, Witness Statement, 5 July 2004, reproduced in Diana Inquest: The Documents the Jury Never Saw, 2010, p440 (UK Edition)

[34] Scott Baker: 31 Mar 08: 9.19.

[35] 20 Nov 07:89.18.

[36] Jean Monceau, Witness Statement, 18 October 2005, pages 2 to 4

[37] Patrick Launay, Witness Statement, 21 March 2006, reproduced in Diana Inquest: The Documents the Jury Never Saw, 2010, pp510-513 (UK Edition)

[38] Jean-Claude Plumet, Witness Statement, 4 November 2005, reproduced in Diana Inquest: The Documents the Jury Never Saw, 2010, pp468-471 (UK Edition)

[39] Gérard Jauze, Witness Statement, 21 March 2006, reproduced in Diana Inquest: The Documents the Jury Never Saw, 2010, pp476-478,485 (UK Edition)

[40] René Deguisne, Witness Statement, 9 May 2005, reproduced in Diana Inquest: The Documents the Jury Never Saw, 2010, p451 (UK Edition)

[41] Jean-Claude Plumet, Witness Statement, 4 November 2005, reproduced in Diana Inquest: The Documents the Jury Never Saw, 2010, p471 (UK Edition)

[42] Martine Monteil, Email Reply sent to DS Easton (in response to undated letter from "Lord Stevens of Kirkwhelpington"), 19 July 2005, page 2

[43] www.lastrights.info/faq.htm

[44] Christy Johnson, Custer-Glenn Funeral Home Gives Green Option, The-Daily-Record.com, 23 November 2008

[45] Arrange for a Green Funeral and Burial

[46] General Price List: Burial Package Options, www.shalomfuneral.com

[47] www.city.neyagawa.osaka.jp/sankakakugo.htm

[48] Personal Touches Reflect Personalities, : http://homefuneral.info/archives/6

[49] http://en.wikipedia.org/wiki/Natural_burial

[50] http://naturalburial.org

[51] Mark Harris, Finding an Eco-Friendly Funeral Director, Grave Matters, http://grave-matters.blogspot.com

[52] The Home Funeral, http://funeralideas.com

[53] Jean Monceau, Witness Statement, 18 October 2005, reproduced in Diana Inquest: The Documents the Jury Never Saw, 2010, p410 (UK Edition)

[54] Jean Monceau, Witness Statement, 18 October 2005, pages 4 to 6, 8 to 9

[55] Martine Monteil, Witness Statement, 15 November 2006, pages 4,6

[56] Jean-Claude Plumet, Witness Statement, 4 November 2005, page 6

[57] Gérard Jauze, Witness Statement, 21 March 2006, page 7

[58] Jean Monceau, Witness Statement, 18 October 2005, pages 6,8

[59] Keith Moss, Witness Statement, 22 October 2004, reproduced in Diana Inquest: The Documents the Jury Never Saw, 2010, pp652-6 (UK Edition)

[60] Keith Moss, Witness Statement, 22 October 2004, reproduced in Diana Inquest: The Documents the Jury Never Saw, 2010, p647 (UK Edition)

[61] Keith Moss, Witness Statement, 22 October 2004, reproduced in Diana Inquest: The Documents the Jury Never Saw, 2010, p654 (UK Edition)

[62] Colin Tebbutt, Witness Statement, 5 July 2004, reproduced in Diana Inquest: The Documents the Jury Never Saw, 2010, p441 (UK Edition)

[63] At 5.4.

[64] Colin Tebbutt, Witness Statement, 5 July 2004, pages 7 to 9

[65] The Operation Paget Inquiry Report into the Allegation of Conspiracy to Murder Diana, Princess of Wales and Emad El-Din Mohamed Abdel Moneim Fayed, December 14 2006, page 544

[66] René Deguisne, Witness Statement, 9 May 2005, reproduced in Diana Inquest: The Documents the Jury Never Saw, 2010, p451 (UK Edition)

[67] René Deguisne, Witness Statement, 9 May 2005, reproduced in Diana Inquest: The Documents the Jury Never Saw, 2010, p451 (UK Edition)

[68] Gérard Jauze, Witness Statement, 21 March 2006, page 2

[69] Jean-Claude Plumet, Witness Statement, 4 November 2005, page 3

[70] Patrick Launay, Witness Statement, 21 March 2006, page 3

[71] René Deguisne, Witness Statement, 9 May 2005, reproduced in Diana Inquest: The Documents the Jury Never Saw, 2010, p450 (UK Edition)

[72] Jean Monceau, Witness Statement, 18 October 2005, reproduced in Diana Inquest: The Documents the Jury Never Saw, 2010, p408 (UK Edition)

[73] Martine Monteil, Email Reply sent to DS Easton (in response to undated letter from "Lord Stevens of Kirkwhelpington"), 19 July 2005, reproduced in Diana Inquest: The Documents the Jury Never Saw, 2010, p54 (UK Edition)

[74] René Deguisne, Witness Statement, 9 May 2005, reproduced in Diana Inquest: The Documents the Jury Never Saw, 2010, pp451,452 (UK Edition)

[75] Jean Monceau, Witness Statement, 18 October 2005, reproduced in Diana Inquest: The Documents the Jury Never Saw, 2010, p411 (UK Edition)

[76] Jean Monceau, Witness Statement, 18 October 2005, reproduced in Diana Inquest: The Documents the Jury Never Saw, 2010, p413 (UK Edition)

[77] Huguette Amarger, Witness Statement, 8 March 2005, pages 3 to 4

[78] Philip Easton, Witness Statement, 19 July 2005, page 1

[79] Philip Easton, Witness Statement, 14 November 2005, page 1

[80] Philip Easton, Witness Statement, 14 November 2005, page 2

[81] Robert Chapman, Witness Statement – Internal Examination, 10 September 1997, pages 11-14

[82] Dr Susan Paterson, Witness Statement, 28 September 2004, reproduced in Diana Inquest: The Documents the Jury Never Saw, 2010, pp615-6 (UK Edition)

[83] Cavity Embalming, www.embalming.net

[84] The Operation Paget Inquiry Report into the Allegation of Conspiracy to Murder Diana, Princess of Wales and Emad El-Din Mohamed Abdel Moneim Fayed, December 14 2006, page 554

[85] Jean Monceau, Witness Statement, 18 October 2005, page 11

[86] David Green, Witness Statement, 13 July 2004, reproduced in Diana Inquest: The Documents the Jury Never Saw, 2010, pp503-4 (UK Edition)

[87] David Green, Witness Statement, 17 September 2004, page 1

[88] Robert Chapman, Witness Statement, 24 February 2005, pages 5,6

[89] Robert Thompson, Affidavit, 13 June 2001, page 3

[90] Robert Thompson, Witness Statement, 9 November 2004, page 6

[91] Dr Susan Paterson, Witness Statement, 28 September 2004, page 2

[92] www.embalming.net under "Arterial Embalming", page 2

[93] Jean Monceau, Witness Statement, 18 October 2005, page 11

[94] Jean Monceau, Witness Statement, 18 October 2005, page 11

[95] Jean Monceau, Witness Statement, 18 October 2005, reproduced in Diana Inquest: The Documents the Jury Never Saw, 2010, p413 (UK Edition)

[96] Jean Monceau, Witness Statement, 18 October 2005, reproduced in Diana Inquest: The Documents the Jury Never Saw, 2010, pp416-7 (UK Edition)

[97] Jean Monceau, Witness Statement, 18 October 2005, reproduced in Diana Inquest: The Documents the Jury Never Saw, 2010, p411 (UK Edition)

[98] Colin Tebbutt, Witness Statement, 5 July 2004, reproduced in Diana Inquest: The Documents the Jury Never Saw, 2010, p442 (UK Edition)

[99] Keith Moss, Witness Statement, 22 October 2004, reproduced in Diana Inquest: The Documents the Jury Never Saw, 2010, p653 (UK Edition)

[100] Keith Moss, Witness Statement, 22 October 2004, reproduced in Diana Inquest: The Documents the Jury Never Saw, 2010, pp655-6 (UK Edition)

[101] Clive Leverton, Witness Statement, 13 July 2004, pages 4 to 5

[102] Patrick Launay, Witness Statement, 21 March 2006, page 7

[103] Jean-Claude Plumet, Witness Statement, 4 November 2005, reproduced in Diana Inquest: The Documents the Jury Never Saw, 2010, p473 (UK Edition)

[104] Gérard Jauze, Witness Statement, 21 March 2006, page 6

[105] Embalming, under Modern Practices, Wikipedia, page 4

[106] 26 Nov 07: 70.15

[107] Colin Tebbutt, Witness Statement, 5 July 2004, reproduced in Diana Inquest: The Documents the Jury Never Saw, 2010, p437 (UK Edition)

[108] 20 Nov 07: 60.16.

[109] 20 Nov 07: 60.14.

[110] 20 Nov 07: 25.20.

[111] 20 Nov 07: 87.22.

[112] Jean-Claude Plumet, Witness Statement, 4 November 2005, reproduced in Diana Inquest: The Documents the Jury Never Saw, 2010, pp470-5 (UK Edition)

[113] Jean-Claude Plumet, Witness Statement, 4 November 2005, reproduced in Diana Inquest: The Documents the Jury Never Saw, 2010, p472 (UK Edition)

[114] Gérard Jauze, Witness Statement, 21 March 2006, reproduced in Diana Inquest: The Documents the Jury Never Saw, 2010, p484 (UK Edition)

[115] Jean Monceau, Witness Statement, 18 October 2005, pages 7 to 9

[116] Jean Monceau, Witness Statement, 18 October 2005, pages 5 to 6, 8 to 9

[117] Jean Monceau, Witness Statement, 18 October 2005, page 12

[118] Jean-Claude Plumet, Witness Statement, 4 November 2005, page 6

[119] Jean-Claude Plumet, Witness Statement, 4 November 2005, page 1

[120] 20 Nov 07:45.2.

[121] Eva Steiner, Witness Statement, 29 September 2006, reproduced in Diana Inquest: The Documents the Jury Never Saw, 2010, pp463-6 (UK Edition)

[122] Included in email from Jean Monceau to Philip Easton (Paget), 19 September 2005, reproduced in Diana Inquest: The Documents the Jury Never Saw, 2010, pp421-3 (UK Edition)

[123] Maud Coujard, Witness Statement, 15 November 2006, reproduced in Diana Inquest: The Documents the Jury Never Saw, 2010, p51 (UK Edition)

[124] Martine Monteil, Witness Statement, 15 November 2006, pages 3 to 4

[125] Dominique Lecomte, Witness Statement, Operation Paget, Paris, 9 March 2005, page 2

[126] Gérard Jauze, Witness Statement, 21 March 2006, reproduced in Diana Inquest: The Documents the Jury Never Saw, 2010, pp481-2 (UK Edition)

[127] The Operation Paget Inquiry Report into the Allegation of Conspiracy to Murder Diana, Princess of Wales and Emad El-Din Mohamed Abdel Moneim Fayed, December 14 2006, page 544

[128] René Deguisne, Witness Statement, 9 May 2005, reproduced in Diana Inquest: The Documents the Jury Never Saw, 2010, p453 (UK Edition)

[129] Lucia Flecha de Lima, Witness Statement, 1 September 2004, reproduced in Diana Inquest: The Documents the Jury Never Saw, 2010, p34 (UK Edition)

[130] Quoted at the inquest by MPS lawyer, Richard Horwell: 21 Nov 07: 44.1

[131] Keith Moss, Witness Statement, 22 October 2004, reproduced in Diana Inquest: The Documents the Jury Never Saw, 2010, p650 (UK Edition)

[132] Patrick Launay, Witness Statement, 21 March 2006, reproduced in Diana Inquest: The Documents the Jury Never Saw, 2010, p512 (UK Edition)

[133] Jean Monceau, Witness Statement, 18 October 2005, reproduced in Diana Inquest: The Documents the Jury Never Saw, 2010, p416 (UK Edition)

[134] Jean Monceau, Witness Statement, 18 October 2005, reproduced in Diana Inquest: The Documents the Jury Never Saw, 2010, p419 (UK Edition)

[135] The full text of this email is included in Philip Easton, Witness Statement, 24 October 2005, reproduced in Diana Inquest: The Documents the Jury Never Saw, 2010, pp421-4 (UK Edition)

[136] Gérard Jauze, Witness Statement, 21 March 2006, reproduced in Diana Inquest: The Documents the Jury Never Saw, 2010, pp481-2 (UK Edition)

[137] Martine Monteil, Witness Statement, 15 November 2006, reproduced in Diana Inquest: The Documents the Jury Never Saw, 2010, p58 (UK Edition)

[138] 22 Nov 07: 90.14.

[139] Robert Chapman, Witness Statement, 24 February 2005, reproduced in Diana Inquest: The Documents the Jury Never Saw, 2010, p585 (UK Edition)

[140] Robert Thompson, Witness Statement, 9 November 2004, reproduced in Diana Inquest: The Documents the Jury Never Saw, 2010, p604 (UK Edition)

[141] David Green, Witness Statement, 13 July 2004, reproduced in Diana Inquest: The Documents the Jury Never Saw, 2010, p504 (UK Edition)

[142] David Green, Witness Statement, 17 September 2004, reproduced in Diana Inquest: The Documents the Jury Never Saw, 2010, p507 (UK Edition)

[143] John Burton, Witness Statement, 16 June 2004, reproduced in Diana Inquest: The Documents the Jury Never Saw, 2010, pp556-562 (UK Edition)

[144] Patrick Launay, Witness Statement, 21 March 2006, reproduced in Diana Inquest: The Documents the Jury Never Saw, 2010, p516 (UK Edition)

[145] Gérard Jauze, Witness Statement, 21 March 2006, reproduced in Diana Inquest: The Documents the Jury Never Saw, 2010, pp481-2 (UK Edition)

[146] Gérard Jauze, Witness Statement, 21 March 2006, reproduced in Diana Inquest: The Documents the Jury Never Saw, 2010, p476 (UK Edition)

[147] Michael Burgess, Witness Statement, 16 August 2004, reproduced in Diana Inquest: The Documents the Jury Never Saw, 2010, p534 (UK Edition)

[148] John Burton, Witness Statement, 16 June 2004, reproduced in Diana Inquest: The Documents the Jury Never Saw, 2010, p558 (UK Edition)

[149] Keith Leverton, Witness Statement, 27 October 2004, reproduced in Diana Inquest: The Documents the Jury Never Saw, 2010, pp499-500 (UK Edition)

[150] David Green, Witness Statement, 13 July 2004, reproduced in Diana Inquest: The Documents the Jury Never Saw, 2010, p504 (UK Edition)

[151] David Green, Witness Statement, 17 September 2004, reproduced in Diana Inquest: The Documents the Jury Never Saw, 2010, pp506-7 (UK Edition)

[152] Jean Monceau, Witness Statement, 18 October 2005, reproduced in Diana Inquest: The Documents the Jury Never Saw, 2010, p418 (UK Edition)

[153] René Deguisne, Witness Statement, 9 May 2005, reproduced in Diana Inquest: The Documents the Jury Never Saw, 2010, p453 (UK Edition)

[154] Jean-Claude Plumet, Witness Statement, 4 November 2005, reproduced in Diana Inquest: The Documents the Jury Never Saw, 2010, pp475 (UK Edition)

[155] Dominique Lecomte, Witness Statement, Operation Paget, Paris, 9 March 2005, reproduced in Diana Inquest: The Documents the Jury Never Saw, 2010, pp141 (UK Edition)

[156] The Operation Paget Inquiry Report into the Allegation of Conspiracy to Murder Diana, Princess of Wales and Emad El-Din Mohamed Abdel Moneim Fayed, December 14 2006, page 2

[157] Michael Jay, Witness Statement, 13 December 2005, reproduced in Diana Inquest: The Documents the Jury Never Saw, 2010, p639 (UK Edition)

[158] Keith Moss, Witness Statement, 22 October 2004, reproduced in Diana Inquest: The Documents the Jury Never Saw, 2010, p656 (UK Edition)

[159] Keith Moss, Witness Statement, 22 October 2004, reproduced in Diana Inquest: The Documents the Jury Never Saw, 2010, pp655-6 (UK Edition)

[160] Keith Moss, Witness Statement, 22 October 2004, reproduced in Diana Inquest: The Documents the Jury Never Saw, 2010, p647 (UK Edition). Confirmed at the inquest: 22 Nov 07: 8.8

[161] Keith Moss, Witness Statement, 22 October 2004, reproduced in Diana Inquest: The Documents the Jury Never Saw, 2010, p655 (UK Edition)

[162] René Deguisne, Witness Statement, 9 May 2005, reproduced in Diana Inquest: The Documents the Jury Never Saw, 2010, p451 (UK Edition)

[163] 2 Oct 07: 79.15

[164] 2 Oct 07: 79.6

[165] Buckingham Palace, Divorce: Status and Role of the Princess of Wales, PR Newswire Europe Ltd, www.prnewswire.co.uk/cgi/news

[166] Tony Blair, A Journey: My Political Life, 2010, p144

[167] Anthony Mather, Witness Statement, 23 August 2005, reproduced in Diana Inquest: The Documents the Jury Never Saw, 2010, pp661,663 (UK Edition)

[168] John Burton, Witness Statement, 16 June 2004, reproduced in Diana Inquest: The Documents the Jury Never Saw, 2010, p557 (UK Edition)

[169] Keith Moss, Witness Statement, 22 October 2004, reproduced in Diana Inquest: The Documents the Jury Never Saw, 2010, p653 (UK Edition)

[170] Location details are based on the general evidence in this chapter. Structure details from: The Role of the Private Secretary, The Lord Chamberlain, The Lord Chamberlain's Office, The Official Website of the British Monarchy, www.royal.gov.uk/TheRoyalHousehold/RoyalHouseholddepartments; Private Secretary to the Sovereign, Wikipedia, http://en.wikipedia.org/wiki

[171] Anthony Mather, Witness Statement, 23 August 2005, reproduced in Diana Inquest: The Documents the Jury Never Saw, 2010, pp660-3 (UK Edition)

[172] Colin Tebbutt, Witness Statement, 5 July 2004, reproduced in Diana Inquest: The Documents the Jury Never Saw, 2010, pp439-441 (UK Edition)

[173] The Operation Paget Inquiry Report into the Allegation of Conspiracy to Murder Diana, Princess of Wales and Emad El-Din Mohamed Abdel Moneim Fayed, December 14 2006, page 544

[174] Clive Leverton, Witness Statement, 13 July 2004, reproduced in Diana Inquest: The Documents the Jury Never Saw, 2010, pp488-491 (UK Edition)

[175] Keith Leverton, Witness Statement, 27 October 2004, reproduced in Diana Inquest: The Documents the Jury Never Saw, 2010, pp497-500 (UK Edition)

[176] David Green, Witness Statement, 13 July 2004, reproduced in Diana Inquest: The Documents the Jury Never Saw, 2010, pp502-3 (UK Edition)

[177] David Green, Witness Statement, 13 July 2004, reproduced in Diana Inquest: The Documents the Jury Never Saw, 2010, p504 (UK Edition)

[178] David Green, Witness Statement, 17 September 2004, reproduced in Diana Inquest: The Documents the Jury Never Saw, 2010, pp507 (UK Edition)

[179] Anthony Mather, Witness Statement, 23 August 2005, reproduced in Diana Inquest: The Documents the Jury Never Saw, 2010, p662 (UK Edition)

[180] Jean-Claude Plumet, Witness Statement, 4 November 2005, reproduced in Diana Inquest: The Documents the Jury Never Saw, 2010, p469 (UK Edition)

[181] Clive Leverton, Witness Statement, 13 July 2004, reproduced in Diana Inquest: The Documents the Jury Never Saw, 2010, p493 (UK Edition)

[182] Clive Leverton, Witness Statement, 13 July 2004, reproduced in Diana Inquest: The Documents the Jury Never Saw, 2010, pp493-4 (UK Edition)

[183] David Green, Witness Statement, 17 September 2004, reproduced in Diana Inquest: The Documents the Jury Never Saw, 2010, pp504 (UK Edition)

[184] David Green, Witness Statement, 17 September 2004, reproduced in Diana Inquest: The Documents the Jury Never Saw, 2010, pp504 (UK Edition)

[185] Keith Moss, Witness Statement, 22 October 2004, reproduced in Diana Inquest: The Documents the Jury Never Saw, 2010, p657 (UK Edition)

[186] Keith Moss, Witness Statement, 22 October 2004, reproduced in Diana Inquest: The Documents the Jury Never Saw, 2010, p658 (UK Edition)

[187] Clive Leverton, Witness Statement, 13 July 2004, reproduced in Diana Inquest: The Documents the Jury Never Saw, 2010, p493 (UK Edition)

[188] Patrick Launay, Witness Statement, 21 March 2006, reproduced in Diana Inquest: The Documents the Jury Never Saw, 2010, p517 (UK Edition)

[189] Clive Leverton, Witness Statement, 13 July 2004, reproduced in Diana Inquest: The Documents the Jury Never Saw, 2010, p488 (UK Edition); Keith Leverton, Witness Statement, 27 October 2004, reproduced in Diana Inquest: The Documents the Jury Never Saw, 2010, p497 (UK Edition)

[190] Clive Leverton, Witness Statement, 13 July 2004, reproduced in Diana Inquest: The Documents the Jury Never Saw, 2010, p491 (UK Edition)

[191] Keith Leverton, Witness Statement, 27 October 2004, reproduced in Diana Inquest: The Documents the Jury Never Saw, 2010, p499 (UK Edition)

[192] Keith Moss, Witness Statement, 22 October 2004, reproduced in Diana Inquest: The Documents the Jury Never Saw, 2010, p657 (UK Edition)

[193] Clive Leverton, Witness Statement, 13 July 2004, reproduced in Diana Inquest: The Documents the Jury Never Saw, 2010, p493 (UK Edition)

[194] Patrick Launay, Witness Statement, 21 March 2006, reproduced in Diana Inquest: The Documents the Jury Never Saw, 2010, p514 (UK Edition)

[195] Keith Moss, Witness Statement, 22 October 2004, reproduced in Diana Inquest: The Documents the Jury Never Saw, 2010, p658 (UK Edition)

[196] Colin Tebbutt, Witness Statement, 5 July 2004, reproduced in Diana Inquest: The Documents the Jury Never Saw, 2010, p444 (UK Edition)

[197] John Burton, Witness Statement, 16 June 2004, reproduced in Diana Inquest: The Documents the Jury Never Saw, 2010, p561 (UK Edition)

[198] John Burton, Witness Statement, 16 June 2004, reproduced in Diana Inquest: The Documents the Jury Never Saw, 2010, pp557-566 (UK Edition)

[199] John Burton, Witness Statement, 29 August 2004, reproduced in Diana Inquest: The Documents the Jury Never Saw, 2010, pp567-8 (UK Edition)

[200] Michael Burgess, Witness Statement, 16 August 2004, reproduced in Diana Inquest: The Documents the Jury Never Saw, 2010, pp534-544 (UK Edition)

[201] The Coroners' System, Coroners, Introduction to the Justice System, Judiciary of England and Wales, www.judiciary.gov.uk/about-the-judiciary

[202] Coroners Office, Her Majesty's Coroners Eastern District of London, www.walthamforest.gov.uk

[203] Lord Chamberlain, Wikipedia, http://en.wikipedia.org

[204] John Burton, Witness Statement, 16 June 2004, reproduced in Diana Inquest: The Documents the Jury Never Saw, 2010, p555 (UK Edition)

[205] John Macnamara, Witness Statement, 3 July 2006, reproduced in Diana Inquest: The Documents the Jury Never Saw, 2010, p518 (UK edition).

[206] Inquests into the Deaths of Diana, Princess of Wales and Mr Dodi Al Fayed, Pre-Hearing 8th January 2007, Before: The Rt Hon Baroness Butler-Sloss, GBE, Point 12.

[207] Anthony Mather, Witness Statement, 23 August 2005, reproduced in Diana Inquest: The Documents the Jury Never Saw, 2010, p662 (UK Edition)

[208] Lord Steward, Wikipedia, http://en.wikipedia.org

[209] Robert Thompson, Affidavit, 13 June 2001, reproduced in Diana Inquest: The Documents the Jury Never Saw, 2010, p598 (UK Edition)

[210] Robert Thompson, Witness Statement, 9 November 2004, reproduced in Diana Inquest: The Documents the Jury Never Saw, 2010, p611 (UK Edition)

[211] Andrew Alderson, Coroner Seeks New Law to Forgo Diana Inquest, Daily Telegraph, April 1 2001

[212] Robert Thompson, Witness Statement, 9 November 2004, reproduced in Diana Inquest: The Documents the Jury Never Saw, 2010, p609 (UK Edition)

[213] Keith Moss, Witness Statement, 22 October 2004, reproduced in Diana Inquest: The Documents the Jury Never Saw, 2010, pp651-2 (UK Edition)

[214] Michael Jay, Witness Statement, 13 December 2005, reproduced in Diana Inquest: The Documents the Jury Never Saw, 2010, p641 (UK Edition)

[215] Michael Jay, Witness Statement, 13 December 2005, reproduced in Diana Inquest: The Documents the Jury Never Saw, 2010, pp635-6 (UK Edition)

[216] Michael Jay, Witness Statement, 13 December 2005, reproduced in Diana Inquest: The Documents the Jury Never Saw, 2010, pp638-9 (UK Edition)

[217] Michael Jay, Witness Statement, 13 December 2005, reproduced in Diana Inquest: The Documents the Jury Never Saw, 2010, pp637-8 (UK Edition)

[218] Michael Jay, Witness Statement, 13 December 2005, reproduced in Diana Inquest: The Documents the Jury Never Saw, 2010, pp639-640 (UK Edition)

[219] Colin Tebbutt, Witness Statement, 5 July 2004, reproduced in Diana Inquest: The Documents the Jury Never Saw, 2010, p437 (UK Edition)

[220] Ingrid Seward, The Queen & Di, HarperCollins, 2000, p14

[221] Keith Moss, Witness Statement, 22 October 2004, reproduced in Diana Inquest: The Documents the Jury Never Saw, 2010, pp657-8 (UK Edition)

[222] Colin Tebbutt, Witness Statement, 5 July 2004, reproduced in Diana Inquest: The Documents the Jury Never Saw, 2010, p441 (UK Edition)

[223] Colin Tebbutt, Witness Statement, 5 July 2004, reproduced in Diana Inquest: The Documents the Jury Never Saw, 2010, pp444-5 (UK Edition)

[224] Patrick Launay, Witness Statement, 21 March 2006, reproduced in Diana Inquest: The Documents the Jury Never Saw, 2010, pp513-6 (UK Edition)

[225] Jean-Claude Plumet, Witness Statement, 4 November 2005, reproduced in Diana Inquest: The Documents the Jury Never Saw, 2010, p475 (UK Edition)

[226] Gérard Jauze, Witness Statement, 21 March 2006, reproduced in Diana Inquest: The Documents the Jury Never Saw, 2010, p483 (UK Edition)

[227] Associated Press, Nightmare Ending to a British Fairy Tale Death of a Princess, Cincinnati Post, 1 September 1997

[228] Andrew Morton, Diana: Her True Story – In Her Own Words, 1997, pages 54-55

[229] Paul Burrell, A Royal Duty, 2003, pages 322-3 and Inquest Evidence Reference INQ0010117.

[230] The Operation Paget Inquiry Report into the Allegation of Conspiracy to Murder Diana, Princess of Wales and Emad El-Din Mohamed Abdel Moneim Fayed, December 14 2006, page 104

[231] Clive Leverton, Witness Statement, 13 July 2004, reproduced in Diana Inquest: The Documents the Jury Never Saw, 2010, pp493-4 (UK Edition)

[232] Keith Leverton, Witness Statement, 27 October 2004, reproduced in Diana Inquest: The Documents the Jury Never Saw, 2010, p500 (UK Edition)

[233] David Green, Witness Statement, 13 July 2004, pages 5 to 6

[234] Alastair Campbell, The Alastair Campbell Diaries: Volume 2: Power and the People: 1997-1999, 2011, page 125

[235] Alastair Campbell, The Alastair Campbell Diaries: Volume 2: Power and the People: 1997-1999, 2011, pages 128-9

[236] Alastair Campbell, The Alastair Campbell Diaries: Volume 2: Power and the People: 1997-1999, 2011, pages 130-1

[237] P267, Part 2.

[238] p257, Part 2.

[239] 12 Feb 08: 3.8.

[240] The Lord Chamberlain's Office, The Official Website of the British Monarchy, www.royal.gov.uk/TheRoyalHousehold

[241] Jean-Claude Plumet, Witness Statement, 4 November 2005, reproduced in Diana Inquest: The Documents the Jury Never Saw, 2010, p469 (UK Edition)

[242] Gérard Jauze, Witness Statement, 21 March 2006, reproduced in Diana Inquest: The Documents the Jury Never Saw, 2010, p477 (UK Edition)

[243] Patrick Launay, Witness Statement, 21 March 2006, reproduced in Diana Inquest: The Documents the Jury Never Saw, 2010, p510 (UK Edition)

[244] Patrick Launay, Witness Statement, 21 March 2006, reproduced in Diana Inquest: The Documents the Jury Never Saw, 2010, p512 (UK Edition)

[245] Alan Puxley, Witness Statement, 16 June 2004, reproduced in Diana Inquest: The Documents the Jury Never Saw, 2010, p462 (UK Edition)

[246] Anthony Mather, Witness Statement, 23 August 2005, reproduced in Diana Inquest: The Documents the Jury Never Saw, 2010, p661 (UK Edition)

[247] Clive Leverton, Witness Statement, 13 July 2004, reproduced in Diana Inquest: The Documents the Jury Never Saw, 2010, p488 (UK Edition)

[248] Keith Leverton, Witness Statement, 27 October 2004, reproduced in Diana Inquest: The Documents the Jury Never Saw, 2010, p497 (UK Edition)

[249] The British Funeral Service, Private Client Adviser Magazine, Volume 5 Issue 2, January 2000

[250] SCI Announces the Appointment of Jerald L. Pullins as Executive Vice-President International, PR Newswire, 14 August 1997, www.prnewswire.com/news-releases

[251] Malcolm Ross (Courtier), Wikipedia, http://en.wikipedia.org/wiki

[252] The Lord Chamberlain's Office, The Official Website of the British Monarchy, www.royal.gov.uk/TheRoyalHousehold

[253] Clive Leverton, Witness Statement, 13 July 2004, reproduced in Diana Inquest: The Documents the Jury Never Saw, 2010, p492 (UK Edition)

[254] Alastair Campbell, The Alastair Campbell Diaries: Volume 2: Power and the People: 1997-1999, 2011, pages 129

[255] Alastair Campbell, The Blair Years, 2007, page 244

[256] David Ogilvy, 13th Earl of Airlie, Wikipedia, http://en.wikipedia.org/wiki

[257] The Lord Chamberlain, The Official Website of the British Monarchy, www.royal.gov.uk/TheRoyalHousehold

[258] Alastair Campbell, The Alastair Campbell Diaries: Volume 2: Power and the People: 1997-1999, 2011, page 127

[259] Defence Services Secretary, Wikipedia, http://en.wikipedia.org/wiki

[260] Defence Services Secretary, Wikipedia, http://en.wikipedia.org/wiki

[261] Defence Services Secretary, Wikipedia, http://en.wikipedia.org/wiki

[262] Lord Steward, Wikipedia, http://en.wikipedia.org/wiki

[263] 13 Dec 07: 100.3

[264] Clive Leverton, Witness Statement, 13 July 2004, reproduced in Diana Inquest: The Documents the Jury Never Saw, 2010, pp488-9 (UK Edition)

[265] Keith Leverton, Witness Statement, 27 October 2004, reproduced in Diana Inquest: The Documents the Jury Never Saw, 2010, p498 (UK Edition)

[266] Anthony Mather, Witness Statement, 23 August 2005, reproduced in Diana Inquest: The Documents the Jury Never Saw, 2010, p661 (UK Edition)

[267] Clive Leverton, Witness Statement, 13 July 2004, reproduced in Diana Inquest: The Documents the Jury Never Saw, 2010, pp492-3 (UK Edition)

[268] Clive Leverton, Witness Statement, 13 July 2004, reproduced in Diana Inquest: The Documents the Jury Never Saw, 2010, pp489-490 (UK Edition)

[269] David Green, Witness Statement, 17 September 2004, reproduced in Diana Inquest: The Documents the Jury Never Saw, 2010, p507 (UK Edition)

[270] Gérard Jauze, Witness Statement, 21 March 2006, reproduced in Diana Inquest: The Documents the Jury Never Saw, 2010, pp484-5 (UK Edition)

[271] Patrick Launay, Witness Statement, 21 March 2006, reproduced in Diana Inquest: The Documents the Jury Never Saw, 2010, pp514-5 (UK Edition)

[272] Alan Puxley, Witness Statement, 16 June 2004, reproduced in Diana Inquest: The Documents the Jury Never Saw, 2010, pp458-9 (UK Edition)
[273] Colin Tebbutt, Witness Statement, 5 July 2004, reproduced in Diana Inquest: The Documents the Jury Never Saw, 2010, p443 (UK Edition)
[274] Jean-Claude Plumet, Witness Statement, 4 November 2005, reproduced in Diana Inquest: The Documents the Jury Never Saw, 2010, p470 (UK Edition)
[275] Jean-Claude Plumet, Witness Statement, 4 November 2005, reproduced in Diana Inquest: The Documents the Jury Never Saw, 2010, pp473-5 (UK Edition)
[276] Gérard Jauze, Witness Statement, 21 March 2006, reproduced in Diana Inquest: The Documents the Jury Never Saw, 2010, pp482-3 (UK Edition)
[277] Gérard Jauze, Witness Statement, 21 March 2006, reproduced in Diana Inquest: The Documents the Jury Never Saw, 2010, p485 (UK Edition)
[278] Jean-Claude Plumet, Witness Statement, 4 November 2005, reproduced in Diana Inquest: The Documents the Jury Never Saw, 2010, pp467-8 (UK Edition)
[279] Martine Monteil, Witness Statement, 15 November 2006, page 4
[280] Clive Leverton, Witness Statement, 13 July 2004, reproduced in Diana Inquest: The Documents the Jury Never Saw, 2010, p489 (UK Edition)
[281] David Green, Witness Statement, 13 July 2004, reproduced in Diana Inquest: The Documents the Jury Never Saw, 2010, p502 (UK Edition)
[282] David Green, Witness Statement, 17 September 2004, reproduced in Diana Inquest: The Documents the Jury Never Saw, 2010, p507 (UK Edition)
[283] Keith Moss, Witness Statement, 22 October 2004, reproduced in Diana Inquest: The Documents the Jury Never Saw, 2010, p657 (UK Edition)
[284] Jean-Claude Plumet, Witness Statement, 4 November 2005, reproduced in Diana Inquest: The Documents the Jury Never Saw, 2010, p485 (UK Edition)
[285] Patrick Launay, Witness Statement, 21 March 2006, reproduced in Diana Inquest: The Documents the Jury Never Saw, 2010, p512 (UK Edition)
[286] Gérard Jauze, Witness Statement, 21 March 2006, reproduced in Diana Inquest: The Documents the Jury Never Saw, 2010, p483 (UK Edition)
[287] Colin Tebbutt, Witness Statement, 5 July 2004, reproduced in Diana Inquest: The Documents the Jury Never Saw, 2010, pp441-2 (UK Edition)
[288] Colin Tebbutt, Witness Statement, 5 July 2004, reproduced in Diana Inquest: The Documents the Jury Never Saw, 2010, p443 (UK Edition)
[289] Keith Moss, Witness Statement, 22 October 2004, reproduced in Diana Inquest: The Documents the Jury Never Saw, 2010, p657 (UK Edition)
[290] Jean Monceau, Witness Statement, 18 October 2005, reproduced in Diana Inquest: The Documents the Jury Never Saw, 2010, p414 (UK Edition)
[291] Gérard Jauze, Witness Statement, 21 March 2006, reproduced in Diana Inquest: The Documents the Jury Never Saw, 2010, p484 (UK Edition)
[292] Patrick Launay, Witness Statement, 21 March 2006, reproduced in Diana Inquest: The Documents the Jury Never Saw, 2010, pp511-4 (UK Edition)
[293] Jean-Claude Plumet, Witness Statement, 4 November 2005, reproduced in Diana Inquest: The Documents the Jury Never Saw, 2010, p475 (UK Edition)
[294] John Burton, Witness Statement, 16 June 2004, reproduced in Diana Inquest: The Documents the Jury Never Saw, 2010, p556 (UK Edition)

[295] John Burton, Witness Statement, 16 June 2004, reproduced in Diana Inquest: The Documents the Jury Never Saw, 2010, p558 (UK Edition)

[296] John Burton, Witness Statement, 29 August 2004, reproduced in Diana Inquest: The Documents the Jury Never Saw, 2010, p568 (UK Edition)

[297] Michael Burgess, Witness Statement, 16 August 2004, reproduced in Diana Inquest: The Documents the Jury Never Saw, 2010, pp534-537 (UK Edition)

[298] Michael Burgess, Witness Statement, 16 August 2004, reproduced in Diana Inquest: The Documents the Jury Never Saw, 2010, p538 (UK Edition)

[299] Helen Smith (Nurse), Wikipedia, http://en.wikipedia.org/wiki; Will Pavia, UK Nurse Helen Smith Buried 30 Years After Death, The Australia, 29 October 2009

[300] John Burton, Witness Statement, 16 June 2004, reproduced in Diana Inquest: The Documents the Jury Never Saw, 2010, pp559,564 (UK Edition)

[301] Michael Burgess, Witness Statement, 16 August 2004, reproduced in Diana Inquest: The Documents the Jury Never Saw, 2010, pp536-7 (UK Edition)

[302] Robert Chapman, Witness Statement, 24 February 2005, reproduced in Diana Inquest: The Documents the Jury Never Saw, 2010, p583 (UK Edition)

[303] Michael Burgess, Witness Statement, 16 August 2004, reproduced in Diana Inquest: The Documents the Jury Never Saw, 2010, pp538-9 (UK Edition)

[304] John Burton, Witness Statement, 16 June 2004, reproduced in Diana Inquest: The Documents the Jury Never Saw, 2010, pp563-4 (UK Edition)

[305] Robert Thompson, Affidavit, 13 June 2001, reproduced in Diana Inquest: The Documents the Jury Never Saw, 2010, pp596-7 (UK Edition)

[306] Robert Thompson, Witness Statement, 9 November 2004, reproduced in Diana Inquest: The Documents the Jury Never Saw, 2010, pp602,605 (UK Edition)

[307] Robert Thompson, Affidavit, 13 June 2001, reproduced in Diana Inquest: The Documents the Jury Never Saw, 2010, p596 (UK Edition)

[308] Robert Chapman, Witness Statement, 24 February 2005, reproduced in Diana Inquest: The Documents the Jury Never Saw, 2010, pp579-580 (UK Edition)

[309] Robert Chapman, Witness Statement, 24 February 2005, p4

[310] Michael Burgess, Witness Statement, 16 August 2004, reproduced in Diana Inquest: The Documents the Jury Never Saw, 2010, p534-5 (UK Edition)

[311] Michael Burgess, Witness Statement, 16 August 2004, reproduced in Diana Inquest: The Documents the Jury Never Saw, 2010, pp539,541 (UK Edition)

[312] John Burton, Witness Statement, 16 June 2004, reproduced in Diana Inquest: The Documents the Jury Never Saw, 2010, p556 (UK Edition)

[313] John Burton, Witness Statement, 16 June 2004, reproduced in Diana Inquest: The Documents the Jury Never Saw, 2010, pp558-9 (UK Edition)

[314] Robert Chapman, Witness Statement, 24 February 2005, reproduced in Diana Inquest: The Documents the Jury Never Saw, 2010, pp580-1 (UK Edition)

[315] Robert Thompson, Affidavit, 13 June 2001, reproduced in Diana Inquest: The Documents the Jury Never Saw, 2010, p595 (UK Edition)

[316] Robert Thompson, Witness Statement, 9 November 2004, reproduced in Diana Inquest: The Documents the Jury Never Saw, 2010, pp601-2 (UK Edition)

[317] John Macnamara, Witness Statement, 3 July 2006, reproduced in Diana Inquest: The Documents the Jury Never Saw, 2010, pp518-9 (UK Edition)

[318] Bill Hunt, Iain West – Obituary, The Independent, 28 July 2001

[319] Email correspondence, John Macnamara to John Morgan, 19 November 2010

[320] Michael Burgess, Witness Statement, 16 August 2004, reproduced in Diana Inquest: The Documents the Jury Never Saw, 2010, p533 (UK Edition)

[321] See Part 3: Hold-Up in Body Transfer in Chapter 16

[322] Michael Burgess, Witness Statement, 16 August 2004, reproduced in Diana Inquest: The Documents the Jury Never Saw, 2010, p541 (UK Edition)

[323] John Burton, Witness Statement, 16 June 2004, reproduced in Diana Inquest: The Documents the Jury Never Saw, 2010, pp556-7,563 (UK Edition)

[324] Robert Thompson, Witness Statement, 9 November 2004, reproduced in Diana Inquest: The Documents the Jury Never Saw, 2010, pp602-3 (UK Edition)

[325] Robert Chapman, Witness Statement, 24 February 2005, reproduced in Diana Inquest: The Documents the Jury Never Saw, 2010, p581 (UK Edition)

[326] Oxford dictionary

[327] The Operation Paget Inquiry Report into the Allegation of Conspiracy to Murder Diana, Princess of Wales and Emad El-Din Mohamed Abdel Moneim Fayed, December 14 2006, pages 628-9

[328] The Operation Paget Inquiry Report into the Allegation of Conspiracy to Murder Diana, Princess of Wales and Emad El-Din Mohamed Abdel Moneim Fayed, December 14 2006, pages 627-8,631-2

[329] The Operation Paget Inquiry Report into the Allegation of Conspiracy to Murder Diana, Princess of Wales and Emad El-Din Mohamed Abdel Moneim Fayed, December 14 2006, pages 636

[330] The Operation Paget Inquiry Report into the Allegation of Conspiracy to Murder Diana, Princess of Wales and Emad El-Din Mohamed Abdel Moneim Fayed, December 14 2006, pages 626, 639

[331] The Operation Paget Inquiry Report into the Allegation of Conspiracy to Murder Diana, Princess of Wales and Emad El-Din Mohamed Abdel Moneim Fayed, December 14 2006, pages 627,638

[332] The Operation Paget Inquiry Report into the Allegation of Conspiracy to Murder Diana, Princess of Wales and Emad El-Din Mohamed Abdel Moneim Fayed, December 14 2006, page 638

[333] Neal Williams, Witness Statement, 1 September 1997, page 1

[334] The Operation Paget Inquiry Report into the Allegation of Conspiracy to Murder Diana, Princess of Wales and Emad El-Din Mohamed Abdel Moneim Fayed, December 14 2006, page 639

[335] Robert Chapman, Post Mortem Exhibits Report, 31 August 1997, page 1; Robert Chapman, Witness Statement, 5 September 1997, page 1; The Operation Paget Inquiry Report into the Allegation of Conspiracy to Murder Diana, Princess of Wales and Emad El-Din Mohamed Abdel Moneim Fayed, December 14 2006, pages 636-8

[336] 26 Nov 07: 39.13

[337] John Burton, Witness Statement, 16 June 2004, reproduced in Diana Inquest: The Documents the Jury Never Saw, 2010, p562 (UK Edition)

[338] Michael Burgess, Witness Statement, 16 August 2004, reproduced in Diana Inquest: The Documents the Jury Never Saw, 2010, p540 (UK Edition)

[339] The Operation Paget Inquiry Report into the Allegation of Conspiracy to Murder Diana, Princess of Wales and Emad El-Din Mohamed Abdel Moneim Fayed, December 14 2006, page 638

[340] Robert Chapman, Witness Statement, 5 September 1997, page 1

[341] 26 Nov 07: 35.4

[342] Robert Thompson, Affidavit, 13 June 2001, reproduced in Diana Inquest: The Documents the Jury Never Saw, 2010, p596 (UK Edition)

[343] Robert Thompson, Witness Statement, 9 November 2004, reproduced in Diana Inquest: The Documents the Jury Never Saw, 2010, pp601-2 (UK Edition)

[344] Colin Tebbutt, Witness Statement, 5 July 2004, reproduced in Diana Inquest: The Documents the Jury Never Saw, 2010, p445 (UK Edition)

[345] Anthony Mather, Witness Statement, 23 August 2005, reproduced in Diana Inquest: The Documents the Jury Never Saw, 2010, pp662-3 (UK Edition)

[346] The Operation Paget Inquiry Report into the Allegation of Conspiracy to Murder Diana, Princess of Wales and Emad El-Din Mohamed Abdel Moneim Fayed, December 14 2006, page 637

[347] The Operation Paget Inquiry Report into the Allegation of Conspiracy to Murder Diana, Princess of Wales and Emad El-Din Mohamed Abdel Moneim Fayed, December 14 2006, page 637

[348] The Operation Paget Inquiry Report into the Allegation of Conspiracy to Murder Diana, Princess of Wales and Emad El-Din Mohamed Abdel Moneim Fayed, December 14 2006, page 637

[349] The Operation Paget Inquiry Report into the Allegation of Conspiracy to Murder Diana, Princess of Wales and Emad El-Din Mohamed Abdel Moneim Fayed, December 14 2006, page 638

[350] The Operation Paget Inquiry Report into the Allegation of Conspiracy to Murder Diana, Princess of Wales and Emad El-Din Mohamed Abdel Moneim Fayed, December 14 2006, page 638

[351] Robert Chapman, Witness Statement, 24 February 2005, reproduced in Diana Inquest: The Documents the Jury Never Saw, 2010, p584 (UK Edition)

[352] Robert Chapman, Witness Statement, 24 February 2005, reproduced in Diana Inquest: The Documents the Jury Never Saw, 2010, pp585-6 (UK Edition)

[353] Robert Chapman, Witness Statement, 24 February 2005, pp7-8

[354] John Burton, Witness Statement, 16 June 2004, reproduced in Diana Inquest: The Documents the Jury Never Saw, 2010, p563 (UK Edition)

[355] David Green, Witness Statement, 13 July 2004, reproduced in Diana Inquest: The Documents the Jury Never Saw, 2010, pp504-5 (UK Edition)

[356] David Green, Witness Statement, 17 September 2004, reproduced in Diana Inquest: The Documents the Jury Never Saw, 2010, p506 (UK Edition)

[357] Alan Puxley, Witness Statement, 16 June 2004, reproduced in Diana Inquest: The Documents the Jury Never Saw, 2010, p462 (UK Edition)

[358] René Deguisne, Witness Statement, 9 May 2005, reproduced in Diana Inquest: The Documents the Jury Never Saw, 2010, p453 (UK Edition)

[359] Jean-Claude Plumet, Witness Statement, 4 November 2005, reproduced in Diana Inquest: The Documents the Jury Never Saw, 2010, p475 (UK Edition)

[360] Jean Monceau, Witness Statement, 18 October 2005, reproduced in Diana Inquest: The Documents the Jury Never Saw, 2010, p418 (UK Edition)

[361] Maud Coujard, Witness Statement, 15 November 2006, reproduced in Diana Inquest: The Documents the Jury Never Saw, 2010, p51 (UK Edition)

[362] Dr Susan Paterson, Witness Statement, 28 September 2004, page 2

[363] Dr Susan Paterson, Telephone Conversation Notes, 11 July 2006, reproduced in Diana Inquest: The Documents the Jury Never Saw, 2010, pp617-9 (UK Edition)

[364] INQ0001800 – on inquest website.

[365] Robert Thompson, Witness Statement, 9 November 2004, reproduced in Diana Inquest: The Documents the Jury Never Saw, 2010, p604 (UK Edition)

[366] The Operation Paget Inquiry Report into the Allegation of Conspiracy to Murder Diana, Princess of Wales and Emad El-Din Mohamed Abdel Moneim Fayed, December 14 2006, page 641

[367] Robert Thompson, Witness Statement, 9 November 2004, reproduced in Diana Inquest: The Documents the Jury Never Saw, 2010, p610 (UK Edition)

[368] Robert Thompson, Affidavit, 13 June 2001, pages 2 to 3

[369] Post Mortem Exhibits (Pathologists Copy) The Princess Of Wales, 31 August 1997, pages 1 to 2

[370] Robert Chapman, Witness Statement, 10 September 1997, p12

[371] Robert Chapman, Witness Statement, 24 February 2005, pp6-7

[372] Rene Delorm, Barry Fox & Nadine Taylor, Diana & Dodi: A Love Story, 1998, pages 159-161

[373] Thomas Sancton and Scott MacLeod, Death of a Princess: An Investigation, 1998, page 134

[374] Frank Klein, Email to John Morgan, 15 December 2010

[375] Dr Susan Paterson, Witness Statement, 28 September 2004, reproduced in Diana Inquest: The Documents the Jury Never Saw, 2010, pp621-3 (UK Edition)

[376] Dr Susan Paterson, Witness Statement, 28 September 2004, reproduced in Diana Inquest: The Documents the Jury Never Saw, 2010, pp614-5 (UK Edition)

[377] Robert Chapman, Witness Statement, 10 September 1997, pp10-11

[378] Dr Susan Paterson, Witness Statement, 28 September 2004, reproduced in Diana Inquest: The Documents the Jury Never Saw, 2010, pp614-5 (UK Edition)

[379] Robert Thompson, Affidavit, 13 June 2001, reproduced in Diana Inquest: The Documents the Jury Never Saw, 2010, p597 (UK Edition)

[380] Robert Thompson, Witness Statement, 9 November 2004, reproduced in Diana Inquest: The Documents the Jury Never Saw, 2010, pp605,610 (UK Edition)

[381] Robert Chapman, Witness Statement, 10 September 1997, reproduced in Diana Inquest: The Documents the Jury Never Saw, 2010, pp574-6 (UK Edition)

[382] Robert Chapman, Witness Statement, 24 February 2005, pp7-9

[383] Richard Wall, Witness Statement, 19 October 2004, pages 1-2

[384] Toby Smith, Witness Statement, 26 June 2006, page 1

[385] Robert Thompson, Witness Statement, 9 November 2004, reproduced in Diana Inquest: The Documents the Jury Never Saw, 2010, pp603-6 (UK Edition)

[386] Robert Thompson, Affidavit, 13 June 2001, reproduced in Diana Inquest: The Documents the Jury Never Saw, 2010, pp596-8 (UK Edition)

[387] Dr Susan Paterson, Witness Statement, 28 September 2004, reproduced in Diana Inquest: The Documents the Jury Never Saw, 2010, pp614-5 (UK Edition)

[388] Robert Chapman, Witness Statement, 5 September 1997, pp11-12

[389] Dr Susan Paterson, Witness Statement, 28 September 2004, reproduced in Diana Inquest: The Documents the Jury Never Saw, 2010, pp621-2 (UK Edition)

[390] The Operation Paget Inquiry Report into the Allegation of Conspiracy to Murder Diana, Princess of Wales and Emad El-Din Mohamed Abdel Moneim Fayed, December 14 2006, page 637

[391] John Burton, Witness Statement, 16 June 2004, reproduced in Diana Inquest: The Documents the Jury Never Saw, 2010, p562 (UK Edition)

[392] John Burton, Witness Statement, 16 June 2004, reproduced in Diana Inquest: The Documents the Jury Never Saw, 2010, p563 (UK Edition)

[393] John Burton, Witness Statement, 16 June 2004, reproduced in Diana Inquest: The Documents the Jury Never Saw, 2010, p565 (UK Edition)

[394] Michael Burgess, Witness Statement, 16 August 2004, reproduced in Diana Inquest: The Documents the Jury Never Saw, 2010, p543 (UK Edition)

[395] Robert Thompson, Witness Statement, 9 November 2004, p5

[396] Robert Thompson, Witness Statement, 9 November 2004, pp7-8

[397] David Green, Witness Statement, 13 July 2004, page 5

[398] Richard Wall, Witness Statement, 19 October 2004, pages 1-2

[399] Roy Green, Witness Statement, 23 November 2006, page 2

[400] Dr Alexander Allan, Witness Statement, 12 December 2006, page 2

[401] Dr Susan Paterson, Witness Statement, 28 September 2004, reproduced in Diana Inquest: The Documents the Jury Never Saw, 2010, pp614,616 (UK Edition)

[402] Richard Wall, Witness Statement, 19 October 2004, pages 1-2

[403] Robert Chapman, Witness Statement, 24 February 2005, reproduced in Diana Inquest: The Documents the Jury Never Saw, 2010, pp580,582 (UK Edition)

[404] Robert Thompson, Witness Statement, 9 November 2004, reproduced in Diana Inquest: The Documents the Jury Never Saw, 2010, p605 (UK Edition)

[405] John Burton, Witness Statement, 16 June 2004, reproduced in Diana Inquest: The Documents the Jury Never Saw, 2010, p557 (UK Edition)

[406] John Burton, Witness Statement, 16 June 2004, reproduced in Diana Inquest: The Documents the Jury Never Saw, 2010, p563 (UK Edition)

[407] John Burton, Witness Statement, 29 August 2004, reproduced in Diana Inquest: The Documents the Jury Never Saw, 2010, p568 (UK Edition)

[408] Robert Chapman, Witness Statement, 24 February 2005, reproduced in Diana Inquest: The Documents the Jury Never Saw, 2010, p586 (UK Edition)

[409] 26 Nov 07: 9.4.

[410] Robert Thompson, Witness Statement, 9 November 2004, reproduced in Diana Inquest: The Documents the Jury Never Saw, 2010, pp606-7 (UK Edition)

[411] Robert Chapman, Witness Statement, 24 February 2005, reproduced in Diana Inquest: The Documents the Jury Never Saw, 2010, pp582,584,590 (UK Edition)

[412] John Burton, Witness Statement, 16 June 2004, reproduced in Diana Inquest: The Documents the Jury Never Saw, 2010, p559 (UK Edition)

[413] Robert Thompson, Witness Statement, 9 November 2004, reproduced in Diana Inquest: The Documents the Jury Never Saw, 2010, pp602-7 (UK Edition)

[414] John Burton, Witness Statement, 16 June 2004, reproduced in Diana Inquest: The Documents the Jury Never Saw, 2010, p563 (UK Edition)

[415] Robert Thompson, Affidavit, 13 June 2001, reproduced in Diana Inquest: The Documents the Jury Never Saw, 2010, pp597-8 (UK Edition)

[416] Dr Susan Paterson, Witness Statement, 28 September 2004, reproduced in Diana Inquest: The Documents the Jury Never Saw, 2010, p614 (UK Edition)

[417] Dr Susan Paterson, Witness Statement, 28 September 2004, reproduced in Diana Inquest: The Documents the Jury Never Saw, 2010, p621 (UK Edition)

[418] Robert Thompson, Witness Statement, 9 November 2004, reproduced in Diana Inquest: The Documents the Jury Never Saw, 2010, pp606,610 (UK Edition)

[419] Robert Thompson, Affidavit, 13 June 2001, reproduced in Diana Inquest: The Documents the Jury Never Saw, 2010, p597 (UK Edition)

[420] Reproduced Figure 17 in Part 2

[421] Reproduced Figure 14 in Part 2

[422] Huguette Amarger, Witness Statement, 8 March 2005, page 3

[423] David Green, Witness Statement, 13 July 2004, reproduced in Diana Inquest: The Documents the Jury Never Saw, 2010, p503 (UK Edition)

[424] John Burton, Witness Statement, 16 June 2004, reproduced in Diana Inquest: The Documents the Jury Never Saw, 2010, p562 (UK Edition)

[425] Robert Chapman, Witness Statement, 10 September 1997, pp3-4,9-10,14-15

[426] Robert Thompson, Affidavit, 13 June 2001, reproduced in Diana Inquest: The Documents the Jury Never Saw, 2010, p598 (UK Edition)

[427] John Burton, Witness Statement, 16 June 2004, reproduced in Diana Inquest: The Documents the Jury Never Saw, 2010, pp564-5 (UK Edition)

[428] Michael Burgess, Witness Statement, 16 August 2004, reproduced in Diana Inquest: The Documents the Jury Never Saw, 2010, pp542-3 (UK Edition)

[429] Michael Burgess, Witness Statement, 16 August 2004, reproduced in Diana Inquest: The Documents the Jury Never Saw, 2010, p533 (UK Edition)

[430] The Operation Paget Inquiry Report into the Allegation of Conspiracy to Murder Diana, Princess of Wales and Emad El-Din Mohamed Abdel Moneim Fayed, December 14 2006, page 515

CPSIA information can be obtained at www.ICGtesting.com
Printed in the USA
LVOW07s1013241014

410338LV00001B/320/P